P9-CER-805

THE BATHROOM READERS' INSTITUTE

Uncle John's

AWESOME

35th

ANNIVERSARY

BATHROOM READER

BY THE BATHROOM READERS' INSTITUTE

PORTABLE
PRESS

Portable Press

San Diego, California

Portable Press / The Bathroom Readers' Institute
An imprint of Printers Row Publishing Group
9717 Pacific Heights Blvd, San Diego, CA 92121
www.portablepress.com • mail@portablepress.com

Copyright © 2022 Printers Row Publishing Group

All rights reserved. No part of this publication may be reproduced, distributed, or transmitted in any form or by any means, including photocopying, recording, or other electronic or mechanical methods, without the prior written permission of the publisher, except in the case of brief quotations embodied in critical reviews and certain other noncommercial uses permitted by copyright law.

Printers Row Publishing Group is a division of Readerlink Distribution Services, LLC. Portable Press, Bathroom Readers' Institute, and Uncle John's Bathroom Reader are registered trademarks of Readerlink Distribution Services, LLC.

Correspondence regarding the content of this book should be sent to Portable Press / The Bathroom Readers' Institute, Editorial Department, at the above address.

Dedicated to our friends and families, because being Mr. Know-It-All is fun, but life would be meaningless without having someone to tell all these useless facts to.

Portable Press
Publisher: Peter Norton • Associate Publisher: Ana Parker
Art Director: Charles McStravick
Senior Developmental Editor: April Graham
Production Team: Beno Chan, Julie Greene, Rusty von Dyl

Producer, Creator, and First Wizard Deluxe: Javna Brothers LLC

Interior, Illustrations, and Infographics Designer: Lidija Tomas
Cover Illustration and Design: Linda Lee Mauri

In memory of Pat Jeffrey

"From the moment I picked your book up until I laid it down, I was convulsed with laughter. Someday I intend to read it." –Groucho Marx

Library of Congress Cataloging-in-Publication data available on request.

ISBN: 978-1-6672-0023-1

Printed in China

26 25 24 23 22   1 2 3 4 5

OUR "REGULAR READERS" RAVE!

If you love trivia, facts, history, or just reading about something
you didn't know a minute ago—this series of books is GOLD!
—John D.

I have been purchasing UJBR's for the men in my family since 1988!
They look for it every year, so I will be in big trouble if they ever stop publishing it!
—Kay T.

I wish I had discovered these wonderful books years ago.
They are by far my favorite read.
—Ross J.

Now I can give my brain food while I take care of nature's call.
—Mike D.

Just a great book and makes a wonderful gift. What's not to like?
—Joanna L.

I love these for my classroom. I can't bring enough
Bathroom Readers in for my students.
—Anne Marie C.

I recently gave my college-bound daughter the *Great Big Bathroom Reader* that my dad
gave me when I went to college. Another generation "going with the flow!"
—Stephen M.

Uncle John's is the best for entertainment, a few valuable insights,
and the periodic laughter it prompts. The other bathroom trivia
books don't hold a candle to this series.
—Jim M.

I love all of these trivia books! Such great information
presented in a positive and funny way!
—Jann H.

I am so happy you've survived as a cool book series in this age.
Paper never has a dead battery.
—Shannon G.

CONTENTS

Because the BRI understands your reading needs, we've
divided the contents by length as well as subject.

Short—a quick read

Medium—2 to 3 pages

Long—for those extended visits, when something a little more involved is required

*   *   *

WATCH THIS

In 2016, a movie critic named Charlie Lyne decided to prank the British Board of Film Classification, which charges filmmakers a fee of £101.50 per movie, plus £7.09 per minute of running time, to rate films (which is required). Lyne crowd-funded £5,936 ($7,389) and then submitted a 10-hour-long feature film he made called Paint Drying...which is exactly that. Per their own rules, the censors had to watch all 607 minutes of it. They gave the film a "U" rating, suitable for all ages.

INTRODUCTION

Hold on to your hats, everybody! Welcome to the 35th annual edition of *Uncle John's Bathroom Reader*. While the team was celebrating our anniversary in the BRI's kitchen with some gluten-free cake, it dawned on us just how much the world has changed since my brother and I (with a lot of help from our friends) put the first Bathroom Reader together back in 1987. One example: There was no such a thing as "gluten-free cake." No smartphones or internet, either. If you were a bathroom reader, and you didn't have a book or a magazine to help you pass the time in there, your options were read the shampoo bottle label (again) or gaze at the shower curtain.

Then the BRI was born, and it revolutionized not only bathroom reading, but the entire humor/trivia publishing genre. And the fact that our little book series is still thriving in the 2020s is, well,

AWESOME!

Not to get too sentimental, but one of the reasons we're still around is because of readers like you, who—like us—have an insatiable curiosity about the world around us...especially when it's mixed with irony, cynicism, and laughter. It's been our great honor to inform and entertain you for 35 years (and counting). And if this is your *first* Bathroom Reader, here's an anniversary bonus: we've included five classic articles from our early editions that we think you'll enjoy.

Over the past three and a half decades, the Bathroom Readers' Institute has been home to hundreds of writers, researchers, editors, and designers (and the world's two best dogs) who've helped us churn out thousands upon thousands of articles. By my guestimate, we've passed along more than 100,000 individual facts. We truly started a movement.

But that was never our goal. We created the first Bathroom Reader so *we'd* have something to read in there. Once it hit big, we decided to go along for the ride. As the great philosopher Yogi Berra once said, "We came to a fork in the road, and we took it."

That reminds me: there's a page of fork facts in this book—proving we will *never* run out of topics to write about—plus facts about ducks, money, firsts and lasts, vomit, carrots, and things that go fast. And that's just scratching the surface. (That phrase, by the way, comes from farming in the early twentieth century; only scratching the surface of the field will not adequately till the soil. That makes 100,001 facts!) More highlights:

Forgotten History: The centuries-long search for Antarctica, how World War I reshaped the marketplace, and the crucial role that a lack of toilet paper played in the Cold War.

Colorful Characters: Hiram Bingham (the real-life Indiana Jones), Carlos Mendoza and his line of mediocrity, Iron Mike Malloy who refused to die, Simon Griffiths (the "man who gave a crap"), and a bunch of people (and a robot) named Johnny.

Origins: Crash test dummies, the electric chair, Newman's Own, the Crockpot, the highway rest area, and that miniature basketball backboard that attaches to an office wastebasket.

Laughs: Funny quotes, funny food origins, the evolution of laughter, and how Monty Python changed the face of comedy (insert obligatory dead parrot reference).

Blunders: The worst Olympic marathon, really bad musicals, game show goofs, mishaps with axes and priceless art, why you should never let your copyright lapse, and H. L. Mencken's bathtub.

Odd Goings-on: The curse of the "Destiny Ring," pets that shot their owners, bizarre buffets, odd podcasts, ghost kitchens, and the tale of the flying pig that shut down London airspace in 1976.

And much, much more!

Here's this year's cast of characters—writers, editors, designers, and inspirers. Thank you, team. We couldn't have done it without you.

Gordon Javna	**Lidija Tomas**	**Charlie Weimer**
John Dollison	**Derek Fairbridge**	**Ann Le Claire**
Jay Newman	**John Javna**	**Greg Weimer**
Brian Boone	**David & Hobby**	**Groucho**
Thom Little	**Thom Hepford**	**Alfred E. Neuman**
J. Carroll	**Paul Stanley**	**Thomas Crapper**

Well, that's a wrap for this edition. Now we all get to take a few weeks off before jumping right back in to Bathroom Reader #36.

Happy reading, and, as ever,

Go with the Flow!

—Uncle John and the BRI Staff

YOU'RE MY INSPIRATION

More examples of how pop-culture architects get their ideas.

Metropolis: Canadian-born comic book artist Joe Shuster went to high school in Cleveland, Ohio, where he and his friend Jerry Siegel created Superman in the late 1930s. For Superman's fictional city, Metropolis, Siegel had to draw on childhood memories from Canada. "Cleveland was not nearly as metropolitan as Toronto was," he explained. "And it was not as big or as beautiful. Whatever buildings I saw in Toronto remained in my mind and came out in the form of Metropolis."

Philip J. Fry: The first name of *Futurama*'s dimwitted protagonist comes from Homer Philip Groening, *Futurama* creator Matt Groening's dad (he'd already used Homer for another character). The name is also a tribute to Phil Hartman, who voiced Troy McClure on *The Simpsons*. The inspiration for Fry's middle initial came from another cartoon character: Bullwinkle J. Moose of *The Adventures of Rocky and Bullwinkle* fame, created by one of Groening's heroes, Jay Ward. No word on where the last name comes from, but on the show it was suggested that Fry was named after a Philips screwdriver.

Hannibal Lecter: "Hello, Clarice." That emotionless, chilling tone of the brilliant serial killer in 1991's *The Silence of the Lambs* came to Anthony Hopkins "on the first reading" of the part. Director Jonathan Demme was "a bit freaked" when he heard it and asked the Welsh actor where it came from. "He's like a machine," said Hopkins. "He's like HAL, the computer in *2001*: 'Good evening, Dave.' He just comes in like a silent shark."

Bob's Big Boy: According to company lore, six-year-old Richard Woodruff was a regular at Bob's Pantry in Glendale, California, in 1937. He cleaned the lot and the ice cream machine in exchange for free food. One day the pudgy boy, who wore checkered pants, asked owner Bob Wian for a hamburger with two patties. Wian added an extra bun between the patties, and the Double Decker Burger was born. A customer named Ben Washam drew a caricature of the big boy with his big sandwich, which became the mascot and, soon after, the name of the fast-food chain.

Gothmog the Orc: This grotesque bulbous-faced Orc shows up at a climactic battle in Peter Jackson's *The Lord of the Rings: The Return of the King* (2003). He's the one that growls, "The age of Men is over. The time of the Orc has come." According to actor Elijah Wood (Frodo), Gothmog's appearance and personality were based on Miramax producer Harvey Weinstein, who reportedly treated Jackson so poorly that the director took his movie to New Line. Wood said that Jackson crafted Gothmog "as a sort of a f*** you" to Weinstein, who was later sentenced to prison for sexual assault.

According to scientists, 40 percent of people have a first memory that didn't really happen.

GAME SHOW GOOFS

Being on a game show may look easy from the comfort of your living room, but under those hot television lights, contestants' mouths sometimes disconnect from their brains.

Richard Dawson: Name a yellow fruit.
Contestant: Orange.
—*Family Feud*

Alex Trebek: It's the southernmost city in the 48 contiguous states.
Contestant: What is West Virginia?
—*Jeopardy!*

Bob Eubanks: In what country will your husband say the last foreign car he rode in was manufactured?
Contestant: The United States.
Eubanks: That's not a foreign country.
Contestant: Um, Texas.
—*The Newlywed Game*

Jeff Foxworthy: Which European country is Budapest the capital of?
Contestant: This might be a stupid question. I thought Europe was a country? I know they speak French there, don't they? Is France a country?
—*Are You Smarter than a 5th Grader?*

Alex Trebek: A Christian hymn and a Jewish holiday hymn are both titled this, also the name of a 2009 Tony-nominated musical.
Contestant: What is *Kinky Boots*?
—*Jeopardy!*

Les Dennis: Name a famous Arthur.
Contestant: Shakespeare.
—*Family Fortunes*

Steve Harvey: Name a fruit that comes in more than one color.
Contestant: Jell-O.
—*Family Feud*

Bamber Gascoigne: What was Gandhi's first name?
Contestant: Goosey?
—*University Challenge*

Bob Eubanks: What will your husband say is his favorite rodent?
Contestant: His saxophone.
—*The Newlywed Game*

Anne Robinson: In the Lord's Prayer, what word beginning with "H," meaning "blessed," comes before "be thy name"?
Contestant: Howard.
—*The Weakest Link*

Todd Newton: What type of vehicles are used to compete in the legendary Tour de France?
Contestant: Uh, uh, SUVs.
—*Whammy! The All-New Press Your Luck*

Jamie Theakston: Where do you think Cambridge University is?
Contestant: Geography isn't my strong point.
Theakston: There's a clue in the title.
Contestant: Leicester.
—*Beg, Borrow or Steal*

In France, the 1975 movie *Jaws* was called *Les Dents de la Mer,* or "The Teeth of the Sea."

THE LAST OF IT

Everything has a beginning...and an end.

THE LAST PRESIDENT WITH FACIAL HAIR

Changing styles and a clear preference for politicians to be clean-shaven means the United States hasn't had a commander in chief with hair on his face in more than a century. The last U.S. president with facial hair: William Howard Taft, serving from 1909 to 1913 underneath a long, thick mustache.

THE LAST CIVIL WAR WIDOW

In 1936, 17-year-old Helen Viola Jackson married James Bolin, who had served in the Union Army with the 14th Missouri Cavalry more than 50 years earlier. At the time of their wedding, he was 93, and the marriage was more of a business arrangement—Jackson worked as a housekeeper for a cash-strapped Bolin, and by marrying her he ensured she'd receive his military pension upon his death. Bolin died in 1939; Jackson lived until 2020.

THE LAST AMERICAN SOLDIER TO DIE IN EUROPE IN WORLD WAR II

On May 7, 1945, the German army surrendered, ending World War II in Europe. It must have taken a while for the news to spread, because a few hours later, in Czechoslovakia, a German Panzer unit attacked the 803rd Tank Destroyer Battalion. Private First Class Charles Havlat of Dorchester, Nebraska, was shot and killed in the melee.

THE LAST PERSON EXECUTED WITH A GUILLOTINE

The guillotine—a machine in which a rapidly descending blade quickly decapitates the condemned—is strongly associated with France, where it was used as capital punishment from the French Revolution in the 1700s until the 1970s. On September 10, 1977, after receiving a death sentence for the murder of his girlfriend, Hamida Djandoubi of Marseilles, France, was executed by guillotine.

THE LAST CIGARETTE AD ON TV

In 1969, the U.S. Office of the Surgeon General released a report with scientific proof of what doctors and scientists had long thought true: that cigarette smoking can lead to health problems, particularly low birth weight if pregnant women light up. Congress passed the Public Health Cigarette Smoking Act, requiring health warning labels on cigarette packs and a ban on cigarette advertising on television. President Nixon signed the order into law on April 1, 1970, and it took effect early the following year. On January 1, 1971, at 11:50 p.m., cigarettes were advertised on American TV for the last time. During a commercial break during *The Tonight Show Starring Johnny Carson*, viewers saw a 60-second spot for Virginia Slims.

Six million years ago, otters were as big as wolves.

IT'S FUNNY MONEY, HONEY

True tales of counterfeit cash.

💰 DEVINE INTERVENTION: Brandy Tuczynski was tending bar at Chumley's in Lafayette, Indiana, when a customer named Earl Devine paid for drinks with a $100 bill. The bill looked phony, so Tuczynski called the cops. Devine was arrested for counterfeiting. Soon after being released on bail a few days later, he was arrested again, for using a fake $100 bill at a drugstore. This time Devine was charged with four counts of forgery. The bills lacked a security thread and were covered in red and blue dots, suggesting they'd been made on a home printer. But there was one other telltale sign: unlike legal $100 bills, they didn't picture Benjamin Franklin. "They all had Abe Lincoln's watermark, which is on the $5 bill," Jeff Rooze of the Lafayette Police Department told reporters.

💰 SWITCHEROO: A Tempe, Arizona, man, Adrian Jean Pineda, worked at a Home Depot from January 2018 to January 2020. Among his daily tasks: rounding up all the cash taken in at the business each day and depositing it at a branch of Wells Fargo bank. Well, most of it. Turns out he regularly pocketed bills from those deposits and replaced them with counterfeit currency of the same denomination. According to federal officials in a news release upon the man's arrest in February 2022, over the two-year period he stole $387,500.

💰 TWO CRIMES FOR THE PRICE OF ONE: In June 2021, police in Waterboro, Maine, were investigating a call about a stolen vehicle when they stopped a pedestrian near the scene. They didn't think the man was involved in the theft, but he was acting suspiciously, so they ran his ID and found an outstanding warrant on a shoplifting charge. The suspect (name not revealed in news reports) had to post $200 in bail. He said he had the money on him, and then handed the bond commissioner two poorly counterfeited $100 bills. Bail denied. The man was taken back to his jail cell, and cops added a charge of forgery to his rap sheet.

💰 ONE BIG CLUE: Authorities in Ontario's Essex County issued an alert in February 2019 warning business owners to look out for counterfeit Canadian $20 notes circulating in the area. According to police, the fake money, used for burning in funeral rituals by members of the area's prominent Chinese community, had been passed at stores, despite lacking metallic strips and other distinguishing characters found on genuine Canadian bills. "These particular bank notes are more noticeably counterfeit, having additional writing prominently displayed on either side of the bills," Essex police said, referring to the fact that the currency is splashed with Chinese characters.

That's using their heads: In the late 1800s, road crews in Argentina filled in potholes with sheep heads.

STRANGE CRIME

Some true crime stories are tough to categorize. They're just...strange. (Shameless plug: For more bizarre stories like these, check out Portable Press's book Strange Crime.*)*

The Choir Boy Robber

From 1998 to 2002, at least 26 seemingly normal bank robberies occurred in the Midwest and California. In each one, a man would walk in wearing regular clothes—his face obscured by sunglasses and a ball cap—and present the teller with a robbery note. (He got the nickname "Choir Boy Robber" for the way he clasped his hands in front of him while waiting for the cash.) By the time police arrived, the man would be long gone, having left no sign of a getaway vehicle. In March 2002, the crook's spree ended after he robbed a bank in Walnut Creek, California, and a responding officer recognized an orange racing bicycle that he'd seen at the site of an earlier robbery. A brief chase ensued, and the crook escaped. But investigators were able to trace the distinctive racing bike and ultimately caught the robber—a 31-year-old Illinois native named Tom Justice.

Here's how Justice did it: After robbing a bank, he would run outside, hide behind something, and quickly remove his pants and shirt to reveal a body-fitting cycling suit. Then he'd stuff the clothes and cash into a messenger bag, hop on his waiting bike, and casually ride away...sometimes waving at cops rushing to the scene.

Justice later told police his crime spree began after a spate of other jobs (including joining the priesthood) didn't pan out. Before that, as a teen, he was an Olympic hopeful for cycling, but that didn't pan out, either. At first he gave away his bank-robbery money to the homeless, but then he got greedy—and sloppy—and spent nine years in federal prison.

Woke Coke

For the discerning cokehead who cares where his drugs come from, "woke coke," as police called it, hit England's black market in 2021. According to UK drug policy expert Neil Woods, the "environmentally friendly sniff" was touted to be "ethically sourced" and was sold to high-end users at posh parties. But it's nothing more than a gimmick, said Woods, as there's no such thing as ethically sourced illegal contraband. He also said that the drugs weren't cheap: "At £200 a gram [$5,670 per ounce], I call it the Woke Coke Con."

Getting Ahead

"Him: what's with the Mellon? Us: it da corona mask." That was the caption below a video uploaded to TikTok in May of 2020. The "Him" refers to the Louisa, Virginia, convenience store clerk who is asking the two men in the video why they are wearing watermelons on their heads. (Earlier that night, they had hollowed out two watermelons and cut eyeholes in them.) The melon heads then proceeded to shoplift some beer, resulting in a call to police (and an APB for two men who might or might not have watermelons on their heads). One melon head was apprehended a few days later (thanks to the TikTok video) and was charged with "wearing a mask in public while committing larceny"; the other melon head remains at large.

Brunk Duffalo

In July 2021, a veterinarian was called to a farm in Gujarat, India, to examine a buffalo that, according to a police report, was "acting strangely" and frothing at the mouth. The vet couldn't figure out what was causing the symptoms, but he did notice that the water in the buffalo's trough was discolored and smelled weird. He later called the police and told them it could be alcohol—which is a big deal in Gujarat, where it's illegal to make, buy, or sell the stuff. The cops raided the farm and discovered 100 bottles of homemade moonshine—worth 3,200 rupees ($400)—hidden on the floor of the trough. A few of the bottles had broken and contaminated the water, which got the buffalo drunk and led to the arrest of three bootlegging farmers.

Orange is the New Birthday Suit

Ruth Bryant was attending her 100th birthday party at her Roxboro, North Carolina, assisted living community when two large sheriff's deputies barged in and said, "Are you Miss Bryant?"

"Depends on what you want."

"We want you." They informed her they had a warrant for her arrest.

"For what!?"

"You went to the fire department and exposed yourself a couple weeks ago." Bryant's family and friends couldn't believe it as the centenarian was handcuffed to her walker and then (slowly) escorted out. When she was placed in the squad car, she kicked at one of the officer's knees. Then, on the ride to the station, Bryant complained that they should arrest whoever made "the low damn seats in all these cars!" At the station, the old woman was booked, had her mug shot taken, and was placed in a holding cell.

> Bryant grinned and started singing, "I'm in the jailhouse now! I finally got here!"

When a cop gave her the standard-issue orange "Person County Jail" T-shirt, Bryant grinned and started singing, "I'm in the jailhouse now! I finally got here!" Turns out that in her century on Earth, Bryant had never gone to jail, so that's what she wanted for her birthday. And the police were happy to oblige. (The fire station incident never really happened.) Only thing: Bryant didn't tell her family that it was all a ruse until after she'd been booked. Her daughter told local reporters that she knew something weird was up, but "I didn't think they'd go *this* far."

Just plane weird: Qatar Airways has a rule
limiting six falcons to a plane's economy class section.

LET ME WRITE SIGN— I SPEAK ENGLISH GOOD

When signs in a non-English-speaking country are presented in English, anything is possible. Here are some real-life examples. Can you figure out what the author meant?

ON A ROAD SIGN IN INDIA:
"Drive carefully:
90% of all People are caused by accidents"

———

AT A GARDEN IN CHINA:
"Do not disturb: tiny grass is dreaming"

———

ON A BANQUET HALL MENU IN PORTUGAL:
"Grilled: Feces, spare ribs, blood"

———

ON A RUSSIAN MENU:
"Sausage in the father-in-law"

———

AT A ZOO IN CHINA:
"The wild monkeys are haunted.
Please keep away."

———

ON A SIGN ON A BEACH IN ISRAEL:
"Noun area bathing adjective forbidden"

———

*FROM A 1962 HONDA
MOTORCYCLE SAFETY GUIDE:*
"Go soothingly on the grease mud, as there
lurks the skid demon. Press the brake foot
as you roll around the corners, and save the
collapse and tie up."

———

AT A BAKERY IN INDIA:
"Pao-Village delivers delicious bread of the
combustion setting up to you. A warm,
fragrant bread becomes happy and full only
because it eats the unit. Please eat it."

———

ON A GUIDE DOG VEST IN CHINA:
"Explosive dog"

*ON A BASEBALL-THEMED DART BOARD
MANUFACTURED IN HONG KONG:*
"Usual ruler of basebalt apply. Three stakes
for an out. A toutball counts as a streic out
not as d third stake any itch that misses
the plate (target zone) is ruled a ball fours
awarbed that past"

———

ON A STORE SIGN IN INDIA:
"Very Suspicious Supermarket"

———

ON A MENU IN EASTERN EUROPE:
"Creamy jail with zucchini, chickpeas,
spinach soy half five"

———

IN A PUBLIC AREA IN PAKISTAN:
"Than 'Q' for not smoking"

———

*ON A CHINESE-MADE STEREO
ADVERTISEMENT:*
"Your ears will get pregnant"

———

ON A DOOR IN JAPAN:
"There is no exit"

———

AT A HOTEL IN SPAIN:
"You should enter dressed and with shoes.
You shouldn't enter wetted."

———

AT A PARK IN THE CANARY ISLANDS:
"We are improving the gardens.
Discuss the discomfort."

———

IN A PUBLIC RESTROOM IN CHINA:
"Toilet button is on your back side"

The original prototype for the television set was called a "shadowgraph."

NAME THAT THING

Uncle John's advice: unless you're willing to accept a satiric, ironic, or funny-but-dumb result, never let the internet vote on naming anything.

NAME THAT MOON: The Search for Extraterrestrial Intelligence Institute, or SETI, held a contest in 2013 to name two moons of the dwarf planet Pluto that had just been discovered. William Shatner, who played Captain Kirk on *Star Trek*, mobilized his fans to cast votes for fictional Trek planets Vulcan and Romulus. Those entries easily won, but a few months later, SETI decided to ignore the contest results and instead named the moons Kerberos and Styx.

NAME THAT SNOWPLOW: In February 2022, the Minnesota Department of Transportation announced the results of its Name-a-Snowplow contest. The top-eight vote getters will appear on new plows stationed across the state. The runaway winner, with more than 40,000 votes: Betty Whiteout, honoring Betty White, the beloved actress who died in December 2021 at age 99. The other winners: Ctrl Salt Delete, The Big Leplowski, Plowasaurus Rex, Scoop Dogg, Blizzard of Oz, No More Mr. Ice Guy, and Edward Blizzardhands.

NAME THAT MUSICAL ACT: "Rickrolling" was a huge, silly internet fad in 2008—online denizens would send someone a link purporting to direct them to an interesting article or site, but instead it would pull up the cheesy music video for Rick Astley's 1988 pop hit "Never Gonna Give You Up." Pranksters pulled off the ultimate "Rickroll" on the 2008 MTV Europe Music Awards. Organizers had added a special category—"Best Act Ever"—to be voted on solely by fans. Viewers could nominate anyone from the history of popular music, and more than 100 million votes were cast via MTV websites. The winner, defeating the Beatles, Britney Spears, Green Day, and U2: Rick Astley.

NAME THAT SPACE STATION MODULE: In 2009, NASA tried to drum up interest in a new space station module by allowing the public to name it. While introducing its own preferred title, Serenity, NASA took any and all suggestions. Stephen Colbert, then host of Comedy Central's *The Colbert Report*, encouraged viewers to vote for "Colbert." After more than 1.1 million votes were collected, Colbert was the overwhelming favorite, garnering 230,500 votes (with Serenity in second place, at 190,000). NASA promptly announced that the poll results were not binding and that it could name the module whatever it wanted, and then announced that the agency had decided on "Tranquility." However, as a gesture of good faith to the ballot-box stuffers, NASA installed a treadmill for astronauts on the space station and named it the Combined Operational Load-Bearing External Resistance Treadmill, or COLBERT.

Athletes who finished outside of the top three in the 1896 Olympics were awarded a bronze medal anyway, as a kind of participation trophy.

ODD PODCASTS

Podcasts have been around since 2004. These days, you can find one on almost any topic that interests you—sports, politics, music, art, news, weather, cooking, pop culture, history, you name it. But if you're in a really weird mood, try one of these.

Where Should We Begin? with Esther Perel. Here's your chance to eavesdrop on complete strangers at their most vulnerable with renowned Belgian psychologist Esther Perel, who records her couples' therapy sessions (with their names left out) and then replays them.

Mish and Zach's Leguizamarama. Two friends (Australian comedians Mish Wittrup and Zachary Ruane) discuss everything that American character actor John Leguizamo has ever been in. They've divided his 40-year-career into stages like "Baby Legs," "Leguizollywood," and "Dadguizamo."

Whatever Happened to Pizza at McDonald's? McDonald's didn't serve pizza in the 1990s, or ever. But that hasn't stopped comedian-turned-investigative journalist Brian Thompson from calling the chain's restaurants and going to their corporate offices to find out what happened to their pizza. The interactions go from polite to surreal as Thompson presses on and on, despite having no evidence to back up his increasingly wild theories. Are there nefarious forces at work trying to make everyone forget that McDonald's served pizza? The answer may shock you.

The WALKING Podcast. Conservationist Jon Mooallem takes long walks in the woods near his home on Bainbridge Island, Washington. He records the audio, but no video, and he doesn't narrate. All you can hear are the sounds of his footsteps, his breathing, the chirping of birds and gurgling of streams, and an occasional hello to another hiker. (And several ad breaks.) It appeared on several "Best Podcasts of 2019" lists.

Keep Classical Weird. Don't think classical music is weird? Check out this podcast from Oregon-based violinist Casey Bozell as she takes a deep-dive with special guests (including "Not Dead Composers") into subjects like "The Fascinating World of Castrati," "Classical and Tik-Tok," "Dirty Mozart," and "Operatic Mad Scenes." Bonus: You'll get bits of inside information from the orchestra, such as what the percussionist sees from the back row, and how difficult it can be to get everyone in tune.

Attention HellMart Shoppers! This serialized horror comedy hearkens back to old radio shows. The setting is a superstore built over the Gates of Hell, where the employees must contend with "psychotic leprechauns, were-chickens, cannibalistic grandmas, incubi, interdimensional pirate attacks, zombie raves, and monkey armies."

Behind the Bastards. Did you know that former Iraqi dictator Saddam Hussein had a second career as a romance novelist? That's the kind of fun fact you'll learn on American journalist Robert Evans's macabre podcast, where he and a guest take a deep dive into the personal lives of infamous figures from the past and present... and then make fun of them. Other targets include Adolf Hitler, Benito Mussolini, Jeff Bezos, and payday loan sharks.

DID YOU KNOW?

Want to start a podcast? You better have a good angle, because it's a crowded field. As of 2021, there are an estimated two million different podcasts available, comprising a total of 48 million individual episodes.

The Pen Addict. In a world overrun by digital, American pen manufacturer Brad Dowdy and British podcaster Myke Hurley team up to celebrate the "analog tools that they love so dearly." Which pen should you use to write the next great novel? What's the current state of the stationary market? Why are colored pencil leads so hard to find? And how should you celebrate Fountain Pen Day (the first Friday of November)? Dive in to the surprisingly rich world of writing things down. Their motto: "There are worse addictions, right?"

Confessions of the Idiots. Australian comedian Sam Peterson and a guest read and react to anonymous online confessions. (Apparently, there are websites where you can post them.) Most of the confessions are too salacious to print here, but they're all really weird—like the young man who habitually snatches butterflies out of the air and eats them whole. "And I can't stop."

Dead Eyes. Delivered with the intensity of a true crime documentary, the "crime" that actor-comedian Connor Ratliff is trying to solve is why he got fired from his small part on the miniseries *Band of Brothers*, an HBO war drama from 2001. Twenty years later, Ratliff seeks out fellow cast and crew members (and celebrity guests) in his quest for the answer. The title was inspired by *Band of Brothers* director Tom Hanks, who remarked that Ratliff has "dead eyes." But maybe there was something else at play.

Song Salad. Shannon (a writer) and her friend Scott (a Broadway composer) pick a random music genre out of a list of 500 and then discuss it. Then they click on Wikipedia's "Random Article" link and learn about a random subject. Then, Shannon pens lyrics about the subject while Scott composes a song in the genre. Result: surprisingly catchy "song salads," like a ska tune about a German model train museum, or an Austropop ditty about Jesus cleansing a leper.

Largest number whose name has only one syllable: twelve.

YOU DIG?

Most of the time when someone digs a hole, all they have to show for their effort is the hole and a mound of dirt. But once in a while someone (or something) gets lucky...

MONEY PIT

Location: A badger den, burrowed into the floor of a cave in Asturias province, northwest Spain

The Hole Story: It's not clear when the badger began digging its den. One guess: January 2021, when a freak snowstorm dumped several inches of snow in the area and sent wildlife scrambling to find food and shelter. Whatever the case, at some point in late 2020 or early 2021 the badger began burrowing into a crack in the floor of the cave.

Discovery! The experience must have been frustrating, because the badger kept hitting metal objects. By the time the den was finished, the badger had dislodged more than 90 objects and scattered them around the entrance to the burrow.

The objects remained there for several months until a local man named Roberto Garcia found them while exploring the cave and quickly recognized them for what they were: a hoard of Roman coins dating between the 3rd and 5th centuries. Garcia reported the find to archaeologists, who discovered more than 100 more coins in the same crack in the cave floor. Because the coins date to the fall of the Roman Empire, when barbarian tribes were driving the Romans out of Spain, it's thought that the owner of the coins may have stuffed them into the crack to protect them from falling into the hands of raiders. It worked—too well. The coins remained safely hidden for some 1,600 years until the badger came along. The cache is the largest hoard of Roman coins ever recovered from inside a cave in Spain. "We've taken out the first deposit, but we think there is a lot more to take out," the lead archaeologist, Dr. Alfonso Fanjul Peraza, told reporters. He plans to explore the cave further to determine whether it was just a hiding place for valuables, or whether people sheltered there as well. "We think it's a reflection of the social and political instability that came along with the fall of Rome—an ideal site to learn more about the people who were living through this transition," he says.

HATCHET MAN

Location: The Tetney Golf Club in northeast England

The Hole Story: In July 2018, workers were using an excavator to dig in a small pond on the golf course.

Discovery! About 12 feet down, the excavator struck something solid—a log, perhaps? Well, sort of. It turned out to be a prehistoric *coffin* made from a

hollowed-out oak log, containing the skeletal remains of a man and a "perfectly preserved axe." The coffin, which was found in pieces, would have been nearly ten feet long and more than three feet wide.

The man in the coffin is believed to have been of high rank, because only important people were laid to rest in hollowed-out logs, and the coffin was interred beneath a large gravel mound, which would have required the efforts of many people to complete. Estimated age of the man and his coffin: about 4,000 years, which dates him to the Bronze Age and the dawn of European civilization. To date, fewer than 70 such coffins and only 12 intact axes from the period have ever been found in Britain. Golf course owner Mark Casswell said he was shocked by the discovery. "My family farmed here for years before opening the golf course," he told reporters. "I'd never imagined that there was a whole other world there buried under the fields...it's certainly something to think about while you're playing your way around the course."

UNDER WORLDS

Location: The basement of the building at 56 Via Ascanio Grandi in Lecce, Italy

The Hole Story: In 2000, a man named Luciano Faggiano bought the building and made plans to turn it into a casual restaurant called a *trattoria*. The only problem: the toilet on the ground floor was connected to a leaky sewer pipe, and the floor was damp. Faggiano, with help from his two sons, began digging up the floor to find the leak in the sewer pipe so that they could repair it. He estimated the repair would take about a week.

Discovery! It ended up taking *15 years*. As he dug, Faggiano discovered a false floor, and beneath that he found a medieval stone floor. Beneath that was a tomb... and a chamber that the ancient Romans used to store grain...and the basement of a Franciscan convent used to prepare dead bodies for burial.

And that was just the beginning. The city of Lecce, located in the heel of the boot of the Italian peninsula, has been described as a "layer cake" of civilizations built one atop another—Greek, Roman, Ottoman, Norman, Lombard—over more than 2,000 years. The basement beneath Faggiano's building, it turns out, was built atop the ruins of just about every one of those civilizations. From 2000 to 2015, he excavated the site at his own expense (but supervised by a government-appointed archaeologist) and recovered more than 5,000 artifacts, including coins, pottery, ceramics, statues, a gold bishop's ring with 33 emeralds, and even children's toys made from terra-cotta.

Faggiano eventually even found the leak in the sewer pipe and repaired the leaky toilet. In 2019, he finally opened his trattoria...in the building next door. The original building, 56 Via Ascanio Grandi, is now the Museum Faggiano, complete with a glass floor and a spiral staircase that lets visitors view and even climb down into the underground chambers. Faggiano and his extended family operate both the museum

All the air on Earth weighs 11 quintillion pounds.

and the trattoria. "My father would prefer once people come visit the museum, then they visit the trattoria," his son Andrea told the BBC. "If they visit both, it's better."

LONG-TERM PARKING

Location: The backyard of a home in the West Athens neighborhood of Los Angeles

The Hole Story: According to news reports, in February 1978, a group of kids were playing in a neighbor's backyard, digging a hole, when they hit a horizontal metal surface. They were so intrigued by what it might be that they flagged down a passing L.A. County Sheriff's Office patrol car and told the deputy what they'd found.

Discovery! The deputy got the permission of the people living in the house to enlarge the hole. With a little more digging, his team of investigators discovered that the flat surface was the roof of a car that had been buried in the backyard. Not just any car, either: it was a 1974 Ferrari Dino that had been reported stolen four years earlier, barely a month after the owner purchased it.

So what was the car doing in the hole? One theory: the thieves stole it to "chop" it and sell the parts on the black market, but could not bring themselves to dismantle such a beautiful car. Instead, they decided to keep it for themselves and buried it with the plan of someday digging it up, stuffing the intake and exhaust pipes with towels to keep out moisture. The car was later sold at auction for less than $9,000 to an auto mechanic, who repaired, repainted, and restored it to running condition. It's still on the road today, and easy to spot if you live in Southern California: it's the metallic green Ferrari Dino with the California license plate DUG UP. Estimated value: between $420,000 and $480,000.

I'M ON SAPPHIRE

Location: The city of Ratnapura, Sri Lanka, a center of the country's precious-stone-mining industry

The Hole Story: In 2021, a Sri Lankan man (identified in press reports only as "Mr. Gamage") hired some workers to dig a well in his yard.

Discovery! Because rubies, sapphires, and other gems are mined in the area, it probably came as no surprise to the workers when they found some precious stones while digging the well. The digging stopped, the stones were collected, and work resumed. That's when Mr. Gamage says they discovered a "sapphire cluster," or giant rock consisting of dozens or perhaps hundreds of sapphires stuck together in clay. The Serendipity Sapphire, as it has been named, weighs more than 1,120 lbs., making it one of the largest such clusters—if not *the* largest—ever found. It still needs to be broken apart to remove the sapphires (unless it's kept intact and put on display in a museum), but if enough of the sapphires are high quality, the giant rock could be worth as much as $100 million.

Dolphins will allow other trusted adult dolphins to babysit their children.

MOUTHING OFF

PARENTHOOD

Having a child is simple; raising one is hard.

"It just occurred to me that the majority of my diet is made up of the foods that my kid didn't finish."
—Carrie Underwood

"If you're not yelling at your kids, you're not spending enough time with them."
—Reese Witherspoon

"You want to know what it's like having a fourth kid? Imagine you're drowning, then someone hands you a baby."
—Jim Gaffigan

"I've noticed that one thing about parents is that no matter what stage your child is in, the parents who have older children always tell you the next stage is worse."
—Dave Barry

"HAVING CHILDREN IS LIKE LIVING IN A FRAT HOUSE—NOBODY SLEEPS, EVERYTHING IS BROKEN, AND THERE'S A LOT OF THROWING UP."
—Ray Romano

"Having a baby dragged me, kicking and screaming, from the world of self-absorption."
—Paul Reiser

"One thing I had learned from watching chimpanzees with their infants is that having a child should be fun."
—Jane Goodall

"Having an infant son alerts to me the fact that every man, at one point has peed on his own face."
—Olivia Wilde

"WHEN YOUR CHILDREN ARE TEENAGERS, IT'S IMPORTANT TO HAVE A DOG SO THAT SOMEONE IN THE HOUSE IS HAPPY TO SEE YOU."
—Nora Ephron

FAMOUS NAME FOOD FLOPS

Just because a restaurant carries a famous name doesn't guarantee success. Here are some very big companies that couldn't make it in the cutthroat world of food service.

MICKEY'S KITCHEN

In the late 1980s, Disney opened a chain of Disney Store mall shops, selling Disney-branded clothing, toys, and collectibles. Business was booming to the point that Disney decided to expand its retail footprint into fast food. In 1990, the company opened two Mickey's Kitchen outlets, one at a Los Angeles mall and the other in a shopping center outside of Chicago. Diners were greeted by a statue of Mickey Mouse in a chef's hat, and ate in a dining room covered in framed movie posters and stills from Disney movies. On the menu: standard family restaurant fare with pun-heavy, Disney-oriented names, such as the Supercalifragi-Chicken Salad (*Mary Poppins*), Salad-in-Wonderland (*Alice in Wonderland*), and Soup-A-Dee-Doo-Dah (*Song of the South*). Mickey's Kitchen also tried to present itself as a healthier alternative to mall food courts, featuring turkey hot dogs and Mickey's Meatless Burgers. But despite the allure of the Disney brand, neither location turned a profit and the company closed both of them down in 1992.

YOGI BEAR'S HONEY FRIED CHICKEN

The fastest-growing fast-food restaurant in the United States in the 1960s: Kentucky Fried Chicken. Naturally, other entrepreneurs tried to get in on the popularity of fried chicken, including a successful chain restaurant operator from South Carolina named Eugene Broome. In 1966, some of his restaurants started offering fried chicken made with a honey-flavored additive, and Broome decided to build a chain around it. To bring attention to his new venture, Broome pursued TV star Jackie Gleason to license his name, image, and catchphrase, pitching Jackie Gleason's Honey Fried Chicken with the marketing slogan "How sweet it is!" Gleason said no, and Broome, after seeing a Yogi Bear cartoon on TV one day, decided to use the cartoon character instead. He licensed the rights from Hanna-Barbera and named the new chain Yogi Bear's Honey Fried Chicken. Amazingly, before a single outlet could open, Hardee's bought the concept from Broome and opened 11 Yogi Bear's Honey Fried Chicken stores in 1968. Less amazingly: by 1971, all but two were closed. Industry analysts blamed the failure on the fact that fried chicken appealed to adults, while the chain's cartoon branding appealed to children. One more Yogi Bear's Honey Fried Chicken shut down in 1979, but as of 2022, there's still one open in Hartsville, South Carolina.

S'not a joke: Parrotfish sleep in a mucus cocoon of their own making to ward off predators and protect against parasites. They make a new one every night; it takes about an hour.

MARVEL MANIA

In the 21st century, movies featuring Marvel superheroes are billion-dollar box office draws. In the late 1990s, comics and superheroes were still a niche entertainment, but that didn't stop Marvel from opening a themed restaurant called Marvel Mania at the Universal Studios amusement park in 1998. As Planet Hollywood was to movies and Hard Rock Cafe was to music, Marvel Mania would be to superheroes, with menu items named after characters—Fantastic Four Cheese Pizza, Doc Ock's Wok Stir Fry, Gambit's Ragin' Cajun Quesadillas (Gambit was an X-Man of Cajun descent)—and memorabilia lining the walls. While the waitstaff zipped around tables and multiple big-screen TVs showed old Marvel Comics Saturday morning cartoons from the 1970s, actors dressed as Wolverine and the Incredible Hulk greeted diners. Marvel Mania lasted slightly more than a year, closing down in September 1999.

KENTUCKY ROAST BEEF

Kentucky Fried Chicken started out in a gas station in North Corbin, Kentucky, where Harlan Sanders sold Southern-style dinners—fried chicken and country ham—out of a tiny dining room in the 1930s. By 1964, when Sanders sold Kentucky Fried Chicken, it numbered more than 600 outlets, and under new management it exploded to 1,700 locations by 1968. To head off rival companies such as Chick-Fil-A and Church's, KFC execs decided to test out serving roast beef and ham at locations separate from the chicken places. The pilot location of Kentucky Roast Beef opened in Las Vegas in 1968 and in its first month sold nearly $100,000 worth of 79-cent roast beef sandwiches (slow-cooked meat with "zestful flavoring" served on a buttered bun), a rousing success that prompted KFC to open 100 more stores over the next two years. But outside of Las Vegas, where money flowed because people were on vacation, the sandwich flopped. True, it cost only 79 cents, but a full chicken dinner with sides at Kentucky Fried Chicken cost only 85 cents. Not only was that a better value for customers, the profit margin on the chicken dinner was better than on the roast beef sandwich. A few Kentucky Fried Chickens in cities where the sandwich had been popular added roast beef to their menus through the 1970s, but Kentucky Fried Roast Beef as a separate entity was gone by 1978.

*   *   *

REJECTS WANTED

The Journal of Universal Rejection is a satire of academic publications. Editors jokingly adhere to a policy of rejecting "all submissions, regardless of quality." Twelve issues of the journal have been published—all of them consisting entirely of blank pages.

A quarter of the world's hazelnut crop is used to make Nutella.

SILLY WORLD RECORDS

Uncle John holds the unofficial record for "Most Books Read in the Bathroom." (He reckons at least a million.) Here are some other strange achievements...that are actually real records.

Largest Ball of Human Hair: His name is Hoss. He's as tall as a human and weighs 225 pounds. Constructed over a period of eight years by Cambridge, Ohio, hairstylist Steve Warden, Hoss is made of liquid glue, hair spray...and hair from the heads and beards of 3,000 client-donors. At last report, the multicolored hair ball—adorned with Mr. Potato Head-esque facial features—was traveling the country with the Ripley's Believe It or Not! Roadshow.

Most Tennis Balls Held in the Mouth by a Dog: In 2003, a golden retriever named Augie set this record with five tennis balls. Nearly 15 years later, another golden retriever, this one named Finley, surprised his owner, Erin Molloy of Canandaigua, New York, when he dropped six tennis balls from his mouth at her feet. Molloy said they didn't train the dog to hoard tennis balls; he just likes to. In 2020, Finley's record of six was verified by Guinness. (Anyone for seven?)

Most M&M's Stacked on Top of One Another: During England's third COVID-19 lockdown in 2021, Will Cutbill alleviated his boredom by trying to beat the world record for M&M's balanced on top of one another. "It's a lot harder than you think," he said. After hundreds of failures, the British engineer's persistence finally paid off: a stack of five perfectly balanced M&M's.

Longest Laugh in TV History: On a 1965 episode of *The Tonight Show*, guest Ed Ames (he played an American Indian named "Mingo" on the TV show *Daniel Boone*) was showing host Johnny Carson the proper way to throw a tomahawk. The target: the outline of a cowboy, drawn onto a piece of plywood. A hush filled the studio as the tomahawk flew across the stage. But Ames's aim was off; the axe struck, as sidekick Ed McMahon recalled, "where no cowboy should be struck." There was a gasp followed by silence...and then the audience erupted into sustained laughter that was kept alive by three perfectly timed Carson quips: "I didn't even know you were Jewish," "welcome to Frontier Bris," and, when Ames asked Carson to try it, "I couldn't hurt him any more than you did!" When the guffaws finally died down, four minutes had passed. It's still regarded as the longest TV laugh of all time.

Longest Run without Going Anywhere: At a long-distance running tournament held in Poland in 2021, the Gold Medals in both the men's and women's categories were won by Ukrainians. Over a 48-hour period, Andriy Tkachuk ran 254.76 miles, and Valentina Kovalskaya ran 210.65 miles, but despite the fact that they were setting world records, the number of actual miles they covered was zero. Reason: it was the Treadmill World Cup.

Largest Underwater Human Pyramid: In 2013, two Americans and an Aussie (Tyler Reiser, Manolo Cabasal, and John Shaddick) recruited 62 scuba divers. They swam to the sea floor in Thailand's Mango Bay and arranged themselves into a pyramid—with 16 on the bottom layer, seven divers high—and held that position for 30 seconds to set this world record.

Most Pencils in a Beard: In September 2021, Joel Strasser of Dupont, Washington, appeared on *Live with Kelly and Ryan* to break his own world record of 450 pencils stuck into his big, burly beard. Throughout the show, cohost Ryan Seacrest was mesmerized by Strasser's progress. "He kept coming over in the commercials," said Strasser, "and he really wanted to touch my pencil-beard. Kelly [Ripa] was like, 'Stop. Get away from him. You're going to mess him up.'" By the time the episode was over, Strasser had successfully stuck 456 pencils into his beard, which he then allowed Seacrest to touch.

> By the time the episode was over, Strasser had successfully stuck 456 pencils into his beard.

Tallest Hat: An eccentric hatmaker from Tampa, Florida, named Odilon Ozare (which might be his stage name) spent a year wrapping white felt around a telephone pole in his backyard to construct a 15-foot, 9-inch stovepipe hat, sparsely decorated with peacock feathers. Ozare's creation set the official world record in 2018 when, as stipulated by Guinness, he walked 10 meters (32 feet, 10 inches) without the hat falling off.

Most Stuffed Animals Tossed Onto the Ice: January 22, 2022, was "Teddy Bear Night" at the Hershey Bears minor league hockey game in Pennsylvania. Fans were asked to bring a teddy bear (or several) to the game and then, when the home team scored its first goal, throw the stuffed animals onto the ice. And that's what they did. The game was delayed for 45 minutes to clean up and count the toys, which were then donated to local charity organizations. Final tally: 52,341 stuffed animals, a new world record.

Longest Stand-up Comedy Routine: The East Room in Nashville, Tennessee, hosted this weeklong record attempt in 2015. Bookended by producers/comedians DJ Buckley and Chad Riden, dozens of local comics signed up for 15- or 30-minute spots—along with a few big names, like Hannibal Buress, Eric Andre, and Ahmed Ahmed. The comics told jokes nonstop for 184 hours and 16 minutes, ending precisely at 4:20 a.m. on 4/20. Afterward, Riden vowed to try it again next year: "I want to break our own record by five minutes just to show that we know how silly and pointless this all is."

Stomach acid can burn a hole through human skin.

THE OFFICE, STARRING JAMES GANDOLFINI

Some actors are so closely associated with a specific role or TV series that it's
hard to imagine he or she wasn't necessarily the producers'
first choice. But it happens all the time.

GROWING PAINS, STARRING BRUCE WILLIS

ABC's answer to NBC's *The Cosby Show*: a sitcom about a psychiatrist who practices from home, where he also keeps an eye on his kids while his wife works as a reporter. Cast as the father, Dr. Jason Seaver, on *Growing Pains*: Alan Thicke, who had hosted a couple of game shows on Canadian TV in the 1970s, and was the host of the hit daytime talk show *The Alan Thicke Show* in the early 1980s. By 1985, ABC wanted the right shows for Thicke and another actor, up-and-comer Bruce Willis. The network had two shows in need of a star: *Growing Pains* and the detective series *Moonlighting*. Thicke got *Growing Pains* because he had great chemistry with the actress already cast as his TV wife, Joanna Kerns; Willis wound up on the Emmy-winning *Moonlighting*.

LAVERNE & SHIRLEY, STARRING GILDA RADNER

Garry Marshall created *Happy Days* and then its spin-off, *Laverne & Shirley*, which centered on two characters from the original show: Laverne, played by Marshall's sister, Penny Marshall, and Shirley, portrayed by *American Graffiti* actor Cindy Williams. But Williams's movie career was starting to take off, so at first she declined the role of Shirley on the spin-off series. After some underwhelming auditions, Penny Marshall set out to find a new Shirley, and in late 1975 she approached Gilda Radner, who had become famous just weeks earlier as one of the original cast members of *Saturday Night Live*. When Radner opted to stay with *SNL*, *Laverne & Shirley* producers reached out to actress Liberty Williams (no relation). She aced a screen test and even shot publicity photos with Penny Marshall...and was then dumped when Cindy Williams decided she wanted to do *Laverne & Shirley* after all.

PUNKY BREWSTER, STARRING MELISSA JOAN HART

To find the plucky, pint-size street kid who would play Penelope "Punky" Brewster, NBC held national auditions, seeing about 3,000 young actresses for the role. Two of the finalists: Soleil Moon Frye and Melissa Joan Hart. Frye got the part, but Hart didn't do too badly, going on to star on the '90s teen sitcoms *Clarissa Explains It All* and *Sabrina the Teenage Witch*. (Frye later joined the cast of *Sabrina* as the teenage witch's best friend, Roxie King.)

SATURDAY NIGHT LIVE, STARRING JOHNNY KNOXVILLE

Aspiring actor Philip John Clapp Jr.—who uses the stage name Johnny Knoxville (he's from Knoxville, Tennessee)—couldn't find much work in the 1990s, so he created a gig for himself: He pitched a piece to skateboarding magazine *Big Brother* in which he would be a living test subject for self-defense gear. Editor Jeff Tremaine ran the piece and also released a video of Knoxville willingly being attacked with a stun gun and pepper spray. The video did so well that Tremaine wanted more, and introduced Knoxville to a group of skateboarders who made videos of themselves performing crazy stunts and pranks. The group then made a pilot episode for a TV series, consisting of themselves performing more dangerous (but entertaining) acts of nihilism, and they pitched it to several shows, including *Saturday Night Live*. The late-night sketch series, which has almost always included some kind of pretaped element, offered Knoxville and his so-called "Jackass" crew a weekly showcase for one of their wild stunts. But Knoxville turned down the spot because MTV offered the group a weekly half-hour standalone *Jackass* series. Then *SNL* producers asked Knoxville to be part of the show's regular cast. He passed on that one too, because unlike on *Jackass*, "none of my friends were really going to be there and I had no control."

THE OFFICE, STARRING JAMES GANDOLFINI

After seven seasons portraying the world's worst boss on *The Office*, Steve Carell left the show, and a high-profile hunt was on for an actor who could possibly replace Carell, who'd racked up six Emmy nominations playing the lovably odious office manager Michael Scott. After Will Ferrell, Idris Elba, Kathy Bates, and James Spader each joined the cast for awhile, playing a succession of idiosyncratic managers, producers promoted cast member Ed Helms, as Andy Bernard, to head Dunder Mifflin's Scranton branch. But according to *Office* writer and costar B. J. Novak, the show aggressively pursued James Gandolfini, who had recently ended his acclaimed role as mob boss Tony Soprano on HBO's *The Sopranos*. "The way Michael Scott will say something very serious but mispronounce a word I feel is a direct descendant of the Tony Soprano sense of humor. I thought he would've been an incredible replacement. I really, really wanted to work with him," Novak told Andy Cohen on TV's *Watch What Happens Live*. Gandolfini—who planned to play the new boss as a tough "blue-collar guy"—wanted the role and NBC offered him a $4 million contract. But HBO made him an offer he couldn't refuse: they paid him $3 million . . . to walk

Wet...dry...wet...dry: In the early 1950s,
airlines wouldn't serve alcohol when flying over states where booze was illegal.

away and *not* take the part. Reason: they didn't want Gandolfini starring on a sitcom, fearing it might tarnish the legacy of *The Sopranos*.

GILLIGAN'S ISLAND, STARRING JERRY VAN DYKE AND RAQUEL WELCH

When the desert island castaway show *Gilligan's Island* premiered in 1964, Bob Denver was the best-known cast member, having starred as beatnik Maynard G. Krebs on the popular sitcom *The Many Loves of Dobie Gillis*. However, he wasn't the first choice to play the marooned bumbling first mate Gilligan—Jerry Van Dyke was. Van Dyke was offered the lead role in two new shows: *Gilligan's Island* and *My Mother the Car*. He took *My Mother the Car*, a show about a man whose dead mother's soul inhabits his car, which was quickly canceled and later named by *TV Guide* as the worst sitcom of all time. Other casting almosts: Future *9 to 5* star Dabney Coleman might have been cast as the Professor if not for his terrible screen test, and producers narrowly selected Alan Hale Jr. over *All in the Family* star Carroll O'Connor to play the Skipper. Silver-screen pinups Jayne Mansfield and Raquel Welch were offered the roles of Ginger and Mary Ann, respectively, and both declined.

FANTASY ISLAND, STARRING ORSON WELLES

Fantasy Island was an anthology series that aired from 1977 to 1984. Each week, new arrivals would come to the tropical island to live out their biggest wishes, only for things to inevitably turn dark and go awry. There were only two recurring characters for most of the show's run: the island's proprietor, Mr. Roarke, portrayed by Ricardo Montalbán, and his assistant, Tattoo, portrayed by Hervé Villechaize. Executive producer Aaron Spelling fought with ABC over the casting of both. The network wanted a bigger star, preferably one from Hollywood's Golden Age, suggesting both John Huston and Orson Welles. And instead of the diminutive, sycophantic Tattoo, ABC executives wanted Mr. Roarke's assistant to be a statuesque blond woman. Spelling got his way...at least initially. When Villechaize left *Fantasy Island* briefly in 1981, his replacement was the young, blond Wendy Schaal, portraying Mr. Roarke's niece, Julie.

* * *

JOHNNY, ROY, AND THE PONYTAIL

In 1988, Johnny Cash made a pact with fellow music legend Roy Orbison, who was terminally ill, that they would both grow their hair long enough to wear in a ponytail. As Cash later admitted, he'd had no intention of actually following through. A few months later, at Orbison's funeral, Cash looked into the casket and started laughing when he saw Orbison's hair was in a ponytail.

Odds that an astronaut who walked on the Moon was born in Texas: 1 in 4.

FLUBBED HEADLINES

Here are some honest-to-goodness headlines, providing that even the most careful editors sometimes make mistooks.

Responsibility to Regulate Open Burning Shits to Village

FILING FOR MUNICIPAL EXECUTIONS OPENS SOON

Our Mother's Panty Provides Some Basic Needs for More Than 200 People a Month

7,000 Cops Undergo Sexual Harassment Training Online

Boil Water Advisory Issued for Potter, Raccoon

Host Remains Deviant after Defending Sex Criminal

11th Annual Online Auction for Children

Antibusing Rider Killed by Senate

Putting Your Baby to Sleep: Some Advice and Good News

TRAMP TAX CUT IS ALREADY WORKING

Uranus to Make a Splash Tomorrow Night

Astronomers Spot X-Rays Coming from Uranus

Kelly Ripa Slammed While Examining Potato Chips in Tight Pants

City Still Working to Get Smart

Man Drives Injured Friend to Hospital in Stolen Caterpillar

State Population to Double by 2040; Babies to Blame

Judge Warns Shoplifter: Think of What's in Store

Cops Say Man Concealed Crack in His Underwear

Canada hosted the Summer Olympics in 1976…and didn't win a single gold medal.

WORD ORIGINS

Ever wonder where words come from? So do we.

VET

Meaning: To evaluate something for possible approval or acceptance

Origin: "*Vet* has only fairly recently become the word du jour among writers and pundits in the United States, but it has been in use in Britain since the turn of the 20th century. Perhaps the most surprising thing about *vet* is its origin, because it seems almost too simple. *Vet*, the verb, like *vet* the noun, is a shortening of *veterinarian*, and *to vet* originally meant 'to have an animal thoroughly examined by a vet.' *Veterinarian*, in turn, comes from the Latin *veterinae*, or 'cattle,' which constituted the bulk of early veterinarians' patients." (From *The Word Detective*, by Evan Morris)

MUSEUM

Meaning: A building where objects of cultural significance are stored and exhibited

Origin: "The Nine Muses were the children of Zeus and Mnemosyne and were originally the goddesses of memory, later to be identified with particular sciences and arts. The word *museum* is literally the home or seat of the Muses. The first building so named was erected by Ptolemy at Alexandria about 300 B.C." (From *Word Origins: The Romance of Language*, by Cecil Hunt)

HELICOPTER

Meaning: An aircraft that derives both lift and propulsion from overhead rotors

Origin: "There's nothing wrong with this evocative word for what is more generically called a rotating-wing aircraft, since it derives, via French—from the Greek words *helix*, 'a spiral,' plus *pteron*, 'a wing.' It's what people have done with it that puts it into the class of false etymology. Understandably enough, the correct division of the word into its elements *helico-* and *pter-* doesn't occur to anyone, a split into *heli-* plus *copter-* being preferred. As a result, a number of compounds have been created—as in *helipad*, *heliport*, and *heliskiing*. This misapprehension is now much too firmly fixed in the language for even the most die-hard of pedants to contemplate countering." (From *Ballyhoo, Buckaroo, and Spuds: Ingenious Tales of Words and Their Origins*, by Michael Quinion)

BELITTLE

Meaning: To make (someone or something) seem unimportant

Origin: "Thomas Jefferson coined the word *belittle* in about 1780 and Noah Webster included it in his 1828 dictionary, but many critics denounced it as an incurably vulgar term, one going so far as to say, 'It has no visible chance of becoming English.' The condemnations went on for almost a century, but needless to say all the belittling of *belittle* failed to ban the word from the language." (From *The Facts on File Encyclopedia of Word and Phrase Origins*, by Robert Hendrickson)

LIVE

Meaning: A performance or event that is listened to or watched at the time of its occurrence

Origin: "Modern recording technology has broken the bond between time and events, posing an existential challenge to the concept 'alive.' Dead performers can now speak on the radio and move on the screen, and need to be distinguished from those who are actually breathing at the moment of transmission. The word first appeared in the 1934 *BBC Year-Book*: 'Listeners have complained...that recorded material was too liberally used...but transmitting hours to the Canadian and Australasian zones are inconvenient for broadcasting "live" material.'" (From *Movers and Shakers: A Chronology of Words that Shaped Our Age*, by John Ayto)

TIDE

Meaning: The alternate rising and falling of the sea and other large bodies of water

Origin: "The words *tide* and *time* are related, both going back to the Indo-European root *da-*, 'to divide,' and were once synonyms, both meaning 'an interval or division of time.' This sense for *tide* is now obsolete. The modern meaning of *tide*, 'the periodic variation in the surface level of the earth's waters,' is a development of the word's original meaning, since the tides rise and fall at predictable times of the day." (From *Word Histories and Mysteries: From Abracadabra to Zeus*, by the Editors of the American Heritage Dictionaries)

MILK

Meaning: An opaque white fluid rich in fat and protein, secreted by female mammals for their young; as a verb, the act of drawing milk

Origin: "The word *milk*, dating from before the 12th century, is from the Old English *meole* and is derived from the Indo-European root *melg*, meaning 'to squeeze out,' as an animal's udder is worked for its fluid. In a sense, a child asking for a glass of milk is asking that an udder be squeezed." (From *Sexy Origins and Intimate Things*, by Charles Panati)

> **DID YOU KNOW?**
>
> What's the difference between "heavy cream" and "heavy whipping cream"? Dairies add a protein to the latter that makes it easier to whip.

LIFE IN THE 2020s

Disappointed that things don't quite measure up to the way you imagined life in "the future" would be? You're not alone. It didn't pan out the way trend watchers, psychics, experts, and imaginative writers thought it would, either. Here are some predictions about the world in the far off year of 2020.

HIGH-SPEED TRANSPORT: According to a 1957 *Popular Science* article about life in 2020, roads were supposed to have been replaced with a massive "network of pneumatic tubes." Like those things that banks use at the drive-up window to send capsules filled with deposit slips and checks to the teller, the pneumatic tube system was supposed to send people (in capsules) shooting along "to any desired destination."

SERVICE TECHNOLOGY: In 1967, the RAND Corporation, an influential research and development think tank ("RAND" actually stands for "research and development"), released a report stating that by 2020 "it may be possible to breed intelligent species of animals, such as apes, that will be capable of performing manual labor." RAND predicted that we'd all have "a live-in ape to do the cleaning" and a chimp chauffeur, which would somehow "decrease the number of automobile accidents."

BRAINPOWER: The 1995 sci-fi movie *Johnny Mnemonic* is loosely based on a 1981 short story by William Gibson about a man living in a dystopian 2021, by which time corporations completely control the world. Johnny Mnemonic works as an information courier—he uploads sensitive data into his brain. His maximum capacity: a massive 80 gigabytes...which is about the same amount of storage as a standard smartphone.

GLOBAL UNITY: Rudy Rucker's 1982 novel *Software* posited that by the time the 2020s began, the people of Earth have united in order to defeat a common enemy: hostile humanoid robots who have built colonies on the Moon.

DRASTIC DIETARY CHANGES: In a 1913 *New York Times* article, American Meat Packers Association president Gustav Bischoff forecasted a future in which meat would be in such short supply that only the super-rich could afford it. Everyone else, he said, would have to adopt a vegetarian lifestyle, subsisting on rice and vegetables, creating a population of "slothful creatures, anemic and without initiative."

EVERYTHING WILL BE METAL: According to a 1911 interview with inventor and industrialist Thomas Edison, the future would be made of steel. Edison predicted that by the 2020s, all home furnishings, from dining tables to baby cradles, would be made from steel, books would be printed on ultra-thin sheets of nickel, and, because scientists

By the 2020s, the average woman would stand more than six feet tall.

would have perfected a process to transmute common metals into precious metals, cars would be made of gold.

LIFE ON MARS: In 1997, the editors of the technology magazine *Wired* predicted that in 2020, humans would arrive on Mars and start building life on a second planet.

THE STRONGER SEX: Dorothy Roe Lewis wrote a popular syndicated column in the mid-20th century and, in a 1950 installment, predicted that women would evolve physically over the following 70 years. By the 2020s, she predicted, the average woman would stand more than six feet tall, wear size 11 shoes, and have the broad shoulders of a wrestler with "muscles like a truck driver."

FEWER TOES: A doctor named Richard Clement Lucas gave a lecture to the Royal College of Surgeons of England in 1911, in which he foresaw the human foot evolving rapidly over the next century. "The small toes are being used less and less as time goes on, while the great toe is developing in an astonishing manner." By around 2020, Lucas believed, "man might become a one-toed race."

MOBILE HOUSES: Arthur C. Clarke, best known for his science-fiction writing (he cowrote the screenplay for *2001: A Space Odyssey*), also wrote extensively about science and technology. And according to a 1966 article, by 2020 technology would have advanced to a point where a house "would have no roots tying it to the ground," with independent water, electrical, and sewer systems. "The autonomous home could therefore move, or be moved, to anywhere on Earth at the owner's whim," Clarke wrote.

DAILY PLEASURES: Inventor Nikola Tesla wrote in 1937 that by the 2020s, "coffee, tea, and tobacco will no longer be in vogue." But alcohol, he said, would remain popular because it is "a veritable elixir of life."

ATOMIC APPLIANCES: Lewyt Vacuum Cleaner Company president Alex Lewyt saw a brave new world ahead for vacuum cleaners. In 1955, he envisioned a 2020 in which "nuclear-powered vacuum cleaners" would be the new standard in cleaning technology.

EVERYTHING IS DISPOSABLE: In 1950, *New York Times* science writer Waldemar Kaempffert imagined life in the early decades of the 21st century. Cities, he wrote, would be arranged around airports, which would be located in the center, surrounded by concentric rings of factories, hotels, and homes. People would travel on double-decker highways that have "hardly any curves" while houses would cost $5,000 and be totally weatherproof but also designed to fall apart within 25 years. Dishes would be disposable, composed of cheap plastics made from oat hulls, soybeans, and fruit pits. In another manufacturing breakthrough, Kaempffert predicted, used rayon underwear would be "bought by chemical factories to be converted into candy."

Can they talk? Falcons are more closely related to parrots than other birds of prey.

ALL-AMERICAN INVENTOR

In August 2021, Ohio-based inventor Don Poynter died at age 96. Never heard of him? He was a prolific inventor, with more than 100 patents, and he made a fortune off his gadgets, almost all of them silly novelty, gift, and junk items. Maybe you remember some of these.

Genuine Rye Whiskey–Flavored Toothpaste (introduced in 1955). It really tasted like whiskey. Why? Because it had a 3 percent alcohol content. It also came in Scotch and bourbon varieties.

Jayne Mansfield Hot Water Bottle (1957). A therapeutic hot water bottle made in the image of bikini-clad bombshell Jayne Mansfield (who actually posed for Poynter).

Little Black Box (1959). A black plastic box with a switch on top. When the user flipped the switch, the box vibrated, and then a mechanical hand emerged from within to flip the switch back off. ("Mysterious! Sinister! Unearthly!") In 1964, Poynter introduced an updated Little Black Box—a licensed version of the disembodied hand (named Thing) from the TV show *The Addams Family*— and sold 14 million units.

The Antmobile (1960). Sold by Ripley's Believe It or Not!, these model building kits produced a car so tiny that you could fit several in the palm of your hand. Kids were told they could capture a carpenter ant and get it to drive the car.

Uncle Fester's Mystery Light Bulb (1965). Another *Addams Family*-branded toy, this novelty light bulb flashed on when placed in an ear or mouth, just the way the creepy Uncle Fester did it on the TV show.

Executive Waste Basket Ball (1966). It's the first-ever (and often imitated) miniature basketball backboard meant to fit over an office trash can.

Mighty Tiny, the "World's Smallest Record Player" (1967). It came with three two-inch-wide records that played 15-second snippets of songs like "Turkey in the Straw."

Go-Go Girl Drink Mixer (1969). Place this Barbie-like doll (dressed in a skimpy go-go dancer outfit) on top of your cocktail glass. With the push of a button, she'd shake, shimmy, and twist her hips to stir the drink.

Golfer's Dream: Hole-in-One Golf Ball (1970). It's a gag gift based on a play on words. It was a golf ball with a hole drilled into it—a *literal* "hole-in-one" ball. (Get it?)

Talking Toilet (1971). A motion-activated device placed on a toilet to prank guests. When somebody sat down, a voice would call out "Hey, you're blocking the light!"

The Thinking Man's Crossword Toilet Tissue (1975). Poynter was the first person to make novelty toilet paper, printing crossword puzzles on a roll, a pre–Uncle John way of providing entertainment to an otherwise captive audience.

Staying power: In 2020, Americans collectively watched 57 billion minutes of *The Office*, which ended production in 2013.

LOCAL HEROES

*Now for some stories that will restore your faith in humanity,
brought to you by the kindness of strangers.*

A SAVE AND A HAIRCUT

In July 2021, a 36-year-old mother (name not released) was carrying her eight-month-old daughter across the street in Yonkers, New York, when a drunk driver came around the corner too fast, hit a parked car, and kept coming. The mom started to run, but there was no time: the car ran her over and then crashed through a barbershop window before coming to a halt. Two police officers having breakfast at a nearby bagel shop rushed over. The mother was badly hurt and calling for her baby girl...who was trapped underneath the vehicle! One officer and several bystanders lifted the car high enough for the other officer to reach underneath it, and, after a tense moment, everyone heard "I got it! I got the baby!" The infant suffered a fractured skull and severe burns, and her mom had a broken femur, but both were expected to make full recoveries. The 43-year-old drunk driver, David Poncurak, wasn't injured, nor was his female passenger. They were both arrested. The actions of the two officers and the people who helped lift the car, said Yonkers Police Commissioner John Mueller, were "nothing short of heroic."

SIX MEN AND A BACKHOE

In August 2020, after tearing a path of destruction from Africa to Florida, Hurricane Isaias became a tropical storm, creating record rainfall and turning tranquil streams into raging rivers as it continued up the Eastern seaboard. In West Marlborough, Pennsylvania, one such stream overtook the low point of a country road. As motorists stopped, debating whether to try to cross the flooded road, one car was already in it. The driver, Dazoh Duwoe, and four children—his two young sons, his little brother, and his niece—tried to make it to the other side, but they couldn't. The rapids were too high and too swift. Then, as onlookers watched helplessly, the water pushed the car backward around a corner before pinning it against a fence. The family was too far away for anyone to reach, and no one knew how long it would be before the car sank or got swept away. That's when Burnett Wilson, a public works employee, arrived in a backhoe. "Call it a miracle, call it an Act of God, call it whatever you want," said one of the rescuers, Dan DiGregorio, "but Burnett was there with a bucket, and we immediately screamed that we have to jump on this." Five men—none of whom knew each other—climbed into the bucket and the backhoe traversed the rapids. The men then formed a human chain, each man holding onto the belt of the man next to him, and rescued the family one by one. At one point, Duwoe's little brother lost his grip...

Champion racehorse Secretariat had a heart almost twice as big as a regular racehorse's.

and DiGregorio caught him by the wrist just in time. Everyone made it out.

A few weeks later, a ceremony was held to honor the six strangers-turned-heroes: Dan DiGregorio and David MacDonald (both from the area), Walter Puddifer and Tom Garner (from England), and two public works employees, Wilson and Hugh Lofting II, who said this was his third water rescue. "It's just part of the job out in West Marlborough. We are lucky we have good people with good hearts around us."

RESCUING THE RESCUES

Keith Walker, 53, was living on the streets of Atlanta in December 2020 when he went to visit his pit bull, Bravo, at the W-Underdogs animal shelter. The shelter's owner, Gracie Hamlin, allowed Bravo to stay there at night. That evening, Walker arrived to find smoke billowing out of the building. Hamlin was out picking up donations, and no one else was there. "I was nervous as hell, I'm not going to lie," Walker told reporters. "My dog is my best friend. I wouldn't be here without him, so I knew I had to save all those other dogs." And not just the six dogs that were trapped in the smoke: he saved ten cats, too—every animal in the shelter. Firefighters extinguished the blaze (caused by an electrical fire in the kitchen), but the building had to be condemned.

The public rallied to help Hamlin find a new home for the shelter (which was already in the works), and a home for Walker as well. A GoFundMe raised nearly $90,000 in less than a month, but as Hamlin explained to donors, "Please understand that the issues surrounding Mr. Walker's homelessness are complex, and we need to proceed with care." On the streets since he was 13, Walker was accepted into a program for the chronically homeless called Georgia Works, which provides three meals a day, therapy, and finance and employment classes. Best of all, he gets to see Bravo every day. Hamlin called Walker her "guardian angel."

THE LITTLEST LIFEGUARD

"I didn't think about nothing," said 10-year-old Rickie August Jr. "I just acted." Junior, as he prefers to be called, was swimming at his apartment complex pool in Houston, Texas, in June 2021 when he saw a little girl lying motionless at the bottom of the deep end. Junior took a deep breath and swam down to the girl—5-year-old Egypt Bradly—and carried her to the surface. He yelled for help as he swam to the side of the pool with Egypt draped over his shoulder. The grown-ups took over and Rickie watched as Egypt's parents desperately tried to revive her...but she wasn't breathing. "I was very scared," he told television station KHOU, "and it was just super sad." Unable to watch, he ran home to his apartment. A little while later, Junior got the good news: Egypt was going to be okay! A few days later, they all had a party, where Egypt and her mom, Diamond, thanked Junior for his good deed. And where many Good Samaritans say they don't want to be called heroes, Junior had no problem with it, telling reporters, "I felt like I was a real hero."

All 50 states of the United States have an official state soil. (Maryland's is sassafras soil.)

BIZARRE BASKETBALL RECORDS

Here are some of the greatest—and weirdest—things to ever happen in hoops.

Least dribbles with the most points: In December 2016, the Golden State Warriors beat the Indiana Pacers 142 to 106 thanks to a career-high 60 points from star Klay Thompson. Over the course of the entire game, Thompson bounced (dribbled) the ball just 11 times.

Shortest professional career: JamesOn Curry was drafted by the Chicago Bulls in 2007, but he wound up playing in the NBA Development League and throughout Europe until 2010, when he suited up for the Los Angeles Clippers. He played in just one game and was on the court for 3.9 seconds. That's the shortest NBA stint of all time.

Most fouls in one game: In the NBA, players can only commit six fouls before they're ejected. Only once in league history did a player commit six fouls, remain in the game, and then commit one more foul. During a 131 to 95 rout by the Portland Trail Blazers, the Atlanta Hawks' Cal Bowdler got away with committing seven fouls because the referees and scorekeepers forgot to record number 6, and realized he'd made one more than legally allowed only *after* the game was over.

Quickest time to fouling out: Hall of Famer Dennis Rodman was an exceptional defensive player, but he was a woefully bad free throw shooter. Opposing teams knew it and would often intentionally foul him whenever he got the ball, sending him to the line to miss those two easy shots. During a 1997 game against Rodman's Chicago Bulls, the Dallas Mavericks' Bubba Wells fouled Rodman six times in just three minutes—fouling out in the shortest period on record.

Least productive on-court appearance: Joel Anthony of the Miami Heat played nearly 29 of the 48 regulation minutes during a January 2011 game against the Portland Trail Blazers. And during those 29 minutes he didn't do *anything*—he didn't register a single point, assist, rebound, steal, block, free throw, or even an attempt at a shot. (He did, however, commit one turnover and four fouls.)

Most points scored with nothing else to offer: On December 2, 2000, Allan Houston of the New York Knicks set an NBA record for most points scored without contributing anything else. He amassed 37 points against the Minnesota Timberwolves but had no rebounds, assists, steals, or blocks.

"Fist" games, similar to "rock paper scissors," originated in China and date back to the 3rd century BC.

1-STAR REVIEWS

Customers have the right to write bad reviews for faulty products or bad service, but these real 1-star reviews are faulty, bad...and funny.

A LEGO SET
★ ☆ ☆ ☆ ☆

"My Lego set was broken when I opened it!"

WOLF URINE TO REPEL DEER
★ ☆ ☆ ☆ ☆

"VERY BITTER TASTE! Was barely able to get through a sip before I felt sick."

MIGHTY MORPHIN POWER RANGERS: THE MOVIE (1995)
★ ☆ ☆ ☆ ☆

"Great movie. GREATEST MOVIE EVER!!! I'm confused, does 1 star mean good??"

A SET OF WEIGHTS
★ ☆ ☆ ☆ ☆

"Weighs too much"

EMERGENCY REFRIGERATOR REPAIR BUSINESS
★ ☆ ☆ ☆ ☆

"We had $300 worth of food at stake... We needed an immediate repair and left our number to please call us back. No one ever did!"
Response from the owner
"Our operations are shut down due to Hurricane Dorian... To leave a business a 1 star review because you didn't get a response while a category 5 storm is hitting our area is incredible."

THE MOVIE *TITANIC* (1997)
★ ☆ ☆ ☆ ☆

"My stupid friend watched this on Saturday night when he logged into my prime account. Jesus, Adam, *Titanic* by yourself on a Saturday night? Really?"

HOMER'S *THE ODYSSEY*
★ ☆ ☆ ☆ ☆

"I haven't actually bought this item yet... It turns out you cannot give something ZERO stars on Amazon. So I am giving it one star but only because I am being forced to do so by the gods."

A GROCERY STORE
★ ☆ ☆ ☆ ☆

"In a time of desperation I tried to walk out of the store without paying for my groceries and the manager himself jumped in front of me and...turned me over to the police."

A PASTA RECIPE
★ ☆ ☆ ☆ ☆

"my wife left me because i made this for her mother i also slept with her sister. i lost the custody battle and she took the kids because of this stupid recipe."

JUSTIN BIEBER: JUST GETTING STARTED (2012) AUTOBIOGRAPHY
★ ☆ ☆ ☆ ☆

"I don't like it because I hate Justin. Write a book about Justin Timberlake."

Helium is the only element that stays liquid when cooled to absolute zero (-459.6°F).

"THE MAN THEY COULDN'T HANG"

*If you're really unlucky, you could end up on the gallows with death seeming imminent.
Then if your luck changes for the better, you could end up with a nickname like
"The Man (or Woman) They Couldn't Hang."*

JOSEPH SAMUEL (C. 1780)

Nickname: "The Man They Couldn't Hang"

Background: Samuel was an Englishman and a convicted robber who was banished to a penal colony in New South Wales, Australia, in 1801. He escaped from the penal colony and joined a criminal gang that robbed the house of a wealthy woman named Mary Breeze in 1803. During the robbery, a policeman named Joseph Luker was killed. (He was the first police officer killed in the line of duty in Australian history.) Samuel and his gang were arrested for the burglary: the other members were acquitted, but Samuel was found guilty and sentenced to death—for the *burglary*. Joseph Luker's murder remains unsolved to this day; it is Australia's oldest cold case.

What Happened: On September 26, 1803, Samuel was loaded into a cart and taken to the gallows, where a large crowd was waiting to watch him and several other condemned prisoners die. The standard procedure for execution in Australia at the time was to stop the cart directly beneath the gallows, tie the noose around the condemned prisoner's head, then drive the cart away, leaving the prisoner to hang from the noose until dead. But when Samuel's cart pulled away, his rope snapped, and he dropped to the ground. The executioner prepared another rope, and Samuel was hanged a second time. This time the rope unraveled from around Samuel's neck, in the process lowering him until his feet touched the ground. A third noose was prepared, and Samuel was hanged for a third time, only to have the rope snap again. At this point the crowd became so unruly that rather than attempt to hang Samuel a *fourth* time, the official presiding over the executions rode off to consult with the governor of the colony, who promptly commuted Samuel's sentence to life in prison. He is believed to have escaped from prison in April 1806, along with seven other convicts; none of them was ever seen again.

ANNE GREENE (C. 1628–1659)

Nickname: "The Woman They Couldn't Hang"

Background: Greene was a domestic servant in the house of a justice of the peace, Sir Thomas Read, in Oxfordshire, England. She was in her early twenties when she was seduced by Read's 17-year-old grandson, Geoffrey Read. Greene became pregnant but apparently didn't realize it until she miscarried. Perhaps because she feared either scandal or losing her job, she attempted to dispose of the fetus without anyone knowing she'd been pregnant. Big mistake: anyone caught hiding the death of an illegitimate child was presumed a murderer under a law called the Concealment of Birth of Bastards Act. Greene was caught and arrested, and prosecuted for murder by her former employer, Sir Thomas Read himself. She was found guilty, sentenced to death, and hanged in December 1650.

> On the assumption that Greene's survival was the result of divine intervention, she was granted a full pardon.

What Happened: Executed criminals were often handed over to physicians for dissection, one of the few legitimate sources of cadavers for medical study at the time. That's what happened to Greene. After the hanging, her body was placed in a coffin and donated to two Oxford University physicians, Drs. William Petty and Thomas Willis. The morning after the execution, they opened the coffin and were preparing to dissect Greene when they discovered that she had a weak pulse and was still breathing. They were able to revive her by administering liqueur, poultices, and enemas and by rubbing her limbs and extremities. After four days she was well enough to eat solid food; a month later she had fully recovered and, fortunately, had no memory of her hanging. On the assumption that Greene's survival was the result of divine intervention on behalf of an innocent woman, she was granted a full pardon. A free woman, Greene later married and had three children before dying in 1659 when she was in her early thirties.

JOHN "BABBACOMBE" LEE (C. 1864–1945)

Nickname: "The Man They Couldn't Hang"

Background: In 1884, Lee, a "known thief," was a live-in servant employed by a woman named Emma Keyse, who lived at Babbacombe Bay in Devon, England. That November, Keyse was brutally murdered in her own home and Lee, who was the only man in the house at the time, was arrested for murder. Lee proclaimed his innocence, but he had a cut on his arm that he could not explain, which prosecutors claimed proved his guilt. Result: Lee lost his case. He was convicted of murder and sentenced to die by hanging in February of 1885.

What Happened: At the appointed hour, Lee was delivered to the gallows at Exeter Prison in Devon. This gallows was the type with a trapdoor that the condemned prisoner dropped into as soon as the trap was sprung—assuming that the trapdoor opened, that is. It didn't for Lee—he stood upon it with the noose around his neck, and the trap was sprung...but the door never opened. He was taken aside, the trap door was tested and found to be working, so he was placed on it again. Once again it failed, and then, after the gallows was inspected and tested a second time, the third attempt to execute Lee failed as well.

At this point, the medical officer overseeing the proceedings refused to participate any further, and the execution was postponed until the gallows could be thoroughly examined and repaired. In the meantime, the British government's Home Secretary, Sir William Harcourt, commuted Lee's sentence to life in prison. "It would shock the feeling of anyone if a man had twice to pay the pangs of imminent death," he explained. Lee served a total of 22 years in prison and was released in 1907. He is believed to have emigrated to the United States, dying there in 1945 at the age of 80.

GORD MANKTELOW (1932–)

Nickname: "The Man the Chinese Couldn't Kill"

Background: Manktelow, 20, was a Canadian lance corporal fighting in the Korean War in 1952. Canada and the United States were part of the United Nations effort to defend South Korea, while China was supporting North Korea. One day in March 1952, Manktelow was serving in a six-man forward observation team when his position came under mortar attack by Chinese soldiers. His unit received orders to withdraw, but Manktelow soon realized he was surrounded. He had little choice but to lay face down on the ground and play dead.

When the Chinese soldiers arrived, they beat his body with their rifle butts to be sure he really *was* dead, then they stabbed him with their bayonets. Manktelow remained still and silent the entire time. Next the soldiers set one of Manktelow's own hand grenades next to his left leg, pulled the pin, and ran away. "The grenade went off and it flipped me in the air and over. I felt no pain. It was just a very great shock in the thigh," Manktelow told Canada's CBC Radio News in 2003. Luckily for him, the soldiers set the grenade next to him in a way that directed the shrapnel away from his body when it went off. He was struck by the base plug of the grenade and a rod called a striker that embedded in his leg, but that was it. Still the young man played dead. Afterward the soldiers returned and kicked Manktelow a few times before leaving for good.

What Happened: Manktelow lay on the battlefield throughout the night with mortar shells exploding all around him. He was rescued the following morning and taken to a field hospital. At first doctors wanted to amputate his badly wounded leg, but instead they gave him a skin graft and were able to save it. Manktelow spent the rest of the war recovering in a rehabilitation hospital in Japan. A Canadian Press reporter named Bill Boss is credited with giving the young man the title "The Man the Chinese Couldn't Kill." "I guess from a news media standpoint and probably from my buddies' standpoint also, they were saying, 'What do they have to do to kill this guy?'" Manktelow says. He made a full recovery and spent another 20 years in the Canadian armed forces before retiring in the 1970s.

Famous forgotten date: August 14, 1936. That was the day the last public execution in the U.S.—a hanging—took place in Owensburg, Kentucky.

PYTHONESQUE

Monty Python's influence is so pervasive that one could say it's the water that today's edgiest comedies swim around in. One could also say that your mother was a hamster, and your father smelt of elderberries. (We apologize for that insult. The introduction writer has been sacked.)

IN ON THE JOKE

Those who aren't well-versed in Monty Python can feel left out of Python quotation fests, which are prone to break out at any time (as just happened above). Python fans will immediately recognize those gags from the 1975 movie *Monty Python and the Holy Grail*. But even if you're not a fan, you've probably heard, "It's only a flesh wound," which also comes from *Holy Grail*. Or maybe you've heard, "This is an ex-parrot!" or, "No one expects the Spanish Inquisition!" Those quotes come from *Monty Python's Flying Circus*, a half-hour BBC sketch-comedy show that aired from 1969 to 1974. And even if you've never watched one minute of Python, if you've seen *Saturday Night Live*, *Airplane!*, *Rick and Morty*, *Deadpool*, and countless more fringe comedies over the past five decades, you've been exposed to Pythonesque humor. *That's* Monty Python's impact—it even has its own adjective.

THE BEATLES OF COMEDY

Formed in 1969 by Graham Chapman, John Cleese, Terry Gilliam, Eric Idle, Terry Jones, and Michael Palin, Monty Python has often been referred to as the "Beatles of Comedy." The Pythons became the benchmark that all subsequent comedy would be compared to. Just as rock 'n' roll was much more predictable before the Beatles came along and redefined the genre (by adding string arrangements and feedback, charting singles that were over five minutes long, and playing concerts in stadiums instead of small theaters or nightclubs), the humor landscape was similarly conventional pre-Python. Although sketch comedy had enjoyed a heyday during the vaudeville era and on variety programs such as *Your Show of Shows* and *Rowan & Martin's Laugh-In*, the jokes—though often very funny—would be considered too safe by today's standards. But something dangerous was brewing in Britain.

HOW THEY MET

The early 1960s saw post–World War II England "turn from black-and-white into color," as Eric Idle put it. He was talking about his country's so-called Satire Boom, which started at the Universities of Oxford and Cambridge and spawned comedy legends such as Peter Sellers, David Frost, and Douglas Adams. It was at Cambridge

Technically, Starburst is a kind of taffy.

that Idle joined a comedy troupe called the Footlights Dramatic Club, where he met Graham Chapman and John Cleese. And then, on a Footlights tour in New York City, Cleese befriended Terry Gilliam, an American animator who moved to England a few years later. Meanwhile, at Oxford University, Terry Jones and Michael Palin were members of a comedy troupe called the Oxford Revue (which also spawned Dudley Moore, Rowan Atkinson, and Maggie Smith).

After college, the future Pythons worked as writers and performers on several BBC programs, including David Frost's parody news show, *That Was the Week That Was* (the first show to overtly make fun of politicians). In May 1969, all six members were together for the first time during a taping of *Do Not Adjust Your Set*, a zany kids show starring Idle, Palin, and Jones, with cartoons by Gilliam. Cleese and Chapman were there that day, and afterward they all went to Cleese's apartment and decided to form a troupe.

Their goal from the start: make unpredictable comedy in the vein of a BBC Radio program called *The Goon Show*. Created by veteran comedian Spike Milligan (who once had a nervous breakdown and nearly murdered costar Peter Sellers), *The Goon Show* was known for its surreal sketches and random interruptions of silliness. "The humor of my parents' generation was radio sitcoms," said Cleese, "they used to leave the room when the Goons' funny voices came on." Now it was their turn to make old people leave the room.

OWL STRETCHING TIME

In autumn of 1969, the BBC offered Cleese and Chapman their own show—with full creative control—which Cleese and Chapman agreed to only if they could include the other four members of their troupe...which was still lacking a name. BBC executives insisted that the words "Flying Circus" be included (mainly because the network had already put that title in the schedule). None of the troupe members liked it. Their top choices were *Owl Stretching Time* and *The Toad Elevating Movement*. No, and no, said the BBC. Palin, pulling the name from a newspaper he was flipping through, suggested *Gwen Dibley's Flying Circus* (thinking it would be funny when whoever Gwen Dibley was found out she had her own show). They ultimately settled on Idle's idea: "Monty," named for the British war hero Field Marshal Montgomery, who must have a "slippery-sounding surname," like "Python." The network didn't like the name but acquiesced after the troupe threatened to change it every week.

AND NOW FOR SOMETHING COMPLETELY DIFFERENT

When *Monty Python's Flying Circus* premiered on Sunday, October 5, 1969, at 10:50 p.m., few people tuned in, and the suits at the BBC never quite knew what to make of it. Clashes with the censors began almost immediately. Over time, mainly through

Oldest running online webcam stream:
San Francisco's FogCam, which has been going since 1994.

word of mouth, *Flying Circus* gained a small but loyal following in the UK, but it was *too* small, and the BBC pulled the plug after the 1974 season (which Cleese had sat out in order to star in his sitcom *Fawlty Towers*).

That could have been the end for Monty Python. Then a syndicator took the tapes (which had nearly been erased) to America, where PBS stations ran all-night *Flying Circus* marathons—propelling the troupe to cult status. Eager to take advantage of the momentum and make the jump into movies, the Pythons borrowed money from British rock acts Led Zeppelin, Pink Floyd, and Jethro Tull to finance *The Holy Grail* in 1975. Four years later, they made what many consider to be their masterpiece, *Monty Python's Life of Brian*, financed by George Harrison, who often remarked, "The spirit of the Beatles has passed onto Monty Python." Then came 1983's *The Meaning of Life*, a movie consisting of irreverent sketches that take on every sacred institution (and subsequently drew fire from all of them). That was the last project completed by the original lineup. Their legacy was set.

Take a silly walk over to page 297 to learn more about Monty Python's revolutionary humor and the lasting effects it's had on modern comedy.

AMERICA'S 6 HOTTEST CITIES

99°

1. Phoenix, AZ
(107 days over 99°F per year)

2. Las Vegas, NV
(70 days over 99°F per year)

3. Riverside, CA
(24 days over 99°F per year)

4. Dallas, TX
(17 days over 99°F per year)

5. Austin, TX
(16 days over 99°F per year)

6. Sacramento, CA
(11 days over 99°F per year)

First person to win an Oscar for playing an Oscar winner:
Cate Blanchett, who portrayed Katharine Hepburn in *The Aviator* (2004).

BAD DENTISTS

Q: *When is the worst time to schedule a dentist appointment?*
A: *2:30. Get it? "Tooth-hurty." Well, that joke is almost as painful as these true stories.*

WHEN THE NAME FITS THE CRIME

In 2015, and despite a "not-guilty" plea, a former Veteran Affairs dentist received a sentence of probation and a $1,000 fine for a crime he committed in the summer of 2013. The dentist entered the VA Medical Center in Omaha, Nebraska, and broke into a locked supply cabinet. He then stole nearly $17,000 worth of medical equipment—primarily gold and other precious metals used in dentistry—put them in a bag, walked out, and drove away. A lab technician witnessed the theft and called police, who stopped the dentist in his car. He denied knowledge of how he came to be in possession of the stolen items and professed his innocence on Facebook, claiming it was part of a plan to bring him down, executed by the "Prince of Darkness." The dentist's name: Randall Toothaker.

DENTISTRY ISN'T FOR EVERYONE

Late one night in May 2021, deputies from the Washoe County Sheriff's Office in Nevada responded to an after-hours alarm at a dental office in the Reno suburb of Sun Valley. They discovered a broken window and an open door, and determined that nearly $23,000 in cash and checks had disappeared from a cash drawer. Dental office management pointed police in the direction of a person of interest: a former employee named Laurel Eich. Deputies arrested Eich, who admitted to previous misbehavior in the dental realm, claiming she stole partially empty anesthesia containers from the office's garbage and used them to perform 13 tooth extractions on one person—all of her own accord and without any dental training. Eich was charged with multiple counts of burglary, grand larceny, conspiracy to commit burglary, and performing surgery without a medical license.

BUT WHO'S COUNTING

In 2013, 21-year-old Christopher Crist booked an appointment at Amazing Family Dental in Indianapolis, for an examination and removal of three teeth that were causing him a great deal of pain. According to Crist, Amazing Family Dental staff removed those three problem teeth...and then kept going. By the time Crist woke up from sedation, *all* of his teeth were gone. "They pulled every last one of them," he told reporters. "I am going to look like a freak now." What's worse, the surgery led to an oral infection that required hospitalization. Crist's family told reporters they were going to file a lawsuit against the dentists, bolstered by testimony by a fellow patient who saw Crist after his teeth were removed and said the victim's face "looked scary."

The U.S. federal government issued Santa Claus a pilot's license in 1927.

ASK UNCLE JOHN

Some questions have no answers. Others, like these, do.

NOT FLUSHED WITH PRIDE

Dear Uncle John, why don't Americans use bidets?

A: Although popular in much of the developed world, most North Americans don't know exactly what a bidet is. Invented in 17th-century France, some bidets are small, freestanding tubs installed next to a toilet, while others are built into the tank itself. You position yourself over it, water whooshes out, and you're all cleaned up. Feeling a bit squeamish? That's the main reason bidets haven't caught on in North America: the perceived "yuck factor." (And, by the way, it's reciprocal—many people from other continents are grossed out by the act of wiping.)

The aversion runs even deeper. Canadian and American soldiers stationed in Europe during World War II associated bidets with the places they most commonly saw them: in the bathrooms at bordellos. Prostitution was a taboo subject in mid-20th-century North America, so unlike pizza and M&M's, bidets didn't come home with the GIs.

In the 21st century, bidets are beginning to catch on in the U.S. and Canada; they're better for the environment and much cheaper in the long run than the 20,000 toilet paper sheets the average American tears through each year. That's why bidet sales rose sharply during the pandemic-induced TP shortage of April 2020... but only briefly. According to a 2021 survey, only 12.1 percent of Americans had access to a bidet.

NOT A DROP TO DRINK

Dear Uncle John, why can't we drink salt water, and how much would you have to drink to die?

A: No one knows how much salt water would kill you, because you'd get too sick to keep drinking long before you reached a lethal amount, but the consensus is about two gallons. How does it kill you? Your blood filters through your kidneys to remove waste products that end up in the toilet. Too much salt will upset the sodium-potassium balance in the kidneys and force the fresh water out through the cell membranes. When the kidneys run out of fresh water, they stop functioning. Then your innards fill up with waste products and *you* stop functioning.

SEAL OF APPROVAL

Dear Uncle John, why doesn't honey ever spoil?

A: Honey, which can last for thousands of years, begins its life on a flower, which lasts for only a few days. The flower secretes a sugary fluid called nectar. Bees collect the nectar on their bodies and in their stomachs and take it back to the hive to make into honey. First, they flap their wings over and over until most of the water in the nectar has evaporated. Then, through the use of an enzyme in the bees' stomachs called glucose oxidase, the nectar is broken down into gluconic acid and hydrogen peroxide, the same stuff you put on a cut so it doesn't get infected. The resulting honey is acidic and, due to its low water content, very thick. Bacteria (the leading cause of food spoilage) need moisture to thrive, which they won't find in honey. That is, unless it isn't sealed: if water does get in, honey will eventually spoil—it'll just take longer than most other foods. But if it's properly sealed in a jar, it doesn't matter if that jar was pried out of the hands of a 5,000-year-old mummy, the honey will taste as fresh as the day the bees made it.

HONEY, WHAT IS MR. S DOING IN OUR CLOSET?

Dear Uncle John, a woman in an illicit affair with a married man is referred to as his "mistress," but is there a word for the male equivalent?

A: Urban Dictionary defines a "manstress" as "a married woman's side piece." But the wordsmiths at *Oxford English Dictionary* and *Merriam-Webster* don't count "manstress" as an actual word. Perhaps it should be, because there really isn't a male equivalent of "mistress." The word "mister" has been used, but it hasn't caught on because it can be confused with "Mr." Attempts at "misteress" have also fallen short. Then there's the word "paramour," but that can be used to describe a "side piece" of either sex. HuffPost senior correspondent Lisa Belkin chalks the omission up to the sexism that's rooted in the English language: "Mostly it says that we still think of *him* as a bit of a stud at best, and a victim of her manipulation, at worst, while we think of *her* as defined in relation to him—something we can label. And label we do."

* * *

"Never follow anyone else's path, unless you're in the woods and lost and you see a path.
Then, by all means, follow that path."

—Ellen DeGeneres

Meatheads: In a 2021 study, 40 percent of American kids
said they thought hot dogs were vegetables.

MONEY TALKS

Everybody has money problems. You can't help thinking about them...so you might as well laugh about them.

"I have enough money to last me the rest of my life, unless I buy something."
—Jackie Mason

"A BANK IS A PLACE WHERE THEY LEND YOU AN UMBRELLA IN FAIR WEATHER AND ASK FOR IT BACK WHEN IT BEGINS TO RAIN."
—Robert Frost

"The only thing tainted about money is 'taint mine' or 'taint enough.'"
—Governor Marvin Griffin

"Don't judge me. I made a lot of money."
—Samantha Bee

"ALL I ASK IS THE CHANCE TO PROVE THAT MONEY CAN'T MAKE ME HAPPY."
—Spike Milligan

"I made my money the old-fashioned way. I was very nice to a wealthy relative right before he died."
—Malcolm Forbes

"If you want to know what God thinks of money, just look at the people he gave it to."
—Dorothy Parker

"I finally know what distinguishes man from other beasts: financial worries."
—Jules Renard

"If making money is a slow process, losing it is quickly done."
—Ihara Saikaku

"Money cannot buy peace of mind. It cannot heal ruptured relationships, or build meaning into a life that has none."
—Richard M. DeVos

"Don't tell me what you value, show me your budget, and I'll tell you what you value."
—Joe Biden

BATHROOM HERO: THE MAN WHO GAVE A CRAP

Sometimes the best ideas are also the crappiest.

BATHROOM HERO: Simon Griffiths, cofounder and CEO of an Australian toilet paper brand with a very unusual name

NOTABLE ACHIEVEMENT: Coming up with a fun way to raise serious money for an important cause

TRUE STORY: In 2009, Griffiths was traveling in Asia and Africa, studying the work of nongovernmental organizations in developing countries. He was looking to start a "social business," a for-profit company that devotes some or all of its profits to addressing important social issues. (The Newman's Own company is a well-known example of a social business. Founded by actor Paul Newman in 1982, the food products company sells cookies, salad dressing, frozen pizza, and dozens of other products. To date, it has donated 100 percent of its more than $550 million in profits to charity.)

During his travels, Griffiths became interested in organizations working in the field of public sanitation—in other words, providing toilets to people who don't already have access to them. It's a big issue: the World Health Organization estimates that more than 2.4 billion people around the world do not have access to a toilet. Griffiths learned that groups building toilets in developing countries spend about 30 percent of their time raising the money they need to do their work, instead of doing the work itself. "I started to think about how I could create a new channel to expand the funding pool and help accelerate development," he told an interviewer.

PAPER TRAIL: It was around this time that Griffiths popped in to use a restroom and saw a pack of toilet paper next to the toilet. He had what he calls his "aha moment"—starting a toilet paper company: "Why don't we sell toilet paper, use half the profits to build toilets, and call it 'Who Gives a Crap,'" he says. "I called three friends, told them about the idea and they all said I had to do it."

GETTING STARTED: Griffiths and his two cofounders, Jehan Ratnatunga and Danny Alexander, spent the next two years developing a business plan, and designing the product and packaging, which were made from 100 percent postconsumer recycled paper. Then they contracted with a Chinese toilet paper manufacturer to begin producing the rolls under the brand name Who Gives a Crap.

Now all they had to do was come up with the $50,000 they needed to place their first bulk order with the toilet paper manufacturer. In July 2012 they launched

The inspiration for Arthur Miller's *Death of a Salesman*
was the author's uncle, Manny Newman, a successful salesman.

a livestreaming campaign on the crowdfunding website Indiegogo, one centered around a clever public relations gimmick: Griffiths livestreaming himself, with his pants down around his ankles, sitting on a toilet in the empty Who Gives a Crap warehouse in Melbourne and refusing to get off until the crowdfunding campaign raised the entire sum. "Basically, we need toilet paper," Griffiths implored visitors to the Indiegogo site. "And like anyone who's waiting for toilet paper, we need someone to help us out. I'm sitting down for what I believe in, and I'm not getting up until I've got some toilet paper—$50,000 worth!"

> Griffiths livestreamed himself, with his pants down around his ankles, sitting on a toilet in the empty Who Gives a Crap warehouse.

ON A ROLL: The gimmick worked—as anyone who viewed the live feed will attest, Griffiths remained perched on the pot for more than 50 hours straight, or just over two days. By the end, he'd raised over $63,000, more than enough to stock the empty Who Gives a Crap warehouse with toilet paper. The company shipped its first rolls to customers in March 2013.

Who Gives a Crap has grown steadily since then; it has expanded its product line to include "forest friendly" facial tissue and paper towels; premium toilet paper made from bamboo fiber; and even its own brand of coffee called Blend No. 2. (Get it? *Number two!*) Fifty percent of the company's profits are donated to organizations working to improve hygiene, sanitation, and access to clean water in developing countries. To date, Who Gives a Crap has contributed more than $10 million to these organizations.

In 2021, Who Gives a Crap raised more than $30 million in venture capital funding to grow the business further, in the hope that a larger company will be able to raise even more money to fund the construction of toilets in the developing world. The best way to order Who Gives a Crap toilet paper and other products is online at the company's website, but as the business continues to grow, the day may soon be coming when you can buy rolls of Who Gives a Crap toilet paper at a supermarket near you. And every time you do, you'll make life a little better for someone living in the developing world.

* * *

CELEBRITY INDUCTEES IN THE WWE HALL OF FAME

You don't have to have actually been a professional wrestler to be honored.

- Pete Rose
- William "The Refrigerator" Perry
- Bob Uecker
- Drew Carey
- Mike Tyson
- Donald Trump
- Mr. T
- Arnold Schwarzenegger
- Snoop Dogg
- Kid Rock
- William Shatner
- Ozzy Osbourne

The Empire State Building cost $24.7 million to build.
At that price, it came in 43 percent under budget.

SMARTPHONE "SOLUTIONS"

In the 2000s and 2010s, countless tech entrepreneurs tried to get rich on supposedly can't-miss "killer apps." Many of these offer real-world services. Some, like Uber and DoorDash, caught on. Most others...didn't.

WASHBOARD. This app appeared in 2014, promising to fix the problem of never having correct change for coin-operated laundry machines. Subscribers to the service received a certain amount of quarters (via mail) on a monthly basis—ten dollars' worth of quarters cost $15; twenty dollars' worth cost $27. Washboard went out of business in about a month.

OUTBOX. The developers thought consumers would pay $5 a month to have someone sort their mail. Here's how it worked. The company would send an "unpostman" to a subscriber's home to grab their mail, take it to another location, and digitally scan it. The Outbox user then received an email detailing all of that day's mail, and would tell the unpostman which pieces to bring back and which ones to throw away. In other words, you still had to sort through your mail, just with the extra step of paying a stranger to snoop through it first. Outbox went out of business in less than a year.

REEFILL. Reefill cost $2 a month and gave users access to special water bottle–filling dispensers around New York City. They simply scanned their phone into the Reefill machine's sensor, placed their own bottle or cup under a spout, and got a refill for no additional charge. Source of the water: it was regular New York City tap water. Reefill machines offered room temperature tap water to non-subscribers free of charge, while app users got theirs "chilled and filtered." Reefill started with eight dispensers around Manhattan...and went out of business after a few months.

TAXI HOLD'EM. There's a tried and true method of summoning a taxi in big cities—you lean out into the street and hold up your hand as a cab approaches, telling the driver to pull over and let you in. Or you could download Taxi Hold'Em, an app that does nothing more than fill the screen with a bright yellow taxi-colored background and the word "TAXI." Users are supposed to hold it up in the air so a taxi driver can see it.

POCKET HEAT. This app promised to mimic disposable hand warmer packets. When triggered, it made the phone get really hot, which felt nice in a cold hand on a wintry day. The effect didn't last for too long, though—Pocket Heat used the smartphone's entire computing power in order to overheat it and drained the battery in a matter of minutes. Apple ultimately made the developers remove that feature, reducing the app to just an illustration of a hand over a furnace vent.

State with the largest portion of its area that's water: Michigan (41.5 percent).

AMERICAN PIZZA

Pizza: It's just bread, sauce, cheese, and maybe some pepperoni, right? Not if you live in one of these places in the United States where they've got their own, distinctive, not widely known take on the world's most popular savory pie.

Location: St. Louis
Style: The crust is very thin and unleavened, with a cracker-like consistency, topped with a tomato sauce that's heavy on the oregano, and Provel cheese. What's Provel? Rarely found outside St. Louis, it's a processed blend of provolone, Swiss, and cheddar. The finished pie is served cut into rectangles, each about four inches wide.

Location: Altoona, Pennsylvania
Style: Altoona-style pizza begins with a thick crust and continues with a sweetened tomato sauce. Standard topping: a ring of bell pepper, a deli-style slice of salami, and a slice of American cheese or Velveeta.

Location: Rhode Island
Style: Bakery pizza has a dough that's thick and spongy, similar to focaccia. It's covered in a spicy tomato sauce—but no cheese—and cooked on a sheet pan, then cut into long strips. Afterward it's just left out, served as a room-temperature snack.

Location: Philadelphia
Style: A cousin to Rhode Island bakery pizza, a Philly tomato pie is a square piece of focaccia drenched in tomato sauce, topped with a sprinkling of Parmesan cheese, and served at room temperature or cold.

Location: Youngstown, Ohio
Style: Named for the Youngstown neighborhood to which it's almost exclusive (although it pops up in the nearby cities of Cleveland and Pittsburgh), it looks like a familiar round, tomato sauce–topped pizza, except that the sauce is very thick, applied sparingly, and it's topped with red and green bell peppers and Romano cheese—no mozzarella.

Location: New Haven, Connecticut
Style: Known locally as "apizza," New Haven's take is made from fermented dough formed into an oval shape, and cooked in a coal oven at around 600° F. That makes for a crust that's crispy and a little charred. The most popular style of apizza: white sauce (no tomatoes) and clams.

Location: Quad Cities
Style: The region comprising Davenport and Bettendorf in Iowa, and Rock Island and Moline in Illinois, is known for pizza that's cut into rectangular strips. It looks

In captivity, cheetahs experience such severe anxiety that zoos often pair them with emotional support dogs.

like a standard pizza, but the crust has a nutty taste thanks to an unusual ingredient: brewer's malt. It's topped with an abundance of cheese and crumbled spicy sausage, heavy on the fennel.

Location: Ithaca, New York

Style: The upstate New York city is home to Cornell University and PMP, or "poor man's pizza." PMP was invented in 1960 by a local food cart owner named Bob Petrillose. What makes it unique isn't the toppings—it's the dough. Instead of raw pizza dough, Petrillose used French bread. Stouffer's copied the idea—reportedly after a former Cornell student suggested it—and introduced frozen French bread pizza in 1974. Within two years, Stouffer's was selling $1 million worth per month.

Location: Colorado

Style: What makes Colorado mountain pie its own thing? The braided crust, laced with honey. The pizza is also very large and piled high (earning the name "mountain") with hefty amounts of toppings; it's so heavy that it's sold by the pound, rather than by size "small, medium, or large." Colorado mountain pie is often served with honey on the side, for drizzling on the pie or dipping the crusts.

Location: Miami

Style: Cuban pizza is named for the city's historically large Cubano population. It starts with a thick crust and some sauce, and is covered edge to edge with Gouda and mozzarella cheeses to create a crispy cheese crust. Diners usually fold a slice in half and handle it as one would a taco.

Location: Detroit

Style: Baked in a two-inch-deep rectangular sheet pan, Detroit pizza is covered entirely in a Midwestern specialty called "brick cheese," a buttery, semisoft variety. After the pizza has mostly finished cooking, it's then topped with several thick spoonfuls of tomato sauce.

Location: New England

Style: This type can be found throughout the region at restaurants that call themselves "pizza houses," such as the spot that popularized the style: George's Pizza House in Harwich, Massachusetts. Pizza bakers take ordinary pizza dough and mix in a generous portion of olive oil, stretch and fit it into an oil-coated round pan, then top the thick, chewy, oily crust with a spicy, chunky tomato sauce and a blend of cheddar and mozzarella cheeses. It's sometimes referred to as a Greek pizza, though the ingredients are seldom Greek. Another New England style is beach pizza, which is rectangular (not round), has a very thin crust (not thick and chewy), sweet tomato sauce (not chunky), and mozzarella and provolone (not cheddar) cheeses.

> **DID YOU KNOW?**
>
> You've probably never heard of Leprino Foods, but if you've ever eaten a pizza from a major American chain, or even a frozen one, you've tasted their product. They're the United States' main supplier of pizza cheese, providing 85 percent of all mozzarella used each year.

STRANGE LAWSUITS

These days, it seems like people will sue each other over practically anything. Here are some real-life examples of unusual legal battles.

THE PLAINTIFF: Jesse Dimmick, 27, of Colorado

THE DEFENDANT: Jared and Lindsay Rowley, newlyweds from Topeka, Kansas

THE LAWSUIT: The Rowleys were at home one evening in 2009 when Dimmick burst in and said that someone was trying to kill him, "most likely the police." Then he said he would pay them "a lot of money" if they let him hide in their house. Fearing for their lives, Jared and Lindsay gave the stranger some snacks and watched movies with him until he fell asleep. Then the couple snuck out and alerted the police, who, it turned out, were looking for Dimmick. He was on the run for a beating death in Colorado. In addition to murder, he was charged with two counts of kidnapping.

The Rowleys later filed a $75,000 civil suit against their kidnapper for emotional distress and Dimmick filed a countersuit against them for breach of contract...because they escaped. From his handwritten lawsuit: "I, the defendant, asked the Rowley's to hide me because I feared for my life. I offered the Rowley's an unspecified amount of money which they agreed upon, therefore forging a legally binding oral contract." He was seeking damages of $235,000 (mostly for medical bills because he'd been shot during his arrest).

THE VERDICT: Case dismissed. "In order for parties to form a binding contract," explained the Rowleys' lawyer, "there must be a meeting of the minds on all essential terms, including and most specifically, an agreement on the price." Dimmick was later sentenced to 11 years in Kansas for the kidnapping, followed by a 37-year sentence in Colorado for the murder.

THE PLAINTIFF: Brandon Vezmar, 37, a political communications consultant from Austin, Texas

THE DEFENDANT: A 35-year-old Austin woman who wished to remain anonymous

THE LAWSUIT: In 2017, Vezmar and the woman went on a blind date (via a dating app) to see the movie *Guardians of the Galaxy Vol. 2*. In a suit that Vezmar later filed in small claims court, he alleged that, during the movie, she "activated her phone at least 10-20 times in 15 minutes to read and send text messages." Then, he said, she refused to stop, which is a violation of the theater's policy and was ruining the movie for him and other patrons. Then the woman left before it was over, leaving him stranded (because she drove). Vezmar sued her...for the price of his movie ticket: $17.31. "While damages sought are modest, the principle is important as defendant's behavior is a threat to civilized society."

All species of octopus are venomous,
but only the blue-ringed octopus's venom is deadly to humans.

Vezmar then contacted several Austin-area news stations and newspapers to complain about his "date from hell." He said he told the woman, "'Listen, your texting is driving me a little nuts,' and she said, 'I can't not text my friend.'" As the odd news story started making the rounds, the blind date called local media stations to tell her side of the story: "His behavior made me extremely uncomfortable, and I felt I needed to remove myself from the situation for my own safety." She said that she only texted "two or three times" (to a friend in need), and that she kept her phone low and dim so as not to bother anyone. She said she left when Vezmar started berating her, and later filed a protective order against him after he contacted her younger sister to get his $17.31 back. "I'm not a bad woman," she said. "I just went on a date."

THE VERDICT: Vezmar dropped the suit. "I feel sorry that I hurt his feelings badly enough that he felt he needed to commit so much time and effort into seeking revenge," she said in a statement. "I hope one day he can move past this and find peace in his life."

THE PLAINTIFF: Paige Stemm of Belleville, Illinois
THE DEFENDANT: Tootsie Roll Industries, a Chicago-based candy company
THE LAWSUIT: In April 2018, Stemm bought a box of Junior Mints only to discover that, despite the "oversized theater box," it was only 40 percent full of candy. She filed a class action suit against the candy company for "misleading, deceptive, and unlawful conduct" because it leads consumers to believe "they're getting more candy than they're actually getting."

Stemm isn't the only litigious candy lover who was left wanting. A New York City woman filed a similar class action suit against Junior Mints in 2017, as did a New Jersey man in 2020. In each case, Tootsie Roll's legal department argued that "slack fill" is a common practice to protect the candy. Stemm's lawyer wasn't buying it—countering that too much air can actually damage the Junior Mints because there's more room for them to shake around. Not only that, but similarly boxed candies don't have nearly as much slack fill: 23 percent for Milk Duds and only 12 percent for Good & Plenty.

THE VERDICT: Stemm's case was dismissed by a judge who said that although the company may be misleading consumers, "That she expected to receive something more than what she got, in and of itself, does not constitute actual damages." The judge wasn't the only one who sided with the Chicago-based candy company. So did the *Chicago Tribune*, which published a scathing editorial that mocked the plaintiff for standing up to misleading business practices: "We are trying to imagine the outrage that gripped Paige Stemm when she opened a box of Junior Mints and found that it was not filled to the brim with the luscious peppermint-filled dark chocolate buttons. Oh, the soul-crushing disappointment!...But is there anyone in America who doesn't know that their boxes of candy, cereal, and other products aren't necessarily filled to the brim? Or that you could jiggle the candy box to determine how much is inside?"

Did something rub off? The mother of '80s rock star Adam Ant worked as the house cleaner for rock star Paul McCartney.

THE QUIRKS OF LANGUAGE

How many languages are there? Which one is the weirdest? Which alphabet has the most letters? The least? And what does an umlaut do? If you find facts like these fascinating, you're speaking our language.

OFFICIALLY SPEAKING: In 1780, future U.S. president John Adams presented a proposal to the Continental Congress to make English the fledgling nation's official language, which would give the language special status above all others. The bill was defeated on the grounds that it was "undemocratic and a threat to individual liberty." The U.S. wasn't settled by only the British but by people from throughout Eurasia and Africa, many of whom who could speak multiple languages. Today, the world's "melting pot" has more than 350 languages spoken. Because English is already used by governments, courts, schools, and financial institutions, there's no real need to make it official. Most individual U.S. states have adopted English officially, though.

THE MOST OFFICIAL LANGUAGES: Following the adoption of Zimbabwe's Constitution in 2013, the southern African nation has 16 official languages—including English, Shona (the indigenous language spoken by three-quarters of the nation's 15 million people), and more than a dozen regional languages spoken by minorities. Why so many? Out of respect for the country's diverse—and often marginalized—ethnic groups. To have their language included in official government business is important not only for the flow of information, but for political representation.

HOW MANY LANGUAGES ARE THERE? The answer is...it's disputed. According to the reference book *Ethnologue: Languages of the World*, there were 7,139 languages in 2021. But other sources put this number at 6,500 or 6,700. It's difficult to calculate because languages are not static. The Language Conservancy, a nonprofit advocacy group, estimates that 40 percent of the world's languages are endangered because so few people speak them. About nine languages go extinct every year, or one about every 40 days. There are new languages, too—some that evolve out of existing languages, and others that are discovered in isolated populations.

> About nine languages go extinct every year ...or one about every 40 days.

A TALE OF TWO DIALECTS: American English and British English are dialects of the same language. Whereas an American might sit in his apartment in his underwear eating potato chips in front of the TV, a Brit would be in his flat in his pants eating crisps in front of the telly. Despite the differences, the "loser" (American) can still communicate with the "plonker" (British) without too much difficulty.

WRITING VIETNAMESE: The only East Asian language with a Latin alphabet is

Vietnamese. Written languages come in three broad categories: *alphabets*, wherein combinations of letters form words (English, Russian); *syllabaries*, wherein symbols represent syllables that are combined to form words (Japanese, Cherokee); and *logographies*, wherein symbols represent entire words or phrases (Chinese, Egyptian hieroglyphs). Vietnam's written script, *Chữ Nôm*, was originally based on Chinese logograms. In the 1600s, Portuguese Jesuit missionaries had difficulty learning the logograms, so they rewrote the entire Vietnamese language using a combination of Latin characters, Portuguese *orthography* (writing conventions), and additional marks to represent the spoken language's sounds. Called *Quốc ngữ* (Vietnamese for "National Language"), French colonists made it Vietnam's official language in 1910. Here's how "go to the toilet" reads in Vietnamese: "đi vệ sinh."

IT'S SNAWING! True or False? The Inuit people of the Arctic have the most words related to snow. False. It's the Scots. Parts of Scotland see snow more than 100 days a year, resulting in 421 different Scottish Gaelic snow-related words. This wintry mix includes *skovin* (a large snowflake), *flindrikin* (a slight snow shower), *spitters* (wind-whipped raindrops or snowflakes), *snaw-breakers* (sheep that clear paths through the snow), and *snaw-ghasts* (snowy spirits).

WHAT'S AN UMLAUT? Represented by two dots over a letter (¨), *umlaut* is a German word that means "changed sound." The only vowels umlauts can be placed over are ä, ö, and ü, and they not only change the sound of the word but its meaning. For example, *schon* means "already" or "previously," whereas *schön* means "beautiful." Other languages such as Swedish, Slovak, and Hungarian use umlauts, but with different rules. In Swedish, the two dots are called a *diaeresis*, indicating that characters that include the dots are unique letters. What about the ice cream company Häagen-Dazs? That name was chosen because it sounds Danish, but it's made up. Danish doesn't use umlauts.

AND THE WORLD'S "WEIRDEST" LANGUAGE IS... Chalcatongo Mixtec, spoken by 6,000 people in Oaxaca, Mexico. This is according to the "Language Weirdness Index" that was calculated in 2013 by data scientists who compared and contrasted 239 languages to determine the most unique. Their criteria included the order in which subjects, objects, and verbs appear in a sentence; the language's sounds (such as "uvular continuants" and "velar nasals"); and how negation is expressed, as in "I don't know what those sounds mean." Then the scientists gave each language an official Weirdness rating. Chalcatongo Mixtec topped the list for such quirks as the verb going at the beginning of the sentence, and providing no way to distinguish questions from statements, which are spoken the same way with no change in structure or tone. "Are you perplexed?" sounds just like "You are perplexed." (English, by the way, is ranked #33.)

The BC and AD dating system was proposed in AD 525,
but wasn't used until more than 300 years later.

ALL YOU NEED IS WAX

What was the Beatles' record company? That's a surprisingly complex question.

BACKGROUND

Electric and Musical Industries, or just EMI, was a British media conglomerate; its subsidiaries included some of the biggest record labels in the world in the 1960s, among them EMI Records, Parlophone, and, in the United States, Capitol Records. At various times, covering different markets and countries around the world, each of them was the home label of the Beatles—and so were a few small, independent American labels that cashed in on Beatlemania just as it was starting to take hold in the early 1960s.

On April 4, 1964, the Beatles achieved an impressive feat: the band occupied positions one through five on the *Billboard* Hot 100 chart. That could only happen because of the perfect storm of intense demand for Beatles content after their American debut on *The Ed Sullivan Show,* and because of a mishmash of different record labels bearing the rights to different Beatles recordings. Nowadays, an act is generally signed to one label, and they'll release one single at a time so as not to cannibalize sales. But in February 1964, everybody with a Beatles song put it out at the same time, and they virtually all did quite well.

That top five:

1. "Can't Buy Me Love" (Capitol Records)

2. "Twist and Shout" (Tollie Records)

3. "She Loves You" (Swan Records)

4. "I Want to Hold Your Hand" (Capitol Records)

5. "Please Please Me" (Vee-Jay Records)

VEE-JAY RECORDS

Capitol Records conducted its affairs independently of its parent company, EMI, and when EMI offered the company first dibs at releasing Beatles records in the U.S., Capitol declined. Reason: Executives thought the band's sound was "too British" to appeal to American listeners. With Capitol opting out, in 1963 EMI next offered its Beatles-in-America business to Vee-Jay Records, a small Chicago label founded by married entrepreneurs Vivian Carter and James Bracken (the "Vee" and "Jay" in the company's name) to release jazz, blues, and R & B records. (The biggest names on Vee-Jay at the time: blues great John Lee Hooker and vocal group the Four Seasons.) The Beatles were virtually unknown in America, and Carter and Bracken weren't sold on them. But they agreed to take on the Fab Four provided they could also have the American rights to "I Remember You," a pop song that singer Frank Ifield had recorded for EMI that was a massive hit across Europe and Australia in 1962.

"I Remember You" hit #5 in the U.S., and at first Vee-Jay's executives' assessment that the Beatles were nothing special proved correct. The company released a few Beatles singles in mid-1963—"Please Please Me," "From Me to You," and "Do You Want to Know a Secret"—that didn't gain much traction. One station in Portland, Oregon, added "From Me to You" to its playlist for a couple of weeks, and that was about it.

But when Beatlemania arrived, Vee-Jay Records rereleased "Please Please Me," and it peaked at #3 on the pop chart. In early 1964, Vee-Jay sold 2.6 million units of Beatles recordings in a single month (mostly "Please Please Me" and the first full-length Beatles album available in the U.S., *Introducing...The Beatles*). The company could have sold more if it hadn't been too small to keep up with demand. Despite the huge sales, however, it failed to pay royalties to its artists...and to EMI. Lawsuits resulted, and EMI ultimately canceled its arrangement with Vee-Jay to distribute its music in the United States. Amount of the payment that Vee-Jay failed to make to EMI, which cost them the Beatles contract: $589.

TOLLIE RECORDS

As Beatlemania started to ramp up in early 1964, Vee-Jay Records set up a subsidiary called Tollie Records to separate the British rock act from its regular lineup of mostly Black blues and R & B acts. The first Beatles release on Tollie was the single of "Twist and Shout," which reached #2 on the *Billboard* singles chart. (The B side, "There's a Place," made it to #74.) Tollie's second single: the Beatles' "Love Me Do" with the B Side "P.S. I Love You." Those songs reached #1 and #10, respectively. Tollie shut down in early 1965 after a year of operation, having released 48 singles, of which "Twist and Shout" and "Love Me Do" were the only hits.

SWAN RECORDS

In the summer of 1963, the Beatles weren't finding much luck in the United States with Vee-Jay Records. Louise Harrison Caldwell, sister of Beatles guitarist George Harrison, was living in America at the time (in Illinois) and wrote a letter to the band's manager, Brian Epstein, expressing her frustration. Realizing the group needed a strategy shift, Epstein withheld the single "She Loves You" from Vee-Jay and, after putting out some feelers, placed it with the Philadelphia-based Swan Records. *American Bandstand* host Dick Clark co-owned the label and used his show to promote acts in whom he had a financial interest. Epstein and EMI hoped Clark would help launch the Beatles in such a manner, but Clark declined. Weeks after the song hit #1 in the UK in 1963, "She Loves You" was released in the United States and it flopped...at first. After the Beatles started getting attention in the U.S., and as "I Want to Hold Your Hand" climbed the charts, Swan reissued "She Loves You" in January 1964. After "I Want to Hold Your Hand" spent four weeks at #1, "She Loves You" replaced it at the top for two weeks.

Dolphins can drown. (They breathe air from the atmosphere through their blowholes, not from the water.)

CAPITOL RECORDS

In January 1964, eight days after Vee-Jay put out the first full-length Beatles record in the U.S., Capitol Records released *Meet the Beatles!* That label would be the primary home for Beatles albums for most of the band's life, with the exception of *A Hard Day's Night* and *Help!*, the soundtrack albums from the films of the same names, because they were released on the film studio's subsidiary, United Artists Records. Capitol, EMI's American division, had decided against releasing Beatles records in the U.S., and probably would have held to that decision forever. But in early 1964, after nearly two years of refusals, EMI ordered Capitol to issue a 45 of "I Want to Hold Your Hand." Capitol finally relented and released the single. Smart move. It was available in stores when the Beatles appeared on *The Ed Sullivan Show* and became virtually overnight superstars in the United States, proving that Capitol had been wrong about the Fab Four being "too British."

Nevertheless, throughout the 1960s, Capitol repeatedly fussed with the Beatles' music before allowing Americans to buy it. Whenever the band recorded an album in England on EMI's British label, Parlophone, Capitol executives would delete a few songs and then, when they had enough, package them together as an entirely new record. (John Lennon complained about this in interviews and told fans to write letters to Capitol to complain about being ripped off.) Example: the 1966 album *Yesterday and Today* included two tracks from the soundtrack of *Help!*, four songs from *Rubber Soul*, two from a single, and three from *Revolver*. When all was said and done, American Beatles fans had to buy 12 albums to get the same songs British listeners got from buying just seven LPs.

APPLE RECORDS

Because of a combination of frustration with Capitol Records' strange handling of its output, and manager Brian Epstein's idea to create a business model that would result in less taxes on the band's earnings, the Beatles formed their own label, Apple Records, in 1968. *The White Album, Yellow Submarine, Abbey Road,* and *Let It Be* were Apple releases, as were recordings by Beatles associates Yoko Ono, Billy Preston, Mary Hopkin, Ravi Shankar, and Badfinger, along with solo efforts by all four members after the Beatles' breakup in 1970.

Individually, each of the Fab Four enjoyed a successful solo career, but the Beatles did reunite briefly . . . sort of. In 1995, 15 years after the death of John Lennon, the surviving band members recorded new instrumental and vocal parts on a couple of the assassinated singer's demos. Released in conjunction with the ABC documentary miniseries *The Beatles Anthology*, those songs, "Free as a Bird" and "Real Love," reached #6 and #11 on the *Billboard* Hot 100, respectively. Both of those singles were issued on Apple Records, the last new music ever released by that imprint.

Michael Jackson's sparkly glove was a golf glove with rhinestones affixed.

HIDDEN IN PLAIN SIGHT

These true stories might make you take a second look at some of those odd items sitting around your house.

THE MASTERPIECE ON THE CUPBOARD

The Find: A rare Chinese vase

Where It Was Hiding: Precariously perched on a cupboard

The Story: In 2019, an octogenarian who lives in a "remote country house in central Europe" (news reports provided no other information about her) hired an Amsterdam-based art consultant named Johan Bosch van Rosenthal to assess some Chinese art pieces that she'd inherited when she was a young woman. Her favorite was a pear-shaped vase. She had a feeling it might be worth something, but she also thought it was pretty, so she displayed it on a cupboard. Amazingly, in the nearly 50 years that it sat there, none of the woman's numerous dogs or cats managed to bump into the cupboard and topple the fragile vase, so it was in near-perfect condition. And when Van Rosenthal dusted it off, he could see, through the intricately carved lower portion of the vase, there was an even more ornate blue-and-white vase *inside.* He sent photos to Sotheby's Asia Chairman, Nicolas Chow, who immediately flew to Europe to see it for himself.

This "lost masterpiece," described as a "double-walled *yangcai* vessel," has been known since the 1950s as the Harry Garner Reticulated Vase, named for the British collector who paid £44 ($56) for it. Garner sold it a few years later for about £100, and whoever bought it left it to the anonymous woman in the 1970s. The vase is much older, though—it was made for China's Qianlong Emperor in 1742. Chow called it a "miracle" that the vase has survived this long. In 2020, the old woman's vase sold at auction for an astonishing $9 million.

TODDLERS AND TIARAS

The Find: A priceless brooch

Where It Was Hiding: On a little girl's Disney Princess dress, and then in Mom's jewelry box

The Story: For about five years, Thea Jourdan, a 31-year-old mom from Hampshire, England, had been eyeing a brooch that was kept under glass on a dusty shelf in a local junk shop. One day in 2011, she decided to shell out the £20 ($31) for the brooch, which has a big pink stone surrounded by smaller clear stones. "I like shiny things," she wrote in a *Daily Mail* article. When Jourdan's four-year-old daughter, Imogen, dressed up as a Disney Princess for a party, Jourdan lent her the brooch, which Imogen insisted on wearing "on the most inappropriate occasions—to the post office, at the school play...she

could easily have lost it countless times. Worse, I probably wouldn't have noticed."

Then one day, when Jourdan was having her engagement ring appraised for insurance purposes, the jeweler saw the brooch in the jewelry box and asked to look at it. Jourdan told him she didn't pay a lot for it, so she assumed the 27 stones on the outside were glass. Not so, said the jeweler, who was inspecting it closely: "Those are diamonds." And the larger pink stone turned out to be a nearly flawless, 20-carat topaz. According to the *Daily Mail,* an appraiser later described the brooch as a "magnificent example of early 19th-century jewelry, possibly part of a tiara or necklace that may have graced the neck of a Russian Czarina." Jourdan was told she might get a "few thousand pounds" for the brooch, but later that year, it sold at auction for £32,000 ($43,000). "Imogen is going to be sad the brooch has gone," she said, "but we are going to put the money it raises in a trust fund for her university fees and buy her a few pearls of wisdom."

PANEL 16

The Find: A culturally significant painting missing from a set

Where It Was Found: Hanging on a wall in a private residence in New York City

The Story: In the 1950s, Jacob Lawrence (1917–2000), an influential Black painter known for his vividly colored cubist depictions of American history, painted a series of 30 panels he titled *Struggle,* which highlight "the struggles of a people to create a nation and their attempt to build a democracy." But the series wasn't kept together; five paintings have been missing for decades. One of them, a panel that depicts Shays' Rebellion (an early American uprising against high taxes), sold in 1960 at a Christmas charity auction for a "modest sum"...and then it disappeared from the public eye.

In 2020, when the incomplete series toured the United States, the missing paintings (of which there are no photographic records) were represented by placards printed with a panel number. During the exhibit's run at New York's Metropolitan Museum of Art, a local visitor saw the panels and wondered if his Upper West Side neighbors' Jacob Lawrence painting might belong to this series. At the visitor's urging, his neighbors—an elderly couple—contacted the museum.

It turned out to be Panel 16 (titled *There are combustibles in every State, which a spark might set fire to. –Washington, 26 December 1786*). The couple bought it in 1960, and hung it in their living room on the other side of Central Park—about a mile away from the Met. The couple loaned it to the museum for the remainder of the exhibit.

Update: In October 2020, the Massachusetts-based Peabody Essex Museum, which organized the exhibit, announced that *another* Jacob Lawrence painting had been found, this one by a nurse who'd had Panel 28 hanging on her dining room wall for 20 years. Perhaps you, or one of your neighbors, is in possession of one of the final three Jacob Lawrence holdouts: Panels 14, 20, and 29.

Which one do you like better? The Swedish equivalent of "born with a silver spoon in one's mouth" is "slid in on a shrimp sandwich."

(B)AD CAMPAIGNS

Companies are always trying to come up with innovative ways to sell their wares (or, as they might put it, to "deepen brand loyalty"). These efforts are notable for achieving the opposite result.

FLUBBED HEADLINE

Brilliant Marketing Idea: It's one of the most iconic—and ironic—photographs of all-time: President-elect Harry Truman, having just pulled off an upset win over Thomas Dewey in the 1948 election, grins as he holds up a newspaper with the erroneous headline, "DEWEY DEFEATS TRUMAN." The irony was apparently lost on Dell Computer's marketing team in 1999, when it parodied the Truman photo in a full-page ad in the *New York Times*. Now, Truman is holding up a newspaper that says, "DELL LOWERS PRICES." Wait a second. Given the context, does that mean that Dell is actually *raising* their prices? People were confused.

Damage Control: "We were a bit more simplistic than that in our approach," explained a Dell spokesperson. "Obviously, everyone knows Harry Truman. We just thought the photo was an eye grabber."

SHADY TACTICS

Brilliant Marketing Idea: Just before noon on April 25, 2015, a magnitude 7.8 earthquake struck Nepal, killing thousands of people. At 1:30 p.m., before the dust had even settled, an India-based eyewear retail chain called Lenskart texted this sale ad to all their customers: "Shake it off like this Earthquake. Get any Vincent Chase Sunglasses up to 3000 rupees for 500 rupees."

Damage Control: Ninety minutes later, Lenskart sent a follow-up text. "We apologise for the accidental choice of words. Our intention was not to hurt anybody's feelings. We are extremely sorry for this error."

HISTORY LESSON

Brilliant Marketing Idea: June 19, 2021, was the first federally observed Juneteenth holiday—which commemorates the emancipation of enslaved Blacks in the United States. Companies across the country marked the occasion with outreach programs, donations to civil rights groups, and other PR-friendly activities. The managers of an IKEA furniture store in Atlanta tried something a little different—they decided to serve employees a Juneteenth-themed lunch. "To honor the perseverance of Black Americans and acknowledge the progress yet to be made," read a company

So why is the name so hard to remember? *Hyperthymesia* is the inability to forget. Fewer than 100 people have ever been diagnosed with it.

email, "look out for a special menu on Saturday which will include: fried chicken, watermelon, mac n cheese, potato salad, collard greens, candied yams."

Delicious though they may be, these particular dishes have long been used to reinforce negative stereotypes of Blacks. Result: 20 IKEA workers called in sick, and the menu made national news. One employee explained to reporters, "You cannot say serving watermelon on Juneteenth is a soul food menu when you don't even know the history—they used to feed slaves watermelon during the slavery time."

Damage Control: "We got it wrong and we sincerely apologize," wrote management in a statement...that went on to imply that it wasn't solely their fault: "The lunch menu was created with the best of intentions, including recommendations from Black co-workers."

NO MEANS NOTHING

Brilliant Marketing Idea: In 2015, as part of Anheuser-Busch's #UpForWhatever ad campaign, the St. Louis–based beer company added little platitudes to Bud Light labels, one of which read, "The perfect beer for removing 'no' from your vocabulary for the night."

A photo of the label went viral, sparking outrage from women's rights and anti-drunk-driving groups alike. Consumer complaints poured in on Twitter: "Budweiser—a proud sponsor of American Rape Culture™ (Removing the 'no' from women's vocabulary since 1876)." And on Anheuser-Busch's Facebook page: "As a woman, as a mother of a girl and a boy, I find this message very disturbing and dangerous. I have been a Bud Light drinker for quite a while, but until this campaign ends, you do not have my dollars."

Damage Control: "The campaign, now in its second year," said a company spokesman, "has inspired millions of consumers to engage with our brand in a positive and light-hearted way. In this spirit, we created more than 140 different messages intended to encourage spontaneous fun. It's clear that this message missed the mark, and we regret it. We would never condone disrespectful or irresponsible behavior." Despite pressure to end the campaign (which had raised eyebrows two years earlier, when the company posted a St. Patrick's Day tweet urging beer drinkers to "pinch people who aren't #UpForWhatever"), Anheuser-Busch said "no." (But they did can that label.)

GLOCK-BLOCKED

Brilliant Marketing Idea: In 2021, Culper Precision, a Utah-based gun store, started selling a GLOCK 19 handgun cover kit called Block 19. The customizing kits, which ran from $549 to $765, came with red, blue, and yellow LEGO blocks that made the

Most types of whales have one blowhole. Baleen whales have two.
They're right next to each other and can look like nostrils.

GLOCK look a lot like a colorful toy gun...and implied that it was officially licensed by LEGO. It wasn't. (Even the "Block 19" text had the LEGO font.) Culper marketed the gun cover as a "childhood dream coming to life." Company president Brandon Scott boasted on social media, "We wanted the second amendment to simply be too painful to tread on." (Possibly because stepping on a LEGO block really hurts.)

A nonprofit gun-control group called Everytown for Gun Safety contacted the LEGO Group in Denmark and shared the statistic that unintentional shooting deaths by American children were up by 31 percent that year. LEGO's legal team sent Culper a cease-and-desist letter.

Damage Control: At first, Scott vowed to fight back, arguing that gun owners "have the right to customize their property to make it look like whatever they want." But after his lawyer informed him that the Danish toy company had a strong case, the Block 19 was discontinued.

THAT'S NOT OKAY, GOOGLE

Brilliant Marketing Idea: In a 2017 Burger King commercial, a restaurant employee explains that there's not enough time to list all the fresh ingredients, so, right before the 15-second spot ends, he says, "Okay Google, what is the Whopper Burger?" The question essentially "hacked" any Google Home console or Android phone within earshot of the TV, activating the Google voice assistant, which said, "According to Wikipedia, the Whopper is a flame-broiled burger..." and then listed all the fresh ingredients.

Turns out, people didn't like it when their TVs talked to their phones.

Turns out, people didn't like it when their TVs talked to their phones. And because the ad agency hadn't thought to change the permissions section of Burger King's Wikipedia page, which allows anyone to edit it, a lot of people went in and edited it. Now, instead of "juicy tomatoes, fresh lettuce, and creamy mayonnaise," Google informed consumers that Whoppers are "far inferior to the Big Mac" and "cancer-causing," with patties that are "100-percent medium-sized child."

Damage Control: Before the ad agency was able to fix the permissions, Google shut down the Whopper search functionality, putting an end to the fun. But aside from that, there was no need for damage control. "Google Home for the Whopper" became Burger King's most talked about commercial of all-time, and the ad agency won numerous awards, including the prestigious Grand Prix in the Direct category at the Cannes Lions festival. The true brilliance of the ad (excluding the pranksters' antics) was explained by Business Insider: "The hack essentially ended up turning the chain's 15-second spot into a 30-second spot—without the additional ad buy. It was both invasive and effective at the same time, with one jury member calling it 'the best abuse of technology.'"

FAST FACTS

Hurryupandreadtheseamazingfactsaboutspeed!

- *Speed,* a movie about a speeding bus on an L.A. freeway pursued by police and news helicopters, was released on June 10, 1994. The "Low Speed Chase," in which fugitive O. J. Simpson rode in a slow-moving Bronco on an L.A. freeway pursued by police and news helicopters, took place exactly one week later, on June 17, 1994.

- Fastest sneeze ever recorded: 103 miles per hour. (Coughs average about 50 miles per hour.)

- The average educated adult can read 200 to 250 words per minute. Six-time world speed-reading champion Anne Jones reads 4,200. To prove it, she read all 607 pages of *Harry Potter and the Deathly Hallows* in 47 minutes, and then answered reporters' questions about basic plot points.

- The National Highway Traffic Safety Administration reports that in a normal year, excessive speed is a factor in 1 of 4 fatal crashes, resulting in 10,000 deaths. But during the COVID-19 pandemic of 2020, even though there were 13 percent fewer drivers, the per-mile death rate increased by 24 percent due to "drivers hitting high velocities on empty roads."

- World's fastest roller coaster: the Formula Rossa at Ferrari World in Abu Dhabi. It travels 150 miles per hour.

- The fastest piloted plane: the Lockheed SR-71 Blackbird, which can reach 2,193.17 miles per hour (Mach 3.3). The fastest unmanned plane: NASA's Hypersonic X-43A. A Pegasus booster rocket pushes it to speeds in excess of 7,000 miles per hour (Mach 9.6).

- The smaller the animal, the higher its *flicker fusion rate* (ffr). That's the number of images (or light flashes) that register on the brain every second. The amount of images required to see the world in continuous motion dictates how animals sense the passage of time. That's why it's so difficult for humans (ffr: 60) to swat a housefly (ffr: 250). As far as the fly is concerned, we're moving in slow motion.

- Who has traveled the fastest? Thomas Stafford, Eugene Cernan, and John Young. On May 26, 1969, these three Apollo 10 astronauts orbited (but didn't land on) the Moon. On the return trip, they hit an out-of-this-world speed record of 24,790.8 miles per hour.

...fermented sorghum. More is drunk each year than all the vodka, rum, tequila, gin, and whiskey combined.

- Twenty-thousand years ago, a group of humans in what is now New South Wales, Australia, sprinted across some drying mud. In 2006, archaeologists measured the size of their fossilized footprints and the distance between them, calculating that one of the humans was running at least 23 miles per hour—perhaps faster. That's as fast as Usain Bolt, who in 2009 sprinted 100 meters in 9.58 seconds for a (modern) world record of 23.35 miles per hour.

- In 2013, a Russian shredder (guitar, not paper) named Sergiy Putyatov played a speedy "lick"—27 notes in one second—and set the world record for fastest guitarist. Guinness has since discontinued the category "due to the fact that the quality of performance (i.e. clarity of individual notes, etc.) is dramatically reduced at these speeds. Unless the performance is flawless, it is not a record."

- Ranging from 6 to 14 feet, Africa's longest venomous snake—the black mamba—is also the fastest. While ambushing its prey, it can reach speeds of 12.5 miles per hour.

- The speed of light is 671,000,000 miles per hour, whereas the speed of sound is only 767 miles per hour. Sound is so much slower because it's a different kind of wave—a pressure wave, which requires a vibration to push it past air molecules. (It goes even slower through water and solids, and can't go anywhere in a vacuum.) Light is an electromagnetic wave made of protons that aren't slowed down by air or a vacuum. (Walls, however, are a problem.)

- At less than two inches long, the aptly named bee hummingbird is the world's smallest bird. It also boasts the fastest wings (80 beats per second) and the second fastest heartbeat in the animal kingdom (1,260 beats per minute). The animal with the fastest heartbeat is a tiny rodent called an Etruscan shrew. Its tiny heart beats 1,500 times per minute.

- The fastest...bird: peregrine falcon (242 miles per hour); mammal: Mexican free-tailed bat (100 miles per hour); fish: black marlin (80 miles per hour); reptile: bearded dragon (25 miles per hour); amphibian: Andean salamander (15 miles per hour).

- At #94 on the AFI's list of 100 Greatest Movie Quotes is the *Top Gun* rallying cry: "I feel the need—the need for speed!"

*   *   *

"If everything seems under control, you're not going fast enough."
—Mario Andretti

First world leader with his own YouTube channel: UK prime minister Tony Blair (2007).

CRÈME *de la* CRUD

The best of the worst of the worst.

WORST MATADOR
"El Gallo" (Raphael Gomez Ortega), an early-20th century bullfighter

El Gallo employed a technique called the *espantada* (sudden flight) that was unique in the history of professional bullfighting— when the bull entered the ring, he panicked, dropped his cape, and ran away. "All of us artists have bad days," he would explain. His fights were so hilarious that he was brought out of retirement seven times; in his last fight in October 1918, he claimed he spared the bull because "it winked at him." (The audience thought it was a big joke, but Ortega's relatives didn't—his brother was so ashamed during that last fight that he entered the ring and killed the bull himself...just to salvage the family's honor.)

WORST DRUG-SNIFFING DOG
"Falco," at the County Sheriff's Office, Knoxville, Tennessee

In August 2000 David and Pamela Stonebreaker were driving through Knoxville in their recreational vehicle when sheriff's deputies pulled them over for running a red light. The cops were suspicious and called for backup: a drug-sniffer named Falco. The dog sniffed outside the vehicle and signalled "positive," so deputies immediately searched the inside of the RV... and found more than a quarter ton of marijuana.

But in court, the Stonebreakers' attorney challenged the search—the dog couldn't be trusted. It turned out that between 1998 and 2000 Falco had signalled "positive" 225 times and the cops found drugs only 80 times. In other words, the dog was wrong nearly 70% of the time. Falco, the defense argued, was too incompetent to justify searching vehicles based on his "word" alone. The judge agreed and the Stonebreakers (their real name) went free.

LEAST-WATCHED TV SHOW IN HISTORY
"In 1978 an opinion poll showed that a French television program was watched by no viewers at all. The great day for French broad casting

---

Most recent disease fully eradicated globally: rinderpest, a viral disease that kills cattle and buffaloes. The last known case was diagnosed in 2001.

was August 14, when not one person saw the extensive interview with an Armenian woman on her 40th birthday. It ranged over the way she met her husband, her illnesses, and the joy of living....The program was broadcast in primetime."

—*The Incomplete Book of Failures*, by Stephen Pile

WORST JOCKEY

Beltran de Osorio y Diez de Rivera, "Iron" Duke of Albuquerque

The duke developed an obsession with winning England's Grand National Steeplechase horse race when he was only eight years old, after receiving a film of the race as a birthday present. "I said then that I would win that race one day," the amateur rider recounted years later.

- On his first attempt in 1952, he fell from his horse; he woke up later in the hospital with a cracked vertebra.

- He tried again in 1963; bookies placed odds of 66–1 against him finishing the race still on his horse. (The duke fell from the horse.)

- He raced again in 1965, and fell from his horse after it collapsed underneath him, breaking his leg.

- In 1974, having just had 16 screws removed from a leg he'd broken after falling from the horse in another race, he fell while training for the Grand National and broke his collarbone. He recovered in time to compete (in a plaster cast) and actually managed to finish the race while still on his horse—the only time he ever would. He placed eighth.

- In 1976 the duke fell again during a race—this time he was trampled by the other horses and suffered seven broken ribs, several broken vertebrae, a broken wrist, a broken thigh, and a severe concussion, which left him in a coma for two days.

- He eventually recovered, but when he announced at the age of 57 that he was going to try again, race organizers pulled his license "for his own safety."

The Iron Duke never did win the Grand National, as he promised himself he would, but he did break another record—he broke more bones trying to win it than any jockey before or since.

You *can* judge a zebra by its stripes: the more it has, the warmer its native climate.

WEIRD ANIMAL NEWS

Wild tales from the wild kingdom.

HEY, FOXY SHOES!

In the summer of 2020, the residents of the forested Berlin suburb of Zehlendorf experienced a quirky crime wave: at night, some thief was sneaking through town, stealing flip-flops and athletic shoes left on porches and doorsteps. After four weeks of ongoing shoe disappearances, one Zehlendorf resident decided to take the law into his own hands. In a vacant lot, he spotted the bandit and caught him in the act. There the thief stood, holding two blue flip-flops in his mouth. The culprit: a fox who apparently had been coming into town from the woods each night to steal shoes and add them to its collection. Authorities found more than 100 shoes in the lot. (But the one belonging to the man who caught the fox was never recovered.)

DON'T GIVE HIM A HAND

Adjacent to Walt Disney World and EPCOT in Florida sits Disney's Animal Kingdom, a wildlife-themed amusement park that includes rides, hiking trails, and live animals that visitors can see up close. In July 2021, one visitor got up a little *too* close. While walking the Gorilla Falls Exploration Trail, which winds through jungle-like primate enclosures, a TikTok user named "lovindisworld" captured video of a gorilla defecating into its own hand...and then throwing it at "lovindisworld." (The gorilla missed, but the video went viral.)

A STORY WITHIN A STORY

In 1991, scientists were curious as to why animal and insect populations were dying off and becoming extinct on Sottunga, a Finnish island in the Baltic Sea. So they released Glanville fritillary caterpillar larvae, seeking to study what would happen after those larvae turned into butterflies and moved about the island. Instead, the researchers inadvertently started another scientific experiment. They were unaware that some of the released specimens had already been infected with *Hyposoter horticola*, a parasitic wasp. The wasp feeds off the growing caterpillar from the inside, and then, before the butterfly transformation process begins, the wasp pushes through the caterpillar's body, killing it. And inside of *those* parasitic wasps was a *second* parasitic wasp, *Mesochorus cf. stigmatizes.* Just before the first parasitic wasp is fully grown and ready to emerge from the caterpillar, the smaller wasp kills that wasp, and, 10 days later, comes out of the caterpillar corpse. Though the original experiment failed, the parasitic wasps remain alive and thriving 30 years after their accidental introduction.

Under the Electoral College system, it's technically possible for a candidate to win the presidency with as little as 23 percent of the popular vote.

HARD TO SWALLOW

Fishing boat captain Michael Packard headed out into the waters off Cape Cod in Provincetown, Massachusetts, in June 2021. He left his boat briefly to dive into the sea and check on a lobster trap when, to his surprise, a humpback whale swam by and gulped him up. "I realized I'm in a whale's mouth, and he's trying to swallow me," Packard later told reporters. "I thought to myself, 'Hey, this is it. I'm going to die.'" Then, after about 30 seconds, the whale spat him out. When he got back to shore, Packard had himself checked out at a local hospital, where he was pronounced completely fine. Marine life experts say the attack was probably an accident, as humpbacks generally don't attack (or eat) people. They gather food by unhinging their jaws and eating whatever gets in their mouths; Packard was merely caught in the whale's feeding area.

> "I realized I'm in a whale's mouth, and he's trying to swallow me."

SAMSON AND GOAT-LIATH

It's tough to take down or kill a grizzly bear, which is why officials of Parks Canada were baffled when a 150-pound grizzly was found dead near the Burgess Pass trail in British Columbia. After an investigation didn't provide much information, Parks authorities ordered a necropsy (an autopsy, but for a nonhuman animal), from which scientists determined that the cause of the bear's death was severe stab wounds to its armpits and neck. "The location of the fatal wounds on the carcass were consistent with the predatory attack behavior of grizzly bears and the defensive response of mountain goats." That's right—the unlikely assailant was a goat, much smaller than the bear, but sporting daggerlike horns able to pierce the skin of a grizzly.

THANK YOU FOR FLYING AIR TURTLE

One day in September 2021, Runway A at the busy Narita Airport outside of Tokyo, Japan, was closed for 12 minutes, delaying five commercial flights. Reason: a pilot about to take off noticed a small turtle slowly making its way across the tarmac. The pilot reported the sighting to airport authorities who immediately shut down the runway and called in an animal control unit. Those officials quickly and easily apprehended the foot-long, four-pound turtle with a net and returned it to its home, a pond about 300 feet from the runway. Oddly, one of the delayed planes was an Airbus A380 painted to resemble a turtle, usually used to take guests on sea turtle–themed tours in Hawaii.

* * *

AMOUNT OF STREAMS IT TAKES
FOR A MUSICIAN TO EARN A $1 ROYALTY

• Apple Music: 128   • Spotify: 315   • YouTube: 1,250

Sigourney Weaver's smoking in *Avatar* is completely CGI.
She puffed on a "cigarette-sized stick," and the smoke was added later.

OPERATION TAMARISK

Here's one of the most unusual spy stories we've ever come across...
and one that seems almost tailor-made for the Bathroom Reader.

DIVIDE AND CONQUER

After Nazi Germany was defeated in World War II, it was occupied by the armed
forces of four of the victorious Allies: the United States, the Soviet Union, Great
Britain, and France. Each of these nations administered its own piece of German
territory or "zone of control." To coordinate activities between the zones, each
country established "military liaison missions" in the other Allies' zones. This
arrangement continued even after Germany was divided into two countries:
West Germany (comprised of the British, American, and French zones), and East
Germany (the Soviet zone). By then, the Soviets were so at odds with their wartime
allies that there wasn't much liaising left for the military liaison missions to do.
Nevertheless, the arrangement remained in place for more than 40 years. Reason:
both sides used the missions as a cover to spy in each other's territories.

BEHIND ENEMY LINES

As Soviet-dominated Eastern Europe cut itself off from the rest of the world and
retreated behind what was euphemistically known as the "Iron Curtain," the military
liaison missions spying in East Germany assumed an ever-greater role in intelligence
gathering. Hundreds of thousands of Soviet troops were stationed all over East
Germany, and if the Cold War ever turned hot, the border between East and West
Germany would have been the front line. Members of the military liaison missions,
which enjoyed a status similar to diplomatic immunity, were virtually the only
Westerners allowed to travel freely inside the country. They collected a great deal of
valuable information simply by driving around and taking photographs of military
installations, troop maneuvers, and anything else of military significance—close-up
whenever possible, and using telephoto lenses from afar when necessary. Taking
pictures of radar antennas, for example, made it possible for intelligence analysts to
determine the systems' operating frequencies; and photographing military maneuvers
helped analysts to understand how the Soviets planned to use their tanks, helicopters,
fighter planes and other military equipment in battle. The Soviets tolerated the spying
because their military liaison mission was doing the same thing in West Germany.

A DIRTY BUSINESS

But the most famous (and by far the most unpleasant) spy mission to come out of this
arrangement was "Operation Tamarisk," the code name for intelligence gathering by

dumpster diving—digging through the Soviet army's garbage and looking for secret documents or anything else that might be of intelligence value. This dirty work paid off big, but as the people doing the digging soon realized, the job was dirtier than they imagined it would be. *Much* dirtier, and it soon became clear why: toilet paper was very scarce in East Germany, and Russian soldiers were rarely issued any. So they used whatever paper was on hand...including, it turns out, lots of sensitive military documents: code sheets, technical drawings, correspondence detailing troop maneuvers and equipment, pages ripped out of equipment manuals, you name it—if the Russians could get their hands on it, they wiped with it.

Office paper makes a poor substitute for toilet paper, not least because it clogs the plumbing if you flush it down the toilet. If the Soviets didn't know this already, they soon figured it out and set up special bins in restrooms that were used for disposing of these papers. These bins were then emptied into dumpsters with the ordinary trash, instead of being burned, shredded, or otherwise destroyed the way sensitive documents usually were. That's how they fell into the hands of the dumpster divers. Ironically, because the soiled papers were often the only secret documents tossed out with the regular trash, they were easy to find: all the dumpster divers had to do was—eww!—follow their noses. The smellier the papers, the more likely they were to contain valuable information.

DID YOU KNOW?

Why was it called the "Cold War"? Because it wasn't "hot," like an actual shooting war. From 1946 until 1991 the U.S. and the Soviet Union avoided direct combat out of fear that any conflict might escalate into a nuclear World War III. This tense period was marked by numerous smaller proxy wars, but the U.S. and the Soviets never declared war against *each other*.

AN OPEN BOOK

One important piece of intelligence pulled from the trash at a military training site near the city of Cottbus, close to the border with Poland, was a set of battle plans that revealed which military units were real, and which ones were phony "decoy" units set up to fool the United States and its allies—information that would have been invaluable in an actual shooting war.

But perhaps the most important intelligence coup came after British photographers took a picture of the term "Article 219," apparently a code name for a military vehicle, written on a status board listing other military vehicles. It wasn't clear what the vehicle was until a dumpster diver rescued a soiled document that revealed it to be a new model of main battle tank, the T-80. Then when the T-80 went on maneuvers near Cottbus, members of the British military liaison mission were on hand not only to photograph it, but also to record the unusually high-pitched whining

The Humpty Dumpty is a 17th-century cocktail made by boiling brandy and ale together.

sound of the engine, revealing it to be the first Soviet tank (and only the second tank in the world) powered by a gas turbine engine. Another soiled document, this time a logbook rescued from the trash near the town of Neustrelitz, provided such a detailed description of the T-80's armor as well as a thorough analysis of the tank's strengths and weaknesses that the British were able to develop a new anti-tank weapon called a "long-rod penetrator" to take specific advantage of the T-80's vulnerabilities. It's unknown how many millions of dollars were spent developing this next-generation main battle tank, but the effort was almost completely undone because the Soviets could not (or would not) spare the funds to provide their own troops a regular supply of toilet paper.

ON AGAIN, OFF AGAIN

When Soviet soldiers didn't have toilet paper, the quality and quantity of the intelligence collected from their trash was tremendous...but when they did get some TP, the yield went down. The correlation between the *unavailability* of toilet paper and the amount of valuable secret information retrieved from Soviet trash piles was so strong that Western spy agencies did whatever they could to disrupt toilet paper supplies whenever the Soviet Army seemed to be getting too much of it. Operation Tamarisk continued through the 1980s, ending only after the Berlin Wall came down and Germany reunited in October 1990, at which point the military liaison missions came to an end. By then, the dirtiest job in espionage had come to be recognized as one of the biggest intelligence successes of the entire Cold War.

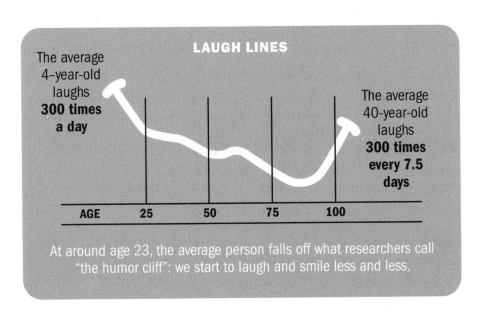

LAUGH LINES

The average 4–year-old laughs **300 times a day**

The average 40-year-old laughs **300 times every 7.5 days**

AGE   25   50   75   100

At around age 23, the average person falls off what researchers call "the humor cliff": we start to laugh and smile less and less.

Sonic the Hedgehog's first name is Ogilvie.

NAKED NEWS

All the nudes that's fit to print.

NUDE SCHOOL

In October 2021, a professor at Hanyang University in China delivered an online class lecture. Intending it to be an audio-only session, the teacher (unnamed in news reports) accidentally turned on his computer's camera, revealing to his students that he was taking a bath, and thus completely naked. He quickly switched off the camera and continued the lecture as if nothing had happened, but students could still hear the sound of water splashing around. "It was an utter shock," one said. "I came in for a lecture, not for a hot bath." The students (all watching remotely) contacted one another about the incident and some recalled hearing clues in previous audio-only classes, such as splashing water and a bathroom-like echo in the professor's voice, indicating that this might not have been their first nude lecture. The professor apologized, blaming the "unfortunate event" on a high fever from receiving his second COVID-19 vaccine shot.

NUDE HARBINGER OF CRIME

Sweetwater, Tennessee, police sergeant Daniel Johnson was patrolling a residential neighborhood in August 2021 when he spotted a man he recognized from previous criminal encounters walking naked through the backyard of one of the houses. Johnson called for backup, and then asked the woman who lived in the house, Samantha Ashley Stephens, if he could search her home, looking for the nude man. She said okay, and almost as soon as the cops started searching, they found a syringe sticking out from under a mattress. The item had methamphetamine in it, leading to Stevens being charged with possession of drugs, possession of drug paraphernalia, and resisting arrest. The officers never did locate the naked man.

NUDE RESTAURANT ADVENTURES

Police in Ocala, Florida, responded to a call in June 2021 reporting that an "out of control" topless woman was flipping over tables in a Mojo's restaurant and had attempted to break into a car. By the time police got there, the woman had stolen a car (a different one) and escaped. Just as they were about to pursue her, they received another call—this one telling them to head to an Outback Steakhouse a few blocks away from the Mojo's. Cops arrived and found the same woman, Tina Kindred, standing in the restaurant's bar area. When police entered the building, Kindred, still topless, threw several bottles of alcohol at them. Police subdued her with a Taser and

Queen Elizabeth II paid for her wedding dress in 1947
with post–WWII clothes-rationing coupons.

took her to a nearby hospital, where she was later arrested. The half-naked woman blamed her behavior on the fact that Mojo's had refused to serve her earlier that day.

NUDE ON TV

NBC's *Today* broadcasts in front of a large picture window from Studio 1A in Midtown Manhattan, and each day fans line up outside with signs, hoping to appear on camera. In September 2021, a naked man ran past during a live segment. "Oh, there's a—there was a naked runner," cohost Craig Melvin nonchalantly said before continuing with the news. "There he goes!" Hoda Kotb shouted, pointing at the nude individual, then asking, "Where are your clothes?" The show then abruptly cut to commercial. (The man wasn't completely naked. Because this was during the COVID-19 pandemic, he was wearing a face mask.)

NUDE INTERFERENCE

In 2021, 18-year-old Myles Abbott fled from police in Dunedin, Florida, climbed the roof of a house, and pointed a gun at the officers who were chasing him. A six-hour standoff resulted, during which time, according to Pinellas County deputies, a woman named Jessica Smith managed to drive a golf cart right through the well-guarded safety perimeter set up around Abbott. Oh, and she was naked. (Authorities pointed out that Smith didn't know Abbott and had nothing to do with that other criminal incident.) "The defendant had a distinct odor of an alcoholic beverage coming from her person," the filed police report read, "and she was completely nude."

NUDE SWIM GONE WRONG

On March 3, 2021, a woman (unnamed in news reports) was reported missing from her home in Delray Beach, Florida. Her boyfriend told police that when he left home at 6:30 that morning, the woman was asleep, but that when he returned, she was gone, having left behind her purse and phone. There was no trace of her and no leads for three weeks...until police received a 911 call that sounded like a person yelling from an underground storm drain. Delray Beach Fire and Rescue and police quickly arrived on the scene and, after removing a grate and lowering a ladder into the drain, found the missing woman in question—dirty, with some cuts and bruises, and totally naked, but otherwise fine. What happened? On the day of her disappearance, she'd gone for a nude swim in the canal behind her apartment complex and saw a trapdoor she thought would make for an easy exit to the street level. Wrong. Instead, it led her into a confusing network of underground tunnels. Unable to find her way out, she stayed in the drain for most of the three weeks, surviving thanks only to a bottle of ginger ale she found. "This was by far one of the most bizarre incidents that our officers have responded to," said Ted White of the Delray Beach Police Department.

MOUTHING OFF

BACK TO NATURE

Remember nature? That place that's outside and far from the road? Here are some reminders.

"If you can't be in awe of Mother Nature, there's something wrong with you."
—Alex Trebek

"The Amen of nature is always a flower."
—Oliver Wendell Holmes Sr.

"I TOOK A WALK IN THE WOODS AND CAME OUT TALLER THAN THE TREES."
—Henry David Thoreau

"In nature, nothing is perfect and everything is perfect. Trees can be contorted, bent in weird ways, and they're still beautiful."
—Alice Walker

"On earth there is no heaven, but there are pieces of it."
—Jules Renard

"Men argue. Nature acts."
—Voltaire

"Nature is pleased with simplicity. And nature is no dummy."
—Isaac Newton

"ONE TOUCH OF NATURE MAKES THE WHOLE WORLD KIN."
—William Shakespeare

"Study nature, love nature, stay close to nature. It will never fail you."
—Frank Lloyd Wright

"I felt my lungs inflate with the onrush of scenery—air, mountains, trees, people. I thought, 'This is what it is to be happy.'"
—Sylvia Plath

"Nature does not hurry, yet everything is accomplished."
—Lao Tzu

"NATURE IS THE ART OF GOD."
—Dante Alighieri

TRULY DEDICATED

Most books open with a dedication, a way for the author to thank someone who inspired them or their work. Some are heartfelt while others, like these, are funny.

"Dedicated to everyone who wonders if I'm writing about them. I am."
—*Insight* by Gary Davies

"For Carley, who was a better person than I am even though she was a dog."
—*This Book Is Full of Spiders* by David Wong

"For Mom (Just skip over the sex scenes, please)"
—*No Way Back* by Matthew Klein

"To Joshua and Noah. Gratitude, my dear boys, for constantly reminding me that age is not something that matters unless you are cheese."
—*Brain Rules* by John Medina

"I want to thank everyone who helped me create this book, except for that guy who yelled at me in Kmart when I was eight because he thought I was being 'too rowdy.'"
—*Let's Pretend This Never Happened* by Jenny Lawson

"This is not for you."
—*House of Leaves* by Mark Z. Danielewski

"For Colin Firth: You're a really great guy, but I'm married, so I think we should just be friends."
—*Austenland* by Shannon Hale

"For everyone who only hears from me when I need something."
—*Admiral* by Sean Danker

"To my parents, I'm sorry for denting the coffee table with my ninja swords. Yes, it was me."
—*The Land of Stories: Beyond the Kingdom* by Chris Colfer

"For my parents, even though they never bought me a robot."
—*Nothing Can Possibly Go Wrong* by Prudence Shen

"To those who inspired it and will not read it."
—*Makbara* by Juan Goytisolo

Myth-understood: Scientists used to believe that kangaroos don't fart. Now it's believed they don't fart *much.*

"To my daughter Leonora without whose never-failing sympathy and encouragement this book would have been finished in half the time."
—*The Heart of a Goof* by P. G. Wodehouse

....

"To my parents, to whom I owe everything (at a relatively competitive rate of interest)."
—*Ostrich* by Matt Greene

....

"To Maris, in hopes that having a book dedicated to her "will make her enemies jealous."
—*Nice Try* by Josh Gondelman

....

"For Phyllis, who made me put the dragons in."
—*A Storm of Swords* by George R. R. Martin

....

"My first stepfather used to say that what I didn't know would fill a book. Well, here it is."
—*This Boy's Life* by Tobias Wolff

"For my parents, who never once to my knowledge tried to kill me."
—*The Doorposts of Your House and on Your Gates* by Jacob Bacharach

....

"To my wife Karen, who is 90% inspiration and 90% patience. No, it doesn't add up to 180%. She multitasks."
—*I Wonder What I'm Thinking About?* by Moose Allain

....

"This book is dedicated to my childhood glasses—you made me who I am today."
—*Everything Is Perfect When You're a Liar* by Kelly Oxford

....

"To my wife Anne, without whose silence this book never would have been written."
—*The Man in the High Castle* by Philip K. Dick

....

"Dedicated to bad writing."
—*Pulp* by Charles Bukowski

* * *

ACCIDENTAL TRENDSETTER

The 1983 hit movie *Flashdance* stars Jennifer Beals as a steel mill worker who dreams of becoming a ballerina. During filming, Beals brought a gray sweatshirt from home for her character to wear, but when she tried to put it on, she realized that it had shrunk in the wash and wouldn't fit over her head. Solution: she cut the entire collar off with a pair of scissors. When Beals put the sweatshirt on, it covered only one shoulder, leaving the other bare. The sexy look became one of the defining 1980s fashion trends.

How do you turn an Indonesian flag into a Polish flag, or vice versa? Turn it upside down.

UPCHUCK SCIENCE

This is a fascinating article, but you may want to keep a bucket handy.

COMING UP...

Call it *puking, upchucking, hurling, spewing, barfing, tossing your cookies,* or *praying at the porcelain altar,* it's all the same thing—vomiting—and everybody does it. But it's important to know a bit about it just in case you experience a serious bout of vomiting and have to describe it to a doctor, and there are a surprising number of varieties.

But first, some basic upchuck info. Vomiting can be caused by a wide range of physical ailments or injuries—such as food poisoning, motion sickness, pregnancy, drinking too much alcohol, and physical injury to the stomach or intestinal tract. But wait, there's more: exposure to toxic chemicals or extreme amounts of radiation, reaction to chemotherapy medications, medical conditions such as migraine headaches and brain tumors, and even intense emotion, such as fright or great surprise.

THE MECHANICS OF VOMITING

According to scientists, there are three distinct phases:

- The *nausea phase*, during which unpleasant sensations are experienced in the stomach, accompanied by dizziness, weakness in the limbs, sweatiness, a buildup of saliva in the mouth, and, ultimately, an urge to vomit.
- The *retching phase*, during which a collection of respiratory muscles—muscles located in the front of the abdomen, and normally involved in the breathing process—go through a series of rapid, involuntary, coordinated contractions.
- The *expulsive phase*, during which the pressure caused by the prolonged contraction of the abdominal muscles finally causes the esophageal sphincters—muscles that form stoppers at the lower end of the esophagus, where it connects with the stomach, and the upper end, near the throat—to relax, thereby allowing for the expulsion of vomit out of the mouth.

VOMIT TYPES

DRY RETCHING. Also known as *dry heaving,* this includes all the phases of vomiting, but without the expulsive phase. Causes include excessive alcohol intake, eating too quickly, exercising on a full stomach, or smelling something gross.

POSSETTING. This is the name for vomiting by very young babies—regurgitating small amounts of food, especially milk, after feeding.

The little sash coming out of a Hershey's Kiss is called the "niggly wiggly."

PROJECTILE VOMITING. Sudden vomiting that can travel several feet. You might know projectile vomiting from its appearance in such movies as *The Exorcist* (1973), *Monty Python's The Meaning of Life* (1983), and *Stand By Me* (1986).

BILIOUS VOMITING. Green- or yellow-colored vomit that contains *bile*, a fluid created in the liver and stored in the pancreas. There are numerous causes, including vomiting on an empty stomach and a blockage in the intestines.

COFFEE GROUND VOMITING. Dark-colored vomit that appears to contain small, brown granules that resemble ground coffee. When the iron in your blood interacts with stomach acid, it undergoes a chemical reaction that causes the iron to *oxidize*—creating the coffee ground appearance. It's most commonly caused by bleeding in the upper gastrointestinal tract—the stomach and esophagus—and can be caused by ulcers, reflux disease, and more serious ailments (meaning you should see a doctor if this ever happens to you).

BLOOD STREAKED VOMIT. Known as *haematemesis*, this is vomit that contains bright red blood. Unlike coffee ground vomit, it's an indication of heavy blood flow in the upper gastrointestinal tract, and should be treated as a medical emergency.

FECAL VOMITING. This severe form of vomiting occurs when a lower intestinal blockage prevents normal elimination via the rectum, and results in the expulsion of fecal material through the mouth.

WAIT...THERE'S A LITTLE MORE

- The scientific term for the act of vomiting is emesis. It comes from an ancient Greek word of the same meaning. "Vomit" derives from the Latin *vomere*, meaning (no surprise) "to vomit."

- The word "upchuck" first appeared in English in the 1930s as slang for "throw" (chuck) "up." "Barf" first appeared in the 1950s and its origin is unknown. (The airline-related term barf bag first appeared in the mid-1960s.)

- The term "puke," as we've noted in previous Bathroom Readers, dates to around the year 1600, but was first recorded in the 1623 play *As You Like It* by William Shakespeare.

- The very young offspring of the Eurasian roller—a colorful, blue jay–sized bird found in Asia and Europe—use an interesting means of defense when confronted by predators in their nests: they puke all over themselves. The orange-colored vomit is extremely foul smelling, and it serves to make predators who thought they were hungry realize they weren't that hungry. (The scent also serves to alert the birds' parents when they return to their nests that a predator may be nearby.)

MYTH-CONCEPTIONS

*"Common knowledge" is frequently wrong. Here are some examples of things
that many people believe...but according to our sources, just aren't true.*

Myth: The first completely digitally created movie was Pixar's 1995 film *Toy Story*.
Fact: In 1990, Disney released *The Rescuers Down Under*, a sequel to its 1977 animated
feature *The Rescuers*. Animators made every aspect of every frame of the film with
a hardware and software combo called Computer Animation Production System,
making *The Rescuers Down Under* the first entirely digital movie; it just "looks" like it
was animated with traditional ink and paint.

Myth: Tear ducts generate tears.
Fact: Tear ducts, technically the nasolacrimal ducts, are just tubes through which the
tears leave the body. Tears are generated in the lachrimal glands just above the eyes, then
travel through the ducts around the nasal bone, to the back of the nose, and then out.
Fun fact: almost all mammals have lachrimal glands. Two that don't: goats and rabbits.

Myth: "Possum" and "opossum" are two different ways to spell the name of one
animal.
Fact: The possum and opossum are two different animals. The possum is native to
Australia and southeastern Asia, while the opossum can be found in North America.
They're both marsupials but are members of different orders, so they're only distantly
related.

Myth: The darker the roast of a coffee, the more caffeine it contains.
Fact: It's actually the opposite. Coffee starts out as raw, green beans and roasting
turns the beans brown. The longer the bean is roasted—into a dark variety like French
or Italian roast, for example—the more caffeine seeps out and is lost. A variety that
has been only lightly roasted, such as a breakfast blend, has way more caffeine than its
bolder cousins.

Myth: Japanese fighter pilots in World War II who sacrificed their lives to attack
and take down American planes did so voluntarily and were trained to be suicide
bombers.
Fact: Such pilots, known as *kamikaze*, were more victims of peer pressure than they
were ready and willing to go on a suicide mission. Japanese commanding officers
would gather large groups of pilots together and ask for volunteers. Not wanting to
look cowardly in front of their fellow airmen, few pilots said no.

Easy on the nutmeg! As little as two teaspoons can be toxic when consumed all at once.
Symptoms include convulsions, palpitations, nausea, and "generalized body pain."

Myth: The remains of a deceased person after cremation are their ashes.

Fact: Those fires aren't hot enough to completely burn every last part of a human body and reduce it to dust. So what's left after a cremation breaks down all of the soft tissue is actually a combination of ash and tiny bone fragments.

"To Protect and to Serve" is a marketing motto that originated in 1955.

Myth: It's the fundamental duty of police officers to protect citizens.

Fact: They take an oath to uphold and enforce laws, and to discharge their duties to the best of their ability. "To Protect and to Serve" is a marketing motto originated in 1955 by the Los Angeles Police Department (and written onto squad cars in 1963).

Myth: Processors at Ellis Island in the late 1800s and early 1990s forced newly arriving immigrants to change their names to sound more "American."

Fact: Clerical errors aside, when names were changed, it was the choice of the individual or family. In starting their lives over in the United States, thousands of people decided to abandon or alter their family names as a way to seem more American, or to more quickly assimilate. If they wanted a change, they reported it to the processors at Ellis Island.

Myth: Bill Clinton won the presidential election of 1992 because it was a three-way race. The third candidate, independent H. Ross Perot, took away votes that otherwise would have gone to incumbent president George H. W. Bush.

Fact: Perot, a political outsider from Texas, won 19 percent of the vote in the general election, the best showing by a non-Democrat, non-Republican candidate in decades. Perot ran as an independent conservative, and some of his ideas were similar to Bush's, leading to the conventional wisdom that without Perot in the picture, Bush would've garnered that 19 percent plus the 37 percent he did capture, leading to an easy victory—56 percent over Clinton's 43 percent. However, nationwide exit polls revealed that Perot voters were almost equally liberals and conservatives, indicating that he took away just as many votes from Clinton as he did Bush, meaning it was a wash and the incumbent president *still* would have lost in a two-man race.

*   *   *

HUH?

In 2014, Jane Mulcahy of England filed suit against her divorce lawyers for failing to explain to her that her impending divorce would result in the termination of her marriage. She claimed that, because they were aware that she's a devout Roman Catholic, they should have suggested she seek a judicial separation, which technically wouldn't terminate the marriage and not put her at odds with her faith. Case dismissed.

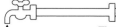

The eggs of the horn shark resemble drill bits. Why?
So the mothers can wedge them into crevices for protection.

THE LAST LAUGH: EPITAPHS

Some unusual epitaphs and tombstone rhymes from around the world.

IN WASHINGTON, D.C.:

Uncle Walter loved to spend.
He had no money in the end.
But with many a whiskey,
And many a wife.
He really did enjoy his life.

. . . .

IN CORNWALL, ENGLAND:

His foot is slipt
and he did fall.
"Help; Help" he cried
and that was all.

. . . .

IN COLORADO:

Here lies a man named Zeke.
Second fastest draw in Cripple Creek.

. . . .

IN NEW YORK:

Underneath this pile of stones
Lies all that's left of Sally Jones.
Her name was Lord, it was not Jones,
But Jones was used to rhyme
with stones.

. . . .

IN VIRGINIA:

She always said her feet were killing her
But no one believed her

IN ARIZONA:

Here lies George Johnson
Hanged by mistake 1882
He was right
We was wrong
But we strung him up
And now he's gone

. . . .

IN NORFOLK, ENGLAND:

Here lies a man that was Knott born,
His father was Knott before him,
He lived Knott, and did Knott die,
Yet underneath this stone doth lie.

. . . .

IN TEXAS:

From their love came five Skidaderones
Who married five Betrojacks
Who had eleven Skiddley Jiddley Gees
Daddy's own language brought us love,
joy, and laughter

. . . .

IN SPAIN:

Here lies Pancrazio Juvenales
He was a good husband,
a wonderful father,
But a bad electrician.

Only European nation with no hospital, and no prison: Vatican City.

POT SHOPS

The preferred term is "cannabis," but it's also referred to as marijuana, pot, weed, herb, bud, flower, and hash. It comes in "strains" like Lemon Kush and Girl Scout Cookie. And now that 18 U.S. states (and counting) and all of Canada have legalized it for medical and/or recreational use, "stoner" entrepreneurs are opening dispensaries and having a field day using cannabis lingo to name them. These are all real.

The Kushery	The Flower Shop	Up N Smoke
KushMart	Euphoros	Magic Show
Pot of Gold	Euflora	Budee
Pot Spot	Gramsterdam	Zippy Leaf
Filabong	Cloud Nine	Urbn Leaf
Hashtag Cannabis	Happy Camper Cannabis	Green Gold Cultivators
Fweedom Cannabis	Happy Green	HaHa Organics
Weed on Wheels	Village Green Society	Hey Bud
Speedy Weedy	Whole Greens	Smokane
We'd	Buds & Roses	Zenganic
Weedery	Purple Lotus	Zen Leaf
Mary Jane on Penny Lane	Tree of Life	Gnome Grown
The Pottery	Island Smoke	Pottersville
Lit Co	Star Buds	Hollyweed
Cannabliss & Co	The Bud Depot	Rocky Mountain High
Grass Station	Spliff Nation	Exhale Nevada
420 Central	Weed Land	The Source
House of Leaves	Electric Lettuce Dispensary	Heaven Scent
House of Flowers	Herbs House	Medicine Man
The Living Room	Cookies	Greenlight Therapeutics
The Basement	Buzz Box	The Green Cross Farmacy
The Treehouse	Bud Hut	A Greener Today
The Joint	ShinyBud	Ye Olde Cronic Shoppe
Green Theory	Buddy Boy	Gram Central Station
Dank's Wonder Emporium	Doctor's Orders	BudaBoom
Herbarium	The Dime Store	Higher Level of Care
It's 4:20 Somewhere	High Q	Herbal Outfitters

REAL-LIFE SUPERHEROES

Have you ever considered sneaking out at night in a weird
costume to fight crime? You wouldn't be the first.

POWER TO THE POWERLESS

The Real Life Superhero (RLSH) movement took off in the 1990s and reached its peak in the early 2010s. Since then, a decade of social unrest followed by the COVID-19 pandemic has put a damper on their heroic efforts, but the "Reals" are still out there. While some take their super-heroism more seriously than others, they all have one thing in common: they say that they felt a calling.

They also insist that they're not vigilantes. As far as the law is concerned, it's legal to dress up as a superhero, but it's illegal to interfere with police business. Police would rather the Reals stay out of danger and simply report crimes, which is what most of them say they do. Besides, there's more than one way for a superhero to make an impact: "Many of the homeless people I work with are from immigrant populations and are fearful of authority figures," explains Chaim Lazaros, a New York City–based RLSH who goes by the name Life. "I put on my mask and say I'm a superhero, and they understand I'm going to do something good for them and not try to take anything in return."

Here are some more stories behind the masks.

THE BLACK RAT (SYDNEY, AUSTRALIA)
Secret Identity: Unknown
Costume: A black chain mail "Rat Suit" with a black face mask and black fedora. The $5,000 costume was designed to withstand bullets, swords, knives, and punches. He also carried a "Rat Pack," which included a first aid kit, fire extinguisher, fire blanket, emergency saw, and headlamp.
Details: Like his inspiration, Batman, the Black Rat witnessed a murder when he was a kid. Then when he was a young man, he was beaten in a random attack. Suffering from PTSD, he discovered within himself an intense desire to help people. "My job is to be an extra set of ears and eyes on the ground...so I can make sure something gets done," he explained in a 2015 documentary. His skills include kung fu, aikido, Japanese martial arts, fencing, and archery—along with "a sensitivity to danger that allows me to see things most others pass by."

The Black Rat claims he's intervened in two domestic violence incidents that led to arrests, and helped bring a serial burglar to justice. He also fought darkness—literally—by spearheading a campaign to bring better lighting to Sydney's sidewalks. At last report, this masked do-gooder is retired. "If you cross paths with The Black Rat," he says, "you probably won't even know."

PURPLE REIGN (SEATTLE)

Secret Identity: Unknown. In fact, little is known about her personal life, except that she is (or was) an accountant, and at some point in the past, she was the victim of domestic abuse.

Costume: A purple-and-black mask and bodysuit with a backward "P" and mirror-image "R" on her chest, Superman style. "Purple is a color which is very often used in domestic abuse awareness campaigns," she explains, "and 'reign' comes from the fact that I now reign over my own life."

Details: In the early 2010s, Purple Reign patrolled downtown Seattle with then-husband Phoenix Jones, a mixed martial arts fighter and leader of Rain City Superhero Movement (until several run-ins with the law—including pepper-spraying some nightclubbers he mistakenly thought were fighting—cut his superhero career short). To be accepted into Rain City, Purple Reign had to had to run two miles in full superhero gear, which wasn't a problem: "I dominate my male counterparts when it comes to physical endurance," she boasted.

No longer associated with Rain City, over the years Purple Reign has spent less time on the streets and more time as a motivational speaker in schools and women's shelters. For her activism, she was awarded the University of Washington Women of Courage honor. (Her heroics can now be found online at www.purplereigncampaign. org, which offers free legal help and counseling for victims of abuse.)

SHADOWVISION (LITTLE ROCK, ARKANSAS)

Secret Identity: Unknown

Costume: A black ninja uniform with a steel motorcycle helmet, armored shoulders, and bulletproof chest plates. He carries handcuffs, two Japanese blocking weapons, and a sword called a katana.

> He claims to have hunted down two serial killers in the 1990s, and thwarted several armed robberies.

Details: Little is known about ShadowVision, except where he's from—Belfast, Northern Ireland—and why he became a superhero: "I got tired of turning on the TV and all I hear is people losing hope." He claims to have hunted down two serial killers in the 1990s, and thwarted several armed robberies.

Since 2013, he's been walking the streets of Little Rock at night, occasionally posing for pictures with passersby that he posts on his Facebook page. ShadowVision made headlines in May 2021 after he issued a public challenge to the "Little Rock Slasher," an assailant wanted for three murders:

> I know that the serial stabber is keeping a eye on my page here. So this is a threat to you when i find you i will show you what i do to serial killers. I am hunting you right now.

A few more things learned from ShadowVision's Facebook page: he's 45, he has over 12,000 followers, and the cops don't seem to mind him. Also, the Little Rock Slasher is still at large.

What's a "cheeper"? A baby partridge.

NYX, THE GREEK GODDESS OF THE NIGHT (NEW YORK CITY)

Secret Identity: Nyx goes by Scarlett Thomas on social media, but is that her real name? "Like the night, I cannot be proven or disproved to certain degrees; and also much like the night, when morning comes there will be no trace of me." (Her real name is Irene.)

Costume: A black body suit with striped leggings, and a red mask that matches her hair.

Details: Nyx was among the first RLSH's to make the news in 2009 after she took photos of Kansas City drug houses and sent them to the cops. After she moved to New Jersey, she married another Real named Phantom Zero. (They later appeared on a 2011 HBO documentary about RLSH's.)

"I feel a certain degree of loyalty to every being that inhabits this earth," says Nyx. Based on press reports, as recently as 2018, she was patrolling Manhattan, giving out food and clothing to people in need. Her social media pages are still open, but for the past few years, there's been no trace of the Greek goddess of the night.

Archenemies

"One could not be a superhero without a supervillain as a foil," declared the Potentate, founder of R.O.A.C.H., short for "The Ruthless Organization Against Citizen Heroes." These RLSV's (the "V" is for "villain") aren't after world domination or anything like that; their beef is with the Reals, whom they deride as "vagabonds and harlequins looking for an excuse to don silly outfits." (To be fair, RLSV's also wear silly outfits.) Their web page is active, but it's unclear what supervillain-y things they actually do. One who calls himself Tamerlane sells T-shirts and reviews fast food restaurants for his 1,000-plus followers.

Whether these men and women are heroes or villains—or both, or neither—they certainly do come up with creative monikers. We'll leave you with some names of these "Reals" and "Arches" gleaned from their respective databases. You can paint your own mental picture of what it would look like if they were to duke it out.

Real-Life Superheroes	Real-Life Supervillains
Hawt Flash	Professor Plague
Blue Potato	Agent Beryllium
Apocalypse Meow	The Baroness
The Komet	Kaptain Blackheart
Bearman	Rex Velvet
Lucid	The Aluminum
Nihilist	Calamity
Nameless Crusader	Fatal Phyllo
Doctor Mystery	Lord Malignance
Mr. Silent	Lord Mole

Midwinter Day, the southern winter solstice, is observed as a holiday on June 21 in Antarctica, and is celebrated with sumptuous meals, such as lobster and rib eye steaks.

FINDING URSULA

Most Disney top-10 lists include The Little Mermaid...*and it's usually near the top. Here's how a minor character in Hans Christian Andersen's 1837 fairy tale became one of the most beloved villains in Disney's history.*

RETURN TO FORM

Walt Disney Animation Studios was reborn in the 1990s, thanks to *Aladdin, Beauty and the Beast, The Lion King, Pocahontas, Mulan,* and many others. The movie that kicked off this "Disney Renaissance" was 1989's *The Little Mermaid.* "Here at last," raved film critic Roger Ebert, "is the kind of liberating, original, joyful Disney animation that we all remember from *Snow White, Pinocchio,* and the other first-generation classics." That was good news for an animation studio mired in a decades-long slump that reached a low point after the 1985 flop *The Black Cauldron.* (It was their first PG-rated animated film and proved to be too dark, even for parents.)

So, for *The Little Mermaid* (which had been on Disney's radar since the 1930s), new CEO Michael Eisner and chairman Jeffrey Katzenberg pulled out all the stops to recapture that first-generation magic. Take the villain, Ursula the Sea Witch, who tricks a little mermaid named Ariel into giving up her beautiful voice in exchange for legs. It took the cream of the crop of writers, directors, composers, and animators four years—not to mention an exhaustive search to find the right voice actor—to develop her. Here's how Ursula came to be.

The Character

In 1985, screenwriters/directors Ron Clements and John Musker decided to base the movie's villain on an unnamed Witch Queen from the original fairy tale. In early drafts, Ursula was a scheming manta ray inspired by Joan Collins, who played the scheming Alexis on the TV soap opera *Dynasty.*

The writing team of Howard Ashman and Alan Menken—known for their 1982 off-Broadway hit musical adaptation of *Little Shop of Horrors*—were hired to compose songs for the movie. They ended up writing most of Ursula's dialogue, and Ashman became a coproducer for the entire film.

At first, Ashman lobbied for Collins to voice Ursula, but she wasn't interested. As Ashman was looking at some other concept illustrations—drawn by Rob Minkoff (future *Lion King* director)—he skipped over the manta ray and instead honed in on a heavy-set woman with big hair, gobs of aquamarine eye makeup, and the body of a shark.

Ashman recognized her right away as having been inspired by Divine, a drag queen (real name: Glenn Milstead) during the 1970s and '80s known for outrageous roles in several John Waters movies (*Pink Flamingos, Polyester, Hairspray*). Ashman came

Jupiter has its own version of the Northern Lights, and it covers an area bigger than Earth.

up in the same Baltimore-area gay scene as Divine, and he loved her for the part of Ursula. The animators started reviewing footage of the drag queen; she served as Menken and Ashman's muse while they wrote the song "Poor Unfortunate Souls."

For the final touch, storyboard artist Matthew O'Callaghan (future director of *Curious George*) had the idea to change Ursula from a shark to an octopus, which is how she ended up. (Though due to budget constraints, they could animate only six arms.)

The Voice

Divine herself might have voiced her undersea alter ego, but Milstead died in 1988. So Musker offered the part to Bea Arthur (*Maude, The Golden Girls*) because that's who he had in mind while writing the character. But Arthur's agent turned it down without even telling her about the "silly" role. Among others who auditioned: jazz singer Nancy Wilson, Nancy Marchand (Tony Soprano's mother on *The Sopranos*), and Roseanne Barr.

The two finalists for Ursula's voice came down to Charlotte Rae (Mrs. Garrett on *The Facts of Life*) and Broadway legend Elaine Stritch (*Bus Stop, Company*). Rae couldn't hit all the notes, so Stritch got the role...and was fired a few weeks later for creative differences with Ashman. After months of casting, they were right back where they started.

Then they auditioned veteran TV and stage actress Pat Carroll (*The Danny Thomas Show*), who could sing so low she sometimes played men on stage. Unlike Stritch, who insisted on singing "Poor Unfortunate Souls" her own way, Carroll asked Ashman to sing it so that she could match his style (and steal some of his ad-libs, such as, "No more talking, singing, zzzip!"). Carroll even studied footage of Divine to mimic the drag queen's trademark guttural growl, and then added her own spin: "I saw [Ursula] as this ex-Shakespearean actress who now sold cars. The voice was very Shakespearean: 'Hello, my dear! Oh, no, dahling.'...but the pitch was a used car salesman."

EPILOGUE

At *The Little Mermaid* premiere in November 1989, Ashman gushed to reporters about the finished product, noting that the end credits "go on forever." He said it goes to show that an animated movie musical "is the most deeply collaborative medium imaginable." (Ashman's tenure with Disney was short: he worked on *Beauty and the Beast* and *Aladdin*, but died of AIDS in 1991.)

The Little Mermaid's $40-million budget (higher than any animated film before it) made $235 million worldwide. And Ursula holds a permanent spot on Disney villain top-10 lists, along with Cruella de Vil (*101 Dalmatians*), Jafar (*Aladdin*), and Scar (*The Lion King*). Not that the scheming Sea Witch would be surprised by her success; after all, she did tell Ariel, "My dear, sweet child. That's what I do. It's what I live for, to help unfortunate merfolk like yourself, poor souls with no one else to turn to." (Spoiler alert: She's lying.)

Parrots, like humans, can get addicted to opiates, and have been known to attack opium poppy fields in India (grown for pharmaceutical firms) to get more of the drug.

RANDOM ORIGINS

Once again, the BRI asks—and answers—the question: Where does all this stuff come from?

HIGHWAY REST STOPS

At the beginning of the automobile age, when long-distance drivers needed a break from the traffic or wanted to eat the lunch they'd packed for the trip, they'd simply pull over to the side of the road. Until 1929. That's the year that a Michigan civic planner named Allan Williams decided, on a whim, to install a picnic table on a patch of grass just off Route 16, three miles south of the town of Saranac. With signs announcing its presence down the road, hundreds of families stopped for a picnic lunch in the tiny roadside park, and many were so delighted they wrote to the Michigan State Highway Department expressing their approval. With public demand demonstrated, the Highway Department started building similar parks all over Michigan, eventually adding public restrooms. Other states soon adopted the model of a small green space plus restrooms, adding vending machines and information kiosks. That, in turn, eventually gave rise to travelers' plazas and truck stops, both of which include gas stations, convenience stores, and fast-food restaurants. Today, there are about 1,900 rest stops along the U.S. interstate highway system.

CROWD-SURFING

If you've been to a rowdy rock concert in the last 30 years—or just seen footage of one—then you likely saw some brave souls get themselves up above the crowd (often by jumping off the stage) and then traveling from one end of the arena to another, moving along the gently pushing outstretched hands of fellow concertgoers. That's called "crowd-surfing," and like "moshing" (fans smashing into each other) or holding lighters aloft during a ballad, it's become a rock tradition. The first guy to do it: singer Iggy Pop. At the Cincinnati Summer Pop Festival in 1970, he jumped from the stage into the crowd, who kept him on his back and surfing along, as if instinctively knowing what to do. The first recorded instance of a fan crowd-surfing happened at a 1980 Bruce Springsteen concert in Tempe, Arizona. While Springsteen played "Tenth Avenue Freeze-Out," a rowdy fan got on the stage, dove off, and "surfed."

MODERN SOCCER BALLS

For decades, the standard ball used in international soccer was made of brown leather. In the 1960s, as more and more games were being aired on television—primarily in black and white—broadcasters found that the ball was difficult to see as it bounded up and down the field. That changed in 1970 in Mexico City at soccer's biggest event, the FIFA World Cup, when sponsor Adidas designed and produced a new ball. Called the Telstar, it featured alternating panels of black pentagons (with five sides) and white hexagons (with six sides). The contrast made it much more visible than a brown leather ball, especially on TV. After its use in the heavily watched World Cup, the black-and-white design became the most common soccer ball style across the globe.

THE WEEKEND

For centuries, employers worked their laborers hard, giving them scarcely more than one day off each week—generally Saturday or Sunday—to be spent at church or engaging in religious activities. The idea of having both Saturday *and* Sunday off originated in industrial northern England in the early 1800s. Factory and mill owners worked out an agreement with workers that they could knock off at 2:00 p.m. on Saturdays (and get all of Sundays off) as long as they reported to work well rested (and sober) on Monday morning. The word "weekend," referring to this concept, which spread around England, was first used in the British publication *Notes and Queries* in the late 1870s. In the United States, the five-day workweek first appeared in the early 1900s, when a New England cotton mill with many Jewish workers gave its employees the Jewish Sabbath off—observed from sundown on Friday until sundown on Saturday. Christian workers were already getting Sunday off, and so from that point on, everyone at the cotton mill got both days to themselves.

THE SLOW COOKER

The Naxon Utilities Corporation of Chicago manufactured heat lamps and laundry equipment in the early decades of the 20th century, until founder Irving Naxon was inspired to build an electrical device that could safely prepare *cholent*, a Jewish meat-and-bean stew that his mother made in her native Lithuania. The recipe required hours to cook the beans until they're soft, and early 20th-century kitchen stoves weren't the safest appliances. So Naxon invented a plug-in, low-heat stewing pot he called the Naxon Beanery All-Purpose Cooker. He received a patent in 1940, but the U.S. war effort used so much of the available raw materials that his company wasn't able to mass produce the All-Purpose Cooker until 1950. By that time, the Industrial Radiant Heat Corporation had introduced a similar machine called the Simmer Crock, named for the clay cooking pot it resembled. Nevertheless, the Naxon Beanery All-Purpose Cooker dominated the market until 1970, when Irving Naxon retired and sold the company to appliance giant Rival. The following year, Rival reintroduced the product under its new name: the Crockpot.

Worldwide, 90 percent of all jury trials take place in the United States.

EVERYTHING'S DUCKY

Long before he got into the book racket, Uncle John was in a band called Quacky Duck and His Barnyard Friends. Seriously. Here are some other facts about ducks (the kind that swim and quack, not the kind that play guitars).

- Part of the reason why ducks can handle living in extremely cold water is because they don't feel the chill in their webbed feet. There are no blood vessels or nerves in duck feet, meaning they literally do not feel icy cold water.

- Ducks do change the appearance of their feet, however. During mating season, a duck's feet turn from brown or orange to bright red, a sign to the opposite sex that they're ready to make babies.

- Speaking of mating: the reproductive organ of a male duck is corkscrew shaped. On average, it's eight inches long, though the Argentine Lake Duck measures in at 17 inches, the lengthiest (in relation to body length) in the entire animal kingdom.

- Ducks swallow little rocks, but not to eat. Stored in their gizzards, the rough stones grind up and make digestible the bones of the fish that ducks eat whole. Once the rocks have been used to the point of being smooth and no longer sharp enough for breaking down bones, the duck vomits them up.

- Fastest duck on record: the Red-breasted Merganser. It's been clocked at speeds of more than 100 miles per hour.

- Male ducks are called drakes, and female ducks are called hens. Only hens quack.

- When ducks fly around their regular habitat, they get only about 200 feet off the ground. When migrating, they'll usually go as high as 4,000 feet. However, an airplane flying near Las Vegas once hit a duck when at an altitude of 21,000 feet.

- Spending all that time in water doesn't keep a duck clean. For that, they *preen*, picking bits of dust, dirt, and bugs out of their skin and feathers with their beaks. And as they peck, they spread an oily wax over their feathers, which keeps them waterproof.

- Ducks sleep in groups, with the idea of safety in numbers in mind. A few of the brood serve as guard ducks and will hang out on the perimeter with one eye open. They're actually half asleep—one closed eye means half of their brain is sleeping.

- Duck eyes are complex. They've got three eyelids on each eye, and because their eyes are located on opposite sides of the head, they offer a field of vision of about 340 degrees. The shape of the duck's eye is such that it can see up close and far off at the same time.

Police in Tokyo learn a special crime-fighting form of martial art called *taiho-jutsu*, which translates as "arrest technique."

LIFE IN 1918

It was more than 100 years ago, but the more things change, the more they stay the same—1918 is also the last time Americans lived through a pandemic. Here's a look back at what day-to-day living was like during the age of the Spanish flu.

IN THE KITCHEN

- Bread: **7¢ per loaf**
- Eggs: **34¢ per dozen**
- Canned tomatoes: **20¢ per can**
- Canned peas: **21¢ per can**
- Ground beef: **25¢ per pound**
- Canned salmon: **25¢ per can**
- Sugar: **12¢ per pound**
- Rolled oats: **10¢ per pound**
- Cornmeal: **8¢ for a one-pound bag**
- Flour: **$1.70 for a 24-pound bag**

- Lard: **$1.60 for a five-pound tub**
- Butter: **36¢ per pound**
- Milk: **9¢ per quart**
- Kellogg's Corn Flakes: **8¢ per box**
- Shortening: **$1.45 per can**
- Beef suet: **$1.20 per can**
- Potatoes: **2¢ each**
- Hershey Bar: **5¢**
- Beer: **10¢ per pint**
- Ground coffee: **48¢ per pound**

AROUND THE HOUSE

- Men's wool suit: **$26**
- Shirt to go with it: **$1.30**
- Women's cotton dress: **$3.50**
- Cotton skirt: **$2.70**
- Toilet paper: **25¢ for two rolls**
- Laundry soap: **30 10-ounce bars for $1.75**
- Oven: One of the first electric ovens on the market, the El Bako, sat on the counter and offered three levels of heat: low, medium, and high. Cost: **$10**.
- Refrigerator: The first mass-produced electric unit, made by Frigidaire, was introduced in 1918. Major innovation: it did not require users to add their own ice every day. However, it cost **$775**, which made it too expensive for most American households.
- Stamps: After the first postage rate increase in more than 30 years in late 1917, it cost **3¢** to mail a first-class letter.

- Communication: An average telegram cost 2¢ per word. That was a lot cheaper than using a telephone—the average cost of a long-distance call was **$4** for the first three minutes, and **$1.35** for each additional minute.
- Children's bicycle: around **$10**
- Newspaper: A weekday edition of the *New York Times* cost **2¢**
- Aspirin: **85¢ for 20 pills**
- Mixing bowls: **$2.00 for a set of five**
- Guitar: Acoustic guitars (the only kind that existed in 1918) started at **$3.95** in the Sears, Roebuck and Co. catalog.
- Wedding: Americans spent about **$400** on a wedding in 1918.
- Home: A new single-family home cost, on average, **$3,300**.
- Apartment: The average rent for a one-bedroom apartment in New York City was **$60 per month**.

Don't believe it? Count 'em. There are 147 windows on the White House.

TRANSPORTATION

- Cars: A brand new Ford Model T Touring Car cost **$450** for the least expensive base model, up substantially from **$360** the year before.
- Gas: A gallon averaged **25¢**.

WHAT PEOPLE EARNED

- The average household earned **$1,518 a year**. A government job at the state or federal level netted an annual average of **$1,160**, while teachers earned **$970**.

NEWS

- **The Great War:** In June 1914, Austro-Hungarian Archduke Franz Ferdinand was assassinated in Sarajevo, at the time part of Serbia. Austria-Hungary believed Serbians were behind it and declared war on Serbia, hoping to regain control of the country. That triggered a number of alliances and treaties, and within six weeks, Russia joined Serbia's side. In August, Germany came to Austria-Hungary's defense, then declared war on France and invaded Belgium, prompting the United Kingdom to declare war on Germany. That involved most of Europe, and the Great War (later known as World War I) began. The United States would send troops in 1917 and 1918. By the time an armistice was signed in November 1918, about 10 million soldiers and 10 million civilians had died, worldwide.
- **Influenza pandemic:** In the most devastating spread of a deadly disease in modern history, influenza infected 500 million people worldwide in 1918 and 1919. Also called the Spanish flu, because Spain was one of the few nations that openly reported on the outbreak, it's believed that one out of every three people on the planet became infected at some point, including about 700,000 in the United States. This all predated viral disease-stopping measures such as vaccines and antibiotics, resulting in the deaths of 50 million people.

BOOKS

- In the early decades of the 20th century, Zane Grey sold 40 million copies of more than 80 Western and adventure novels. In 1918, his book The *Roaring U.P. Trail* was the most popular novel of the year. It's a fictionalized telling of the Union Pacific Railroad into the West, with workers constantly besieged by Sioux warriors.

DID YOU KNOW?

Zane Grey is still one of the most successful American authors of all time. He wrote 89 novels, primarily set in the Old West, and he appeared on the yearly bestseller lists every year from 1915 to 1924. His most enduring work: *The Lone Star Ranger*, adapted into *The Lone Ranger* radio program (1933–56), movie (1938), and TV series (1949–57).

MUSIC

- Some of the most popular recorded songs of the year include "Tiger Rag" by the Original Dixieland Jazz Band, "I'm Always Chasing Rainbows" by Charles

Yeah, but it tastes better: Gram for gram, vanilla costs more than silver.

Harrison, and "Hello Central! Give Me No Man's Land" and "Rock-A-Bye Your Baby with a Dixie Melody" by Al Jolson. The year 1918 also marked the first time that annual sales of phonograph records topped 100 million units.

MOVIES

- It cost between 7¢ and 10¢ for a ticket to see a feature-length film, all of which were in black and white...and silent. The most popular movie of 1918, with an $8 million box office gross, was *Mickey*. The comedy, produced by and starring Mabel Normand, is about an orphan who inherits a lucrative mine, and all of her distant relatives appear to try and swindle her. Another big hit, with a $1 million gross: *Tarzan of the Apes*. It was the first-ever movie adaptation of Edgar Rice Burroughs's 1912 novel.

SPORTS

- While the Stanley Cup had been awarded since 1893, 1918 marked the first time it would go to an NHL champion, in this case the Toronto Arenas. In football, the Pittsburgh Panthers won the national college championships. In baseball, the Boston Red Sox beat the Chicago Cubs to win the World Series. The Red Sox star player: Babe Ruth, who led all of major-league baseball in home runs that season, with 11.

VITALS

- Life expectancy for an American born in 1918 was estimated at 54 years for men, and 47 years, three months for women. Population of the United States (consisting of 48 states) in 1918: 103.21 million. That's 60,000 fewer people than in 1917, the first decline in population in American history, attributable to the Spanish flu pandemic.

NAMES

- The most popular names for baby boys born in the U.S. in 1918: John, William, James, Robert, and Charles. For girls: Mary, Helen, Dorothy, Margaret, and Ruth.

* * *

A BATHROOM LAWSUIT

In 1976, *The Tonight Show* host Johnny Carson sued a company called "Here's Johnny Portable Toilets, Inc." for trademark infringement. The judge sided with Carson, but company owner Earl Braxton spent the next 30 years appealing. He finally lost the case in 2010, five years after the King of Late Night's death, and ended up keeping the temporary name, Toilets.com. But if Braxton really wanted "Johnny" in the name, he could have taken inspiration from Port 'O' Jonny, a portable toilet company serving eastern Iowa since 1990, or Johnny on the Spot, founded in Chico, California, in 1998.

Tyrannosaurus rexes nuzzled each other.

THE GREAT FAST-FOOD FAKE OUT

Early 2020 was marred by widespread lockdowns to curb the COVID-19 virus. Some of the bigger restaurant chains found a sneaky way to stay open: pretend to be small, humble eateries on delivery apps—taking up multiple spots when customers browsed their options. Perhaps you ordered food from...

Pasqually's Pizza and Wings. The food at Chuck E. Cheese was always secondary to the restaurant's real attraction: video and arcade games. With no on-site eating allowed, Chuck E. Cheese hit delivery apps like Uber Eats and DoorDash as Pasqually's Pizza and Wings. (Pasqually P. Pieplate is the restaurant's fictional head chef, and the drummer in the Chuck E. Cheese in-house animatronic rock band.)

Buster's American Kitchen. Dave & Buster's is like Chuck E. Cheese for adults—they've got loads of video games, but also have big-screen TVs to air sporting events and they serve beer and cocktails. Shutdowns meant a loss of gaming and alcohol revenue, so the chain rebranded itself for delivery apps, selling its pub food (burgers, sandwiches, fries) as Buster's American Kitchen.

Pasta Americana. In late 2020, family restaurant Ruby Tuesday introduced four "old world recipe" pasta entrées, which it sold online under the name Pasta Americana. Ruby Tuesday also offers bags of crawfish online. For that, it lists itself as The Captain's Boil.

Market Fresh. As an alternative to its standard roast beef, Arby's sells a line of "Market Fresh" sandwiches made from hand-carved turkey and chicken. Market Fresh is also the name the company used to bolster its presence on delivery apps.

Guy Fieri's Flavortown Kitchen. The famous TV chef has developed and opened numerous real restaurants, but this one involved slapping his name on food prepared by the kitchens of the Bravo! Italian Kitchen chain.

Mariah's Cookies. Pop superstar Mariah Carey launched a collection of high-end cookie bakeries in 2020. Not really—they were all baked at Bravo! Italian Kitchen outlets.

Twisted Mac. Another Italian American food chain, Romano's Macaroni Grill, presented itself on delivery apps both as itself and as a hip pasta joint.

Rotisserie Roast. The signature menu item at Boston Market is chicken roasted rotisserie-style. It's also the signature menu item of Boston Market's online identity, Rotisserie Roast.

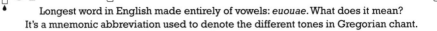

Longest word in English made entirely of vowels: *euouae*. What does it mean? It's a mnemonic abbreviation used to denote the different tones in Gregorian chant.

I'M STUCK!

Now you're stuck reading this article about people who got stuck!

MY THUNG IS THUCK!

In 2019, Clare Woof, of Lancaster, England, was driving along when her six-year-old son, Riley, suddenly started yelling from the back seat. His tongue was stuck in the lid of his water bottle. Clare pulled over and tried to help, but Riley's tongue was too firmly wedged in the half-inch straw hole in the center of the lid. He was now screaming in pain, so she rushed him to the nearest hospital. The staff there was flummoxed. A doctor managed to unscrew the lid from the cup, but the tip of Riley's tongue had become severely swollen. At first, the surgeons determined they could remove the lid safely only with special equipment, but the hospital that had the equipment was an hour and a half away, and with the swelling increasing, threatening to clog Riley's airway, they couldn't risk the trip. They prepped for emergency surgery. "This is really serious," a doctor told the family. "We need to warn you: Riley could die." (His throat could have closed up or he could have had a heart attack when all the blood from his swollen tongue flowed back into his body.) The scared-but-brave boy was sedated and the surgery, which lasted well into the night, was a success. Afterward, the tip of Riley's tongue was black and too big to fit in his mouth, leaving him with a temporary speech impediment.

> Originally, Huse had intended to hang by her ankle from a rope tied to a branch...naked.

HANG IN THERE

Hilde Krohn Huse was one of 37 contemporary artists (out of thousands who applied) to be selected for the prestigious 2015 Bloomberg New Contemporaries exhibition. Her work, an 11-minute video entitled "Hanging in the Woods," was described as "the breakdown between performance and reality as the intended performance goes wrong." That's an understatement. Originally, Huse had intended to hang naked by her ankle from a rope tied to a branch and film a few seconds that would be edited into a longer piece. But as the 26-year-old Norwegian was hanging there in the buff, with her head just above the grassy ground, her "safety knot" tightened around her ankle. The more she struggled to get free, the tighter the rope got. After 11 minutes, she stopped filming, swallowed her pride, and started calling for help. She was on a small island with other artists, not far from a house. Surely someone would come. Her friends later said they heard something that they mistook for "the cries of a distant seagull." Three hours later, a friend (a female one) finally found the naked artist and freed her. Huse's ankle hurt so much she thought she might lose it. (She didn't.) When she watched the video for the first time, she said, "I felt sick. I experienced everything anew."

There's a specific Antarctica accent shared by people who live and work there for several months on end.

BEHIND CLOSED DOORS

In 2019, a woman was stepping onto the Tube (London's subway) when she turned to say to goodbye to someone on the platform...at the same time the doors were closing...on her neck. The doors are designed to open on contact with any obstacle, but they malfunctioned. Result: the woman's head was outside the train; the rest of her was inside. Bystanders on both sides of the metal doors tried to pull them open, but they wouldn't budge. "Please help me, please help me," the woman kept repeating. Because this was happening several cars from the front, there was little time to alert the driver, and the train could start moving at any second. Who knew what would happen when it reached the tunnel? After nearly two minutes, despite a dozen heroic passengers working together, the doors *still* wouldn't budge. With the woman starting to panic, a passenger pulled the emergency alarm. The doors stayed closed. The train driver asked over the speaker why the alarm was triggered. The passengers were trying to respond, but it was apparently a one-way communication. According to a witness named Ruth Rubin, who detailed the account, at that point everyone yelled in unison: "Open the [bleep]ing door!" A moment later, the doors finally opened. The woman was unhurt, but badly shaken. A London Underground spokesperson apologized and said they would "look into all the circumstances surrounding this particular incident."

YOU'RE IN THE JAILHOUSE NOW

On June 5, 2019 (a Wednesday), at around 8:00 a.m., an unidentified Missouri woman was released from the St. Louis Justice Center. "Go down the hall to the elevator," a staffer told her. "Go down to the first floor, make a right turn. Walk out of jail." Once in the elevator, instead of pressing "1," the woman pressed every button and ended up on the fifth floor. She wandered until she found an emergency exit door to the fire stairwell. When she opened it, the alarm didn't sound because it had been shut off for maintenance. The door shut (and locked) behind her, so she walked down five flights, only to find the outside door locked from the inside. *All* the doors were locked. The woman knocked and banged and yelled for help, but as a corrections commissioner later explained, "The jail is a noisy place." Over the next two days, staffers said they could hear strange noises moving from floor to floor but were unable to pinpoint their source. It wasn't until Friday at around 6:30 p.m. that someone finally traced the noises to a fire stairwell door and saw the woman's eyes peering through the small window. She'd spent two and a half days in there with no food or water. Staffers fed her and offered to take her to a hospital. "I just want to go home," she said.

Worldwide, 60 percent of all sandwiches sold are burgers.

WEIRD WAYS TO DIE

Sometimes the Grim Reaper likes to make things interesting.

SWALLOWED BY A DINOSAUR

In May 2021, a 39-year-old Spanish man (unnamed in news reports) appeared to have accidentally dropped his phone inside a papier-mâché stegosaurus that was on display outside an office building in a Barcelona suburb. He climbed in head first through a small gap above the statue's leg...and got stuck. A few days later (but only a few hours after the man's family had reported him missing), a father and son were looking at the dinosaur when they noticed a foul smell. The dad looked through a crack and discovered the deceased man. Firefighters had to cut the dinosaur open to retrieve the body.

UP, UP, AND AWAY

In 2021, two Iranian fighter pilots were sitting in the cockpit of their F-5 when their ejection seats activated. Only problem: the plane was still in the hangar. According to Iranian State TV, the two men lost their lives "due to a severe impact with the roof of the hangar." The pilots were hailed as national heroes. The incident, which occurred at Dezful's Vahdati Air Force Base near the Iraq border, was blamed on a "technical problem."

SPUN QUITE A YARN

In 1987, Paul Thomas was working at the textile mill he co-owned in Thompson, Connecticut. He was all by himself operating a pinwheel dresser machine, which transfers yarn from a small spool to a large spool. At about 3:45 p.m., Thomas, 47, lost his footing and fell onto the small spool as the industrial machine kept spinning. By the time his fellow workers found him, Thomas had been wrapped up in 800 yards of yarn. Cause of death: suffocation.

THE GATEKEEPER

In August 2020, a man named Paul Lloyd Harvey was vacationing with his family at Antshill Caravan Park in Wales. After a day of relaxing and fishing—and a bit of drinking—Harvey decided to take a walk after his partner went to bed, which he'd done many times before. But when his partner woke up at 4:00 a.m., Harvey wasn't back. She called his phone but got no answer. A few hours later, he still hadn't returned, so she called police. Meanwhile, at around 6:30 a.m., a neighboring farmer found an unresponsive man—Harvey—with his head tangled up in the chain on his livestock gate. Next to him were two beer cans—one empty and one full. Attempts

First time Santa Claus was used in advertising: in a 1915 ad for White Rock mineral water.

to revive Harvey failed. No one knows exactly what he was trying to do when he got stuck in the chain, but an official inquiry ruled out foul play. "It seems to me," said coroner Paul Bennett, "that this appears to have been a completely freak accident."

MOOD KILLER

What happens when you throw dry ice into a wet pool? Disaster. That's how it played out in Moscow, Russia, in February 2020 for the 29th birthday party of a popular Instagram influencer named Yekaterina Didenko. Reports conflict as to exactly why Didenko's husband added 55 pounds of dry ice to the indoor pool—some said it was to cool the water, others said it was because he wanted to add a "visual effect" to the party. Whatever the reason, after the dry ice had created a moody mist above the pool surface, about a dozen partiers jumped in...and immediately started choking on carbon dioxide. (That's what dry ice is—carbon dioxide in solid form. It should be dispersed only in ventilated areas.) Seven partiers were hospitalized. Three—including Didenko's husband—didn't make it.

HOT! HOT! HOT!

In 2019, an English wedding planner named Darren Hickey, 51, was sampling some food for an upcoming affair. One of the sample items was a freshly-cooked fishcake, hot out of the oven—so hot that it burned Hickey's throat. Later that day, his windpipe started to swell, so he went to an urgent care ward in Lancashire. Doctors couldn't see any damage to Hickey's mouth or tongue, so they gave him acetaminophen to relieve the pain, and sent him home with instructions to return if it got worse. It got worse... but he never made it back to the hospital. The swelling continued, and within less than 12 hours after eating the fishcake, Hickey had choked to death.

MMM...GLYCYRRHIZIN

Health professionals warn that the chemical glycyrrhizin, when consumed in high doses, can rob your body of potassium and cause high blood pressure. This plant extract is commonly used as a sweetener, and is one of the main ingredients in black licorice, so it's recommended that you limit your licorice intake. Someone should have told that to a 54-year-old construction worker who was rushed to Massachusetts General Hospital in January 2019 after losing consciousness in a restaurant. Doctors were unable to save the man, nor could they figure out what had killed him. After an investigation, *The New England Journal of Medicine* released the official cause of death: cardiac arrest triggered by extremely low potassium levels after the man had eaten "one or two large bags of black licorice every day for three weeks." One of the attending physicians, Dr. Jacqueline B. Henson, remarked, "We almost didn't believe it when we figured it out."

Senator comes from the Latin word *senex*, which means "old man."

FUNNY FOLKS

Laugh at them, will we?

"Some people have a way with words, and other people...oh, uh, not have way."
—Steve Martin

"ACCEPT WHO YOU ARE. UNLESS YOU ARE A SERIAL KILLER."
—Ellen DeGeneres

"There's two positions in snowboarding. One is looking cool and the other is DEAD!"
—Eddie Izzard

"I'm over 40 years old and I've never used essential oils, which makes me wonder just how essential they really are."
—Stephen Cookson

"What is it about magicians that gives them ponytails?"
—Sarah Silverman

"We started off trying to set up a small anarchist community, but people wouldn't obey the rules."
—Alan Bennett

"My mom was a ventriloquist and she always was throwing her voice. For ten years I thought the dog was telling me to kill my father."
—Wendy Liebman

"I HAD A ROMANCE NOVEL INSIDE ME, BUT I PAID THREE SAILORS TO BEAT IT OUT OF ME WITH STEEL PIPES."
—Patton Oswalt

"When I asked my personal trainer at the gym which machine I should use to impress beautiful women, he pointed outside and said the ATM machine."
—Trevor Noah

AMAZING LUCK

*There's really no way to explain it. Call it good fortune or
dumb luck—sometimes some people just get lucky.*

LOTTERY NEWS

Just the Ticket: The chances of winning a big lottery jackpot are so low that it's literally almost impossible. And there's no way to skew the results, so drawing a ticket with the right numbers is entirely based on luck. But sometimes fate steps in. In September 2021, a woman from Clare, Australia, stopped at a local pharmacy to buy a Lucky Lotteries ticket for her mother. She usually bought two—one for mom and one for herself—but this time she decided to skip hers. Then, after she purchased her mom's ticket, the console randomly awarded her a free ticket...which turned out to be a winner, netting the woman a prize of $72,300.

Double Double: Some people buy lottery tickets every week, as part of their regular routine—an item that's always on their "to-do" list. But that means they can occasionally forget whether they took care of that item or not, which is what happened to Scotty Thomas, a dump truck operator from Fayetteville, North Carolina, in 2021. "I was just laying in bed watching a basketball game on TV and I couldn't remember," Thomas told reporters. So he filled out an online lottery form and played his usual numbers. Turns out Thomas *had* already bought a ticket and, as an email revealed, it was a winner, with Thomas poised to receive $25,000 a year for the rest of his life. However, because he absentmindedly played the same numbers again (and they were still *winning* numbers) Thomas received another email, telling him that his second ticket was a jackpot-winner, too. Thomas effectively won the lottery twice.

WHEN BAD TRAFFIC IS GOOD

Sony Setiawan works as an official for Indonesia's federal finance ministry, a job which requires a lot of travel. About once a week, he flies from the capital city of Jakarta to Pangkal Pinang Airport in the Bangka Belitung Islands. He routinely took Lion Air Flight JT 610 out of Jakarta, but one day in October 2018, he missed it. Traffic jams in Jakarta are common, even in the middle of the night, and this time cars were backed up so far that Setiawan arrived at the airport more than three hours late, at 6:20 a.m., not 3:00 a.m. as he'd planned. He had to take another, later, plane, which was a good thing for him. Lion Air Flight JT 610 crashed 13 minutes after

Only 1 in 10 professional film critics is a woman.

takeoff, killing all 189 people on board. Had Setiawan not gotten stuck in traffic, he would have been on that flight and probably would have died. "My family was in shock and my mother cried," Setiawan told reporters, "but I told them I was safe, so I just have to be grateful."

THE HEART OF THE MATTER

During a transatlantic flight from Manchester, England, to Orlando, Florida, 67-year-old Dorothy Fletcher suffered a life-threatening heart attack. Fletcher's daughter immediately summoned a flight attendant, who went on the PA system to ask the passengers if any of them was a doctor. Somebody was. It turned out that Fletcher was sharing her flight with 15 cardiologists—doctors who specialize in treating heart disease—on their way to a medical conference in Florida. They quickly began administering care to Fletcher and, following a short hospital stay after the plane was diverted to North Carolina, she made a full recovery. "All these people came rushing down the aircraft towards me," Fletcher told reporters. "The doctors were wonderful. They saved my life."

A VERY GOOD DOG

When Nicole Grimes of Marianna, Pennsylvania, was ten years old, her grandmother gave her a scruffy black-and-gray puppy that she named Chloe. The two were inseparable, but when Grimes was 14, Chloe's incessant barking threatened her father's work-from-home customer service job, so the family had to get rid of the dog. Rehoming attempts didn't work out, so Chloe wound up at a local animal shelter. Grimes understood, but remained "really sad because I loved the dog." Flash-forward seven years to 2018. Grimes was now 21, married and with a baby daughter and living half an hour away from home in Brownsville. After deciding that the ideal gift for her daughter's first birthday would be a dog, Grimes saw one she liked on Facebook, offered by a friend looking to rehome. The dog looked a lot like Chloe, so she adopted her. Not only did this dog look like Chloe, but she was named Chloe, was 11 years old like Chloe, and behaved like Chloe, too. A veterinarian's scan of the dog's ID microchip confirmed the obvious—it *was* Chloe, reunited with Grimes after seven years apart. "I felt like I won the lottery," Grimes said. "I never thought I'd see her again."

*   *   *

"Sometimes you lie in bed at night and you don't have a single thing to worry about. That always worries me!"

—Charlie Brown

Total number of nuclear bombs detonated since 1945: more than 2,000.

THE BOTTOM LINE

Everybody wants to be remembered. It's only human. And, ideally, you'd probably like to be remembered for being the best at something. But what if you could be memorable...for being the worst ever to do what you did?

A SHORT STOP IN MEXICO

Mario Mendoza might have been one of the greatest baseball players of all time—if one were to consider only fielding abilities and none of the other, many elements of the game. In a major-league career as a shortstop that would span nine seasons, he committed only 85 errors—about 9.5 errors per year. But baseball also involves offense, and while Mendoza was a great fielder, he was among the worst long-term batters to ever step up to the plate.

In 1970, the 19-year-old Chihuahua, Mexico, native was playing shortstop for the Diablos Rojos del Mexico (the Mexico City Red Devils), a team in the Mexican League. A scout for the Pittsburgh Pirates attended a Red Devils game to check out another prospect, but was taken aback when he saw Mendoza quickly and stylishly field a difficult ground ball. For a lesser shortstop, the ball probably would've gotten through and the batter would've landed on first base. The scout was so impressed with Mendoza's sparkling fielding that he signed him to a contract and enrolled him in the Pirates' farm team system. After four years of working his way up, Mendoza got called up to Pittsburgh.

BIG LEAGUE BUST

It took Mendoza so long to make it to the top because, while his fielding was great, his batting was awful. In his rookie season with the Pirates in 1974, Mendoza played in 91 games and racked up a batting average of .221 with 35 strikeouts, just about matching the 36 times he got a hit. And of those meager 36 hits, all but three were singles. His fielding percentage, however, was a stellar .964, which is how he managed to make it onto the Pirates roster the following year, 1975. Over his career, Mendoza's work at shortstop consistently ranked among the best in baseball; his hitting did not. In the 1975 season, Mendoza's batting average dipped to a sorry .180. It improved to .185 in 1976, and a bit higher, to .198, in 1977.

Four years of bad batting proved too much to ignore. At or near the top of the National League East in the 1970s, the Pirates knew they needed to shake things up if they wanted to make it to the World Series. So following the 1978 season, they traded Mendoza to the Seattle Mariners...and in 1979, their first season without Mendoza, the Pirates won the World Series. The Mariners, however, didn't get close. In 1978, they'd won 56 games and lost 104—one of the worst records in baseball history. With Mendoza on the squad in 1979, the team won just 11 more games than they had the

Over the course of the seven books in the *Where's Waldo* series,
Waldo actually got harder to find. Reason: The...

previous year. Perhaps Mendoza's fielding helped (his fielding average that season was .968, fifth-best among American League shortstops). But at the plate, Mario Mendoza was still Mario Mendoza, hitting just .198 over 148 games, a record for the player with the lowest average over the most games played.

HOLD THE LINE

All told, Mario Mendoza would hit below .200 in five of his nine major-league seasons. There's actually a name for the numerical barrier of a .200 batting average: the Mendoza Line. The term started to appear around the baseball world in 1980, the year in which, ironically, Mendoza put up his best numbers, hitting a relatively robust .245. It was also the year that future Hall of Famer George Brett hit .390 with the Kansas City Royals, the highest average since Ted Williams's .406 in 1941.

> The term started to appear around the baseball world in 1980, the year in which, ironically, Mendoza put up his best numbers.

That September, Brett suffered a hitting slump for about a week. When a reporter asked him about it, Brett deflected. "The first thing I look for in the Sunday papers," he said, referring to a then-common practice of newspapers listing full stats once a week, "is who's below the Mendoza Line." That Mendoza, of course, was Mario Mendoza. Players whose batting averages are above the Mendoza Line are considered at least okay batters; below it, they're mediocre.

Brett may have introduced the term "Mendoza Line" to the public...but he didn't invent it. Mendoza himself later told *Sports Illustrated* that his Mariners teammates Tom Paciorek and Bruce Bochte came up with it while teasing him one day when his batting average was right around .200. Not long after, when the Mariners played the Royals, Paciorek and Bochte jokingly warned the slumping Brett that if he weren't careful, he'd "sink down below the Mendoza Line." The phrase spread through baseball, where it was heard by ESPN sportscaster Chris Berman, who used it on the air in the early 1980s. The Mendoza Line is Mario Mendoza's lasting legacy, and it's a term that's made its way into business, finance, politics, and entertainment to describe the line between barely acceptable and completely unacceptable.

BAD AS ALWAYS

More about Mario Mendoza:

- Playing for the Texas Rangers in 1982, his last season in the majors, Mendoza hit .118, his personal worst.
- Mendoza appeared in the postseason just once, when the Pirates played in the National League Championship Series (and lost to the Los Angeles Dodgers). In five at-bats, he made it on base once, working out to an average of .200—right on the Mendoza Line.

...illustrator made him smaller. By the seventh book, Waldo was one-fifth the size he was in the first.

- In 1977, the Pirates let Mendoza pitch a couple of innings. During his time on the mound he walked two batters and gave up three hits, including a home run.

HOMECOMING KING

Waived by the Texas Rangers following the 1982 season and still of prime playing age at 32, Mendoza returned to his home nation and played in the Mexican Summer League. He was a bona fide star in that organization, hitting .291 in seven seasons and earning the nickname "Eleganté" for his smooth style of play.

In 2000, Mendoza was awarded one of the highest honors in Latin American sport—he was elected to the Mexican League Hall of Fame. That's for his contributions to baseball before and after his time in U.S.-based Major League Baseball. That's pretty good for someone who may go down in history as baseball's worst of all time.

WHAT'S MY LINE?

Other terms that baseball players have come up with to mock bad batters:

- In the late 1800s, poor hitters were said to have "tapperitis" for their tendency to give the ball little taps with their weak swings, rather than manly wallops.
- By the 1930s, batters who couldn't hit above .200 were said to not be able to "hit their weight," seeing as how the average ball player weighed in at around .200.
- In the 1950s, "banjo hitter" and "ukulele hitter" were hurled at players who couldn't hit for power, implying that their hitting was so weak they were using a hollow wooden instrument and not a solid bat.
- In the 1960s, before Mario Mendoza's time, the San Francisco Giants used the term "Lanier-Mason Line" to refer to the chasm of bad averages between .228 hitter Hal Lanier and .205 hitter Don Mason.
- By the time Mendoza entered the big leagues in the 1970s, it was customary to say that bad batters were "on the Interstate." Meaning: When a player's average was displayed on a scoreboard, a .180, for example, would look like I-80 (short for Interstate-80).

* * *

A WARNING FROM PHYSICIST STEPHEN HAWKING

"The real risk with artificial intelligence isn't malice, but competence. A super-intelligent AI will be extremely good at accomplishing its goals, and if those goals aren't aligned with ours we're in trouble. You're probably not an evil ant-hater who steps on ants out of malice, but if you're in charge of a hydroelectric green-energy project and there's an anthill in the region to be flooded, too bad for the ants. Let's not place humanity in the position of those ants."

Confetti is the Italian name for Jordan almonds, those almonds with a hard sugar coating. It's a tradition in Italy to throw the almonds during carnivals.

BATHROOM STYLES OF THE RICH AND FAMOUS

The price of fame, for these celebrities at least, is that even your bathroom habits make headlines.

Dwayne "The Rock" Johnson. In 2017, Johnson posted a video on Instagram featuring himself in the weight room he calls his "Iron Paradise." At one point in the video he shows off a training shoe...but next to it is a water bottle containing a suspicious yellow liquid that definitely *isn't* water. That's when the Rock fessed up about an unusual habit: during his long, intense workouts he doesn't usually take bathroom breaks. "I just realized you all just saw my big bottle of pee," he explains. "Look, I go hardcore when I train. I don't have time to go to the bathroom. I find a bottle, I pee in it, and I keep training like a beast."

Ed Sheeran. The chart-topping English folk-pop singer-songwriter best known for hits such as "Thinking Out Loud" (2014) and "Shape of You" (2017) will do just about anything to avoid using a public urinal (except, perhaps, pee into a water bottle à la the Rock). Why is he so particular? Well, let's just say his fans can be a little *too* curious when he's too indisposed to do anything about it: "There will be twenty urinals, and I will stand at an end one, and someone will come and stand right next to me just to have a look," he explained on the *Armchair Expert* podcast in 2021. "So my rule is I usually don't."

Gisele Bündchen. You'd think a Brazilian supermodel and wife of NFL quarterback Tom Brady would have access to great health care...and you would be correct. But when she was getting ready to deliver her son, Benjamin, in 2009, she opted to give birth at home, in the bathroom, in the *tub*. The bath was filled with warm water heated to match Bündchen's body temperature, to "ease the transition" of the baby from his mother's womb into the world. Bündchen says she was inspired to give birth in her bathtub after watching *The Business of Being Born*, a documentary hosted by TV personality Ricki Lake. Brady was initially opposed to the idea, fearing it was too risky. "He was like, 'Who has a kid at home in 2000...?'" Bündchen says. But he eventually came around, and the bathroom birth went off without a hitch. "I think we brought this boy into the world in the most precious way," the proud papa told *People* magazine in 2021.

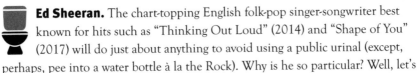

If you're healthy, your stomach is home to more than 400 different bacteria strains.

Madonna (and Mary J. Blige). When on tour, their contract riders require that their dressing room toilets be fitted with brand-new, never-used toilet seats at each concert venue. (Jennifer Lopez travels with a special toilet seat cover and won't use a toilet without it.)

Frank Sinatra. When Sinatra performed at the Golden Nugget Hotel and Casino in Atlantic City in the 1980s and '90s, he stayed in a special "Chairman's Suite" built just for him, complete with an Italian marble toilet and a golden clamshell toilet seat. Sinatra died in 1998, but it wasn't until 2020 that some of the contents of the Chairman's Suite, including Sinatra's toilet, were sold at public auction. How much would you have paid for the prestigious pot? The winning bidder got it for $4,250. Similar secondhand toilets not graced by Old Blue Eyes's backside typically sell for about $2,000; if you want a brand new one, it'll set you back as much as $27,000.

Barbra Streisand. Fact? Fiction? You be the judge: one *unauthorized* biography of Streisand claims that she requires her assistants to scatter fresh rose petals in the toilet bowls in her home. Similarly, *Vanity Fair* magazine reported in 2002 that Streisand "has a contract rider demanding rose petals be strewn in backstage toilet." What does Babs have to say about all of this? "Absolutely false," she writes on her website. "This is one of those dreamed-up stories where a journalist figures, 'if it's whacky enough, people will believe it.'"

Liberace. Here's another story you can judge for yourself: in a 1981 interview with *Rolling Stone* magazine, the flamboyant pianist claimed to have invented and patented a disappearing toilet that "rotates on an axis and folds neatly into a wall" when not in use. "There's just no reason why you should walk into a bathroom and see a toilet. It's unglamorous," he told the magazine. But a search of the U.S. Patent Office's database shows no such toilet patent (or any other, for that matter) awarded to Liberace. Apparently, no photos of the toilet exist; pictures of other toilets in Liberace's homes show that he was more inclined to decorate them and turn them into thrones than hide them from view.

* * *

THE POOP ON WHALE POOP

Krill swim through the oceans in huge hordes, making an easy meal for blue whales, who swallow around four tons' worth of these tiny creatures every day. Krill are shellfish, and those shells have to go somewhere. Krill shells are bright orange...and so is whale poop.

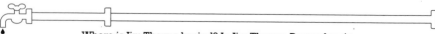

UNCLE JOHN'S PAGE OF LISTS

Random bits of information from the BRI's bottomless files.

11 Odd Cookbooks
1. *Microwave Cooking for One*
2. *Cookin' with Coolio*
3. *White Trash Cooking*
4. *Mosh Potatoes: Recipes...from the Heavyweights of Heavy Metal*
5. *The Pyromaniac's Cookbook*
6. *Feeding Hannibal: A Connoisseur's Cookbook*
7. *Tastes Like Schitt: The Unofficial Cookbook of Schitt's Creek*
8. *Cooking in the Nude*
9. *Cooking for Your Evil Twin*
10. *Prison Ramen: Recipes and Stories from Behind Bars*
11. *Reasons Mommy Drinks*

5 Oldest MLB Franchises That Never Moved
1. Chicago Cubs (1876)
2. Pittsburgh Pirates (1882)
3. Cincinnati Reds (1882)
4. St. Louis Cardinals (1882)
5. Philadelphia Phillies (1883)

8 Celeb Moms Who Ate Their Placentas
1. Hilary Duff
2. Alicia Silverstone
3. Chrissy Teigen
4. January Jones
5. Kim Kardashian
6. Kourtney Kardashian
7. Khloé Kardashian
8. Mayim Bialik

8 Most Popular Passwords (2018)
1. 123456
2. Password
3. 123456789
4. 12345678
5. 12345
6. 111111
7. 1234567
8. sunshine

7 Language Lessons in Weird Al's "Word Crimes" Song
1. Could care less vs. couldn't care less
2. It's vs. its
3. Espresso vs. "expresso"
4. Who vs. whom
5. Irony vs. coincidence
6. Are you vs. RU
7. Literally vs. figuratively

8 Strange Things Left in Ubers
1. Pink leopard-print bikini
2. FBI bulletproof vest
3. Rabbit legs
4. Painting of Kate Middleton
5. Catheter
6. Cooler of breast milk
7. Part of an ankle monitor
8. Toilet seat

Top 10 Instagram Hashtags (July 2021)
1. #love (1.835B)
2. #instagood (1.15B)
3. #fashion (812.7M)
4. #photooftheday (797.3M)
5. #beautiful (661M)
6. #art (649.9M)
7. #photography (583.1M)
8. #happy (578.8M)
9. #picoftheday (570.8M)
10. #cute (569.1M)

4 Words With 4 S's
1. Weightlessness
2. Sassafras
3. Lossless
4. Assassin

"SORRY, WRONG _____."

In which one person or thing is inexplicably mistaken for another person or thing.

WRONG CAR: One summer night in 2021, a man (unidentified in press reports) was walking to his car at the Walton Lighthouse parking lot in Santa Cruz, California. At least, he thought it was his car, and he thought it was his wife sitting in the driver's seat with the engine running. But his wife was in the next car over, which looked just like his. Meanwhile, the woman who was sitting in the closer car panicked when her passenger door opened and a stranger started to get in. She hit the gas, drove over some grass, and crashed through a metal fence before plunging 20 feet down to a rocky beach. The man wasn't injured, and except for the woman's foot (and probably her pride), neither was she. Investigators determined that the mishap was "truly an accident."

WRONG IDENTITY: A rookie police officer was driving on the M8 motorway in Glasgow, Scotland, one night in 2021 when she called the station to report that a drone was following her squad car. No matter how fast she went, she couldn't shake it. Dispatchers ordered her to return immediately. As she approached the police station, she said the drone was continuing its pursuit—even on the side streets. When her fellow officers reached the parking lot, the rookie was already out of her vehicle, crouched on the ground with her hood pulled over her head. She pointed to a bright light just above the horizon and said, "It's right there." The officers all looked over and one of them said, "That's Jupiter." Case closed. After the incident was shared on social media (without mentioning any names), a police spokesperson said the officer was very embarrassed, but can now tell the difference between a small unmanned aerial vehicle and a gas giant that's 365 million miles away. "This is going to haunt her," he said.

WRONG ORB: In October 2020, Scottish soccer fans were left scratching their heads, and yelling at their TVs, during a live telecast of an Inverness Caledonian Thistle Football Club game. At several points during the match, the TV camera, aimed down at the field from the top of the stadium, would drift away from the action on the field and follow the assistant referee up and down the sideline. As the game wore on, it kept happening, at one point even missing a goal scored by the home team. Fans went online to complain, and they knew who to blame: Caledonian's brand-new, highly publicized, state-of-the-art Pixellot camera system "with in-built, AI, ball-tracking technology." Caledonian had replaced the human camera operators with Pixellot a few weeks earlier, and the AI system had thus far performed adequately, keeping the white soccer ball in the center of the TV picture... until it was unable to distinguish between the ball and the referee's bald head. ("Get that man a toupee!" tweeted one fan.)

WRONG BRAD: When *Batman* actor Michael Keaton isn't acting, he likes to ride horses on his Montana ranch. One day he decided to purchase a handmade saddle from one of the best in the business: Brad "Cash" Cooper, saddlemaker to the stars (and nonstars). After visiting Cooper's California shop to look at samples, Keaton continued the conversation via a series of emails, asking detailed saddlemaking questions. But Keaton was growing increasingly frustrated with Cooper's replies: they were taking days to arrive, and when they did, they were short and cryptic, such as, "Yeah. OK. Ha!" This went on for a few weeks until Keaton looked at his contacts list and realized it wasn't saddlemaker Cash Cooper that he'd been emailing, but friend and fellow movie star Bradley Cooper. "[Bradley] was on the other end," Keaton recalled, "going, 'What the **** is he even talking about?'"

WRONG NOISE: Xi Yan of Jurong West, Singapore, called the animal welfare group ACRES in 2021 to report a snake in her house. She hadn't seen the snake, but she sent them a recording of it hissing, and the wildlife experts said that it sounded just like a black spitting cobra—not aggressive but highly venomous. So they sent a team right over. Wearing protective clothing and carrying snake tongs, the rescue officers methodically searched every crevice of every room. They could hear the hissing intermittently as it reverberated through the house. "At one point we thought there might be two or three cobras," said one of the rescuers. An hour into the search, they'd traced the hissing to the third floor bathroom. Wearing thick gloves, the lead rescuer went in and reached into a wastebasket. He pulled out an Oral-B electric toothbrush, turned it off, and the hissing stopped. The relieved homeowner explained that water had gotten inside the toothbrush, and it must have short-circuited. "I should really buy a new one," Xi said. "I don't want to go through this again."

WRONG GATOR: Early one morning in July 2021, a woman described as "hysterical" called the Vancouver, B.C., police to report that a large alligator was on the loose in her high-rise condominium, and it had her trapped in a stairwell! Officers rushed to the scene and slowly approached the animal in a dimly lit corridor. It really did look like a large alligator—it had scales, webbed feet, and a mean snarl. Upon closer inspection, however, it was shiny and gold and...it was a sculpture. In a police tweet about the odd call, Constable Jason Doucette said the sculpture even fooled his officers, and pondered what it must have been like for the woman "running up that secluded stairwell, rounding the corner and suddenly coming face to face with this...'clean up, aisle one' for me."

There are no green mammals; mammal hair can develop only in black, brown, yellow, or reddish colors.

BEHIND THE HITS

Here's another spin of a longtime Bathroom Reader *golden oldie—the secret stories and facts behind popular songs.*

The Song: "Everybody Loves Somebody" (1964)

The Artist: Dean Martin

The Story: By the mid-1960s, gentlemanly, tuxedo-wearing crooners such as Dean Martin were considered passé—the kind of singers whose work was oriented toward the older, less hip generation. Along with Frank Sinatra, Tony Bennett, and Perry Como, Martin was one of the more successful traditional pop-standards singers, but he hadn't had a top-10 hit since "Return to Me" in 1958. One day in early 1964, at the peak of Beatlemania and rock 'n' roll's "British Invasion," Martin heard his 12-year-old son, Dean Jr., listening to a Beatles record, and it filled him with such resentment that he reportedly told his son, "I'm gonna knock your pallies off the charts." And he did. He went into the studio and recorded a new version of "Everybody Loves Somebody," a song that had been a minor hit for Sinatra in 1948, but had been largely forgotten by 1964. That comeback single reached #1 on the *Billboard* pop chart, displacing "A Hard Day's Night" by the Beatles. More good news: the song, sung in Martin's classic style, reinvigorated his career. In 1965, he was asked to host a weekly TV variety show, which lasted for nine years, and during every episode of *The Dean Martin Show*, its star sang "Everybody Loves Somebody."

> He reportedly told his son, "I'm gonna knock your pallies off the charts."

The Song: "(Everything I Do) I Do It For You" (1991)

The Artist: Bryan Adams

The Story: Michael Kamen, who started his career as part of the New York Rock & Roll Ensemble and later became an orchestral arranger for Pink Floyd and Queen, moved into scoring movies in the 1980s, writing for films such as *Lethal Weapon*, *Brazil*, and *Die Hard*. When he started to compose for *Robin Hood: Prince of Thieves*, he remembered a melody that had popped into his head more than a decade earlier, but for which he'd never found a use. After seeing a rough cut of the scene where Robin Hood (Kevin Costner) smolders passionately at Maid Marian (Mary Elizabeth Mastrantonio), Kamen thought his old riff could form the basis of the movie's "love theme," a radio-friendly pop song to encapsulate—and promote—the movie. Kamen figured it should be sung from Marian's point of view, so he approached a few major female vocalists. Kate Bush said no, Lisa Stansfield's record label wouldn't let her, and

Annie Lennox of Eurythmics said yes...as long as she could perform the song in the style of an Olde English ballad (which Kamen refused). Then Kamen decided a man could sing it and recruited Peter Cetera of Chicago (and singer of "Glory of Love," the #1 hit love theme from *The Karate Kid Part II*). Cetera wrote a song around Kamen's original melody, but Kamen rejected it because he thought it lacked edginess. Finally, gravelly voiced Canadian pop-rocker Bryan Adams signed on, and, with producer Mutt Lange, wrote "(Everything I Do) I Do It For You" in about an hour. They used Kamen's melody, and for lyrical inspiration, they took a line from the movie, when Marian says to Robin, "I do it for you." The producers of *Robin Hood: Prince of Thieves* didn't much care for the song; they wanted something more medieval sounding, with lutes and similar instruments, rather than a modern-day pop song. Result: they buried the song over the credits of the movie...but it took off anyway. It went to #1 in 30 countries, including the United States, where it became the best-selling single of 1991.

The Song: "I Can Help" (1974)

The Artist: Billy Swan

The Story: At 16, Billy Swan wrote a song called "Lover Please" for Mert Mirly and the Rhythm Steppers, his garage band from the small town of Cape Girardeau, Missouri. The group recorded the song in 1958 and it became a regional hit. But it was R & B singer Clyde McPhatter's recording of the song in 1962 that made "Lover Please" a top-10 hit nationally. Swan tried to make it as a songwriter, first in Memphis and then in Nashville, where he wrote tunes for Mel Tillis, Waylon Jennings, and Conway Twitty, before joining Kris Kristofferson's band as a bass player in the early 1970s. During a break in touring, Swan and his wife converted a closet in their home into a makeshift recording studio, where they placed a drum machine and the organ Kristofferson had bought them as a wedding present.

> **DID YOU KNOW?**
>
> The year 1974 set a record for the 52-week period with the most #1 hits on the American pop chart—36 songs in all went to #1. Among that long list are the last #1 hit for former Beatle Ringo Starr ("You're Sixteen") and the first two disco songs to top the charts: "Rock the Boat" by Hues Corporation and "Kung Fu Fighting" by Carl Douglas.

Using one of the presets on the machine, a shuffling rockabilly beat, he played a song called "I Can Help," about a man attempting to win the favors of a woman by presenting himself as a friend. Kristofferson helped Swan get a contract with Monument Records, where producer Chip Young decided to make a full studio recording of "I Can Help," because 1) Swan's voice kind of sounded like Ringo Starr's, and 2) the song's early rock 'n' roll sound fell in line with the 1950s revival going on in music at the time. Young's instincts were correct: "I Can Help" went to #1 on the pop chart in 1974.

The Song: "Blame It on the Bossa Nova"

The Artist: Eydie Gormé

The Story: In the early 1960s, after the rise of Elvis Presley but before the arrival of the Beatles, Americans enjoyed a brief—but big—fascination with bossa nova, the exotic (at the time) form of jazz-influenced dance music from Brazil. Two of the biggest bossa nova hits of the era: "The Girl from Ipanema" by Stan Getz and João Gilberto, and "Blame it on the Bossa Nova," as recorded by Eydie Gormé. Gormé usually worked as a duo with her husband, Steve Lawrence, and she hadn't had a solo hit in years when Lawrence's producer, Al Kasha, offered her the song. Gormé had recorded many Latin-flavored songs before "Blame It on the Bossa Nova" (written not by Brazilian musicians but by the American songwriting team of Barry Mann and Cynthia Weil, whose credits also include "You've Lost That Lovin' Feelin'" and "On Broadway"), but Gormé hated the new song and refused to sing it...until her record label, Columbia Records, forced her to. Still, she tried to sabotage the recording by intentionally singing slightly off key. Good move. It wound up being Gormé's first (and only) top-10 hit as a solo artist, peaking at #7 in 1963.

The Song: "Lookin' Out My Back Door" (1970)

The Artist: Creedence Clearwater Revival

The Story: Creedence had more #2 hits than any other act in rock history (and they never did score a #1) with five songs reaching the runner-up position on the pop charts. One of those was the lighthearted "Lookin' Out My Back Door," which wasn't as gritty as the band's usual "swamp rock." Reason: CCR lead singer and songwriter, John Fogerty, wrote the song for his three-year-old son Josh. The song describes a surreal parade that the narrator witnesses going down the street as he looks out his back door. He sees elephants playing instruments, spoons flying, ghosts, magicians, and a giant doing cartwheels, among other sights. The lyrics fit in nicely with the drug-addled psychedelic music of the time, but Fogerty's inspiration wasn't some hallucinogenic episode—it was Dr. Seuss's 1937 children's book *And to Think That I Saw It on Mulberry Street*, which details a similarly silly parade. Fogerty read the book to his son, who enjoyed it so much that Fogerty decided to write a song about it.

*   *   *

AN IRONIC DEATH

The first known mention of Russian Roulette (a "game" where the player puts a revolver to his head, fires, and hopes there's no bullet in the chamber) was by writer Mikhail Lemontov, in his 1840 book, *A Hero of Our Times*. A year later, Lemontov died in a duel.

Bees can fly to an elevation of 29,525 feet. (That's higher than Mount Everest.)

WHEN WORLDS COLLIDE

Humans and animals occupying the same place
at the same time, with memorable results.

THERE WAS BLOOD EVERYWHERE!

Micheline Frederick was standing on her front stoop in Queens, New York, in December 2020, when a squirrel jumped on her left arm and sank its teeth into her skin. "We're wrestling in the snow and there's blood everywhere and my fingers [are] getting chewed and it won't let go!" she told WCBS-TV. A few days later, a neighbor named Licia Wang was mauled on the arm by another squirrel. Then came more reports of stark-raving-mad squirrels. The Centers for Disease Control reassured the public that rabies is very rare in squirrels, but urged bite victims to see a doctor immediately. Wildlife officials still don't know what caused the normally docile rodents to turn savage. None of the squirrels were captured, so the residents have no answers and were left to fend for themselves. "I came out of the house with a shovel after the first few days," said Frederick, "but now I think 'I have the vaccine, I'm wearing heavy gloves, bring it on.'"

BREAKING AND ENTERING

In the middle of the night in June 2021, a Thai woman named Ratchadawan Puengprasoppon was awakened by strange noises in her kitchen. She and her husband ran downstairs to investigate. "I saw this elephant [had] poked its head into our kitchen where the wall was broken," she told CNN. It was using its trunk to rifle through their cupboards. How did the hole in the wall get there? It had been made a month earlier by another hungry Asian elephant. "I have seen elephants roaming around our town looking for food since I was young, but this is the first time they actually damaged my house," said Ratchadawan. A wildlife expert explained that the pachyderms—which live in a nearby national park—were probably looking for salt, adding that as more elephant habitat is encroached upon, more of these kinds of interactions will occur.

WHAT A BUTTHEAD

In September 2020, a Douglas County, Georgia, sheriff's deputy was driving around town serving civil papers. At one of her stops, while she was standing at the front door of a farmhouse, she saw a goat grazing in a nearby field. "I hope that goat don't get in my car," she said to herself. The deputy had left her driver's side door open—a habit she picked up after she was chased by dogs a few times. Sure enough, when she got back to her car, the goat was standing on the driver's seat munching on stacks of legal documents in the passenger seat. The goat ignored her commands to exit the vehicle, so she tried to push it out from behind. That didn't work, so she went around and tried to pull it out by its head. The animal wouldn't budge. A long moment later, it finally hopped out on its own volition with a stack of papers in its mouth. When the exasperated deputy tried to retrieve them, the goat headbutted her and she tumbled to the ground. After that, it left her alone while she scooped up all the slobbery, chewed-up legal documents and then scuttled to the safety of her squad car. The entire kerfuffle was captured by the deputy's body camera and then posted on the department's Facebook page as "a little Friday humor."

TOILET COBRA!

The siege began in late 2016 in a Pretoria, South Africa, apartment building when a female tenant made a terrifying discovery during a nighttime bathroom visit: a six-foot-long snouted cobra poking its head out of her toilet. The woman escaped unscathed, but the cobra was soon spotted in another tenant's toilet. Then another. The tenants called in a snake catcher named Barry Greenshields, who tried grabbing it with his snake hook, but it was able to wiggle back down the drain. "It's big and strong," Greenshields told reporters. "It's by far the biggest I have seen." Local herpetologist Johan Marais explained that the tenants have every reason to be scared: "Snakes do go up drain pipes and there have been a few cases of people going to the toilet and getting bitten." His advice to tenants: "Keep your toilet lids closed when not in use." Two long weeks later, the cobra was finally removed by another professional snake handler, Hencke Marais, who reached into the toilet and grabbed it: "You have to get your hand behind its head and gently pull it out bit by bit. It uses its tail like an arm or leg and will grab hold and not let go." The cobra was taken to a wildlife reserve far away from any toilets.

> His advice to tenants: "Keep your toilet lids closed when not in use."

A BIRD IN THE FACE

In 2019, at Warner Bros. Movie World amusement park in Queensland, Australia, 10-year-old Paige Ormiston was riding one of the fastest, tallest "hyper coasters" in the world. While traveling at 70 miles per hour, Paige's face struck a large, white bird called an ibis, known for its long, curved beak...which left a long, curved scratch on her shoulder and feathers all over her seat. "I didn't know what to do because I was stuck in a chair," she later told TV reporters. Paige avoided serious injury, but staffers were unable to find the bird. (Interestingly, this happened almost exactly 20 years after the actor and model Fabio, while riding a Virginia roller coaster, struck and killed a goose with his face.)

According to one estimate, it would take about 23 bales' worth of hay to break a camel's back.

CLASSIC BRAINTEASERS

Time to test your mental fortitude with these tricky conundrums.
(Answers are on page 401.)

1. How many seconds are there in a year?

2. During which month are you most likely to get the least amount of sleep?

3. What do these famous names have in common: Britney Spears, Fred Armisen, Denzel Washington, Jack Handey, and John Leguizamo?

4. How can you remove two letters from a four-letter word and still have four left?

5. Imagine you are in a room full of water. There are no windows or doors. How do you get out?

6. Arnold Schwarzenegger has a long one. Michael J. Fox has a short one. Madonna doesn't use hers. Joe Biden always uses his. The Pope never uses his. What is it?

7. Two parents have six sons and each son has one sister. How many people are in the family?

8. Four cars, approaching from four different directions, arrive at a four-way stop sign at the same time. No one goes...and then everyone goes. Yet no cars hit each other. How is this possible?

9. When does 8 + 8 = 4?

10. How can you add eight 8s to get the number 1,000?

11. Tommy, Timmy, and Tammy need to cross a river, but their boat can hold only 200 pounds. Tommy weighs 175 pounds. Timmy and Tammy each weigh 100 pounds. How do they cross?

12. The timepiece with the fewest moving parts is the sundial. Which timepiece has the most?

13. Two ducks in front of a duck, two ducks behind a duck, one duck in the middle. How many ducks are there?

14. The word "startling" is the only nine-letter word that allows you to...what?

15. A patch of lily pads floats in a lake. Every day, the patch doubles in size. If it takes 48 days for the patch to cover the entire lake, how long would it take to cover half of the lake?

16. A utility worker fell from a 50-foot ladder onto hard concrete without getting injured. How?

17. Guess the next three letters in the series: G-T-N-T-L...

18. At noon, the big hand is on the 10 and the small hand is on the 3. What time is it?

Alice's Adventures in Wonderland author Lewis Carroll was briefly suspected of being Jack the Ripper. Who knows? Since the murderer was never caught, maybe he was.

SKELETONS IN THE NEWS

Skeletons are creepy, weird, and interesting—no bones about it.

PASSENGER SKELETON: In February 2022, Washington state trooper Rick Johnson pulled over a driver from the carpool lane on Interstate 405. But as he approached the vehicle, he realized that the occupant of the passenger seat wasn't a person—it was a fiberglass skeleton dressed in construction worker clothes (including a neon sweatshirt with the hood pulled up), propped up in the seat, and buckled in with a seat belt. Johnson cited the driver for misuse of the carpool lane. In a Twitter post, Johnson reminded readers that to use the HOV, or high-occupancy vehicle, lane, everyone in the car "must be alive."

OBSCENE SKELETON: According to Cuyamungue, New Mexico, resident Diana Hogrebe, shortly after Joseph Downs moved into her neighborhood, he started harassing her family. He would play loud music at night and fired off a propane cannon, a noisy tool used by farmers to scare away scavengers. Their feud reached its peak when, Hogrebe says, Downs placed an artificial, anatomical skeleton outside of his house and posed it so that its middle finger was raised. "It just put me to the boiling point," she told reporters. "It was like the last straw that broke the camel's back." Hogrebe's response to the skeleton flipping the bird: she snuck onto Downs's property and stole the skeleton. She admitted her guilt to police (probably because she was caught on surveillance video), but refused to say what she did with it. Police charged Hogrebe with one count of larceny, but the skeleton, worth about $1,500, was never recovered.

MUSICAL SKELETON: Tampa-based heavy metal musician Prince Midnight, who claims to be "half demon" and "supreme ruler of the abyss," showed off his homemade guitar to reporters in 2021. Why is that even remotely newsworthy? Because Prince Midnight built the guitar out of the remains of his "Uncle Filip," who was killed in an auto accident in Greece in 1996. Filip wanted his body donated to science, but he died right around the time that Greek medical schools stopped using human cadavers for study. So his remains were interred in a cemetery, and his family was charged an excessive monthly rental for the plot. Refusing to pay the high fees any longer, Prince Midnight arranged to have his uncle's skeletal remains exhumed and shipped home to Florida. He wasn't sure what he was going to do with the body at first. "It just popped into my head. 'I'm going to turn Uncle Fil into a guitar,'" Midnight told reporters. "And I was like, that is the best way to honor him." The body of the guitar is made out of Uncle Fil's ribcage and spinal cord, with the fretboard, pickups, and strings attached. Prince Midnight named it "The Skelecaster," a pun on the famous Fender Stratocaster. According to the musician, it "plays perfect and sounds awesome."

A CELEBRITY SAVED MY LIFE

For these people, their brush with fame was literally a matter of life and death.

HANDS OF AN ANGEL

A nine-year-old actor and dancer named Talia Hill landed a small part in the 2020 Netflix holiday film *Christmas on the Square*. On the busy downtown location, while she was at the hot chocolate station, the actors were directed to return to their starting positions. "So I started walking," Talia told *Inside Edition*, "and there was a vehicle moving, and then somebody grabbed me and pulled me back, and I looked up and it was Dolly Parton!" Afterward, Talia said she was shaking so hard that the 74-year-old country superstar "hugged me and shook me and said, 'I saved your life.' And my mom was crying, like, 'Yes you did, Dolly Parton, yes you did.'" Parton's response: "Well, I am an angel, you know." (She was actually playing an angel in the movie.)

IS THERE A DOCTOR IN THE STREET?

"Are you famous?" asked 17-year-old Weston Masset, who was trapped in his overturned Ford Mustang. "Yeah," said Patrick Dempsey. "I'm a doctor." Well, not really, but Dempsey did play one on TV: Dr. Derek Shepherd, aka Dr. McDreamy, on the hit ABC drama *Grey's Anatomy*. The accident happened in April 2012 outside of Dempsey's home in Malibu, California. After rolling three times, Masset had a concussion and was in and out of consciousness. Dempsey didn't know if the car would catch fire, but rather than wait for first responders, he grabbed a fire extinguisher and a crowbar and pried the door open just enough to pull the teenager out. Later, as Dempsey waited with Masset until paramedics arrived, he called the injured boy's mother, Mary Beth, to tell her what happened. "He had a certain authority in his voice," she later told ABC News. "I asked if he was a paramedic, and he said, 'No, this is Patrick Dempsey.' I thought, 'McDreamy?'"

MYSTERY SOLVED

Agatha Christie always did her research. For example, in her 1961 book *The Pale Horse*, the mystery writer described in great detail the effects that thallium poisoning has on the human body. Thallium wasn't particularly well known back then, so it's unlikely a Scotland Yard detective would have deduced that a serial killer named Graham Young—who killed three people between 1962 and 1971—was using thallium to poison his victims...unless that detective had read *The Pale Horse*. (Although some

Joe Dougherty, the original voice of stuttering Porky Pig, was eventually fired by
Warner Bros. Reason: he couldn't control his stutter.

critics, including *The Daily Mail*, blamed Christie for giving the killer the idea, Young claimed that he never read her books.) In 1975, a woman from South America told Christie in a letter, "Had I not read *The Pale Horse* and thus learned of the effects of thallium poisoning," a friend who was being poisoned by his wife "would not have survived." In 1977, a year after Christie's death, a British nurse saved a thallium-poisoned baby (who drank insecticide) because, out of all the other doctors and nurses, she was the only one who'd read *The Pale Horse*.

DAN THE MAN

Danny Trejo might play some of Hollywood's toughest characters, but in real life, he's known as an all-around nice guy for saying things like this: "Everything good that has happened to me has happened as a direct result of helping someone else." And for performing good deeds like this: In August 2019, after Trejo witnessed a car accident in Los Angeles, he ran over to the overturned vehicle and discovered a baby trapped in a car seat. Trejo tried to get in through a broken window, but he was too big to reach the seat belt. So he and another motorist, Monica Jackson, worked together from the other side of the car and were able to get the baby free. Downplaying their heroism, Trejo said, "The only thing that saved the little kid was his car seat, honest to God."

HOW INTERESTING

Even if you don't recognize the name Jonathan Goldsmith, you probably know who "The Most Interesting Man in the World" is. That's Goldsmith. The then-69-year-old actor (he's appeared in more than 300 TV shows) beat out hundreds of other hopefuls in 2007 to become Dos Equis's new beer spokesman. Turns out, he *is* pretty interesting. "[Being in] a commercial does not top my other experiences one bit," he said in a 2020 interview. What does? "Saving a man's life on Mt. Whitney in a snowstorm, saving a little girl from drowning in the ocean, as well as [saving] a dog who fell through the ice. [Those are] much more important to me."

TERROR AT 35,000 FEET

In June 2018, a man (unnamed in press reports) was flying from Houston to L.A. on his way to Vietnam to visit his ailing mother. About an hour into the flight, the man—who doesn't speak much English—needed to use the restroom, so a flight attendant pointed him toward one in business class. Confused, he ended up at an emergency exit door...and tried to open it. With both hands on the lever, he probably would have succeeded had actor Michael Rapaport (*Boston Public*, *The War at Home*, *Justified*) not sprang out of his seat and restrained the man just in time. "Everyone did say I was brave and heroic," Rapaport said on his podcast. "I consider myself a common man who does uncommon things."

All in the family: Globally, 10 percent of all marriages are between cousins.

CAN I WRITE IT OFF?

Everybody has something they spend money on that they're entitled to claim as a deduction on their tax returns. Uncle John, for example, lists his fancy Japanese talking toilet as a business expense. (Note to IRS: Just joking.) Here are some other things—bizarre but totally legitimate—that people have successfully deducted from the amount they owe to Uncle Sam.

BREASTS: Exotic dancer Cynthia Hess performed as Chesty Love, so to make that stage name more appropriate (and to potentially grow her clientele), she underwent breast augmentation surgery. Arguing that a larger chest would lead to increased income, she deducted the cost of the cosmetic surgery from her taxes as a work expense. The IRS initially refused the deduction, until she successfully sued for the right to do so in 1994, and won.

CAT FOOD: In 2001, junkyard operators Samuel and Carol Seawright of Columbia, South Carolina, petitioned the Tax Court to allow them to deduct from their taxes the $300 they'd spent on cat food...and won. The Seawrights used the food to attract stray and feral cats, hoping the animals would chase off the dangerous rats and snakes that tended to congregate around a junkyard, thus making the place a safer and more welcoming business for their customers.

BODY OIL: Professional bodybuilder Corey L. Wheir set a legal precedent when the Tax Court allowed him to deduct the hundreds of dollars he spent each year on body oil. It made his muscles shine and glisten, which made him more likely to impress judges at bodybuilding contests. Because bodybuilding was his chief source of income, he was allowed to list the body oil as a business expense.

WHALING: It makes sense that the costs of repairing and maintaining a boat used for commercial purposes are tax deductible, even on whaling vessels. In 2004, the federal government added a clause to the tax code allowing whaling boat captains to write off as much as $10,000 annually in this fashion. Why is this weird? Commercial whaling is illegal in the United States.

CLARINETS: Some parents have successfully written off the costs of buying a clarinet for their child and paying for lessons. In 1962, the Tax Court ruled it legitimate after an orthodontist testified that playing the clarinet helped correct overbite, so the costs associated with playing the instrument could be considered tax-deductible medical expenses.

Why does Samuel L. Jackson use the "MF" word so much?
He says it helps prevent him from stuttering.

MOVING PETS: If the proper criteria are met, the IRS allows taxpayers to deduct the cost of moving when relocating for a new job. If you meet the IRS's criteria for the distance of your new home from your old home and the number of weeks you work at the new job in the first year, you can also deduct the cost of moving your pets.

DRUG DEALING MATERIALS: Just because you do something illegal for a living doesn't mean the income isn't taxable. Drug dealers who earn income by selling illegal substances and then get caught may also face charges of tax evasion. There are even sections in the U.S. tax code about what costs related to illegal drug dealing are tax deductible. For growers of marijuana in places where it's not legal, things like soil and pots aren't deductible, but the cost of raw materials—marijuana seeds and mature plants to be distributed and sold—are.

> Just because you do something illegal for a living doesn't mean the income isn't taxable.

SPECIAL TREES: The state of Hawaii allows individuals to deduct as much as $3,000 from their taxes if the money was spent on caring for one of a handful of legally designated "exceptional trees," deemed rare or vital to an ecosystem. A couple of state-approved trees that provide tax shelter: the Indian Banyan at Iolani Palace, and the Kapok tree at the corner of Young and Ke'eaumoku Streets, both in Honolulu.

KIDNAPPING VICTIMS: Until 2009, the parents of children who were kidnapped—but never recovered—could claim the victim as a dependent only in the year they were abducted. The law was amended to allow the deduction every year until the missing child's 18th birthday.

GAMBLING PROFITS: Standard tax rate in the U.S. for gambling winnings: 30 percent. Exception: you don't have to pay the tax if you won the money in the U.S., but you're not a U.S. citizen.

GREEN HOMES: The federal government encourages households to "go green" by allowing ecological or energy-saving house improvements to be a tax write-off. One example: installing solar panels on your roof.

RANSOMWARE: "Ransomware" is a kind of online hacking attack in which cybercriminals threaten to release sensitive data about an individual or a corporation unless they're paid a substantial ransom, either in money or in cryptocurrency. Authorities generally recommend that ransomware victims not pay the ransom, but if they do—and they have a police report to prove that they were the victims of extortion—they can write off the payout on their tax return.

In 2015, Japan made Godzilla an honorary citizen and tourism ambassador.

DO WE REALLY NEED TO READ THE ARTICLE?

These days, most people get their news by scrolling through headlines. Result: headline writers try to squeeze in as much info as possible—so much that it might make you wonder if what you're reading is a typo. It's not. We assure you these headlines are 100 percent real.

Cards Against Humanity Sells 30,000 Boxes of Poop for Black Friday

Dozens of Camels Barred from Saudi Beauty Pageant for Using Botox

A Robot Promising to Destroy Humans Will Be Mass Produced

No Foul Play Suspected in Death of Missouri Man Kept in Freezer for Nearly a Year

RHINESTONE VEST-WEARING PIGEON REUNITED WITH FAMILY

Transport Canada Says It Wasn't Feces That Fell Onto People and Cars

Little Girl Lost at Sea Found Floating on a Unicorn

The Strange Job of Spanish Ham Sniffers

Recent Research Shows That Imaginary Numbers Are Needed to Explain Reality

"Sprinklegate": British Bakery Reported for Using "Illegal" US Sprinkles

Zookeeper Mates with Murderous Crane for Life

New Zealand Discontinues Payroll of Its Official Wizard after 23 Years

Florida Weather: "Falling Iguana" Alert Issued

Meatball Sandwich Horseplay Leads to Two Deaths, Family Betrayal, Two Trials

Woman Who Married Tree Is Happy to Share with Boyfriend

"Large, Pink & Elusive:" S. Carolina Police Seek Ruinous Pig

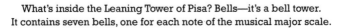

What's inside the Leaning Tower of Pisa? Bells—it's a bell tower.
It contains seven bells, one for each note of the musical major scale.

Marvel Superheroes Doomed to Heart Trouble and Dementia, Scientists Say

In Brazil, a Mayor and an Opponent Face Off in an MMA Ring

Total Lunar Eclipse Will Be Broadcast Live on
Northwoods Public Radio

FLORIDA MAN RESCUED FROM GIANT FLOATING
HAMSTER BALL—AGAIN

NASA HIRES RELIGIOUS EXPERTS TO PREPARE FOR ALIEN CONTACT

Policeman Loses Nose in Circumcision Ceremony

Man Sets New World Record after Lifting
Lady Using His Beards

Oops—Ignore That Email Invitation to a Cookie Monster
Cat Party, U.S. Embassy Says

METALLICA-LOVING FINNISH CROSS-COUNTRY SKIER SUFFERS
FROZEN PENIS AT OLYMPICS

Eel Bursts Out of Flying Heron's Stomach "Alien"-Style

**Former Model Claims Drinking Own Urine for
17 Years Has Maintained His Six-Pack**

FIREFIGHTERS RESCUE COW STUCK IN TREE

Is Your Meth Contaminated with Coronavirus?
This Florida Police Dept. Will Test It for Free

* * *

FINGER LICKIN' BAD

In 1987, KFC became the first American fast food chain to open a franchise in China. But the first impression wasn't that appetizing. Why? A botched translation changed the phrase "finger-lickin' good" to "eat your fingers off."

Though rivals during the Cold War, the U.S. and Soviet Union
were on the same side of the Nigerian Civil War (1967–70).

EPONYMS

The English language is loaded with eponyms—terms derived from people's names. You had a Caesar salad for lunch? Caesar is the name of the guy who invented that kind of salad. Your boss is a narcissist? "Narcissist" comes from the name Narcissus, the mythological character who was in love with his own image. Your Aunt Nina lives in Pennsylvania? Pennsylvania is named for William Penn, the man who founded the state. Get the idea? You could describe a fun article full of fascinating trivia like this as "Unclejohnian." (Let's make this a word, people.)

LYNCHIAN

Meaning: A fictional work (usually a movie) that juxtaposes the mundane aspects of life with the darkest elements of humanity, woven together to create a dreamlike sense of dread.

Details: David Lynch's surname has been an adjective at least since 1984, when a *Cinefantastique* article predicted that the writer-director's first feature-length film, 1977's *Eraserhead* (in which a man must care for a grotesquely deformed alien baby), would probably "remain his most distinctive, purely Lynchian film." It wouldn't, because Lynch had yet to make *Twin Peaks*, *Blue Velvet*, and *Mulholland Drive*. And "Lynchian" has since been used to describe other auteurs' macabre films—including Richard Kelly's *Donnie Darko*, David Cronenberg's *Naked Lunch*, and Darren Aronofsky's *Requiem for a Dream*.

How does Lynch himself feel about his eponym? He asked to change the subject when a biographer brought it up. Nevertheless, in 2018, the *Oxford English Dictionary* added "Lynchian" to its official list of words (along with "Tarantinoesque" and "Kubrickian," for Quentin Tarantino and Stanley Kubrick, whose films have also been described as Lynchian).

Use It in a Sentence: "To state the obvious, nobody is going to watch *Cooking with Paris* to sharpen their culinary skills. The new Netflix series piggybacks on last year's bizarre, almost Lynchian YouTube video where Paris Hilton cooked what can only be described as an anti-lasagne." –*The Guardian*, from the article "Kitchen Nightmares: Do We Need More Celebrity Cooking Shows?"

MACHIAVELLIAN

Meaning: Cutthroat, unprincipled; wanting to acquire and retain power by any means necessary—including manipulation, corruption, and other unscrupulous means.

Details: Niccolo Machiavelli was an Italian Renaissance-era author and diplomat. His 1532 treatise, *Il Principe* ("The Prince"), is considered one of the first modern books on political philosophy. Even in its own time, this how-to guide for princes was controversial for suggesting that immoral tactics are justified as long as you win. Examples: "Never attempt to win by force what can be won by deception"; "If an injury has to be done to a man, it should be so severe that his vengeance need not be feared."

In politics, Machiavellianism is the creed that the end justifies the means—even if the means are lying and cheating. In business, workplace psychologists have developed a test to determine if employees are "high Machs" (those who have questionable ethics but thrive in sales and management roles) or "low Machs" (who are more submissive and work better in groups). Psychologist Annette Towler warns that high Machs can "prey on the good nature of colleagues through a mixture of soft and hard tactics, such as seduction and bullying."

Use It in a Sentence: "I found out that a male colleague...was making significantly more money....I went into my boss's office with no plan and started crying. It was the worst possible approach. I had every reason to cry. But if I had been more Machiavellian, I would have thought, 'How can I use this information?'" —Stacey Vanek Smith, author of *Machiavelli for Women: Defend Your Worth, Grow Your Ambition, and Win the Workplace*

KAFKAESQUE

Meaning: A hopeless, illogical predicament that feels more like a nightmare than real life.
Details: Franz Kafka (1883–1924) was a German-speaking Bohemian author known for mind-boggling stories such as *Die Verwandlung* ("*The Metamorphosis*"), about a man who wakes up as a giant cockroach and lets himself starve to death so as not to inconvenience his family, and *Der Prozess* ("*The Trial*"), about a man who is arrested for a crime, though neither he nor the reader is ever told what the crime was. "Kafkaesque" first appeared in English in 1946, to describe books and films reminiscent of Kafka's works. These days, the meaning has been expanded to describe any seemingly unsolvable real-life predicament.

Use It in a Sentence: "In the formal petition asking for the 'suspension and removal' of Jamie [Spears, Britney's father] as conservator of Britney's estate, the 'Oops!...I Did It Again' singer's new lawyer said his client has been living in a 'Kafkaesque nightmare' that has left her traumatized while lining Jamie's pockets." —*New York Daily News*, from the article "Britney Spears files petition to boot dad from estate, says he pays himself $16K a month, while she only gets $14K"

CHAUVINISM

Meaning: Excessive bias for one's own cause, group, or gender.
Details: "Chauvinism" originally referred to someone who is extremely—and annoyingly—patriotic. That someone was Nicolas Chauvin, who may—or may not—have served in Napoleon Bonaparte's army at the turn of the 19th century. (Historians can't find any evidence that Chauvin actually existed.) According to legend, Chauvin was wounded 17 times and permanently disfigured, but remained fiercely loyal to

Napoleon even after the emperor was exiled in 1815. In the 1831 satirical play *La Cocarde Tricolore* ("*The Tricolor Cockade*"), the character of Nicolas Chauvin is a young, jingoistic soldier, who bellows to the audience: "I am French, I am Chauvin!" The eponym entered English in the 1870s, still referring to overzealous French soldiers. Over time, its meaning expanded to include nationalists from any country.

The eponym's first link to sexism goes back to the 1930s (in a play by Clifford Odets), but it went mainstream a few decades later during the women's liberation movement—as evidenced by a 1970 *Playboy* magazine article titled "Up Against the Wall, Male Chauvinist Pig!" (This use of "pig," by the way, began as a civil-rights era epithet first directed at police, inspired by the tyrannical pig Napoleon, who ruled George Orwell's *Animal Farm* like Joseph Stalin ruled the Soviet Union.)

Since 2000, the term "male chauvinist" has fallen into disuse in favor of the more clinical-sounding "misogynist" (from the Greek words *misos*, "hatred," and *gunē*, "woman"). But they have different meanings—male chauvinists don't necessarily hate women, they just deem them inferior. Technically, "chauvinism" can be used to describe a member of any group that believes they are superior.

Use It in a Sentence: "Everybody in charge of the galaxy seemed to look like us. I thought there was a large amount of human chauvinism in it." —Carl Sagan, telling *The Tonight Show* host Johnny Carson what he didn't like about *Star Wars*

ORWELLIAN

Meaning: Authoritarian control through sinister means—including disinformation, propaganda, and surveillance—suggestive of the dystopian society described in George Orwell's 1948 novel, *1984*, in which he coined the phrases "Big Brother" and "thought police."

Details: Orwell lived for only two more years after his most celebrated novel was published. But even by 1950, "Orwellian" was already in use. In 2003, linguist Geoffrey Nunberg called it "the most widely used adjective derived from the name of a modern writer." And it's also one of the most politicized. Why? People on the left side of the political spectrum believe Orwell spoke for them...and so do people on the right.

One key to understanding Orwell's intentions in *1984*: He wasn't predicting the future so much as he was describing the authoritarian governments gaining ground in post–World War II Europe—especially in the Soviet Union, where Joseph Stalin's Communist regime spied on citizens and weaponized language. Orwell saw the seeds of this happening in the UK, and his novel was meant to serve as a warning.

Use It in a Sentence: "All politicians operate within an Orwellian nimbus where words don't mean what they normally mean, but Rovism posits that there is no objective, verifiable reality at all. Reality is what you say it is." —Karl Rove, President George W. Bush's senior advisor, who failed to make "Rovism" a word

In 2010, Finland made internet access a legal right for all citizens.

STRANGE MEDICAL NEWS

We probably should have called this Gross Medical News, because that's what these stories are. If you're squeamish about diseases, parasites, or the bizarre things that some people do to their own bodies, maybe you should skip this one. Or maybe not.

WHO WEARS SHORT SHORTS?

In 2021, a 25-year-old woman from North Carolina identified in news reports only as "Sam" posted a TikTok video about having worn a pair of high-cut, very short jeans shorts on a date in 2018. Why is this newsworthy? Because the shorts were so tight that they landed her in a hospital's intensive care unit. During the date, Sam said, her shorts were uncomfortable, but she just ignored it. That night, she was sore all over and feeling ill. The following day, she noticed some chafing on her buttocks, which quickly turned into "throbbing, stabbing pain." The next morning, her mother rushed her to the emergency room, where she was diagnosed with a bacterial skin infection (cellulitis) and septic shock (the body sometimes responds to an infection by attacking soft tissue and organs)—all caused by an eight-hour wedgie. Sepsis can lead to death, so Sam spent four days in the ICU recovering from the effects of her atomic wedgie and at one point, doctors considered surgically cutting off the infected part of her buttock. Fortunately, though, surgery was not needed and Sam recovered.

SHE REALLY BLEW IT

Emma Cousins of Sheffield, England, was treated in 2018 for *mesenchymal chondrosarcoma*, a rare type of cancer that manifests as a slowly growing tumor behind the eye. When Cousins saw and felt her left eye bulging out of the socket, she sought medical help, which consisted of the diagnosis and surgical removal of the tumor. An MRI revealed that the cancer had spread to her eye, so doctors removed that as well, leaving behind an empty socket. There's a tiny hole in the skin that covers the socket—probably a result of her radiation treatments—and that hole leads directly to Cousins' lungs...which gives her a unique ability: she can blow out candles with her eye socket.

BEAN THERE

An issue of the medical journal *Urology Case Reports* featured the tale of a 30-year-old Michigan man (unnamed in the story) who sought medical attention at Sparrow Hospital in Lansing to remove a foreign object stuck in a narrow pathway in his body. Actually, there were six foreign objects—six kidney beans that he'd placed into his urethra in hopes they would provide extra stimulation during bedroom activities. But then they became uncomfortable...and the man couldn't get them out. Using a special tool, the emergency department staff was able to extract one bean, but the rest had to be removed surgically. (One bean had made its way all the way to the bladder.)

Making the cut: Only about 29 percent of Americans aged
18–24 are eligible to join the military.

Amazingly, the man was discharged from the hospital on the day of his surgery and made a full recovery.

NOT EELING WELL

A man identified in news reports only as hailing from Xinghua, in the eastern Chinese province of Jiangsu, suffered from a painful and long bout of constipation in July 2021. With other methods not getting things moving again, he resorted to what he'd heard was a surefire old folk remedy: inserting a live eel into his rear end. The man procured an eight-inch eel and allowed it to swim inside of him. Theoretically, the eel is supposed to just kind of loosen things up, but this eel apparently didn't know that. It bit a hole in the man's colon, crawled through it, and lodged itself in the abdomen. A full 24 hours after beginning to suffer severe stomach pain, the man went to the local hospital, where doctors surgically removed the still-living eel.

TOO COLD

Prolonged exposure to cold without proper protection can be deadly—if the body's internal temperature falls too far, organs can't function, and the body dies. That's a different fate entirely than cold urticaria—an allergic reaction to cold, be it chilly air or freezing water. According to a report in *The Journal of Emergency Medicine*, in 2020, a 34-year-old Colorado man emerged from a hot shower into a cold bathroom. He collapsed almost immediately as his skin broke out in hives and anaphylaxis set in—his blood pressure fell, and his airways narrowed, making him almost completely unable to breathe. After being rushed to the hospital, the patient was diagnosed with cold urticaria and treated with common allergy treatments, including steroids and antihistamines.

THE TALE OF THE TAPE(WORM)

According to a study published in *The New England Journal of Medicine* in 2021, a wife checked her husband into Massachusetts General Hospital in Boston earlier that year. The 38-year-old man was reportedly in reasonably good health up until one evening when his wife found him lying on the ground in the middle of the night, shaking and babbling. Doctors treated the man for what appeared to be a seizure, his first ever and unrelated to anything in his medical history. Seizures are usually indicative of another health issue, so doctors conducted more examinations, including blood testing and brain scans, and determined that the man had neurocysticercosis—tapeworms in the brain. Doctors had to go back more than 20 years in the man's personal history to figure out where he'd acquired a parasite. It turned out that as a child and teenager, he'd lived in an area of rural Guatemala where parasite-caused illnesses are common, usually spread by eating undercooked meat or by poor hygiene. Tapeworms generally remain in the digestive system and quickly cause issues like abdominal pain and weight loss. Rarely do they travel to other areas of the body, such as into the brain via the bloodstream, or lie dormant for years, let alone decades.

The world's shortest scheduled commercial flight is between two Scottish islands. It's 1.7 miles. Actual flying time: about a minute.

EDWARD SCISSORHANDS, STARRING TOM CRUISE

Some roles are so closely associated with a specific actor that it's hard to imagine that he or she wasn't the first choice, but it happens all the time. For example, could you picture...

Ben Stiller as Marty McFly (*Back to the Future*, 1985)

It's common knowledge among movie buffs that Michael J. Fox was director Robert Zemeckis's first choice to play the time-traveling teen, but Fox couldn't get time off from his sitcom *Family Ties*, so Eric Stoltz (*Mask*) was cast. He filmed a few scenes... and was fired for not being funny enough. By then, Fox had become available and arguably gave one of the most iconic film performances in history. ("You built a time machine...out of a DeLorean?") But a 35th-anniversary Blu-ray edition revealed that, in between Fox and Stoltz, director Robert Zemeckis auditioned a who's who of past and future superstars, including 19-year-old Ben Stiller, whose only screen credit was a bit part in the TV soap opera *Guiding Light*. "I actually think I blocked out that memory," Stiller said of his audition in 2020. Others who read for Marty were Jon Cryer, Charlie Sheen, Ralph Macchio, C. Thomas Howell, Billy Zane, John Cusack, and Johnny Depp, but none of them inhabited Marty like Fox did. Other considerations for Christopher Lloyd's equally famous role of Doc Brown: John Lithgow (to whom it was first offered), Steve Martin, Jeff Goldblum, Gene Wilder, and Eddie Murphy.

Jon Lovitz and Dana Carvey as Mike Lowrey and Marcus Burnett (*Bad Boys*, 1995)

This odd pairing was undone by a clash of personalities—namely, the timid Dana Carvey and producer Don Simpson, notorious for his hard-partying and rampant cocaine use. Simpson and his partner Jerry Bruckheimer (*Flashdance*, *Beverly Hills Cop*, *Top Gun*) invited the *Saturday Night Live* stars to Las Vegas to celebrate their casting in what was originally called *Bulletproof Hearts*, which *Variety* described as "an action comedy about two cops, one a rich kid bachelor (Carvey), the other a South Miami family man (Lovitz), who through a series of incidents have to change places." But Carvey, who became an A-lister thanks to 1992's *Wayne's World*, was reportedly revolted by Simpson's lewd behavior. He also didn't like George Gallo's script. In the end, the rewrites took too long to keep Carvey from bailing to make *Wayne's World 2*. As a result, Lovitz lost his role, too. And he *really* wanted it: "It was disappointing."

After the retitled *Bad Boys* went from Disney to Columbia, director Michael Bay decided to cater it to a younger audience. He changed the setting from New York to

There are 46 aircraft and helicopter carriers in the world. The U.S. Navy owns 20 of them.

Miami and started reworking the screenplay (which he said was "written so white") for two Black actors. When the budget proved to be too small for his first choices, Wesley Snipes and Eddie Murphy, Bay offered the leads to talk show host Arsenio Hall and sitcom star Martin Lawrence. Hall declined (and later regretted it), so Bay suggested they look at rapper turned *Fresh Prince of Bel-Air* star Will Smith, who'd be much cheaper than Murphy or Snipes. Columbia was nervous about two sitcom stars, but they trusted Bay, and he solved the script problems by letting Smith and Lawrence improvise most of their dialogue. (Example: nobody wrote, "No, you freeze, b*tch! Now back up, put the gun down, and get me a pack of Tropical Fruit Bubblicious." Smith ad-libbed it.) The quick dialogue and over-the-top action sequences—not to mention the shaky, handheld camera work—established Bay as a Hollywood director. (Before *Bad Boys*, he'd only directed commercials and music videos.)

Tom Cruise as Edward Scissorhands (*Edward Scissorhands*, 1990)

Tim Burton's "gothic autobiography" was inspired by a picture he drew as a teenager: a sad man with knives for hands. Following the success of his first three movies—*Pee-wee's Big Adventure*, *Beetlejuice*, and *Batman*—Burton was able to bring his picture to life. Some of show business's biggest names expressed interest in the lead role, including Tom Hanks and Gary Oldman (who reportedly turned it down). William Hurt, Robert Downey Jr., and Jim Carrey were also considered. But the suits at Fox were pushing hard for Hollywood's most bankable name to play Edward: Tom Cruise. It came down to the *Top Gun* star and Burton's first choice, Johnny Depp, who was just starting to become a star on TV's *21 Jump Street*. So, at the studio's behest, Burton met with Cruise...who lost the part, recalled screenwriter Caroline Thompson, because of his incessant questioning about Edward's daily regimen. "Part of the delicacy of the story was not answering questions like, 'How does he go to the bathroom? How did he live without eating all those years?' Tom Cruise was certainly unwilling to be in the movie without those questions being answered." Depp was another story. Whereas Cruise wanted to play a more manly Edward, someone who fights back and gets the girl, Depp said he cried when he read the script. Burton knew right away he was perfect, "Just meeting him, I could tell..." At first, Depp didn't really get Edward either, until he looked at Burton's drawing: "I instantly fell for the character—he made his way into my body."

Gene Hackman as Hannibal Lecter (*The Silence of the Lambs*, 1991)

Thomas Harris's 1988 horror novel, which pits an incarcerated psychiatrist–serial killer against a young FBI agent, became an instant best seller. That usually ignites an intense bidding war for the movie rights...but it didn't happen in this case. Why? Because a movie based on Harris's first Hannibal Lecter book—1981's *Red Dragon* (retitled *Manhunter*, starring Brian Cox as "Hannibal Lecktor")—received mixed reviews and underperformed at the box office. Result: few serious filmmakers were willing to take the risk on *Silence of the Lambs*.

But Oscar-winning actor Gene Hackman (*The French Connection*) thought it was the most "cinematic" book he'd ever read, and decided to make the movie himself. Already regarded as Hollywood royalty, Hackman teamed up with Orion Pictures to option the movie rights for $500,000. He had planned to write the screenplay, direct the film, *and* play Lecter. A few months later, he quit.

Exactly why is a bit of a mystery. Hackman himself chalked it up to his lack of writing experience, telling reporters, "I was so respectful of the book that I was into it 100 pages, and had about 300 pages of the script! So I let the project go, kinda regretfully." But was something else at play? According to some sources, Hackman abandoned *Lambs* because of its grim content. He visibly cringed at the 1988 Academy Awards ceremony when clips of his violent movie *Mississippi Burning* were shown, and he was wary of taking on another "dark role." Whatever his reasons, once Hackman was out, Ted Tally took over the screenplay, Jonathan Demme took over as director, and Anthony Hopkins took over as Lecter. All three won Oscars, *Lambs* won Best Picture, and Hackman never directed a movie.

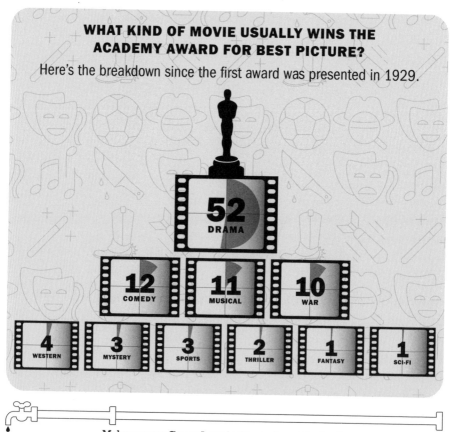

WHAT KIND OF MOVIE USUALLY WINS THE ACADEMY AWARD FOR BEST PICTURE?

Here's the breakdown since the first award was presented in 1929.

52 DRAMA

12 COMEDY

11 MUSICAL

10 WAR

4 WESTERN

3 MYSTERY

3 SPORTS

2 THRILLER

1 FANTASY

1 SCI-FI

Makes sense: Grope Lane in Glastonbury, England, used to be where the brothels were located.

A YULE LOG LIKE NO OTHER

Some Christmas logs are burned in the fireplace, and others are eaten for dessert.
As for Tió de Nadal, well, he (or she) is just a little bit different...

MADE IN SPAIN

If you trace your ancestry back to the UK or Scandinavia, there's a good chance a Yule log is part of your Christmas tradition. In some places, the custom originally called for an entire tree trunk—one long enough to burn for the entire 12 days of Christmas—to be dragged into the house on Christmas Eve. One end of the log was shoved into the fireplace and set alight; as it burned away the rest of the log would be pushed into the fireplace until the log was completely consumed. That tradition eventually gave way to burning a smaller log either on Christmas Eve or Christmas Day; then, when homes began to be built without fireplaces, people baked and ate special cakes shaped like logs instead.

In Catalonia, in the northeastern corner of Spain, they have an entirely different tradition around a log called *Tió de Nadal*, or "Christmas Log." If you've never heard of this tradition, you're in for a treat. (Or if you're squeamish, maybe not...)

LOG ROLE

Tió de Nadal is a cartoonish character. It's usually made by painting a smiling face on one end of a real log. The face end is propped up on two stick legs, almost as if the log were doing push-ups. It wears a floppy red hat that is sometimes made from a sock, and it may have a protruding nose made from a piece of wood stuck into the face of the log. There are male and female versions: sometimes the male version smokes a pipe, and if the log is female, she will have long hair that is sometimes braided.

The log is brought out and set up on December 8, the evening of a religious celebration called the Feast of the Immaculate Conception. From that day until Christmas morning, the children of the household are responsible for caring for the log. This involves placing a blanket over it so that it's kept warm, and "feeding" it fruits, nuts, vegetables, and water in the evening, in much the same way that North American kids leave cookies and milk for Santa and carrots for his reindeer. By morning the food is gone.

PUTTING THE LOG IN SCATALOGICAL

This is where the tradition really gets different: like Santa, Tió de Nadal brings presents to kids on Christmas, but with Santa the kids must be *good* if they want to get presents. With Tió de Nadal, kids get their presents through coercion, threats, and violence: they beat the log with sticks until (we kid you not) it *poops* the presents out. Here's how it works:

- On Christmas morning, Tió de Nadal, still covered by the blanket with his (or

---

There's an award ceremony for obituary writers called the Grimmys.

her) head poking out, is placed in or next to the fireplace, or in some other special place. While the kids are out of the room, the adults hide candies, nougats, nuts, dried figs, pieces of cheese, and small presents—the kinds of things that American parents would put in a Christmas stocking—under the blanket. (Big presents are brought by the Three Wise Men, who don't arrive until January 5.)

- The children are then brought into the room. They beat Tió de Nadal with sticks while singing a special song. There are many variations of the song, but they all go something like this:

DID YOU KNOW?

The American Christmas tradition Elf on the Shelf started in the 1940s, when parents displayed elves as decorations at Christmas-time and warned kids not to misbehave in front of "Santa's helpers." In 2005, the best-selling book *The Elf on the Shelf* helped cement the tradition; to date, more than 11 million copies have been sold.

"Poop, log,
Poop nougats,
Hazelnuts and mató cheese.
Do not poop herrings,
They are too salty.
Poop nougats
They taste better.
If you don't have more,

Poop money.
If you don't have enough,
Poop an egg.
Poop, log,
Almonds and nougats,
And if you don't poop well
I will hit you with a stick!
Poop, log!"

(The first line of the song—in Catalan Spanish—is "Caga, tió." So, because of these lyrics, Tió de Nadal is also known as *Caga Tió*, which translates to "Poop Log" or "S*** Log.")

FIGS IN A BLANKET

The kids give Tió de Nadal one last hard whack while shouting, *"Caga Tió!"* Then they lift the blanket to discover all the wonderful treats and gifts that Tió de Nadal defecated during the beating. Sometimes an onion or a smelly piece of herring is placed among the treats as a sign that Tió de Nadal is literally pooped out and has no more treats to give. (When kids are bad, Tió de Nadal poops only the onion and/or herring, the Catalan equivalent of placing a lump of coal in a Christmas stocking.)

How did this tradition come about? One theory: the log represents nature, which is asleep in winter. Hitting the log wakes it up, and the food and presents the log poops out represent the abundance that nature will provide in the Spring.

OUT OF THE FRYING PAN...

If Tió de Nadal is lucky, after the presents have been collected, he or she is put away and saved for next Christmas. But if the unfortunate log's owners are sticklers for tradition, not long after having its presents beaten out of it, it is thrown into the fireplace and burned for warmth.

Merry Christmas!

One spelling, two meanings: the word *theist* can refer to someone who:
1) believes in God (or gods); or, 2) is addicted to coffee or tea.

MONEY FACT$

Even in today's world, where debit cards and cryptocurrency have become increasingly important parts of our financial lives, cash is still king. Here are a few random facts about money—the one item that really does make the world go 'round.

- The word "money" comes from Moneta, another name for the Roman goddess Juno, who was the protector of finances. The first Roman mints were in her temple and the coins were called "Moneta."

- George Washington's annual presidential salary (1789): $25,000. Joe Biden's (2022): $400,000.

- The average ATM in the United States can hold up to $100,000, but typically holds no more than $10,000.

- The pyramid on the back of the one-dollar bill is framed by two mottoes: *Annuit Coeptis*, meaning "God favors our undertakings," and *Novus Ordo Seclorum*, meaning "A new order of the ages."

- All standard credit cards have the same measurements: 3-3/8" x 2-1/8".

- The word *bankruptcy* comes from "bank" (from banca, a 16th-century word for "bench") + "rupture," referring to an old Italian custom of destroying the moneylender's bench when one's business failed.

- Other names for money: bread, dough, cabbage, lettuce, long green, clams, cream, bank, bucks, ducats, shekels, wherewithal, smackers, loot, moolah, scrill, scratch, and simoleons.

- How much is a billion dollars? If a billionaire spent $100,000 a day for 15 years, they'd still have close to half a billion left. If they gave away $1 every second, their billion would last more than 30 years.

- U.S. coins have no numerals on them. All the numbers are spelled out. (One cent, five cents, etcetera.)

- Every year, millions of dollars in abandoned savings accounts, payroll checks, insurance and tax refunds, royalty payments, utility deposits, and other cash assets are turned over to state treasuries as unclaimed property. It's estimated that $49 billion sits waiting to be claimed.

The red-colored water in Antarctica's Blood Falls is so salty it never freezes.

- All U.S. coins are produced with a "coin turn"—when the image on one side is right side up, the image on the other side is upside down.

- Q: If you find a very rare old $20 bill in your grandmother's attic and you turn it in to the government, how much will they give you for it? A: $20.

- In the United States, all bills feature portraits of men. That's not the case elsewhere. Some women who appear on paper money in other countries: *Out of Africa* author Karen Blixen (Denmark), actress Greta Garbo (Sweden), businesswoman Mary Reibey (Australia), President Corazon Aquino (the Philippines), painter Frida Kahlo (Mexico), First Lady Eva Perón (Argentina), singer Cesária Évora (Cape Verde), poet Leah Goldberg (Israel), and Queen Elizabeth II (Canada, Australia, the Bahamas).

- Angelina Quirion and Adam Jalbert went to Androscoggin County Jail in Auburn, Maine, to bail out a friend. They paid in cash, then waited outside in their car. While processing the friend's release, cops realized the cash was all counterfeit money. So they searched Quirion and Jalbert's car and found cocaine, fentanyl, methamphetamine, and a handgun. The couple was promptly arrested.

- In 2020, the U.S. Treasury Department minted 7.6 billion pennies. (Canada discontinued production of its penny in 2012.)

- Minimum wage in 1938, when the first federal minimum wage law was passed: 25 cents an hour.

- The first plastic credit cards were introduced in 1959 by American Express. Before that, they were made of paper.

- The symbol for the British pound (£) looks like a stylized "L." That's because it derives from the Latin phrase *libra pondo*, the most common unit of weight in ancient Rome.

- The word "penny" does not appear anywhere on a U.S. penny.

- World's most valuable coin: the 1794 "Flowing Hair" U.S. dollar, featuring a bust of Liberty (with flowing hair). It's believed to be the oldest American coin in existence, which could be why it sold at auction for $10 million in 2013.

* * *

"That money talks, I'll not deny, I heard it once: It said, 'Goodbye.'"
—Richard Armour

A mother platypus lactates, but it doesn't have nipples, so the milk just oozes out of her abdominal skin.

SCANDALOUS MUSIC VIDEOS

Singers and bands still make music videos today to promote their music, but they don't quite have the same cultural impact or visibility as they did in the 1980s and 1990s, when entering the rotation on MTV or VH1 could guarantee success. Videos weren't always tiny movies or long commercials—they sometimes had an impact on the world at large.

"THIS NOTE'S FOR YOU"

In 1986 and 1987, several classic rock acts, including Eric Clapton, Steve Winwood, and Genesis, filmed ads featuring their music for Michelob beer. Singer-songwriter Neil Young was so offended by what he perceived as crass commercialism that he wrote a seething critique of selling out called "This Note's for You" (a play on the Budweiser slogan "This Bud's for you"). The video, directed by filmmaker Julien Temple, was designed to look like one of those Michelob ads, and included a sneering Young pretending to endorse products mixed in with appearances by Whitney Houston and Michael Jackson impersonators. (Houston had made a Coke commercial and Jackson pushed Pepsi.) After Jackson threatened to sue MTV, the channel banned Young's video, but when competitors such as the Canadian channel MuchMusic aired "This Note's for You" without complaint, MTV put it into heavy rotation...and even gave it the 1989 award for Video of the Year.

"IF I COULD TURN BACK TIME"

Music video director Marty Callner received permission from the U.S. Navy to film the video for Cher's 1989 single "If I Could Turn Back Time" aboard the battleship USS *Missouri*. The navy didn't have a TV advertising budget, so naval officials thought the clip, planned to be a simple shoot of Cher and her band performing for a big assembly of sailors, could help boost recruitment. Cameras rolled at the Long Beach Naval Shipyard in southern California on the night of June 30, 1989, and Cher did perform...except that she was almost naked, dressed in a mesh body stocking and a skimpy black swimsuit that left her tattooed buttocks fully visible. Her partial nudity didn't bother MTV—they just aired the video late at night. The navy, however, was incensed. Officials were under the impression that Cher was going to wear a more modest jumpsuit, because that's how she was dressed in the storyboards. But in spite of Cher's surprise outfit choice, they had to let her go on with the show because hundreds of sailors were already in place. Result: the navy received hundreds of complaints from angry veterans who felt Cher's display (in one scene, she sat on one of the ship's guns with its barrel between her legs) was disrespectful to the USS *Missouri*'s historical significance—it's where Japan surrendered in 1945, ending World War II.

"WHEN THE LADY SMILES"

The Dutch band Golden Earring made their first record in 1965, but didn't score a top-10 hit in the United States until 1982, with "Twilight Zone"—a success in part due to heavy exposure on MTV. In early 1984, Golden Earring was back with a new album and a video for the single "When the Lady Smiles." The music video format was still in its infancy, and clips were often little more than some footage of a band lip-synching to their song, but the video for "When the Lady Smiles" has a plot: singer Barry Hay gets on a subway, tries to assault a nun, and then a dog eats his brain. That imagery was too shocking for mid-1980s television, and MTV banned the video. The song (and album) flopped, and Golden Earring never had another American hit.

> That imagery was too shocking for mid-1980s television, and MTV banned the video.

"COMA WHITE"

Shock rocker Marilyn Manson was often met with protestors when his violent, provocative stage show toured in the 1990s, and politicians blamed Manson's music for inspiring the Columbine High School massacre in April 1999. That was right around the time when Manson released the music video for "Coma White," a single off his *Mechanical Animals* album. Manson and his girlfriend at the time, *Charmed* star Rose McGowan, portrayed John F. Kennedy and Jacqueline Kennedy in a graphic reenactment of the November 1963 JFK assassination. After Manson announced the video, claiming his intention was to call out America's "unquenchable thirst for violence," MTV refused to air it because of the recent Columbine shootings. The network then delayed its release again in the summer of 1999 due to the sudden death of John F. Kennedy Jr., and finally aired it a few times in late 1999, by which point *Mechanical Animals* was no longer actively being promoted by Interscope Records.

"JUSTIFY MY LOVE"

Madonna has frequently acted as an envelope-pushing provocateur, but she went too far for a lot of people with the 1990 release of "Justify My Love." The song is an experimental piece of music in which Madonna breathily mutters romantic musings like "I wanna kiss you in Paris" over droning synthesizers. The video was an erotic short film, shot in black and white and featuring Madonna wandering through a hotel and spying on its scantily clad guests doing what scantily clad people do. MTV found it far too explicit to air, and because banning a video by a star of Madonna's caliber was newsworthy, ABC's *Nightline* covered the story and aired the video in full around midnight on December 3, 1990. The public's appetite was thoroughly whetted, so Madonna released "Justify My Love" as a "video single"—a VHS tape with just the one clip. It sold more than a million copies and helped propel "Justify My Love" to the #1 position on the *Billboard* pop chart in early 1991.

Science quiz: Earth has one moon; Mars has two. How many moons does Venus have? A: None. (Mercury doesn't have any either.)

THE CURSE OF THE DESTINY RING

Italian American actor Rudolph Valentino, the original "Latin Lover," was one of the biggest movie stars of all time, even though his career lasted barely a decade, entirely within film's silent, black-and-white era. A smoldering, charismatic figure, he starred in many hits like The Four Horsemen of the Apocalypse, The Sheik, Blood and Sand, *and* The Eagle. *Valentino died in 1926 at age 31, a death so sudden and shocking that some people attribute it to a cursed ring.*

VICTIM #1: RUDOLPH VALENTINO

In 1921, Valentino went into a jewelry store in San Francisco, where he'd lived in the mid-1910s, before his movie career took off. One piece of jewelry caught his eye—a simple silver signet ring inset with a brown and black tiger's-eye crystal. The store owner told the movie star that he wouldn't sell him the ring—supposedly named the "Destiny Ring"—claiming it was cursed and had brought bad luck or utter doom to whoever had owned it previously. Dismissing all that as superstitious nonsense (and a way for the owner to jack up the price), Valentino persisted and bought the Destiny Ring anyway.

But not long after he bought the ring, Valentino's personal life began to collapse. In 1921, his wife, actress Jean Acker, sued for divorce. He then married another actress, Natacha Rambova, but their wedding occurred less than a year after his divorce, which under California law, constituted bigamy. As the result of a well-publicized, scandalous trial, the marriage was annulled and Valentino and Rambova were legally forced to separate for a year. During that period, Valentino starred in *The Young Rajah*, the first and only box office bomb of his career. (He blamed the film's failure on his own poor performance, which he attributed to distraction and stress from the trial and his marital issues.)

In August 1926, Valentino collapsed at the Hotel Ambassador in New York and was rushed to the hospital. Doctors diagnosed gastric ulcers and appendicitis, and performed the appropriate surgeries. He appeared to be recovering, but six days later he developed pleuritis, a severe lung inflammation, followed by sepsis, a fatal blood infection. Two days after that, he died, and doctors discovered that he'd never had appendicitis at all; his gastric ulcers had been perforated, a rare condition that presents like appendicitis and is frequently misdiagnosed. (This diagnosis soon began to be called Valentino's syndrome.) On his deathbed, Valentino was wearing the Destiny Ring.

In 1972, the CBC held a contest to find the Canadian equivalent of "As American as apple pie." The winner: "As Canadian as possible under the circumstances."

VICTIM #2: POLA NEGRI

Valentino's personal effects, including the Destiny Ring, were given to his partner at the time, Polish actress Pola Negri, who'd been linked to Valentino since they met at a costume party thrown by newspaper tycoon William Randolph Hearst in 1924. Valentino's death was a major news event that attracted a lot of media attention, and Negri exploited it, dramatically fainting several times at the funeral and paying for a floral arrangement spelling "POLA" to be placed on her deceased lover's coffin. She also wore Valentino's tiger's-eye ring, in his honor...until she fell mysteriously ill for a few months. Upon recovering from the illness, Negri resumed her film career briefly and then retired in 1928. But she came out of retirement a few months later. Reason: she needed the money after her husband, an Eastern European prince named Serge Mdivani, squandered her fortune on failed businesses and investments.

VICTIM #3: RUSS COLUMBO

After that run of misfortune, Negri got rid of the Destiny Ring, handing it off to a friend, crooner Russ Columbo, who'd had a hit song with "Paradise," from Negri's 1932 film, *A Woman Commands*. Why Columbo? She thought he and Valentino resembled one another, and so she gave him her late boyfriend's ring, quipping, "From one Valentine to another."

In September 1934, a few days after receiving the ring and putting it on, Columbo visited the Los Angeles home of his friend, photographer Lansing Brown. Brown invited Columbo to look at his gun collection, and while handling a dueling pistol, Brown accidentally pulled the trigger, unaware that the gun was loaded. It went off; the bullet struck a nearby table and ricocheted into Columbo. It hit him in the face, above his left eye, and entered his brain. Surgeons at L.A.'s Good Samaritan Hospital were unable to remove the bullet and Columbo died.

VICTIM #4: JOE CASINO

Columbo's cousin, with whom he was very close, thought the singer's possessions should go to his best friend, an aspiring singer named Joe Casino. Because it was a piece of memorabilia that belonged to a legendary movie star, Casino put the ring in a glass case and displayed it in his home. He kept it locked up that way for two years and then, deciding that the curse was an exaggeration and that all the deaths and misfortune that came to those who'd owned it were just coincidence, he put the ring on and wore it out of the house. Within a week, Casino was hit by a truck, and he died instantly. Casino's brother, Del, inherited the ring, and, not wanting to tempt fate, locked it in a safe in his home, occasionally taking it out to wear.

All in the Family: Every golden retriever is a descendant of a single pair—Nous, a flat-coated retriever, and Belle, a tweed water spaniel.

VICTIM #5: JAMES WILLIS

Del Casino didn't suffer any notable bad luck, injury, or death while wearing the ring, nor did the Valentino memorabilia collector to whom he loaned it. But shortly after the collector returned it in early 1938, Casino's home was burgled. The Los Angeles Police arrived, and one officer spotted a suspect running from the scene. He fired his service revolver at the robber, whose name was James Willis, striking and killing him. Among the few things Willis had managed to steal from Casino's home: Valentino's ring.

VICTIM #6: JACK DUNN

News of the burglary reignited interest in Valentino, and movie producer Edward Small thought the time was right to make a movie about the fallen star. It also seemed to be the ideal project for Jack Dunn, a former figure skater turned actor who had appeared in two movies, and who bore a resemblance to Valentino. In July 1938, just ten days after signing his contract (and being temporarily gifted Valentino's ring, borrowed from Casino by Small), 21-year-old Dunn died of tularemia, a bacterial disease found mainly in rabbits that humans can contract if they handle an infected animal—and Dunn had just been on a rabbit hunting trip in Texas.

VICTIM #7: ALFRED HAHN

Del Casino started to believe that the Destiny Ring might be cursed after all, so he placed the artifact in a vault in a bank in downtown Los Angeles. About a year after the ring was deposited, the bank was robbed by a gang, who made off with $200,000 in cash and a few other items from the vault, including Valentino's ring. A police chase ended in a shootout; two of the suspects, as well as two innocent bystanders, were shot. The leader of the gang, Alfred Hahn, was caught and later sentenced to life in prison. "If I'd known what was in that vault apart from money," he said upon sentencing, "I'd have picked myself another bank."

THE RING REMAINS

Casino returned the ring to the bank vault, and after his death, his heirs kept it there, rarely, if ever, disturbing it. That Los Angeles bank, however, has endured another robbery, a labor strike, and multiple fires. Some of the contents of the vault were destroyed in one of those fires, which means the Destiny Ring could have been destroyed, too. Or maybe it's still there, just waiting to be placed on some unlucky soul's finger.

* * *

"I hope life isn't a big joke, because I don't get it."

—Jack Handey

Queen Elizabeth II bought six Big Mouth Billy Bass toys for her Balmoral estate.

COACH MADDEN

As a football coach, John Madden never had a losing season. As a broadcaster, he won 16 Emmy Awards. And his namesake video game, Madden NFL, lauded for its realism, has sold over 130 million units. So when he spoke, people listened.

"Coaches have to watch for what they don't want to see and listen to what they don't want to hear."

"Football isn't nuclear physics, but it's not so simple that you can make it simple. It takes some explaining to get it across."

"Knowing his coach likes him is more important to a player than anything else."

"I've always said winning's the great deodorant, and conversely, when you have a bad record, everything stinks, and everything starts to unravel, and everything falls apart."

"THE ONLY YARDSTICK FOR SUCCESS OUR SOCIETY HAS IS BEING A CHAMPION. NO ONE REMEMBERS ANYTHING ELSE."

"If you can't run with the big dogs, stay on the porch."

"A coach is just a guy whose best class in grammar school was recess and whose best class in high school was P.E. I never thought I was anything but a guy whose best class was P.E."

"THE ROAD TO EASY STREET GOES THROUGH THE SEWER."

"If you think about it, I've never held a job in my life. I went from being an NFL player to a coach to a broadcaster. I haven't worked a day in my life."

ACCORDING TO THE LATEST RESEARCH

It seems like every day there's a report on some scientific study with dramatic new info on what we should eat, or how we should act, or who we really are. Did you know, for example, that science says...

YOU PROBABLY LEAN TO THE RIGHT WHEN YOU KISS

Researchers: Psychologists at the University of Bath in England and the University of Bangladesh

Who They Studied: Married couples in Bangladesh. The scientists chose that country because, as lead researcher Michael J. Proulx explained in 2017, Bangladesh isn't "W.E.I.R.D."—which stands for "Western, Educated, Industrialized, Rich, and Democratic." Kissing, which is commonplace in so-called weird countries, is considered taboo in Bangladesh to the point that it's censored from movies and shows. Result: people there must rely on instinct when going in for a kiss.

Methodology: The couples were instructed to kiss each other, and then go to separate rooms to answer a questionnaire.

Findings: Kissing is more of an instinct than a learned behavior. The test subjects reported that, not surprisingly, right-handed people tend to lean right when they kiss, and lefties lean left. Also, husbands are 15 times more likely to initiate the kiss (also not surprising in a patriarchal society). However, regardless of who leans in first, or to which side, the one being kissed will almost always match the direction of the kisser. And most of the world—around 90 percent—is right-handed. Just as fetuses in the womb tend to turn to the right, and infants tend to roll to the right, kissing is "likely innate and determined by the brain splitting up tasks to its different hemispheres, similar to being either right- or left-handed." In this case, nature wins over nurture, and Proulx says that's a good thing: "It turns out that humans are similar, even if our social values, and the habits we are exposed to, differ."

RIDING ON A ROLLER COASTER CAN HELP YOU PASS A KIDNEY STONE

Researcher: Dr. David Wartinger at Michigan State University

What He Studied: A silicon model of a kidney and a urinary tract. The original—and unwitting—test subjects were several people who reported that their kidney stones (hard deposits of minerals) became dislodged after riding Disneyland's Big Thunder Mountain Railroad. After reading about these reports, Dr. Wartinger decided to test it out for himself.

Despite how the Sahara Desert is pictured in movies, only 15 percent of it is sand dunes.

Methodology: His team took their model kidney (hidden in a backpack) on that same roller coaster for 240 rides. They used three real kidney stones and urine, and sat in different seats on the coaster, which can reach speeds of 35 miles per hour and has numerous drops and sharp turns.

Findings: The study "supports the anecdotal evidence that a ride on a moderate-intensity roller coaster could benefit some patients with small kidney stones"—especially if you sit toward the back, where there was a 64-percent success rate, compared to less than 17 percent in the front.

PLANTS SQUEAL WHEN YOU HURT THEM

Researchers: Biologists from Tel Aviv University in Israel

What They Studied: Tomato and tobacco plants

Methodology: In 2019, the researchers "tortured" the plants by not watering them and cutting their stems. Sensitive microphones were placed a few inches away to record the reactions.

> Researchers "tortured" the plants by cutting their stems.

Findings: Though not discernible to the human ear, the plants make a high-frequency "distress sound" (or "squeal," as it's described in news reports) between 20 and 100 kilohertz. In one test, after a researcher snipped a tomato stem, the plant "emitted 25 ultrasonic distress sounds over the course of an hour." The control plants that weren't tortured emitted about one sound per hour. The researchers also noted that plants make different sounds at different intensities, depending on the type of stress inducer. (Tobacco plants squeal louder when they're denied water than when they're pruned.)

Are these plants really screaming in pain? Or are they warning their neighbors that danger is near? The jury is still out, but the scientists speculate that not only can other plants and trees hear these squeals but so too can insects and other animals. And if farmers can better learn to listen to their crops, this study could lead to improved agriculture...and happier plants.

YOUR REACTION TO BODY ODOR CAN PREDICT HOW YOU'LL VOTE

Researchers: Psychologists at Stockholm University

Who They Studied: This three-year study surveyed thousands of people from all over the world. The portion of the study that garnered the most headlines was conducted in 2016, when questions about the presidential election were added to the U.S. version of the survey.

Methodology: Disgust is an evolutionary survival mechanism that helped our prehistoric ancestors avoid eating spoiled food and swimming in festering swamps. The researchers wanted to see how this reaction affects modern humans. The study's first objective was to identify people with a strong sense of "Body Odor Disgust

In the UK, the Big Dipper is called the Plough (because it looks like a wagon).

Sensitivity," or BODS, and then determine if that has any bearing on how they want society to be structured. The 169 American respondents with a strong sense of BODS were asked about their social values, including who they were going to vote for in the upcoming presidential election.

Findings: According to lead researcher Jonas Olofsson, "There was a solid connection between how strongly someone was disgusted by smells and their desire to have a dictator-like leader who can suppress radical protest movements and ensure that different groups 'stay in their places.' That type of society reduces contact among different groups and, at least in theory, decreases the chance of becoming ill." In the U.S., the study found that people who were more disgusted by smells were also more likely to vote for Donald Trump.

BEER MATS MAKE LOUSY FRISBEES

Researcher: Johann Ostmeyer, a physicist at the University of Bonn in Germany

What He Studied: The flight pattern of flat, round, cardboard coasters (called beer mats), when tossed

Methodology: Inspired after a night at the pub during a 2017 physics conference, Ostmeyer simulated beer-mat throwing in a lab setting. In order to eliminate the randomness of hand-throwing, his team modified two treadmills into disc launchers that could adjust the angle, spin, and force of the throws, which were then recorded with high-speed cameras.

Findings: Whereas a skillfully thrown Frisbee can fly a long distance, a similarly thrown beer mat will maintain its trajectory for only 0.45 seconds before flipping sideways. The Frisbee has a curved lip that, much like a plane's wing, acts as an airfoil—creating lift underneath the center that keeps it afloat. A beer mat can also generate lift, but without that lip, the lift quickly shifts to the edge and the mat flips over. In the study's footnotes, Ostmeyer offered his sincere apologies to "everyone hit by a beer mat" in the course of his "silly experiment."

* * *

THE 7 TYPES OF LOVE

The ancient Greeks believed there are seven distinct types of love, and they named them.

1. **Eros.** Passionate, romantic, lusty love.
2. **Philia.** Intimate, emotionally close, soul mate love.
3. **Ludus.** Playful, flirty, early stages of a romantic relationship love.
4. **Storge.** Undying, unconditional, familial love.
5. **Philautia.** Self-esteem, self-care, and other forms of self-love.
6. **Pragma.** Committed, everlasting companionship love, the kind between a couple that grows out of eros.
7. **Agape.** A love for one's higher power, nature, the universe, and humanity.

Makes sense: The man who grew the largest chili pepper on record
(10 inches, .63 pounds) is named Ed Curry.

HIS LOUSY HIGHNESS

Throughout history, many leaders were given lofty nicknames—Catherine the Great or Richard the Lionhearted, for example. But not everyone could be Great or Magnificent. Some rulers got strange, and strangely specific, nicknames.

ALFONSO THE SLOBBERER

King Alfonso IX ruled Leon (now part of France) from 1188 to 1230. He was prone to fits of rage, and anytime he got especially angry, especially while in battle, he drooled uncontrollably, sometimes to the point of foaming at the mouth.

PIERO THE GOUTY

Heir to the powerful Medici family, which ruled Florence, Italy, in the 1500s, Piero suffered from gout, a form of arthritis commonly characterized by a large, painful sac of uric acid that forms somewhere inside the body. In Piero's case, it was in his big toe.

HARALD THE LOUSY

At the age of 12, Harald vowed to found a kingdom for the Norwegian people. He also vowed not to cut his hair until he achieved that goal. By 872, he'd founded the kingdom, but in the 10 years since he'd made his vow, Harald's hair had grown extremely dirty and was riddled with lice. This earned him the nickname "the Lousy," meaning "full of lice," not "inadequate." (Oh, that's better.)

IVAR THE BONELESS

Historians believe that the ninthcentury Danish Viking chieftain suffered from osteogenesis imperfecta, or extremely brittle bones. That, however, didn't stop him from becoming a Viking warlord and leading successful invasions into northern England.

IVAN I DANILOVICH, MONEYBAGS

In the 14th century, Ivan was the grand prince of Muscovy, now part of Russia. He earned his nickname not only from his wealth but also because he was a tax collector for the Tatar Empire, which required him to haul around big bags of money.

In the 1994 movie, Forrest Gump ran across the U.S. for 3 years, 2 months, 14 days, and 16 hours.

CONSTANTINE THE DUNG-NAMED

Eighth-century Byzantine Emperor Constantine V got his nickname from political opponents, who started a rumor that as a baby, he had pooped in a baptismal font. (He might have—he was a baby, after all.)

PTOLEMY VI THE MOTHER-LOVER

Ptolemy was the king of Egypt in the second century B.C. He ascended to the throne at age six and ruled jointly with his mother, the queen— Cleopatra I. Since kings and queens are generally married to each other, Ptolemy became know as "the mother-lover." But he didn't really love his mother. (He did, however, marry his sister.)

ETHELRED THE UNREADY

Although Ethelred was just 10 years old when he became king of England in 978 C.E., that's not where the nickname originates. "Unready" comes from an Anglo-Saxon word that meant "ill-advised," which reflects the unpopular decisions made by his advisors.

ERIC THE PRIESTHATER

King Eric II of Norway (1280–99) earned his nickname from his (successful) efforts to keep the Catholic Church from garnering special favors and obtaining land from the Norwegian government.

LONGSHANKS

Edward I of England (reigned from 1272 to 1307) had very long "shanks," or legs. Standing at more than 6', he was extremely tall for that era.

BOLESLAW THE WRY-MOUTHED

A Duke of Poland in the 12th century, Boleslaw III was a scheming dictator who assumed power after forcing out his brother. "Wry" means "cleverly humorous" as well as "physically crooked," and by historical accounts, Boleslaw possessed both kinds of wry mouth.

IVAILO THE CABBAGE

A rebel leader and briefly the emperor of Bulgaria in the 1270s, Ivailo probably got the name because, before becoming a politician, he was a peasant farmer. According to some translations, Ivailo was also known as "Radish" and "Lettuce."

The average leech has 32 brains, 10 stomachs, 18 testicles, and 2 ovaries.

YES! IT'S JORDAN!

Remember the "I ❤ NY" and "Virginia Is for Lovers" ad campaigns? You probably do... because they worked! The tourism bureaus of many countries around the world have created similar slogans to attract English-speaking travelers. Some are funny, some are outlandish, and some are so strange it's hard to believe that anybody would think they'd work.

"I wish I was in Finland" *–Finland*

"There's nothing like Australia" *–Australia*

"Incredible India" *–India*

"Get natural" *–Switzerland*

"Good people, great nation" *–Nigeria*

"Go your own way!" *–Albania*

"Much mor" *–Morocco*

"Experience it!" *–Haiti*

"It's all about U" *–Ukraine*

"Your Singapore!" *–Singapore*

"My Serbia" *–Serbia*

"Live your unexpected Luxembourg" *–Luxembourg*

"I feel SLovenia" *–Slovenia*

"I feel like Tunisia!" *–Tunisia*

"Visit Armenia, it is beautiful" *–Armenia*

"Happiest place on Earth!" *–Denmark*

"Europe's West Coast" *–Portugal*

"The 45 minute country" *–El Salvador*

"The original cool" *–The Netherlands*

"The heart shaped land" *–Bosnia and Herzegovina*

"All of Africa in one country" *–Cameroon*

"UKOK" *–United Kingdom*

"Everything is here" *–Honduras*

"The only risk is wanting to stay" *–Colombia*

"Move your imagination" *–Poland*

"Djibeauty" *–Djibouti*

"See it! Feel it! Love it!" *–Lithuania*

"Yes, it's Jordan" *–Jordan*

"The place to be" *–Belgium*

"Happiness is a place" *–Bhutan*

"Where happiness finds you" *–Fiji*

"You have to feel it!" *–Paraguay*

"You're welcome" *–Uganda*

"All you need is Ecuador" *–Ecuador*

"Feel the friendship" *–Tajikistan*

"Ours. Yours. Bahrain." *–Bahrain*

"Explore the Carpathian garden" *–Romania*

"Travel in Slovakia–good idea" *–Slovakia*

"For travelers" *–Kiribati*

"Think Hungary–more than expected" *–Hungary*

"Experience princely moments" *–Liechtenstein*

"Keep exploring" *–Canada*

"Best enjoyed slowly" *–Latvia*

"No stress" *–Cabo Verde*

Netflix bought the hit show *Stranger Things* only after 15 other outlets turned it down.

THE HOLDOUTS

*World War II ended with the unconditional surrender of Japan on August 15, 1945,
but some Japanese "holdouts," as they became known, remained
at "war" for years afterward.*

DOWNFALL

Even if you don't know a lot about World War II, you probably do know that the war
ended abruptly after the United States dropped atomic bombs on the Japanese cities of
Hiroshima and Nagasaki. The "A-bomb" was the most powerful weapon ever invented,
and the Manhattan Project, the crash program set up to bring it into existence, was the
most secret program of the entire war. How secret? Fewer than a hundred people knew
the bombs existed until after they were dropped on Japan. Not even President Harry
S. Truman—who ultimately gave the order to drop the bombs—knew about them until
after he became president following the death of Franklin Roosevelt in April 1945.

The terrible destruction the bombs wrought shocked the Japanese government
into concluding that continuing the war was pointless. Within 24 hours of the
Nagasaki bombing, the government signaled its intention to surrender, and on August
15 it made its surrender official. The formal signing of the Japanese Instrument of
Surrender, aboard the battleship USS *Missouri* in Tokyo Bay, followed two weeks later.

Before Hiroshima and Nagasaki, Japanese military planners had assumed that
the war would drag on for years. An estimated 3.5 million of the country's soldiers,
sailors, and airmen were still stationed abroad, and after the war ended it took more
than three years to bring everyone home. *Nearly* everyone, that is. Partially because of
the nature of the war, which was waged across much of Asia and on dozens of remote
islands in the Pacific, and also because of the way the soldiers had been trained, some
Japanese soldiers either *could not* or *would not* surrender. One Japanese government
estimate put the number of holdouts at 3,600, only a handful of whom ever returned
home. Here are some of the most famous cases.

THE ANATAHAN ISLAND 21

During the U.S. invasion of the Japanese-held Pacific island of Saipan in June 1944,
American bombers sank three Japanese supply boats off the small island of Anatahan,
65 miles to the north. Thirty-one crew members survived that attack and swam
ashore. There they met a Japanese woman named Kazuko Higa, who lived on one
of the island's coconut plantations. With the battle for Saipan underway (it soon
claimed the life of Higa's husband), she and the castaways retreated into the jungle,
where, cut off from the outside world, they did not learn of the war's end until
months after the fact. Even when the news did reach them, they could not believe it.

Anatahan became a U.S. possession after the war, and repeated attempts were made to contact the castaways and persuade them to lay down their arms and return to Japan. The castaways dismissed these entreaties as the tricks of an enemy still at war, and remained hidden in the island's interior, surviving on fish, crabs, lizards, bats, coconut milk, and moonshine made from tropical fruits while they waited for the Japanese navy to rescue them.

The rescue never came. *Five years* later, in June 1950, Mrs. Higa, dressed in a kimono she'd made from a silk parachute salvaged from the wreckage of a plane, walked out of the jungle alone and left the island aboard a fishing boat. She did so out of fear for her own life, after several of the castaways had killed one another fighting for her affections. In Saipan, Mrs. Higa supplied the names of the remaining holdouts to the American authorities, who forwarded the information to Japan, where wives, mothers, and other family members were encouraged to write letters in a final attempt to convince them the war really was over. The letters were collected and in June 1951 were deposited on a beach on Anatahan where the castaways were likely to find them. That did the trick: a few days later, following a surrender ceremony in which the leader of the group apologized for being "ignorant" of the war's end, the 20 surviving castaways evacuated Anatahan and returned home to their families in Japan.

SHOICHI YOKOI

Yokoi was a 28-year-old infantry soldier stationed on the island of Guam in the western Pacific in 1944. Japan had captured the island from the U.S. in 1941 following the bombing of Pearl Harbor, but in the summer of 1944, the U.S. invaded and took it back. Some 5,000 Japanese soldiers refused to surrender following the battle and fled into the jungle. Over the next year, nearly all of them were captured or killed; Yokoi and two companions were among a handful who remained at large. The three men hid out for 20 years. Then, in 1964, the two other men drowned in a flood, leaving Yokoi alone.

Yokoi "lived like a badger in the jungle," as he put it. He spent the daylight hours hiding inside a cave that he'd dug eight feet underground. The single chamber was three feet high and ten feet long—about the size of a human grave—and was accessed via a hole in the ground no wider than Yokoi's shoulders. At night he climbed a bamboo ladder out of the cave and scavenged for food, including nuts, edible plants, fish, eels, birds, snail, frogs, and rats. At first light he returned to his cave, the entrance of which he concealed from view with a bamboo mat. An apprentice tailor before the war, he wove plant fibers into fabric and made the fabric into clothes. He marked the passage of the years by observing the phases of the moon.

Yokoi might have gone on like this for decades more had he not gotten a little sloppy one evening in January 1972 and allowed himself to be spotted by two men

What's an *acersecomic*? Someone who's never had a haircut.

checking their shrimp traps on a riverbank. They were the first human beings Yokoi had seen in several years. Fearing for his safety, he attacked the two men but was quickly overpowered, dragged out of the jungle, and handed over to the Guamanian authorities. He was so ashamed of having been captured that he begged the two fishermen to kill him instead of handing him over to the police.

When interviewed by the authorities, Yokoi admitted that he'd known since 1952 that the war was over, but he was afraid that if he surrendered, he might be court-martialed and executed upon his return to Japan, where—at least during the war years—there was no shame greater than falling prisoner to the enemy. "We Japanese soldiers were told to prefer death to the disgrace of getting captured alive," he later explained. Even suicide was more honorable than being captured.

When he arrived in Japan, Yokoi famously admitted to reporters, "It is with much embarrassment that I return home." He expected to be treated as a pariah but was astonished to see that 5,000 people were waiting at the airport to welcome him home... as a hero. He became a celebrity of sorts: he wrote a best-selling memoir titled *Road to Tomorrow*, made frequent appearances on television, ran for parliament (and lost), and toured the country giving lectures about his years in the jungle. When Yokoi died from a heart attack in 1997 at the age of 82, he was laid to rest in the empty grave his mother had purchased for him 40 years earlier after giving him up for dead.

HIROO ONODA

In December 1944, Onoda was a 22-year-old intelligence officer and second lieutenant in the Japanese Imperial Army stationed on the island of Lubang in the Philippines. His mission: sabotage the airfield and port facilities to make it harder for the U.S. and its allies to invade the island; then if an invasion and occupation did come, to wage guerilla warfare against the occupiers from the jungle. Onoda's commanding officer, Major Yoshimi Taniguchi, gave him strict orders not to surrender, not to kill himself, and to continue the fight until he was killed or relieved of duty. "Whatever happens, we'll come back for you," Taniguchi assured him.

Onoda took his orders to heart. When the Allies seized the island in February 1945, rather than surrender like most Japanese troops who survived the battle, he and three other soldiers retreated into the jungle and began their guerilla campaign. In October 1945, the holdouts saw the first flyer telling them that the war had ended the previous August. They dismissed it as a fake. A few months later, an airplane dropped leaflets signed by a Japanese general, ordering them to surrender, but the message was apparently translated into Japanese by someone who was not a native speaker. "The leaflets they dropped were filled with mistakes, so I judged that it was a plot by the Americans," Onoda later explained. The holdouts remained hidden in the jungle for years and survived by hunting, fishing, and stealing livestock from local farmers.

One of the four holdouts, Yuichi Akatsu, surrendered in March 1950 and returned home to Japan; a second, Shoichi Shimada, was killed in 1954 in a shootout with locals who were searching for Japanese soldiers to tell them the war had been over since 1945. The surviving holdouts took the skirmish to mean that the war was still on, and their guerilla campaign was working.

Eighteen years after that, in 1972, a third holdout named Kinshichi Kozuka was killed by police while trying to burn a farmer's rice fields. Onoda was now alone. Kozuka's death received a great deal of press coverage in Japan, where it had long been assumed that all the holdouts—on Lubang and in other places—must have died off long ago. How could any of them still be alive?

The coverage inspired an eccentric 24-year-old college dropout named Norio Suzuki to go to Lubang and begin looking for Onoda, the only holdout on the island still unaccounted for. Suzuki's goal in life was "to find Lieutenant Onoda, a panda, and the Abominable Snowman, in that order," he would later explain to reporters. After arriving on Lubang, it took him just four days to find Onoda, who felt so unthreatened by this peculiar young man that he came out from hiding and revealed himself to a pursuer for the very first time. What made him comfortable enough to do it? Socks. "This hippie boy Suzuki...had on these thick woolen socks, even though he was wearing sandals," Onoda later explained. "If he had not been wearing socks, I might have shot him."

"If he had not been wearing socks, I might have shot him."

But once again, Onoda refused to surrender. "I still need an order from my senior officer before making a decision to give myself up," he told Suzuki, who returned to Japan and passed word to the authorities that Onoda was alive and waiting to be relieved of duty. The authorities tracked down Onoda's wartime commanding officer, Major Taniguchi, who was still alive and now working as a bookseller. Taniguchi agreed to go to Lubang and in March 1974, he officially relieved Onoda, still dressed in his Imperial Army uniform and cap, and still carrying his sword, of his duties.

Just as Shoichi Yokoi had been warmly welcomed on his return to Japan two years earlier, Onoda, too, was treated like a hero. (When Onoda's older brother was asked by a reporter how he planned to greet his brother, he answered, "I don't know whether to shout, 'You damn fool!' or 'Well done!'") The Philippine government even granted Onoda a full pardon for the 30 Filipinos he and the other holdouts had killed over the decades during their guerilla campaign.

But unlike Yokoi, Onoda never quite fit in in modern Japan, and for the rest of his life he divided his time between Japan and Brazil, where he purchased a cattle ranch. He had few regrets about the decades he'd spent in the jungle. "I do not consider those thirty years a waste of time. I was ordered to go there, and I carried out the orders to the best of my ability," he explained.

Before he was a rapper, Tupac Shakur danced ballet.

Onoda lived another 40 years and died in Tokyo in 2014 at the age of 91. Norio Suzuki, who'd set out to find Onoda, a panda, and the Abominable Snowman, was not so lucky. He eventually did find his panda, but in November 1986 he was killed in an avalanche while searching for the Abominable Snowman in the Himalayas. He was 37. Today the "Onoda Trail and Caves" on Lubang Island are operated as a tourist attraction.

SHIGEYUKI HASHIMOTO AND KIYOAKI TANAKA

Hashimoto and Tanaka were defense-industry workers at a Japanese steel mill in Malaya (modern-day Malaysia) who joined the Japanese Imperial Army during the war. One of the ways Japan justified its wars of aggression against its neighbors in Asia was by "freeing" them from domination by the Western colonial powers. Hashimoto and Tanaka were such enthusiastic supporters of this policy that when Japan surrendered in 1945, they and 13 other Japanese soldiers fled into the jungle and joined up with communist guerillas fighting for Malay independence from Great Britain. "Japan may have surrendered, but we were still fighting a war against Britain...I was never a communist, but we fought for a common goal," Hashimoto later recalled. Over the years, the Japanese soldiers battled British, Australian, Thai, and Malaysian forces, and all but Hashimoto and Tanaka were killed.

Malaya achieved full independence within the UK's Commonwealth of Nations in August 1957, but that wasn't independence enough for the Malayan communists or for Hashimoto and Tanaka, who kept on fighting. Then when they became too old to fight, they made weapons, ammunition, and booby traps at a guerilla camp hidden in the jungle. It wasn't until 1990, when the Malaysian Communist Party signed a peace treaty with the Malaysian government, that the two men, now in their seventies, walked out of the jungle and returned home to Japan, *45 years* after the end of World War II. At the time of their return, the Japanese government was actively investigating 48 other cases of former Japanese soldiers from World War II that it believed might still be alive.

> **DID YOU KNOW?**
>
> The atomic bombing of Hiroshima and Nagasaki in 1945 brought World War II to an end...and also devastated both cities. The first flower to bloom again in the blackened earth: the oleander. Today it's the official flower of Hiroshima, a living symbol of "both the dangers of nuclear war and the hope of a more peaceful future."

* * *

"Strength does not come from winning. Your struggles develop your strengths. When you go through hardships and decide not to surrender, that is strength."
–Arnold Schwarzenegger

Unless you're a member of a Native American tribe, it's illegal to possess eagle feathers.

FOUNDING FATHERS

You know the names. Here's a look at the people behind them.

JOHN LEA AND WILLIAM PERRINS

Lea & Perrins—the world's oldest brand of Worcestershire sauce—is named for its place of origin: the English city of Worcester. But pharmacists John Wheeley Lea and William Henry Perrins didn't invent the condiment—they were trying to imitate *garum*, a fermented anchovy sauce widely consumed in ancient Rome. According to company lore, Lord Marcus Sandys tasted a garum-inspired sauce while serving as governor of the Bengal region of India in the 1830s, and, upon his return to Worcester, asked Lea and Perrins to re-create it. They spent months on the recipe, combining malt vinegar, molasses, sugar, salt, tamarind, onions, garlic, anchovies, and spices. But when they tasted it, they thought it was awful. They apologized to Lord Sandys, but they kept a barrel in their basement...then opened it 18 months later. Bravely tasting it, they found that it had fermented, matured, and mellowed into something more palatable. Lea and Perrins marketed the sauce, and by the end of the 1840s it was available throughout the British Empire. In 1897, the company opened a factory in Worcester, which is where most bottles of Lea & Perrins Worcestershire Sauce are still produced today.

DAVE CORRIVEAU AND BUSTER CORLEY

In the late 1970s, 24-year-old David Corriveau opened his first business, an adult video arcade and bar called Cash McCool's in a hip neighborhood of Little Rock, Arkansas. Right next door was a bar and grill called Buster's, owned and operated by James "Buster" Corley. Both businesses thrived, but Corriveau and Corley noticed a lot of foot traffic between their hangouts, with patrons going back and forth to play games and guzzle beers at Cash McCool's, and then to grab a burger or a steak at Buster's. Corriveau and Corley decided to just combine their businesses, but in a much bigger way. They pinpointed Dallas's bustling "Restaurant Row" for their venture, leased a 40,000-square-foot empty warehouse, put in a bar, restaurant, and video arcade, and opened Dave & Buster's in December 1982. (Why Dave & Buster's instead of Buster & Dave's? Corriveau won a coin toss, so his name went first.) The concept worked and, as of 2022, there are more than 100 Dave & Buster's gigantic arcades around the country.

PHILIP CASWELL AND WILLIAM MASSEY

What's the oldest consumer brand in the United States? It may surprise you to learn that it's Caswell-Massey, a direct predecessor to brands like Bath & Body Works and Crabtree & Evelyn. In 1752, Scottish doctor William Hunter opened Dr. Hunter's Dispensary, a pharmacy in Newport, Rhode Island. At the time, Newport was a

Garlic attracts leeches.

vacation destination for the colonial elite, so Hunter added high-end cosmetics, essential oils, perfumes, and other luxury items to his inventory. When Hunter retired, the Dispensary went to his son, William Hunter Jr., then to Charles Feke, then to Rowland Hazard, and then, in 1833, to Hazard's partner, Philip Caswell. In 1876, propelled by sales of European soaps and hand creams, Caswell opened a branch in New York City, where he brought in Canadian businessman Dr. William Massey. That's when the firm took on the name Caswell-Massey. It's no longer owned by the Caswell or Massey families, but it's still called Caswell-Massey; still sells high-end soap, oils, and perfumes; and still caters to the elite.

WILLIAM MURPHY

In the early 20th century, it was considered unseemly for an unmarried woman to be in a man's bedroom. That was a problem for men who lived in boarding houses in big cities like San Francisco, and that was inventor William Murphy's situation. He rented a room at the same house as opera singer Gladys Kaighin, yet they could never spend any alone time together. It just wasn't respectable. Then Murphy realized that if he could get rid of his bed, then it was technically no longer a bedroom. So he designed a contraption consisting of a mattress on a hinged metal frame, that folded up vertically into a closet. When needed, one simply opened the closet doors and lowered the bed. Called the In-a-Dor Bed, Murphy patented his design in 1911 (the same year he married Kaighin). He didn't trademark the name "Murphy Bed," but that's what everyone called it, to the point that it became a genericized trademark... until 1985, when the courts ruled that the term had entered common usage and was no longer entitled to trademark protection.

JOHN TYSON

In 1931, early in the Great Depression, 25-year-old John Tyson moved from his hometown, Mound City, Missouri, to Springdale, Arkansas, because that's where he could find a job to support his family. Working primarily on poultry farms, he learned that chicken commanded a higher price in big cities, so, in 1935, he borrowed money from relatives and started Tyson Foods, buying chickens from other farmers and then driving truckloads of them to sell in Kansas City, St. Louis, and Chicago. Each trip earned a bit more money than the last, and Tyson put the proceeds back into the business, eventually opening his own poultry farm and a mill where he produced chicken feed. In the early 1940s, Tyson and associates started crossbreeding chickens to create a meatier product, which was perceived as a better value during World War II, especially since chicken was not subject to wartime rationing. By the time Tyson died in 1967, Tyson Foods had grown into one of the largest chicken producers in the United States, and is now one of the largest meat producers in the world.

Useless information: According to experts, didgeridoo players snore far less than people who don't play the instrument.

"PECKED BY TURKEY"

Most hospitals around the world use the International Statistical Classification of Diseases and Related Health Problems—a system of diagnostic codes, established by the World Health Organization, to indicate what situation required the patient to seek medical attention. It makes medical records easier to navigate and assists in billing insurance companies, and they're also very specific...which, despite the fact that they're describing serious, potentially fatal injuries, makes them kind of funny. All of these are real codes.

W21.32: Struck by skate blades

X52: Prolonged stay in weightless environment

W09.2: Fall on or from jungle gym

Y65.0: Mismatched blood transfusion

X15.1: Contact with hot toaster

X00.4: Hit by object from burning building

X05: Exposure to ignition or melting of nightwear

V91.35: Hit by a falling object due to a canoeing accident

W55.21: Bitten by a cow

V91.07: Burn due to water skis on fire

X32: Exposure to sunlight

X36.0: Collapse of dam or man-made structure causing earth movement

W62.1: Contact with nonvenomous toads

W61.43: Pecked by turkey

V00.83: Accident with motorized mobility scooter

W05.2: Fall from non-moving motorized mobility scooter

W20.0: Struck by falling object in cave-in

Y37.52: Military operations involving indirect blast effect of nuclear weapon

Y27.1: Contact with hot tap water, undetermined intent

W61.01: Bitten by parrot

W40.1: Explosion of explosive gases

V70.7: Person on outside of bus injured in collision with pedestrian or animal in traffic accident

V00.22: Sled accident

T84.02: Dislocation of internal joint prosthesis

S30.862: Insect (nonvenomous) bite on penis

W56.12: Struck by sea lion

W51: Accidental striking against or bumped into by another person

T61: Toxic effect of noxious substances eaten as seafood

W26.1: Contact with sword or dagger

W29.1: Contact with electric knife

T53.1: Toxic effects of chloroform

T63.2: Toxic effect of venom of scorpion

T16.2: Foreign body in left ear

T14.9: Unspecified injury

If the Earth wasn't curved, a human eye would be able to see for 30 miles.

COPYWRONG

This page is copyright 2022 by Uncle John's Bathroom Reader. Consequently, it may not be reused or reprinted without permission. But please feel free to use any of the intellectual properties in this article in any way you see fit, because they're all in the public domain, and not subject to copyright and trademark laws.

CHARADE

Stanley Donen's 1963 romantic chase movie *Charade* is a classic comic thriller, and earned Golden Globe nominations for its stars, Cary Grant and Audrey Hepburn. And due to a typographical error, it's been in the public domain since the day it was released. The final print of the film bears the credit: "MCMLXIII by Universal Pictures Company, Inc. and Stanley Donen Films, Inc. All rights reserved." But producers inadvertently left the word "copyright" off, meaning there *is* no copyright on *Charade*.

PETER PAN

The most famous creation of Scottish author J. M. Barrie—and one of the most enduring characters of all time—is Peter Pan, the magical boy from Neverland. Barrie introduced the character in his 1902 novel *The Little White Bird*, and used him as the central figure in his 1904 play *Peter Pan*, adapted into the novel *Peter and Wendy* in 1911. All of those works are in the public domain in the United States, because of their age. In the UK, however, the play *Peter Pan* was granted a special dispensation by Parliament in 1995 to hold onto its copyright forever. That's mainly because in 1929, Barrie bequeathed the rights to the Great Ormond Street Hospital, which still derives much of its operating income from the royalties.

NIGHT OF THE LIVING DEAD

Writer-director George Romero kicked off the zombie movie genre in 1968 with *Night of the Living Dead*, a low-budget independently produced film. For a copyright to be valid in the United States at the time, a filmmaker had to register the work and then provide notice of that copyright in the film, such as in the credits. *Night of the Living Dead* was a shoestring, quickly produced film, and its makers forgot to include that copyright notice, putting it into the public domain immediately upon its release.

JAMES BOND

Nearly 180 nations adhere to the Berne Convention for the Protection of Literary and Artistic Works, an international copyright law that makes standard (with many exceptions) the rule that literary and musical works remain copyrighted for at least 50 years after the death

That means Fleming's most lucrative literary creation, James Bond, is free to use in Canada.

Makes sense: A group of cockroaches is called an "intrusion."

of their author. Because of that rule—but with other copyright rules complicating matters—in 2014, Ian Fleming's works entered the public domain...in Canada. That means Fleming's most lucrative literary creation, James Bond, is free to use in that nation, and Canadian producers Lee Demarbre and Ian Driscoll plan to take advantage of the rule by making a Canadian version of *For Your Eyes Only*, set and filmed entirely in Canada and with a cast that potentially includes Canadian actors Ryan Reynolds, Donald Sutherland, and Michael Ironside.

THE GOLD RUSH

Among the most famous and enduring of Charlie Chaplin's silent film comedies is *The Gold Rush*. Chaplin wrote, directed, produced, and played his "Little Tramp" character in the 1925 film, which Chaplin said was his personal favorite of all his works. At that time, a film's copyright lasted 28 years, meaning copyright for *The Gold Rush* came up for renewal in 1953. Chaplin failed to update that original theatrical cut, so it entered the public domain. In 1995, after numerous video producers had released the film in the VCR-crazy 1980s, Chaplin's estate found a legal loophole that restored the copyright...only to have *The Gold Rush* revert back to the copyright-free "fair use" category in 2020. Reason: under current public domain laws, a film loses its protection 95 years after its initial release.

A STAR IS BORN

Four movies about a tragic old entertainer mentoring and falling in love with a younger talent bear the name *A Star Is Born*: the 2018 Lady Gaga version, the 1976 Barbra Streisand version, the 1954 Judy Garland version, and the original 1937 version starring Janet Gaynor and Frederic March. Part of the reason it's been remade so often is that the copyright on the original film lapsed at some point. The 1937 *A Star Is Born* was a production of Selznick International Pictures, which fell apart by 1940. The rights to the movie were sold to Film Classics, Inc., which, after theatrically rereleasing the film a few times to diminishing returns, sold the package to Edward L. Alperson, who planned a remake. He didn't, and then sold the property to Warner Bros., which made the version with Garland. By the time the 1976 movie went into production, the copyright on the original *A Star Is Born* had lapsed 11 years earlier.

ATARI JAGUAR

Once the leading company in home video-game systems, Atari nearly went out of business during the video game crash of 1983. In an attempt to come back and to compete with the more popular state-of-the-art Nintendo and Sega console systems, Atari introduced the XEGS console in 1987 and the Lynx handheld system in 1989, but neither was enough for Atari to regain its share of the gaming market. In 1993, Atari unveiled what would be its final system, the Atari Jaguar. Despite advanced

The Japanese equivalent of a "shotgun wedding" is *dekichatta kekkon*, or an "oops we did it marriage."

graphics comparable to those of Super Nintendo or Sega Genesis, only 150,000 Atari Jaguars were sold, not enough to save the company. Atari discontinued the Jaguar in 1996, and began negotiations to sell the company to Hasbro. When Hasbro completed the purchase in 1999, it released its patents on the Jaguar and declared the software "open platform." Reason: Hasbro recognized that there were a lot of passionate, diehard Jaguar fans, but the company had no intention of investing any resources in the product. So as a goodwill gesture (and an excellent public relations move), they put the product into the public domain, making it possible for anyone to develop new games for Jaguar, free of royalties.

"ROCKIN' ROBIN"

Early rock 'n' roll singer Bobby Day had the biggest hit of his career with "Rockin' Robin," which sold a million copies and went to #2 on the *Billboard* pop chart in 1958. Written by Leon René under the pseudonym Jimmie Thomas, a copyright renewal that would have protected the music and lyrics (but not the recording) wasn't filed, meaning anyone can record it without paying artist's royalties.

"THE HOUSE OF THE RISING SUN"

The best-known version of the song is the spooky, anthemic, hard rock version recorded by the Animals, a #1 hit in 1964. That recording is still well under copyright, but the rights to the underlying music itself—the song's melody and lyrics—belong to the public domain because, like many folk songs, the original author is unknown. "The House of the Rising Sun" derives from music that dates back to the 16th century. The first recording of the song was in 1933, by singer-guitarist Clarence "Tom" Ashley, who said his grandfather taught it to him.

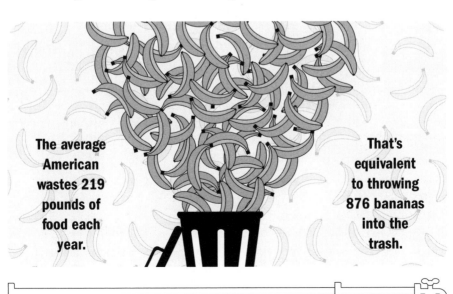

The average American wastes 219 pounds of food each year.

That's equivalent to throwing 876 bananas into the trash.

About half of all humans born before 1800 died before the age of 5.

THE WORST OLYMPIC MARATHON EVER

How much of a disaster was the marathon at the 1904 St. Louis, Missouri, Olympic Games, the first ever held in North America? Let us count the ways:

Stifling heat. The 24.85-mile race took place on August 30, in the middle of summer. It started at 3:03 in the afternoon; the temperature was above 90°F, though because the course wasn't shaded and the humidity level was high, it felt like well over 100°F. Of the 32 runners, John Lordon, who was favored because he'd just won the Boston Marathon, was first to drop out—he started vomiting from the heat right away, within the first half-mile.

Impossible course. It was laid out on dirt roads around the stadium, prompting one official to call the course "the most difficult a human being was ever asked to run over." There were seven steep hills, rising as high as 300 feet, and the athletes had to pound over jagged rocks while dodging pedestrians, cars, and trains on the busy road.

Racism. James E. Sullivan, chief organizer of the 1904 Olympics, structured events to try to prove that white American men were superior to all other people. He created "Anthropology Days," during which indigenous peoples from around the world were exhibited, much like a human zoo, and competed in a variety of athletic contests. He also invited two Black South Africans (they were part of an anthropology exhibit) to participate in the marathon—despite the fact that they'd never run one before—in order to publicize their expected failures.

Sexism. Although women had competed in some events in the 1900 Olympics in Paris, Sullivan and his cohorts barred them from the 1904 marathon—and *all* events except archery.

Lack of water. Believing that drinking or eating during exercise would upset athletes' stomachs and hurt their performance, Sullivan used the marathon to test the effects of "purposeful dehydration." Result: there were only two places to get water—at mile 6 and mile 12. There were *no* liquids in the brutally hot second half of the race. But many people never got that far anyway.

Dust. Inches of dust covering the roads were kicked up not just by competitors, but by horses and cars being driven next to them. Some athletes threw up, but for William Garcia of San Francisco, California, it was much worse. Garcia had been in fourth place until he collapsed, having swallowed so much dust that it coated his esophagus and damaged his stomach lining. Rushed into emergency surgery, he suffered hemorrhaging that would have killed him in the next hour.

Feral dogs. Some wild dogs got on the path, forcing at least one competitor to run for his life as he was chased a mile off course.

Food poisoning. Having eaten nothing all day, Cuban athlete Félix Carvajal got so hungry while running that he stole peaches from a group of spectators. He was still hungry, so, according to some reports, he stopped at an orchard where he accidentally ate a bad apple and, plagued by stomach cramps, laid down and took a nap.

Rat poison. American runner Thomas Hicks became desperately dehydrated, and within seven miles of the finish, his trainers revived him in a dangerous way. They fed him egg whites mixed with one milligram of strychnine sulfate—sometimes used as a stimulant, but more commonly used to poison rats. The trainers must have given Hicks too much because he started to hallucinate. Begging for water or tea, he was instead given brandy. The combination of drugs and alcohol left him ashen, limp, and barely able to lift his legs.

Cheating. New Yorker Fred Lorz was so exhausted by mile nine that he quit...sort of. He hopped in his manager's car, rode several miles, then got dropped off near the finish line and jogged across it. He'd won! Just as President Teddy Roosevelt's daughter Alice was about to award him the gold medal, he was called out and disqualified. Lorz later claimed that he wouldn't have accepted the medal and that it was all "just a joke."

Slowest winning time ever. Hicks, still running, but still in agony from the strychnine and brandy, was dragged over the finish line by his handlers and became the actual winner. His time of 3 hours, 28 minutes was about a half hour slower than any Olympic Marathon winner before or since. Then he collapsed and, near death, had to be treated by four doctors before he could leave the grounds.

Record-breaking failure rate. Only 14 people finished the race. The abysmal 34 percent completion rate, including nine runners who bowed out before it began, is the lowest in Olympic history.

The expected losers were winners. Carvajal, having slept off his food poisoning, came in fourth. Sullivan's white supremacy ploy backfired: the two Tswana tribesmen who were first-time marathoners finished ninth (even with a mile detour fleeing a dog) and twelfth. They made history as the first Black Africans to compete in the Olympics.

It's a "man-killing event." That's what the *St. Louis Post-Dispatch* called the Olympic marathon. Critics—including Sullivan, who told reporters that the race was "asking too much of human endurance"—almost got the race banished from the Olympics. But it survived, becoming a 26.2-mile course with a record time of 2 hours, 6 minutes, 32 seconds. Today, the use of drugs and alcohol are not allowed—but women and water are.

WHAT'S IN A NAME?

The study of proper names—their origins, meanings, and usage—is called onomastics or onomatology. Here are some more fun facts and trivia about what we call ourselves.

- The most popular baby names in the United States in 2020: Liam and Olivia.

- Most first names in English begin with the letters J, M, S, D, and C. Most surnames begin with S, B, H, M, and C.

- Q: Which common first name originally meant "farmer"—from the ancient Greek words for "earth worker"? A: George (geo, "earth," and ergon, "work").

- Parents in Iceland have to choose their babies' names from a government-approved register of 1,712 boy names and 1,853 girl names.

- Three Native American names and their meanings: Sacajawea, "Bird-woman" (Shoshone); Pocahontas, "playful one" (Powhatan); Geronimo, "the one who yawns" (Chiricahua Apache).

- Longest modern celebrity name: Kiefer William Frederick Dempsey George Rufus Sutherland.

- Longest all-time celebrity name: Pablo Diego José Francisco de Paula Juan Nepomuceno María de los Remedios Cipriano de la Santísima Trinidad Martyr Patricio Clito Ruíz y Picasso.

- "Proto-names": Jiahu Symbols are an early form of proto-writing found on tortoise shells and shards of clay pottery dating to ancient China. These 8,000-year-old symbols most likely denote ownership, which anthropologists consider the earliest known examples of names:

- The closest modern equivalent: in 1993, when the artist known as Prince changed his name to The Artist Formerly Known as Prince, represented by this symbol:

- Meet Kushim: He (or she) was a Mesopotamian accountant who lived 5,000 years ago. This was before paper existed, so wheat farmers paid Kushim to keep track of their financial records on clay tablets. That moniker has been found on 18 tablets so far, making it the earliest known example of anyone's name appearing in a written language.

- In most Asian languages, the family name comes first. This created confusion for basketball star Yao Ming: "To my Chinese friends, I was Ming." When he entered the NBA in 2002: "Everyone called me Yao—they thought it was my first name. I never corrected them. I was too shy."

The first year that celebrities received more mentions in newspapers than elected officials: 1901.

- Shared by more than 150 million people, the world's most popular name has at least 14 spellings: Muhammad, Mohammed, Mohammad, Muhammed, Mohamed, Mohamad, Muhamad, Muhamed, Mohamud, Mohummad, Mohummed, Mouhamed, Mohammod, and Mouhamad.

- National Middle Name Pride Day is observed on the Friday of the first full week of March. Possible activities: share your middle name with friends and coworkers; find out how you got your middle name (or why you didn't get one); and study the history of middle names. (Fun!) The middle name "holiday" was the brainchild of amateur onomatologist Jerry Hill, who also came up with Unique Names Day, Learn What Your Name Means Day, and Name Tag Day.

- Middle names became popular in 15th-century Italy among the aristocracy. The first ones were the names of saints, in the hope that they would protect the child.

- According to marine biologists, dolphins have names, or "signature whistles," that they use to keep track of each other.

- On family gravestones in Japan, the names of deceased family members are engraved in black, while the names of those who are still alive are red. That's why in Japan, it is considered bad luck to write anyone's name in red ink.

- In 2001, expectant parents from California, Maggie Baird and Patrick O'Connell, saw a documentary about conjoined twins Katie and Eilish Holton. Inspired, they decided to name their baby daughter Eilish. Her brother Finneas, 4, convinced them to name her Pirate. But before she was born, her grandfather Billie died. Result: the singer's legal name is Billie Eilish Pirate Baird O'Connell.

- American boy and girl names with the most spellings: Caden, at least 52; and Aaliyah, 89.

- Michael J. Fox? Cecil B. DeMille? George W. Bush? Research shows that if you include your middle initial in your name, you're more likely to be perceived as intelligent and intellectual.

- In 1950, only five percent of American parents picked a baby name that wasn't in the top 1,000. In 2020, more than 25 percent did.

- According to the U.S. Census Bureau, at the turn of the 21st century, Americans collectively had more than 150,000 unique surnames.

- In 2020, Australia's Registry of Births, Deaths and Marriages Victoria released a list of 46 illegal baby names—including Admiral, Princess, Dame, Seaman, Chief, Lord, Major, Majesty, Lucifer, Satan, Messiah, and Christ.

There are no stop signs in Paris.

FEAR ITSELF

Don't be afraid to read these quotations.

"Nothing in life is to be feared. It is only to be understood."
—**Marie Curie**

"Fear has a large shadow, but he himself is small."
—**J. Ruth Gendler**

"To fear is one thing. To let fear grab you by the tail and swing you around is another."
—**Katherine Paterson**

"The enemy is fear. We think it is hate; but, it is fear."
—**Mahatma Gandhi**

"So many of us chose our path out of fear disguised as practicality."
—**Jim Carrey**

"Anxiety does not empty tomorrow of its sorrow, but only empties today of its strength."
—**Charles Spurgeon**

"The dogs with the loudest bark are the ones that are most afraid."
—**Norman Reedus**

"Fear is never a reason for quitting; it is only an excuse."
—**Norman Vincent Peale**

"A champion is afraid of losing. Everyone else is afraid of winning."
—**Billie Jean King**

"The greatest mistake you can make in life is to continually be afraid you will make one."
—**Elbert Hubbard**

"It is the strange fate of man, that even in the greatest of evils the fear of the worst continues to haunt him."
—**Johann Wolfgang von Goethe**

"The scariest moment is always just before you start. After that, things can only get better."
—**Stephen King**

"People living deeply have no fear of death."
—**Anaïs Nin**

"If you're afraid to fail, then you're probably going to fail."
—**Kobe Bryant**

"Thinking will not overcome fear but action will."
—**W. Clement Stone**

"The timid are afraid before the danger, the cowardly while in danger, and the courageous after danger."
—**Jean Paul Richter**

"A lot of people are afraid to say what they want. That's why they don't get what they want."
—**Madonna**

Only three people have ever died in outer space: three Russian cosmonauts in 1971.

THE STRANGE (AND DISTURBING) HISTORY OF THE ELECTRIC CHAIR

It may seem like a relic from the distant past, but the electric chair is still employed as a means of execution in some U.S. states. Here's the odd story of how it came to be. (Warning: parts of this story are not for the faint of heart.)

BUZZED

One afternoon in 1881, a 30-year-old dockworker named George Lemuel Smith and some friends took a tour of the Brush Electric Company's power plant in Buffalo, New York. The power plant supplied electricity to the powerful carbon arc street lamps that illuminated the city at night, and it was a popular tourist attraction. Touring a power plant may sound strange today, but in the 1880s it was a fun and interesting thing to do: electric arc light technology was very new and, for many, scary. Buffalo was one of the earliest cities to have it. To combat the public's fear of electricity, companies like Brush Electric invited people inside their power plants to see how the electricity was produced.

Just inside the door of the plant, behind a metal railing that kept the public from getting too close, sat a huge generator. One of the entertaining parts about a visit to the plant was that when the generator was operating, people who touched the railing would get a bit of an electric shock—not enough to do any harm, but enough to tickle the skin and give them a buzzing sensation unlike anything they'd ever felt before. Smith enjoyed the experience so much that later that same evening, after spending hours drinking with his friends in a saloon, he made his way back to the power plant in order to do it again.

Was the alcohol to blame? Or was it that electricity was so new that Smith didn't understand the danger? Whatever it was, after dodging the security guards who repeatedly turned him away, Smith snuck right up to the generator. He laid one hand upon it, then another, giving it a sort of drunken hug. At least that's what he tried to do: the moment his second hand made contact with the generator, his body shot up from a boozy slouch to a fully upright stance in a single violent spasm as the powerful electric current flowed through him. He remained frozen in this position until the guards shut off the generator, at which point his body went limp and he fell to the ground, dead.

SILENT BUT DEADLY

According to eyewitnesses, Smith did not scream out in pain when he received the shock, nor did he give any sign that he was even still alive. No sparks flew, he did not burst into flames, nor was there any smoke or smell of burning flesh. When his body was autopsied, the physician, Dr. Joseph Fowler, found no burns or other tissue damage on the body. He concluded that Smith had died the instant he received the electric shock.

Not long afterward, Fowler discussed his findings in a lecture he gave to a group of science enthusiasts. One person who attended the lecture was a dentist named Alfred P. Southwick. Southwick had worked as an engineer before switching to dentistry, and he had long been interested in electricity. He was already experimenting with it in his dental practice, using low-voltage electrical current as anesthesia during dental procedures. He was fascinated with the idea that Smith had been killed instantly—and, as far as anyone could tell, painlessly—and he wondered if electrocution might provide a more humane way of executing criminals who had been sentenced to death.

ON THE ROPES

In the 1880s, the primary method of execution in the United States was hanging, usually on a raised platform called a gallows. If you're a fan of Western movies then you can already picture the scene: The condemned prisoner stood on a trapdoor on the gallows platform, then a hangman tied a noose around his neck and placed a hood over his head. When a signal was given, the trapdoor was sprung and the prisoner dropped through the hole, only jerking to a stop when the noose pulled taught, breaking the prisoner's neck and killing him relatively quickly and painlessly. (Relatively.)

That was how the gallows was *supposed* to work, but if the rope was too short, the drop wasn't far enough and the prisoner's neck wouldn't break. In such a case it might take 20 minutes or more for a prisoner to die by slow strangulation. Conversely, if the rope was too long, the prisoner dropped too far and could be decapitated—a quick death, but one that horrified onlookers. A number of botched hangings in the state of New York and elsewhere had caused growing public opposition to hanging; there was even talk of getting rid of capital punishment altogether.

NEW AND IMPROVED

Just as the incandescent light bulb, the telephone, and the transcontinental railroad had transformed life in America in recent years, Southwick became convinced that electrocution could transform death, by replacing an archaic and often brutally violent form of capital punishment with something modern, scientific, almost clinical, and virtually painless. He tested this theory and refined his electrocution technique by experimenting on hundreds of stray dogs at the Buffalo dog pound until he was satisfied that he had perfected the killing process.

Next, Southwick had to adapt his technique for a human being. As the idea of death by electrocution began to grow in popularity, other proponents suggested

Safety fact: You're less likely to be injured on a rectangular trampoline than on a round one.

executing condemned prisoners while they were standing, perhaps by shocking them as they stood barefoot on a metal plate. People stood on the gallows to be executed, and they also stood when facing a firing squad; it seemed natural that they should also stand to be electrocuted. But Southwick was a dentist: he was used to working on patients while they were seated in a chair. He saw no reason why they couldn't be executed in an "electric chair" as well.

FRIENDS IN HIGH PLACES

In 1886, the Governor of New York, David B. Hill, formed a three-person commission to conduct a comprehensive review of capital punishment methods and make recommendations for a more humane alternative to hanging. Southwick, who by now had written a number of articles proposing his electric chair as a replacement for the gallows, was one of the three men appointed to the commission. He advocated for electrocution from the beginning, but the two other members, Elbridge Gerry and Matthew Hale, were open to other possibilities such as firing squads, lethal injection, and inhalation of lethal quantities of chloroform gas, which at the time was used as a general anesthetic. Gerry and Hale soon rejected lethal injection as "*too* painless," and therefore unlikely to have the desired deterrent effect. But they remained undecided about other forms of capital punishment. So in November 1887, Southwick wrote a letter to Thomas Edison, the inventor of the incandescent light bulb and the founder of the Edison Electric Light Company, and asked for his support.

Edison, one of the most famous and admired Americans of the age, declined. He explained to Southwick that he opposed the death penalty and believed that life in prison was preferable to any form of killing, no matter how humane. But when Southwick wrote Edison a second time just one month later, this time Edison wrote back saying that he was willing to help.

> Gerry and Hale soon rejected lethal injection as "too painless," and therefore unlikely to have the desired deterrent effect.

AC/DC

What caused the change of heart? At the time Edison, a proponent of DC, or *direct current*, electrical power systems, was locked in a battle with another inventor–industrialist George Westinghouse—over the future of the American electricity infrastructure. Westinghouse's company favored AC, or *alternating current*, electrical systems, which had the technological advantage over DC of being able to transmit electricity over great distances using high voltage power lines. This meant that electricity could be generated at a handful of large, efficient power plants that would serve customers over a wide area. Edison's DC power plants, by contrast, could supply customers within only a one-mile radius of where the electricity was generated.

Sharks have been on Earth longer than trees.

This meant that small power plants would have to be built in just about every neighborhood that wanted electricity.

As the advantages of alternating current became increasingly clear, Edison was desperate to prevent Westinghouse and other competitors from dominating the electricity industry. It dawned on him that if he could promote AC as a deadlier form of electricity, customers might feel safer installing DC systems in their homes, giving him the advantage. And what better way to do that than by endorsing an electric chair powered by alternating current? Edison wrote back to Southwick and explained that he still opposed capital punishment, but as long as it was still in effect, he was in favor of finding the "most humane method available." To that end, he recommended the use of "alternating machines" manufactured by Westinghouse. "The passage of the current from these machines through the human body, even by the slightest contacts, produces instantaneous death," he advised.

Now that the greatest inventor of the age had vouched for electrocution, Gerry and Hale, the other two commission members, came around to Southwick's point of view. When the commission issued its report in January 1888, it recommended the electric chair.

LIGHTS OUT

Edison's campaign against alternating current didn't help him win the AC/DC "current war," as it came to be known. It didn't even help him hang onto his own electric companies: a series of mergers between Edison's companies and many rival firms resulted in the creation of a single large company called Edison General Electric in 1889. But the mergers diluted Edison's ownership stake, and he no longer had a controlling stake in the company that bore his name. Then in 1892, the financier J. P. Morgan orchestrated yet another merger between Edison General Electric and another rival, the Thomson-Houston Electric Company, to create a giant new company called General Electric.

Edison was not told of the merger until a day before it was announced. He was so angry about it and about the fact that his last name had been dropped from the company's name that he resigned from the board of directors and moved on to other projects. Edison, the inventor of the incandescent light bulb, was out of the electricity business—for good. With him out of the way, GE moved aggressively into AC power generation, a field that it still dominates: today, roughly one-third of all the electricity generated on earth is generated in GE power plants.

For Part II of this electrifying history, turn to page 345.

Busy guy: Saint Julian the Hospitaller is the patron saint of ferry workers, hotel keepers, carnival workers, fiddlers, jugglers...and murderers.

TOILET TECH

Better living through toilet technology.

MAKING A STATEMENT

Product: Magic Secret Message Urinal Screens

How It Works: If you find a trip to the public restroom boring, this may be for you. The Secret Message signs are rectangular pieces of black plastic, a little smaller than a credit card, that are attached to a vinyl screen that sits over the drain of the urinal. When peed upon, the warmth of the urine causes the black layer to become opaque, revealing a hidden message beneath. Two popular sellers: "Employees must wash their hands" and "Drink more. She's still ugly." When the urinal is flushed, the cold water turns the sign black again...until the next person uses it. "Whether you want to have fun or need to communicate an important message, this urinal screen will capture attention and be remembered," says the manufacturer, Drain-Net Technologies.

Special Bonus: "These screens are cherry scented!"

THE FACE IS FAMILIAR

Product: Stanford University's Precision Health "Anal Recognition" smart toilet seat

How It Works: You've heard of facial recognition software? It turns out your rear end is as unique as your face, and the Precision Health Smart Toilet Seat takes advantage of this fact: It attaches to a standard toilet and is equipped with an array of gadgets and sensors that analyze urine and stool samples for signs of prostate, urological, and colorectal cancers, plus a host of other maladies. The only problem: making sure the data collected is matched with the correct "end user." That's where the anal recognition software comes in—a special digital camera takes a picture of your rear when you sit down, then any data collected is matched to you, instead of someone with a different "anal print."

The health data—*not* including any images of your butt, which the inventors insist are never seen by anyone—is uploaded to the cloud. Anything that suggests you may be suffering from illness is automatically forwarded to your health care provider for follow-up. "We know it seems weird, but as it turns out, your anal print is unique," says Stanford University's Dr. Sanjiv Gambhir, leader of the team that developed the toilet seat. "Everyone uses the bathroom—there's really no avoiding it—and that enhances [the toilet seat's] value as a disease-detecting device."

PAY TOILET

Product: The BeeVi Toilet

How It Works: Why poop for free when you can get paid to do your business? The BeeVi toilet, installed in a restroom in South Korea's Ulsan National Institute of Science and Technology (UNIST), allows a person to do just that. It collects the fecal matter and sends it to an underground tank where soil microorganisms break down the waste and produce methane gas which is then used to power a gas stove, a hot water tank, and other devices in a nearby laboratory.

The average UNIST student produces enough methane in a single day's pooping to drive a car three-quarters of a mile. The methane has a cash value, and students who do their business in the BeeVi toilet are paid in a virtual currency called *Ggool* (Korean for "honey") for their trouble. They can use their honey money on campus to buy coffee, instant noodles, and even books. "I had only ever thought of feces as dirty, but now it is a treasure of great value to me," Heo Hui-jin, a UNIST postgraduate student, told the Reuters news agency. "I even talk about feces during mealtimes to think about buying any book I want."

QUITE A VIEW

Product: Transparent public restrooms in Tokyo, Japan

How It Works: The restrooms, which have been installed in two parks in the city's popular Shibuya district, feature exterior walls made of transparent glass that allows park goers to see inside the restrooms—sinks, toilets, and all—before stepping inside. Then as soon as someone enters and locks the door behind them, the walls turn opaque, giving the user privacy. Why build see-through facilities? To break down the stigma of the city's public restrooms being "dark, dirty, smelly and scary," say the organizers of the Tokyo Toilet Project, which built the restrooms. "There are two things we worry about when entering a public restroom, especially those located in a park. The first is whether it is clean inside, and the second is that no one is secretly waiting inside. This allows users to check the cleanliness and whether anyone is using the toilet from outside."

Special Bonus: "At night, the facility lights up the park like a beautiful lantern."

* * *

AND NOW FOR A WELSH JOKE

Two American tourists, traveling through Wales, stop at a restaurant in the town of Llanfairpwllgwyngyllgogerychwyrndrobwllllantysiliogogogoch and ask the waitress, "Before we order, could you pronounce the name of where we are, very slowly?"

The waitress answers, "Burrrr Gerrrrr Kiiinnng ."

Male wasps can't sting.

OBSCURE PRESIDENTIAL FIRSTS

Every U.S. president makes history, but few were the first in their positions to do something really *important—like, for example, owning a Siamese cat or hosting a presidential sleepover.*

- The first documented Siamese cat in the United States belonged to President Rutherford B. Hayes. The American consul in Bangkok, Thailand (formerly called Siam), sent one as a gift to Hayes and his wife, Lucy, in 1879.

- In 1958, more than 25 years after he left the White House, former President Herbert Hoover published *The Ordeal of Woodrow Wilson*. It was a best-seller...and the first presidential biography written by another president.

- During a visit to Portland, Oregon, in November 1974, President Gerald Ford sat courtside at a game between the Portland Trail Blazers and the Buffalo Braves, the first time an American president ever attended an NBA game.

- In April 1976, President Ford made history again. Making a cameo appearance in a pretaped video, he became the first—and, so far, only—sitting president to appear on *Saturday Night Live* (which was still in its first season).

- First president to shake hands with guests: Thomas Jefferson. His two predecessors, George Washington and John Adams, took a more formal approach to visiting dignitaries and luminaries, greeting them with a bow.

- Richard Nixon resigned the presidency in 1974 after it became clear that he was connected to the 1972 Watergate break-in. He initially denied any involvement, angrily proclaiming in 1973 that he was "not a crook." Nixon made those defiant remarks to a group of newspaper editors at Walt Disney World—which was also the first presidential visit to the resort and amusement park.

- An autopen is a mechanical device that replicates a signature, which put an end to the elaborate presidential signing-a-bill-into-law ritual—or at least it did once. In 2011, President Barack Obama authorized his staff to use an autopen to sign a bill extending the Patriot Act, the first time a president signed a bill without actually being on site.

- When Herbert Hoover was born in West Branch, Iowa, in 1874, he became the first future president to be born outside of the Eastern Seaboard states.

Barbie's hometown: Willows, Wisconsin.

- While filming a movie during his acting days, a prop gun was discharged near Ronald Reagan's head, resulting in almost total hearing loss in one ear. In 1983, he was outfitted for a hearing aid, making him the first sitting president to wear such a device.

- The United States Secret Service was established in 1865. Their most public duty today: to protect presidents and their families from harm. For security reasons, each president is assigned a code name. But the tradition didn't start until 1945, when President Harry S. Truman became the first chief executive to get one: "General."

- California entered the Union in 1850, but it still took a while for any U.S. president to see it. In 1852, future president Ulysses S. Grant visited San Francisco and saw the Pacific Ocean, the first Commander-in-Chief to do so.

- In September 1993, President Bill Clinton hosted the first-ever presidential slumber party. He invited former presidents George H. W. Bush and Jimmy Carter to the White House for an informal meeting of the minds and they accepted, enjoying cocktails, dinner, and chatting late into the night. (President Ronald Reagan was also invited, but had other plans.)

- Former president Bill Clinton won back-to-back Grammy Awards in the spoken word category for his memoir *My Life* (2003) and for *Wolf Tracks and Peter and the Wolf* (2004). Jimmy Carter and Barack Obama have also won Spoken Word Grammys, but Clinton was the first.

- When Calvin Coolidge was born on July 4, 1872, he became the first—and so far, only—president to be born on the Fourth of July. (Oddly, three ex-presidents have died on the Fourth of July. John Adams and Thomas Jefferson, who both passed on July 4, 1826, and James Monroe, who died on July 4, 1831.)

- In 1881, four months into his presidential term, James A. Garfield was shot. The assassin's bullet would eventually claim his life, but to keep the president comfortable as he lay dying in a hospital bed, doctors concocted a rudimentary cooling contraption. Made up of a fan, a wet cloth, and a large box of ice, it was the first time a U.S. president experienced air-conditioning. (Garfield was also the first left-handed president.)

- For his many appearances at and longtime association with the popular World Wrestling Entertainment franchise, future president Donald Trump was inducted into the Celebrity Wing of the WWE Hall of Fame in 2013—the first and only commander in chief enshrined by that organization.

Unlike the 50 stars on the American flag, the 12 stars on the European flag represent "the peoples of Europe in a form of a circle,...

LUCKY FINDS

Ever stumble upon something valuable? It's an incredible feeling. Here's the latest installment of one of the BRI's regular features.

THE POPE'S SWEATER

The Find: A vintage sweater that once belonged to a legend

Where It Was Found: A thrift store in Asheville, North Carolina

The Story: In 2014, Rikki and Sean McEvoy of Knoxville, Tennessee, were on vacation when they stopped in a Goodwill store to see what they could find. Normally, the married couple wouldn't have gone "thrifting" so late in the day. Their primary source of income was reselling vintage clothes online, so they usually hit the stores in the morning. But they went in anyway. While flipping through the men's shirts, Rikki saw a sweater with "West Point" on it. Judging by its vintage zipper, she pegged it as from the 1940s. She threw it in her cart and paid 58 cents for it.

The McEvoys' original plan was to resell the vintage sweater for a tidy profit, but it had a few moth holes, so Rikki decided to patch it up for Sean to wear. As she prepped the garment for sewing, she saw, written on the tag, "Lombardi 46." She put the sweater aside, but not because she recognized the surname of Vince Lombardi, the famed Green Bay Packers coach who won five NFL championships in the 1960s. (Rikki's a baseball and hockey fan, not a football fan.) It was simply that "I had this feeling in my gut that I'm really gonna regret altering this piece," she told NPR.

Coincidentally, the next day, Sean, who *is* a football fan, was watching a Vince Lombardi documentary and saw a photo of "The Pope" (a nickname bestowed by Green Bay fans upon the deeply religious Lombardi) wearing a similar West Point sweater during his assistant coach days in the early '50s. Sean said to his wife, "Wouldn't that be crazy if that sweater was Vince Lombardi's?" Rikki looked up and said, "That's the name! Lombardi!" And then she ran and got the sweater.

After verifying that it was indeed the genuine article, their lucky find was auctioned a few months later for $43,000. Heritage Auction House donated the $4,000 buyer's fee to the Goodwill store that had sold the sweater for 58 cents.

BOWLED OVER

The Find: A porcelain bowl from the Ming Dynasty

Where It Was Found: At a yard sale near New Haven, Connecticut

The Story: "It's always really exciting for us as specialists when something we didn't even know existed appears seemingly out of nowhere," said Chinese antiques expert Angela McAteer of Sotheby's Auction House. Sotheby's receives dozens of emails per

...a sign of union," and not the Union's member states.
(There are currently 27 countries in the European Union.)

week from people who believe they have a valuable artifact, and most of the time, it's not. But when McAteer saw photos of this six-inch blue-and-white porcelain bowl with a floral design, "it was immediately apparent...that we were looking at something very, very special."

The bowl, purchased at a yard sale in 2020 by an unidentified antiques enthusiast, turned out to be a Chinese porcelain, made in the 1400s for the Yongle emperor. There are only six others like it in the world, all in museums. The appraisers didn't know how a 15th-century Chinese bowl could have ended up at a Connecticut yard sale in pristine condition, but they assumed it was passed down through generations of the same family who had no idea how unique it was. The yard sale price of the bowl: $35. Sotheby's estimated its value at $300,000 to $500,000...and they were wrong. It sold to the highest bidder for $721,800.

> **DID YOU KNOW?**
>
> In the 1700s, European men gave their fiancées *gimmel* rings. Derived from the Latin word for "twin," a gimmel ring was separated into two hoops, one worn by each partner. Once married, the hoops were rejoined and worn by the bride as her wedding ring.

WITH THIS RING, I THEE WEED

The Find: A lost wedding ring

Where It Was Found: In a garden in Sweden

The Story: In 1995, Lena Påhlsson was baking Christmas cookies with her daughters when she noticed her wedding ring was missing from her finger. They looked and looked and couldn't find it. She'd designed the expensive ring herself; it had a gold band inset with seven small diamonds. A few months later, when they pulled up the floorboards during a kitchen remodel, the ring still hadn't shown up. "I had given up hope," Påhlsson said.

Sixteen years later, in 2011, she was in her garden and pulled a carrot out of the ground. There was something shiny around the top of it. Could it be...? The wedding ring! And it was in remarkably good shape (although Påhlsson had to get it resized because that carrot wasn't the only thing that had gotten bigger). She surmises that she lost the ring while she was baking the cookies, and that it fell into a pile of food scraps that were later fed to their pet sheep. Then the sheep probably "deposited" the ring in the Påhlsson's compost pile, and sometime later it found its way to the garden, where it was surrounded by dirt until a carrot grew downward, right through the middle of it. (Neat trick.)

A VELLUM IN THE ROUGH

The Find: A historic U.S. document

Where It Was Found: In a house in Scotland

The Story: By 1820, the original print of the Declaration of Independence was over 40 years old and in tatters. Secretary of State John Quincy Adams commissioned a printer

named William J. Stone to meticulously re-create the print onto a copperplate. After three painstaking years, Mason had a near-perfect replica. He printed a few copies onto paper and then about 200 onto vellum, a kind of parchment that's made from calfskin. In 1824, the vellum prints were distributed to state houses, to institutions, and to the three surviving signers themselves— Thomas Jefferson, John Adams, and Charles Carroll of Maryland. Carroll gave both of his copies to his grandson-in-law, a Scottish diplomat named John MacTavish. One ended up with the Maryland Historical Society, and the other went missing.

Tucked inside was a folded-up vellum document—a copy of the Declaration of Independence.

In 2021, Cathy Marsden, a rare book specialist for the auction house Lyon & Turnbull, was at a client's Scottish ancestral home looking through the attic when she came across a box of old papers. Tucked inside was a folded-up vellum document—a copy of the Declaration of Independence. Most of the time, these kinds of documents end up being cheap Victorian knockoffs, especially in Europe. But Marsden had a feeling about this one. "When I got back to the office and started doing some research I became really excited as its significance became clearer," she told the BBC. "After extensive research we confirmed it was indeed one of the 201 copies made by William Stone, of which only 48 of them are known to still exist."

When the document was auctioned off in Philadelphia later that year, it was expected to fetch between $500,000 and $800,000. An intense bidding war between buyers from all over the world pushed the price higher and higher until it sold for over $4.4 million.

SOFA, SO GOOD

The Find: A 500-year-old painting
Where It Was Found: Inside a piece of furniture
The Story: In 2007, a German college student bought a used sofa bed for $215 at a Berlin flea market. She'd been using it as a couch for a while until one day when she needed the bed. When she pulled out the mattress, tucked between the folds was an old oil painting. The 10"-by-15" baroque-style work depicts two nude, winged figures flying above a lake while people on the ground shoot arrows at them. Intrigued, the student had it appraised. Good move. Painted in Italy in the early 1600s, it's called "Preparation to Escape Egypt," and even though the artist's name is lost to history, the artwork fetched $27,630 at auction.

* * *

"I told Roland Hemond to go out and get me a big-name pitcher. He said, 'Dave Wehrmeister's got 11 letters. Is that a big enough name for you?'"
—**Eddie Eichorn**

Boanthropy is a real psychological disorder in which the sufferer believes they are a cow.

ALL THE POOP

Some trivial pieces about the fascinating feces of various animal species.

- Waste not, want not: Rabbits metabolize food so quickly that they don't get all the nutrition out of their vegetarian diet before their bodies process it. So rabbit poop pellets, or *cecotropes*, retain valuable nutrition that the rabbit gets by consuming it a second time.

- Dogs also engage in the act of poop eating, or *coprophagia*. According to scientists, about a quarter of all pet dogs will eat their feces at least once in their lifetimes, and it's a carryover from pooches' ancestral days. Thousands of years ago, when dogs traveled in packs, a dog would eat their poop if they sensed that it contained parasites, protecting the rest of their clan from getting sick.

- Many species of animals—particularly plant eaters and specifically koalas, pandas, elephants, and rhinos—eat their *parents'* feces, but only when they're newborn babies. Reason: they haven't yet developed the necessary bacteria for proper digestion, so they get it from their parents' poop.

- Vultures poop on their legs. It cools them, and mimics the same principle as perspiration (sweating) in humans. As the liquid in the poop evaporates it also pulls away heat, making vulture skin notably cooler.

- Whale poop is vital to the health of the ocean. Waste explodes out of sperm whales in big clouds, which spreads clouds full of iron that the microscopic, bottom-of-the-food-chain-of-the-ocean phytoplankton feed upon.

- Two odd facts about demodex mites: 1) they're tiny beings that live on almost every human being's face; 2) they don't poop. Nature made them without an anus, and with nowhere for the poop to go, it just stays in their bodies until they die after about two weeks of life.

- Caterpillar poop is called *frass*. It's plant matter that comes in a chunk roughly the size of an oat flake, and it comes bursting out of the creature's rear. Blood pressure builds up behind the anus, blasting the feces out and as far away as 40 times the length of the caterpillar itself. By sending it so far away, the poop is less likely to attract predatory ants.

- Ah, the beautiful pristine beaches of Pacific Ocean islands covered in gleaming white sand. Turns out that white sand is made up largely of parrotfish dung. How? Parrotfish eat, process, and excrete coral, which becomes sand in the end.

Cellophane was invented in 1908 as a tablecloth protector.

I SPY...AT THE MOVIES

You probably remember the kids' game "I Spy, with My Little Eye..."
Filmmakers have been playing it for years. Here are some in-jokes and
gags you can look for the next time you see these movies.

TWILIGHT ZONE: THE MOVIE (1983)

I Spy... Neidermeyer from *Animal House*

Where to Find It: At the end of the 1978 comedy *National Lampoon's Animal House*, each main character gets a freeze-frame and some text about what happened to them after college. For ROTC enrollee and antagonist Doug Neidermeyer (Mark Metcalf), he was "killed in Vietnam by his own troops." *Animal House* filmmaker John Landis also directed one of the stories in *Twilight Zone: The Movie*. During a sequence set in the Vietnam War, an American soldier in danger shouts, "We shouldn't have shot Lieutenant Neidermeyer!"

HALLOWEEN KILLS (2021)

I Spy... a man named Bob

Where to Find Him: In this movie, the eleventh sequel of the original *Halloween* (1978), producers wanted to show a TV news clip about a character named Bob Simms, one of the victims of serial killer Michael Myers. But they couldn't get the rights to use an image of John Michael Graham, the actor who played Bob, so they found a picture of someone who looked a lot like him and actually *is* named Bob. The picture: the yearbook photo of *Better Call Saul* actor Bob Odenkirk, who agreed to be Bob Simms.

THE HARDER THEY FALL (2021)

I Spy... a salute to Chadwick Boseman

Where to Find It: Boseman, best known for portraying Black icons Jackie Robinson in *42*, James Brown in *Get on Up*, and Black Panther in *Black Panther*, died from cancer in 2020 at the age of 43. In 2021, the makers of the Western *The Harder They Fall*, which features a predominantly Black cast, paid tribute to the deceased actor. As two of the main characters walk past a train in a dusty Western town, the audience can see a name painted on the side of a passenger car: "C.A. Boseman."

THE DEPARTED (2006)

I Spy... an ominous X

Where to Find It: In Martin Scorsese's epic crime story about the Massachusetts

Mongolia may be a landlocked nation, but it does have a navy...
consisting of seven sailors and one seaworthy vessel (a tugboat).

State Police, Irish American gangsters, and the moles both sides have installed in their rival's camps, almost every main character dies. Just before each death, every character appears in a scene next to a giant X.

SOUL (2020)

I Spy... a Nine Inch Nails shout-out

Where to Find It: Joe Gardner (Jamie Foxx) walks out of a hardware store. There's a small sign on the window advertising a sale on "9 inch nails." In real life, Nine Inch Nails is the name of the rock band fronted by *Soul* soundtrack co-composer Trent Reznor.

BEVERLY HILLS COP II (1987)

I Spy... Sylvester Stallone

Where to Find It: Before producers hired Eddie Murphy to play fish-out-of-water Detroit detective Axel Foley in the 1984 action comedy *Beverly Hills Cop*, Sylvester Stallone was attached to the project. Then Stallone rewrote the script to remove all the humor and make it a straightforward police movie; his rewritten script became the basis for another movie, *Cobra*, which Stallone made in 1986. In a scene in *Beverly Hills Cop II*, Murphy goes into Billy's (Judge Reinhold) room and closes the door. Behind the door: a *Cobra* movie poster.

SPIDER-MAN: HOMECOMING (2017)

I Spy... The Incredible Hulk

Where to Find It: When Peter Parker (Tom Holland) is sitting in a science classroom at school, posters of important scientists line the wall behind his teacher. Among them are portraits of Nikola Tesla, Sir Isaac Newton, Marie Curie...and Mark Ruffalo—the actor who plays scientist Bruce Banner, aka the Incredible Hulk, in other Marvel Comics movies.

THE BREAKFAST CLUB (1985)

I Spy... the younger version of the janitor character

Where to Find It: In establishing shots of the empty Shermer High School at the beginning of the movie, there's a plaque with photos of past students voted "Man of the Year." One of them is actor John Kapelos, who appears later in the movie as the high school janitor.

Most profitable independently released cartoon of all time: the X-rated *Fritz the Cat* (1972).

YOU BROKE MY ART

It's been said that after a work of art goes on display, it no longer belongs to the artist but to the public. Judging by these folks, the public should be more careful.

NAPOLEON'S SISTER'S PLASTER TOES

One of the most prized sculptures at Rome's Borghese Gallery is *Venus Victrix*, a provocative marble statue of Princess Pauline Bonaparte (Napoleon's sister) sculpted by Antonio Canova in 1808. Wearing nothing but a sheet on her lower half, the princess is depicted "in the guise of Venus"—reclining on a couch with her legs outstretched and her bare feet exposed. The original plaster cast that Canova sculpted in 1805 and used as a model for the marble statue is on display at the Gypsotheca Museum in northern Italy. A World War I air raid damaged the plaster figure's head, hands, and feet in 1917, and it wasn't fully repaired until 2004. But the sculpture remained unscathed...until July 2020, when a 50-year-old Austrian tourist decided to sit down alongside the topless princess so his wife could take a photo. When he stood back up, he looked down at Pauline's feet and realized he'd broken off three of her toes. The couple hurried out, but they were easy to find because they'd left their information for possible COVID-19 contact tracing.

THE THREE SPLOTCHES

A crowd gathered at Lotte World Mall in Seoul, South Korea, in 2016 to watch renowned American graffiti artist JonOne (real name: John Andrew Perello) create one of his colorful abstract expressionist works. Titled *Untitled*, it measures 8 feet by 22 feet. As he often does, JonOne left his used paint cans and brushes on the floor below the graffiti. That's part of the installation, and for five years, no one touched it. In March 2021, a young couple saw the art supplies and assumed it was a "participatory work." When they were done participating, there were three dark green splotches near the center of the $440,000 painting. The couple was later tracked down and are said to be very embarrassed for what police say was an honest mistake. For now, the splotches remain, and a "Do Not Touch" sign has been placed among the art supplies. JonOne was upset at first and wanted it fixed, but the press generated by the blunder renewed interest in his painting. "With just three brush strokes on my canvas," he said, "they have managed to cause a planetary buzz? There is strength in that." He also said he'd like to join the couple for tea someday.

THE CURSE OF TUT'S BEARD

In August 2014, staffers at Cairo's Egyptian Museum were cleaning one of the most famous artifacts in the world: King Tut's golden burial mask. Exact details are scarce,

Women with third-class passage on the *Titanic* had a
32 percent likelier chance of surviving than men in first class.

but at one point the pharaoh's "imperial goatee" became detached from the mask. Staffers panicked and instead of taking the 3,000-year-old mask to the conservation lab, they sloppily reattached the 5.5-pound goatee with industrial-strength epoxy. When they were through, the goatee was off-center and not even touching Tut's chin—and there was a substantial gap of yellowish epoxy. Worse yet, some epoxy had dried on the mask, so they used a spatula to get it off and left scratch marks.

> **King Tut's mask was put back on display in the hopes that visitors wouldn't notice. They noticed.**

Looking like it lost a fight, King Tut's mask was put back on display in the hopes that visitors wouldn't notice. They noticed. The ensuing scandal led to the Egyptian government charging eight museum workers—including four senior restoration experts and the former director of restoration—with "negligence of the artifact." It took two painstaking months for restorers (who actually knew what they were doing) to repair the "repair." Still, some scratch marks remain. The dumbest part: The ancient Egyptians had attached Tut's goatee with a wooden dowel. The museum staffers should have known that the dowel needs to be changed every 20 years or so. If they had, it would have been a simple procedure, requiring neither epoxy nor a spatula.

CROWNING ACHIEVEMENT

Hypercaine was part of a huge art project conceived in collaboration by artists Simon Birch, Gabriel Chan, Jacob Blitzer, and Gloria Yu, and held in 2017 at the 14th Factory in Los Angeles. The vast warehouse was divided into 14 different exhibitions and this one, *Hypercaine*, consisted of 64 crowns placed on free-standing white pedestals. As visitors were wandering through the grid of crowns, a young woman kneeled down for a selfie...and stumbled backward into a pedestal. An entire row came crashing down, dominoes-style. Some crowns were undamaged, a few received nicks and scratches, and three were beyond repair. Reported value of the damage: $200,000. Surveillance footage of the incident went viral, leading some to wonder if this was just a publicity stunt. Gallery spokesperson Jocelyn Ingram denied it, saying "It would be pretty irrational for the artists...to intentionally inflict harm on their own work hoping to gain any benefit." (One benefit: we get to include it in an *Uncle John's Bathroom Reader*.)

BAD REVIEW

Influential Mexican contemporary artist Gabriel Rico gathered some "found objects"—including a tennis ball, a soccer ball, a rock, and a feather—and set all of them into a pane of glass, which he then stood vertically on a brass base. He called it *Nimble and sinister tricks (To be preserved without scandal and corruption)*. In 2020, Galería OMR made it the centerpiece of the Zona Maco contemporary art fair in Mexico

Ancient Incas built Machu Picchu to be earthquake-proof.
The mortar-free stone walls "dance" during a quake, then resettle back as they were.

City. Rope barriers kept visitors a safe distance away from the fragile work, but critics were allowed a closer look. One such critic, Avelina Lésper—who'd made her views known in her 2015 book, *The Fraud of Contemporary Art*—approached Rico's piece while openly mocking it. Then, as she stepped back to take a photo...the pane of glass suddenly shattered and millions of tiny shards rained onto the floor along with the found objects, some of which rolled away. At first, Lésper was unrepentant and even suggested they keep it that way. But she apologized after learning that Rico's sculpture had been valued at $20,000. The incident made headlines in the art world, with some in the media calling Lésper a hero for destroying the overpriced work. The gallery owner called it an "enormous lack of professionalism and respect." It's still a mystery as to exactly how the sculpture shattered. Lésper's theory: "It was like the work heard my comment and felt what I thought of it."

* * *

UNCLE JOHN'S HOUSEHOLD HACKS

- To deep-clean your dryer's lint trap, put an empty toilet paper or paper towel roll on the end of your vacuum hose, and squeeze it in flat to get it into narrow spaces.
- Need to freshen the air in your bathroom? Put a few drops of essential oil on the inside of the cardboard toilet paper tube.
- To clean a microwave of dried food particles, fill a large bowl with water, a slosh of white vinegar, and a sliced lemon. Heat it in the microwave for five minutes, then let the bowl sit in there for another five. Remove the bowl and everything will wipe off easily.
- To dust Venetian blinds, use a clean, dry 3-inch paintbrush.
- To prevent grit from building up between your shower tiles, keep a soap-dispensing dish brush in your shower caddy, and give the walls a quick, soapy scrubbing every time you shower.
- If you want your stainless-steel sink looking new again, give it a good wash and dry, and then sprinkle it with flour. Buffing will bring the shine back.
- To clean your kitchen exhaust fan filter, add a scoop of Oxiclean to a bucket of boiling water, then dunk the filter in the mix for a few minutes, rinse, and dry flat on a towel. All the grease will be gone.
- To tame flyaway hairs, spray a little hairspray on a toothbrush and use it to smooth those hairs down.
- Don't have time to iron your clothes? Wet and wring out a washcloth and throw it in the dryer with your wrinkled garment. Dry it for 5 to 10 minutes. Most of the wrinkles will be gone.

How do kangaroos cool off? By licking their forearms.

UNCLE JOHN'S CYNIC-TIONARY

If the standard dictionary is a bit too ordinary for your taste,
delight in these darker definitions of common words.

ADVERTISING: "The rattling of a stick inside a swill bucket." –*George Orwell*

ALCOHOL: The only drug on earth you have to justify not using.

ASKING: "Polite demanding." –*Max Headroom*

BARGAIN: "Something you can't use at a price you can't resist." –*Franklin Jones*

BLONDE JOKE: A joke short enough for most men to understand.

CELEBRITY: Someone who spends the first half of their life trying to become famous, and the second half wearing dark sunglasses so no one recognizes them.

CENSORSHIP: "An excuse to talk about sex." –*Fran Lebowitz*

CHARITY: "Something you do for people while other people are watching." –*Bob Odenkirk*

COAT: Something you wear when your mom gets cold.

CONSCIENCE: "What hurts when all your other parts feel good." –*Kevin Dutton*

CRICKET: "Baseball on valium." –*Robin Williams*

CYNIC: "One who never sees a good quality in a man, and never fails to see a bad one." –*Henry Ward Beecher*

DEATH: "What politically correct doctors call a 'negative patient outcome.'" –*John Koski*

DIET SODA: A drink you buy along with a half-pound bag of peanut M&M's.

DNA: "A complex organic molecule characterized as the building block of life and appropriately shaped like a spiral staircase to nowhere." –*Rick Bayan*

DOCTOR: One who kills your ills with pills and then kills you with bills.

ENGLISH TEACHER: Someone who puts more thought into a novel than the original author ever did.

ETERNITY: The last two minutes of a football game.

FIDDLE: "An instrument to tickle human ears by friction of a horse's tail on the entrails of a cat." –*Ambrose Bierce*

FLUSHABLE WIPES: Unflushable wipes.

GRADUATION CEREMONY: "Where the commencement speaker tells thousands of students dressed in identical caps and gowns that 'individuality' is the key to success." –*Robert Orben*

GRUOP: "A collective term for a group of proofreaders." –*Tom Gauld*

HELL: "Other people." –*Jean-Paul Sartre*

HOPE: The first step toward disappointment.

IDEALIST: "One who, on noticing that a rose smells better than a cabbage, concludes that it is also more nourishing." –*H. L. Mencken*

INTERNET: Why you're not getting anything done at work.

IRONING BOARD: A surfboard that gave up on its dreams and got a real job.

LIBERAL: A fellow who could get into an argument with himself and lose.

LIFE: "Nasty, brutish, and short." –*Thomas Hobbes*

MEETING: It could have been an email.

NATIONAL SECURITY AGENCY: A government organization that actually listens to you.

PAPER CLIP: A staple for people with commitment issues.

PATIENCE: Something you admire in the driver behind you and can't stand in the driver ahead of you.

PESSIMIST: A well-informed optimist.

POLITICIAN: Someone who shakes your hand before an election, and your confidence after it.

SEX: A man's definition of a romantic evening.

SIBLING: One to whom you'd donate a kidney but wouldn't lend your charger.

SYNONYM: A word used in place of the one you can't spell.

UNEMPLOYMENT: "Capitalism's way of getting you to plant a garden." –*Orson Scott Card*

USER: "The word computer professionals use when they mean 'idiot.'" –*Dave Barry*

WATER: "Stupid juice." –*Bob*, Bob's Burgers

WATERPROOF MASCARA: Mascara that comes off if you cry, shower, or swim, but not when you try to remove it.

WRITER'S BLOCK: "A fancy term made up by whiners so they can have an excuse to drink alcohol." –*Steve Martin*

Most stolen artist: Pablo Picasso. More than 1,000 of his paintings have disappeared.

PET SHOTS

Millions of American homes have pets, and millions of American homes also have guns. Once in a while, those two things collide—with a few unlucky humans getting shot (accidentally, probably) by their four-legged friends.

SHOT BY A YELLOW LABRADOR

At about 2:30 p.m. one day in October 2019, 79-year-old Brent Parks stopped his car in front of some train tracks in Enid, Oklahoma, and waited for a train to pass. As the train neared, Parks's seven-month-old yellow Lab puppy, Molly, got so startled by the noise that she jumped up from the backseat onto the center console that separated the driver's and passenger's seats. The pressure bore down on some fabric in the compartment, which caught on the trigger of the .22-caliber handgun Parks had stored inside. Result: the handgun fired, and put a bullet into the left thigh of Parks's passenger, his 44-year-old caregiver, Tina Springer. Parks managed to slow Springer's profuse bleeding by wrapping his belt around her thigh, until first responders arrived and took her to the hospital, where she made a full recovery. The gun "wasn't normally loaded," Parks told police.

SHOT BY A ROTTWEILER

Sonny "Tex" Gilligan was headed out to hunt jackrabbits in the desert outside of Las Cruces, New Mexico, in October 2018. He was sitting behind the wheel of his pickup truck with his two dogs in the backseat, when he suddenly heard a gunshot and felt tremendous pain in his back and neck. For a moment, Gilligan thought he'd been shot by a passerby, then quickly realized it was Charlie, his 120-pound rottweiler mix, who'd fired on him, stepping on a firearm next to him on the seat. "Charlie got his foot in the trigger of the gun and I leaned forward and he slipped off the seat and caught the trigger—and it shot," Gilligan told reporters. Gilligan called 911 and then passed out (he was clinically dead). But paramedics revived him with CPR and transported him to an El Paso hospital, where doctors treated him for broken ribs, a broken collarbone, and organ damage that left him in critical condition...and he survived. "Poor Charlie, he's a good dog," Gilligan said. "A big, loving dog who would never hurt anybody on purpose."

SHOT BY A CHOCOLATE LABRADOR

Allie Carter, a resident of northern Indiana, went on a waterfowl hunt in 2015 at a designated public spot called the Tri-County Fish and Wildlife Area. She brought along her chocolate Labrador retriever, who, after Carter placed her shotgun on the ground (with the safety off), accidentally stepped on the gun. It went off, shooting a round at point-black range into Carter's foot. The guilty dog's name: Trigger.

A baby puffin is a *puffling*.

SHOT BY AN EXCITED DOG

In December 2014, 46-year-old Richard Fipps of Sheridan, Wyoming, stopped his truck on the side of a snowy road to help a stranded driver. Along with two coworkers, Fipps was going to remove the snow chains from his vehicle to put them on the stuck truck in hopes of freeing it. As he got out of his truck, he told his dog to get into the backseat, which it did...and then it jumped onto the trigger of a loaded .300 Winchester Magnum rifle. The rifle discharged; the bullet went through the passenger side window and into Fipps. Fipps was rushed to a hospital, and while his injuries were not life-threatening, he narrowly avoided amputation of the lower part of the arm where the bullet had lodged. "It appeared to be an accident," a sheriff's deputy told reporters.

SHOT IN SELF-DEFENSE

In 2004, 37-year-old Pensacola, Florida, man Jerry Allen Bradford was in possession of seven puppies—a litter of German shepherd mixes. As the dogs approached three months old and Bradford couldn't find any homes for them, he decided the best thing to do would be to put down the unwanted animals...by shooting them. While Bradford was holding two of the little dogs, one in his left hand and the other in his arms—right next to his .38-caliber handgun—the puppy in his left hand wiggled loose and placed its paw directly on the trigger of the gun. The weight of the little dog managed to pull the trigger, which discharged a bullet into Bradford's wrist. He was treated for a gunshot wound (and the sheriff's office took the dogs away).

SHOT BY A CAT

A cat? It happened while Joseph Stanton was cooking dinner in his Bates Township, Michigan, kitchen one night in 2005. As he stood at his stove, one of his cats started walking around the kitchen, and, while padding across a counter, knocked Stanton's 9mm pistol to the ground. And as it hit the floor, the loaded pistol went off, sending a bullet into the lower part of Stanton's chest. The man was treated for internal injuries at a nearby hospital, but survived.

SHOT FROM BEHIND

A 46-year-old man from Brigham City, Utah, went on a duck hunt in 2011, bringing along his dog, as he always did. (He later told the local sheriff's office that the pooch was his "best friend" and a "loyal canine.") After rowing into a marsh, the man got out of the boat to set up decoys, and left his 12-gauge shotgun resting on the bow, whereupon the dog jumped up to follow the man and, in the process, stepped on the gun and pulled the trigger. That unleashed a load of bird shot, of which precisely 27 pellets ended up lodged in the man's buttocks. (He made a full recovery—from the gunshot wound, but probably not the embarrassment.)

Oldest door in Great Britain: one in Westminster Abbey dating to 1032.

ARE YOU A POLYGLOT?

That's not an insult: a polyglot is someone who can speak several languages.
English has incorporated words from many other cultures, so you've
probably been speaking other languages without even knowing it.
Below are a few examples of everyday words that came to
English from elsewhere. Can you match them to their
original language? (Answers on page 401.)

1.	Ketchup	**a)**	Hawaiian
2.	Emoji	**b)**	Persian
3.	Robot	**c)**	Japanese
4.	Cafeteria	**d)**	Dutch
5.	Avatar	**e)**	French
6.	Chocolate	**f)**	Chinese
7.	Boss	**g)**	Spanish
8.	Wiki	**h)**	Tsogo
9.	Zombie	**i)**	Tongan
10.	Checkmate	**j)**	Sanskrit
11.	Taboo	**k)**	Czech
12.	Restaurant	**l)**	Nahuatl

*   *   *

3 REAL HISTORICAL PLAQUES

"On this exact spot in the afternoon of April 27, 1968, a marital argument was won by the husband."
—in Laona, Wisconsin

"On this empty lot stood the nation's only combination sushi and cigar bar."
—in Arlington, Virginia

"On this site in 1874, Julio Richelieu, bartender, served up the first Martini when a miner came into his saloon with a fistful of nuggets and asked for something special. He was served a 'Martinez Special.' After three or four drinks, however, the 'Z' would get very much in the way. The drink consisted of 2/3 gin, 1/3 vermouth, a dash of orange bitters, poured over crushed ice and served with an olive."
—in Martinez, California

The Mall of America in chilly Minnesota has no central heating.
It's warmed by skylights, lighting fixtures, and the body heat of shoppers.

RANDOM BITS ABOUT '80S HITS

Inside the, like, totally tubular making of, like, those songs you,
like, couldn't escape when you were playing Pac-Man.

Steve Miller Band, "Abracadabra" (1982)

An experiment with synthesizers and New Wave sounds turned into a comeback hit for the Steve Miller Band, a bluesy, hard rock group best known for its late 1960s and early '70s output. "Abracadabra" went to #1 in 1982, and is still one of the top 100 biggest hits of all time, according to *Billboard*. Inspiration: Diana Ross. Miller told a reporter that he wrote the song after seeing Diana Ross at a luxury ski resort, recalling the crush he'd developed on her years earlier when he met her backstage on the 1960s musical TV show *Hullabaloo*. Those memories, he confessed, fueled "Abracadabra," a song about a man with a powerful, lustful crush.

Toni Basil, "Mickey" (1981)

The cheerleader chant-like song about a guy named Mickey is a gender-swapped cover of "Kitty," a song released in 1979 by the British power-pop band Racey. When Basil decided to cover it, she changed the title and lyrics, and based them on her celebrity crush of more than a decade: Monkees singer and drummer Micky Dolenz.

Rick Springfield, "Jessie's Girl" (1981)

Springfield emerged from Australia as a teen idol in 1972 with the hit "Speak to the Sky," but when his record sales underperformed, he turned to acting, peaking with a role on the U.S. soap opera *General Hospital* in the early 1980s. He parlayed that fame into another go-round as a musician, and in 1981 released "Jessie's Girl," a song about coveting a friend's girlfriend. A few years earlier, Springfield had enrolled in a stained glass–making class where he got to be friends with a man named Gary...and he soon developed a crush on Gary's girlfriend. When he wrote the song, Springfield didn't think "Gary's Girl" sounded very good, so he changed it to Jessie (lifting the name from NFL player Ron Jessie). As for the "girl"? Springfield doesn't remember her name. Even the expert research team at *The Oprah Winfrey Show* couldn't find her in the late '90s, when Springfield appeared on that show as a guest.

Hall & Oates, "Private Eyes" (1981)

Many of Hall & Oates's songs were written individually by guitarist John Oates, or by lead singer Daryl Hall, either alone or with Janna Allen, younger sister of Hall's girlfriend, Sara Allen. "Private Eyes" developed differently. It was pitched to Janna Allen by a friend, Los Angeles studio musician Warren Pash, and was inspired by a billboard for the 1980 Tim Conway and Don Knotts movie *The Private Eyes*. Pash made a demo with Allen singing lead, but when they realized it would be a better song if performed by a man, they offered it to Hall & Oates. Hall rewrote and rearranged the song with the Allen sisters. Pash still received a songwriting credit—which netted him a small fortune when the song hit #1 on the pop charts.

> **Van Halen figured the song would disappear into obscurity.**

Michael Jackson, "Beat It" (1983)

When Michael Jackson was recording the hard-rocking "Beat It" for his *Thriller* album, producer Quincy Jones decided it needed a hot guitar solo and that the ideal musician to play it was the music industry's premier rock guitarist at that time: Eddie Van Halen. After initially thinking that somebody was prank calling him pretending to be Jones, Van Halen agreed to meet the producer at his studio, where he listened to a demo of "Beat It" and improvised two searing guitar solos. Amount of time Van Halen spent on the song: about half an hour. The guitarist refused royalty payments on the future #1 hit from the eventual best-selling album of all time because he considered it a favor to Jones; Van Halen figured the song would disappear into obscurity.

Christopher Cross, "Arthur's Theme (Best That You Can Do)" (1981)

In 1980, Christopher Cross became an unlikely pop sensation. His sweetly sung, ultra-laid-back brand of soft rock struck a chord, and after "Sailing" went to #1, he became the first act to win all four major Grammy Awards (Record of the Year, Song of the Year, Album of the Year, and Best New Artist) and was asked by producers of the Dudley Moore–Liza Minnelli romantic comedy *Arthur* to provide the film's score. Director Steve Gordon didn't want to deal with someone who'd never written a score before, so veteran composer Burt Bacharach got the job. But Cross was still invited to sing the film's big love theme, and to cowrite it with Bacharach and lyricist Carole Bayer Sager. According to Cross, he wrote the melody with Bacharach; according to Bayer Sager, she and Cross wrote the lyrics. However, they all agree on one thing: the song's most memorable line, "When you get caught between the moon and New York City," came from Peter Allen, with whom Bayer Sager had previously collaborated (and who, coincidentally, was Minnelli's ex-husband). One night in the 1970s, Allen had been stuck in an airplane circling a New York airport, and the line popped into his head. He and Bayer Sager used it in a song they wrote but never released, and Bayer Sager thought it would be perfect for the movie's theme song. She asked him if she could use it and he said yes. Result: for that one line, Allen wound up with a cowriting credit for "Best That You Can Do," which hit #1 and won the Academy Award for Best Original Song.

Naming your kid? Consider this: if your first, middle, or last name is Lyndon, you can get into the Lyndon Johnson Presidential Library for free.

IRONIC, ISN'T IT?

*There's nothing like a good dose of irony to put the problems
of day-to-day life into proper perspective.*

COLD, HARD IRONY

The Titanic Museum Attraction in Pigeon Forge, Tennessee, lets you explore a
half-scale replica of the *Titanic*. There's also a half-scale replica of the iceberg that sank
the luxury cruise ship in 1912. In August 2021, part of the iceberg collapsed, injuring
three visitors and forcing a temporary closure of the Titanic Museum.

THE IRONY IS ACCUMULATING

A freak snowstorm blanketed Vancouver's University of British Columbia in January
2020, causing widespread cancellations—including the annual campus snowball fight,
which had to be rescheduled for a day when there wasn't as much snow.

IRONY IN THE COURT

In 1938, a 21-year-old man was charged with reckless driving. When he didn't show
up for his court date (he was representing himself), he was charged for both the traffic
offense and for failure to appear. His name: Raymond Burr, who later in life would
play TV's most trusted lawyer, Perry Mason.

REPTIRONY

The common lancehead snake is a pit viper that lives in the lowland east of the Andes
Mountains. In 2021, an international group of researchers announced the discovery
of a glue-like enzyme in its venom that causes severe blood clotting. With some
modifications, the deadly snake venom can be turned into a lifesaving field medicine
that can close wounds that won't stop bleeding (such as one from a snakebite) in less
than a minute.

POISONING THE IRONY

Smallmouth bass are considered an invasive species in Miramichi Lake in New
Brunswick, Canada, where they're crowding out the native Atlantic salmon. In
a bid to save the salmon, a coalition of environmental groups came up with an
unusual plan to eradicate the bass: pour thousands of gallons of a toxic chemical
into the lake. "Unfortunately," reported the local newspaper, the *River Valley Sun*,
"Noxfish Fish Toxicant II, with the active ingredient rotenone, will kill almost all
fish, regardless of species."

Countries with the most Spanish speakers:
1) Mexico; 2) Colombia; 3) Argentina; 4) Spain; 5) the United States.

BLUB BLUB IRONY BLUB BLUB

In August 2021, the mysterious British graffiti artist Banksy (or a Banksy copycat) installed a multimedia art piece on a stone wall in East Suffolk, England: on the ground was a piece of scrap metal bent in the shape of a small boat; painted on the wall behind the boat were three children that, depending on where you stood, look like they're onboard. One kid is using a bucket to drain water. Painted above the kids in huge letters: "WE'RE ALL IN THE SAME BOAT." The installation was removed a few days later because the scrap metal was blocking a storm drain. Heavy rains were in the forecast, and officials were concerned that the "boat" would cause a flood.

A MATCH MADE IN IRONY

In the early days of the internet, people were dubious that it could help singles find a romantic match. In 1993, a developer named Gary Kremen came up with the idea of a website where each user creates his or her own "online dating profile," and Match.com was born. One of the first people Kremen recruited to create a profile was his girlfriend. Not long after, she was wooed by another man's profile and left Kremen for a better match.

AN IRONIC KISS-OFF

Halfway through Kiss's 2021 "End of the Road" farewell tour, the glam metal band's lead singer, Gene Simmons (age 72), fired the opening act, David Lee Roth (age 66), citing that the former Van Halen front man was "past his prime."

CONVINCING IRONY

"I track down the people who scam others on the Internet," wrote Jim Browning, who hosts a YouTube channel called Tech Support Scams. But the channel disappeared in July 2021. Reason: A scammer sent Browning a phishing email from "google.com." Posing as Google Chat, the scammer convinced him to delete his channel while moving it to a new YouTube account. Browning said it just goes to show that "anyone can be scammed."

IRONY REACHES ITS BOILING POINT

It was a tense situation at a Blackpool, England, warehouse in 2013 when a worker who'd just been fired punched his boss in the face and then—holding a knife in each hand—threatened his fellow coworkers, repeating, "I will cut you up!" Thankfully, the workers were able to calm him down, and no one was seriously injured. Up until that point, the man's job had been packing stress balls.

Worldwide, 90 percent of all refined metal is made from iron.

WAR STORY: "WE ARE ALL JEWS HERE"

Have you ever wondered what you would do if you were in a situation where you had to risk your life in order to save the lives of others? We'd like to think we'd act with bravery, but who knows? Fortunately, that's a choice most of us will never have to face. But here's the amazing story of someone who did.

DOWNFALL

By December 1944, World War II had entered its final stage, and only Adolf Hitler himself was delusional enough not to see it. On the Eastern Front, the Red Army had driven the German Wehrmacht (Armed Forces) out of the Soviet Union and westward across Poland all the way back into eastern Germany. On the Western Front, six months had passed since the D-Day landings in northern France. Since then, the Allies had also landed in southern France and had taken back much of the country from the Nazis. In October, the Allies pushed into the German city of Aachen, just across the border from Belgium and the Netherlands. Aachen was the first major German city to fall to the Allies. It would not be the last. After years of invading and brutalizing its neighbors on all sides, now Nazi Germany was fighting its enemies on its own soil and losing badly.

Hitler was desperate to turn the tide of the war. In December, he launched the Ardennes Offensive, which would turn out to be the last major German offensive of World War II. It was an attempt to break through the Allied lines in the West and retake the port city of Antwerp, Belgium, which, since being captured in September, was being used to deliver troops and supplies in support of the Allied advance. Hitler hoped that if he could retake the port and encircle the Western armies now streaming into Germany, he might force the Allies into a negotiated peace that would save him from total defeat.

Even Hitler's own generals knew this grandiose plan was doomed. They suggested a more modest offensive that had a greater chance of success, but the führer dismissed their concerns and at 5:30 a.m. on the morning of December 16, the Ardennes Offensive got underway.

ENCIRCLED

Because the offensive was directed against a lightly defended section of the Western Front and the Germans had retained the element of surprise, for several days they were able to drive deep into Belgian territory, creating a bulge in the front lines that gives the Ardennes Offensive its famous nickname: "the Battle of the Bulge." In the fighting, the Germans also managed to surround two regiments of the U.S. Army's 106th Infantry Division, forcing their surrender. That's how Roddie Edmonds of Knoxville, Tennessee, at age 25, then the youngest master sergeant in the U.S. Army, ended up as a prisoner of war at the Stalag IX-A, a POW camp in Ziegenhain in western Germany.

MAN OF THE HOUR

Edmonds was the senior noncommissioned officer in the American sector of the camp, and that made him the leader of the American POWs. His leadership was put to the test the day he arrived in the camp in January 1945. That day, orders came over the loudspeaker that all American Jews in the camp—and only the Jews—were to fall out and report to roll call the following morning. Everyone else was to remain in their barracks, and anyone who failed to obey the order would be shot.

The Holocaust was still underway, and its full scale and horror had yet to be revealed to the outside world. But it was well known that the Nazis had been murdering Jews by the thousands. On the Eastern Front, Jews in the Red Army who were captured by the Nazis were shot on the spot or sent to extermination camps and murdered in the gas chambers. Jews serving in the U.S. military had been warned by their commanding officers to destroy any evidence of their religion in case they too fell into German hands. Edmonds feared the worst for his men and decided on the spot that he would not obey the order. Nor would anyone else. "We are not doing that, we are *all* falling out," he told the POWs. He passed word to the five barracks of American POWs that every single soldier was to report to roll call the following morning, no matter how sick, no matter how injured. Every single one.

And the following morning, they all did.

Major Siegmann, the German officer conducting the roll call, was incredulous when he saw all 1,292 of the American POWs lined up. "Only the Jews! They cannot all be Jews!" he screamed at Edmonds.

"We are all Jews here," Edmonds coolly replied.

At this, Siegmann drew his Luger pistol and pressed it against Edmonds's forehead between his eyes. "Sergeant, you will order the Jews to step forward or I will shoot you right now," he ordered.

Silence.

Then Edmonds told Siegmann, "According to the Geneva Convention, we only have to give our name, rank, and serial number. If you shoot me, you will have to shoot all of us, because we know who you are, and you will be tried for war crimes when we win this war. And you will pay."

Siegmann paused for a moment, then holstered his weapon and stormed off. The

Something to ponder: At some point in your life,
your parents put you down and never picked you up again.

date was January 27, 1945. There were more than 200 Jews at roll call that day, and every one of them survived the war. That same day, in Poland, the Red Army liberated Auschwitz.

The war in Europe had three months to go. The Battle of the Bulge was already over: it had ended on January 25 with the Germans in full retreat—not just there but on every front, a retreat that ended only after Adolf Hitler committed suicide in his Berlin bunker on April 30. Germany surrendered unconditionally to the Allies a week later, on May 8.

A QUIET MAN

> **Some things, he told them, were too painful for him to talk about.**

After the war, Roddie Edmonds returned home to his family in Knoxville. There he worked as a salesman for everything from mobile homes to cable television subscriptions, raised his family, and, as far as anyone knows, never spoke of the Siegmann incident to anyone again. In his wartime diaries he gives the incident three words: "before the commander." That's it. He did tell his family that he'd been captured during the Battle of the Bulge and had spent 100 days in German POW camps, but he never said much more than that. Some things, he told them, were too painful for him to talk about.

Edmonds's son, Chris, inherited the diaries when Edmonds died in 1985. Then in 2008, Chris's daughter, Lauren, then in college, received an assignment to write a family history. Chris suggested she make it about her grandfather, and after she completed a video for the class, he became curious to know more about his father's wartime service. So he did the first thing anyone did in 2008 when they wanted to research something: he googled his father's name to see what came up. The first link led him to a 2008 article in *The New York Times* about President Richard Nixon's purchase of a Manhattan townhouse in 1979. The seller was a man named Lester J. Tanner, and in that 2008 article he related how he'd been a prisoner in a German POW camp during the war, and how, as a Jew, his life was in grave danger until the ranking officer, one Master Sgt. Roddie Edmonds, risked his own life to save the lives of the Jews under his command.

LONG OVERDUE

The *Times* article made only a brief mention of Tanner's story, but when Chris Edmonds left a comment online identifying himself as Roddie Edmonds's son, Tanner reached out to Edmonds and invited him to come to New York for a visit. There he gave Chris Edmonds a full accounting of his father's bravery in the POW camp, and it is because of this that we know the story today.

Roddie Edmonds may have been reluctant to tell his story, but Tanner and the other men he saved that day were not so reticent. They were determined that

Edmonds be recognized for the bravery he showed that day. As Chris Edmonds continued to research the details of his father's story, he was pleasantly surprised when Tanner and others called him repeatedly asking for more details—*specific* details—about his father's life. Chris Edmonds didn't know it at the time, but Tanner and some friends of his had recommended Roddie Edmonds for consideration as one of the "Righteous Among the Nations," the highest honor that the State of Israel bestows upon non-Jews who risked their lives to save Jews during the Holocaust. Researchers at Yad Vashem, Israel's national Holocaust memorial, spent hundreds of hours confirming the details of the story; then on June 6, 2015, the Israeli consulate in Atlanta telephoned Chris to let him know that his father had been chosen for the honor. This phone call was the first inkling that Chris Edmonds had that his father was even up for consideration for the award.

The following December, Chris Edmonds made his first trip to Israel and to Yad Vashem to accept the honor on his father's behalf. To date, more than 27,000 non-Jews have been honored as Righteous Among the Nations; of these, only five are Americans and just one is a U.S. service member: Master Sergeant Roddie Edmonds, the youngest master sergeant in World War II, who is also the first person—and to date the only person—honored for saving the lives of American Jews.

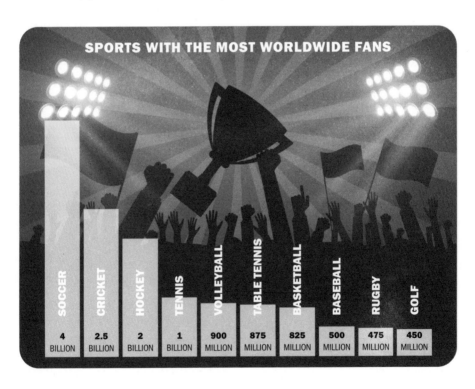

SPORTS WITH THE MOST WORLDWIDE FANS

SOCCER	CRICKET	HOCKEY	TENNIS	VOLLEYBALL	TABLE TENNIS	BASKETBALL	BASEBALL	RUGBY	GOLF
4 BILLION	2.5 BILLION	2 BILLION	1 BILLION	900 MILLION	875 MILLION	825 MILLION	500 MILLION	475 MILLION	450 MILLION

The weights in a public gym have more than
300 times more bacteria than the toilet seats in the restroom.

 **MOUTHING OFF**

HOPE QUOTES

We really hope you like this page.

"Our hopes, often though they deceive us, lead us pleasantly along the path of life."

—François de La Rochefoucauld

"Hope is the feeling you have that the feeling you have isn't permanent."

—Jean Kerr

"HOPE SMILES ON THE THRESHOLD OF THE YEAR TO COME, WHISPERING THAT IT WILL BE HAPPIER."

—Alfred, Lord Tennyson

"The important thing is not that we can live on hope alone, but that life is not worth living without it."

—Harvey Milk

"He that lives upon hope will die fasting."

—Benjamin Franklin

"What oxygen is to the lungs, such is hope to the meaning of life."

—Emil Brunner

"Hope is a good breakfast, but it is a bad supper."

—Francis Bacon

"THREE GRAND ESSENTIALS TO HAPPINESS IN THIS LIFE ARE SOMETHING TO DO, SOMETHING TO LOVE, AND SOMETHING TO HOPE FOR."

—Joseph Addison

"All human wisdom is summed up in two words; wait and hope."

—Alexandre Dumas

"Don't ever underestimate the importance you can have because history has shown us that courage can be contagious and hope can take on a life of its own."

—Michelle Obama

"Hope is patience with the lamp lit."

—Tertullian

UNIDENTIFIED AERIAL PHENOMENA

We're not saying that aliens are visiting Earth—and neither is the U.S. military—but based on recently declassified reports of the U.S. Navy's encounters with UFOs (or UAP, in Pentagon-speak), if aliens aren't behind these incidents, then the alternative might be even scarier.

THE FLYING TIC TAC

It was "the strangest, most obscure thing I've ever seen flying," Cmdr. Dave Fravor told NBC News in 2021. That was the first time the retired U.S. Navy fighter pilot was allowed to speak in public about his close encounter with an Unidentified Aerial Phenomenon (UAP). He said the incident took place in November 2004 during a training mission over the Pacific Ocean. Fravor and another pilot, Lt. Cmdr. Alex Dietrich, were ordered to investigate an area of churning white water, about the size of a football field, in the open sea. Dietrich remained at a higher altitude while Fravor flew his F/A-18F Super Hornet fighter jet toward the anomaly. He saw what he described as a "little, white Tic Tac" flying swiftly above the churning waters. "It's pointing north-south, and it's just going forward, back, left, right...like a ping pong ball." Fravor estimated the object was about the length of his own plane, but there were no markings or any visible means of propulsion. When he flew to within a half-mile of it, the Tic Tac flew right at him and then darted away at such a high rate of speed that Fravor lost sight of it.

Dietrich's plane didn't get as close, but he witnessed it as well. In 2021, he told *60 Minutes* that the encounter was "so unsettling" because "we couldn't classify it." And because their planes weren't carrying live ammunition, they couldn't defend themselves. What the pilots didn't know at the time: a nearby aircraft carrier's radar team had been tracking a number of these fast-moving UAP in that area for several days. The one that sped away from Fravor and Dietrich was reacquired on radar a few seconds later...60 miles away. Even more unsettling, this incident took place about 100 miles southwest of San Diego.

NARROWING THE SCOPE

Rumors of American service members encountering UAP have been flying around for decades, and you can find dozens of grainy videos of alleged military encounters online. But it wasn't until 2020 that the Department of Defense (DoD) officially confirmed that UAP exist. The revelation elevated the UFO debate from the fringes of conspiracy websites to the front pages of news outlets worldwide. That's one reason

Most endangered marine mammal: the vaquita porpoise. Fewer than 10 remain.

for the Pentagon's abrupt about-face: "to clear up any misconceptions by the public on whether or not the footage that has been circulating was real, or whether or not there is more to the videos."

Confirmation that these videos are not fiction brings us one step closer to knowing what they are. Ruling out pilot error or hallucinations, radar or camera malfunctions, or a cyberattack (all possible, given the sheer number of incidents), the DoD lists five possible explanations for UAP: 1) naturally occurring phenomena, such as static electricity that creates balls of light; 2) weather balloons, satellites, or other benign man-made objects; 3) secret technology owned by foreign governments or agents; 4) secret American technology that even the military is unaware of; and 5) "other." Though not mentioned by name, "other" includes extraterrestrial technology.

"INCREASINGLY CLUTTERED AIR DOMAIN"

In the late 2010s, as these videos started showing up on the nightly news, Congress called for an investigation to determine whether UAP pose a risk to national security. A Pentagon task force studied 144 incidents that took place from 2004–21 and presented them in a report titled "Preliminary Assessment: Unidentified Aerial Phenomena."

Most of the incidents could be explained by the first two reasons outlined above, but 18 UAP demonstrated "unusual flight characteristics" that are, as yet, unexplainable. Without drawing any conclusions, the nine-page report confirmed that the UAP events in question "probably do represent solid objects" (as opposed to sensor goofs)...and that it's not good that they're here:

> Safety concerns primarily center on aviators contending with an increasingly cluttered air domain. UAP would also represent a national security challenge if they are foreign adversary collection platforms or provide evidence a potential adversary has developed either a breakthrough or disruptive technology.

PERMISSION TO SPEAK FREELY

Government officials are so concerned with these potential threats that, for the first time, they're urging current and former service members to come forward with any unreported eyewitness accounts. In the past, service members were often ridiculed for speaking out about "little green men." Some even say they were silenced. That was the culture for more than half a century, and it left in its wake a troubling lack of data to be analyzed. As stated in the report: "The limited amount of high-quality reporting hampers our ability to draw firm conclusions about the nature or intent of UAP." But now some retired navy pilots are freely sharing their stories on national news programs.

The Pentagon's new policies also explain the terminology change to "UAP"; it's a more neutral term that they hope won't carry the same stigma as "UFO." It's the same reason that, back in the 1950s, the navy chose "UFO" over "flying saucer." U.S. military intelligence officials were mostly concerned that flying saucers were secret Russian technology, whereas pop culture (especially the movie industry) preferred to push the alien narrative. And "UFO" sounded more earthly than "flying saucer."

WE WANT TO BELIEVE

It didn't matter; the alien narrative persisted. So it wasn't surprising that the 2021 UAP report's lack of firm conclusions led a lot of people to come to their own conclusions. As the *New York Times* put it, "Because the government has offered no explanation for so many of the episodes, the new report is sure to fuel the enthusiasm of those who believe they could be." Just as the *Times* predicted, the mere prospect that unidentified aerial phenomena could be visitors from another world—and not an earthly national security risk—has been used as clickbait. Case in point: this NBC News headline. "UFO report: No evidence of alien spacecraft, but can't rule it out." (If you're like us, you read "can't rule it out" as "the aliens are here!")

Whatever these things are, they're more prevalent than one might think. According to the National UFO Reporting Center, there were 7,200 UFO sightings—by civilians—during the first full year of the COVID-19 pandemic, up by more than a thousand from 2019. (And most sightings, they say, go unreported.)

THE TRUTH IS NOT NOT OUT THERE

Final note: A navy video (recorded at night with an infrared camera) captured this chilling incident in July 2019 off the coast of San Diego. A sphere about six feet in diameter is flying at a high velocity and then hovers above the choppy sea. A few seconds later, the sphere slowly descends...and then disappears below the surface. A subsequent search for wreckage turned up nothing. Where did the sphere go? How can it fly *and* swim? And who or what was in control of it? Given the Pentagon's recent push to revamp its data collection protocols—which, for the first time, includes reaching out to the scientific community to analyze this data—we may have these answers sooner rather than later. Then things could really get interesting.

* * *

"WHAT THE [EXPLETIVE] IS THAT?"

Here's the chilling transcript of an undated UAP encounter released by the U.S. Navy.

[radio transmission] "Whoa, got it—woo-hoo!" "Roger —" "What the [expletive] is that?" "Did you box a moving target?" "No, I took an auto track." "Oh, OK." "Oh my gosh, dude. Wow!" "What is that, man?" "There's a whole screen of them. My gosh." "They're all going against the wind. The wind's 120 knots from west." "Dude." "That's not—is it?" "[inaudible]" "Look at that thing."

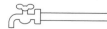

The worldwide human-to-ant ratio is one person for every 1.6 million ants.

A BIG FORKIN' PAGE OF FORK TRIVIA

Bite-sized nuggets of trivia about the utensil you use every day.

- The word *fork* derives from Latin *furca*, which referred to the farming tool we today know as a pitchfork.

- Technically speaking, the ends of a fork that stick into food are called tines, the tips are called points, and the area between tines are slots.

- Forks were used by ancient Chinese, ancient Romans, and ancient Egyptians, but primarily as cooking utensils, not eating utensils. Who introduced the fork to the dining table? The Byzantine Empire, around the 4th century.

- When Byzantine princess Theodora Doukania married the Doge of Venice in the 11th century, her dowry included gold forks. It caused a scandal. Venetians considered it an affront to God because humans are given natural eating utensils: their fingers. Soon after, forks became all the rage among wealthy Venetians.

- The two-tined deli fork was invented in Italy and has one use: to eat thin slices of prosciutto.

- Forks didn't catch on in daily use in Europe until the 16th century. Italy adopted them first, followed by Spain and France over the next 100 years.

- Early fork makers tried many different designs before settling on the three or four tines that ultimately became the standard. (Two-tined forks didn't work well because people accidentally stabbed either their hands or faces.)

- There are about 35 different types of forks in use, most of them used only in royal or state dinners. Among them: snail fork, crab fork, carving fork, pastry fork, fruit fork, and cocktail fork.

- The proper setting of cutlery at a formal dinner goes, from left to right: salad fork, dinner fork, fish fork, (dinner plate), salad knife, dinner knife, fish knife, soup spoon or fruit spoon (depending on if the first course is soup or fruit), and oyster fork. The butter knife is placed on its own, diagonally across the butter plate.

Ostriches have three stomachs. (Alligators and kangaroos have two.)

- In 2019, Ricky Eggins of North Orange, Australia, attempted to stop his friend, Darryle Tailford, from driving home drunk from a party. Tailford objected, and then stabbed Eggins repeatedly. Tailford received a seven-year prison sentence for manslaughter. The murder weapon: a carving fork he'd taken from the party host's kitchen.

- In Victorian England, when ice cream became a delicacy among the wealthy, the ice cream fork was added to formal table settings. It's similar to the modern-day spork— it was a metal spoon with three short tines on the edge.

- The plastic spork was patented in 1970, soon thereafter introduced internationally by Kentucky Fried Chicken.

- Lizards and snakes in the reptilian taxonomic order of Squamata have forked tongues, which are split down the middle and resemble the eating utensil. The two "tines" at the top help the animal smell better, and aid in determining the direction from which the odor emanates, allowing them to more effectively hunt prey.

- Springfield, Missouri, is the home of the world's largest fork. The 11-ton stainless steel sculpture stands 35 feet tall in front of the building that houses the Food Channel.

- Ever see a spaghetti fork? It looks like a standard fork except the tines have tiny ridges to hold twirled pasta in place.

*   *   *

WHAT'S SO FUNNY?

In 1922, a New York City jazz label called Okeh Records released a three-minute novelty song that had been recorded a few years earlier in Germany. The record begins with a somber melody played by a cornet (a brass instrument similar to a trumpet). About 15 seconds in, a woman starts to laugh, softly at first, and then louder. The cornet player stops, then resumes, and then stops again after a man starts laughing along with the woman. The cornet then resumes its somber melody, only for the laughter to overtake it. He tries once more and gives up. The final minute is just the man and woman (two famous German opera singers) laughing hysterically. The "Okeh Laughing Record" was one of the most popular novelty songs of its time, selling over a million copies in the United States. (We challenge you to listen to it online and not start laughing yourself.)

The legal voting age in Bosnia is 18, but 16-year-olds can vote if they've got a job.

FIVE ANCIENT FINDS

Just like your missing sock, these fossils and artifacts were lying
around waiting to be discovered.

What a Trip. A nine-year-old boy was hiking in the New Mexico desert in 2016 when he tripped on something sticking out of the ground and fell. As he started to get up, he came face-to-face (or face-to-skull) with a jawbone and tusks that resembled an elephant's. Actually, it was *much* rarer: it was the skull of a prehistoric elephant called a *Stegomastodon*. Because the upper part of *Stegomastodons*' skulls are mostly hollow and very thin, previously discovered examples were so fragile that they had largely disintegrated over the years. This skull, exposed after a recent storm, was intact—held together only by the sediment around it—and was painstakingly extracted by a team of 10 university researchers. It's one of the only complete *Stegomastodon* skulls ever found...and it survived for 1.2 million years.

Hungry, Hungry Gators. In 2021, a company that "processes" (butchers) wild game animals in Yazoo City, Mississippi, found two ancient artifacts from different eras in the same place: inside the stomach of a 13-foot-long, 750-pound alligator. One was a plummet, a heavy object with two holes that Native Americans made from the mineral hematite around 1700 BC. Its purpose is a mystery. The other artifact was even older—a stone dart point of a prehistoric spear, dating to 5000 or 6000 BC. But how did they end up there? Gators eat sand and rocks to help them digest food, and most likely those items were mixed in.

Cave of Horror. After rappelling 260 feet down a cliff, archaeologists accessed a cave in Israel's Judean Desert. Though it had been excavated before, the scientists had begun a new quest to find antiquities in 2017. Smart decision. Inside it they found fragments of biblical scrolls from the Old Testament (from the books of Zechariah and Nahum) and rare coins left by Jewish rebels fleeing the Romans 1,900 years ago. They also discovered the remains of a 6,000-year-old child who'd been mummified naturally in the cave—that's in addition to the 40 skeletons found there in the 1960s, earning it the name "Cave of Horror." The skeletons are believed to belong to families who probably died of starvation while hiding. But wait, there's more. In a nearby cave, the researchers made another discovery: possibly the world's oldest intact woven basket, believed to be 10,500 years old. And their search of the desert continues.

Ill-Gotten Fossils. When Brazilian police busted a "fossil trade operation" in 2013, they recovered a staggering 3,000 specimens. The fossils had been stolen

The only complete fossil of its kind, it contains the pterosaur's fragile head crest.

from a quarry in northeastern Brazil's Araripe Basin, which is rich with fossils embedded in limestone, and were bound for the United States, Europe, and other places to be sold to museums or collectors. In 2021, scientists announced the most impressive find in the lot: a four-foot-tall pterosaur skeleton preserved in limestone slabs. At 115 million years old, it's a remnant of a flying reptile that went extinct with the dinosaurs. The only complete fossil of its kind, it contains the pterosaur's fragile head crest, the flap under its beak, and even soft tissue, allowing researchers to draw some new conclusions about the creature. For example, because this type of pterosaur had a disproportionately large head crest, a long neck and legs, and short wings, scientists now believe that the "flying reptile" could fly for only short periods and actually spent most of its time...walking.

A Royal Mystery. For centuries, people have sought the final resting place of England's Queen Cynethryth of Mercia, thought to be located near a monastery where she served as abbess. When she ruled in the late 700s, she shared equal status and power with her husband, King Offa, and is likely the only Anglo-Saxon queen who had coins issued in her honor. The disappearance of the monastery was perplexing because it was well-known and geographically important, sitting on a contested border between two kingdoms. In 2021, archaeologists finally unearthed the monastery next to a church in Cookham, in southeastern England, though it's unknown how it became buried. It was along a stretch of the River Thames where artifacts are rare and little is known about life back then, making the discovery of everyday items important. In the ruins, they've already discovered food remnants, pottery, window glass, and jewelry that likely belonged to Queen Cynethryth, although they haven't found her tomb...yet.

*   *   *

3 PRODUCTS WITH MISLEADING NAMES

HBO Max. Warner Media's streaming video service's name implies a "maximum" amount of content from cable channel HBO. But it's actually a portmanteau of two networks whose programs appear on the service: HBO and Cinemax.

Price Club. The warehouse-style store (which would eventually merge with Costco) had a name that indicated low or fair prices. That was just a lucky coincidence for founder Sol Price.

Ab Doer. Hundreds of thousands of this sit-up aid and abdominal exerciser sold via TV infomercial in the 1990s and 2000s. While it can "do" one's "abs," it's the invention of fitness guru John Abdo.

Charlotte Brontë (author of *Jane Eyre*) could read better in a darkened room than she could in one that was well lit.

ALL-YOU-CAN-ACK!

Apparently unlimited access to mountains of food isn't the only pressing danger at a buffet-style restaurant.

SHE SNARFED SUSHI

In December 2021, 24-year-old Danielle Shapiro and a friend each plunked down $50 for an All-you-can-eat Sushi 85 restaurant in Mountain View, California. Intending to get the biggest bang for her buck, Shapiro consumed far more than $50 worth of food, finishing off a round of appetizers—including miso soup, gyozas, edamame, and jalapeño poppers—and then went all in on the sushi. Shapiro ate eight green dragon rolls, eight snow rolls, eight California rolls, and eight wakame rolls, for a grand total of 32 plates. The meal lasted two hours because, Shapiro said, she and her companion "were so stuffed we had to keep taking breaks," and then they sat in the car for 30 minutes because they were too full to drive. "My stomach felt very firm from all the sushi and probably the rice that expanded in my stomach," Shapiro said in a TikTok viral video. Later that night, Shapiro awoke with chest and stomach pain so severe that she checked into a hospital, where she was diagnosed with acid reflux. "This experience has not ruined sushi for me, or the all-you-can-eat sushi experience," Shapiro said. "I did learn that next time I need to listen to my body and take things slower."

FOOD FIGHT

Police in Pinellas Park, Florida, responded to a call at the Hibachi Buffet restaurant in November 2021. The manager of the eatery called them, alleging that customer Paul Mitchell became angry and violent when the buffet didn't have what he wanted. According to a police report, Mitchell walked up to the sushi section of the buffet line, and, seeing that the kind of sushi he liked wasn't ready to go, became enraged and started picking up plates and throwing them, breaking about $250 worth of dishware. Then, allegedly, Mitchell walked up to the manager and started slapping his hands because he was trying to record Mitchell's meltdown on his phone. Mitchell was charged with criminal mischief and battery.

HOLD THE LINE

Carl Sanderson took his girlfriend out for a meal at the Ocean Garden Buffet in Toledo, Ohio, in January 2014. Something happened after a visit to the seafood table. "As I was eating the crayfish, I felt something tickling in the bottom of my throat," he told reporters. "I felt something on the side of my lip, so I reached for it and I pulled it out." The object: a foot-long piece of fishing line, likely used to catch that crayfish. Sanderson complained to a server, who claimed that it was the diner's fault, suggesting that he'd planted the line in order to get a free meal. (Sanderson wasn't charged for his meal, but the restaurant made him pay for his girlfriend's.) An Ocean Garden manager told Toledo TV station WTOL that the line's presence wasn't their fault, because all their fish arrives at the restaurant precooked. "We do our best to prevent anything from happening to our food. I know that something probably happened in this case, but no other customers had this problem," the manager said. (He apparently forgot that a few months earlier, another Ocean Garden customer had reported finding a large chunk of plastic in their food.)

PRAWNS GONE

A man who goes by the name "Mr. Kang" is an online celebrity in China for posting live streaming videos of himself consuming huge amounts of food. On two occasions, he made videos at the Handadi Seafood BBQ Buffet in Changsha, Hunan Province. On his first trip to the buffet, Mr. Kang ate more than three pounds of pork trotters (pigs' feet). On a second visit, he ate nearly nine pounds of prawns. That was too much for the manager of the Handadi Seafood BBQ Buffet, who, in November 2021, banned Mr. Kang from ever setting foot in the restaurant again. "I can eat a lot, is that a fault?" Mr. Kang rhetorically told a Hunan TV reporter. "Every time he comes here, I lose a few hundred yuan," the manager explained. "When he eats the pork trotters, he consumes the whole tray of them. And for prawns, usually people use tongs to pick them up. He uses a tray to take them all."

> **DID YOU KNOW?**
>
> The first modern competitive eating event was held in 1916, when Nathan's Famous staged its first annual hot dog eating contest on Coney Island in New York on the Fourth of July. Winner: James Mullen. He ate 13 hot dogs in 12 minutes.

RUNNING, AWAY

Jaroslav Bobrowski is a competitive triathlete from Germany, and he adheres to a strict eating plan for maximum energy retention, fasting for 20 hours a day and then gorging for the other four, in order to fuel up. One day in July 2018, he took his daily eating session to Running Sushi, an all-you-can-eat buffet restaurant in the Bavarian city of Landshut. Paying about €16 ($18.50), Bobrowski virtually inhaled more than 100 servings of sushi in less than half an hour, consuming the equivalent of 18 pounds of fish and rice. He took so many plates off of the sushi carousel—entire batches as they came out of the kitchen—that other customers thought the restaurant was cheaping out. "The other guests asked if we had skimped on the fish," the owner, identified in reports as Tan, said, adding that Bobrowski ordered one cup of tea during his meal, leading to further lost income, because drinks have a high profit margin. Bobrowski was a regular at Running Sushi, but this visit was the last straw for Tan, who banned the triathlete from the restaurant permanently. The diner, nicknamed "Sushi Man" by the German media after the story went viral, promised to eat a little less when he goes to another local buffet, China City.

Avocados are toxic to lemurs.

NICE STORIES

*Every now and then we like to lock our inner cynics in a box
and share some stories with happy endings.*

That's Some Fine Print

Donelan Andrews of Barnesville, Georgia, was nearing retirement in March 2019, capping off a 25-year-career as a high school teacher. To celebrate that milestone—and her 35th wedding anniversary—she booked a vacation to Scotland. Then she bought travel insurance. Unlike almost everyone else, Andrews always reads every single word of the contracts she signs. Midway down page 7 was a peculiar heading: "Pays to Read." The paragraph beneath that heading stated that only 1 percent of consumers read the fine print, and "the first person who makes it this far will win $10,000." Andrews contacted the insurance company (Florida-based Squaremouth Inc.) and sure enough, she'd won $10,000! The company had sold 73 policies with the special contest clause that day; Andrews was the only one to respond. The prize money (mostly) paid for her vacation, and Squaremouth donated $5,000 to each of the two schools where Andrews taught. The company explained that its secret contest had a purpose: to remind everyone to read the contract.

A Lotto Help

"I was paying more attention to my cellphone," said Mike Weirsky at a press conference. The unemployed, recently divorced father had just bought $20 worth of Mega Millions tickets at QuickChek in Phillipsburg, New Jersey, in 2019. He thought he'd lost the tickets at home, but after looking all over and failing to find them, he drove back to the store and asked if anyone had turned them in. Someone had. A QuickChek clerk named Phil Campolo found the tickets on the counter where Weirsky absentmindedly left them. By law, he could have kept them, but he didn't—he put them aside for Weirsky. Two days later, one of the tickets won the $273 million jackpot. "I was very thankful there was an honest person out there because I thought it was gone," Weirsky said.

"I was doing the right thing," said Campolo, "and I'd do it again."

The Return of Batgirl

"While we agree with you that girls are certainly as capable as boys, and no doubt would be an attractive addition on the playing field, I am sure you can understand that in a game dominated by men, a young lady such as yourself would feel out of place in a dugout." That's from a rejection letter that 10-year-old Gwen Goldman received in 1961 from New York Yankees general manager Roy Hamey after asking if she could serve as batgirl for her favorite team.

In 2020, the Pacific island nation of Palau banned sunscreen containing ultraviolet light–absorbing chemicals. Reason: when it gets in the water, it can damage coral reefs.

Sixty years later, with that letter still posted on the wall of her Connecticut home, Goldman's daughter, Abby McLoughlin, sent her mom's story to the Yankees, and it found its way to general manager Brian Cashman. Then Goldman received a letter of acceptance (on Vimeo) from the Yankees: "It's not too late," said Cashman, "to reward and recognize the ambition you showed in writing that letter to us." At a June 2021 home game, the 70-year-old batgirl got to meet her favorite players and even throw the ceremonial first pitch wearing the famous Yankees pinstripes. "Walking in the front door of the stadium," she said to reporters, "a locker with my name on it, Gwen Goldman, and suiting up, and walking out onto the field. It took my breath away."

"Hello Again"

After an early childhood marred by "haunting, horrific times," siblings Kitt and Tasha spent the early 1980s in Oklahoma's foster care system. The brother and sister clung to each other for survival, but—as is too often the case—they were split up. Kitt was only five, and Tasha was four. But they never forgot each other. "On a regular basis," said Kitt, "she was on my mind, where's she at, what's she doing?" Tasha had been wondering the same thing. In 2021, she finally found the answers she was looking for.

Forty years after he watched his crying little sister being taken away from him, Kitt received a Facebook message from a woman named Tasha Henderson: "I'm your sister." At first, Kitt was skeptical. He didn't remember his sister being Black. She was biracial, she explained, but they didn't notice things like that when they were kids. Tasha told him that as soon as she saw his smiling photo on Ancestry.com, she knew it was him. Still wary, Kitt asked Tasha some questions that only his little sister would know. She knew. Not long after, they met up at a restaurant. "Oh, I just almost melted when I touched him," she told reporters.

Getting caught up, Tasha said she was a stay-at-home mom. Then she learned that her big brother is Christian rocker Kitt Wakely, a chart-topping multi-instrumentalist and songwriter with a dedicated following. (Kitt later wrote a song for Tasha called "Hello Again.") Making it even more amazing: the two of them had been living within a mile of each other in Edmond, Oklahoma, for years. At last report, Kitt and his wife Melissa were planning to adopt three little kids—siblings—to ensure they'd never be torn apart.

A Nice Story with a Perfect Ending

Herbert Delaigle was so late to his own wedding in 1948 that he and his bride Frances had to beg the preacher to perform the ceremony. Their marriage wasn't always easy—Herbert often had to be gone for long periods of time during his 20 years in the Army. But their bond never weakened while they raised six children and gobs of grandchildren in Augusta, Georgia, where Frances owned a flower shop. In July 2019, their love story became national news: After 71 years of wedded bliss, Herbert died at 2:20 a.m. on a Friday morning. Exactly 12 hours later, Frances followed him home.

Makes sense: The stage before frostbite is called frostnip.

WHAT'S THE DIFFERENCE BETWEEN...

Uncle John knows pretty much everything—even the subtle nuances that separate common, similar, and frequently confused things.

...GREAT BRITAIN AND THE UNITED KINGDOM? Great Britain is an island, a landmass divided into three nations—England, Scotland, and Wales. Those countries comprise three of the four constituents of the United Kingdom. The fourth is Northern Ireland, which shares the *island* of Ireland with the *country* of Ireland.

...A COLLEGE AND A UNIVERSITY? Size. In the United States, colleges are generally much smaller than universities in terms of real estate, faculty, and student body. Colleges seldom confer anything besides undergraduate degrees while universities offer graduate studies and have more facilities, which is where staff and students can conduct more studies and research.

...A TABLET AND A CAPSULE? Tablets begin with a substance, chemical, or compound that has been pulverized into a powder, then machine-compressed into a solid shape, usually a circle or a rounded rectangle. Capsules consist of a tiny container, a water-soluble shell filled with particles of medicine. You can cut a tablet in half, which you can't do to a capsule, but the medicine in a tablet takes longer to enter the bloodstream. Other differences: tablets are generally less expensive and have a longer shelf life than capsules.

...MUFFINS AND CUPCAKES? Their ingredients are basically the same. Muffins are thought of as "healthy" because they've been marketed as a wholesome breakfast food, but they're really just sweetened quick breads...or cake. Cupcakes are also cake, but they are prepared slightly differently than muffins are. Cupcakes start by "creaming" the butter and sugar together before adding the dry ingredients, which makes smooth, fluffy batter; muffin batter is briefly mixed prior to baking, which makes it denser than a cupcake. But what *really* sets them apart from each other? Cupcakes have frosting (or icing).

...A DONKEY AND A MULE? Both are beasts of burden that somewhat resemble and behave like horses, only smaller. A donkey is its own species of animal, while a mule is a hybrid—the offspring of a male donkey and a female horse. (A female donkey and a male horse produce a "hinny.")

...DRESSING AND STUFFING? When served alongside a turkey on Thanksgiving, dressing and stuffing are the same food—bread crumbs mixed with spices, vegetables, and stock. What it's called depends on how it's prepared. If it's cooked inside the bird, it's stuffing. If it's cooked on its own, it's dressing.

...JEALOUSY AND ENVY? According to psychologists, jealousy is what you feel when you're in possession of something (often a relationship) and you fear that someone (often a third party) wants to take it from you. Envy occurs when you just plain want something that someone else has.

...A GRAVEYARD AND A CEMETERY? Both are where the dead are buried, but a graveyard is land that sits on the property of or adjacent to a church, while a cemetery is a freestanding nondenominational burial ground.

...FOG, MIST, AND HAZE? When the air temperature drops suddenly, airborne moisture cools and the droplets collect, creating low-lying clouds called fog. In air travel, fog describes a condition in which a pilot can't make out anything more than 1,000 meters away. In scientific circles, fog describes low cloud cover that cuts off visibility at 200 meters. Meteorologically speaking, mist is fog, just not as dense; if you can still see a few dozen meters ahead of you, *that's* mist. Haze is a lot like fog (or mist), but it's made of pollution particles rather than water droplets.

...AN EMOJI AND AN EMOTICON? Emojis are the little animated pictures commonly used to communicate feelings in text messaging programs. For example, the little yellow smiley face, the "thumbs up," or the brown, googly-eyed "poop." Emoticons, from which emojis were derived, are formed by combining letters, numbers, or other typographical characters to form what look like pictures. For example, a smiling face :-), a frowning face :-(, and a winking face ;-).

...A BISCUIT AND A COOKIE? In the UK, they call a biscuit what Americans would call a cookie—a sweet, crispy, baked wafer. However, not all foods in that category are called biscuits. If it's soft and fluffy like an American-style chocolate chip cookie, the Brits call it a cookie, too. The food known in America as a biscuit—fluffy, savory, served alongside fried chicken—is rarely served in the UK, but when it is, it's called a scone, which can be sweet or savory.

...BOATS AND SHIPS? If the seaworthy vessel has at least three masts, and the room and use for all those sails, it's a ship. If it doesn't, it's a boat. Ships are designed for traversing oceans and other deep waterways; boats are for getting around ponds, lakes, and shallower, restricted waterways.

...ALPACAS AND LLAMAS? They are closely related, being two of the four *lamoid* species. (The other two: vicuña and guanaco.) The llama and the alpaca are both fluffy members of the camel family, and while their names are often used interchangeably, there are some physical differences between these two kinds of pack animals. Alpacas are smaller—about 35 inches tall at the shoulder and weighing an average of 130 pounds; llamas are a foot taller and around 100 pounds heavier. Additionally, an alpaca's face is small and squat, while a llama's is longer.

Good work! Dolly Parton wrote "Jolene" and "I Will Always Love You" on the same day.

ANIMALS FAMOUS FOR 15 MINUTES

When Andy Warhol said, "In the future, everyone will be famous for 15 minutes," he probably didn't have animals in mind. But even critters can't escape the relentless publicity machine.

HEADLINE: *Mischievous Crow Flies Into Homes, Trains, McDonald's...and One Man's Heart*

THE STAR: Canuck, a Northwestern crow from Vancouver, British Columbia

THE STORY: Canuck was a local celebrity from 2016 to '19, primarily for his antics around town but also for his friendship with Shawn Bergman. Originally found as an orphaned crow by a little boy, when Canuck became well enough to fly, he landed on Bergman's back fence, and the middle-aged man and the crow soon became companions.

As for those famous antics, Canuck once stole a knife from a crime scene, swiped tickets from a horse-racing track, and "attacked" a kid on a bike (to play with his shiny backpack). He often made himself at home in McDonald's, frequented local soccer games, and even rode on Vancouver's SkyTrain. He was the talk of the city.

The crow became so well known—he amassed more than 120,000 Facebook followers—that Canadian wildlife officials gave him special protected status. But tragedy struck one day in 2019 when a soccer referee accidentally hit the bird with a stick and knocked him unconscious. Bergman set up a GoFundMe that raised $1,500 for vet bills, but not long after Canuck recovered, he disappeared. A $10,000 reward was offered for the return of the "federally protected crow."

AFTERMATH: Canuck's disappearance remains a mystery. Barely halfway through his lifespan of seven to eight years, it's unlikely he died of natural causes. Despite calls for a police investigation, there wasn't one. Bergman knows he can "potentially be facing my whole life with no answer." At least he was able to capture their unique bond in the 18-minute documentary, *Canuck and I.*

HEADLINE: *Royals' Prayers Answered by the Mantis Upstairs*

THE STARS: Rally and Rally Jr., two praying mantises that lived in Major League Baseball stadiums in 2016

THE STORY: It was mid-summer and the defending World Series champion Kansas City Royals' playoff hopes were fading fast. Then, during a night game in early August, a praying mantis flew into the team's dugout and landed on outfielder Billy Burns. The Royals won the game, so Burns decided to adopt the insect, naming it

Rally Mantis. When the Royals won five of their next six games, the media credited the praying mantis and Rally became a local celebrity. Energized, the team took the bug on their next road trip...and it died in its cage. Then the team went on a losing streak. "We need another one," said teammate Edinson Vólquez.

> **Energized, the team took the bug on their next road trip... and it died in its cage.**

As luck would have it, a second praying mantis appeared during an away game in the Detroit dugout. Burns took the new mascot—named Rally Mantis Jr.—under his wing, vowing to take better care of it...and lo and behold, the Royals won nine out of their next ten games and were suddenly back in playoff contention. The mantises became Kansas City's feel-good story of the fall: the team sold Rally Mantis T-shirts and gave away Rally Mantis beanbags to fans, many of whom showed up at the stadium wearing Mantis masks.

AFTERMATH: Whatever mojo the insect had, it wasn't enough to carry the Royals into the playoffs; they were eliminated with four games left in the season. A few weeks later, on November 2, the team's front office issued a somber tweet: "Sad news: #RallyMantis Jr. has passed away at Lakeside Nature Center after a long and plentiful life."

HEADLINE: *Beloved Turkey Wreaks Havoc, Becomes Less Beloved*

THE STAR: Gerald the Turkey, a large tom from Oakland, California

THE STORY: For years, Gerald had an amicable relationship with the humans at Morcom Rose Garden—until April 2020, when a COVID-19 lockdown took effect in Oakland. With so many of the area's entertainment venues closed, the eight-acre rose garden saw a massive uptick in visitors...and in the number of visitors who were feeding the wild turkey population, despite signs prohibiting it. Making matters worse, it was Gerald's mating season and, not one to practice social distancing, the three-foot-tall turkey went on the attack. One victim likened Gerald to "the velociraptor in *Jurassic Park*...'cooing' at me, sizing me up." With Gerald's preferred targets being elderly women and little kids, he became so dangerous that officials closed the park. A wildlife team tried to tame him, but when the park reopened, the attacks resumed. California Department of Fish and Wildlife officials felt they had no option but to "lethally remove" Gerald. When word of the death sentence got out, people from all over the world came to the turkey's defense. A fan from Illinois amassed 13,000 signatures on a Change.org petition to have Gerald relocated.

AFTERMATH: It worked! Officials agreed to move Gerald to a less-populated area... provided they could catch him. It took well into autumn until the turkey was finally apprehended. A wildlife expert named Rebecca Dmytryk dressed up as an old lady and used "blueberries, kibble, and sunflower seeds" to coax Gerald out of his hiding place. When she pretended to be scared, he charged her. "Oh, you want a piece of

Not the worst way to go: In an average year, 200 people die while taking a sea cruise.

this?" Dmytryk said as she grabbed Gerald. Her team released him into a forest in the East Bay hills, where he strutted off into the underbrush.

HEADLINE: *Penitentiary Pup Peps up Prisoners*

THE STAR: Pep, a black Labrador retriever sentenced to life in prison for murder

THE STORY: In 1925, the *Boston Daily Globe* reported that Pennsylvania Governor Gifford Pinchot's dog, Pep, killed a cat that belonged to Cornelia Pinchot, the governor's wife. Accompanying the article was the dog's mug shot (he was inmate no. C2559), along with a report that he'd been sentenced to life at Eastern State Penitentiary, one of the largest prisons in the country. More articles about Pep followed, but they weren't all fluff pieces. Many criticized the Republican governor for dealing too harsh a sentence to a dog that didn't know any better.

AFTERMATH: A few years later, Cornelia came clean to the *New York Times,* confessing that the cat-killing story was made up by a reporter. In reality, the couple had donated one of their Labradors to improve sagging morale at the overcrowded prison. (Pep's only real crime: he chewed the cushions.) The governor, it turns out, was way ahead of his time in his feeling that hardened criminals could be reformed rather than tossed away in solitary confinement, and that animals could play a positive role in their rehabilitation.

"Pep the Black," as the inmates liked to call him, lived out the rest of his days at Eastern State, and he was buried on the grounds. The penitentiary closed for good in 1971, but the practice of using therapy animals in prisons is commonplace today.

*   *   *

A *FAMILY FEUD* MOMENT

Steve Harvey: Name something that follows the word "pork."

Contestant: Cupine.

The sun orbits the galaxy. According to scientists, since the beginning of time, it's made 20 full trips.

OOPS!

*Everyone makes outrageous blunders from time to time. So
go ahead and feel superior for a few minutes.*

HOT SUPPORT

In November 2021, the Toronto Transit Commission (TTC) was hit with a ransomware attack that compromised the personal information of 25,000 current and former employees, who learned about the breach in a memo, which included a phone number for a legal support line. But someone goofed, and the number was off by one digit. It took callers to an adult chat hotline. One of those callers was union president (and former TTC worker) John Di Nino. "I had it on speakerphone at my house, and my grandchildren heard it."

NEGLIGENT DISCHARGE

The Dutch aviation magazine *Scramble* reported in 2018 about a fighter jet at a Belgian air force base that "had just been refueled and prepared, together with another F-16, for an afternoon sortie." At some point, a mechanic accidentally fired the plane's cannon, which was loaded. "After impact of the 20mm bullets, the [plane] exploded instantly and damaged two other F-16s." No one was killed, but two mechanics suffered hearing damage.

THE WRONG BROTHERS

The Wright Brothers built their airplane at their bike shop in Dayton, Ohio, but they needed the constant winds in Kitty Hawk, North Carolina, to get it airborne. That was in 1902. To this day, both states still lay claim to the "Birthplace of Aviation" title. That phrase was printed on Ohio's new license plate design in 2021, specifically on a banner being pulled by the Wright Brothers' famous plane. Within a day of the license plate's unveiling—via a tweet from Ohio Department of Transportation (ODOT)—dozens of Ohioans commented that the Wright Flyer was facing the wrong direction, as if it were "pushing" the banner. ODOT tweeted an apology, and promised to recycle the 35,000 license plates they'd already made. North Carolina's DOT noticed too, tweeting, "Y'all leave Ohio alone. They wouldn't know. They weren't there."

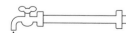

Most popular dog names in the English-speaking world: Molly and Max.

LEADER OF THE PACK

Tyler Pence won the 2021 Quad Cities Marathon, a 26.2-mile Boston Marathon Qualifier that takes place in Illinois. Running a personal best (2 hours, 15 minutes, and 6 seconds), Pence became the first American to win the race since 2000...even though he kind of came in third. Near mile 14, the two leaders and heavy favorites—Elijah Mwangangi Saolo and Luke Kibet of Kenya—followed a race volunteer riding a bicycle who absentmindedly went straight when the route turned right. The goof ended up giving the Kenyans a four-mile shortcut. They made it to the finish line, thinking they'd won, only to learn that they'd been disqualified. The volunteer was also there, nearly in tears, repeating, "I messed up royally." Race organizers pointed out that the turn was well marked, and the runners had been briefed about the course the day before. Pence took home the $3,000 prize, and the Kenyans, who support their families by running, were still given $2,000 each. Some people cried foul play, but *Quad City Times* called it "a human mistake that the volunteer feels terrible about."

ROCK YOU LIKE A HURACÁN

While at a party on the night of February 15, 2020, a 26-year-old British man named Ali Zaman decided to take his friend's $265,000 Lamborghini Huracán for a joyride around Bradford, West Yorkshire, without the owner's permission. Zaman slyly lifted the keys from the friend's pocket, and he and his wife snuck out of the party and got in. Despite the fact that a historic windstorm was battering the UK, the drive was uneventful at first. Then, while stopped at a traffic light, Zaman revved the engine, challenging the driver in the next lane to a race. When the light turned green, Zaman floored it...and lost control of the Huracán. He swerved and hit the other car, totaling them both. It gets worse. Zaman wasn't insured to be driving the Lamborghini. It gets even worse. Zaman and his wife had gotten married only a few hours earlier. (The car's owner had been a wedding guest.) They spent their wedding night in the hospital, and a lot of time after that in court.

*   *   *

A BIZARRE WORLD RECORD

Mihailo Tolotos was born in Greece in 1856 and never saw his mother because she died during childbirth. He was raised in a monastery on top of Mount Athos where females are not permitted. After living for 82 years as an Orthodox monk, Tolotos died in 1938...without ever once talking to or even *seeing* a woman.

There are 80 percent fewer nuclear arms in the world today than there were in the mid-1980s.

THE VAN GOGH AWARDS

Vincent van Gogh is universally acknowledged as one of the greatest painters in history, and his works have sold for tens of millions of dollars. But he never got to enjoy the accolades or the money, because his success came long after his death. Here are some more bittersweet success stories—people who found fame and fortune...but only after they were gone.

EVA CASSIDY

Cassidy, a soul and blues singer who played clubs in and around Washington, DC, released just one album during her lifetime—*The Other Side*, in 1992. The following year, she had a cancerous mole removed from her back, and by 1996, the cancer had spread to her bones and lungs. Cassidy died that year at the age of 33. In 1998, a few songs she'd recorded here and there were compiled into a second album called *Songbird*. Sales of that one were poor...until BBC radio personality Terry Wogan played it on his highly rated morning show in 2000. By the end of that year, *Songbird* topped the UK album charts and would eventually sell nearly two million copies in that country. Another collection, *Imagine*, also went to #1, as did her live cover of "What a Wonderful World," the last song Cassidy ever sang in concert, at her own benefit concert six weeks before her death.

STIEG LARSSON

The *Millennium* trilogy of crime novels by Swedish author Larsson were a publishing phenomenon in the 2010s. The plot: an antisocial punk hacker named Lisbeth Salander helps reporter Mikael Blomkvist track down (and punish) some truly evil criminals. Translated into many languages, *The Girl with the Dragon Tattoo* (2005), *The Girl Who Played with Fire* (2006), and *The Girl Who Kicked the Hornets' Nest* (2007) sold more than 100 million copies altogether and spawned film franchises in Sweden and the United States. Larsson didn't get to enjoy any of that, though. Shortly after submitting all three manuscripts to his publisher in 2004, he died of a heart attack at age 50.

JOHN KENNEDY TOOLE

Toole completed two manuscripts, one of which was *A Confederacy of Dunces*, a comic, meandering novel about the pompous, overeducated, overweight Ignatius J. Reilly, a 30-year-old man who lives with his mother in colorful, character-filled, hard-partying 1960s New Orleans. Kennedy couldn't find any publisher willing to take on the novel, however, and, suffering from severe clinical depression triggered in part by his professional failure, he committed suicide in 1969 via carbon monoxide poisoning. A few years after his death at age 31, Toole's mother, Thelma Toole, took it upon herself to get *A Confederacy of Dunces* published. Louisiana State University Press accepted the manuscript and published it in 1980. In 1981, John Kennedy Toole, dead for 12 years, won the Pulitzer Prize for Fiction.

JONATHAN LARSON

Larson waited tables in New York for more than a decade to pay the bills while he waited for his career as a playwright to take off. He produced some works in tiny, off-Broadway theaters, but struck big with *Rent*, a rock musical version of the opera *La Bohème*, concerning artists and musicians coping with poverty and AIDS. On January 25, 1996, *Rent* was set to make its Broadway debut. Hours before showtime, Larson died of an aortic aneurysm at age 35. *Rent* went on as planned, and won Larson the Pulitzer Prize as well as three Tony Awards, including Best Musical.

SYLVIA PLATH

Plath's poetry and prose dealt extensively with sadness, depression, and feelings of dissatisfaction. In February 1963, the writer committed suicide at age 30. Her autobiographical novel *The Bell Jar* had hit stores only weeks before, and went on to become an international best-seller by the end of the 1960s. In 1982, almost two decades after her death, Plath became the first posthumous winner of the Pulitzer Prize for poetry, for her book *The Collected Poems*.

EMILY DICKINSON

Heralded as one of the great poets and a pioneering woman in the male-dominated literary world, Dickinson is an American icon. She died at age 55 in 1886, having written more than 1,800 poems but only ever publishing 10. Friends, family members, and famous writers with whom she was acquainted started compiling her work in 1890, and the first collection, *Poems*, was a best-seller and went back to print 10 times. The follow-up, *Poems: Second Series*, reprinted five times, permanently establishing Dickinson as a major poet.

ROBERT JOHNSON

Johnson was probably the single most influential figure in the history of blues music, a singer and guitarist whose style has been imitated by most blues musicians, not to mention those who adapted the blues into rock in the 1950s and '60s. So little is known about Johnson (only three photographs of him exist) that the mystery, combined with his greatness, gave rise to legends—especially one that says he made a deal with the devil at a crossroads in rural Mississippi, trading his eternal soul for untouchable musical ability. That (probably) didn't happen, but it is known that he played on street corners and in bars in Mississippi in the 1930s, and sat for two

There are about 350 million individual products available on Amazon (including this book).

recording sessions in Texas in 1936 and 1937, which resulted in a preserved body of work consisting of 29 poorly recorded songs. Some of those tunes were released as 78-rpm records, but by the time the last ones hit stores in 1938, Johnson was dead at the age of 27. (No cause was listed on his death certificate.) His stature grew among musicians and blues fans, but the general public didn't take notice until Columbia Records issued the compilation *King of the Delta Blues Singers* in 1961. Another collection followed in 1970, and in 1990, Columbia released a box set of everything Johnson recorded. It sold a million copies, the first blues album to reach that milestone.

HERMAN MELVILLE

In his lifetime, Melville was a literary one-hit wonder. His debut book, *Typee: A Peep at Polynesian Life*, a memoir of his time living in the Marquesas Islands, was a modest best-seller upon its release in 1846. Struggling to produce a successful follow-up, Melville wrote four books before finally publishing the novel *Moby-Dick* in 1851. British critics gave middling reviews to the novel about a whaling-ship captain's single-minded quest to exact vengeance on the titular whale, while American critics' reviews were uniformly negative. The book flopped, and by the time Melville died in 1891, *Moby-Dick* had fallen out of print. In the 1920s, literary critics started to reconsider Melville, and by the mid-20th century, *Moby-Dick* was required reading in thousands of American schools; now, it is often considered *the* Great American Novel.

* * *

SYLVESTER STALLONE'S ANALYSIS OF A
HYPOTHETICAL FIGHT BETWEEN ROCKY AND RAMBO

"If the fighters were to remain upright Rocky would prevail. His body punches and right hooks would eventually beat Rambo. If the fight goes to the ground, Rambo will prevail in a bloody brutal fight to the end. Rethinking this scenario, I believe that upon initial contact, since they will not be in the rain but fighting outside, basically a street fight, then Rocky will land the first five or six blows. If that does not incapacitate Rambo, which I don't think he will unless he's caught clean, Rambo's skill set will definitely be in full display, which means incredibly vicious assaults on the eyes, the throat, every vulnerable part of the body eventually leading to being pulled to the ground and most likely mauled. Then again Rocky is incredibly resilient and pretty good on the ground too!!! That's my opinion in this fictional world. Final result is neither man will ever be the same."

On average, identical twins live longer than fraternal twins. No one knows why.

THE NATURAL GAS REPORT

"Breaking wind," as some people politely call it, is a natural and inevitable part of life. So it's not surprising that farts occasionally make the news.

A WINDY DAY AT THE GOLF COURSE

On the first hole of the first day of the 2020 Travelers Championship golf tournament, Australian golfer Greg Chalmers hit a solid shot down the fairway. And then somebody let another one rip—not a ball, but a very loud fart, so loud that the Golf Channel's sound equipment picked it up and shared it with the people watching at home. Chalmers was on screen when the flatulence sounded, but he wasn't responsible. Who was? Fellow Australian Ian Poulter, who was a few feet away, ready to tee off next, when he broke wind. "Did you get that?" Chalmers asked the camera crew, and then told Poulter, "Stay over there."

YOU ARE GETTING VERY FARTY...

Xandra Samson worked as a nurse at Ealing Hospital in London until 2019 when she filed a complaint against the National Health Service, alleging the "inappropriate use of hypnosis / ideomotor phenomenon" at her workplace. What is "ideomotor phenomenon"? It's an obscure type of hypnosis that controls the subjects' use of their own bodies. In this case, Samson claimed, it was creating "gastrointestinal disturbance," making her "fart against her will." She said the hypnotic effect was being caused by poor heating and bad ventilation at Ealing Hospital, and she believed it was intentional. After she refused psychiatric assistance, the NHS fired her. Samson then sued for wrongful termination, but in 2021 a judge ruled in favor of the NHS.

FROM INK TO STINK

Model Tracey Munter checked into the Good Tattoo Emporium in Rotherham, England, in 2016, for the final touches on an elaborate tattoo depicting the chariot race scene from the 1959 movie *Ben-Hur*. That tattoo was on one of Munter's buttocks, requiring tattoo artist Jason Burns to get very close to the model's rear end. As she lay on a table while Burns worked, Munter inadvertently let out a very small fart. Burns happened to be smoking a cigarette at the time, and as farts are comprised of methane, the gas quickly found the flame. "Before I know what's happening, there's a flame shooting from her a**," Burns recounted, "and my beard's gone up like an Aussie bushfire." Burns put out the fire at the parlor's sink while Munter used a wet towel to extinguish her thong-style underwear, which had also caught on fire. Both parties were briefly hospitalized for minor burns (Munter on her tattoo, and Burns around his eyebrows) and shock.

Half of all solar power generated in the U.S. comes from California.

THE AIR UP THERE

According to University of Copenhagen clinical researcher Jacob Rosenberg, people tend to fart more during flights, and he set up a whole study to pinpoint why, exactly, that's true. During a long flight from Europe to New Zealand, he suffered from stomach bloating and noticed that his empty water bottle had similarly expanded with air. Following the flight, his stomach issue went away and the bottle re-crumpled. Both are the result of the change in the plane's cabin pressure. After takeoff, "the pressure drops and the air must expand into more space," Rosenberg told reporters. The internal gas, which can expand the stomach's area by as much as 30 percent, has to go somewhere— and quickly. Result: much to the chagrin of their row-mates, most people fart it out. Rosenberg said that while this is a scientific phenomenon that can't really be eliminated, eating less fiber before the flight can help cut down on the farts.

> The internal gas, which can expand the stomach's area by as much as 30 percent, has to go somewhere.

RAISING A STINK

Farting is not a crime—or at least it isn't when it's an isolated incident. If wind is broken within the context of other illegal activity, or brandished as a weapon with hostility, farts can get a person into serious trouble. In June 2020, a man (unnamed in reports) was sitting on a park bench in Vienna, Austria, when some police officers came over and asked to see his ID. After some antagonizing words, the man stood up, stared at the officers, and "let go a massive intestinal wind apparently with full intent," the Vienna police department wrote on its Twitter page. "And our colleagues don't like to be farted at so much." For behaving "provocatively and uncooperatively," the farter was fined €500 ($560). The man appealed on the grounds that it was a mere "biological process," and that he was exercising his freedom of expression. The court reduced the fine to €100 (because the man had no criminal record), but ruled that farting as a form of communication "transcends the boundaries of decency."

* * *

COUNTRY ROCK

Elvis Presley is one of 11 artists who've been inducted into both the Rock and Roll Hall of Fame and the Country Music Hall of Fame. Here are the other ten:

- Chet Atkins
- Johnny Cash
- Floyd Cramer
- The Everly Brothers
- Brenda Lee
- Bill Monroe
- Sam Phillips
- Jimmie Rodgers
- Hank Williams
- Bob Wills

Felix Hoffmann, a German chemist who worked for Bayer, invented aspirin and heroin two weeks apart in 1897.

CELEBRITY ANAGRAMS

Rearranging the letters of these celebrities' names may not really provide better descriptions of the people...but they are pretty funny.

ROD STEWART	becomes...	WORST DATER
TAYLOR SWIFT	becomes...	WITTY FLORAS
FRANK ZAPPA	becomes...	FAN PARK ZAP
MATTHEW BRODERICK	becomes...	BATTERED HICK WORM
DAVID LEE ROTH	becomes...	HOT DAREDEVIL
NEIL YOUNG	becomes...	ONLINE GUY
JOHN CUSACK	becomes...	COACH'S JUNK
SANDRA BULLOCK	becomes...	BAD ACORN SKULL
HULK HOGAN	becomes...	LAUGH HONK
LEONARDO DICAPRIO	becomes...	A PERIODICAL DONOR
ADAM SANDLER	becomes...	REAL DAMN SAD
AVRIL LAVIGNE	becomes...	GRAVE VILLAIN
DIANE KEATON	becomes...	KINDA ATE ONE
CHRISTOPHER WALKEN	becomes...	CRANK THE LOWER HIPS
AL PACINO	becomes...	PAIN COLA
RON HOWARD	becomes...	DRAW HONOR
DREW BARRYMORE	becomes...	MERRY WARDROBE
MAYA ANGELOU	becomes...	YOGA ALUMNAE
MEG RYAN	becomes...	GERMANY
STEVE HARVEY	becomes...	HAS EVERY HAT
CHARLIE CHAPLIN	becomes...	CHINCHILLA PEAR
SUSAN ORLEAN	becomes...	NEURON SALSA
BLAKE SHELTON	becomes...	HOT KNEE BALLS
ERNEST HEMINGWAY	becomes...	MY THINNER SEWAGE
CHRISTIAN BALE	becomes...	ANARCHIST BILE
BEN AFFLECK	becomes...	BAFFLE NECK
BEN STILLER	becomes...	I'LL BE STERN
CLIVE OWEN	becomes...	NICE VOWEL
STEVE MARTIN	becomes...	TAVERN ITEMS
CATE BLANCHETT	becomes...	BATCH TENTACLE

More than half of all the spacecraft sent to Mars never arrived.

STRANGE LAWSUITS

More real-life examples of unusual legal battles.

ARE YOU SITTING DOWN FOR THIS?

Lawsuit: The German word *sitzpinkler* is a slang term for "wimp" or "unmanly," but its literal meaning is "a man who sits down to urinate." Such a practice is actually encouraged in Germany; public toilets frequently display large red signs requesting that men have a seat when they use the facilities. Reason: men who stand are likely to leave a few drops on the floor, which is no fun for the custodians or the property owners—chemicals in urine can severely damage floors over time. In 2015, an apartment complex owner (not named in press reports) in Düsseldorf sued a former tenant for €1,900 (about $2,200), the cost of replacing his bathroom floor. The resident reportedly refused to sit down to urinate in his rented home, and according to expert testimony, the uric acid in the traces of urine left behind eroded the floor tiles to the point where they had to be replaced.

Outcome: The non-sitzpinkler didn't have to pay. In his ruling, Judge Stefan Hank declared that men have the right to pee while standing up.

A TWISTED TALE THAT'S HARD TO BEAR

Lawsuit: John Donaldson of Davis, California, was vacationing in Lake Tahoe, Nevada, in 2019, and he rented a condo in the Incline Village area. He took his dog out to do its business one morning, bagged up the waste, and went over to a dumpster to throw it out. According to legal documents, Donaldson had difficulty opening the latch and when he finally did, he discovered a bear inside. Donaldson instinctively tried to run away, but tripped, fell, twisted his ankle, and landed hard on his back. (The bear lumbered away into the woods behind the complex.) Donaldson needed surgery for an Achilles tendon tear and a spinal cord compression. He then sued the condo association and the waste management company that owns the dumpster for $15,000, claiming their poor maintenance of the trash bin led to his injuries.

Outcome: The case was settled out of court.

THE WINNER TAKES IT ALL

Lawsuit: 2021 was a big year for the 1970s Swedish pop supergroup ABBA. They reunited nearly 40 years after splitting up, released an acclaimed new album, earned a Record of the Year Grammy nomination...and sued some of their most ardent fans. The defendants: ABBA MANIA, an ABBA "tribute band," whose members perform ABBA songs in sparkly jumpsuits like the group wore in the '70s. In December 2021, ABBA filed suit, calling the British cover band's activities "parasitic" and in "bad

Smart animal, sad fact: Octopuses in captivity can get so bored
and distressed that they'll eat their own arms.

faith," because they intentionally gave the impression that they were endorsed by the real ABBA, which they were not. "Defendants include the term 'official' and 'original' in many of their marketing materials, website pages, and social media handles, which gives consumers the impression that there is some kind of association, affiliation, or sponsorship," ABBA's lawyers wrote in a UK court filing. ABBA gave ABBA MANIA a chance to avoid a lawsuit by asking the group to use a less ABBA-centric name, as other tribute acts, such as Arrival from Sweden, Dancing Dream, or Bjorn Again, had. **Outcome:** As of press time, the case is still pending.

PROCEED GINGERLY
Lawsuit: For years, cans and bottles of Canada Dry ginger ale have been emblazoned with the slogan "Made from real ginger." In 2018, a British Columbia man named Victor Cardoso initiated a class action lawsuit against the soda's Canadian manufacturer, alleging false advertising. Cardoso claimed that his family consumed heavy amounts of Canada Dry assuming it was healthy, because it said "Made with real ginger," and ginger has well-known benefits. Cardoso's lawyer, Mark Canofari, argued that Canada Dry is only barely "made from real ginger." "They do buy actual ginger, but then what they do is boil it in ethanol, and that essentially destroys any nutritional or medicinal benefits," Canofari said. That solution is made into a concentrate, he explained, one drop of which is dispersed into 70 cans of the soda. **Outcome:** Canada Dry settled the lawsuit for $200,000, but didn't have to admit any wrongdoing. (And it didn't remove "Made from real ginger" from its packaging.)

ONE SUIT TO RULE THEM ALL
Lawsuit: What's the biggest craze in the financial world over the last few years? The buying and selling of cryptocurrency—a form of completely digital money not tied to any central government or bank. The most popular and biggest news-making cryptocurrencies are Bitcoin and Dogecoin, but there are dozens of others, and in 2021, an American developer named Matthew Jensen introduced a new one called "JRR Token." The name is a play on words; "token" is a common term to indicate a denomination of cryptocurrency, but the whole thing is meant to evoke J. R. R. Tolkien, the author of The Lord of the Rings and The Hobbit. In promotional materials, Jensen drove the pun home, proclaiming JRR Token to be "the one token that rules them all," a reference to the famous line "one ring to rule them all" from The Lord of the Rings. One day after JRR Token went on sale, the estate of J. R. R. Tolkien sued Jensen for illegal use of and association with the author's name. Jensen defended himself, claiming that the "JRR" actually stood for "journey through risk to reward." **Outcome:** The World Intellectual Property Organization didn't buy it. It sided with the Tolkien estate, immediately cutting off sale of JRR Token, which the trademark group said was "clever but not humorous."

Holy roller: Pope Francis once worked as a bouncer.

MOUTHING OFF

WANDERLUST!

Some thoughts about exploring our Big Blue Marble.

"Perhaps travel cannot prevent bigotry, but by demonstrating that all peoples cry, laugh, eat, worry, and die, it can introduce the idea that if we try and understand each other, we may even become friends."

—Maya Angelou

"One's destination is never a place, but a new way of seeing things."

—Henry Miller

"THE WORLD IS A BOOK AND THOSE WHO DO NOT TRAVEL READ ONLY A PAGE."

—St. Augustine

"I haven't been everywhere, but it's on my list."

—Susan Sontag

"Broad, wholesome, charitable views of men and things cannot be acquired by vegetating in one little corner of the earth all of one's lifetime."

—Mark Twain

"Stuff your eyes with wonder, live as if you'd drop dead in ten seconds. See the world. It's more fantastic than any dream made or paid for in factories."

—Ray Bradbury

"NATIONALISM IS CURED BY TRAVELING."

—Shakira

"Traveling—it leaves you speechless, then turns you into a storyteller."

—Ibn Battuta

"Go as far as you can see; when you get there, you'll be able to see further."

—Thomas Carlyle

"A mind that is stretched by a new experience can never go back to its old dimensions."

—Oliver Wendell Holmes Jr.

SCIENCE IS AMAZING

In case you haven't noticed, there have been some game-changing scientific discoveries in recent years. (They tend to get buried in the news.) So, unless you're a scientist or a science nerd, you'd be forgiven if you hadn't heard that...

NO HUMAN BEING HAS EVER LEFT EARTH'S ATMOSPHERE

Where does space begin? What most people think of as the Earth's atmosphere is actually the *biosphere*. From the Latin words for "life ball," it's a thin life-sustaining layer that extends 40 miles above and 12 miles below the surface. By contrast, the *atmosphere* ("gas ball") is comprised of five layers: the troposphere (up to 7 miles), stratosphere (31 miles), mesosphere (50 miles), thermosphere (440 miles), and exosphere, which extends to the far reaches of the *geocorona*, a gaseous cloud of hydrogen atoms that escaped the inner atmosphere.

Since the 1960s, scientists assumed the geocorona's boundary fell well within the orbit of the Moon. Then, in December 2019, French planetologist Jean-Loup Bertaux and Russian physicist Igor Baliukin made a stunning announcement: "The Moon flies through Earth's atmosphere." Their results are based on data that Bertaux had collected in the 1990s during a NASA/ESA (European Space Agency) mission to monitor the effects of solar wind on our planet. Using a specialty camera, Bertaux measured Lyman-alpha radiation, a frequency of ultraviolet light made up of the hydrogen atoms in the geocorona. He calls Lyman-alpha "the color of hydrogen."

After Bertaux retired from the ESA, he and Baliukin analyzed the data and determined that the geocorona extends to 391,000 miles (50 times the Earth's diameter). The Moon, by comparison, is 238,900 miles away. As such, because space technically begins where the atmosphere ends, the first humans to truly put Earth in their rearview mirror will most likely be on a spaceship to Mars. But even more amazing: only a planet with abundant water in its inner atmosphere can emit a large Lyman-alpha glow like ours. Now that astronomers know what to look for, and how to detect it, this could lead to the discovery of an Earth-like planet beyond our solar system.

FISH ARE SELF-AWARE

The "mirror test" was conceived in 1970 by a graduate student named Gordon Gallup. (The idea came to him while he was shaving.) He devised a cognitive test to determine if apes and monkeys could recognize their own reflections. The chimps and other higher apes passed the test; the macaques and other monkeys did not. Since then, the mirror test has been one of science's main determinants of an animal's self-awareness. (Humans can't pass the mirror test until toddlerhood.)

In 2019, researchers from the Max Planck Institute for Ornithology and Osaka

---

The U.S. president has Air Force One, and the Pope's plane is called Shepherd One.

City University announced that a species of fish (cleaner wrasse fish, to be exact) had passed the mirror test. Like Gallup's chimpanzees, the fishes' first reaction to the "fish" in the mirror was aggression. Eventually, the fish became accustomed to the reflection and seemed, to the researchers, to be looking at themselves. The next step: place a bit of brown material on the fish near its mouth. After some (not all) of the fish looked at their reflection, they swam down to a rock and scraped off the material, and then swam back to the mirror to confirm it was gone, thus passing the test. "The finding suggests that fish might possess far higher cognitive powers than previously thought," conclude the researchers, "and ignites a high-stakes debate over how we assess the intelligence of animals that are so unlike ourselves."

TIME TRAVEL IS POSSIBLE

The "grandfather paradox" is the theory that you can't travel back in time and kill your grandfather, because it means you would have never existed in the first place. Scientists have long used this paradox to argue that traveling to the past is not possible, even though Einstein's general theory of relativity—which posits that "space-time can be bent by a massive gravitational field"—suggests that it is. In 2014, a team of physicists from the University of Queensland, Australia, used photons to disprove the grandfather paradox. The researchers put the photons (tiny particles of light) through a simulated "closed timelike curve," wherein, according to physicist Andrew Zimmerman Jones, the photon "follows a curious path where it eventually returns to the exact same coordinates in space and time that it was at previously." While we probably won't be visiting our great-great-grandparents anytime soon, *Scientific American* reported that the study "offers tentative support for time travel's feasibility—at least from a mathematical perspective."

MEMORIES DON'T NECESSARILY REQUIRE BRAINS

In 2021, German biologists Mirna Kramar and Karen Alim studied a bright-yellow slime mold called *Physarum polycephalum*. This forest dweller looks like a fungus but is actually a multi-cellular "social amoeba." Previous experiments on slime molds revealed that they can seek out nutrient sources *and* remember their locations—a considerable feat considering they have no eyes, brain, or central nervous system. Slime molds are a network of *tubular tendrils* that can branch out in different directions. Looking through a microscope, the scientists observed a slime mold making some of its tubes thinner and some thicker when it found a food source. Result: "Memory about nutrient location is encoded in the morphology of the network-shaped organism." In other words, the organism's shape *is* its memory. This discovery could theoretically could be used to develop biomaterials that utilize artificial intelligence. (Talk about memory foam...)

Mickey Mouse's first words of dialogue, in the 1929 short *The Karnival Kid*: "Hot dogs!"

THE DUSTBIN OF HISTORY: THE GOODIES

In our Triumphant 20th Anniversary Bathroom Reader, *we wrote about a British bricklayer who died in 1975 after laughing for 30 straight minutes at a TV show called* The Goodies. *That's about the only time the comedy troupe the Goodies (and that bricklayer) have shown up in our books. But the Goodies' contemporaries, Monty Python, pop up often. Here's why.*

ANYTHING, ANYTIME

In the early 1970s there were two groundbreaking off-the-wall comedy shows on British television—*The Goodies* and *Monty Python's Flying Circus*. One was hugely popular and the other was constantly in danger of getting canceled. Which was the popular show? Surprisingly, it was the one you've probably never heard of: *The Goodies*.

Part sitcom and part sketch show, *The Goodies* aired on the BBC from 1970 to 1982. Stars Tim Brooke-Taylor, Graeme Garden, and Bill Oddie play three men for hire who ride a three-person "trandem" bicycle (and fall off a lot). Their motto: "Anything, anytime." One week, the Goodies are trying to save London from a gigantic, rampaging kitten. Another week, they're getting tortured by rabbits on the Moon.

A TALE OF TWO TROUPES

If this all sounds Pythonesque, it's because it is. The Goodies and Monty Python share the same DNA: both comedy troupes included members from the Cambridge University Footlights (Eric Idle and Graeme Garden both served as president), and they roomed together and later worked on many of the same programs in the 1960s. When the BBC wanted to put more comedy on the air at the end of the decade, the Pythons and the Goodies broke off into separate groups and got their own shows.

On the surface, their humor looks and sounds a lot alike: funny voices, strange costumes, fantasy elements, and absurd plotlines. As Oddie said in 2007, "There's some Python stuff that any of us would have felt comfortable doing, and some of the Python people would have felt comfortable doing Goodies stuff." But their trajectories couldn't have been more different: When *Monty Python's Flying Circus* premiered in 1969, it drew mediocre ratings and was constantly at the risk of cancellation. *The Goodies* premiered a year later, and they soon became household names in England, topping out at 15.2 million viewers for a 1975 episode. The Goodies also wrote and recorded novelty pop songs such as "The Inbetweenies," "Funky Gibbon," and "Black Pudding Bertha (The Queen of Northern Soul)" that broke the UK Top 10 charts. *The Goodies* remained on television until 1982, and then...that was about it.

What's a *nibling*? A gender-neutral word to refer to a niece or nephew.

INTO THE DUSTBIN

It wasn't just blind luck that one of these two troupes became woven into the fabric of society, while the other became a footnote. There were a lot of factors in play.

The Pythons Were Better Self-promoters: Oddie recalled getting a call from Idle one day in the late '70s: "Come over, I've got some friends 'round." Those friends were Paul Simon and Mick Jagger. Other Python friends-turned-financiers were Hugh Hefner and George Harrison. Though not necessarily shy, the Goodies were more reserved. Besides, there wasn't much they could do on their own while under contract with the BBC.

Monty Python Was Edgier: Python member John Cleese once dismissed the Goodies as a "kids' program." Oddie put it this way: "I saw the Pythons as the Stones, slightly dangerous and slightly naughty, and we were more like the Beatles because we were family friendly and appealed to the widest possible audience." Both shows featured surreal sketches, but Python was more violent and cynical, whereas the Goodies were more slapstick and whimsical. It's like the difference between *America's Funniest Home Videos* (Goodies) and *Jackass* (Python).

The Goodies Were Too Topical: The Goodies scripts were set in the modern world and often touched on controversial subjects, such as apartheid and pollution. But for that reason, a lot of their more preachy comedy hasn't aged as well as Monty Python's, which attacked broader targets, such as the upper classes and bureaucrats. In fact, when viewed through a modern lens, a few of the Goodies' sketches are downright cringeworthy. They spoke out against racism...but in doing so, they used racially charged language, and in one sketch, Oddie wore blackface and spoke in an exaggerated African accent. Was *Flying Circus* squeaky clean? Not by a long shot. This was the '70s, after all. Monty Python members also wore blackface and mocked foreign dialects. If the *Flying Circus* sketch called "Prejudice" were to air on network TV today, the introduction would sound like: "*Prejudice*: the game show that gives you a chance to have a go at the [bleep], [bleep], [bleep], [bleep], [bleep], bubbles, [bleep], [bleep], [bleep], jocks, [bleep], [bleep], and [bleep]." (We can't tell you what the bleeps are.) Why is that acceptable, while the Goodies' take is not? Maybe it's because Python was trying to be satirical, not "relevant," and in doing so, their comedy came off as irreverent, not racist. But for whatever reason, Python got away with it.

The Network Held the Goodies Back: The BBC kept them on the air until 1981 (their final season aired on ITV in '82). That was too long for a show like *The Goodies*—they'd run out of ideas, the novelty had worn off, and their brand of slapstick had gone stale. Result: Oddie, Garden, and Brooke-Taylor could only watch from the sidelines as Monty Python—after getting axed by the BBC in 1974—made the jump to movies and became household names in America. It almost happened for the Goodies: In 1979, Steven Spielberg approached them to make a Goodies movie. They would have jumped at the offer, but the BBC had them under contract and wouldn't allow it. (Spielberg made *Raiders of the Lost Ark* instead.) Worse yet, the Goodies never got the chance for a resurgence in England because the network refused to air the show in reruns—citing different reasons over the years, from it not being progressive enough to a lack of demand. (That's odd, considering all the other '70s shows the network has re-aired.) *The Goodies* TV show didn't get its first home video release until 2007, and it played on only "Region 2" DVD players, which are not sold in the United States.

DID YOU KNOW?

> **DID YOU KNOW?**
>
> A BBC pamphlet called *The Green Book*—issued to all writers, editors, and broadcasters in 1949—prohibited on-air jokes about "lavatories, effeminacy in men, immorality of any kind... suggestive references to honeymoon couples, chambermaids, fig leaves, prostitution, ladies' underwear, animal habits, lodgers, and commercial travelers."

GOODIE 'NUFF

Even though their TV show didn't leave a lasting mark, the Goodies themselves did okay.

Bill Oddie went on to become England's "4th most trusted figure," according to a public poll, as host of a popular nature program called *Springwatch*. Tim Brooke-Taylor and Graeme Garden spent 50 years as panelists on the popular Radio 4 quiz show *I'm Sorry I Haven't a Clue*. All three were awarded OBEs (the Most Excellent Order of the British Empire)—Oddie for wildlife conservation, and Brooke-Taylor and Garden for "services to light entertainment."

And to be fair, they haven't been completely forgotten. Famous Goodies fans (or "Giddies") include Simon Pegg, Mike Myers, Martin Freeman, and Prince Charles, who once commented, "Monty Python is good, but I prefer the Goodies." One place that *Goodies* reruns did air was Australia in the 1980s, five nights a week at dinnertime. They gained a huge following Down Under, and reunited there in 2005 for a sold-out stage tour.

Do the Goodies feel bitter about being overshadowed by the Pythons? Quite the opposite, said Garden in 2015, calling it a "good-natured rivalry." If there's anyone the Goodies are angry with, it's those BBC executives (we can't print what the Goodies called them). And if the Monty Python members had gone their separate ways in 1975, who is to say they wouldn't be a silly footnote as well?

* * *

RIDDLE ME THIS

Q: A man went around the world in a ship, yet he was always in sight of land. How is this possible?

A: It was a spaceship.

In 1886, the year it was invented, an average of nine servings of Coca-Cola were sold each day.

SAD? I'M MIDAS?

Palindromes are words or phrases that are spelled the same way backward and forward. Here are some of the best we've found.

Emil peed deep lime.

Deb, smash Sam's bed!

Dairy myriad.

A nut for a jar of tuna.

Kayak salad, Alaska yak.

No, slang is a signal, son.

Borrow or rob?

St. Simon sees no mists.

Pull up if I pull up.

Tangy gnat.

Gold log.

He stops spots, eh?

Saw tide rose, so red it was.

Wonton on salad?
Alas, no, not now!

Yawn a more Roman way.

But Anita sat in a tub.

Denim axes examined.

Mirror rim.

Slap my gym pals.

Bombard a drab mob.

Mix a maxim.

Tessa's in Italy, Latin is asset.

Sad? I'm Midas!

Dr. Awkward.

Lee had a heel.

As I pee, sir, I see Pisa!

No pet so tragic as a cigar to step on.

Panda had nap.

Son, I sack casinos.

Naomi, did I moan?

Ten animals I slam in a net.

Bird rib.

Name now one man.

Sup not on pus.

Don did nod.

Swap for I, a pair of paws?

Timid as Ma, I am sad I'm it.

Oh, cameras are macho.

Never a foot too far, even.

Sat in a taxi, left Felix at Anita's.

Drowsy baby's word.

Niagara, O roar again.

Pets never even step.

Wet rare paper art, ew!

Revenge my baby, Meg? Never!

'Tis Ivan on a visit.

Roy, am I mayor?

Trade ye no mere moneyed art.

Won't lovers revolt now?

Ed is a trader; cast sacred art aside.

I prefer pi.

A Santa dog lived as a devil god at NASA.

A lot not new I saw as I went on to L.A.

Eva can ignite virtuosos out riveting in a cave.

Only animal with opposable thumbs that doesn't also have thumbnails: the opossum.

THE REAL-LIFE INDIANA JONES

Stories about a handsome professor who climbs over clouded mountaintops and down into the jungle looking for lost Inca villages seem too Hollywood to be true. Yet there really was such an explorer. His name was Hiram Bingham III, and, he explored Peru on just such a quest.

EMPIRE BUILDERS

One of history's most fascinating and mysterious civilizations is the Inca. In the early 1500s, their 2,400-mile-long empire in the Andean region of South America was one of the world's largest, incorporating what's now Peru with parts of Ecuador, Colombia, Bolivia, Argentina, and Chile. With fewer than 40,000 members, the tribe presided over 12 *million* people. How? They were well-organized, diplomatic, and had *lots* of gold. The Inca assimilated other tribes—usually peacefully—then tracked and redistributed their goods using an advanced accounting system.

Because they had no written language with which to record their story, much of their culture remains an enigma. Yet we do have some remnants of the Inca: their structures. As master builders, they paved 14,000 miles of roads, wove massive bridges (using methods still used today), and built aqueducts to supply water. From 1438–72, their emperor, Pachacuti, directed these impressive projects, expanding the empire beyond the capital of Cuzco (in present-day Peru) and rebuilding Cuzco into the shape of their most revered animal, the puma. The Incas had labor, resources, military power, and so much treasure that they made a garden out of precious metals and soled their nobles' shoes with silver.

THE CONQUISTADORS

Everything changed after Spanish conquistadors came along. In 1532, the European invaders massacred 5,000 unarmed Incas, kidnapped the king, and later took 24 *tons* of gold and silver as ransom for his release. Then they murdered the king anyway and captured Cuzco. The surviving Incas fled into the Andes Mountains—to the remote capital city of Vitcos—and, according to legend, took the tribe's remaining treasure with them. From Vitcos, and later from a town called Vilcabamba, even deeper in the jungle, the surviving Incas rebelled against Spanish rule for decades. But their defeat by the technologically superior, disease-carrying conquistadors was inevitable, and the Inca empire finally collapsed in 1572. Their last capital, Vilcabamba, came to be called "the Lost City of the Inca." For centuries, people wondered...where was Vilcabamba? And where was Vitcos? And what happened to the Incas' riches? Enter Professor Hiram Bingham III.

THE SWASHBUCKLER

As a mountaineer and scholar, Hiram Bingham III was the most successful adventurer you've probably never heard of. In 1900, he married an heiress to the Tiffany & Co. fortune and was soon traversing South America on her money, studying local history. He overcame altitude sickness and other dangers as he climbed old trade routes through the Andes, the highest mountains in the Americas, while writing about the Venezuelan revolutionary Simón Bolívar. And when he became Yale University's first Latin American history professor in 1907, he was one of the only experts in the field. More daring than a typical lecturer, Bingham returned to the wild in Peru, often donning a white shirt, brown fedora, leather jacket, and boots—a look later copied by the costume designer for the character of Indiana Jones.

INTO THE CRADLE OF GOD

In 1909, Bingham met a persuasive magistrate in Abancay, a city in southern Peru. The man insisted that Bingham check out an ancient Inca town to the west. Other men the magistrate had sent there had tried (and failed) to reach the town, but the mission required someone who could navigate a torturous ascent *and* understand the site's historical value. Someone like Bingham. But Bingham refused. With his interest in post-Columbian history (the history of the Americas after the arrival of Christopher Columbus), he said he was "not on the lookout for new Inca ruins." The magistrate, assuring Bingham he'd be the first non-Peruvian to visit, organized and outfitted the expedition anyway.

Riding on muleback, Bingham set off in the cold, dreary February of 1909. Soon the verdant river valley gave way to cliffs so perilous that some mules refused to continue. In heavy rain they kept traveling through what Bingham described as, "well nigh impassable bogs, swollen torrents, avalanches of boulders and trees," and at one point, he had to jump his mule over a chasm, under a waterfall. A condor with a 12-foot wingspan circled the travelers so closely that they feared it would attack. Finally, their efforts were rewarded. On a ridge nearly 10,000 feet high and surrounded by precipices was the impregnable citadel of Choquequirao, which means "cradle of gold" in the indigenous language *Quechua*.

In case you were wondering: The Harry Potter book series consists of exactly 1,090,739 words.

BARELY RUINED RUINS

Spanning nearly 4,500 acres, the stone city had been commissioned by the emperor, Pachacuti. The buildings were intricately built with trapezoid-shaped doorways, nooks to display mummies, built-in shelves under the windows to keep food cold, and stone rings that scholars believe were used to tether pumas. Amazingly, all of it was untouched by the conquistadors, who began destroying every remnant of the Inca people in 1532. Though the city had been overtaken by the jungle, Bingham was able to identify buildings made of stone and clay, and artifacts, including mummies and an ancient spinning wheel. To his dismay, Bingham also discovered evidence that he was not the first foreigner there—the first was a Spanish explorer who'd stumbled on the site around 1710.

> Archaeologists hailed it as the most spectacular find, even calling it the Lost City of the Inca.

Bingham's trip was life-changing and, on his return to the United States, he shifted his focus to pre-Columbian history. Although he wasn't Choquequirao's discoverer, he became its publicist. Archaeologists hailed it as the most spectacular find, even calling it the Lost City of the Inca. Bingham disagreed, writing, "Personally I did not feel so sure that [Choquequirao] was the Inca town of Vilcabamba. The ruins did not seem fine enough for an Inca's residence. There were certainly no 'sumptuous palaces' all 'built of marble,'" as a Spaniard had described in 1610. To prove the experts wrong, he got Yale and *National Geographic* to sponsor additional expeditions...to search for Vitcos and the real Vilcabamba.

UNDER SIEGE

But where to start? All Bingham had to go on were the Incan towns somewhere near Cuzco. On old maps, many sites had more than one name or were misidentified, and *Vilcabamba* is the name of several places, including a modern city in Peru (which he ruled out). Because the Inca didn't write, old texts were mostly from Spaniards who weren't experts in or even very respectful of the natives' history. Still, Bingham pieced together that in 1537, the king, Manco Inca Yupanqui, withdrew his tribe to a "most inaccessible" region. Even if the Spanish knew where the cities were, they'd need a lot of manpower, supplies, and audacity to venture there. From his strongholds of Vitcos and Vilcabamba, Manco directed sneak attacks to kill the foreigners.

Meanwhile, Spain cracked down on its conquistadors and outlawed their enslavement of indigenous people. The conquistadors weren't having it. In 1544, they killed both Manco and the Spanish viceroy. Manco's sons ruled for decades after that, while the foreigners tried, unsuccessfully, to lure the Incas out of hiding. Then, in 1571, the tribe was startled by something never seen in Vilcabamba: Spanish soldiers.

Incredibly, the Spaniards survived the treacherous journey and river crossings, then broke past the warriors guarding the bridges, the only way to enter the region. Facing invasion, the natives set their city on fire and fled. But the soldiers tracked them down and, in 1572, murdered the last Inca ruler and mounted his head on a pike, ending the civilization. With that, the empire's last two capitals were lost.

PIECING TOGETHER THE PUZZLE

There were bound to be clues, though. Bingham learned, for example, that Vilcabamba was supposedly a two or three days' journey from the village of Pucyura, about 10 miles northwest of Cuzco. It was in the rain forest and had tropical crops, including coca and sugarcane. Southwest of that was Vitcos, which contained Manco's stunning White Palace built of white rock. Vitcos was on a high mountain that had a giant white boulder overhanging a stream.

In 1911, Bingham returned to southern Peru with a new strategy. He asked everyone he met if they'd heard of any old stone buildings, and he followed all leads no matter how small—or how exaggerated, which was often the case. Then he matched each site against what he knew about the lost cities. Although other people were looking too, Bingham's historical knowledge, climbing skills, and vast resources made him uniquely qualified to find both cities.

One day Bingham got a tip from a prospector about ruins in the same river valley where he'd found Choquequirao. In his 1922 memoir, Bingham wrote of the man, "Those who knew him best shrugged their shoulders and did not seem to place much confidence in his word. Too often he had been over-enthusiastic about mines which did not 'pan out.'" Yet he recalled that in 1875, a French explorer, Charles Wiener, also heard about the place the miner mentioned...but couldn't find it. Bingham wrote, "Could we hope to be any more successful? Would the rumors that had reached us 'pan out' as badly as those to which Wiener had listened so eagerly?"

There was one major difference now. Crews had spent years blasting a mule trail through the unnavigable river canyon, granting access to uncharted areas. Taking that new road, Bingham set off on what would be the most grueling trip of his life.

Grab your machete and swing over to page 377 to continue the adventure.

* * *

"I don't mind doing interviews. I don't mind answering thoughtful questions. But I'm not thrilled about answering questions like, 'If you were being mugged, and you had a light saber in one pocket and a whip in the other, which would you use?'"
—Harrison Ford

The word *oxymoron* is itself an oxymoron, or a contradictory combination of words. It derives from the Greek words for "sharp" and "stupid."

THAT'S FINAL!

Everything must come to an end eventually, even phenomenally
popular sources of entertainment and amusement.

THE LAST CLASSIC TV WESTERN

Western movies were cheap to produce and very popular, which made the genre perfect for television. By the end of the 1950s, when TV ownership exploded, there were 30 Western series airing on the big three TV networks. The heyday of the small-screen Western lasted through the 1960s and even into the 1970s. The two longest-running and most popular Westerns were NBC's *Bonanza*, which ended in 1973 after 14 seasons and 431 episodes, and CBS's *Gunsmoke*, which premiered in 1955 and was canceled in 1975 after 20 seasons and 635 episodes.

THE LAST 78

What's a 78? You can ask your grandparents, but unless they're record collectors, they probably won't know either. Introduced in 1925, 78s—so named because they rotated 78 times per minute—were the predominant form of physical music media in the United States for 30 years. Each one held only a few minutes of music, so they were made obsolete soon after the introduction of the 33-1/3-RPM LP (short for "long-playing") in 1948. By 1958, 78s accounted for only 2 percent of all records sold. A year later, every major record label had phased them out. The last big 78 release: the 1959 hit "Fannie Mae" by Buster Brown. (The last 78 produced in the United States, overall: "Ole Pappy Time," by Cousin Fuzzy and His Cousins, made in 1962 by the tiny Midwestern label Polkaland Recording Company.)

THE LAST BOB HOPE SPECIAL

Hope made more than 270 "Bob Hope Specials" for NBC starting in 1954, often featuring the comedian performing for the troops on USO tours. His final special, *Laughing with the Presidents*, aired in 1996. (Hope was 93 at the time.) Cohost Tony Danza emceed, introducing old clips of Hope either hanging out with American presidents (from Eisenhower to Clinton) or telling jokes about them.

THE LAST RODGERS AND HAMMERSTEIN MUSICAL

Although they collaborated with others, neither composer Richard Rodgers nor lyricist Oscar Hammerstein II had as much commercial or cultural impact alone as they did together. The duo wrote 11 Broadway musicals together, starting with *Oklahoma!* in 1943, and ending with *The Sound of Music* in 1959.

Number of attendees at Jane Austen's funeral: four.

THE LAST SILENT FILM

The first feature-length, major movie with synchronized sound and dialogue: Al Jolson's *The Jazz Singer*, released in 1927. Studios adopted sound quickly but still produced a decreasing number of silent movies over the next few years as they waited for movie theaters to install sound systems. The final Hollywood-produced silent film was Paramount's 1935 release *Legong: Dance of the Virgins*. Filmed on location in Indonesia, it was a tale of forbidden love between two young people from warring families. Its main selling point (because a silent movie would need one to compete with "soundies"): it featured footage of topless native Indonesian women.

THE LAST RADIO DRAMAS

Once TV was widely adopted, the scripted dramas that ran on CBS and NBC radio networks in the 1940s and '50s couldn't compete. NBC pulled the last of its dramas off its radio feed in 1960 while CBS kept two on the audio airwaves—the mystery anthology *Suspense* and detective show *Yours Truly, Johnny Dollar*. After runs of 22 years (*Suspense*) and 13 years (*Johnny Dollar*), both shows aired their final installments on the same day: September 30, 1962.

THE LAST CATSKILLS RESORT

From the 1920s to the early 1960s, the Catskill Mountains in upstate New York (a three- or four-hour drive from Manhattan) was home to nearly 500 vacation resorts. Geared primarily toward Jewish families from New York City, hundreds of thousands of people would spend a weekend, a week, or even the entire summer staying in a cabin or bungalow, eating prepared meals in a dining hall, swimming, canoeing, and enjoying nightclub-style variety entertainment at night. As many as 150,000 people would summer in the Catskills, until the increased availability of lower-cost air travel opened up new vacation options for middle-class New Yorkers. All 500 resorts but one closed by the mid-1980s. The last one, Grossinger's Catskill Resort Hotel, closed at the end of the 1986 summer season.

THE LAST GUEST ON...

- *The Ed Sullivan Show* (1948–1971): Gladys Knight and the Pips
- *The Muppet Show* (1976–1981): Shirley Bassey
- *American Bandstand* (1952–1989): The Cover Girls
- *The Tonight Show Starring Johnny Carson* (1962–1992): Bette Midler
- *The Late Show with David Letterman* (1993–2015): Foo Fighters
- *Late Night with Conan O'Brien* (1993–2009): The White Stripes

European country that sleeps the most:
France, with the average person resting for 8.83 hours a day.

THE GREAT BATHTUB HOAX

While digging through a history book recently, Uncle John found a terrific story about the first bathtub in the United States. "Perfect for the Bathroom Reader," he thought. Then he did a little more research and discovered that this bathtub story didn't hold water.

"A NEGLECTED ANNIVERSARY"

December of 1917 was a bleak time for Americans—the U.S. had just entered World War I and thousands of American troops were being shipped to Europe; back home, more and more municipalities were banning alcohol in response to a growing national prohibition movement. A few days after Christmas, newspaper columnist H. L. Mencken, a commentator known for his critiques of democracy and religion, attempted to lighten the mood (and test how gullible people are) in an article called "A Neglected Anniversary" that ran in the *New York Evening Mail*. It began:

> On December 20 there flitted past us, absolutely without public notice, one of the most important profane anniversaries in American history, to wit, the seventy-fifth anniversary of the introduction of the bathtub into These States. Not a plumber fired a salute or hung out a flag. Not a governor proclaimed a day of prayer. Not a newspaper called attention to the day.

Mencken explained that the Public Health Service of Washington, DC, had been preparing for a 75th-anniversary celebration of the bathtub, but the event was canceled after DC outlawed alcohol on November 1. The 1,800-word article laid out in great detail the controversial history of the bathtub. Here are some of the highlights:

Made from mahogany and lined with lead, the bathtub was invented in 1828 by England's Lord John Russell. It was introduced to the U.S. in 1842 by a Cincinnati man named Adam Thompson. After doctors warned that bathtubs cause "rheumatic fevers, inflammation of the lungs, and the whole category of zymotic diseases," they were banned in Philadelphia and Boston. At the same time, populist politicians convinced lower-income voters that "undemocratic" bathtubs were a symbol of vanity, reserved for only the wealthy, and therefore should not be trusted. It was only in 1850, after President Millard Fillmore installed "a tub of thin cast iron, capable of floating the largest man" in the White House, that Americans began to warm up to the idea of a hot bath. By 1860, every hotel in New York had a tub. And soon after, the nation.

A TISSUE OF ABSURDITIES

It's a fascinating story, but none of it is true. If Mencken had thought the majority of his readers would laugh along with what he thought was an obvious fabrication, he was sorely mistaken. A few weeks later, the *Boston Herald* reprinted an abridged version of the article without mentioning (or possibly even knowing) that it was satire; that version of the article was then reprinted by dozens more papers across the country. After that, Mencken's fabrication started appearing in medical journals, and then in history and reference books.

In 1926, eight years after he wrote "A Forgotten Anniversary," Mencken came clean: "This article, I may say at once, was a tissue of absurdities, all of them deliberate and most of them obvious...Readers, it appeared, all took my idle jocosities with complete seriousness."

IT'S A FACT!

But it was too late. No matter how many times Mencken tried to set the record straight over the next 20 years, a lot of people flat-out refused to believe him (because they'd read somewhere that Millard Fillmore introduced the bathtub). Even after his confession, Mencken's own newspaper, *The Baltimore Evening Sun*, published it as fact on more than one occasion. In the late 1940s, President Harry Truman routinely told the faux Fillmore history when he gave tours of the White House—and continued to do so after he was informed the story was false. "Scarcely a month goes by," lamented Mencken in 1949, "that I do not find the substance of it reprinted, not as foolishness but as fact, and not only in newspapers but in official documents and other works of the highest pretensions."

It persists, even in the 21st century. A 2004 *Washington Post* article shared the Fillmore fact in its "Bet You Didn't Know That" column (and later retracted it). Fillmore's hometown of Moravia, New York, has been hosting annual bathtub races since 1975. The townsfolk all know—and don't seem to care—that Fillmore didn't install the first White House bathtub. So who did?

GREAT (TRUE) MOMENTS IN BATHTUB HISTORY

The Middle Ages: The poor bathe in bathhouses (if they bathe at all), while the wealthy do so at home in wooden tubs, lined with linen to protect from splinters.
1720: The first known European-style bathhouse in the New World is installed for Lord Dunmore at the Governor's Palace at Williamsburg, Virginia.
1810: The fourth president, James Madison, is the first president to bathe in the White House in a tub made of tin, painted green, and lined with canvas to protect his skin.
1881: The shiny, white bathtub is invented in Detroit by David Buick, who patents a method to coat cast iron with vitreous enamel. (In 1899, he'll start the Buick Motor Company.)

Mencken could have included some of those facts in his article (they were known in 1917), but the tale he told was far more interesting. So interesting that it hardly mattered that it was a lie. His takeaway: "The majority of men prefer delusion to truth. It soothes. It is easy to grasp."

GROANERS

Don't say we didn't warn you.

I swallowed a book of synonyms and got thesaurus throat I've ever had.

I shot a man with a paintball gun just to watch him dye.

I went bald, but I kept my comb. I just can't part with it.

I wrote a poem about a tortilla. Actually, it's more of a wrap.

I'm sorry, I can't share the Indian restaurant's bread recipe. I signed a naan disclosure agreement.

Q: Where do rainbows go when they break the law?
A: Prism, but it's usually a light sentence.

Q: How do you make antifreeze?
A: Steal her blanket.

In Athens, no one wakes up before noon. Dawn is tough on Greece.

Q: Why are the littlest beaches the warmest?
A: All the microwaves.

My girlfriend owns a Taser. She's stunning!

Q: Where do boats go when they get sick?
A: To the dock.

Doctor: I'm sorry to tell you, but you're color-blind.
Patient: Well, that came out of the green.

Patient: I had an accident while playing peekaboo.
Doctor: Quick, to the ICU!

Did you hear about the kitten that finished three bowls of milk in one minute? He set a new lap record.

Did you hear about the two elephants that got thrown off the beach? Only one pair of trunks.

My bakery burned down last night. My business is toast.

I had to reschedule my yoga lesson. Good thing the teacher is flexible.

I switched from eating venison to eating pheasant. Absolute game changer.

I took a pole and found out that 100 percent of people in the tent were angry when it collapsed.

I just don't get that towel's jokes. His sense of humor is so dry.

Jan: My boyfriend doesn't like fruit puns.
Jen: You gotta let that mango.

Should I marry the man who makes the pancakes, or the poet? I guess it's for batter or for verse.

Q: Why did it take so long for the construction worker to propose?
A: He was building up to it.

Some people believe babies come from storks, but that's a misconception.

I should really write a book about what I want to do with my life. It'll be my ought-to biography.

The Dog Star is moving closer to Earth every second. In a few million years, we could be in Sirius trouble.

My wife rotates playing her guitar, drum, or flute once a month. It's part of her minstrel cycle.

CARROTS!

Orange you glad we rooted around and found a few cool facts about carrots?

- The oldest fossilized carrot was found on the island of Madeira, off the coast of Portugal in the Atlantic Ocean, in 2019. Age: 1.3 million years. The earliest evidence of carrots being eaten as a foraged food: ancient carrot seeds that were discovered in Central Asia in the early 20th century. Archaeologists believe the seeds were used as a spice and the greens as medicine.

- Carrots are *taproots*, meaning they are the carrot plants' large, central roots, utilized primarily as water storage containers. Many familiar plants use this taproot strategy, including beets, parsnips, radishes, and turnips. And oak, elm, hickory, and pine trees.

- The earliest confirmed evidence of carrots being domesticated as a food source dates to the 10th century, when ancient farmers began cultivating carrots in what is today Iran and Afghanistan. These carrots were very different from the vegetables we know today—they were likely quite thin, and were probably white, pale yellow, or purple in color.

- Carrots are members of the *Apiaceae* family, making them close relatives of many common edible plants, including parsley, celery, caraway, anise, coriander, cumin, dill, fennel, and parsnip. Note: they are also closely related to hemlock, which is highly toxic—and very *unedible*.

- As carrots became more popular, they were carried by trade routes away from Central Asia, eventually making it to Europe in about the 12th century. Over the following centuries, carrots were selectively bred to make the taproots larger and easier to digest, and to develop breeds that grew to maturity more rapidly. At some point along the way, this selective breeding led to carrots that were more yellow, and with a sweeter flavor. These became the most popular type, and were spread throughout Europe, until around the 17th century, when the carrots we know today—bright orange—first came to be.

- Four hundred years later, orange remains the most common carrot color, though many other varieties are still grown today, including white, black, purple, and red ones. Some carrot varieties you may—or may not—be familiar with:

Nantes. Developed around the Atlantic coastal town of Nantes in western France in the late 1800s. Nantes carrots are bright orange, medium sized (6-8 inches), and cylindrical (meaning they keep their thickness throughout their length, ending with

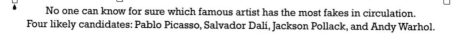

a blunt tip, rather than tapering to a point), with very smooth skins and a crisp, crunchy texture. There are a number of varieties of Nantes carrots, just as there are with all the varieties mentioned here. Some notables: *scarlet, bolero, white satin,* and *touchon*—a small, stout, juicy (and sweet) Nantes variety that you'll probably have to grow yourself, because they're very hard to find in stores.

Imperator. Imperator carrots are long (8–11 inches) with a deep orange color, and bodies that taper from their tops to a point at the bottom. They have thin skins that are easy to peel; they have a sweet, mild flavor; and they are very easy to cultivate. And they're especially easy to pick with machinery (due to their strong stems and leaves, which mechanical pickers latch onto in the picking process)—as a result, Imperator is the most common type found in North American grocery stores. Some cultivars: *atomic red, yellowbunch,* and *viper*—a very long (12–14 inches), skinny, bright orange carrot known for its crisp texture.

Danvers. Medium-sized carrots with skinny, tapered bodies, popular with gardeners because they are easy to grow, even in poor soil. The name of this carrot type comes from the town in which it was first developed—Danvers, Massachusetts—in the 1870s. Danvers varieties include the *half-long* (named for its short growing time), and the *Danvers 126*—first introduced in 1947 as a sweet-flavored, heat-tolerant carrot that grows well in clay-heavy soils.

Chantenay. Developed in the Chantenay region of France in the mid-1800s, they're stout, short, pointy carrots with light orange skin and red-orange cores. Varieties include *royal Chantenay, Hercules,* and *kuroda nova*—noted for its very high sugar content and tender texture, and considered one of the best carrots for making carrot juice.

Parisian carrot. Also known as the Paris market carrot, it's a popular type of *ball carrot*: unlike normal carrots, they grow in the shape of balls, about the size of large radishes. Tender and sweet, Parisian carrots are perfect for popping in your mouth and eating fresh. (But they're very good cooked, too.)

BONUS FACT: Wild carrots—known as the species *Daucus carota*—can still be found growing in many parts of the world today. They are a popular item among wild food foragers, although most recommend that these very fibrous carrots be used for flavoring in dishes like stews, and not actually eaten.

EXTRA FACT: Every domestic carrot grown and eaten around the world today is a descendant of a subspecies of *Daucus carota* that grew in the wilds of Central Asia millennia ago.

EXTRA BONUS PLUS: "Wild Carrot" is also the name of a popular band in the city of Cincinnati, Ohio. They play *roots* music.

IMPOSTOR SYNDROME

These confessions of self-doubt were really easy to find. We're not sure if that's comforting or troubling. Does ANYONE know what they're doing? (We sure don't.)

"I have written 11 books, but each time I think, 'uh oh, they're going to find out now. I've run a game on everybody, and they're going to find me out.'"
–Maya Angelou

"There are days when I know that 3 o'clock tomorrow afternoon I am going to have to deliver some degree of emotional goods, and if I can't do it, that means I'm going to have to fake it. If I fake it, that means they might catch me at faking it, and if they catch me at faking it, well, then it's just doomsday."
–Tom Hanks

"I still sometimes feel like a loser kid in high school and I just have to pick myself up and tell myself that I'm a superstar every morning so that I can get through this day."
–Lady Gaga

"Now when I receive recognition for my acting, I feel incredibly uncomfortable. I tend to turn in on myself. I feel like an imposter. Any moment, someone's going to find out I'm a total fraud, and that I don't deserve any of what I've achieved."
–Emma Watson

"I am not a writer. I've been fooling myself and other people."
–John Steinbeck

"I've been in the car when one of our songs has come on the radio and I've been the color of, as we say in Dublin, scarlet. I'm just so embarrassed."
–Bono

"I spent the first two weeks of *Ed Wood*, and *Scissorhands*, and in fact *Sleepy Hollow* thinking that I was going to be fired— that I was going to be replaced. Because, I just thought, 'There's no way I can get away with this. There's just no way.'"
–Johnny Depp

"Today, I feel much like I did when I came to Harvard Yard as a freshman in 1999. I felt like there had been some mistake, that I wasn't smart enough to be in this company, and that every time I opened my mouth I would have to prove that I wasn't just a dumb actress."
**–Natalie Portman,
giving a commencement speech**

"I went to a lot of events this year because of Deadpool, so you get into the tux and try and look like a grown-up. But to be honest, I still feel like a freckle-faced kid, faking it until I make it."
–Ryan Reynolds

"What's talent but the ability to get away with something?"
–Tennessee Williams

LEFT-HANDED FACTS

We considered doing a piece about left-handedness for several years, but the question always came up—are there enough left-handed bathroom readers to make it worthwhile? After six years, we decided it didn't matter—we just wanted to use the info. So here's a section for you southpaws.

A re you left-handed? If so, you're not alone—but you're definitely outnumbered; lefties make up only 5% to 15% of the general population. If you're a female southpaw, you're even more unusual—there are roughly 50% more left-handed males than females. For centuries, scientists have tried to figure out what makes people left- or right-handed, and they still aren't sure why. (They're not even sure if all lefties are that way for the same reason.) Here are some theories:

WHAT MAKES A LEFTY?

- Scientists used to think that left- and right-handedness was purely a genetic trait, but now they have doubts. Reason: In 20% of all sets of identical twins, one sibling is left-handed, and the other is right-handed.
- Some scientists think the hand you prefer is determined by whether you're a "right-brained" person or a "left-brained" person. The right half of the brain controls the left side of the body, as well as spatial / musical / aesthetic judgment and perception; the left half controls the right side of the body, plus communication skills. Lefties are generally right-brained.
- Support for this theory: Most children begin demonstrating a preference for one hand over the other at the same time their central nervous system is growing and maturing. This leads some scientists to believe the two processes are linked.
- According to another theory, before birth all babies are righthanded— which means that the left side of their brain is dominant. But during a stressful or difficult birth, oxygen deficiency can cause damage to the left side of the brain, making it weaker and enabling the right side to compete against it for dominance. If the right side wins out, the baby will become left-handed.
- This theory also explains, researchers claim, why twins, any child bom to a smoker, or children bom to a mother over 30 years old are

more likely to be left-handed: they are more prone to stressful births. Children of stressful births are also more likely to stammer and suffer dyslexia, traits that are more common in lefties.

LEFT-HANDED HISTORY

No matter what makes southpaws what they are, they've been discriminated against for thousands of years—in nearly every culture on Earth. Some examples:

- The artwork found in ancient Egyptian tombs portrays most Egyptians as right-handed. But their enemies are portrayed as lefthanders, a sign they saw left-handedness as an undesirable trait.

- Ancient Greeks never crossed their left leg over their right, and believed a person's sex was determined by their position in the womb—the female, or "lesser sex," sat on the left side of the womb.

- The Romans placed special significance on right-handedness as well. Custom dictated that they enter friends' homes "with the right foot forward".. .and turn their heads to the right to sneeze. Their language showed the same bias: the Latin word for left was sinister (which also meant evil, or ominous), and the word for right was dexter (which came to mean skillful, or adroit). Even the word ambidextrous literally means "right-handed with both hands."

LEFT-HANDED MISCELLANY

- Lefties are more likely to be on the extreme ends of the intelligence scale than the general population: a higher proportion of intellectually disabled people and people with IQs over 140 are lefties.

- Why are lefties called "southpaws"? In the late 1890s, most baseball parks were laid out with the pitcher facing west and the batter facing east (so the sun wouldn't be in his eyes). That meant lefthanded pitchers threw with the arm that faced south. So Chicago sportswriter Charles Seymour began calling them "southpaws."

- What did traditional Christians believe was going to happen on Judgment Day? According to custom, God blesses the saved with His right hand—and casts sinners out of Heaven with His left.

- Why do we throw salt over our left shoulders for good luck? To throw it into the eyes of the Devil, who, of course, lurks behind us to our left.

ZOO-LEBRITIES

Some of the most famous people to ever walk this world aren't people at all—they're animals who lived at zoos, who became the pride of their cities and subsequently became well-known all over the world.

PACKY

In April 1962 at the Portland Zoological Gardens (later renamed the Oregon Zoo), an Asian elephant named Belle gave birth to a 226-pound baby boy. For a few weeks of his life, he was called Fuzzy Face. But then a local radio station held a naming contest and the winning entry, which came from a suburban Portland teacher, was "Packy," short for *pachyderm*, another term for elephant. Because he was going to be the first elephant born in North America since the 1930s, Packy was famous even before his birth. And in his first year alone, more than a million people filed through the gates of the zoo to see him. He was, by far, the most visited animal at the Portland facility, which became the birthplace of more than two dozen calves in the following decades. The busiest day every year for more than 50 years: the day the zoo held a birthday party for Packy, presenting him with a birthday cake (made of veggies) and conducting a mass sing-along of "Happy Birthday to You." When Packy died in 2017 at age 54, he was the oldest male Asian elephant in North America.

Packy was famous even before his birth.

FIONA

When a hippopotamus named Fiona was born six weeks prematurely at the Cincinnati Zoo in January 2017, she weighed a light 29 pounds and required an oxygen tube—and she wasn't expected to survive. But she did, with hundreds of thousands of supporters watching her improve via social-media updates. Within months, Fiona was at a healthy weight (500 pounds), and soon became the most popular attraction at the Cincinnati Zoo. Fiona made news again in October 2017, after Nick Kelble proposed to Hayley Roll in front of Fiona's tank. An amazing photo of the baby hippo pressed up against the glass, watching the romantic moment, was posted on Instagram. It went viral. More accolades: two Cincinnati companies, Listermann Brewing and Graeter's Ice Cream, have Fiona-inspired flavors—Team Fiona IPA and Chunky Chunky Hippo.

KNUT

Tosca, a polar bear rescued from an East German circus by the Berlin Zoo, gave birth to two cubs in December 2006. For reasons zookeepers could never ascertain, Tosca rejected her babies and abandoned them on a rock in her enclosure. One of them

The babies of some turtle species "talk" to each other from inside their eggs before they hatch. This helps them all to hatch at the same time.

died of an infection days later; the other, Knut, became the first polar bear to survive to adulthood at the Berlin Zoo since the early 1970s. Undersized—weighing about the same as a guinea pig—Knut was stuck in an incubator for more than 40 days. Then zookeeper Thomas Dörflein gave the bear constant care, sleeping next to him in his crate at night, and bottle-feeding him a mixture of baby formula and cod liver oil (until he graduated to milk and cat food). Knut would appear briefly in the daily polar bear shows at the Berlin Zoo, and became famous around Germany as the media tracked his growth and his continually-improving health. It spawned a phenomenon labeled "Knutmania," inspiring Knut books, Knut toys, and Knut T-shirts, making Knut the most profitable and merchandisable animal ever at the Berlin Zoo. Sadly, four-year-old Knut died suddenly in 2011, of a seizure caused by encephalitis.

E.T.

While working off the coast of Alaska in 1982, oil rig workers found an orphaned young walrus. Because he was brown and looked kind of like the star of the blockbuster hit of the year, *E.T. the Extra-Terrestrial*, that's what they named him. The closest major zoo with aquarium facilities, the Point Defiance Zoo and Aquarium in Tacoma, Washington, agreed to adopt and care for E.T., and because he had a huge personality, he became very popular as an attraction and star of a daily show. E.T. loved to interact with zookeepers and he seemed to be able to carry on conversations, grunting, braying, whistling, and even learning how to imitate the sound of a bell. By 2015, E.T. was almost 40 years old, elderly for a walrus. Experiencing several health problems, he didn't survive surgery on his voice box. But E.T. remains at the Point Defiance Aquarium in a way—there's a life-size bronze sculpture of the walrus at the facility's entrance.

COOKIE

Chicago's Brookfield Zoo opened its gates in 1934, and one of the animals awaiting visitors on day one was a Major Mitchell's cockatoo named Cookie. Imported from Australia, Cookie was believed to be about a year old at the time. He lived in the keepers' offices near the Bird House as more of a pet than a caged animal, but appeared in daily shows at the zoo for decades, wowing guests with his chatty personality and impressive plumage—white feathers with pink ones on the neck, and a rust crest atop his head. Every year, the Brookfield Zoo held a well-attended birthday party for Cookie, who became one of the most famous and long-lived zoo animals in the United States. In 2014, *Guinness World Records* certified Cookie as the oldest living parrot, and at 80 years (or possibly more), he was one of the oldest living birds in recorded history. By the time Cookie died in 2016 at age 83, euthanized after a rapid decline in health, he was the last animal remaining from Brookfield's opening day.

Count 'em: Bald eagles have about 7,000 feathers.

THE SPINSTER PRIZE

Marriage is a basic part of civilization. It crosses all cultures and all periods of human history. But it's not for everyone. As actress Mae West once said, "Marriage is an institution, but who would want to live in an institution." More than a century ago, a British magazine asked single women to tell why they were unmarried. We found their answers fascinating.

STILL SINGLE

Tit-Bits was a British weekly magazine that was published for more than a century, from 1881 until 1984. Its specialty was, as the name suggests, providing readers with entertaining tidbits of information on a wide variety of subjects, printed in an easy-to-read format. (Sounds familiar...though no word on whether people read it in the bathroom.)

It also invited readers to write in and share their opinions on various topics. In 1889, for example, it asked unmarried female readers to write in and explain why they were spinsters, or unmarried. The term *spinster* dates back to the days when single women supported themselves by spinning yarn, mending clothes, and doing other low-paying jobs, and the stereotype was that such women were "childless, prissy, and repressed." The magazine offered a prize for the best entry: 5 shillings, or about $25 today. The editors received so many good entries that rather than print only one, they printed an entire pageful and awarded the 5 shillings to each entrant featured. Here are some of our favorite responses:

> "Because I have other professions open to me in which the hours are shorter, the work more agreeable, and the pay possibly better."
>
> *–Miss Florence Watts, 29 High Street, Fulham*

....

> "My reason for being a spinster is answered in a quotation from the 'Taming of the Shrew': 'Of all the men alive I never yet beheld that special face which I could fancy more than any other.'"
>
> *–Miss Lizzie Moore, 12 Foulser Road, Upper Tooting*

....

> "Because I am an English lady, and the Americans monopolize the market."
>
> *–Miss Jessie Davies, 16 Claremont Road, Birmingham*

What's a *zugzwang*? It's a chess term for a situation in which any move you make will make your situation worse.

"John, whom I loved, was supplanted in his office by a girl, who is doing the same amount of work he did for half the salary he received. He could not earn sufficient to keep a home, so went abroad; consequently, I am still a spinster."

—Miss E. Jones, 32 St. Peter's Street, Mile End, London

....

"Like the wild mustang of the prairie that roams unfettered, tossing his head in utter disdain at the approach of the lasso which, if once round his neck, proclaims him captive, so I find it more delightful to tread on the verge of freedom and captivity, than to allow the snarer to cast around me the matrimonial lasso."

—Miss Sarah Kennerly, Newton Road, Ashton-on-Ribble

....

"Because matrimony is like an electric battery, when you once join hands you can't let go, however much it hurts; and, as when embarked on a toboggan slide, you must to the bitter end, however much it bumps."

—Miss Laura Bax, 29 Pelham Road, Wood Green, London

....

"Because (like a piece of rare china) I am breakable and mendable, but difficult to match."

—Miss S. A. Roberts, The Poplars, Ocker Hill, Stafford

....

"Because men, like three-cornered tarts, are deceitful. They are very pleasing to the eye, but on closer acquaintanceship prove hollow and stale, consisting chiefly of puff, with a minimum of sweetness, and an unconquerable propensity to disagree with one."

—Miss Emaline Lawrence, Abbey Gardens, St. John's Wood

....

"Because I am like the Rifle Volunteers: always ready, but not yet wanted."

—Miss Annie Thompson, No 2A, Belmont Street

....

"Because I do not care to enlarge my menagerie of pets, and I find the animal man less docile than a dog, less affectionate than a cat, and less amusing than a monkey."

—Miss Sparrow, 9 Manor Place, Paddington W.

**World's biggest individual seller of chocolate:
the Brussels Airport in Belgium (it sells 800 tons per year).**

UNREAD, UNPUBLISHED, UNSEEN

Uncle John can tell you firsthand that writing a book takes a lot of time and a lot of work, which is why we found it mind-boggling that these famous authors put countless hours into writing these works...and then abandoned them.

Author: Harper Lee

Book: *The Long Goodbye*

Details: Lee published her first novel in 1960—the Pulitzer Prize–winning, Deep South–set best seller *To Kill a Mockingbird*. A few years later, millions of readers (and her publisher) were ready for a follow-up, and she reportedly nearly completed a new novel called *The Long Goodbye*. Lee wouldn't share many details about it, except to say that it was set in a small town in Alabama. She subsequently abandoned that book, but in the mid-1980s, she drew on similar themes for another attempted novel, about a murderous Alabama minister. Lee abandoned that one, too, and published only one more book before she died: *Go Set a Watchman*, a first draft/sequel to *To Kill a Mockingbird*, in 2015.

Author: John Steinbeck

Book: *Murder at Full Moon*

Details: Steinbeck was awarded the 1962 Nobel Prize in Literature, primarily for his works about American life during the Great Depression, such as *Of Mice and Men* and *The Grapes of Wrath*. But in 1930, when he'd published only one book (the novel *Cup of Gold*), Steinbeck wrote *Murder at Full Moon*, a murder mystery set in a fictional California coastal town, where a string of brutal killings is believed to be the work of a werewolf. Steinbeck never published the work, and in his will (he died in 1968), he instructed his heirs to prevent the supernatural horror tale from ever being printed.

> **DID YOU KNOW?**
>
> Only two authors have declined the Nobel Prize for Literature. In 1958, Soviet authorities forced Russian author Boris Pasternak (author of *Dr. Zhivago*) to turn down the award, and in 1964, existentialist Jean-Paul Sartre said "No," concerned that accepting the prize would diminish the impact of his work.

Author: Stephen King

Book: *The House on Value Street*

Details: Not only one of the top-selling American novelists of all time, King is also very prolific, with 63 novels (so far) since the 1970s. Among his best known works: *Christine*, *Cujo*, *Misery*, *The Dark Tower*, and *The Stand*. He got the idea for *The Stand*,

The hooded nudibranch is a type of sea slug that smells like watermelon.

a 1,200-page epic about a worldwide plague and the battle of good versus evil that develops in its wake, in 1974, while working on another novel—*The House on Value Street*. *House* is loosely based on the kidnapping of newspaper heiress Patricia Hearst, and how she was brainwashed by her captors into participating in a bank robbery and then evading authorities for months. King got so wrapped up in *The Stand* that he lost interest in *The House on Value Street* and never picked it up again.

Author: Herman Melville

Book: *The Isle of the Cross*

Details: *Moby Dick* (1851) is widely regarded as one of the best American novels of the 19th century, but it was a commercial bomb, as was Melville's next book *Pierre; or, The Ambiguities*, published in 1852. Melville believed his fortunes would change with his next work, *The Isle of the Cross*. During a trip to Nantucket, Massachusetts, Melville had heard a story about Agatha Hatch, daughter of a local lighthouse operator who married a sailor and bore his child, only to have the man leave her and then return 17 years later. Melville thought the story was so compelling that he expanded it into a novel, but his publisher, Harper's, turned it down, on the grounds that the Hatch family would sue. The manuscript was destroyed.

Author: Karl Marx

Book: *Scorpion and Felix*

Details: The writings of philosopher Karl Marx, particularly *The Communist Manifesto* (1848) and *Das Kapital* (1867–83), became the basis for the brand of Communism that would lead to the Russian Revolution and the formation of the Soviet Union. But Marx wrote more than just political polemics. In 1837, at the age of 19, he composed *Scorpion and Felix*, a comedic novel about three bumbling idiots trying to figure out their family origins. It was never published and most of it was destroyed, with only a few disjointed chapters surviving.

Author: Michael Chabon

Book: *Fountain City*

Details: In 2001, Chabon won the Pulitzer Prize for his novel *The Amazing Adventures of Kavalier & Clay*, about two teenage cousins who create comic books in the mid-20th century. His other most famous book: *Wonder Boys*, which is about Pittsburgh academic and novelist Grady Tripp struggling to finish his long-awaited next work, which has become a sprawling, unmanageable 2,611-page monster that he ultimately abandons. Chabon loosely based *Wonder Boys* on himself. Like Grady Tripp, Chabon was a Pittsburgh-based academic and he also wrote an epic novel (1,500 pages), entitled *Fountain City*. Chabon published the first four chapters of *Fountain City* in a magazine and threw away the rest.

Hair you go: Foxes have whiskers on their face and on their legs.
(The leg whiskers help them navigate.)

THE PROVERBIAL TRUTH

You know that "a watched pot never boils," but there are countless other proverbs that you've probably never heard. Here are some of BRI's favorites from around the world.

There seldom
is a single wave.
—Icelandic

The bigger a man's
head, the worse his
headache.
—Persian

A half-truth
is a whole lie.
—Yiddish

Not knowing is not
shameful, not asking is.
—Turkish

Trusting men is like
trusting water in a sieve.
—Egyptian

An army of sheep
led by a lion would
defeat an army of lions
led by a sheep.
—Arabic

If you chase two hares at
the same time, you will
catch neither of them.
—Ukrainian

Let not your own hands
contribute to your
destruction.
—The Koran

Honey on the tongue;
ice in the heart.
—Slovenian

A wise man adapts
himself to circumstances
as water shapes itself
to the vessel that
contains it.
—Chinese

You do not really
know your friends
from your enemies until
the ice breaks.
—Icelandic

Lock your door and
keep your neighbor
honest.
—Chinese

He who holds the
ladder is as bad as the
thief.
—German

"O, sheep, if I do not
eat you, you will eat
me," said the hyena.
—Ethiopian

When you are rich, you
are hated; when you are
poor, you are despised.
—Ghanaian

Who gossips to you will
gossip of you.
—Turkish

It is better to be a
coward for a minute
than dead the rest of
your life.
—Irish

Whoever saves a life,
it is considered as if he
saved an entire world.
—The Talmud

Beware of the man of
one book.
—Latin

Two make an army
against one.
—Icelandic

Wait until nightfall
before saying it has been
a good day.
—French

If your beard's on fire,
others will light their
pipes on it.
—Turkish

When a thief kisses
you, count your teeth.
—Yiddish

After he hit it big with "Ice Ice Baby," rapper Vanilla Ice
became a professional jet ski racer and was ranked #6 in the world.

HARRY POTTER AND THE LAWYER WHO WENT ROGUE

Here's a weird story about a folk singer, a lawyer, a fictional band, and some rock stars. The backdrop: the second-highest grossing movie of 2005.

WYRD OF THE DAY

"The Weird Sisters [are] all extremely hairy and dressed in black robes that had been artfully ripped and torn." That's how J. K. Rowling describes the all-male rock band that plays at a school dance in *Harry Potter and the Goblet of Fire* (2000), the fourth book in her best-selling series. Rowling took the band's name from William Shakespeare's Three Weird Sisters, the prophetic witches in *Macbeth* (1606) who whip up "double, double toil and trouble." Variously referred to as the Fates, the Weird Sisters, and the Wyrd Sisters, Shakespeare's witches have appeared in dozens of books and movies. A handful of musical groups have also gone by that name. This particular tale is about one of them—a folk act from Winnipeg, Manitoba, called the Wyrd Sisters.

INTELLECTUAL PROPERTY

In late summer 2005, while the film version of *Harry Potter and the Goblet of Fire* was in postproduction ahead of a highly anticipated Thanksgiving release, the Warner Bros. legal team sent a letter to the Wyrd Sisters requesting permission to use the name "Weird Sisters" in the movie. The studio offered $5,000 in return. Singer-songwriter Kim Baryluk said no. As the band's founder and owner of the Canadian trademark for "Wyrd Sisters," Baryluk had spent 15 years—and about a million dollars, she said—recording albums, touring, and building a regional fan base. Her all-female band had been nominated for three JUNO Awards (Canada's equivalent to the Grammys), and she felt they were on the cusp of hitting the big time.

Warner Bros. upped their offer to $50,000. Baryluk's answer was still no. Unsure how to proceed, she was referred to a Toronto-based copyright lawyer named Kimberly Townley-Smith, who lived more than 1,200 miles away. Townley-Smith agreed to take the case and promptly filed a $40-million lawsuit against Warner Bros (in Baryluk's name) demanding that *Goblet of Fire* be halted from release in Canada if the name "Weird Sisters" appeared in the movie. "The problem is, [Kim] was first. She has the right to use [the name]," Townley-Smith told CBC News. "She's the Wyrd Sisters; and now, when she goes out, people are going to think...who is this person ripping off Harry Potter?"

LAWSUIT EXPELLIARMUS!

With the lawsuit making headlines, the Warner Bros. legal team decided to play it

Former Soviet Union leader Mikhail Gorbachev recorded an album of romantic songs in 2009. Called *Songs to Raisa,...*

safe and just cut the name "Weird Sisters" from *Goblet of Fire* altogether. The studio even flew an executive to Toronto to show Townley-Smith that there were no visual or spoken mentions in the final cut. Even so, the lawyer refused to drop her case.

On November 4, a Toronto judge denied Townley-Smith's motion to halt the film and dismissed her "highly intrusive" lawsuit. And that's where most stories like this usually end. Goliath had squashed David, leaving the filmmakers free to re-add the band's name. But Townley-Smith wouldn't be squashed. She threatened to appeal, pointing out that her client still owned the Canadian trademark. With the North American release only weeks away, Warner Bros. decided that restoring "Weird Sisters" wasn't worth the risk.

INTO THE CAULDRON

> "The whole story is just a couple of people in a band trying to get some money."

This decision riled a lot of people. Reason: the filmmakers had cast a musical supergroup to perform in the movie as the Weird Sisters, including Pulp lead singer Jarvis Cocker and Radiohead members Jonny Greenwood and Phil Selway. There were even plans for a Weird Sisters album and a tour that would include Franz Ferdinand, Jack White, and Iggy Pop. Those plans were scrapped—not just because "Weird Sisters" had been deleted from the movie, but because of the threat of litigation: the Wyrd Sisters lawsuit had specifically named Cocker, Greenwood, and Selway as defendants.

Losing the band's name angered "Potterheads" too, who obsessed over every detail of the books and movies. "The debacle created so much tension," wrote a Harry Potter news site after the London premiere, "that Cocker was escorted down the red carpet to avoid reporters' questions on the subject." An unnamed member of Radiohead's management told the press, "The Wyrd Sisters are just trying to sue them for namesake. The whole story is just a couple of people in a band trying to get some money."

As for Baryluk, she let her lawyer do most of the talking in public, but she did tell an interviewer: "I've been getting hate mail, death threats. It's insane. This is not good publicity."

THE LAWSUIT THAT LIVED

On Friday, November 18, 2005, *Harry Potter and the Goblet of Fire* opened in the U.S. and Canada and made more than $100 million that weekend, the highest non-May opening ever. True to Townley-Smith's word, in 2006, she refiled her $40-million lawsuit and included a demand for "the destruction of DVDs, compact discs, video games, and other paraphernalia that contain references to a musical act named The Weird Sisters." Ontario Superior Court Justice Colin Campbell denied the appeal—pointing out that the name had already been omitted. He then ordered the Wyrd Sisters to cover Warner Bros. legal costs, totaling $140,000. (In similar cases of dismissal, the plaintiffs usually don't have to pay retribution.)

...it was named in honor of his wife. (The proceeds went to charity.)

Townley-Smith managed to keep the lawsuit going for five *more* years. In 2010, news outlets reported that it had been settled out of court. The details were sealed.

CHAMBER OF SECRETS

In 2010, an exposé in *Maclean's* magazine revealed that there was more going on behind the scenes than previously reported. The real battle wasn't between a folk group and a movie studio, but between a lawyer and her client...and some judges. "Townley-Smith went rogue," Baryluk told *Maclean's*. She accused her now ex-lawyer of filing motions and appeals without consulting her. She said she didn't even know about the motion to destroy any DVD, compact disc, video game, and other paraphernalia until she saw it in a 2008 news story.

Baryluk was also unaware that in addition to Warner Bros., Townley-Smith had sued two judges in her name (including Justice Campbell) for $21 million each, charging "case fixing, abuse of public office, and fraud." That explains that $140,000 in punitive damages Campbell leveled against the Wyrd Sisters. Baryluk also told *Maclean's* that when she tried to fire Townley-Smith, the lawyer threatened to demand immediate payment-in-full of all her legal fees. "She kept me at financial gunpoint," Baryluk said.

Townley-Smith denied the claims: "At every juncture, Ms. Baryluk chose to go on."

Baryluk did hire a new lawyer (in 2008) and then sued her former lawyer for negligence and breach of contract. Townley-Smith filed a countersuit against Baryluk for $20 million. A judge dismissed the countersuit, calling Townley-Smith's litigation tactics "threatening, contemptuous, abusive, and largely without substance." In 2012, Townley-Smith was disbarred. (The fact that six years had elapsed from the first complaint to disbarment prompted calls for legal reform in Canada.)

MISCHIEF MANAGED

In 2018, Townley-Smith posted an article on the online publishing platform Medium about a new business venture in adult education. And although she didn't mention the Potter case, she did shed a bit more light on how she felt about being an attorney: "I began looking into leaving law pretty much as soon as I began. (Hey, law school was interesting, but this practice crap? Why didn't anyone warn me that this is what I would be doing?)"

As for Baryluk, she says the case left her in "financial ruin." As of this writing, the Wyrd Sisters' website is still active, but there hasn't been any activity for years.

To this day, if you look up the lawsuit online, you couldn't be faulted for thinking that Baryluk was the one stirring the pot the entire time. But she insists that she never wanted to halt the movie or sue for $40 million; in fact, she later said that she would've been content with a line in the credits that read, "The real Wyrd Sisters band lives in Canada." Instead, her quest to protect the Wyrd Sisters' name left her with nothing but the name.

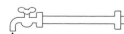

Do you have *geomelophagia*? It's the compulsion to eat raw potatoes.

THE WORLD WAR I EFFECT

The Great War, retroactively referred to as World War I after the 1940s, was a relentless onslaught of death and devastation across Europe from 1914 to 1918. That four-year period, and all the fighting that took place, also accelerated certain industries and trends. Here are some things that became a common, pleasant part of everyday life that grew out of World War I.

CHOCOLATE BARS

The chocolate bar, as a commercial product, began life in the United Kingdom in 1847, when Bristol candymaker Joseph Fry introduced it. Two other British candymakers, Cadbury and Rowntree's, popularized the treat by the late 19th century. During World War I, the mayor of York, England, where Rowntree's was based, sent tins of chocolates to frontline troops, as a morale booster. The U.S. Army Quartermaster Corps thought it was a nice gesture, and got several American candy companies to donate giant blocks of chocolate, which were then cut into individual portions, wrapped by hand, and packed into ration kits. When the troops returned home after the war, they brought back a taste for chocolate bars. By the end of the 1920s, the American chocolate bar market exploded, with 40,000 different bars being manufactured in the United States over the course of the decade.

CIGARETTES

At the outset of the 20th century, tobacco use was common in the United States, but the method of consumption was strongly tied to race and social status. "Respectable" people favored cigars or pipes, while cigarettes, popular in Europe for decades, were associated with the large numbers of recently arrived immigrants. But cigarettes were cheap and portable, and in 1917, the tobacco industry successfully lobbied Congress to make a huge purchase and begin including cigarettes in the ration kits of American soldiers fighting in World War I in Europe. They argued that smoking provided a bit of comfort and pleasure in an otherwise unpleasant situation, and that cigarettes might also help prevent troops from engaging in worse forms of recreation. Result: when soldiers returned home, they were literally hooked on cigarettes. By 1920, cigarettes had grown from 7 percent of the tobacco market to 20 percent.

BLOOD TRANSFUSIONS

In the late 1800s and early 1900s, transferring blood from a healthy person to a desperately needy or dying patient was done only in controlled medical settings, and only directly from the donor to the patient. Transfusions weren't possible on a large scale until the development of refrigeration, which meant donated blood could be stored and transported to, say, World War I field hospitals. The world's first blood bank was established by the British Army, working with U.S. Army doctor Oswald Robertson, on a World War I battlefield in western Europe. Robertson could safely store blood for as long as 28 days by keeping it on ice and adding sodium citrate as a preservative and anticlotting agent. Because he could keep blood on hand for wounded soldiers, countless lives were saved. Robertson's technology made blood transfusions a standard medical procedure after the end of the war.

WRISTWATCHES

Before World War I, wristwatches were made and marketed almost exclusively to women; men carried pocket watches. But those timepieces were wildly impractical for combat—a soldier who was holding his rifle with both hands could not glance at his pocket watch. American troops began to imitate British Army troops, who'd started using wristwatches during the Boer War in the late 19th century. Soldiers could now check the time with a flick of the wrist, and pilots could use them too, because in those days, flying a plane required two hands at all times. When American soldiers came home in 1918, wristwatches were no longer seen as feminine, but rather as a symbol of macho pride—a subtle fashion choice that sent the message that the man wearing it was a war veteran.

SANITARY PADS

In 1914, engineers with the Kimberly-Clark paper goods company developed a cotton-like material made from wood pulp that was five times as absorbent as cotton, but cost half as much to produce. With cotton scarce during World War I, the U.S. military contracted with Kimberly-Clark to supply surgical dressings made from this new material, which the company called "Cellucotton." It worked great for dressing and wrapping wounds, but the Red Cross nurses working in those facilities discovered that Cellucotton also made an excellent replacement for sanitary pads, hard to find due to the wartime cotton shortage. After World War I ended, Kimberly-Clark bought back the military's surplus of Cellucotton and formalized what nurses had used it for, marketing a product made from 40 individual sheets of the paper as Kotex (short for "cotton-like texture") sanitary pads.

* * *

"Ben Franklin may have discovered electricity, but it's the man who invented the meter who made the money."
—**Earl Warren**

Record for most words in a hit single: Eminem's "Rap God" (2013), with 1,560.

WHO IS BLACK WIDOW?

Whether or not you're a fan of comic book movies, when you hear the name Black Widow, you probably think of Scarlett Johansson. But she wasn't the director's first choice, and if it had been someone else, the face of Marvel's cinematic universe would be very different.

TO BE BLUNT

In 2006, British actress Emily Blunt got her big Hollywood break, appearing as Meryl Streep's assistant in *The Devil Wears Prada*. One of the many filmmakers who wanted her as their next leading lady was Jon Favreau. He hit it really big with 2008's *Iron Man*, which relaunched Robert Downey Jr.'s career *and* the Avengers film franchise. For the sequel, Favreau planned to introduce Black Widow, a redheaded Russian superspy named Natasha Romanoff who first appeared in the comic books in 1964. Favreau and screenwriter Justin Theroux tailored the role for Blunt; she wouldn't even have to audition.

Blunt wasn't much of a comic book fan, but she *was* a Robert Downey Jr. fan, so she accepted the offer and began negotiations. One big problem: Blunt's *Prada* contract, which she'd signed three years earlier, included an "optional picture deal" that obligated her to appear in any movie that 20th Century Fox chose for her. And they wanted her for their big-budget Jack Black comedy, *Gulliver's Travels*. Scheduling conflicts can often be worked around, but Marvel Studios gave Favreau less than two years to make *Iron Man 2*, and he needed Blunt to start right away. "I didn't want to do *Gulliver's Travels*," she told talk-show host Howard Stern in 2021, but Fox was pressuring her to do it.

SCAR JO

With Blunt on the fence, Marvel brought in a who's who of leading ladies to read for Black Widow—including Jessica Biel, Gemma Arterton, Natalie Portman, Jessica Alba, Angelina Jolie, and Scarlett Johansson, who wanted to play Black Widow so much that she dyed her hair red for the screen test. But Johansson didn't get it. Knowing the role was still Blunt's to turn down, the *Lost in Translation* actress kept her foot in the door by telling Favreau, "If this doesn't work out, I'm an actor for hire, so call me anytime."

A few weeks later, when it became obvious that Blunt couldn't get out of *Gulliver's*, the Black Widow role was offered to Johansson. "The best call you can receive is after you are rejected for something and then you get it," she told *Parade* magazine. "You appreciate it more."

EPILOGUE

Iron Man 2 was a critical flop; the filmmakers later admitted to focusing more on introducing new characters than telling a good story. And Johansson complained that Black Widow was "sexualized" and "treated like a piece of meat" in that first appearance. But over time she and the writers were able to give the character more depth. In all, Johansson appeared in nine Marvel movies in eleven years, culminating in 2021's standalone *Black Widow*, which she announced would be her last.

As for Blunt, she followed up the poorly received *Gulliver's Travels* with the well-received sci-fi action film *Edge of Tomorrow*. Ironically, if Blunt had been able to take the Black Widow role and become an Avenger, she wouldn't have been available for standout roles in films like *The Young Victoria*, *The Girl on the Train*, and *Mary Poppins Returns*.

In that 2021 interview, Stern teased Blunt about rumors that she and husband John Krasinski (who starred together in the horror franchise *A Quiet Place*) would be costarring in yet another Marvel reboot of *The Fantastic Four*. Resisting Stern's bait that she's "too good an actor" for a comic book movie, Blunt said that "superheroes are just not for me," and that the entire genre is "exhausted."

PIE-EYED!

The world's largest invertebrate, the colossal squid (*Mesonychoteuthis hamiltoni*), also has the biggest eyes, with a diameter of up to 16 inches, the same size as a large pizza.

16"

THERE'S A MUSEUM FOR THAT!

Museums—they're not just paintings and historical artifacts anymore.

PEZ: The PEZ Visitor Center (Orange, Connecticut)

Details: Crammed into this 4,000-square-foot space is the world's largest publicly viewable collection of PEZ dispensers—those toys that dispense bricks of fruit-flavored candy from of the neck of a pop culture character. Thousands of items are on display, including most of the 1,500 dispensers or so produced since the 1960s—along with a PEZ-themed motorcycle, the world's largest PEZ dispenser, vintage PEZ posters, and discontinued and obscure flavors to sample.

Be Sure to See... The PEZ production facility next door. It's closed to tours, but museum guests can peek through a window to see how PEZ candy is made.

BAKED BEANS: The Baked Bean Museum of Excellence (Port Talbot, Wales)

Details: Until 1986, Barry Kirk worked for British Petroleum. Then the Welsh native made it into Guinness World Records for sitting in a bathtub full of canned baked beans—naked—for 100 hours. At that point, Kirk legally changed his name to Captain Beany and now he's a minor celebrity in the UK, dressing up like a superhero and performing stunts, most of them baked bean related, to raise money for charities.

> He sat, naked, in a bathtub full of baked beans for 100 hours.

In 2009, he turned his third-floor, two-bedroom apartment into the Baked Bean Museum of Excellence. On display are baked bean cans from various brands, old and contemporary advertisements, promotional merchandise, and some wearables, including a pair of cuff links designed to look like pots of baked beans.

Be Sure to See... Captain Beany baked bean–themed bathroom and his kitchen, which is devoted to honoring the UK's baked bean industry leader, Heinz.

MATCHBOX LABELS: The Tumanyan Matchbox Label Museum (Tumanyan, Armenia)

Details: It's a tiny museum—one small room—in a tiny town, devoted to the study and preservation of a tiny thing: the labels affixed to boxes of matches in the early 20th century. Matchbox label collecting was a common hobby in the Soviet Union—the items were easily obtainable and inexpensive, and match companies would print extras solely for *phillumenists* (matchbox label collectors). The Matchbox Label Museum has over 10,000 labels on display, mostly from Soviet brands, along with representatives of matchboxes made in India, Japan, and Australia. The labels

Average cost of a room in New York's Plaza Hotel when it opened in 1907: $2.50 per night. In 2022: $640.

are arranged by theme, including PSAs, national flags, coats of arms, space images, regional costumes, traffic signs, aircraft, children's artwork, wine classes, and puzzles.
Be Sure to See... The series of 28 labels showing the 28 faces in a set of dominoes.

MARZIPAN: The Niederegger Marzipan Museum (Lübeck, Germany)
Details: Marzipan is a sweet combination of ground almonds, sugar, honey (or corn syrup), and egg whites that is used in candy and baked goods. The Marzipan museum is situated above a marzipan-themed cafe in the German town of Lübeck (owned by almond paste manufacturer Niederegger). Wall panels give a full timeline of marzipan's history, from when it was invented in the Middle East in the 1800s up to the present day.
Be Sure to See... The 12 life-size statues of historical figures, all made out of marzipan. There's German author Thomas Mann (who wrote about Lübeck in *Buddenbrooks*) and Holy Roman Emperor Charles IV, who once declared the city one of the empire's "Five Glories." (Can't make it to Lübeck? There's another marzipan museum in Szentendre, Hungary, and they have a life-size marzipan statue of Michael Jackson.)

DENTAL TOOLS: The Sindecuse Museum Of Dentistry (Ann Arbor, Michigan)
Details: In 1991, Gordon H. Sindecuse, a retired dentist who trained at the University of Michigan's School of Dentistry, bequeathed a fortune to the institution to open a museum devoted to American tooth care, from the early 1800s to the mid-20th century. Visitors can witness the evolution of dentistry tools from what look like steel torture devices into modern medical devices. Among the oddities: foot-powered tooth drills, dangerously unsafe early X-ray machines, and smithing tools used to carve artificial teeth out of gold.
Be Sure to See... In addition to 13 displays on dentistry and dentistry tools, there's a shrine to Apollonia, the patron saint of dentists and dentistry.

PSYCHEDELICS: The Institute of Illegal Images (San Francisco, California)
Details: Mark McCloud converted his Victorian-style row house into a slyly named museum celebrating the history of lysergic acid diethylamide, aka LSD, the mind-bending psychedelic drug made famous by the hippie counterculture movement in the 1960s (and inspired a lot of the era's music). The drug was surreptitiously distributed after it was soaked into small, postage-stamp-sized pieces of paper—called "tabs"—many bearing illustrations of cartoon characters (Snoopy, Felix the Cat, the Mad Hatter from *Alice in Wonderland*), religious symbols, occult images, political messages, animals, and psychedelic art. McCloud has 30,000 tabs of LSD in his museum. Why haven't the police shut it down? LSD is still illegal, but the drug-laced papers are all so old that they're no longer viable.
Be Sure to See... Soviet-era LSD tabs bearing the image of Communist Party General Secretary Mikhail Gorbachev.

Benjamin Franklin invented the "pros and cons" list.

AXE-IDENTS

An axe, like its smaller cousin, the hatchet, is a sharp and dangerous tool, and it should be handled with care. The people in the following stories must have known that...but apparently didn't believe it.

A BAD AXE AT BAD AXE

Common sense would suggest that combining axe throwing with alcohol is a terrible idea, but facilities where patrons can throw axes at a wall (like a more dangerous version of darts) and drink beer became very popular in the U.S. in the late 2010s. In 2019, Ainsley Rae went to such a place in Denver, called Bad Axe Throwing. She stepped up to throw an axe at a target, but instead of hitting the target, it bounced off the wall and ricocheted all the way back to her. She had to duck and run to avoid getting sliced in the head. (Most axe bars have an "impact board" that absorbs the throws and prevents bouncing; this one didn't.) A video of the moment (uploaded to the internet by Rae's boyfriend) went viral. "At first, I didn't know what actually happened but then over time, watching it over and over again, I just started laughing at myself," Rae told *Inside Edition*. "I am so glad I didn't get hit in the head."

THIS ONE IS FOR THE FANS

At an agricultural fair in Christchurch, New Zealand, in 2011, Timbersports competitors put on a show for spectators. (Timbersports is a woodcutting competition involving axes or chain saws.) In one event, contestants had to cut a notch into the side of a wooden pole, jam a short wooden board into the notch, climb up onto the board, and then repeat the whole process, in a race to reach the top. During the contest, the blade came loose from contestant Gordon Smith's axe and flew into the crowd. It struck a 50-year-old man (unnamed in news reports) at the intersection of his leg and groin. He was taken to the nearest hospital for emergency surgery. All other Timbersports events were canceled for the rest of the day. Smith was devastated. "We're all feeling pretty numb," he said.

CUT FROM THE BROADCAST

On a June 2015 segment of the cable news show *Fox and Friends*, host Pete Hegseth promoted an upcoming Stihl Timbersports event. On an outdoor stage surrounded by spectators, Hegseth demonstrated one of the event's tasks, axe tossing. He threw an axe at a target...but missed wildly. The tool sailed over the target and into an area where members of the U.S. Army Hellcats marching band were playing. That axe struck drummer Jeff Prosperie on his outer elbow, leaving a few deep cuts that extended down to his wrist. "I was hit by an axe while performing a drum solo live on

Top four causes of U.S. deaths in 2020:
1) heart disease; 2) cancer; 3) COVID-19; 4) unintentional injuries.

national TV," Prosperie wrote on his social media accounts. "My leadership told me they were told there would be no axe throwing. I think the anchor person went rogue and decided to throw it."

HE DIDN'T AXE NICELY

It wasn't an accident, but it was a shock: At about 8:30 p.m. one evening in September 2021, Seattle police responded to a call from a woman reporting that a hammer-wielding man had tried to steal her car. She said he'd walked up to her window and demanded the car, but instead of giving it to him, she drove off. Fifteen minutes later, another call came in from a woman who reported that a man with a hammer had successfully stolen her car. Within the hour, cops located the car, crashed near the site of the first robbery. The suspect ran from the scene before officers arrived and also before they fielded three calls from area residents who reported seeing a man wandering around the neighborhood with an axe trying to gain entry to an occupied home. The man (unnamed in reports) was caught, and booked on charges of robbery and felony harassment.

AXING AND DRIVING DON'T MIX

The King County Sheriff's Office in Washington state recorded a road rage incident in July 2021. The driver of a Jeep had repeatedly honked at another driver as they both tried to merge onto a highway, in the same lane and at the same time. Scared of the angry Jeep driver, the other motorist pulled over to the side of the road. Then the Jeep pulled over and, as surveillance video showed, the driver (he was shirtless) grabbed an axe from his vehicle and threw it at the other car's windshield. And then he drove away. Police were able to discern the man's identity from the footage and made an arrest within three days.

SMELLS LIKE TROUBLE

A different kind of an axe caused chaos on a Texas freeway in 2018. A truck carrying a load of Axe Body Spray (the aerosol deodorant that's marketed mostly to young men and teenage boys) caught fire on Interstate 35, 60 miles north of Austin. The driver was unaware of the fire...until he heard explosions and pulled over, only to see thousands of cans of Axe blow up and launch like missiles onto and over the road. No one was injured, but authorities closed the freeway for more than four hours to pick up the hundreds of charred Axe cans and repair the highway, which was reduced to gravel. "When a trailer catches on fire, we usually have to do repairs on the shoulder and maybe the lane next to it," a Texas Department of Transportation spokesperson told reporters. "But because of all those flying aerosol cans, the pavement all the way across the highway has to be redone. I don't remember another occasion where we've had it all the way across. This is just an unusual situation."

At any given time, there's an estimated $70 million to $200 million worth of counterfeit bills circulating in the U.S.

THE DEFECTORS

General Benedict Arnold is infamous for defecting to the British side during the Revolutionary War. He may be the best-known defector in American history, but he's not the only one. Here are some others.

CLARENCE ADAMS (KOREAN WAR)

When the signing of an armistice in 1953 ended hostilities in the Korean War, one of the terms of the agreement that the U.S. and its allies in the United Nations insisted upon was that prisoners of war who did not want to return home would not have to do so. More than 14,000 POWs from North Korea and China decided not to return home...and so did 23 Americans and one British soldier, who preferred to start new lives in the People's Republic of China.

Clarence Adams was one of the American POWs who refused to come home. A Black U.S. Army corporal from Memphis, Tennessee, he was captured in December 1950 and spent three years in a North Korean POW camp. When the armistice was signed, rather than return home to the racially segregated American South, he decided to try his luck in China. "I might not have known what China was really like before going there, but I certainly knew what life was like for blacks in America and especially Memphis," he later wrote. "I went to China because I was looking for freedom and a way out of poverty and I wanted to be treated like a human being." Adams lived there for 12 years, married a Chinese woman, fathered two children, earned a master's degree, and worked as a translator. During the Vietnam War, he made propaganda broadcasts for Radio Hanoi urging Black soldiers to lay down their arms. But he grew homesick and in 1966 he re-defected to the West, returning home to Memphis with his wife and kids in tow. There were calls to court-martial Adams, but because Adams had already been discharged from the Army under "other than honorable conditions," he could not be court-martialed. He and his wife opened the first of what eventually became a chain of four Chop Suey House restaurants in Memphis that were famous for what Adams liked to call its "Chinese Soul-food cuisine." Adams died from emphysema in 1999 at the age of 69. Chop Suey House is still in business, but under different ownership.

JOHN RILEY (MEXICAN-AMERICAN WAR)

Riley, an Irish immigrant, enlisted in the U.S. Army in 1845, not long after arriving in the United States. He deserted in 1846, then went to Mexico and joined the

French composer Olivier Messiaen's 1949 symphony *Turangalîla* inspired the name of the *Futurama* character Leela. (Her first name: Turanga.)

Mexican Army just before the outbreak of the Mexican-American War, which lasted from 1846 to 1848. There he formed the St. Patrick's Battalion, a unit of some 175 former Europeans, most of them Irish, to fight on the Mexican side. The battalion saw action in several battles and made its last stand at the Battle of Churubusco in August 1847. Riley and more than 70 other members of the battalion were captured by the Americans. Fifty of them, soldiers who'd deserted from the U.S. Army *after* the declaration of war, were hanged in the largest mass execution in U.S. history. Because Riley had deserted *before* war was declared, he escaped the noose. Instead, he was given 50 lashes and was branded on his cheek with the letter *D* for deserter. He then served a sentence of hard labor until the end of the war. Upon his release, he served again for a time in the Mexican Army, then in 1850, he retired on medical grounds after contracting yellow fever. After that, he disappeared into history. When, where, or how he died is unknown, but it is believed he is buried somewhere in Mexico.

MARTIN JAMES MONTI (WORLD WAR II)

In October 1944, Monti, a pilot in the U.S. Army Air Force, went AWOL from his base in Karachi in what is now Pakistan. He made his way to the Pomigliano Airfield in Italy, where, on October 13, 1944, he stole a Lockheed F-5E Lightning reconnaissance plane and flew it to Milan, which was still in the hands of the Germans. There he surrendered. It took some doing to convince the Nazis that he was a genuine defector, not a spy or someone who had gotten lost and landed at the wrong airport. But once his story was believed, he went to Berlin and began broadcasting radio propaganda for the Nazis under the name "Captain Martin Wiethaupt" and other pseudonyms. He also joined the Waffen-SS.

At the end of the war, when Germany was on the verge of defeat, Monti fled Berlin and made his way back to Milan, where he surrendered to the U.S. forces claiming he was an escaping American POW. Under questioning, he admitted stealing the airplane but claimed he did so to *fight* the Nazis, not join them. He did not reveal his propaganda activities or membership in the SS. Court-martialed for desertion and stealing the plane, he was sentenced to 15 years in prison. That sentence was soon waived, along with those of other deserters, by President Harry S. Truman. In 1947, Monti rejoined the U.S. Army Air Force. By 1948, the FBI had discovered that he was the mysterious "Martin Wiethaupt," and they arrested him on the day he was discharged from the military. Charged with 21 acts of treason, Monti pled guilty and was sentenced to 25 years in prison and fined $10,000, the equivalent of about $118,000 today. He was paroled after serving 11 years of his sentence and lived out the rest of his life in Fort Lauderdale, Florida, where he died in 2000 at the age of 78.

What is the Grumman LLV? The make and model of U.S. Postal Service mail trucks. LLV stands for "Long Life Vehicle"—they're built to last 30 years.

MCKINLEY NOLAN (VIETNAM WAR)

Nolan, a Black U.S. Army rifleman, went AWOL for two months in 1967. He was jailed for two days and then disappeared. It wasn't clear what had happened to him until a few months later, when North Vietnam began broadcasting radio propaganda in which Nolan called for other Black American soldiers to lay down their arms. Nolan reportedly joined the Viet Cong, the communist guerilla movement fighting the U.S. and its ally South Vietnam; married a Cambodian woman; and fathered a child. In 1973, he was said to be living in Cambodia under the communist Khmer Rouge, which ruled the country from 1975–79. After 1977, the trail goes cold. Nolan, his wife, and their child may have been killed during the Cambodian genocide in which 25 percent of the nation's entire population was wiped out by the Khmer Rouge. But over the years there have been repeated unconfirmed sightings of Nolan in Cambodia, Vietnam, and even in Cuba. One journalist has described him as "like Bigfoot," in that "he's spotted everywhere." Unless his remains are discovered or a confirmed sighting is made, his true fate may never be known.

* * *

ONE HEN, TWO DUCKS

Thinking of taking up voice acting? Then master this "Announcer's Test" for radio announcer trainees, originated in the 1940s. It's structured like a cumulative song (like "The Twelve Days of Christmas"). First, you say, "one hen." Then you repeat "one hen" and add "two ducks." Then you repeat those phrases and add another: "one hen, two ducks, three squawking geese." And so on. There are ten phrases in all—they become harder to remember and even harder to say. Make it through without flubbing a word and you might have a future in show business. Here's the full test:

- One hen
- Two ducks
- Three squawking geese
- Four limerick oysters
- Five corpulent porpoises
- Six pairs of Don Alverzo's tweezers
- Seven thousand Macedonians in full battle array
- Eight brass monkeys from the ancient sacred crypts of Egypt
- Nine apathetic, sympathetic, diabetic old men on roller skates, with a marked propensity towards procrastination and sloth
- Ten lyrical, spherical, diabolical denizens of the deep who all stall around the corner of the quo of the quay of the quivery, all at the same time

Five banned wagers on the game show *Jeopardy:* $666 (satanic), $69 (suggestive), as well as $14, $88, and $1488 (a white supremacist symbol).

MOUTHING OFF

DUMB JOCKS

Playing sports is hard. Talking is harderer.

"The referee is the most important man in the ring besides the two fighters."

—George Foreman, boxer

"Why should we have to go to class if we came here to play football. We ain't come to play school. Classes are pointless."

—Cardale Jones, college football player

"RIGHT NOW, I FEEL THAT I'VE GOT MY FEET ON THE GROUND AS FAR AS MY HEAD IS CONCERNED."

—Bo Belinsky, baseball player

"I definitely want my son to be Christianized, but I don't know yet what religion."

—David Beckham, soccer player

"Violence is never the answer, but sometimes it is."

—Matt Barnes, basketball player

"It's only puffy when it's swollen."

—Charlie Hough, baseball player, referring to his broken finger

"My teeth weren't that good to begin with, so hopefully I can get some better ones."

—Duncan Keith, hockey player

"We must have had 99 percent of the match. It was the other three percent that cost us."

—Ruud Gullit, soccer player

"I MEAN THE REASON WHY I LOVE SWIMMING IS BECAUSE RACING."

—Ryan Lochte, swimmer

"OUR CEILING IS THROUGH THE ROOF."

—Josh Smith, basketball player

"Defensively, I think it is important to tackle."

—Karl Mecklenburg, football player

BATHROOM NEWS

Going to the bathroom is a completely normal part of nature.
But sometimes what happens is so strange and gross that...
well, you don't want to know. (Yes, you do!)

CHECK FOR SNAKES

According to a 2021 article in the medical journal *Urology Case Reports*, a 47-year-old man from the Netherlands (unnamed in reports) was vacationing at a South African nature preserve. While there, he used the facilities, which he had no reason to believe would be dangerous. Wrong. From inside the toilet bowl, an unseen cobra leapt up and attacked the man, biting him and attaching its fangs to his private parts. The preserve was so remote that it took three hours for a helicopter to arrive and take him to a hospital more than 200 miles away. During the trip, he experienced pain and burning that spread from his genital area to his chest and abdomen, along with profound swelling and purple discoloration at the bite spot. Despite several doses of antivenom and antibiotics, he was diagnosed with scrotal necrosis (tissue death) and required reconstructive skin graft surgery in the first ever documented case of "snouted cobra envenomation of the genitals."

DO HAVE A COW

In 2021, a team of scientists in Germany successfully potty-trained cows. Using a treat made of molasses (cows reportedly have a strong taste for sweets), researchers would lure a cow out of its enclosure, and then coax it to urinate into a special receptacle. It took the scientists just over two weeks to train 11 test subjects to use what they called a "MooLoo." "The cows are at least as good as children, age two to four years," said study senior author Lindsay Matthews. Not only is this a breakthrough in animal behavior science, it's good for the planet. Cow urine is high in nitrogen, and when it's exposed to cow feces, it unleashes ammonia, an environmental toxin. One cow produces as much as eight gallons of urine per day, so if some of that could be collected and disposed of properly, the world's water and air supplies would benefit.

> In 2021, a team of scientists in Germany successfully potty-trained cows.

CAN'T BEAR IT

In 2021, the Fawn fire in Northern California leveled more than 100 structures and thousands of people had to evacuate their homes. Officials believed the fire was caused by human effort, and they found and arrested the culprit: a self-described shaman named Alexandra Souverneva. Facing a nine-year prison sentence,

Souverneva entered a not-guilty plea because while she admits to starting the fire, she claims it wasn't intentional. While hiking through Northern California on her way to Canada, she said, she became thirsty and didn't have enough drinking water. Then she came across a puddle of what she determined to be bear urine, and collected it and boiled it in an attempt to purify it into potable water. But she didn't completely put out the embers before moving on, and it quickly became a wildfire. How did authorities catch her? Souverneva called an area fire department for help after getting lost in brush. (And she was carrying a lighter.)

KLOP'S PLOP FLOP

"Fecal microbiota transplantation" is a cutting-edge medical procedure that involves taking the poop from healthy people, extracting the bacteria and microbes, and consolidating them into a capsule, which is then taken by a person with digestive issues. (Taken orally, or, um, the other, more direct way.) The hope is that the patient's gut will then be newly repopulated with the helpful microscopic organisms. FMTs are subject to a lot of restriction in the U.S. and in Canada, which is where Jason Klop got himself in trouble with the College of Naturopathic Physicians of British Columbia. Klop reportedly set up a not-quite-legal operation in his Abbotsford, B.C., home, making bacteria capsules out of donated material from his nephews, who, according to court documents, "bring their stool down to the basement and someone down there freeze dries it" and turns it into pills. Klop was ordered to cease operations because not only did his process involve zero quality control or safety measures, he was selling the poop pills in Mexico—claiming they could help cure autism—at $15,000 a treatment.

METAL TOILET

Florida musician "Prince Midnight" (more about him on page 114), records heavy metal songs with his vibraphone-based band. He also runs Hellmouth Plumbing Supply, a custom bathroom fixtures company whose primary business is making toilet seat lids bearing the images of famous heavy metal albums. In 2021, he became a viral sensation for his most elaborate bathroom appliance to date: a life-size toilet in the image of one of his favorite musicians, Metallica drummer Lars Ulrich. He got the arms and legs down by casting his own body parts in resin, and then, using several hundred pounds of natural clay that he bought at an art supply store, he sculpted Ulrich's torso and head based on photos from the 1980s. It took Prince Midnight two months to make the toilet, in which man and appliance are fused together. A pants-less Ulrich, holding drumsticks, is positioned between the tank and the bowl, which sits between Ulrich's open legs. "Make no mistake, this is not me taking a jab at Lars," Prince Midnight told reporters. "This is my way to honor Metallica."

Rarest naturally occurring element: astatine, the most stable form of which has a half-life of just 8.5 hours. It gets its name from the Greek word *astatos*, meaning "unstable."

UNHEARD ALBUMS

Some of the most famous and popular musicians in the world have recorded albums that, for one reason or another, were never shared with the general public.

JOHN FOGERTY'S *HOODOO*

Creedence Clearwater Revival was one of the most successful bands of the late 1960s and early 1970s, selling more than 20 million albums and scoring nine top-10 hit singles, including "Bad Moon Rising" and "Proud Mary." After CCR dissolved in 1972, John Fogerty, the group's lead singer and songwriter, seemed primed for a big solo career. Neither *The Blue Ridge Rangers* (1973) nor *John Fogerty* (1975) sold very well, and his losing streak continued with the song "You Got the Magic," which petered out at a lowly #87 on the *Billboard* Hot 100 in 1976. That song was supposed to be the leadoff single for Fogerty's third album, *Hoodoo*. Consisting of nine songs, it was recorded in early 1976 and then submitted to Asylum Records, which even gave it a catalog number and printed up a few thousand copies. But after the poor performance of "You Got the Magic," Fogerty and Asylum president Joe Smith decided *Hoodoo* wasn't a very good album, and pulled the record before it shipped to stores. Fogerty asked Asylum to destroy the masters, but they didn't—though it has never been officially released, bootleg copies of *Hoodoo* have popped up in record stores for years. Fogerty didn't record a new album until *Centerfield*, in 1985, which went to #1.

KISS'S FIRST ALBUM

Before Kiss became one of the 1970s' most popular rock bands with anthems like "Rock and Roll All Nite" and a stage show that involved pyrotechnics, fake blood, and its members in elaborate face makeup, half of the band's members fronted a folk-influenced hard rock group called Wicked Lester. Guitarist Paul Stanley and bassist Gene Simmons formed the group in 1970 and within a year were signed to Epic Records and recording their debut album. Sessions dragged out over months; when the album was finally finished, Epic rejected it, finding it too mediocre to release. Stanley and Simmons were so disheartened that they disbanded Wicked Lester and formed a new band: Kiss. After Kiss became successful in the late 1970s, Stanley and Simmons feared that Epic would try to cash in by releasing the long-abandoned Wicked Lester album (with liner notes that included hard-to-find photographs of Stanley and Simmons without their

DID YOU KNOW?

In 1982, Kiss guitarist Ace Frehley quit, and the band auditioned replacements. Vinnie Vincent got the job, beating out future stars Richie Sambora (of Bon Jovi) and Slash (of Guns N' Roses), as well as Eddie Van Halen...who discovered Kiss and helped them get a record deal in the early 1970s.

trademark Kiss makeup). So, with help from their label, Casablanca Records, they bought the rights to the Wicked Lester recordings from Epic for $138,000...just so they could bury it and prevent it from ever being released.

ADELE'S MOTHERHOOD ALBUM

In terms of albums sales, there's no musician more popular since the late 2000s than Adele. Her first three albums sold a combined 63 million copies. Her soulfully sung torch songs are far from the music of youth-skewing rappers or rock bands, and a vast swath of her listeners are people middle-aged or older, because they relate to her approachable songs of love, heartbreak, and regret. In 2012, Adele gave birth to a son, Angelo, and soon thereafter wrote an entire album's worth of songs about another personal experience: the joys and trials of motherhood. But that record never came out. Instead, Adele released *25* in 2015, and while promoting it, she revealed that she'd totally scrapped the motherhood project. "I did write an album about being a mum," she told *BBC One*, but canceled it because she thought it would be "too boring" for other people.

SEAL'S *TOGETHERLAND*

Seal broke out in 1990 as a singer on thumping, techno dance club music. His first single, "Killer," a collaboration with DJ Adamski, hit #1 in England, while the similar "Crazy" became a hit in the United States. Over the next few years, Seal changed his sound to a mix of soul, pop, and soft rock; in 1994, his "Kiss from a Rose" topped the pop and adult contemporary charts and won Song of the Year at the Grammys. All of Seal's subsequent work had the same laid-back feel, to the point where when he tried to go back to his dance club sound, he found that he couldn't. In 1999, he recorded *Togetherland* at his home studio in Los Angeles, a record with an edgy, electronic sound. It was so different from a typical Seal album that he considered releasing it under a fake name. He and producer Henry Jackman tried to transform *Togetherland* into a more mainstream pop record, but his label, Warner Bros., still didn't like it. Result: they shelved it. Only one song from *Togetherland* ever saw a formal release—a remixed version of "This Could Be Heaven," which was on the soundtrack of the 2000 movie *The Family Man*.

* * *

3 CORONAVIRUS SLANG TERMS

Chin diaper: When someone wears a protective mask, but on their chin instead of over their nose and mouth.

Covidiot: A pejorative term for someone who doesn't take COVID precautions seriously.

Maskne: A combination of "mask" and "acne," it refers to the pimples and skin irritation that can result from wearing a mask many hours a day.

In 1979, a woman named Elvita Adams jumped off the Empire State Building's 86th floor observation deck...

DUMB CROOKS

We've been bringing you stories of hapless criminals for 35 years. You'd think they'd have learned by now.

Here's Your Reward

In July 2021, the Tulsa (Oklahoma) Police Department's Facebook page posted their "Fugitive of the Week": Lorraine Graves, who was wanted for accessory to a murder. One of the comments was from Graves herself: "Where's the reward money at?" Another commenter warned, "Giiiiirl you better stay off social media they can track you!!" But it was too late, they'd already tracked her.

Picture This

One morning in May 2020, a camera store owner was walking to his Riverside, California, shop when 25-year-old Johnny Angel Robles asked if he wanted to buy, according to police, "several hundred dollars' worth of camera equipment." The store owner said no, but when he got to his shop and noticed signs of a break-in, he quickly called the police. Robles, who was on probation, was still in the area when squad cars arrived. He ran but didn't get far. In short order, the cameras went back on the shelves and Robles went back to jail.

Don't I Know You?

Vincent Vinny Marks was driving in Napoleonville, Louisiana, one night in June 2021 when he started flashing his headlights at the car in front of him. When the car pulled into a parking lot, Marks blocked it in, got out, and flashed a badge at the other driver. One problem: Marks wasn't a police officer. Another problem: the other driver was, and he knew Marks wasn't a cop because he remembered him from a recent domestic incident. Marks was later charged with false imprisonment and impersonating a police officer (badly).

Oh "Deer"

In November 2021, three men were poaching deer in rural Massachusetts, sitting in their pickup truck, using a spotlight to stun the deer and a crossbow to kill them. On one productive evening, they had already killed three, when they spied a fourth one standing in a nearby patch of woods. They shined their light at the deer, the shooter aimed his crossbow, and...THUNK! It was a wooden deer. The men tried to drive away but didn't make it very far before they were surrounded by Massachusetts Environmental Police officers, who'd been watching the decoy. The poachers were charged with "firing of a crossbow within 150 feet of a road; illegal hunting with a crossbow; hunting with the aid of a vehicle; hunting with artificial light; hunting after hours; tagging violations, and hunting on public land without permits." The reports ended with, "Additional charges are forthcoming."

The Heat Is On

In November 2021, residents in a Winnipeg, Manitoba, neighborhood called police to report a break-in at a vacant house. They also reported a gas leak coming from the same house. Officers went in and found a man and a woman, both in their 40s, passed out on the floor next to the furnace they were trying to steal. Officers carried the couple outside, waited until they regained consciousness, and then arrested them. A neighbor turned off the gas.

Out-of-Towner

In May 2019, Lincoln (Nebraska) police officers, responding to a report of domestic assault, found a man sitting in a car outside of the house that made the 911 call. The man denied having anything to do with domestic assault and said his name was Deangelo Towns. The sharp-eyed officer noticed that the name he gave—Deangelo Towns—didn't match the name printed on his work ID—Markel Towner...which he was wearing. After a minor kerfuffle, Towner was charged with resisting arrest, providing a false name, and domestic assault.

Going Undercover

In November 2021, police in the small town of Stanfield, Oregon, reported on their Facebook page that, over the previous weekend, they had captured not one, but two, fugitives with outstanding warrants—both of whom were hiding under blankets. One was a 54-year-old man who tried "to be part of a lumpy blanket" on the back seat of his car. The other was a 26-year-old man who was found in a van: "His effort to be one with the blanket was not victorious."

36 Seconds of Fame

During the aftermath of an October 2021 earthquake, an Egyptian reporter named Mahmoud Ragheb was giving a live report from a busy bridge in Cairo. Speaking into his phone, he had just started his report when the 2,000 people who were watching it live saw the picture shake and then freeze for a second, and then resume. Suddenly, instead of the reporter, the screen showed the face of a man—the view is looking up from his lap as he's casually smoking a cigarette—speeding away on his motorbike, having just stolen the reporter's phone. One commenter wrote, "The whole world is watching you." The thief turned off the camera after about half a minute, but there was more than enough footage to lead police right to him.

Anatomy quiz: Can you name the only muscle in your body that's attached at just one end? A: Your tongue.

THE ANTARCTICA TIMELINE

Roughly 100,000 years ago, Homo sapiens (us) became a separate species that wandered out of Africa and then spread to every corner of the Earth...that is, almost every corner. No human being even saw the southernmost continent until about 200 years ago. But a lot has transpired down there in the short time since–including an alarming discovery: that Antarctica may hold the key to our species' very survival...or demise.

EARTH'S BOTTOM

The world's southernmost continent is also the coldest, driest, windiest, and–at an average elevation of 8,200 feet above sea level–the highest. Ninety-eight percent of Antarctica is covered in a layer of ice up to three miles thick in some places; the other 2 percent consists of rocky shores and mountains. At 5.4 million square miles, this treeless tundra is so vast that the continental U.S. could easily fit inside it. Most of Antarctica is classified as a desert–the world's largest. But long ago, this barren land was green and lush. Here are Antarctica's origins:

- According to geologists, our planet had one massive continent now called Pangaea. About 250 million years ago, it split into two parts–Laurasia and Gondwana.
- Driven by plate tectonics, Laurasia drifted north, and Gondwana drifted south.
- About 180 million years ago, Gondwana broke apart into what became the Indian subcontinent, the Arabian Peninsula, South America, Africa, Australia, and Antarctica.
- Since then, the Southern Ocean's circumpolar current has kept the isolated continent cold enough for the snow to never melt. For the past 14 million years or so, it's been covered in glaciers. There's no evidence that humans visited Antarctica before the 19th century, but its existence had been speculated for millennia.

325 BC	The ancient Greeks become the first known European explorers to travel far enough north to reach the ice-covered Arctic peninsula. They're also the first to deduce that Earth is spherical, and they further deduce that because the northernmost continent is covered with ice, then chances are there's a southern continent to "balance" the planet. But will it be barren or verdant?
Circa AD 100	Greek geographer Marinus of Tyre, noting that the brightest star in the northern sky is called Arcturus ("Bear Guardian"), names this hypothetical southern land Ant-Arktos ("Opposite of Bears"). He was correct, without even knowing it, that there are polar bears in the Arctic but not in the Antarctic.

William Shakespeare wrote 37 plays. The shortest: *Comedy of Errors* (14,701 words). The longest: *Hamlet* (30,557 words).

1500s	In the "Age of Sail," merchant ships and warships search for new lands to explore and conquer. Abraham Ortelius's 1570 atlas, *Theatrum Orbis Terrarum* ("Theatre of the Orb of the World"), includes a continent called Terra Australis Incognita ("Unknown Land of the South"). He can only guess as to its size and shape—both of which he gets wrong—and Australia isn't even on the map. (It won't be "discovered" until 1606.)
1675	English merchant Anthony de la Roché's ship blows off course, and he unwittingly discovers the Antarctic Convergence—also known as the Antarctic Polar Front—where the Southern Ocean meets the warmer waters of the Atlantic, Pacific, and Indian Oceans. He doesn't get close enough to see the southern continent, but word soon gets out that this thin band of water is teeming with whales and seals that feed on tiny crustaceans called krill. The first half-century of Antarctic exploration will consist of more than 1,000 whaling and sealing expeditions and only 25 devoted to science.
1772–1775	England's Captain James Cook circumnavigates the Antarctic Circle. Although he won't get within 150 miles of the continent, he proves that if there is a Terra Australis, then it certainly isn't connected to South America or Australia, as some have theorized. However, because the islands that he does discover are nothing but rock and ice, hopes are slim that Terra Australis will have any forests or farmable lands. "The world will derive no benefit from it," Cook writes.
1820	On January 28, Russian explorer Thaddeus Bellingshausen writes in his journal that his crew has sighted an "icefield covered with small hillocks." This is believed to be the first time humans lay eyes on mainland Antarctica.
1821	On February 7, the American ship *Cecilia* anchors offshore, and its captain, John Davis, sends a boat to what's now called Davis Point on the Antarctic Peninsula. The crew spends an hour hunting seals and then heads back. The mainland is of little interest, and although it's suspected that Davis is the first person to visit the continent, the visit is unverified, leaving the "official" discovery for someone else.
1838	A French scientist named Clément Adrien Vincendon-Dumoulin sails to Antarctica in search of the South Magnetic Pole (SMP). Unlike the fixed geographic South Pole, the SMP is constantly shifting. Using compasses from his ship, Vincendon-Dumoulin is able to calculate that the SMP is somewhere over the mainland, but he doesn't go ashore. (The SMP has

Makes sense: Mastercard's HQ is on Purchase Street, in Purchase, New York.

shifted so much that today it's located off Antarctica's coast, about 1,780 miles from the South Pole.)

1840   British Royal Navy captain James Clark Ross sails two heavily fortified warships to Antarctica, the *Erebus* and *Terror*, in a failed attempt to find the SMP. After the ships get stuck in pack ice and barely make it out, Ross discovers the ice shelf that will be named after him. He writes that it is "between one hundred and fifty feet and two hundred feet above the level of the sea, perfectly flat and level at the top, and without any fissures or promontories on its even seaward face."

1895   Seventy-five years after John Davis's unverified landing, the Swedish steamship *Antarctic* anchors a few hundred yards off Cape Adare. Seven men take a boat to the shore. New Zealander Alexander von Tunzelmann will claim that he jumped off first. Norway's Carsten Borchgrevink says he was first. His only "evidence," however, is this picture that he drew.

"Ha ha, I'm first!" Whether he was or not doesn't matter—Antarctica was now inhabited, marking the beginning of a new age of exploration.
To explore that, turn to page 362.

In German, *backpfeifengesicht* is "a face that needs to be punched."

RANDOM FIRSTS

You read it here first, folks.

FIRST SITCOM

The first sitcom was a "Britcom" called *Pinwright's Progress* that ran on the BBC for 10 half-hour episodes—performed in front of a studio audience—premiering on November 29, 1946. As this plot synopsis shows, sitcoms haven't changed that much: "J. Pinwright owns the world's smallest variety-store, but life is far from easy. His attractive daughter, fierce rival, Ralph the octogenarian messenger boy, and members of staff (trying to be helpful) hinder him day-by-day." (The first American sitcom, *Mary Kay and Johnny*, debuted on the DuMont Television Network a year later, in November 1947.)

FIRST U.S. CABINET APPOINTEE

When George Washington became president of the newly founded United States in 1789, one of his first acts was to establish his cabinet. (The term comes from England; a "cabinet council" was a small room where noblemen advised the royalty.) Washington's first cabinet nominee, Alexander Hamilton, was quickly approved by the U.S. Senate. Hamilton's first task as Secretary of the Treasury: figuring out how to pay back the debts incurred during the Revolutionary War.

FIRST JAZZ RECORD

In February 1917, the Original Dixieland Jass Band—six white Chicago musicians playing New Orleans–style blues and ragtime music—went to New York City to record two toe-tapping instrumentals, "The Original Dixieland Jass Band One-Step" and "Livery Stable Blues." The latter, which features a refrain where the horns imitate farm animals, is considered the first jazz song ever commercially recorded. The sound was so novel that even the Victor Talking Machine Company was at a loss for words in advertisements:

> **A brass band gone crazy!**
>
> *That's the way a wag described the original Dixieland "Jass" Band. Beyond that description we can't tell you what a "Jass" Band is because we don't know ourselves. As for what it does—it makes dancers want to dance more—and more—and yet more!*

The song was a huge hit, and by the end of the year, the two *s*'s in the band name were replaced by *z*'s, ushering in the Jazz Age of the 1920s.

FIRST TEXT MESSAGE

On December 3, 1992, a 22-year-old software architect named Neil Papworth, working from his computer, texted "MERRY CHRISTMAS" to Richard Jarvis (who was at a holiday party). Jarvis, a director at Vodafone, the British telecommunications

The little bits of fur inside a cat's ear that help keep out dirt are called "furnishings."

company developing SMS (Short Message Service) technology, received the text on his Orbitel 901 handset, one of the first mobile phones. At a 2021 auction, an anonymous buyer bought an NFT (Non-Fungible Token) of the computer code that was used to transmit that SMS. Winning bid: €133,000 ($150,000).

FIRST ANIMAL IN SPACE

It wasn't Ham the chimpanzee, sent up by NASA in 1961. It wasn't one of the Russian dogs, Laika (1957) or Tsygan and Dezik (1951). Nor was it a rhesus monkey named Albert II, who went up aboard a U.S. rocket in 1949. The first living creatures to leave Earth's biosphere, launched on a U.S. rocket in 1947 to an altitude of 68 miles, were fruit flies. They all survived the flight.

FIRST COVID-19 VACCINE RECIPIENT

After all the trials were completed, 90-year-old Margaret Keenan of Coventry, England, became the first person in the world to receive a fully tested government-approved COVID-19 vaccine (from Pfizer) on December 8, 2020. A year later, when reporters asked her how she was faring, she said it was the best thing she ever did. "I'm so happy I got the jab!"

FIRST NOBEL PEACE PRIZE(S)

The first Nobel Prizes were awarded in 1901. That year had two Peace Prize recipients: French economist Frédéric Passy, a lifelong activist for democracy and peace among European nations, and Swiss businessman and activist Henry Dunant, founder of the International Committee of the Red Cross. Both men were elderly and infirm at the time and neither attended the award ceremony.

FIRST LAND VEHICLE TO BREAK THE SOUND BARRIER

In October 1997—50 years and one day since American fighter pilot Chuck Yeager broke the sound barrier in the air—a British fighter pilot named Andy Green climbed into *Thrust SSC* in Nevada's Black Rock Desert. Basically a rocket on wheels, the 10-ton, 54-foot-long "supercar" zoomed across the playa, causing a sonic boom when it hit the speed of sound (767.26 mph) on its way to setting a measured land-speed record of 763.035 mph. No other land vehicle has broken the sound barrier since, but more advanced supercars are in development, with their sights set on the next big hurdle: being the first car to reach 1,000 mph.

> Basically a rocket on wheels, the 10-ton, 54-foot-long "supercar" zoomed across the playa.

* * *

"Whoever said the pen is mightier than the sword obviously never encountered automatic weapons."

—General Douglas MacArthur

Members of the UK Parliament eat more Kit Kats than any other snack. (Twix is #2.)

ROBOTS IN THE NEWS

One day, they'll enslave and then probably kill us all. Until then,
let's just enjoy these stories about (mostly) harmless robots.

ART-BOT (NOT SPY-BOT): Aidan Meller runs an art gallery in Oxford, England. He's also a roboticist, having created Ai-Da, an android that looks almost exactly like a real human woman. Meller programmed the android to draw, paint, and sculpt from what it "sees," claiming on his website that Ai-Da (named for 19th-century mathematician Ada Lovelace, and for artificial intelligence, or A.I.) is the "world's first ultra-realistic humanoid AI robot artist." In October 2021, Meller and Ai-Da were scheduled to participate in an exhibition near the pyramids in Giza, Egypt, but upon arriving in Cairo, they were detained by border guards. Because the robot's "eyes" are cameras, Ai-Da was suspected of being part of a spying operation. Security forces demanded that Meller remove the eyes for inspection, but he refused, claiming they're integral to the robot's art technique and that "she would look weird without them." Ten days later, Ai-Da was declared innocent and released into Meller's care.

PROPER BEHAVIOR-BOT: The tiny city-state of Singapore is one of the most surveilled locations on Earth. Most public areas are tracked by a network of 90,000 closed-circuit security cameras and lampposts fitted with facial recognition technology, all designed to spot any illegal behavior. In 2021, the government took surveillance to a new level, with a three-week trial run of a team of security robots. Two bots, outfitted with seven cameras each—to capture video footage in every direction—were sent to patrol a large housing complex and a shopping mall. Special software allowed the robots to pinpoint illegal activity and "undesirable social behavior," including smoking in areas where it's banned, improper parking of a bicycle, or violating COVID-19 social-distancing rules. The robots then issued loud warnings. Example: when one of the bots came across a group of elderly people watching a chess game, it ordered them to "Please keep one-meter distancing, please keep to five persons per group."

REAL-LIFE CARTOON-BOT: Gigantic humanoid robots figure prominently in Japanese culture, such as in the TV series *Voltron*, *Mighty Morphin Power Rangers*, and *Mobile Suit Gundam*, an animated show that first appeared on Japanese TV in the 1970s and has spawned numerous offshoots and spin-offs. *Mobile Suit Gundam* is such a popular franchise that Yokohama, Japan, will be the site of Gundam Factory, an amusement park devoted to the brand and its giant robot characters. Engineers even constructed a remarkably real-looking robot based on one from the original cartoon series. With fully movable arms and legs, the Gundam robot took six years to design and build. It stands 60 feet tall and weighs 55,000 pounds.

Most shelter dogs are mutts, but, surprisingly, approximately 5 percent are purebred.

BAD SANTA, STARRING JAMES GANDOLFINI

Grab the popcorn. Here are some memorable movie roles that were almost played by other actors. As these stories prove, there really should be an Academy Award for casting directors.

David Letterman as Ted Striker (*Airplane!*, 1980)

Surely we can't be serious. It's true: In 1977, Letterman was a 30-year-old former Indiana TV weatherman looking for his big break in Hollywood. One of the parts he auditioned for was a news anchorman in the raunchy sketch spoof *The Kentucky Fried Movie*, written by Jim Abrahams, David Zucker, and Jerry Zucker. They passed him over, but for their next spoof, *Airplane!*, they wrote the lead role of the disgraced war pilot with Letterman in mind. His audition (which can be seen on YouTube) wasn't bad...but he didn't quite have the deadpan delivery that they were looking for. With Letterman out, the search for the lead actor was on. Paramount suggested singer Barry Manilow; *SNL* stars Bill Murray and Chevy Chase were also considered. *Real People* host Fred Willard said he turned down the part ("too many puns") and later regretted it. Olympic champion Bruce (now Caitlyn) Jenner auditioned for the Ted Striker role as well, but it was a TV actor named Robert Hays (*Angie*) who nailed the deadpan delivery. Hays starred alongside another newcomer, stage actress Julie Hagerty, who won the role of Elaine over Shelley Long (*Cheers*) and Sigourney Weaver (*Alien*). The filmmakers' casting persistence paid off: *Airplane!* has a 97 percent score on Rotten Tomatoes, the highest score ever attained by a spoof comedy. (Sorry for calling you Shirley.)

Burt Reynolds as George Spahn (*Once Upon a Time...in Hollywood*, 2019)

Quentin Tarantino's tale of Tinseltown in the Charles Manson era had its own share of tragedy when it came to casting. Burt Reynolds, 82, a tough guy known best for the *Smokey and the Bandit* movies, was all set to play the blind rancher who let the Manson Family live on his land, but Reynolds died of a heart attack shortly before filming began. (The part went to Bruce Dern.) And Tarantino originally wrote the role of James Stacy (played by Timothy Olyphant) for Bill Paxton (*Apollo 13*), but Paxton died suddenly (from complications from surgery) shortly before Tarantino finished the script, which took him five years.

Extra: In 2021, Macaulay Culkin (*Home Alone*) revealed that he auditioned for a part in *Once Upon a Time...in Hollywood* (he didn't say which one). How'd it go? "It was a disaster. I wouldn't have hired me."

James Gandolfini as Willie T. Soke (*Bad Santa*, 2003)

Gandolfini had a supporting role in the Coen Brothers' gritty crime neo-noir, *The Man Who Wasn't There* (2001), which starred Billy Bob Thornton. When the Coens were executive-producing *Bad Santa* two years later, they told screenwriters Glenn Ficarra and John Requa to craft the lead role of the disgruntled, alcoholic safecracker who poses as a mall Santa (so he can rob malls) for Gandolfini—best known for his TV role as mob boss Tony Soprano. But Gandolfini's audition for *Bad Santa* "didn't work out," said Requa. Director Terry Zwigoff (*Crumb, Ghost World*) offered the part to Bill Murray, who was reportedly in final negotiations for the movie before he "stopped returning the Coens' calls" and made *Lost in Translation* instead. The script was then sent to Robert De Niro, Jack Nicholson, Sean Penn, Nicolas Cage, and Billy Bob Thornton. "I'd read maybe a third of it," said Thornton, "and I called [my manager] and said, 'We've gotta do this.'" Thornton got the part.

Ironic Quote: "I asked a Universal executive, 'Why'd you guys pass on it?' And he said, 'It was the most foul, disgusting, misogynistic, anti-Christmas, anti-children thing we could imagine.' That's exactly why I bought it." —Harvey Weinstein, *Bad Santa* producer

Debra Winger as Dottie Hinson (*A League of Their Own*, 1992)

Director Penny Marshall was initially interested in hiring Demi Moore, fresh off the success of *Ghost*, to play the on-field leader of a 1940s all-women baseball team. But Moore had to decline—she was pregnant—so Oscar-nominee Debra Winger (*Terms of Endearment*) was cast as Dottie. To prepare for the role, Winger spent three months training with the Chicago Cubs. Then, as filming was about to begin, Marshall cast her friend Madonna to play an outfielder. Winger was not a fan of the hyper-sexualized pop singer's lack of acting experience, so she told Marshall that she didn't want to be in an "Elvis film" and left the project (but still got paid for it). So when Winger walked, Marshall called in another heavy hitter: Geena Davis, fresh off the success of *Thelma & Louise*. The director invited Davis to her backyard and handed her a baseball. Davis recalled, "I threw the ball, competently got it to her, she caught it and said, 'OK.' That was the whole audition." Davis was nominated for a Golden Globe for *A League of Their Own*, which was a huge summer hit and spawned one of the most quoted movie lines in history: Tom Hanks's "There's no crying in baseball!"

Extra: In a 2021 interview, Winger said that Davis "did okay" as Dottie. As for Madonna? "I think her acting career has spoken for itself."

* * *

We let him in, so he came in with his donkey.

—Egyptian proverb

The world's biggest padlock was made by Russian students in 2003. It weighs 916 pounds.

WARNING LABELS

Some things in life should go without saying, but it seems there's always somebody who needs to be told not to step into an empty elevator shaft.

ON A CHAINSAW:
**Do not hold the wrong
end of a chainsaw**

...

ON AN ELEVATOR:
**PLEASE MAKE SURE
ELEVATOR IS THERE
BEFORE STEPPING IN**

...

ON A CANDLE:
Caution: Tin may be hot

...

ON A CACTUS:
PLEASE DO NOT SIT

...

ON A DRILL:
**The light of this power tool is
intended to illuminate the power
tool's direct area of working operation
and is not suitable for household
room illumination**

...

ON A GAS TANK:
**NEVER USE A LIT MATCH OR OPEN
FLAME TO CHECK FUEL LEVEL**

...

ON A MALE PERFORMANCE ENHANCEMENT DRUG:
Do not use if pregnant or nursing

...

ON A HAIR DRYER:
DO NOT EAT

...

ON A CAN OF FLAT-TIRE FIXING SPRAY:
Not to be used for breast augmentation

...

ON A POLE:
**BEWARE OF POLE
WHEN REVERSING**

ON A COMPUTER DRIVE:
Do not consume

...

ON AN INFLATABLE KIDDIE POOL:
**NOT FOR USE
WHILE RIVER
RAFTING**

...

ON SHOWER CLEANER:
Not to be used as body wash

...

ON BATTERIES:
**DO NOT USE
BATTERIES AS
TOOTHPASTE**

...

ON DETERGENT BOOSTER:
Not for drug use

...

ON A SCARF:
**Do not wrap around
baseball bat and
hit on head**

...

ON DECORATIVE STRING LIGHTS:
**FOR INSIDE OR
OUTSIDE USE ONLY**

...

ON AN ASTHMA INHALER:
For oral use only

...

ON A CAN OF CLEANER:
**IF YOU ARE BLIND
OR CANNOT READ
ENGLISH, DO NOT USE
THIS PRODUCT UNTIL
THE RISKS HAVE BEEN
EXPLAINED TO YOU**

Warren Buffett's company, Berkshire Hathaway, has a line of menswear.
Its top model: Warren Buffett.

LET'S DO AN AUTOPSY!

Oh no, did you die? We're so sorry to hear that. Did you die under...mysterious circumstances? Well, that's even worse. But fear not: a pathologist, a medical examiner, or a coroner will get to the bottom of your demise by performing an autopsy on your now-lifeless corpse. Here's everything they'll do, step by step. (Warning: if you're prone to queasiness, you might want to move on to another article.)

JUST CHECKING

1. The body arrives at the morgue, where a technician or coroner's assistant assigns it an identification number and writes the number on a toe tag, along with as much basic information as is known about the person, including name, age, race, and sex. The toe tag is tied around one of the body's big toes.

2. The body is thoroughly photographed, both in its state as it arrives and then after morgue personnel remove any and all clothing.

3. Once the body is naked, it's weighed, measured for overall length, and fingerprinted. (If any hands, fingers, toes, or other parts are notably absent, this is when the pathologist notes that in the deceased's official record.)

4. The pathologist now looks at any imperfections and body modifications—moles, open wounds, tattoos—as well as toenails and hair. Why? They're on the lookout for any external signs of infection or disease that could have led to death. The professional will also search for more indicators of a possible cause of death, including flaky skin, deep cuts, scratches, and gunpowder residue. They're also looking at the arms for syringe marks—signs of recreational use of intravenous drugs, particularly heroin—and at the genitals for signs of sexual assault.

5. The body may be subject to a full-body X-ray, or a battery of smaller scans. This is to find bone abnormalities or deadly foreign objects in the body. At this point, the coroner may take hair and nail samples for further testing.

CUT IT OUT

6. Now begins the thorough, internal examination part of the autopsy. The body is placed on a rubber mat atop a gurney or table, which keeps the patient from sliding around. That also stretches out the body slightly, allowing for more surface area to make for easier cutting...because there's going to be *a lot* of cutting.

7. The pathologist uses a special postmortem scalpel to make a large, Y-shaped incision across the torso, down from each shoulder, across the sternum, and all the way to the pubic bone.

According to the comics, Batman's favorite food is mulligatawny soup.

8. That incision allows full access to the chest cavity, exposing the rib cage. With the skin flapped open, the pathologist uses a bone saw to remove the rib cage and take it off, like a lid. It's set aside, and all the organs within are now fully accessible.

9. All the organs are removed, physically examined, and weighed. (Too heavy or too light indicates the presence of specific disease.) The pathologist also takes samples of blood along with tissue cut from each organ—the heart, lungs, liver, stomach, and spleen—and examines them under a microscope in search of disease or infection indicators.

10. Special attention is paid to the stomach. Tracking the state of digestion of what food remains behind gives the pathologist an idea of the time of the patient's death.

11. In addition to blood, the pathologist may collect samples of other bodily fluids—urine, bile, and eye fluid—in order to run pertinent and revealing tests for drugs, chemicals, and genetic composition.

12. When the examination is complete, the organs are returned to the body (or preserved for teaching and research purposes, or for further study).

THE BRAIN GAME

13. After looking at the organs in the chest and abdomen, the pathologist takes a look at the brain. First, they have to cut in to the skull, either by making an incision from ear to ear in the back, or a triangular cut on the top.

14. That allows the pathologist to pull the skin and hair aside and, with a special cranial saw, cut through the skull. They'll look at the brain inside the head to see if there are any immediate signs of a head trauma (if necessary). To get a better handle on it, they'll next cut the brain out of the head and slice off tissue samples for testing.

> That allows the pathologist to pull the skin and hair aside.

15. If the pathologist finds evidence of trauma or disease that warrants further study, they'll save the brain, placing it in a preservative called formalin for three to four days. That firms up the brain and makes for an easier and more precise dissection. (They'll do this with any other questionable internal organ, too, at their discretion or suspicion.)

16. Once all the organs have been placed back in the body or into a container of formalin, the pathologist and their assistants will put everything back together, placing the organs (in thick plastic bags, to prevent leakage) back into their original homes and then replacing the rib cage. Once stitched up, the body is sent along to a funeral home to prepare for a memorial service and final disposition—usually burial, immurement (above-ground internment), or cremation.

The term *peacock* refers only to male birds of the species.
The females are *peahens*, and together they're *peafowl*.

ASK THE EXPERTS

Everyone's got a question they'd like answered–basic stuff like "Why is the sky blue?"
Here are a few questions, with answers from the world's top trivia experts.

SCATTERED SHOWERS

Q: *Why is the sky blue?*

A: "It can't be that the atmosphere has a blue color like the blue of a tinted windshield. In that case, going outside in the daytime would be like walking around inside a blue glass bottle, with a blue sun shining blue light everywhere, and blue stars and a blue moon at night. The blue can't be from dust, because the air over gravel parking lots and quarries is whitish, not bluish. The blue can't be the result of water droplets. Clouds are made of water droplets, and clouds are white. It's not a matter of relative humidity, either; a dry sky over Arizona can be just as blue as a humid sky over Minnesota. Blue is not the color of outer space. The background of space is black. So, the sky is black at night—it's blue only during the daytime, when the sun is shining on the atmosphere.

"The sun shines with all the colors of the rainbow—blue, yellow, red, and all the rest—mixed together to make white light. The reds and yellows pass through easily, but some of the blue portion of sunlight is scattered in every direction by air molecules. When you look to the sky on a clear day, you can see blue light scattered from sunbeams by molecules of nitrogen, oxygen, and carbon dioxide.

"The more air, the more scattering. In early morning and late afternoon, the sun's light passes through so much air that most of the blue has been scattered away by the time the light reaches you. The reds and yellows remain and the sun looks reddish."
(From *How the World Looks to a Bee*, by Don Glass)

HI-YAH!

Q: *How do people who practice martial arts break concrete blocks with their bare hands?*

A: "In a face-off between hand and block, the hand has a surprising advantage: Bone is significantly stronger than concrete. In fact, bone can withstand about forty times more stress than concrete before reaching its breaking point. What's more, the surrounding muscles and ligaments in your hands are good stress absorbers, making the hand and arm one tough weapon. So if you position your hand correctly, you're not going to break it by hitting concrete.

"The trick to smashing a block is thrusting this sturdy mass into the concrete with enough force to bend the block beyond its breaking point. The force of any impact is determined by the momentum of the two objects in the collision. Momentum is a multiple of the mass and velocity of an object.

Can you name the only American state flag with a British Union Jack in its design? It's Hawaii.

"When striking an object, the speed of your blow is critical. You also have to hit the block with a relatively small area of your hand, so that the force of the impact is focused in one spot on the block—this concentrates the stress on the concrete. As in golf, the only way for a martial arts student to hit accurately with greater speed is practice, practice, practice." (From *Why Do Guys Like Duct Tape?*)

HOWL YA DOING?

Q: *Cats and dogs are both predators with super-sensitive hearing, so how come dogs howl at sirens, but cats don't even seem to notice them?*

A: "The reason dogs howl when emergency services go by may be that to the dogs, the siren sounds like other dogs howling, and they respond by howling back. This goes back to the time they hunted in packs and signaled to one another when searching for prey. Even if the screaming siren does not mimic exactly the sound of another dog, they can probably pick out a component part of the siren that does. Cats, on the other hand, hunt alone, are not pack animals, and so do not respond to the sirens." (From *Does Anything Eat Wasps?*, by Anne Bloomberg for *New Scientist*)

PITCH PERFECT

Q: *Why do they pitch baseball overhand and softball underhand?*

A: "Softball was invented [in Chicago in 1887] as a way for professional baseball players to practice during the winter. Because they couldn't practice in ice and snow, they decided to play the game indoors. To accommodate the small playing area, they used a larger ball and put more players in the outfield. Because they played indoors, there was no pitching mound. Had they used a mound and pitched in the normal way, the speed of the ball over such a short distance could hurt them. If they didn't use a mound, they would get into bad habits so they would not do as well when playing on a regular playing field. Therefore, it became common for a manager or the coach to simply lob the ball underhand to the batter to get the game started. Eventually, the team's pitcher started throwing the ball underhand.

"When softball gained popularity in the 1930s, it became a summer sport as well and was moved outdoors. Because of the smaller field, a mound would have given the pitcher an advantage, so it wasn't used. Pitchers were not allowed to use a windup and had to pitch underhand." (From *What Makes Flamingos Pink?*, by Bill McLain)

STREET LIGHTS

Q: *Why is the road always wet in nighttime scenes in movies?*

A: "Because dry streets don't photograph. Film crews use fire hoses to wet them. The streets are often wet in night scenes even in films set in desert climates." (From *Questions for the Movie Answer Man*, by Roger Ebert)

After portraying Tarzan in 12 movies, Johnny Weissmuller appeared in 13 Tarzan knockoff *Jungle Jim* movies.

RIP, BOB

Q: *Why do dead bodies float?*

A: "You're in your first year of gangster college…Professor Fat Anthony tells you that if you don't weigh down a body properly before you throw it into a waterway, it can float to the top…It's crazy, but true: Bodies that are laden with weight that is equivalent to or greater than the body's shouldn't float to the top. However, bodies that aren't weighted may float for a while. Why? For the most part, it comes down to gas—and not the type that gangsters would use to torch a rat's house. We're talking about gases that form from bacteria in the body during decomposition, including methane, hydrogen sulfide, and carbon dioxide.

"Bacteria in our bodies love to eat. When we're alive, they eat the food in our systems; when we die and there is no food left in our systems, they eat us. Bacteria break down what they eat and produce gas. The gas has no way of being expelled from a corpse, so it causes the body to bloat and, thus, float (if it happens to be in water). Once you have a floater, it's going to remain on the water's surface until there is enough decomposition of the flesh to allow the gas to escape.

"Not all parts of the body inflate at the same rate. The torso, which is home to the most bacteria, becomes more bloated than the arms, legs, and head. This is partly why a body always floats face down. The arms, legs, and head can only fall forward from a dead body, so the corpse tends to flip, with the less-gas-filled limbs dangling beneath the giant gas ball of the chest and abdomen.

"Depending on the situation, the speed of the decomposition process can vary. For instance, cold water slows down decomposition considerably, while warm water speeds up the bacteria feast. It's a gory sight. Not even the fishes want to sleep with such a thing." (From *Why Do Men Leave the Seat Up?*)

*   *   *

TECH-NO

British author and satirist Douglas Adams came up with "a set of rules that describe our reactions to technologies."

1. "Anything that is in the world when you're born is normal and ordinary and is just a natural part of the way the world works."

2. "Anything that's invented between when you're fifteen and thirty-five is new and exciting and revolutionary and you can probably get a career in it."

3. "Anything invented after you're thirty-five is against the natural order of things."

Squid brains are doughnut shaped and they surround the esophagus.

STAMP FLOPS

You wouldn't think that something as low-key and practical as a postage stamp could wreak social and financial havoc, or inspire strong opinions... but you'd be as wrong as leaving a stamp off a letter.

☐ THE SIMPSONS

In 2009 and 2010, the U.S. Postal Service sold a series of first-class, 44-cent postage stamps featuring *The Simpsons*. Commemorating the 20th anniversary of the series debut in 1989, five stamps were offered, each one featuring a portrait of Homer, Marge, Bart, Lisa, or Maggie. Following successful rollouts of stamps that featured Elvis Presley and Marilyn Monroe (each sold around 500 million), the USPS assumed that the characters from the longest-running TV show would move a lot of stamps. They were wrong. A 2012 Postal Service inspector general report revealed that the office had printed a whopping one billion *Simpsons* stamps. By the time it had to discontinue them (when postage went up to 45 cents in 2011), only 318 million had sold, leaving a surplus of more than 680 million stamps that had to be destroyed. The USPS lost more than $1.2 million on the promotion.

☐ ALCOHOLISM

In 1981, the Postal Service released a special 18-cent stamp bearing the words "Alcoholism: You can beat it!" in large blue letters on a stark white background. The idea was to raise public awareness about alcoholism and highlight the fact that it is a medical problem, not a moral one...but it had the opposite effect. Postal customers didn't want to put such an aggressive message on their letters for fear of making it seem like they were calling the addressee an alcoholic. Result: of the 100 million stamps printed, very few were sold. Within a few months of its release, the stamp was withdrawn from circulation and tens of millions of them had to be destroyed.

☐ DINOSAURS

Referred to in promotional materials as "dinosaur stamps," the Postal Service's 1989 "Prehistoric Animal Series" pictured some of the most famous and impressive beasts to ever walk the Earth. Two of the four 25-cent first-class stamps bore major historical errors. One featured a Brontosaurus, a name not used by paleontologists since the mid-1970s—a Apatosaurus is now the preferred term. Another depicted a Pteranodon, which isn't technically a dinosaur at all, but a lizard that flies. (Paleontologists had no issue with the other two stamps, celebrating the Tyrannosaurus and the Stegosaurus.)

President Barack Obama has a phobia of snowmen.

☐ RICHARD NIXON

Traditionally, all American presidents are honored with their face on a postage stamp, some time after their death. In 1995, following the demise of Richard Nixon, the Postal Service issued a 32-cent stamp bearing the ex-president's image. Nixon was a controversial figure, to say the least—he's the only president to ever resign from the office, which he did in 1974 to escape being impeached for his role in the burglary of the Democratic Party's offices in the Watergate building. How controversial could he be 20 years after those events? Very. Hundreds of post offices around the country reportedly sold close to zero Nixon stamps, such was the lingering resentment for the disgraced politician. One place where Nixon stamps did move briskly: Santa Cruz, California. That's where *Santa Cruz Comic News* publisher Thom Zajac created a special envelope (which sold in the tens of thousands) that when affixed with the Nixon stamp, made it appear as if the face of the president was behind the bars of a jail cell. (The envelopes circulated for years; Uncle John claims to have received a letter from a friend in one as recently as 2020.)

☐ ATOMIC BOMBS

In 1995, to commemorate the 50th anniversary of the end of World War II, the U.S. Postal Service announced a series of memorial stamps, including images of U.S. Marines raising the American flag on Iwo Jima, Allied troops liberating Holocaust survivors, a sailor kissing a nurse on V-J day...and a mushroom cloud with the caption: "Atomic bombs hasten war's end," referring to the bombs dropped on the Japanese cities of Hiroshima and Nagasaki in August 1945. The Japanese government quickly protested the planned stamp, decrying it as a callous celebration of mass death. Result: President Bill Clinton asked the Postal Service to *not* release the stamp, and they didn't, replacing it with an image of President Harry Truman announcing Japan's surrender and the end of the conflict.

☐ JUST MOVE

Most First Ladies of the United States have a particular social issue or cause to which they devote a great deal of their public life. For Michelle Obama, it was childhood fitness. In conjunction with Let's Move (Obama's official campaign to get kids to exercise more), the Postal Service worked up a series of 15 stamps depicting kids being active and having fun. Obama's office rejected three of them because they might have encouraged children to engage in unsafe practices. The "Swim" stamp showed a kid doing a potentially dangerous cannonball-style dive, "Stand" depicted a child standing on their head without wearing a helmet, and "Ride" featured a skateboarder with no kneepads. Ultimately, the entire Just Move stamp collection was canceled.

On average, a person or vehicle in the U.S. is struck by a train every three hours.

THE MOST FAMOUS FACE IN THE SUPERMARKET

People over age 40 remember Paul Newman (1925–2008) as a movie star,
but younger people may know him only as the face on Newman's Own
food labels. Here's the story of how that company came to be.

SALAD DAYS

If you ever had the good fortune of dining out with the actor Paul Newman, or even if you just happened to be eating in the same restaurant, the most memorable part of the experience may not have been seeing one of the world's most famous movie stars up close. It might have been watching him whip up his own salad dressing right at the table, using ingredients brought to him by the waiters.

Newman was not a fan of house dressings, not even in gourmet restaurants. He especially hated bottled dressings, with their artificial coloring, artificial flavoring, and preservatives. Because of this, whenever he ate out, no matter where he was, he'd order a salad without dressing and ask the waiter to bring him some olive oil, red wine vinegar, mustard, fresh pepper, and a bowl. Then he'd whip up the dressing in the bowl and pour it over his salad.

And if someone slipped up and brought him his salad with the dressing already on it? A minor inconvenience. "On one occasion," his friend and neighbor, the writer A. E. Hotchner wrote in his memoir *Shameless Exploitation in Pursuit of the Common Good*, "when the restaurant mistakenly served the salad with its own dressing, Paul took the salad to the men's room, washed off the dressing, dried it with paper towels, and, after returning to the table, anointed it with his own, which he concocted with ingredients brought to him from the kitchen."

LEFTOVERS

At home, Newman whipped up large batches of the stuff and poured it into old wine bottles. Then, whenever his kids left to go to college, they'd take some bottles back to school with them. The star was proud of his creation and enjoyed sharing it with his friends. In December 1980, he and Hotchner went into Newman's barn and whipped up a huge batch in an old washbasin, stirring it with a paddle from Newman's canoe. "It was [Newman's] notion that the olive oil and vinegar had a sort of hygienic effect so that one didn't have to wash anything thoroughly," Hotchner joked.

Newman and Hotchner planned to give away the dressing to neighbors when they went Christmas caroling that year. But they accidentally made much more than they needed. What to do with the rest? Rather than toss it out, they decided to bottle it

The word *she* appears in J. R. R. Tolkien's novel *The Hobbit* only once.

On a lark, Newman and Hotchner decided to go into the salad dressing business.

and sell it in a few local supermarkets.

Why stop with just that batch? On a lark, Newman and Hotchner decided to go into the salad dressing business on a very small scale—as more of a hobby than a business, something they could do for fun when they had the time. Kind of like how some people keep bees in their backyard and sell the honey at farmers markets.

JUST FOR FUN

Each man pitched in $20,000 as seed money. They had no business plan, no marketing campaign, no advertising budget, and no idea how to run a business. They weren't even going to make the dressing themselves, just hire an existing salad dressing bottler to make the dressing for them using Newman's recipe. Then they'd sell it in a few local supermarkets, and hopefully eke out a small profit or at least break even. Neither man needed the money (Hotchner was a successful editor and novelist, his best-known book being *Papa Hemingway*, a biography of his close friend Ernest Hemingway)—the main thing was to have fun, then quit when the $40,000 ran out. That was it.

Other than the recipe itself, the only idea they'd come up with was a name for the salad dressing: Newman's Own. That was what they'd planned to call a restaurant they had considered opening in Westport, Connecticut, where they both lived. But a friend of a friend had warned them that restaurants were surefire money-losers, and talked them out of it. Newman's Own became the name of the salad dressing instead.

THANKS...BUT NO THANKS

Selling an all-natural salad dressing with no artificial ingredients or preservatives, named for the famous movie star who invented it, may sound like a license to print money (at least it does to us). But that's because we don't own supermarkets, and we've never lost our shirts trying to sell celebrity-endorsed food products like Mickey Mantle's Barbeque Sauce, Sylvester Stallone's High Protein Pudding, or Richard Simmons Salad Spray. In the early 1980s, celebrity-endorsed products were introduced from time to time, but they were usually cheap gimmicks: mediocre products propped up by a famous person's name, which was the only reason you would buy them. Even Newman himself dismissed celebrity product endorsements as taking the "lowest of the low road" to make money off the public. People typically bought such products once, tasted for themselves how unremarkable they were, and never bought them again, leaving grocers stuck with merchandise they could not sell.

Newman and Hotchner believed their salad dressing was better than that. When retailers understandably expressed skepticism at the idea, the two men arranged for a caterer friend of theirs named Martha Stewart—yes, *that* Martha Stewart—to conduct a blind taste test of Newman's Own against 19 other popular bottled salad dressings.

Twenty people participated in the test: in 18 of the ballots, Newman's Own dressing was ranked #1; in the other two, it was ranked #2.

FACE FACTS

Newman and Hotchner shared the results with their friend Stew Leonard, who owned a chain of supermarkets by the same name. Leonard was skeptical, but he said that if the product was as good as Newman said it was, it had a good chance at success "because your face is on the label."

Huh?

"Whoa!" Newman exclaimed, "my *face* is on the label?!" He was willing to put his *name* on the label, but not his face. "Not a chance in hell!" he said. He didn't want people to think he was cashing in on his fame to peddle condiments to his fans. But Leonard argued that without the star's face on the label, the customers probably wouldn't connect "Newman's Own" with Paul Newman. For all they knew it might be "Seymour Newman from Newark," he explained.

The business might have ended right then and there, had it not occurred to Newman that no one would be able to accuse him of cashing in on his fame if he *gave the money away*. Why not use the salad dressing to raise money for charity? Under those conditions he *was* willing to put his face on the label. "Shameless exploitation for charity, for the common good—now there's an idea worth the hustle," he joked.

That's right: one of the best-known features of the Newman's Own brand, "100% Profits to Charity," as it says right on the label, was an afterthought, something that Paul Newman did to feel more comfortable about putting his face on his salad dressing.

> **DID YOU KNOW?**
>
> One of Paul Newman's best-known features: his blue eyes, which looked sexy on the silver screen. Ironically, Newman was color-blind, and because of it had to drop out of a U.S. Navy pilot training program during World War II. He served as a turret gunner instead.

DRESSED FOR SUCCESS

Stew Leonard agreed to buy 20,000 cases of Newman's Own salad dressing for his supermarket chain. On the strength of that first order, a bottler agreed to make the salad dressing. It was the first all-natural salad dressing on the market, and if Leonard ever worried that he'd ordered too much of the stuff, that fear soon went away—his stores sold 10,000 bottles in the first two weeks alone. And now that the profits were all going to charity, Newman happily promoted his dressing anytime he gave an interview, went on TV, or made a public appearance. The company didn't spend a cent on advertising, but the free publicity was worth millions, and the public responded.

What was supposed to be a regional product sold only in New England soon attracted the interest of retailers all over the country, and they began stocking it on their shelves as well. Suddenly, the bottler had to add extra shifts to keep up with the demand and even then, the bottles sold as fast as they rolled off the production line.

Official bean of the Nation of Islam: the navy bean. (All other beans are forbidden.)

The salad dressing went on sale in September 1982, and by the end of December the company had sold hundreds of thousands of bottles, in the process earning more than $920,000 in profits, every penny of which it donated to charity.

SMORGASBORD

You don't have to spend much time in a supermarket to realize that salad dressing was just the beginning for Newman's Own. One night, when Paul Newman came home to an empty house and found nothing in the refrigerator but a jar of store-bought pasta sauce, he made some spaghetti and was so disgusted by the taste that he decided to expand beyond salad dressing. Newman's Own Industrial Strength All-natural Venetian-style Spaghetti Sauce hit store shelves in February 1983, followed later by Newman's Own Old Style Picture Show Popcorn (the star *hated* Orville Redenbacher's popcorn), then Newman's Own lemonade (based on his wife Joanne Woodward's secret family recipe), then salsa, steak sauce, pretzels, cookies, frozen pizza, fruit juices, coffee, chocolate bars, breath mints...you name it, one product after another, year after year. Why stop at human foods? Today the company sells several kinds of dog food.

As the number of products increased from one year to the next, so too did total sales, profits, and charitable contributions. So far, the company has donated some $550 *million* to more than 600 different charities in the United States and around the world (including one set up by Newman and Hotchner, the Association of the Hole in the Wall Gang Camps, which builds and operates a network of summer camps for children too sick to go to ordinary summer camps). Not a bad return on a $40,000 investment.

As of 2022, Newman's Own is still going strong, still developing new food products, and still donating every penny of its profits to charity. It has outlived both its founders: Newman died in 2008 at the age of 83, and Hotchner passed away in 2020 at the age of 102. "Our little joke, our whimsical $40,000 adventure, was like a character in a play or characters being developed in a book who suddenly take off and run away from the writer," Hotchner wrote in 2003. "All you can do is say, 'Look at that little bugger go.'"

*   *   *

6 TERMS FOR VORACIOUS READERS

1. Bookworm (English)

2. Book caterpillar (Finnish)

3. Book moth (Hungarian)

4. Library mouse (Romanian)

5. Library rat (French)

6. Book swallower (Welsh)

World's oldest bank still in operation:
Italy's Banca Monte dei Paschi di Siena, founded in 1472.

MORE QUIRKS OF LANGUAGE

Here's another round of unusual linguistic facts and anomalies. (Part I is on page 51.)

THAT'S HIGHLY IRREGULAR: Almost every language has irregular verbs—verbs that don't follow the normal grammatical rules of their language when conjugated. In English, for example, verbs denoting past tense commonly end in -d or -ed. Now consider the word "choose," which would sound quite odd if you "choosed" to use it incorrectly. What language has no irregular verbs? Esperanto. It was invented in 1887 by a Polish ophthalmologist named L. L. Zamenhof. Troubled by ethnic violence in his country, he came up with a universal "simple language" that has 16 basic rules and takes its root words from languages familiar to half of the world's population. Even though Esperanto never caught on en masse, there are two million *Esperantophones* around the globe. (English: "Where's the bathroom?" Esperanto: *"Kie estas la necesejo?"*)

ALPHABETICAL EXTREMES: The biggest alphabet: Khmer (Cambodian), which has 74 letters. The smallest is Rotokas, spoken by about 4,000 people in Papua New Guinea. It has 12 letters.

THE LANGUAGE OF FOOD: From *hors d'oeuvres* to *bon appétit*, more culinary terms come from French than any other language. Credit for that goes to French chef François Pierre La Varenne. His 1651 recipe book, *The French Cook*, standardized his country's culinary methods with easy-to-follow directions, making it the first cookbook to receive international acclaim. After the French Revolution in 1799, French chefs emigrated to English-speaking countries, taking with them their techniques and terminology, which soon became the gold standard of cooking worldwide.

THE LARGEST CITY WITH A FRENCH-SPEAKING POPULATION IS... Not Paris. It's Kinshasa, the capital of the Democratic Republic of Congo. From 1908 to 1960, the southeastern African country was ruled by Belgium (it was known at the time as the Belgian Congo), which has three official languages: Dutch, French, and German. (The city was called Léopoldville, after Belgium's king.) After the Congo achieved independence, many French speakers remained. Today, Kinshasa's indigenous groups use French as a common language to talk to each other. It's estimated that 68 percent of Kinshasa's 12.7 million people are francophones (people who speak French). *Fait Bonus:* Paris, with about 12 million residents, is the second-largest city of French speakers, followed by Abidjan in Africa's Ivory Coast, then Montreal.

THE ROYAL VOCABULARY: The Thai language has what's called *rachasap* or *rajasap*. This "royal vocabulary" is reserved exclusively for talking to—or more commonly, about—the king, his family, and other aristocrats. In Thailand's monarchy, which began in 1238, anyone who disrespects the king may be jailed. To show reverence, the Thai people replace the royal family's names, pronouns, actions, and belongings with honorific titles and words from the royal vocabulary. For example, one of the approved references to the king is *Prachao Yu Hua*, meaning "Lord Above Your Head."

MULTILINGUAL: According to poll results, 53 percent of Europeans can speak English and another language, compared to just 18 percent of Americans.

LANGUAGE ISOLATES: That's the term given to rare languages that have no protolanguage (parent language). Linguists postulate there are between 88 and 120 languages that lack roots in any known language. Examples: Zuni, which is spoken in the American Southwest, and Basque, spoken only in the Pyrenees mountains between France and Spain (it even has its own numbering system). The country with the most language isolates is Papua New Guinea, in the southwestern Pacific, whose 9 million people speak about 840 languages. It's the world's most rural country, with only 13 percent of residents living in cities. The extreme landscapes—mountains, active volcanos, swamps, and dense jungles—keep villages secluded and their languages uninfluenced by outsiders.

SIGN HERE: Only 4,000 people live in the small Bedouin village of al-Sayyid in Israel, and about 150 of them are deaf. That's 50 times the average. (This is due, first, to a genetic condition from the 19th century that spread throughout the isolated community and, second, to a law that forbids marrying outsiders.) In the 1940s, ten deaf villagers invented al-Sayyid Bedouin Sign Language (ABSL). It's a simple language, unlike Arabic or Israeli Sign Language, which are also spoken there. Today, nearly all the villagers can speak ASBL, meaning there is no separate deaf culture like there is in most other places.

THE MOST WORDS: Determining which language is the "biggest" is difficult. The *Oxford English Dictionary* says it's "probably" English, with more than one million words, but many are conjugations of a single word, so linguists differ on whether those should count. If the number of words is determined by entries in the dictionary (depending on what dictionary you use), then the winner is Korean with 1,100,373 words, followed by Portuguese (818,000), Finnish (800,000), Swedish (600,000), English (575,000), and Italian, Japanese, and Lithuanian (500,000).

WHISTLE WHILE YOU TALK: From Siberia to Brazil to Turkey, there are at least 80 cultures whose spoken languages include whistling. This makes sense in mountainous regions where dense forests and steep terrain can make it difficult to hear one another. Whistles, aided by the fingers, can travel up to 10 times farther with less echo and exertion than shouting does. (Even so, it's a good bet that most kids still say they "didn't hear" that stop-playing-and-come-home-for-dinner whistle.)

Until 1904, when the *New York Times* moved its headquarters there, Times Square was called Longacre Square.

THE RIDDLER

Time to test your deductive reasoning with some classic and some not-so-classic riddles. (Answers are on page 403.)

1. What is always in front of you but can't be seen?

2. How can a leopard change its spots?

3. In what sport do the winners move backward and the losers move forward?

4. Why couldn't the man marry his widow's sister?

5. What is every living person in the world doing right now?

6. In my three lives I can crack stone, stop traffic, and fly high. What am I?

7. Tread where they're freshly dead and they won't even mumble. Tread where they're long dead and they'll mutter and grumble. What are they?

8. The more there is, the less you see. What is it?

9. What coat is best put on wet?

10. What can you add to your pocket to make it empty?

11. What regal word of six letters has one left when three are removed?

12. What has words but does not speak?

13. What can you catch but not throw?

14. Always open, my tiny eye. Pierce it, and I won't cry. What am I?

15. Tool of thief, toy of queen. Always used to be unseen. Sign of joy, sign of sorrow. Giving all a likeness borrowed.

16. A union of two, one dark and one light. Shake them hard, and they'll spice up your night.

17. I can't be bought, but I can be stolen with a glance. I'm worthless to one, but priceless to two. What am I?

18. What two symbols will make you young?

Well, the shoe fits: Experts say Uranus smells like farts.

TOILET (LOW) TECH

Who says all toilets need to be high tech like the ones on page 165?
Sometimes the simple solutions work the best.

HERE, THERE, EVERYWHERE

Product: The MOH, short for "Moveable Outhouse"

How It Works: Designed by a New Hampshire plumbing supply company executive named Gunnar Baldwin, the MOH is intended for use in developing countries where many people have little or no access to toilets, and clean drinking water is scarce. According to the World Health Organization, nearly half of the world's people have no access to reliable sanitation, and one in three can't get safe drinking water.

The MOH is like an ordinary outhouse, except that it's designed to be moved around fairly frequently rather than remaining fixed in one place. Unlike traditional outhouses, which are usually built over a pit several feet deep, Baldwin's MOH sits on a shallow trough that's dug only six inches deep. The dirt removed from the trough during digging is placed in buckets, and after a person uses the outhouse, they scoop out some of this dirt and put it back into the trough, on top of their waste. Microbes in the dirt help the waste biodegrade more quickly, and as soon as the dirt in the buckets is used up, the outhouse is moved to another location, where another shallow trench is dug. Spreading the waste around this way instead of collecting large quantities in a single pit makes it much less likely to contaminate groundwater, leaving it safe to drink.

THE BILL GATES SPECIAL

Product: The Tiger Toilet

How It Works: This toilet, developed with a $4.8 million grant from the Bill and Melinda Gates Foundation, is also intended for use in the developing world. It's "powered" by *Eisenia fetida*, or tiger worms, which is how the toilet gets its name. Tiger worms typically live in cow, horse, and other manures, which make them a natural for these toilets. The worms are placed in a chamber beneath the toilet. After someone uses the toilet, they flush it by pouring a bucket of water into the bowl. The waste then flows into the chamber, where the worms break it down into compost, water, and carbon dioxide. Converting the waste reduces its volume by 85 percent and kills 99 percent of pathogens, or disease-causing organisms. The worm chamber needs to be emptied only once every eight to ten years, and when it is, the compost can be used as fertilizer. Bonus: the U.S. Agency for International Development has found that users prefer the Tiger Toilets to ordinary outhouses. Reason: "Because the worms break down the solid waste, the toilets emit fewer odors and attract fewer flies," says

Ha! Pro golfer Lucas Glover doesn't wear a golf glove.

a USAID report. The Gates Foundation has pledged to spend $200 million bringing this and other toilet technologies to the developing world.

TWO IN ONE

Product: The GreenPee Sustainable Urinal

How It Works: Is it a large potted plant that people pee into? Or is it a urinal with plants growing out the top? It's actually a little of both—and it's one Dutch company's answer to the problem of after-hours public urination ("wild peeing") on the streets of Amsterdam. The large planter contains native plants and during the day it functions *only* as a planter. In the evenings, when wild peeing is more of a problem, covers are removed from the sides of the planter to reveal urinal-shaped openings. When people pee into them, a chamber stuffed with hemp fibers soaks up the urine, and over time the hemp/pee mixture biodegrades into phosphate-rich organic fertilizer that is collected and can be used to fertilize city parks and gardens. In districts where the GreenPees have been installed, public urination rates have dropped as much as 50 percent.

YOU GO, GIRL!

Product: The Peequal Female Urinal

"We had to choose between going to the loo or getting food."

How It Works: It's the UK's first female urinal designed for use at open-air concerts and other outdoor gatherings. The problem with most public urinals, including the GreenPee mentioned above, is that they're designed for men and are almost impossible for women to use. Two University of Bristol grad students, Amber Probyn and Hazel McShane, came up with the idea for the Peequal after spending too much time standing in line for portable toilets at music festivals. "We had to choose between going to the loo or getting food, because the queues for the Ladies was just insane," McShane told the BBC in 2021.

The Peequal looks a lot like an ordinary urinal, except that instead of being mounted on a wall, it's set into the floor and women stand or squat over it to use it. And instead of being enclosed inside a cubicle like a portable toilet, it sits behind waist-high privacy screens, kind of like an old-fashioned French *pissoir*. Women step behind the screen, use the urinal, then step back out again. Because their heads poke up above the screens during use, it's easy for the next woman in line to see when one of the urinals is free. Using a Peequal takes about one-sixth the time of a portable toilet, reducing lines and wait times dramatically. Bonus: the touchless, open-air design is ideal for use during the COVID-19 pandemic. "We realize this is a shift in behavior, but it's a more efficient way of doing things," Probyn says. "At the start of the day you might look at this woman's urinal and be like, 'I'm not sure about that,' but after a few [drinks], and after you've waited in the queue for about fifteen minutes already, this option suddenly becomes much more appealing."

Right on! Kea parrots have been known to "high-five" each other in midair.

WEIRD VIDEO GAME ACCESSORIES

In the early days of video games, all you needed to play was a joystick or a controller. But as gaming became a multi-billion-dollar industry, companies started introducing peripherals to "enhance" the experience. Some, like virtual reality goggles or a laser gun for shooting games, actually did enhance it; others, like these, didn't.

SNES EXERTAINMENT LIFE CYCLE

In 1994, Nintendo teamed up with exercise equipment manufacturer Life Fitness to make the Exertainment Life Cycle—a stationary bike that connected to the Super Nintendo console. Cost: $800. It came bundled with a racing game called *Mountain Bike Rally*, where players traversed virtual hills and valleys (to which the bike would respond by changing resistance levels) and a program manager to track workouts and set fitness goals. Nintendo also released a limited-edition run of *Speed Racer*, which was the only other game that worked with the Life Cycle. The bike was endorsed by Arnold Schwarzenegger, and Nintendo planned to roll out stair climbers, recumbent stationary bikes, treadmills, and fitness-themed games based on *Tetris* and *Pac-Man*. None of them were ever released. Reason: sales of the original Exertainment Life Cycle numbered in only the low thousands.

PALMTOP CONTROLLER

In the late 1990s and early 2000s, one of the most popular arcade games was *Dance Dance Revolution*. Players would dance across a floor unit, stepping on different spots in rapid succession, as dictated by the game. *DDR* and other "dance rhythm games" were a hit on home video game consoles too, provided players bought a special plastic floor mat for the dancing at a cost of about $80. Or, for about $50, they could buy the Palmtop Controller—a handheld, miniaturized *Dance Dance Revolution* floor mat that fit in the palm of the hand and allowed (lazy) players to just tap with their fingers instead of moving their feet and bodies.

WII INFLATABLE KART

One of the Wii system's biggest successes in the 2000s was *Super Mario Kart*. Utilizing the console's wireless joystick, players controlled an on-screen race car (driven by Mario, Luigi, Donkey Kong, or another Nintendo character). Upgrade: Players could purchase a small, $20 plastic driving wheel into which the cordless Wii controller was placed, creating a more natural-feeling virtual driving experience. And for $100 more, *Super Mario Kart* players could buy the Wii Inflatable Kart—a car-shaped

How much does it cost to produce the wine in a $10 bottle of wine? About a dollar.

blow-up device (it resembled a swimming pool float) that fit one child (although ads claimed the weight limit was 300 pounds). Users could sit in it in front of the TV and play *Super Mario Kart* with their fake steering wheel, thus enhancing the fake-driving experience.

GAMELINE

William von Meister, an early computer entrepreneur, started a company called Control Video Corporation in 1983. CVC's sole product: a service called GameLine. Using a special modem (a device that sends and receives computer data over regular phone lines), GameLine let users of the popular Atari 2600 game console download video games. The service offered a rotating selection of Atari games, plus one GameLine-exclusive title called *Save the Whales*. The video game industry bubble burst later in 1983, and GameLine went offline, although it never did turn a profit because it couldn't find enough subscribers willing to pay $60 for the modem, a $15 monthly fee, and $1 every time they wanted to download a game...which self-deleted after 10 plays.

SUPER GAME BOY

Introduced in 1989, Nintendo's Game Boy—the handheld, battery-powered console that allowed players to take their games to go—was an instant hit. Nintendo sold tens of millions of Game Boys, despite rudimentary graphics, a tiny two-inch, black-and-white (green-tinted) screen, and the fact that very little data could fit on a Game Boy cartridge. When the novelty wore off a few years later, Nintendo found a way to keep it going. In 1994, it introduced the Super Game Boy—a $60 adapter that allowed gamers to play Game Boy cartridges on their Super Nintendo systems, hooked up to a TV. And a few years after that, when Nintendo phased out the Super Nintendo in favor of a new console called the GameCube, it offered *another* new accessory (cost: $40)—the Game Boy Player—that let users play the Game Boy games they'd played on the Super Game Boy on the GameCube.

KID VID VOICE MODULE

In the early 1980s, video game sound consisted almost entirely of bleeps, bloops, and electronic music—the technology just wasn't advanced enough to put actual human voices into games. The Kid Vid Voice Module offered a workaround—it was an audio cassette deck that played special tapes packaged with a handful of games for the Atari 2600. For example, a kid who bought *The Smurfs Save the Day* would insert the game cartridge into their Atari, then press play on the audio cassette in the Kid Vid Voice Module, and little Smurf voices would punctuate the game. Only two games worked with the Kid Vid, and it was discontinued in 1983, the same year it was introduced.

Number of spectators at the first 1900 Olympic croquet match: one.
(Organizers canceled it for the 1904 Olympics.)

KOALA HUNTERS AND LAB MONKEYS

As we get endless rounds of movie reboots, recycled fashion trends (leopard print again?), and history repeating itself, we wonder if anything is new anymore. Yes, it is! The natural world still holds many discoveries...including new species like these.

DOES SIZE MATTER?

In the rain forest of northern Madagascar in Africa, scientists found two chameleons in 2012—a male and a female—so tiny they can fit on the end of your finger. At about only one inch long including the tail, the species was named *Brookesia nana*, or nano-chameleon, and it's thought to be the world's smallest reptile. But oddly, the male's genitals, a pair of organs called *hemipenes*, are nearly 20 percent of its body size. When researchers compared that to 51 other species of chameleon, they found that the nano-chameleon's was the 5th largest. If you're wondering why the scientists would study *that*, it turns out the shape of a reptile's genitals is often specific to each species, which helps them to classify the reptile. Because the female they found is larger than the male, herpetologists suspect the size of the male's hemipenes allows it to mate with larger females.

MONKEY SEE, MONKEY POO

Langurs are long, slender, leaf-eating monkeys, some of which have light-colored patches of fur around their eyes that make it look like they're wearing glasses. The 2020 discovery of a new species called a Popa langur in Myanmar, southeast Asia, is significant for three reasons. First, though new species of amphibians and insects are identified fairly frequently, it's much less common to find a new mammal—there are only about 5,400 mammal species, compared to an estimated one million insect species. Second, it's even rarer to discover new primates, especially as deforestation and hunting decimate their numbers. Third, researchers identified the Popa langur not by catching one in the wild, but by studying records and doing lab research. Because no one was able to track down what was suspected to be a novel species of langur in central Myanmar, scientists undertook an unusual task: They collected all the poop they could find from wild and captive langurs. From those samples, the team then extracted DNA to determine what species each came from. Finally, they studied records, measurements, and DNA from specimens of langurs held at natural

Swedish became the official language of Sweden in 2009.

history museums across the world. One century-old skeleton and skin stored in London were the key. DNA technology, which hadn't existed when the skeleton and skin were acquired, now revealed them to be from a separate species with different-shaped teeth, a longer tail, and different fur coloration than its relatives...*and* its DNA matched some of the recently collected langur poop. With this data, primatologists have now confirmed sightings of Popa langurs, with their white eye patches and a crest of fluffy gray fur on their head. Many live on Mount Popa, the ancient volcano they're named after, but sadly, they're critically endangered. It's estimated that there could be as few as 200 Popa langurs left.

EAGLE SCOUTS

Not all recently recognized species are alive today. In September 2021, paleontologists published findings that a fossil unearthed in the remote outback of southern Australia is a new species of raptor...specifically, an eagle that lived *25 million* years ago. While most ancient bird fossils consist of only a few bones, this one was nearly complete with 63 bones, prompting one of the report's authors to call it "the most exquisite fossil we have found to date." From the skeleton, they concluded that the bird had short wings, long legs, and 6-inch-long talons with which it ambushed prey from up close rather than from soaring heights like longer-winged raptors do. Called *Archaehierax sylvestris*, the bird's name comes from ancient Greek, meaning "ancient hawk of the forest." Forest? The fossil was found in barren sand dunes, so where's the forest? Answer: the scientists hypothesize that millions of years ago, the eagle hunted koala bears, prehistoric possums, and probably ducks and flamingos—which were abundant when that part of Australia was covered in dense rain forest and even had lakes with dolphins!

SNAKE EYES

Because they are cold-blooded, few reptiles can survive the frigid temperatures and low oxygen levels of the high-elevation regions in and around southwestern China. Yet, surprisingly, the plateau has five kinds of pit vipers, a category of venomous snake that senses the body heat of warm-blooded animals (prey and predators) through pits in their faces. In 2021, not one, but two new species of pit vipers were discovered there. The Nujiang pit viper has been found in only one remote village; the Glacier pit viper was located only near Dagu Glacier National Park. Researchers think glaciers play a role in keeping the plateau's vipers isolated, which prevents them from breeding with other species. That could explain why the area has so many types of pit vipers to avoid—even though all of *them* can find *you*...even in the dark.

How about you? The average person has 13 secrets that they won't share with anyone.

TRUTH BOMBS

Pearls of wisdom from today and ages past.

"There's no such thing as bad weather, only inappropriate clothing."

—Sir Ranulph Fiennes

"Art is the closest we can come to understanding how a stranger really feels."

—Roger Ebert

"Life can only be understood backwards, but it must be lived forward."

—Søren Kierkegaard

"There are only two races on this planet—the intelligent and the stupid."

—John Fowles

"Sometimes the road less traveled is less traveled for a reason."

—Jerry Seinfeld

"If it ain't one thing, it's two."

—Mulgrew Miller

"Everybody has a heart. Except some people."

—Bette Davis

"The worst you can do about a situation is nothing."

—Ice Cube

"NOTHING WISE WAS EVER PRINTED UPON AN APRON."

—Demetri Martin

"To live is so startling it leaves little time for anything else."

—Emily Dickinson

"ADVERSITY HAS A WAY OF INTRODUCING A MAN TO HIMSELF."

—Shia LaBeouf

"Perseverance is failing nineteen times and succeeding the twentieth."

—Julie Andrews

PYTHONESQUE, PART II

If you already know everything there is to know about how Monty Python formed,
how they came up with their name, and who their biggest influences
were, then you can just start reading here. If not, go to page 37.

WHAT MAKES HUMOR PYTHONESQUE?

"There was no predecessor for what we were doing," said Michael Palin. "We knew it was a bit of a gamble." That's because Python's comedy was so different from anything that came before it—like, what's so funny about a giant cartoon foot crushing an old lady? Whatever it was, the Pythons' irreverent, postmodern approach to comedy—"unbound by the tyranny of the punchline," said John Cleese—appealed to a hip, young audience that cared little for social norms. Nerds liked Python, and so did rock stars; even Elvis Presley was a fan. Though not meant for kids, Python did manage to corrupt a few of them: "The reason I became a comedian," said *Borat* star Sacha Baron Cohen, "was really from seeing *Life of Brian* when I was about eight years old."

Terry Jones's explanation for Python's unparalleled success: "We weren't concerned with making anyone but ourselves laugh." Because there's nothing less funny than trying to explain why something is funny, we'll show you the hallmarks that make a sketch show, sitcom, or movie Pythonesque.

IT'S REALLY GROSS

Python: In *The Meaning of Life*, the gluttonous Mr. Creosote (played by Jones in heavy makeup) eats so much food at a posh restaurant that his body inflates into a huge ball until he explodes, covering everyone in guts and partially digested food chunks.

Pythonesque: On HBO's *Mr. Show with Bob and David* (1995–98), one of the more disgusting sketches features former *Saturday Night Live* writer Bob Odenkirk as a plane crash victim who, like Mr. Creosote, "balls up" after eating every other crash survivor (but he doesn't explode). "Monty Python became my religion when I was 10," said Odenkirk. "It led me out of the depths of darkness." (In *Rolling Stone*'s "40 Greatest Sketch Comedy TV Shows of All Time," *Mr. Show* came in third behind *SNL* and *Flying Circus*.)

IT'S GOT CARTOONS FOR GROWN-UPS

Python: Terry Gilliam's cut-out-style animated segments (called "bumpers" in the TV business), were an important element in the show. In addition to giving *Flying Circus* its distinctive look, they kept the show moving along when a sketch lacked an ending. Many of Gilliam's cartoons are violent even by cartoonish standards—limbs detach,

Huh? Escaping from prison isn't a punishable offense in Mexico.

> "I just liked shocking people because, to me, television was this sedentary, dulling experience."

people get smooshed—and they're quite peculiar. In one short, dogs, cats, chickens, and other animals tumble into a large shredder that emits a paste that transforms into a woman's long, flowing hair. The lone American of the group, Gilliam (who went on to become an acclaimed film director) explained his approach: "I just liked shocking people because, to me, television was this sedentary, dulling experience, do[ing] anything you could do to shock the audience and wake them up was a good thing as far as I was concerned."

Pythonesque: *The Simpsons'* ultraviolent cartoon-within-a-cartoon *The Itchy & Scratchy Show* is basically *Tom and Jerry* if Terry Gilliam had made it. *Simpsons* creator Matt Groening credits Python as a major influence, especially its "whimsical surrealism with just a hint of cruelty" and the "high-velocity sense of the absurd and not stopping to explain yourself."

IT TAKES ON SACRED INSTITUTIONS

Python: In *Life of Brian*, which a critic at the BBC once described as "the most blasphemous film ever made," a peasant named Brian (Chapman) is mistaken for Jesus, who was born one stable over. The more Brian tries to convince his followers he's not the messiah, the more they're convinced he is. They even worship a gourd that Brian has dropped. "It's not heresy," said Cleese in defense of the film. "It's making fun of the way that people misunderstand the teaching."

Pythonesque: *South Park* creators Trey Parker and Matt Stone bonded in college over their mutual love of Monty Python. A 2002 *South Park* episode called "Red Hot Catholic Love" sees the clergy fooled into believing that, if parishioners stick food up their butts, they will literally "spew crap from their mouths" (which the episode calls "interorectogestion"). Like *Life of Brian*, "Red Hot Catholic Love" drew protests from religious groups.

IT SKEWERS MUSICAL COMEDY

Python: Before the 1970s, sketch comedy characters didn't suddenly break out into song, and when songs were performed on TV, they were rarely risqué or off-kilter. Then came the Pythons and their ludicrous yet catchy (and still popular) tunes like "The Lumberjack Song" and "SPAM Song" from *Flying Circus*; "Knights of the Round Table" from *Holy Grail*; and, from *The Meaning of Life*, "Always Look on the Bright Side of Life," "The Galaxy Song," and "Every Sperm Is Sacred."

Pythonesque: Another show unafraid to thumb its nose at sacred institutions—in song form—is Seth MacFarlane's animated Fox sitcom *Family Guy* (originally created in 1998 as shorts for the sketch show *Mad TV*). "I view Monty Python as the great

What are "Mad Dog," "The Drowned Chicken," and "Spaniel's Ears"?
Eighteenth-century women's hairstyles.

originator of that combination," said MacFarlane. "'Every Sperm Is Sacred' is so beautifully written, it's musically and lyrically legit, the orchestrations are fantastic... It's treated seriously." MacFarlane tries to give the same treatment to his songs, like when a forlorn Santa Claus and his elves sing "Christmastime Is Killing Us," or when Peter (the dad) sings about censorship by the "Freakin' FCC": "Make a joke about your bowels and they order in the troops."

IT SHATTERS THE FOURTH WALL

Python: Before Monty Python, "breaking the fourth wall"—when a character talks directly to the audience during a scripted, filmed performance—was rare (although George Burns, Groucho Marx, and *The Monkees* mastered it). But the general rule was: don't remind the audience they're watching a show. Then came *Flying Circus*, where at any time a colonel played by Graham Chapman might barge into a sketch and deem it "too silly" to continue. One memorable fourth-wall break comes at the end of *Life of Brian* when Brian is tied to the cross, and one of the other crucified victims (Idle) starts cheerfully singing "Always Look on the Bright Side of Life." Between verses, Idle turns to the camera and says, "It's the end of the film. Incidentally, this record's available in the foyer."

Pythonesque: Mel Brooks (whom Gilliam once called the "closest thing to Monty Python in the U.S.") included a scene in his 1987 *Star Wars* spoof *Spaceballs* that has the bad guys watching the VHS tape of *Spaceballs* to find out what happens next. More recently, in *Deadpool* (2016), Wade (Ryan Reynolds) breaks the fourth wall so many times that in one scene he points out that he's making a "fourth-wall break *inside* a fourth-wall break? That's like 16 walls!" (Sharp-eyed viewers will catch several nods to Monty Python in *Deadpool*.)

IT PUTS THE SILLY IN PHYSICAL COMEDY

Python: Physical comedy is as old as comedy itself—perfected by the likes of Charlie Chaplin and Buster Keaton...and John Cleese. One of the best-known *Flying Circus* sketches, "The Ministry of Silly Walks," features the 6'5" Cleese as a stiff-upper-lipped bureaucrat who breaks out in a high-stepping gait that's still imitated today.

Pythonesque: Another smart-meets-silly sketch show was Comedy Central's *Key & Peele* (2012–15). Starring former *Mad TV* castmates Keegan-Michael Key and Jordan Peele, one oft-imitated sketch features the duo playing hotel doormen who become increasingly excited over their mutual love of action-movie star Liam Neeson—to the point where they're running in circles, jumping up and down, and performing an Irish stepdance, all while screeching "LEEM NEESONS" over and over. *Key & Peele* executive producer Ian Roberts, who cofounded the Upright Citizens Brigade, yet another Python-influenced troupe (that begat Amy Poehler, among others), says that both *Key*

Those who know say that the brain has a similar texture to warm scallops when touched.

& Peele and Monty Python "love to undercut secret weaknesses and the things that are humiliating about human nature...They love to go after machismo and manhood."

Python: A famous *Flying Circus* sketch (which also appears in their 1971 compilation movie, *And Now for Something Completely Different*), stars Idle as a man who asks a stranger in a pub, "Is your wife a goer, eh? Know what I mean? Know what I mean? Nudge nudge. Wink wink. Say no more. Know what I mean?"

Pythonesque: That kind of humor was too risqué for American television. That is, until Python devotee Lorne Michaels created *Saturday Night Live*. In a 1998 Ana Gasteyer–penned *SNL* sketch, she and Molly Shannon play soft-spoken NPR cooking-show hosts who interview Alec Baldwin, playing Pete Schweddy. "Over at Season's Eatings," says Pete, "we have balls for every taste...No one can resist my Schweddy Balls."

THE FUTURE'S SO BRIGHT

Python's influence is alive and kicking. Nowhere is that more apparent than with Australian sketch comedy troupe Aunty Donna, considered by many comedy veterans (including Ed Helms and Bob Saget) to be "the second coming of Monty Python." Take one of Aunty Donna's most popular sketches (1.5 million YouTube views and counting) that features a shop teacher (Broden Kelly) telling two students (Zachary Ruane and Mark Bonanno): "Don't get in the kiln!" But all the dim-witted students keep hearing is, "Get in the kiln." It wouldn't be funny in the hands of lesser comedians, and brings to mind a scene from *The Holy Grail* where the King of Swamp Castle (Palin) orders two guards (Idle and Chapman) to, "Stay here, and make sure the prince doesn't leave." Every time the king leaves the room, the guards follow him out, despite his repeated pleas and explanations.

In the same way that the young Pythons came of age listening to *The Goon Show*, Aunty Donna grew up watching *Mr. Show*, *SNL*, and *Flying Circus*. And they're just one of countless young sketch troupes keeping alive that dangerous brand of comedy that the Pythons pioneered: profane, silly, and satirical, with a healthy disdain for authority and a knowing wink to the audience. (Nudge nudge.)

* * *

MONUMENTAL MOUTHFUL

In 1995, a Beijing dentist named Yu Qian wanted to warn his patients about the dangers of poor dental hygiene, so he built an eight-foot-tall sculpture depicting five huge teeth, made out of 28,000 rotten teeth he'd extracted from 100,000 patients over more than 30 years. It took him two years to glue the rotten teeth into place.

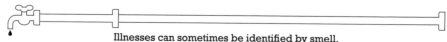

Illnesses can sometimes be identified by smell.
Typhoid fever sufferers smelled like freshly baked bread, diabetics smell fruity...

HEADACHE CURES THROUGH HISTORY

Over-the-counter pain relievers in pill form have been available for more than a century—aspirin became available in 1899, followed by Tylenol in 1955 and ibuprofen in 1983. It's a modern medical miracle how quickly they can cure a headache—especially considering the treatments available in the centuries before their discovery and invention.

CLAY CROCODILE

The Ebers Papyrus, named for Egyptologist Georg Ebers, who translated it in 1874, dates to 1550 BC and discusses several ancient medical remedies, including one for head pain. According to the Ebers Papyrus, a headache could be cured by forming a crocodile out of "medicinal clay" (primarily ochre, which is clay and ferric oxide) and placing grains in its mouth, then strapping it to the sufferer's head with a strip of linen with the names of gods that could intervene written on it. (Present-day medical historians say this actually could have helped with a headache, because the tightly held crocodile put pressure on the scalp, which would have relieved the distended blood vessels that lead to pain.)

BILE VOMIT

Around 2,000 years ago, the prominent ancient Roman physician Galen wrote that headaches could be attributed to an imbalance in the four "humors"—the driving liquids of the body. Of the humors—blood, phlegm, black bile, and yellow bile—Galen believed that headaches were caused by an excess of yellow bile, and could be cured by vomiting up as much of it as possible.

FIRE

Aretaeus of Cappadocia, a Roman province in what is today Turkey, was one of the empire's most esteemed physicians in the late 2nd century—but his recommended treatment for headaches was still pretty extreme. He advised patients to shave off all their hair and then apply fire to their scalps until the muscles and bones were exposed.

But that wasn't Aretaeus's only remedy. Bloodletting was his go-to for many problems, including headaches. He wrote of sharpening the spine of a goose feather and inserting it all the way up the nose and moving it up and down until blood started gushing out of the nostrils. Getting rid of all that blood would, theoretically, relieve pressure on the brain.

...and yellow-fever sufferers smelled "like a butcher's shop."
The sweat of schizophrenics can smell like the spray of a skunk.

GARLIC

Al-Zahrawi, personal surgeon and doctor to the caliph Al-Hakam II of Spain in the late 900s, advocated applying a hot iron to the head. If that didn't work, he recommended taking a head of garlic, peeling it, slicing it at each end, and then surgically inserting it into the head.

DEAD MOLE

Ali ibn Isa al-Kahhal was an astronomer and the pre-eminent ophthalmologist of the Medieval Muslim world. In the late 10th century, he suggested that the way to cure a headache was to find a mole, kill it, and then bind it to the part of the head that hurt.

HONEY BATH

Moses ben Maimon, better known as Maimonides, was a prominent physician in the Spanish city of Córdoba in the 12th century, when it was the capital of a Muslim caliphate and a major educational hub. He treated patients who had persistent headaches by submerging them in a bath of warm and honey-sweetened water, believing that the concoction drew out "the vapors" which he said were the cause of headaches.

VINEGAR, OPIUM, FLOUR

In the 1300s in Europe, a commonly prescribed treatment in England and France was the application of a *poultice*, a gloopy mixture made from linseed or flour, thought to relieve infection or inflammation. For headaches, the proper poultice was one that had been soaked in vinegar and opium. (It might have worked—vinegar can open the pores on the head, which would allow opium, a powerful pain reliever, to soak in through the skin.)

ELECTRIC EELS

The Dutch Society of Sciences published a report in 1762 calling for a natural remedy for headaches that one of its members had picked up on their travels in South America: electric eels. According to that scientist, slaves with headaches were told to put one hand on the affected part of their head and to use their other hand to grab an eel, which would send its electrical impulses into the person and would relieve pain "without exception."

SPINNING

In the 1770s, Erasmus Darwin (grandfather of explorer and evolution proponent Charles Darwin) advocated the medical theory of centrifugation, particularly as a treatment for headaches. In short, he thought that a person suffering from an aching head would experience relief if they were spun around as quickly as possible, and for as long as it took to force the blood (thought to be causing the headache) from the skull down to the patient's feet.

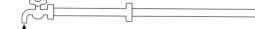

#overload: Every second, 995 photos are uploaded to Instagram.

MORE GROANERS

Uncle John loves jokes that are so bad they're good (but are also still pretty bad).

I just bought a new chimney and I can't believe how much it cost me. The price was through the roof.

My only plans for today are to go buy some new glasses with my wife. After that, we'll see.

Did you hear about the guy who invented a clock with 10 dials? He had a lot of time on his hands.

They say I'm addicted to stealing batteries out of watches, but I can stop anytime I want.

If you turn over a canoe you can wear it as a hat. Because it's capsized.

Poor Phillip lost his lip in an accident. Now we just call him Phil.

It looked like nobody showed up to the first meeting of the Camouflage Club.

I think I might be psychic. I've thought so ever since next Tuesday.

I just found the absolute worst page in the entire dictionary. The words I saw were disgusting, dishonest, disingenuous, and disgraceful.

I always wanted to be an archaeologist. Now my career is in ruins.

I've seen a lot of chiropractors, but that's just my back story.

Two silkworms had a race. But they ended in a tie.

A farmer bought a dairy cow he was convinced would produce milk, but it didn't. Talk about an udder failure.

Q: What do you call a typo on a tombstone?
A: A grave mistake.

Great housekeepers aren't born. They're maid.

Did you hear about the explosion at the clothing store? There were many casual tees.

I failed math so many times I can't even count.

A dolphin strapped on a fake fin and swam near the beach and scared everyone away. It was a killer whale impression.

I accidentally gave my wife a glue stick instead of her lipstick. She's still not talking to me.

Q: What sound does a 747 make when it bounces?
A: Boeing Boeing Boeing!

Did you know that you can lose a lot of weight by wearing bread on your head? It's a loaf-hat diet.

Q: How do you think the unthinkable?
A: With an itheberg.

A third of all American cats are stray or feral.

DECODING OBITUARIES

Obituary writing can be tricky. In not much space, the writer has to convey the entire life of the deceased individual while also announcing the circumstances of their death...but without revealing too much, so as to not offend the readers' sensibilities and also protect the privacy of the dead person's family. But there are certain aspects of that ended life that can't not be mentioned, so writers developed these euphemisms. They don't much appear in obituaries anymore, but they were common from the late 19th century to the late 20th century.

Tireless raconteur: long-winded

Gave colorful accounts of his exploits: a liar

Consummate professional: workaholic

Didn't suffer fools lightly: cranky and unpleasant

Utterly carefree: had a mental illness

Ladies' man: serial adulterer

Generous with his affections: a man who aggressively hit on women

Vivacious: hard drinker

Fun-loving: hard drinker

Lived life to the fullest: hard drinker

Died of natural causes: not an accident or overdose, likely a heart attack or after a long period of illness

Lifelong bachelor: gay

Never married: gay

Flamboyant: gay

Eccentric: a social outcast without many friends

Died unexpectedly: the death was due to a violent crime, drug overdose, or suicide

Died at home: in Victorian times, it explicitly meant the deceased took their own life

Died after a long struggle: succumbed to the effects of a long-term addiction or alcoholism

Died surrounded by family: the death wasn't painful, and it was expected, following a long illness

Respiratory failure or pneumonia: if this appeared in the obituary of a young man in the 1980s, it often meant he had died of HIV or AIDS

Strongly principled: stubborn

Free spirit: unreliable, flaky, unemployed, or unemployable

Colorful character: a jerk

OGs: The earliest historical evidence of dreadlocks are murals depicting people of the Minoan civilization (in what's now Greece) wearing them around 1600 BC.

WHY WE LAUGH

Now for a somewhat serious examination of the evolutionary origins of smiling, laughing, and telling jokes. Each behavior came separately, and millions of years apart.

WANNA HEAR A JOKE?

What does a caveman do on a Friday night? He goes clubbing! Sorry for the "low-brow" humor, but if it made you smile, it might surprise you to know that humor could be "the most complex cognitive function in the animal kingdom." That's according to evolutionary psychiatrists Joseph Polimeni and Jeffrey Reiss. "Even a simple joke," they say, "can utilize language skills, theory-of-mind, symbolism, abstract thinking, and social perception." As it turns out, the act of telling jokes is only the most recent development in our uniquely human sense of humor, which originated long before there was language...or cavemen. So why *do* we laugh?

IT'S A DEFENSE MECHANISM

• Say cheese. Seriously, say it loudly, without smiling, and you'll feel your teeth clench and your lips separate. That awkward "proto-smile" predates modern humans by about 30 million years, when our primate ancestors started baring their teeth (perhaps mimicking tigers or wolves) as a display of dominance. But merely showing one's teeth wasn't enough, so the display came with aggressive body language: standing tall while puffing out the chest and waving the arms around.

• How did all that lead to the smile? When a weaker primate was cornered, the aggressive body language would gradually subside, leaving only the display of teeth—which elicited a response in the aggressor along the lines of, "You've got to be kidding me."

• Teeth-baring sans body language is what's known as an appeasement display. It means "I'm no threat" to others in the group as well as to strangers. Janice Porteous, who studies humor at Vancouver Island University, observed this behavior in rhesus monkeys: "Subordinate members...flash that bared-teeth expression to the dominant member when they are occupying a spot that the dominant wants to occupy. The expression seems to deflect the dominant's aggression, so it's a sign of submission... resulting in the dominant leaving them alone."

• This defense mechanism allowed our weaker ancestors to live long enough to reproduce. It further took hold as a method for parents and children to establish a nonverbal connection. Result: Smiling became an innate part of our behavior, and not just when we're amused. We also smile when we're nervous—a modern form of appeasement display.

The peace sign is a combination of the semaphore symbols for
N and *D*, which stand for "nuclear disarmament."

IT'S A BONDING TOOL

- By studying modern primates and comparing them to the fossil record, researchers have narrowed the origins of laughter to somewhere around 13 million years ago.
- In 2009, Marina Davila Ross, a psychologist at the University of Portsmouth, reported that orangutans, gorillas, chimpanzees, and bonobos exhibit laughter, or, as she describes it, "tickle-induced vocalizations." How did she arrive at this conclusion? She tickled them.

> Orangutans, gorillas, and chimpanzees exhibit "tickle-induced vocalizations."

- Her study found that laughter most likely began during playtime between juvenile monkeys. As with human babies, nonhuman primate infants first learn to laugh by mimicking it, after which it becomes an involuntary response—not unlike blushing (another quirky human trait that began as a primate appeasement display).

IT'S A SOCIAL NETWORK BUILDER

- *Homo sapiens* (us) showed up between 200,000 and 300,000 years ago. An unprecedented time of accelerated brain growth followed, including the development of language, which started to take hold around 150,000 years ago.
- The "social brain hypothesis" posits that the brain got so big in such a short time, not because we needed to learn how to survive by making tools, but because we needed to learn how to live with each other in rapidly expanding, complex social groups. According to Pedro Marijuán and Jorge Navarro at the Health Sciences Institute of Aragon in Spain, laughing—or as they describe it, "this unusual sound feature of our species"—played an integral part in both language building and social development because it allowed for people who weren't part of the conversation to still take part in it.
- So crucial was laughing to social stability, say Marijuán and Navarro, that it evolved to become a built-in, involuntary response, like smiling. "Laughter, far from being a curious evolutionary relic or a rather trivial innate behavior," they conclude, "should be considered as a highly efficient tool for inter-individual problem solving and for maintenance of social bonds."

IT'S THE GLUE OF HUMANITY

- According to Polimeni and Reiss in their 2006 article, "The First Joke: Exploring the Evolutionary Origins of Humor," telling jokes spurred language along by teaching prehistoric people how to think "outside the box" in order to "get" the joke. Because comedy requires shared experiences, humor helped early modern humans learn to talk to each other.

Football fact: Until 1897, a field goal was worth five points, and a touchdown, four.

- For example, the caveman joke requires rudimentary knowledge of both anthropology (cavemen hit things with clubs) and modern lifestyles (people go "clubbing" at nightclubs). Utilizing abstract thinking, your brain might paint a mental picture of a club-wielding caveman in a nightclub, or it might see two pictures—a caveman and a nightclub—connected by a play on words. Either way, you've visualized an incongruous situation so absurd that it elicits involuntary convulsions...otherwise known as laughter.

- The big takeaway is that our sense of humor isn't merely a quirk of being human; without it, we most likely wouldn't have become the dominant species on the planet. And ever since that quirk of nature happened, we haven't stopped trying to crack one another up. Here's the oldest known joke, etched into a tablet by a cheeky Sumerian circa 1900 BC: "Something which has never occurred since time immemorial; a young woman did not fart in her husband's lap." (We've gotten funnier.)

Bonus Facts

- Unlike speech, laughs are symmetrical—recordings of laughter sound the same whether played forward or in reverse.

- Another mammal that researchers have observed making "tickle-induced vocalizations": rats. When tickled, they emit chirping sounds, and will even follow the scientist's hand around for more tickling. Studies of rodent emotions show that they're remarkably similar to human emotions, and these studies may lead to improved treatments for depression.

DID YOU KNOW?

Next time you're in a bad mood, try smiling. Don't pretend—actually smile. According to psychologists, the simple act actually tricks your brain into thinking you're happy, releasing chemicals that really do lift your spirits.

- Some benefits of laughing regularly: it increases your oxygen intake, makes it easier to relax, boosts your immune system, lowers your heart rate, and reduces blood pressure.

- A recent survey asked 2,500 workers from various industries if they would accept a pay cut if it meant having more fun at work. More than half said they would.

- A study proved that laughter really is contagious, or rather, a *behavioral* contagion. When test subjects heard the sound of laughter, it activated the premotor cortical region of the brain, which prepares the facial muscles to move. "It really seems to be true," said lead researcher Sophie Scott, "laugh and the whole world laughs with you."

- Do you suffer from no sense of humor? Good news! Unlike smiling and laughing—which are innate—a sense of humor is a learned behavior that can be nurtured. The first step: identify whatever it is that you find even remotely funny (like, perhaps, this book) and then surround yourself with as much of that humor as you can. (In other words, buy more *Uncle John's Bathroom Readers!*)

Hey, fathead! Your brain makes up about 2 percent of your body weight but uses 20 percent of the calories you consume.

BATHROOM NEWS

Come one, come all for another commodious collection of chronicles from the can!

SLIP SLIDING AWAY

Ultimate Slip 'N Slide was intended to be a lighthearted summertime reality series for NBC in 2021. It featured teams of adult contestants running around a water park competing in challenges and stunts with names like "Body Bowling," "Bocce Fall," "Cornhole," and "The Big Slipper," which a press release called "a colossal slide meant for only the bravest and boldest players." Production was suspended indefinitely and then canceled following an on-set outbreak of *giardia*, a microscopic parasite that, if swallowed, causes severe and violent diarrhea. A crew member tested positive after falling ill and 40 other crew members were affected, some of whom collapsed on set with diarrhea and were seen running for the portable toilets.

TOP FIVE BATHROOM NO-NO'S

In 2019, the British home-improvement retail company B&Q polled 2,000 people about their bathroom pet peeves. Tying for fourth and fifth place at 17 percent each: bathroom hogs and dirty clothes on the floor. In third place at 18 percent: wet towels left behind. In second place at 21 percent: hair in the drain. And at 33 percent, the number-one pet-peeve: the empty toilet paper roll wasn't replaced.

TRUE INTIMACY

Pop singer Meghan Trainor—winner of the 2016 Grammy Award for Best New Artist for her hit "All About That Bass"—married former child star Daryl Sabara (*Spy Kids*) in 2018. In 2021, Meghan's brother, Ryan Trainor, appeared on the podcast *Why Won't You Date Me?* and talked about wanting a relationship, but not one as close as his sister and brother-in-law's. "They poop together! She's pooping and Daryl's like, 'I'm going to go hang out with you now!'" he said. Meghan confirmed on *The Today Show* that she does indeed have a bathroom outfitted with two toilets, which comes in handy because they've got a newborn baby. "A lot of times in the middle of the night when we're with the baby, we gotta pee at the same time. So I was like, 'Can we please have two toilets next to each other?'" She added that they use their his-and-hers potties often, but clarified on Twitter that they've only gone number two together once, "and we laughed and said never again."

Does it operate on a need-to-know basis?
There's a CIA Museum in Virginia...but it's not open to the public.

PINK FLOYD'S PIG

At the BRI, we each have our preferred music to listen to while we write. For one of our veteran writers, it's Pink Floyd...and he had their 1977 album Animals *playing on repeat for weeks while he was researching this story about the British band's mascot: a giant inflatable pig.*

🐷 CRASS MENAGERIE

"Big man, pig man, ha-ha, charade you are!" sings Roger Waters on Pink Floyd's 10th studio album, *Animals*. Released in January 1977, the progressive rock album is an angry diatribe—in the vein of George Orwell's 1945 novel *Animal Farm*—that uses pigs, dogs, horses, and sheep as metaphors for the deceit and decay wrought by capitalism. In the 1970s, album covers were a much bigger deal than they are today. Their high-concept artistry and elaborate packaging were pored over by fans and critics nearly as much as the music. The design firm behind some of the most iconic covers from this era—for bands like Led Zeppelin, Genesis, T. Rex, AC/DC, Paul McCartney and Wings, and dozens more—was called Hipgnosis, best known for their collaborations with Pink Floyd (including the triangle-and-prism-themed *Dark Side of the Moon*).

In late 1976, Floyd hired Hipgnosis to create the cover for the album *Animals*. Hipgnosis cofounder Storm Thorgerson pitched the cover idea of a little boy walking in on his parents while they're making love in bed. Pink Floyd rejected it.

🐷 WHEN PIGS FLY

The band's lyricist and bass player, Roger Waters, and Hipgnosis's other cofounder, Aubrey Powell, had already come up with another cover idea: a photograph of a giant pig flying between the four smokestacks on top of Battersea Power Station. Built in the 1930s along the River Thames, this seven-story coal-burning plant could be seen for miles around the city—including from Waters's apartment. As he recounted to *Rolling Stone*, he was drawn to the London landmark's strange architecture: "It had four legs. If you inverted it, it was like a table. And there were four bits to it, representing the four members of the band."

Thorgerson wasn't as enthusiastic about the idea of flying a pig over Battersea. "Despite serious misgivings about such a notion (shades of Monty Python and the Goodies—was it not intrinsically silly?) we offered to shoot the pictures and put the cover together," he wrote in his book *The Work of Hipgnosis*. Their original plan was to take two separate photos—the power station, and a balloon in the air—and then combine them on the cover, but the band was insistent that it not be achieved by any kind of trickery. So Hipgnosis commissioned acclaimed Australian artist Jeffery Shaw to design a 40-foot-long inflatable pink pig (technically a sow), which was then manufactured by the German zeppelin airship company, Ballon Fabrik. Waters named her Algie; the cover shoot was scheduled for December 2, 1976.

🐖 TAKE 1

Hipgnosis and Pink Floyd arrived at Battersea on that cold, windy morning with the proper permits, a deflated pig, a ground crew, three film crews (to shoot a video for the song "Pigs on the Wing"), eleven photographers, and a helicopter. There was also a rifle marksman on hand, ready to shoot the pig out of the sky if the cables failed. The conditions were ideal for Powell, who was in charge of the production, to get a dramatic photo of the power station lit by the low winter sun beneath billowing clouds. Now they just needed the pig. The plan was to secure a steel cable to the balloon, fill the balloon with helium, raise it with a winch (from the back of a truck), and then tether it between two of the 338-foot-tall smokestacks. But it took the crew so long to inflate the balloon that it was getting too dark to raise it. Everyone was sent home.

🐖 TAKE 2

They all came back the next day...except for the marksman. Recollections differ as to why: either he was too expensive, or Hipgnosis simply forgot to rebook him. The second time, the balloon inflated just fine and the crew was able to raise it into position, but only for a moment. "Suddenly, there was a communal gasp," Powell recalled in the book *The Love of Vinyl.* "The cable had snapped in a fierce gust of wind and the pig drifted up and away into the flight path to Heathrow airport." The helicopter pilot couldn't follow the balloon into air traffic, and everyone on the ground could only watch helplessly as it floated out of sight. Meanwhile, the Civil Aviation Authority (CAA) started getting strange calls from pilots about a gigantic pig. Once the CAA realized the pilots weren't joking, they diverted and grounded all flights.

The balloon couldn't be tracked by radar (no metal parts), so a police helicopter pilot named David Voy was sent to find it, which he said wasn't too difficult: "It was the size of a bus." Voy flew below the pig for several minutes, while the CAA used the helicopter's transponder to track it until it left Heathrow airspace and headed east toward the English countryside. (Algie was rumored to have reached an altitude of 18,000 feet, and there are conflicting reports that the British Royal Air Force scrambled fighter jets.)

Back at Battersea, the band had long since fled the scene when police arrested Powell and told everyone else to go home and remain there. The band members called radio DJs, who asked listeners to keep their eyes out for "Pink Floyd's missing pig." At 9:30 p.m., Powell received a phone call from an angry farmer in Kent, more than 30 miles away: "Are you the guy looking for a pig? It's in my field scaring my cows to death!"

The U.S. Treasury has a "Conscience Fund"—a fund to which people can contribute money if they feel bad about cheating on their taxes.

🐖 TAKE 3

After retrieving and repairing the balloon, they all came back the next day—including the marksman—and the third attempt went off without a hitch...kind of. "As if the whole event hadn't been enough of a fiasco, and very funny at that," Thorgerson wrote, "the band liked the sky and power station from Day 1 (but there was no pig) and the pig from Day 3, but the sky was boring." Result: Pink Floyd reluctantly gave Hipgnosis permission to cut and paste the Day 3 pig onto the power station photo from Day 1. "It is true," said Thorgerson, "that we were seen to smile somewhat when they decided to do that."

🐖 A WIN FOR CAPITALISM

"Pink Floyd couldn't have got better publicity if they tried," added Powell. But it wasn't all good publicity—as many critics pointed out, they were lucky they didn't cause a plane crash. But the band hadn't, as many had charged, released the pig on purpose. The record company, EMI, capitalized on the controversy by holding the album-release press conference in front of the power station. (The band did not attend.)

Animals went multiplatinum, selling over four million copies. And the cover—along with the wild story of its creation—further solidified Battersea Power Station as a London icon. In the 2010s, after the building and crumbling smokestacks were scheduled for demolition (to put in luxury condos), Battersea was saved as a historical landmark. As of this writing, the four smokestacks are being painstakingly restored. The 42-acre grounds will be turned into a multi-use, gentrified riverfront property, where tourists can catch a show and get a bite to eat, and locals can walk their dogs (or pigs or sheep).

> **DID YOU KNOW?**
> Pigs have surprisingly complex methods of communicating with each other—including by scent, body language, and at least 20 different grunting vocalizations. Studies have shown that they're more intelligent than dogs, chimpanzees, and three-year-old humans.

🐖 PIG TALES

After the album came out, Algie became a permanent fixture at Pink Floyd concerts, flying over the arena or stadium suspended from a cable. Then it all came crashing down. In the early 1980s, Waters and his bandmates went through a "bitter divorce," as the press called it. The other three members—David Gilmour, Nick Mason, and Rick Wright—got to continue using the name "Pink Floyd," and Waters won the rights to the pig. He stipulated that if the new Pink Floyd wanted to fly their own pig, they'd have to pay him $800 for every concert. The band had no intention of paying. "Someone suggested that if we altered the design," David Gilmour recalled, "then Roger couldn't claim it." Result: on Pink Floyd's 1987-89 tour, the pig had testicles.

Since then, Pink Floyd–inspired pigs have been popping up in the oddest of places—in movies like *Children of Men* and *Nanny McPhee Returns*, in the video game *The Sims 2*, and on *The Simpsons* (guest star Peter Frampton said he bought his pig at Pink Floyd's yard sale). But for Roger Waters, who came up with the original concept behind the *Animals* album, the pig has never lost its political meaning.

- On a 2006 Roger Waters tour, the helium-filled pig had "Impeach Bush" printed on it.
- Two years later, it said "Obama." During Waters's 2008 tour, the pig escaped several times—twice in Texas, once in Argentina, and most famously at the 2008 Coachella music festival in California, where the anti-capitalist symbol came to rest in a country club.
- In 2017, Waters gave a Chicago architect permission to float four gold pigs in front of Trump Tower so they blocked out the name "Trump."
- On Waters's 2017 tour, the pig was emblazoned with the message: "Bombs and Death Come From Here"...with an arrow pointing to its butt.

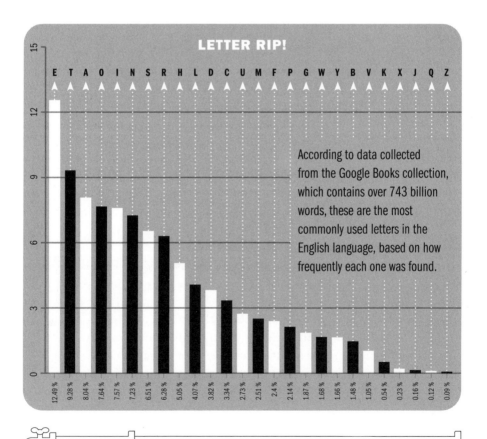

LETTER RIP!

According to data collected from the Google Books collection, which contains over 743 billion words, these are the most commonly used letters in the English language, based on how frequently each one was found.

E	T	A	O	I	N	S	R	H	L	D	C	U	M	F	P	G	W	Y	B	V	K	X	J	Q	Z
12.49%	9.28%	8.04%	7.64%	7.57%	7.23%	6.51%	6.28%	5.05%	4.07%	3.82%	3.34%	2.73%	2.51%	2.4%	2.14%	1.87%	1.68%	1.66%	1.48%	1.05%	0.54%	0.23%	0.16%	0.12%	0.09%

The first World Series grand slam home run and first World Series unassisted triple play both occurred in the same game: Game Five of the 1920 World Series.

RANDOM ORIGINS

Once again, the BRI asks—and answers—the question:
Where does all this stuff come from? origins

EGG CARTONS

For centuries, eggs were delivered from the chicken coop to the marketplace in baskets cushioned with grass or straw. That was never a perfect method, and broken eggs were common. In 1906, a British inventor named Thomas Bethell created the Raylite Egg Box. It was a wooden chest with strips of wood (or cardboard) arranged in a crisscross pattern, creating small compartments for each of the eggs. The Raylite was intended for farmers, though, not shoppers, so broken eggs remained a problem. In 1911, a Canadian newspaper publisher named Joseph Coyle overheard a hotel manager arguing with his supplier about broken eggs. Seeing dollar signs, Coyle sold his paper and got to work designing a cheap, effective way to solve the problem. In 1918, he patented the Coyle Egg Safety Carton, a cardboard box with separate, oblong divots that each held one egg. The cartons haven't changed much since, except for the materials: recycled cardboard egg cartons came along in 1952, and Styrofoam ones were introduced in 1967.

ADJUSTABLE WRENCH

Swedish industrialist Johan Petter Johansson obtained more than 100 patents in the late 19th century for machine parts, tools, lamps, and even a pair of sugar tongs. While toiling away at his workshop, he was often annoyed at having to switch between different wrenches for the varying sizes of nuts and bolts. In 1888, he patented the "Iron Hand," a wrench with a wheel connected to the jaw that could adjust to the size of the nut. It debuted in 1892, available in six sizes. Thanks to a distribution deal with a major European tool company, more than 100 million of Johansson's adjustable wrenches were sold by 1900.

"THE STAR-SPANGLED BANNER" AT SPORTING EVENTS

After witnessing the bombardment of American forces during the War of 1812, Francis Scott Key wrote "The Star-Spangled Banner." In 1916, President Woodrow Wilson signed an executive order making it the national anthem. Its association with sports began in 1862 when a band played it as a patriotic overture during the Civil War at a baseball game at the Capitoline Grounds in New York City. The national anthem showed up again in Chicago at the 1918 World Series. To commemorate the loss of 116,000 American troops in World War I, a military band (who only played at ballparks during special events) spontaneously played it during the seventh-inning stretch. Boston Red Sox third baseman, Fred Thomas, playing while on furlough from the U.S. Navy, saluted, prompting other players—and many fans in the stands—to place their hands on their hearts. When the Series moved to Boston, the Red Sox' front office hired a band to play "The Star-Spangled Banner" before the game. It didn't become a pregame ritual until the late 1940s when PA systems allowed for a singer with a microphone to belt out the tune (or try to, it's notoriously difficult to sing).

HEADPHONES

The first personal listening devices were headsets worn by telephone switchboard operators in the 1880s. These cumbersome contraptions weighed about 10 pounds each and attached to a headband. The following decade, Londoners could subscribe to a service called Electrophone. For £5 a year (three weeks' wages for an average worker), customers got a similar device that connected to their telephone and piped in live classical music. The first comfortable headphones were invented in 1910 by a Utah engineer named Nathaniel Baldwin, who took the earpieces from two telephone receivers and glued them to an arched headband. The U.S. Navy ordered 100 pairs, which Baldwin assembled himself on his kitchen table. In 1958, Wisconsin businessman John Koss devised the first stereo headphones: the SP/3. That same year, he and engineer Martin Lange developed a portable record player that came in a set with the headphones. Their timing was terrific: the rise of rock 'n' roll created a market for parents who didn't want to hear their kids' loud music.

PORTABLE ELECTRIC HAND DRILL

Inspired by large (but slow-turning) industrial rock-drilling machines, in 1895, German engineers Wilhelm and Carl Fein invented a miniature drill that weighed 17 pounds. The size of a briefcase, workers had to grip two handles and force their body weight against a chest plate to propel the weak motor. In 1910, two friends who worked at the Rowland Telegraph Company in Baltimore quit their jobs and pooled their money to open a workshop dedicated to building a better portable drill. S. Duncan Black took out a second mortgage on his home, and Alonzo Decker sold his car, and it took them seven years to perfect their invention. Inspired by a revolver, Black and Decker's drill was shaped like a gun and it operated like a gun—the power switch was a trigger, enabling the user to hold it and operate it with one hand. Inside was a powerful motor that could run off of AC or DC power. First available in 1917, Black and Decker built a manufacturing facility to meet demand, and by 1919 they'd sold more than 200,000 electric drills.

*   *   *

"When the going gets weird, the weird turn pro."

—Hunter S. Thompson

Who is Zelda Wynn Valdes?
The African American fashion designer who created the original Playboy Bunny costumes.

MYTH-CONCEPTIONS

"Common knowledge" is frequently wrong. Here are some more examples of things that many people believe...but according to our sources, just aren't true.

Myth: Polar bears are white.

Fact: Their fur can be yellow, gray, orange, or even green. The outermost layer of polar bear fur is both hollow and transparent, and so when light hits it, it appears white. Looking white (while not really being white) helps polar bears blend in with their snowy and icy climate, making them more effective predators.

Myth: Until a vaccine was developed, a polio diagnosis guaranteed either certain death or a lifetime of paralysis.

Fact: In the 20th century, before the Salk and Sabin vaccines eradicated the disease, polio's mortality rate was quite low. About three-quarters of people diagnosed with polio didn't even experience any symptoms. About 25 percent endured a short and mild illness, and 1 to 5 percent had serious symptoms that required hospitalization. The reason polio was so feared and looms so large in history is because: 1) it was mysterious—no one knew what caused it or how to treat it; and 2) those who got serious cases suffered greatly—about 1 percent of polio patients were permanently paralyzed, and for 5 to 30 percent of *that* group, the disease was fatal.

Myth: President William Howard Taft once got stuck in the White House bathtub.

Fact: At six feet tall and 340 pounds when he was inaugurated in 1909, President Taft had everyday objects custom-made to fit—such as the extra-wide, extra-long bathtub in the ship he used to oversee construction of the Panama Canal in the early 1900s. That's the tub he moved into the White House, and it was plenty big enough for "Big Bill." The rumor that he got stuck in there was probably started by toilet and tub manufacturers, who were out for revenge after President Taft broke up a porcelain price-fixing ring.

Myth: In 1854, Henry David Thoreau wrote *Walden*, a meditation on the joys of living in nature. He wrote it in self-imposed isolation, living far away from civilization in a cabin near Walden Pond in Massachusetts.

Fact: The woods around Walden Pond weren't home to just Thoreau. They housed a small but sizable loose-knit community consisting primarily of runaway slaves, people too poor to live in towns, ex-cons, and other misfits who lived on the fringes of society.

Myth: A bite from a black widow spider can and will kill a human being.

Fact: A bite from a black widow spider is almost never fatal. In a six-year period in the 2000s, there were about 23,000 documented black widow bites. Number of people who died from those bites: zero.

Priests in ancient Egypt were not permitted to eat onions.
Reason: it was believed onions increased a man's libido.

THINKING BIG BY THINKING SMALL

Do you have a "Little Free Library" in your neighborhood? If you don't already, there's a good chance that you will soon.

LEMONS

In 2009, Todd Bol of Hudson, Wisconsin, had a lot of free time on his hands. More than he'd expected, and probably more than he would have liked. A former schoolteacher and self-described "social entrepreneur," his passion was creating businesses that tried to do good in the world. His most recent company, called the Global Scholarship Alliance, addressed the nursing shortage in the United States by arranging scholarships for foreign nurses to study and work in the U.S. But when Bol brought in outside investors in an attempt to grow the business, the investors cut costs...by throwing him out of *his own company.*

Bol's mother had recently passed away, so he was also grieving his loss while trying to figure out what to do next. One way he kept busy was by doing projects around the house, including replacing his garage door with a new one. A dedicated "repurposer," rather than throw out the old garage door, he saved the wood for other projects. He also had a lot of other materials lying around that he scrounged from junkyards, garage sales, and other places.

LEMONADE

It wasn't long after the garage door was done that Bol came up with a use for some of the wood: building a memorial to his mother. June Bol had been a schoolteacher and was the kind of woman who always seemed to be tutoring one or more neighborhood kids at the kitchen table. She was also an avid reader, so Bol decided to honor her by building a dollhouse-sized "library" that looked like an old-fashioned one-room schoolhouse. He put a belfry on the roof, complete with a little metal bell, and mounted a door with a glass window on the front of the schoolhouse so that people could see the books he placed inside. Which books? More than a dozen of his mother's favorites, including *The Greatest Generation*, by Tom Brokaw, about the generation of Americans who came of age during the Great Depression and fought in World War II.

When Bol finished the schoolhouse, he installed it on a post in his front yard next to the curb facing the street, kind of like a mailbox. A painted sign on the schoolhouse read, "Free Book Exchange." He hoped his neighbors would get as much

George Carlin was arrested seven times for his
"Seven Words You Can Never Say on Television" routine.

pleasure from borrowing and reading his mother's books as she had, and he left some space in the library so that his neighbors could share their own favorite books. "It was a spiritual gesture," he explained.

WELCOME TO THE NEIGHBORHOOD

Just as Bol had hoped, his neighbors did take an interest in the books. But what surprised him was how much interest they took in the *schoolhouse*. "I put up my library and noticed my neighbors talking to it like it was a little puppy. And I realized there was something magic about it," he told *The Washington Post* in 2013. A few of his neighbors asked if he would build them little libraries that they could put in their yards, too. Then, when Bol and his wife held a garage sale, he was pleasantly surprised to see that the people who came by spent more time looking at the library and talking about the books inside it than they did looking at the stuff that was for sale. Some people even offered to buy the little libraries if Bol built any more of them. So he did build more—by the end of the year he'd constructed about 30 from his pile of scavenged materials. But he didn't sell them. Instead, he gave them away to friends, neighbors, and anyone else who wanted them.

THINKING INSIDE THE BOX

It was around this time that Bol attended a seminar given by a man named Rick Brooks, who was also interested in social entrepreneurship. Brooks had cofounded a youth newspaper, a community food and gardening network, and other ventures. One afternoon he paid a visit to Bol's house to brainstorm some ideas the two might work on together. It was a short conversation: when Brooks saw the little schoolhouse in Bol's front yard he was so enthusiastic about it that the two men decided to focus on spreading the "Little Free Libraries," as they decided to call them, across the American Midwest and beyond.

Way beyond: Bol and Brooks were inspired by the example of Andrew Carnegie, the 19th-century steel tycoon. Carnegie, who died in 1919 at the age of 83, devoted the last 20 years of his life to donating nearly his entire $380 million fortune (the equivalent of about $6.4 billion today) in support of philanthropic projects—including the building of 2,509 free public libraries in the United States and around the world. The two men set the goal of building 2,510 Little Free Libraries, one more than the number of libraries that Carnegie built, by 2014. They planned to sell the libraries, but only for about what it cost to build them, so that the program would fund itself.

A NECESSARY GOOD

The Little Free Libraries project was a fun one, but it also served an important need. In the United States, it's estimated that over 30 million adults are unable to read

Juicy conversation: Ants communicate by swapping saliva.

beyond the third-grade level. Many kids also struggle to learn how to read, especially if they're poor. Two out of every three children living in poverty in the United States have no books of their own. By putting their Little Free Libraries in places where both adults and kids could access them, Bol and Brooks believed, they would encourage people to read.

The two men started small: for the first two years Bol built the structures himself on his deck, using materials pulled from his salvage pile. He typically built them 24-inches tall (any taller and they wouldn't fit in his station wagon), and 23-inches wide (or they wouldn't fit in the shipping box). "And if they get any bigger, I hurt my back carrying them," he joked.

ON THE MAP

In addition to building the library boxes, Bol and Brooks set up a Little Free Library website to promote the cause. On the site they sold completed library boxes, both painted and unpainted, as well as kits for people who wanted to put the boxes together themselves. They soon discovered that about 65 percent of people would forgo the boxes and kits entirely, preferring to build their own structures from scratch—often in the shape of dogs, cats, spaceships, dragons, robots, castles, haunted mansions, food trucks, you name it—even the TARDIS box from the *Doctor Who* TV show. Some people created Little Free Libraries out of phone booths, old canoes, and front-loading washing machines.

The website also provided guidance on how to give each new Little Free Library its best chance for success. People were encouraged to set up their libraries in a location near a lot of foot traffic, so that people would have easy access to the books. The organization also encouraged each location to designate a volunteer "steward" responsible for looking after the library and stocking it with everything from children's books to classic novels, thrillers, romances, even cookbooks, textbooks, and auto repair manuals—whatever they think will be popular with the people living in their area, with the idea being that the most fun and interesting books will attract and be enjoyed by the most people. Each Little Free Library is registered with the organization, and its location is displayed on a map on the website, so that anyone can use the map to find Little Free Libraries near them.

ON SALE

As demand for the boxes grew, Bol hired an Amish carpenter named Henry Miller to help with the work; Miller himself is estimated to have built more than 2,000 of the boxes entirely by hand. Then, when even the two of them could not keep up with demand, they worked with Wisconsin's Prairie du Chien Correctional Institution to set up a program where the inmates learned vocational carpentry skills by building

Closer to home: In the German-language version of *The Muppet Show*, the Swedish Chef is...Danish.

the libraries. In 2012, Bol and Brooks established Little Free Libraries as a nonprofit organization so that it would continue to grow. And grow it did. In August of that year they accomplished their goal and registered their 2,510th Little Free Library—a year and a half ahead of schedule, making them, as Bol put it, "the largest network of libraries in the world."

UP, UP, AND AWAY

Interest in the project spread far beyond the Midwest—not just because of the positive press from newspapers, radio, and television (NBC's *Today* show set a Little Free Library up near the network's headquarters in New York City's Rockefeller Plaza—but also through word of mouth, just as it had from the moment Bol installed the first Little Free Library in his own front yard. Every time a library was installed in a new location, people who saw it were inspired to set up Little Free Libraries of their own, which in turn encouraged still more people to do the same. Why stop at front yards? Little Free Libraries have popped up in parks, cafes, prisons, hospitals, subway stations, and even refugee camps. In Siberia, the coldest and most remote region in Russia, a Little Free Library was set up especially for reindeer herders. Have you ever seen a Little Free Library in the trunk of a police car? The organization even has a program that assists police departments in turning squad cars into rolling bookmobiles.

> Little Free Libraries have popped up in parks, cafes, prisons, hospitals, subway stations, and even refugee camps.

BOOK REPORT

Brooks retired from Little Free Libraries in 2014, and Bol passed away from cancer in 2018, but the Little Free Libraries movement has continued to grow far beyond the 2,510 locations they set as their original goal. How far beyond? As of 2022, there are more than 100,000 Little Free Libraries in more than 100 countries around the world; they have shared an estimated 250 million books over the years. Dozens more Little Free Libraries are added every week. "The reason Little Free Library has been successful is that people tell us, constantly, 'I've met more neighbors in a week than I've met in thirty years,'" Bol said in a TED Talk in 2013. "It engages and brings neighborhoods together, and folks talk to each other more than they ever have."

* * *

OOPS!

The Statue of Liberty was built in France and shipped across the ocean in pieces. When American workers put her together, they attached her head two feet off-center from where it was supposed to be. The goof wasn't repaired until a 1984 restoration.

What's the "anal sampling mechanism"? That sense you have that lets you tell whether you can fart at a particular given time without, shall we say, "making a mess."

MATCH THE ROCK STAR TO THE SUPERMODEL

It seems like the only people rock stars marry are famous fashion models, and vice versa. Can you match the musician to the professional pretty person they, at one point, married? Answers are on page 403.

ROCK STAR	SUPERMODEL
1. Mick Jagger	**a)** Christie Brinkley
2. Rod Stewart	**b)** Elaine Irwin
3. Ric Ocasek	**c)** Erin Everly
4. Seal	**d)** Pattie Boyd
5. John Mellencamp	**e)** Jerry Hall
6. Jack White	**f)** Kate Moss
7. Billy Joel	**g)** Heidi Klum
8. Axl Rose	**h)** Liv Tyler
9. George Harrison	**i)** Paulina Porizkova
10. Scott Weiland (Stone Temple Pilots)	**j)** Karen Elson
11. Royston Langdon (Spacehog)	**k)** Rachel Hunter
12. Jamie Hince (The Kills)	**l)** Mary Forsberg
13. John Legend	**m)** Behati Prinsloo
14. David Bowie	**n)** Iman
15. Harry Connick Jr.	**o)** Patti Hansen
16. Simon Le Bon (Duran Duran)	**p)** Yasmin Parvaneh
17. Keith Richards	**q)** Heather Mills
18. Caleb Followill (Kings of Leon)	**r)** Chrissy Teigen
19. Adam Levine (Maroon 5)	**s)** Jill Goodacre
20. Paul McCartney	**t)** Lily Aldridge

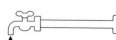

In 2015, President Barack Obama legalized private asteroid ownership.

SPEAKING OF LAUGHING

Some heavy thoughts on why levity is important.

"Laughter is the sun that drives winter from the human face."
—Victor Hugo

"I've always thought that a big laugh is a really loud noise from the soul saying, 'Ain't that the truth.'"
—Quincy Jones

"The truth is, laughter always sounds more perfect than weeping. Laughter flows in a violent riff and is effortlessly melodic. Weeping is often fought, choked, half strangled, or surrendered to with humiliation."
—Anne Rice

"Laughter is much more important than applause. Applause is almost a duty. Laughter is a reward."
—Carol Channing

"Smiling is definitely one of the best beauty remedies."
—Rashida Jones

"Laughter is the tranquilizer with no side effects."
—Arnold Glasgow

"LOVE MAY MAKE THE WORLD GO AROUND, BUT LAUGHTER KEEPS US FROM GETTING DIZZY."
—Donald Zochert

"THEY LAUGHED WHEN I SAID I WAS GOING TO BE A COMEDIAN. THEY'RE NOT LAUGHING NOW."
—Bob Monkhouse

"There's only one true superpower amongst human beings, and that is being funny. People treat you differently if you can make them laugh."
—Jeff Garlin

FALSE ALARMS

These three weird news stories begin with a bang and end with an eye roll.

SOOT YOURSELF: In 2016, Michigan first responders were called to the aid of a 14-year-old boy who had fallen into a campfire. When they arrived on the scene, both of the teen's legs were pitch black, he was screaming in pain, and his parents were frantic. They alerted the hospital to prep for a patient with severe burns over 30 percent of his body. Once there, nurses started cleaning the soot from the teen's legs to assess the damage. They kept cleaning until they found...nothing. Turns out it was almost all soot. He did have one burn on his ankle, but that could have been treated at the scene. "I think his anxiety was contagious and made everyone think he must be really, really injured," said a hospital spokesperson, adding that next time they'll probably withhold judgment until they determine the true severity of a patient's injuries.

SUSPICIOUS PACKAGE: One afternoon in March 2018, a mysterious box was discovered in a hallway on the ninth floor of a Jacksonville, Florida, condominium. It was addressed to the condo, and the return address belonged to a former tenant who was embroiled in a lawsuit with the condo's owners. All 42 apartments were evacuated, and police called in the bomb squad. It took them nearly five hours to determine that the box contained a sex toy, not a pipe bomb. The bomb squad pronounced the package "not hazardous" and allowed residents to return to the building.

RED DAWN: Just before dawn after Halloween night, 2019, a motorist on an Ohio freeway stopped at the scene of a single-vehicle accident. He approached the wrecked car and discovered 20-year-old Sidney Wolfe sitting behind the wheel. She was drenched in blood—her hair, her face, all the way down her white prom dress. "He looked horrified," she told reporters. A few minutes later, three ambulances and two fire trucks arrived. "They thought I was dead." Wolfe explained to the terrified first responders, just as she had to the driver that stopped, *and* to the 911 operator she called (who failed to relay this information), that she was fine—just a bruise on her leg. Wolfe told them she was going 55 miles per hour when a deer darted into the road, and she couldn't avoid it. Prior to that, she'd spent the evening at a haunted house in costume as Carrie, the bloodied teenager from the Stephen King novel, to promote a local stage production of the book. (The makeup *was* convincing.) As Wolfe was explaining all of this for the third time, another firefighter walked up and said, "I hate to interrupt, but don't you guys think she needs medical assistance?"

Doing it wrong? The makers of Post-it Notes claim the correct way to use Post-its is to peel them with the sticky strip running *vertically*, not across the top.

IT'S A WEIRD, WEIRD WORLD

The weirder the world gets, the harder it is to find weird stories. We hope these are weird enough for you.

IT CAME FROM THE...?

On a quiet afternoon in October 2018, a loud boom reverberated through a Jersey City neighborhood, followed by an explosion. A moment later, residents saw smoke rising from a house and called 911. By the time the owner, Arlene Silvestri, got home, the fire department had already extinguished the flames. Then they all tried to piece together what happened. There were two large holes in an exterior wall—which was made of cinder block—and the living room was ransacked. On the ground outside was an oblong object about six feet long. It was made of fiberglass and seemed to be part of a larger...thing. Investigators determined that the first hole was made when the object hit the house; then it bounced around inside and made the second hole on its way out. The only lead they had was a scrapyard located a quarter mile away, but the owner denied the object came from there. In the absence of an official cause, the rumors started flying: "Could this mystery object be related to the others that recently fell from the skies in the Carolinas?" pondered one paranormal website. "Do these cases have anything to do with the weird mystery booms and looming war in space?" As of this writing, the flying object was still unidentified.

PATH OF DESTRUCTION

During morning rush hour in Blaine, Minnesota, in 2019, several commuters reported a Hyundai Santa Fe driving slowly and erratically on a busy four-lane road. The odd thing was, there didn't seem to be anyone driving it. A few

> The odd thing was, there didn't seem to be anyone driving it.

minutes earlier, the large SUV had pulled on to the road from a neighborhood, where it knocked down some mailboxes and clipped a few vehicles and a tree. Police cars followed the slowly swerving SUV as it lumbered into a convenience store parking lot and parked (poorly). The driver's door sprang open, and out popped four-year-old Sebastian Swenson. He was apprehended without incident. Sebastian told police that earlier that morning, he got the key fob off the wall (with the aid of Grandpa's walker) and then went outside and climbed into the SUV without anyone noticing. Even though he couldn't see out the windshield and operate the pedals at the same time, Sebastian managed to back out of his driveway and navigate the mile-and-a-half route. No one was injured. When a reporter asked the little boy why he drove all the way to the store, he answered, "Because I wanna have Reese's!"

How about you? One percent of all Americans work for Walmart.

QUIET DESPERATION

In July 2020, COVID-19 was making its way through Japan, forcing a one-year delay to the Olympics. Desperate to resume normalcy, the government allowed some amusement parks to reopen—albeit with some contingencies. For example, at the Fuji-Q Highland park near Tokyo, signs went up at their fastest roller coaster urging riders not to make any vocal utterances, so they wouldn't spread the virus. To prove that it's possible, park officials issued a video of two stone-faced company executives riding the coaster in complete silence. What garnered the biggest reaction was the final line of the sign telling riders to "Please scream inside your heart." As *Wall Street Journal* reporter Alejandro Lazo tweeted in response, "It took us six months, but we have our motto, 2020."

THE HOLE STORY

After finding a hole underneath a sidewalk in October 2021, Danny Wolverton, 36, of Brooklyn, New York, became a viral TikTok sensation in for his "Mole Man" videos. In one, while wearing a lifelike mole mask—with a bald head, pointy ears, buck teeth, and stylish sunglasses—the lanky performance artist climbs through a narrow opening in the dirt between a tree well and the sidewalk...and disappears into the hole. Other videos show Wolverton throwing loud parties in the hole, which fits three people (sitting down). Out on the sidewalk, he'd record videos of the same "levitation" trick that made him quasi-famous seven years earlier on *America's Got Talent*. With each of Wolverton's videos amassing millions of views, crowds began to gather. "A hole is there to be filled with anything you want," he told a local news reporter. "I decided to fill it with performance and joy." But Wolverton's neighbors were not enjoying it. It wasn't just the parties and crowds, or all the rats that he'd displaced. They were worried that impressionable kids would climb in to the unstable sinkhole when Wolverton wasn't in there. "You come to our block," charged one neighbor, "to exacerbate an already existing problem for your own benefit." Wolverton vowed to film more videos (making a statement about gentrification or something), but a few days later, city workers showed up and filled in Mole Man's hole.

* * *

RULING FROM THE GRAVE

A *necrocracy*—from the Greek words for "death" and "government"—is a government ruled by a dead person. The only one in the world: North Korea. Its founder, Kim Il-sung (1912–94), was named "Eternal President of the Republic" in 1998. His dead son Kim Jong-il (1941–2011) was named "Eternal General Secretary" in 2012.

The north pole of Saturn is blue.

CAMEL FACTS

What day is it? If you're reading this page about the imposing but adorable animals found throughout the Middle East and Africa, it's hump day.

- Some camels have one hump; others have two. The one-humped camels are dromedary camels (also known as Arabian camels) and the two-humped camels are Bactrian camels. There are two kinds of Bactrians: Asian camels and wild Bactrian camels (which are found in a few regions of China and Mongolia and are endangered, with less than 1,000 alive today).

- Besides their humps, the main difference between dromedaries and Bactrians: height. Bactrians stand about seven feet tall, a foot more than the average dromedary.

- Because they live in desert areas, camels evolved to having three sets of eyelids and a double row of eyelashes to help keep sand from getting in their eyes.

- Camels' lips are thick and calloused to protect their mouths while foraging. That's a good thing because they often eat plants covered in thorns.

- Their humps do not store water. Camel humps store fat, which they can live off when food is scarce. They can go as long as two months without food because of this reserve.

- Because water can be scarce in their natural habitat, camels are capable of drinking a lot to hydrate themselves until their next watering opportunity. A camel will drink up to 40 gallons at one time.

- They don't thrive only in hot climates. Camels are native to some of the coldest areas of Asia, and can handle temperatures as low as 20°F.

- A camel's top speed: around 40 miles per hour, just slightly slower than the average thoroughbred racehorse.

- Camels are used as beasts of burden because they're more than capable of carrying big loads. The average camel can haul 900 pounds for around 25 miles before it gets tired.

- All camel varieties are born hump-free.

- A group of camels is called a caravan, flock, or train. They naturally form a family unit of as many as 30 individuals with one alpha male in charge.

- Camel milk is widely consumed in the Middle East, and has more vitamin C, potassium, and calcium than cow milk.

Weird world record: 1,502 authors signed their books simultaneously at the Sharjah International Book Fair in the United Arab Emirates (2019).

COVID IN THE NEWS

These surreal news reports from the first two years of the COVID-19 pandemic show just how much this insidious virus took the world off guard.

BARBERSHOP STRING QUARTETS

In January 2022, after a monthlong lockdown, Dutch officials reopened the cities of Amsterdam and the Hague, but only partially. So-called close-contact businesses, such as gyms and hair and nail salons, could open their doors, but cultural venues—concert halls and museums—could not. Calling the measures inconsistent and unfair, dozens of curators and stage managers joined forces with hairstylists and personal trainers to mount a one-day protest in both cities (following safe COVID-19 protocols, of course):

- At the "Hair Salon at the Concertgebouw," a full orchestra performed "Symphony No. 2" by Charles Ives while two hairdressers worked on clients up on stage.

- The Hague's Mauritshuis gallery held fitness classes, so that patrons could achieve their maximum heart rate while taking in Johannes Vermeer's *Girl with the Pearl Earring.*

- A hair and nail salon opened at the Van Gogh Museum in Amsterdam, giving attendees an opportunity to get their nails done under the watchful eye of a wall-sized Vincent van Gogh self-portrait.

One other profession (not known for its social-distancing practices) that got to reopen its doors: brothels.

LOCKDOWN VS. "LOCKDOWN"

Australia's two biggest cities—Melbourne and Sydney, located in the neighboring states of Victoria and New South Wales (NSW)—both went into lockdown in the summer of 2021, allowing only essential businesses to remain open. Victoria's government provided a list of what types of businesses could be classified as essential; NSW's did not. Result: Two very different kinds of lockdown. Melbournians were allowed to go shopping for basic supplies, such as groceries and prescriptions, whereas Sydneysiders could swing by the Gucci store to pick up some luxury fashion items before popping into Louis Vuitton for a designer handbag. Other "essential" retail outlets that stayed open in Sydney included Skechers, Vans, Dr. Martens, H&M, and EB Games. Responding to complaints—mostly from frustrated Melbournians—NSW Premier Gladys Berejiklian explained that their health officials had to "rely on common sense" and hope that businesses would regulate themselves, adding, "It is so, so difficult to have a precise rule for every single thing."

First scheduled passenger airline: The St. Petersburg-Tampa Airboat Line. It operated for just five months, in the first half of 1914.

LOOK WHO'S WALKING

Spain declared a national COVID-19 emergency in March 2020, setting off some of the strictest lockdown restrictions in Europe. Spaniards were allowed to leave their homes only on foot and only to walk their dogs. That left a lot of people out (or rather, in), leading to some interesting workarounds:

- Dog owners ran classified ads offering to rent their dogs for €15 per walk.
- Some dog-less people tried walking other pets—including reports of people walking leashed cats, goats, a potbellied pig, a chicken, and a crab.
- One man was fined for walking his stuffed toy dog.
- Several people put on dinosaur costumes and took walks (and were fined).
- A dad posted a photo of him getting ready to "walk" his daughter...who's wearing a dalmatian costume.

BRAZILIAN CROCODILES

Why did dozens of people in Brazil, including 60-year-old Leila Fernandes of Fortaleza, wear a crocodile costume to get the COVID-19 vaccine? "As a way of expressing my horror," she told reporters. She said she'd lost several family members to the virus, and she and the other protesters blamed Brazil's president, Jair Bolsonaro. According to critics, Bolsonaro's downplaying of the virus and his delays in purchasing doses of the vaccine contributed to more than a half-million deaths in Brazil in the pandemic's first year (second only to the United States). But why crocodiles? Because of this bizarre warning issued by Bolsonaro in December 2020: "In the Pfizer contract it's very clear: 'We're not responsible for any side effects.' If you turn into a crocodile, it's your problem."

#BESTMUSEUMBUM

When all the museums closed down in 2020, the curators and experts who maintain the displays found a novel way to engage with their absent patrons. England's Yorkshire Museum started it with this tweet, accompanied by a photo of a statue...from behind:

> IT'S TIME FOR #CURATORBATTLE! Today's theme is #BestMuseumBum! This cracking Roman marble statuette depicts an athlete at the peak of fitness! It may have decorated the town house of one of Eboracum's wealthier residents. Has someone taken a bite out of this? BEAT THAT!

The game was afoot. "We raise your athlete and instead give you the bum of a drunken fish," tweeted the York Art Gallery, which entered a figurine depicting a fish with human legs bending over (it's wearing pants). After that, entrants started coming in from around the world, including a macro photograph of a bumblebee's bum, a skeletonized "plesiosaur bum," a painting of a sumo wrestler from behind, and an alluring nude statue called *Sleeping Hermaphroditus*. Victoria and Albert Museum in London entered the most famous bum of them all: "Whilst the cast of Michelangelo's *David* caused quite the stir because of his very exposed front parts (cue fig leaf), the real cause for commotion is actually his butt."

The website Bored Panda let people vote for their favorite rear end. Coming in first place: the firm buttocks of a Hercules sculpture.

THEY DIDN'T EVEN APPLAUD

One of the countless coronavirus cancellations in early 2020 was the upcoming season at Barcelona's Gran Teatre del Liceu opera house. In May, after three long months of darkness, the theater reopened and Spain's famed string ensemble, the UceLi Quartet, took the stage to perform Puccini's "Crisantemi" ("The Chrysanthemums") in front of a full house...of houseplants (2,292 of them, to be exact). Eugenio Ampudia, a Spanish conceptual artist who came up with the idea during lockdown, said the performance was as much for the "Swiss cheese plants, ficus, and palms" as it was for human listeners streaming it from home. "I don't know what the plants say, because we have not yet managed to decode the reverse dialogue," pondered Ampudia, "but I know that each of them will have undergone a change by being at that concert." Afterward, the houseplants were donated to area health care workers (no doubt thrilled to have something else to take care of).

BUTT OUT

Every month since 2007, researchers at University College London have polled 10,000 cigarette smokers about their habit. In the first half of 2020, the number of respondents who quit smoking jumped by a third—the largest increase since the study began. Nearly half of them said they quit due to fears of COVID-19, which attacks the lungs, putting them in the high-risk category. In all, it's estimated that more than one million English people gave up cigarettes at the start of the pandemic.

SEEMS LIKE OLD TIMES

Nearly 700 years before the COVID-19 pandemic took an estimated 5.6 million lives in 2020 and '21, the bubonic plague pandemic (known as the Black Death) killed 75 million Europeans in the mid-14th century. Once people realized that the plague was being spread by close human contact (it was actually being spread by infected fleas that jumped from person to person), social distancing measures took hold all over the continent. In Italy, that begat the *buchette del vino*, or "wine windows"—little counter-height doors that were cut into the stone facades of wineries and eateries, allowing merchants to safely pass their wares to customers without touching them. After the plague ended, wine windows gradually fell out of use. Most were filled in or built over. Then came COVID-19, which, once again, created the need to keep businesses open

John Walker, creator of Johnnie Walker scotch whisky, was a teetotaler—he never touched the stuff.

while keeping people apart. In the city of Florence, dozens of wine windows were restored, many of which hadn't been used in centuries.

> An anonymous crew member reported that COVID-19 safety measures "went out the window."

SOMETHING ROTTEN THIS WAY COMES

The first movie about COVID-19, *Songbird*, was also the first one to start filming in Los Angeles during the first lockdown of 2020. Produced by Michael Bay, this dystopian thriller takes place in the not-so-distant future of 2024, when the pandemic has brought chaos, and millions of people are imprisoned in "quarantine camps." And speaking of chaos, the production was reportedly fraught with it. In July, the actors' union SAG-AFTRA shut down the shoot for a day because of unsigned contracts and unsafe working conditions. A few weeks later, *The Hollywood Reporter* quoted an anonymous crew member who reported that COVID-19 safety measures "went out the window" when the shoot got behind schedule. Was it worth the risky behavior? Despite some respected names in *Songbird*'s cast—Bradley Whitford, Demi Moore, Craig Robinson, and Peter Stormare—the direct-to-video release scored only a 9 percent on Rotten Tomatoes. Sample review: "Derivative, dull and has a plot that's so stale it really should also feature a tornado full of sharks."

UNMASKED

On July 1, 2020, the board of health in Knox County, Tennessee, voted 7-to-1 to enforce a mask mandate inside government buildings. The lone dissenter was Knox County Mayor Glenn Jacobs. Ironically, before Jacobs entered politics, he was a WWE professional wrestling superstar known as Kane, who rarely appeared in the ring without his mask.

'PAUSE FOR THE CAUSE

In 2021, hundreds of anti-vaccine protestors showed up at the Television Centre in West London to demonstrate against BBC News for its perceived pro-vaccine agenda. They chanted slogans and held up signs, while a handful of protesters forced their way in to the building. Only problem: BBC News operated out of another building, five miles away. No one from that network was even in the breached building, and hadn't been for a decade, since the BBC moved out and rented the studios to ITV. Security officers prevented anyone from entering the studios, where the morning shows were being taped. "Not sure what protesters were hoping to achieve," said Charlene White, cohost of the daytime talk show *Loose Women*, "but all they would've found was me, Jane, Nadia, and Penny talking about the menopause."

* * *

"I am kind of paranoid in reverse. I suspect people of plotting to make me happy."

–J. D. Salinger

It figures: The most commonly used noun in English is "time."

ASK UNCLE JOHN

Some questions have no answers. Others, like these, do.

DON'T STOP

Dear Uncle John, why do dogs and cats like to be petted... and why do people like to be caressed?

A: When something touches your arm, you may think you feel it on your arm, but really you're feeling it in your brain. Signals from your nerve endings tell your brain what kind of touch it is—negative, positive, or neutral—and then your brain reacts accordingly. If you're punched, pinched, prodded, or poked, an array of neurons is activated that tell your arm to recoil. But there's one specific type of touch—alternately called caressing, stroking, and petting—that stimulates only the nerve endings at the bases of hair follicles, causing only one subset of neurons (called MRGPRB4+) to activate. (When lab mice were injected with these neurons artificially, their stress level was reduced.) So the reason that being caressed feels good is because it activates feel-good neurons. Furthermore, because caressing requires trust, this behavior began as an evolutionary tool not only for social bonding but also for proper hygiene. Think about how relaxed monkeys and apes look when they are grooming each other.

When it comes to dogs and cats, they get even more out of petting than a few feel-good neurons. For cats, petting helps them spread their scent, and the reason they enjoy top-of-the-head scratches is because that's where their mother licked them when they were kittens. For dogs, which are pack animals by nature, petting reinforces trust and gives structure to your relationship, which reduces their stress. As for the person who is petting, that activity also activates calming neurons.

ON THE ROCKS

Dear Uncle John, why are oceans salty but lakes and rivers aren't?

A: Lakes and rivers—aka fresh water—do contain trace amounts of salt, but it's very little compared to seawater (which happens to have roughly the same salt content as your urine, sweat, and tears: 35 parts per 1,000). Those trace amounts of salt are carried to the ocean by streams and rivers. But where did the salt come from? The rocks located near shores and riverbanks. Raindrops—made up of two hydrogen atoms and one oxygen—pick up carbon dioxide from the atmosphere, making the rain slightly acidic. As that "acid rain" erodes the rocks, the CO_2 dissolves minerals

It's a long story: Giraffes sleep no more than half an hour per day, mostly through tiny naps.

on the rocks, which contain the building blocks of salt: sodium and chloride. They bond together to form tiny salt crystals and then ride the fresh water to the sea. Then, as part of Earth's hydrologic cycle, seawater near the surface evaporates and rises into the atmosphere. The salt and other impurities not chemically bonded to the seawater remain behind in the ocean, so only hydrogen and oxygen—the building blocks of fresh water—form clouds. When those clouds move over land, the raindrops pick up more rock-dissolving CO_2 to keep the process going.

JUST GET TO IT ALREADY!

Dear Uncle John, why do online food recipes always begin with a story?

A: Haven't we all been in this situation? You're scrambling to make dinner and you need a quick recipe for mashed potatoes. So you turn to Google and click on the first "Buttery Mashed Potatoes" recipe, and it begins with something like, "Haven't we all been in this situation? You're scrambling to make dinner and you need a quick recipe for mashed potatoes. That reminds me of the buttery mashed potatoes my grandma used to make for our family's traditional holiday dinners."

There are two reasons for the story. First, the U.S. Copyright Office has determined that the recipes themselves are "factual statements" and are therefore not copyrightable. You know what is copyrightable? A "substantial literary expression"—i.e., an article, a book...or a story. So if a recipe is contained within a literary expression, it's protected. Alone, it's fair game and can be copied without fear of plagiarism.

Another reason for the culinary verbosity: Google's algorithms give preference to what it considers the foremost experts in any given field. So the biggest food sites pepper their prose with time-tested SEO (search engine optimization) words that will help the article rise to the top. And have you ever wondered why there are ads between each paragraph of the story? They sustain the site. Whether you like it or not, says SimplyRecipes.com founder Elise Bauer, "The dynamics aren't going to change any time soon. So when people ask, 'Why don't you put the recipe first?' the answer is that we won't make money and won't be able to create new recipes."

* * *

ATOMIC BOY

Six years after the U.S. defeated Japan in World War II, the first American athletic event to invite Japanese athletes was the 1951 Boston Marathon. The winner: Shigeki Tanaka, a Japanese runner who'd survived Hiroshima. The press called him "Atomic Boy."

What's *vertical contamination*? When particles flow up a stream of water, rather than down.

YOU'RE MY INSPIRATION

*It's always interesting to see where the architects of pop culture
get their ideas. Some of these might surprise you.*

The Cable Guy: One night in the early 1990s, an L.A. prosecutor named Lou Holtz Jr. (son of classic-era Hollywood actor Lou Holtz, no relation to the football coach) saw a cable repairman in his mother's apartment building. "What's he doing here so late?" Holtz asked himself. He answered that in the form of a screenplay—the only one he ever wrote—that became the 1996 hit *The Cable Guy*, for which Jim Carrey was paid a then-unheard-of $20 million.

Elizabeth Swann: No mere damsel in distress, Keira Knightley's character in *Pirates of the Caribbean* (2003) can hold her own in a fight—even when she's forced to wear a white dress and her only weapon is a butter knife. Elizabeth's personality—and those two plot points—were borrowed from Marion Ravenwood (Karen Allen) in *Raiders of the Lost Ark*.

The Ents: When British author J. R. R. Tolkien first read Shakespeare's *Macbeth* as a schoolboy, he was excited by the witches' prophecy that the king "shall never vanquished be until Great Birnam Wood to high Dunsinane Hill shall come against him." Tolkien pictured actual trees going to war. As he later explained, it was to his "bitter disappointment and disgust" that the "trees" turned out to be soldiers carrying branches. When Tolkien grew up and wrote *The Lord of the Rings*, he treated his trees as he thought the Bard should have. Result: the Ents, a race of talking trees that march off to war.

The Pittsburgh Pirates: *Aye, matey, there be pirates in Pennsylvania?* Not those kind of pirates. In the early days of organized baseball, the Alleghenys (from the north side of Pittsburgh) lost most of their best players to a rival team, resulting in a dreadful 23–136 season in 1890. That winter, the Alleghenys started trying to rebuild by poaching good players from other teams around the league. The Philadelphia Athletics filed an official complaint, calling the team's actions "piratical." The following season, the renamed Pirates won twice as many games.

Zelda: In the 1980s, Shigeru Miyamoto knew that his new video game about a "princess with eternal beauty" would be called *The Legend of* ____, but he couldn't think of a name until an associate told him about an early 20th-century American novelist and socialite named Zelda Fitzgerald (wife of F. Scott), who was known for her "eternal beauty."

Average cost of a slave in the Aztec empire:
100 cacao beans, the amount in a quarter pound of chocolate.

UNCLE JOHN'S STALL OF FAME

We're always amazed by the creative ways people deal with bathroom-related emergencies. To honor them, we've created Uncle John's Stall of Fame.

Honoree: Tamara Torlakson, who ran in Southern California's Mountains 2 Beach Marathon in 2018

Notable Achievement: Making a pit stop that was all pit...and no stop

True Story: Torlakson makes a point of going to the bathroom *before* running in a marathon, and this race was no exception. Even so, when she was about halfway through the 26.2-mile race, she realized she had to go again (number *two*). Portable toilets were set up at various points along the route...but Torlakson was making great time, and she didn't want to let a bathroom break slow her down. Her solution: "I thought, 'I don't know if it's possible to poop while running, but I'll try,'" she told reporters.

Well, it turns out you *can* poop while running. Torlakson ran the second half of the race in soiled shorts, completing the marathon in three hours and seven minutes, a personal record, beating her previous record by one minute and 20 seconds. "If I had stopped in a Porta Potty," she says, "who knows what would've happened?"

Honoree: Ludivine, a two-and-a-half-year-old bloodhound in Elkmont, Alabama

Notable Achievement: Taking a long bathroom break—13.1 *miles* long

True Story: Ludivine's family lives near the spot that serves as the starting line of Elkmont's Trackless Train Trek Half Marathon. On the morning of race day in 2016, she was let out to pee, but rather than just doing her business and going back inside, she got excited by the commotion at the starting line and crawled under the garden fence to get a better look. Suddenly the starting gun fired, and the runners were off! And so was Ludivine. She took off after the runners and chased them all the way to the finish line more than 13 miles away, stopping only to sniff a dead rabbit, investigate some cows in a field, and run through streams. Result: she came in 7th— and was awarded a medal by race organizers, who also renamed the race Elkmont's Hound Dog Half Marathon in Ludivine's honor. "All I did was open the door, and she ran the race on her own accord," her owner, April Hamlin, told *Runner's World* in 2017. "My first reaction was that I was embarrassed and worried that she had possibly gotten in the way of the other runners. I can't believe she ran the whole half marathon because she's actually really lazy."

Honoree: Shannon Stevens

Notable Achievement: Escaping the outhouse with her butt intact

True Story: In February 2021, Stevens, her brother Erik, and Erik's girlfriend rode on snowmobiles out to a spot in the wilderness 20 miles northwest of Haines, Alaska, where Erik has a Mongolian-style tent called a yurt. About 150 feet from the yurt is Erik's outhouse, and not long after arriving Shannon went to use it. "Something bit my butt right as I sat down," she said. "I jumped up and I screamed." Was it a squirrel? A rat? The bite wasn't severe—it was more of a nip, really, and Stevens and her brother assumed the critter was small. They were wrong: when they peeked down through the hole in the outhouse seat, they saw a fully grown black bear staring back up at them. They ran back to the yurt and hid inside it until the next morning. By then the bear had climbed out of the outhouse and was gone. The privy is used only when Erik visits the yurt, so the bear may have been hoping to shelter there until spring. It apparently climbed into the pit through a small door in the back of the outhouse. "I'm going to be better about looking inside the toilet before sitting down," said Stevens.

Honoree: Bob Meeley of Des Moines, Iowa

Notable Achievement: Turning a "Little Free Library" into a TP library

True Story: As a family man with two teenage sons at home, Meeley knows how difficult it can be to keep the house stocked with toilet paper and other necessities. When the COVID-19 pandemic sparked a run on toilet paper, hand sanitizer, and other necessities that left store shelves empty, he thought back to a time in 2008, when he and his family were displaced from their home during a flood. He decided to share what little he had with his neighbors, some of whom were elderly or immunocompromised and couldn't go to the stores at all. "I know the feeling intimately, that sort of helplessness," he told the *Newton Daily News* in March 2020.

A few years earlier Meeley had built a box called a "Little Free Library" near his mailbox and stuffed it full of free books to share with the community. Now that a new, more pressing need had arisen, he removed the books and replaced them with toilet paper, gloves, masks, wet wipes, and bottles of hand sanitizer. Then he posted a notice on the Nextdoor neighborhood app, inviting people to help themselves. "I don't care who you are, where you're from, what you're taking or why," he wrote, "it's none of my business as long as it helps."

Within days Meeley's Library became a community chest, with some people taking things they needed, and others restocking those supplies with donations of their own. There are some 80 Little Free Libraries in Des Moines, and Meeley hopes the others will stock COVID-19 supplies as well. "You lead by example and let everything else fall into place," he says. "Share what you can and we'll get through it somehow."

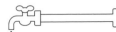

Cold water can give manatees frostbite.

HERE COMES TROUBLE

Troubles sure are troubling, aren't they?

"One trouble with trouble is that it usually starts out like fun."
—**Ann Landers**

"The trouble with most people is that they think with their hopes or fears or wishes rather than with their minds."
—**Will Durant**

"The trouble with being punctual is that nobody's there to appreciate it."
—**Franklin P. Jones**

"The trouble with the future is that it usually arrives before we're ready for it."
—**Arnold H. Glasow**

"The trouble with life sometimes is that we are all in it together."
—**Mary Balogh**

"That's the real trouble with the world, too many people grow up."
—**Walt Disney**

"The trouble with having an open mind, of course, is that people will insist on coming along and trying to put things in it."
—**Terry Pratchett**

"The trouble with people is not that they don't know but that they know so much that ain't so."
—**Josh Billings**

"The trouble with life is that there are so many beautiful women and so little time."
—**John Barrymore**

"The trouble with the rat race is that even if you win, you're still a rat."
—**Lily Tomlin**

"The trouble with most of us is that we would rather be ruined by praise than saved by criticism."
—**Norman Vincent Peale**

"The trouble with the world is that the stupid are cocksure and the intelligent are full of doubt."
—**Bertrand Russell**

"The trouble with unemployment is that the minute you wake up in the morning you're on the job."
—**Slappy White**

"The trouble with a kitten is that eventually it becomes a cat."
—**Ogden Nash**

"The trouble with men is that they have limited minds. That's the trouble with women, too."
—**Joanna Russ**

"The trouble with life isn't that there is no answer, it's that there are so many answers."
—**Ruth Benedict**

"One trouble with the world today is that there are too many people in it who are willing to put in their oars but not willing to row."
—**Hugh Allen**

Eggo frozen waffles were originally going to be called Froffles.

FULL MOON FEVER

Werewolves aren't real, of course, but the idea that these hairy man-wolves are out there, stalking humans, has persisted for centuries. Here's a look at the "origins" of werewolves.

- Werewolf-like creatures appear in many ancient Greek writings. Historian Herodotus wrote of the Neuri, an ethnic group that lived in Scythia (an area that stretched from modern-day Eastern Europe to Iran) and had the power to turn from human to wolf and back, at will. Ancient Greek champion boxer Damarchus was rumored to be so strong and agile because he was a secret werewolf. Greek mythology tells of a king named Lycaon, who went mad and murdered and ate a child. The god Zeus then punished him by turning him into a wolf-man.

- The name of that Greek king-turned-werewolf, Lycaon, is the root of the term for werewolfism: *lycanthropy*. The word "werewolf" comes from the Old English *werewulf*, in which "*were*" meant "man" and "*wulf*" meant "wolf."

- Clinical lycanthropy is a real, recognized health condition—a mental illness categorized by one's steadfast belief that they are a werewolf. It was first diagnosed in the 2nd century by Greek physician Galen of Pergamon.

- *The Epic of Gilgamesh*, a Mesopotamian poem dating back to 2100 BC and believed to be the oldest extant writing in the Western world, includes a werewolf. The hero, Gilgamesh, turns down a potential mate because she transformed her previous lover into a wolf-man.

- Classical Roman poet and chronicler Virgil (*The Aeneid*) wrote about Moeris, a figure who supposedly could transform from human to wolf (and back again) by consuming a series of herbs.

- Those herbs were likely hallucinogenic, as were whatever Gilles Garnier used. In 16th-century France, Garnier became known as the Werewolf of Dole. He was burned at the stake for several murders, which he claimed took place during a werewolf state, brought on by an ointment he'd rubbed on his skin.

- Between 1764 and 1767 in the southern French region of Gévaudan, the "Beast of Gévaudan" reportedly mauled as many as 200 people and killed 100. The French Army finally tracked it down and killed it. Locals believed it was a werewolf, but historians think it was probably a hybrid wolf-dog with rabies.

- Peter the Wild Boy was a popular member of the courts of King George I and King George II of Great Britain in the 1700s. Discovered nude and walking on all fours in a German forest, he ate with his hands, couldn't speak, and suffered seizures,

The official shade of the spacesuits worn by NASA astronauts is "international orange."

leading to the belief that he was some kind of werewolf. In all likelihood, Peter the Wild Boy's symptoms were the result of Pitt-Hopkins syndrome, a rare genetic developmental disability identified by scientists in 1978.

- Another obscure medical malady that may have confounded Europeans hundreds of years ago, and wound up conflated with werewolf myths: hypertrichosis. It causes an abnormal amount of hair to grow all over the body and face, giving sufferers a wolflike appearance.

> It causes an abnormal amount of hair to grow all over the body and face, giving sufferers a wolflike appearance.

- According to movies and werewolf fiction, the only way to kill one of these monsters is with a silver bullet. That's a modern adaptation of mistranslated European folklore. For hundreds of years, people thought that the only way to put down a werewolf, should one need to, was with quicksilver, the liquid form of mercury. (It's poison, so it would kill anyone—human or werewolf.)

- In 1996, when a wolf pack in Uttar Pradesh, India, attacked a village, locals were convinced it was the work of werewolves.

- More "common knowledge" from the Middle Ages concerns how people turn into werewolves: getting bitten by a werewolf, being the seventh son of a seventh son, eating wolf meat, making a pact with the devil, mating with a werewolf, or being murdered under a full moon.

- A common part of werewolf mythology is that the presence of a full moon causes humans with latent werewolfism to transform into their beastly state. This may have something to do with the fact that humans actually do get a bit loony during full moons. A study conducted at Calvary Mater Newcastle hospital in Australia in 2008 and 2009 noted a 25 percent uptick in attacks on doctors by patients—in which they'd bite, scratch, and spit...almost like an animal.

- Other "were" creatures (human-animal hybrids) that appear in various myths and legends: were-panthers, were-foxes, and were-owls.

- The first werewolf movie: The Werewolf, a 1913 silent film based on an 1898 short story. It's about a Navajo witch who teaches her magic skills to her daughter, who uses her powers to turn into a werewolf and fight off white settlers. Then, 100 years later, she comes back to kill the descendants of those white settlers. All prints of the movie were destroyed in a 1924 fire in the warehouse of its producer, Universal Studios.

*   *   *

Report makes the wolf bigger than he is. —**German Proverb**

JUNK FOOD RECIPES

Take packaged snack food...and turn it into something else with one of these weird recipes. (Warning to healthy eaters: DON'T LOOK!)

- **Twinkie Sushi.** Cut Twinkies into inch-long pieces and wrap them in strips of green Fruit Roll-Ups. The result looks like sushi. Serve with dried mango strips (which look like pickled ginger).

- **Pringles Candy.** Mix three cups of crushed Pringles potato chips into a melted package of almond bark. Stir in a cup of Spanish peanuts. Pour onto wax paper; cool, dry, and break into pieces.

- **Kool-Aid Pickles.** Soak some dill pickles in a pitcher filled with equal parts vinegar and cherry or tropical punch-flavored Kool-Aid. The result is a pickle that's sweet, sour...and bright red.

- **Chicken McBigMac.** Not getting enough meat in your diet? Try this: Buy a McDonald's Big Mac and three McChicken sandwiches. Remove the three bun slices on the Big Mac and replace them with the fried McChicken chicken patties.

- **Coke Seafood Au Gratin.** Combine two tablespoons of butter and two of flour. On low heat, add in a cup of milk and a half cup of grated parmesan. As it thickens, add a half cup of Coca-Cola. Pour the sauce over a half pound each of cooked shrimp, crab, lobster, and sole. Top with bread crumbs and bake for 20 minutes. Peppers With Creamy Sauce. Remove the seeds from six green (or red) bell peppers that have been cut in half. Melt a package of marshmallows. Fill the peppers with the creamy marshmallow sauce and bake until brown.

- **Funyun Onion Rings.** Grind a bag of Funyons in a blender. (Funyuns are made from cornmeal that's formed into rings and heavily seasoned with onion powder.) Dip slices of real onions in the Funyun crumbs, then dip in egg whites and cook in a deep-fryer.

- **Maple Bacon Donut.** If you like bacon with your waffles and you've ever dipped the bacon in maple syrup, you'll love this simple treat: Take a maple bar (a donut with maple frosting, also known as a maple longjohn) and place two strips of extra-crispy bacon on top...and hope you have good health insurance.

The good old days: At the 1924 Olympics in Paris,
marathon runner rehydration stations offered wine.

REALITY VS. FANTASY

In this otherworldly edition of "Strange Lawsuits," let Uncle John be your Dungeon Master as you delve into these lurid tales of lawyers and litigants waging war against witches and warlocks...and aliens and Time Lords and whatever Gollum is.

YVONNE EKENSKJÖLD VS. *THE HOBBIT*

The Lawsuit: When Peter Jackson's 2012 adaptation of J. R. R. Tolkien's 1937 book, *The Hobbit*, was shown on movie screens in Sweden, the subtitles listed Dwarf leader Thorin Oakenshield as Torin Ekenskölde. "It's like a slap in the face," said Yvonne Ekenskjöld, 68, of Katerineholm, and she sued to have the character's surname changed. Although the names actually differ by two letters (hers has a *j*), she claimed that her noble surname shouldn't be associated with a fairy-tale figure. "I actually feel violated, and it's offensive that they didn't even bother to call and ask if it was alright." Turns out there is precedent for this kind of case, because noble Swedish family names are forbidden to be used commercially without permission.

Acknowledging that precedent, Stefan Klockby, head of the Swedish Film Institute, which translated the dialogue, pointed out, "It's not a noble family name anymore; that family died out 200 years ago. We're not really sure what she's talking about." He also explained that the Torin Ekenskölde translation first appeared in a 1947 Swedish version of *The Hobbit*. Perhaps most damning for Ekenskjöld's case: it's not even her actual family name. "She just made it her name ten years ago," said Klockby.

The Verdict: There were no further reports about this suit, but the Dwarf king's Swedish surname remains Ekenskölde.

ROGER DEAN VS. *AVATAR*

The Lawsuit: If you saw James Cameron's first *Avatar* film in 2009, and you said to yourself, "This movie looks like a Yes album cover," you wouldn't be the only one. The comparisons started immediately: a tree that English artist Roger Dean painted for the cover of the 1973 album *Yessongs* looks a lot like Hometree in *Avatar*, and the planet Pandora's floating mountains are also very Dean-like. In 2013, the artist—who has created album covers for Yes, Asia, Uriah Heep, and many others—filed a $50 million lawsuit against 20th Century Fox and Cameron's production company, claiming the art designers plagiarized 14 of Dean's paintings. In court, he provided side-by-side comparisons of those paintings with still shots—and in some cases it really does look like the filmmakers were using Dean's paintings for their storyboards. And this isn't some obscure artist: Dean's collective works have sold more than 150 million copies.

In a 2010 interview, Cameron was asked if he got the idea for the floating mountains from a Yes album cover: "'It might have been,' the director said with a laugh, '...back in my pot-smoking days.'" And in court, his art team even admitted that they were inspired by Dean's works.

The Verdict: U.S. District Court Judge Jesse Furman dismissed the suit, going so far as to accuse Dean of altering and cropping some of his paintings to make them look more like the movie stills. He ruled that a static painting can't be compared to a still from a moving image in which lighting and perspective are changing constantly. "No reasonable jury could find that Defendants' and Plaintiffs' works are substantially similar," the judge said, adding that they "bear little or no relation to one another beyond 'style.'" This was one of five intellectual-property-theft lawsuits that other writers and creators had filed against Cameron for *Avatar*. He won all of them.

LONDON'S METROPOLITAN POLICE DEPARTMENT VS. *DOCTOR WHO*

The Lawsuit: The BBC debuted the science-fiction show *Doctor Who* in 1963. Because the show's budget was too small to build a spaceship, the Doctor flies through time and space in a "bigger on the inside" blue police box (a prop borrowed from a BBC cop show) called the TARDIS. In the 1970s, as *Doctor Who* was gaining in popularity, the network sold a line of TARDIS toys, TARDIS lunch boxes, and the like. In '96, the BBC was granted a trademark for the TARDIS.

Soon after, lawyers for London's Metropolitan Police department (referred to locally as the Met) appealed, arguing that the Met had been using blue police boxes since the 1920s—and should thereby be granted the trademark. From the appeal: "The shape of the [BBC's] police telephone box, the wording 'police public call box' and the color blue all so closely mimic the shape, format, and style of the [official] police telephone box as to be likely to deceive."

A few problems: The police boxes, which once totaled over 500, hadn't even been in use in London since the 1960s, so what would viewers confuse the TARDIS with? And a judge said that even if the Met did attain the trademark, it would apply in only the scope of its official policing uses, not for lunch boxes. Nevertheless, the public and the media seemed to side with the Doctor. The *Guardian* compared the TARDIS's interior to the police box's and described the latter as containing "at worst a phone (for the purpose of dialling 999) and at best a bored copper with flat feet and an untried truncheon."

The Verdict: The BBC won. The police were ordered to pay a fine of £850, plus legal costs (no doubt considerably higher than the fine). Hearing officer Mike Knight said in his ruling, "I bear in mind that for most of the period since the police call box was taken out of service, the only sight the public at large would have had of this item of street furniture has been in the TV program *Doctor Who*."

Ronald Reagan's first job: lifeguard. In seven summers, he saved 77 people from drowning.

RECEP TAYYIP ERDOĞAN VS. *THE LORD OF THE RINGS*

The Lawsuit: Erdoğan, who's served as president of Turkey since 2014, has been widely mocked for not being able to take mockery. In fact, several people—including journalists—have been fired, jailed, or even beaten for "insulting the president," which is a crime in that country. Bilgin Çiftçi, a doctor at the Public Health Institution of Turkey, learned that the hard way after posting a meme on his Facebook page showing side-by-side photos of Erdoğan and Gollum, the skulking creature from *The Lord of the Rings* films, with similar facial expressions. Çiftçi was fired from his job and arrested, with a possible four-year prison sentence if found guilty of insulting the president.

But the case hit a snag when the judge admitted that he'd never seen *The Lord of the Rings*. So he called for a recess and then watched all nine hours of the trilogy in order to determine if the comparison to Gollum was indeed an insult. As the case made international headlines, it caught the attention of the *Rings* director and cowriter Peter Jackson. In a joint statement with the other two screenwriters, Jackson tried to diffuse the situation by explaining that the character has two personalities:

> If the images below are in fact the ones forming the basis of this Turkish lawsuit, we can state categorically: none of them feature the character known as Gollum. All of them are images of the character called Sméagol. Sméagol is a joyful, sweet character. Sméagol does not lie, deceive, or attempt to manipulate others. He is not evil, conniving, or malicious—these personality traits belong to Gollum, who should never be confused with Sméagol.

The case pivoted to the question of whether or not Gollum/Sméagol was a good guy. If the doctor was comparing the president to Sméagol, then it wouldn't necessarily be an insult.

The Verdict: The judge ruled it *was* an insult and sentenced Çiftçi to a one-year suspended prison sentence and the loss of parental custody.

LUCIEN GREAVES VS. *CHILLING ADVENTURES OF SABRINA*

The Lawsuit: Greaves is a satanist, but not the sacrificing-animals kind of satanist—more the nontheistic, First Amendment–activism kind of satanist. In 2014, the group he cofounded, the Massachusetts-based Satanic Temple, crowdfunded the commission of a nine-foot-tall bronze statue called "Baphomet with Children." Based on a drawing by a 19th-century occultist, the statue portrays a winged, goat-headed deity (Baphomet) sitting on a throne with one hand raised, while two children look up at him adoringly. The Satanic Temple made national news in 2015 for its unsuccessful campaign to place Baphomet next to the Ten Commandments at the Oklahoma State House. By 2018, the Temple was billing itself as a force for "Empathy, Reason,

First movie translated into a Native American language:
the original *Stars Wars* (1977). It was dubbed into Navajo in 2013.

When his request went unanswered, Greaves filed a $150 million suit against both Netflix and Warner Bros.

Advocacy." Then, said Greaves, it was "all at once entirely eclipsed by some Netflix show production department who did a Google Image Search."

On the show, Sabrina (a teenage witch) battles a murderous satanic cult that worships...the exact same statue of Baphomet—even down to the male breasts. (Classic depictions of Baphomet have female breasts.) Because this particular design was copyrighted by the Satanic Temple, Greaves sent a letter to Netflix, asking them to change it. When his request went unanswered, Greaves filed a $150 million suit in New York District Court against both Netflix and Warner Bros.—not just for copyright infringement, but for damaging the Satanic Temple's brand. "A lot of people who haven't heard of us...recognize that monument as the 'Sabrina' monument, which denigrates the entire project."

The Verdict: Greaves wrote on his blog that the suit had been "amicably settled." Though he didn't divulge whether any money changed hands, he said Netflix agreed to provide a line in the credits acknowledging the Satanic Temple. "So ends one of the most overpublicized of copyright claims," wrote Greaves. "So, too, hopefully ends the parade of stupidity from online amateur legal experts."

* * *

DUMB DOGGY DEVICES

Product: BowLingual Dog Translator ($50)

Details: Ever wonder what your dog would tell you if it could talk? The BowLingual Dog Translator is a special collar fitted with a microphone that records barks and sends a signal to a handheld device that analyzes the sound. Then it delivers a text message informing you if your furry friend is happy, sad, or scared. (Not a dog person? There's MeowLingual, too.)

Product: Hot Doll ($70)

Details: Does your dog have a humping problem? This French product, marketed as a nonsurgical alternative to neutering a male dog, is essentially a doggy love doll. Molded out of plastic in the shape of a small, faceless female dog, it has a cone-shaped silicone "receptacle" in the back that can be removed for cleaning. Available in black or white.

Product: Bowser Beer ($30 for a six pack)

Details: What's a best friend if you can't share your beer with it? Bowser Beer tastes like regular beer but with dog-friendly flavors added. It comes in Beefy Brown Ale, Porky Pug Porter, and chicken-based Cock-a-Doodle Brew. And it doesn't contain any alcohol.

Seventy percent of all carrots sold are baby carrots.

WHEN JOHN EATS FOOD GETS THROWN

"Garden path" sentences are one of our favorite—and most mind-bending—wordplay games. Identified by linguist Henry Watson Fowler in his 1926 book A Dictionary of Modern English Usage, *they deceive the reader into thinking the speaker is going one place...and then they end up going someplace completely different. They're called "garden path" sentences because the reader is being "led down the garden path," which means "being tricked." Commas could be added to make the meanings clearer, but they're grammatically correct without them—as well as being a lot trickier and more fun to read. Here are some of our favorite garden path sentences—which you'll probably have to read a couple of times.*

THE MAN WHISTLING TUNES PIANOS.

She told me a little white lie will come back to haunt me.

I know the words to that song about the queen don't rhyme.

THAT JAY IS NEVER HERE HURTS.

The old man the boat.

We painted the wall with cracks.

The prime number few.

WHILE THOM WAS WASHING THE DISHES FELL ON THE FLOOR.

The horse raced past the barn fell.

The man who hunts ducks out on weekends.

WHEN JOHN EATS FOOD GETS THROWN.

A person's fingerprints are formed by their 17th week in the womb.

After the young New Yorker had visited his parents prepared
to celebrate their anniversary.

When I dressed the baby stayed in the crib.

THE MANAGEMENT PLANS TO CUT VACATION DAYS ARE REJECTED.

Wherever John walks the dog chases him.

The government plans to raise taxes were defeated.

While I was surfing the internet went down.

The sour drink from the ocean.

I convinced her children are noisy.

An old friend just dropped by his girlfriend was happy to see her.

WITHOUT HER CONTRIBUTIONS WOULD BE IMPOSSIBLE.

I told the girl the cat scratched Kim would help her.

While the man hunted the deer ran into the woods.

FAT PEOPLE EAT ACCUMULATES.

When Brendan called his old mother was happy.

The complex houses married and single soldiers and their families.

Because he always jogs a mile seems a short distance to him.

AFTER OLIVER DRANK THE WATER PROVED TO BE POISONED.

* * *

"Grammar is a piano I play by ear."
–Joan Didion

Planet with the fastest-moving winds: Neptune.

THE HISTORY OF THE ELECTRIC CHAIR, PART II

Here's the second installment of this shocking story. Warning: some of the descriptions are a bit grisly, so if you're squeamish, you might want to turn to the next article. (Part I is on page 161.)

THE CHAIR

In June 1888, Governor Hill signed legislation that established the electric chair as the official method of execution for New York State beginning on January 1, 1889. The chair constructed for this grim task was made of oak and had a high back that sloped back at an angle. Sturdy leather straps on the back, arms, and feet of the chair secured the condemned prisoner in place. Another leather strap secured the head, covering the face. There were two "electrodes," or conductors of electricity—one for the top of the head and one for the back. The one for the head consisted of a rubber skullcap that held a natural sea sponge in place on top of the prisoner's head. An electrical cable passed through a hole in the skullcap and attached to the sea sponge, which was soaked in saltwater or another liquid to ensure that it was a good conductor of electricity. The electrode for the back was similar: it, too, made use of a rubber cap and a sea sponge saturated with saltwater.

During an execution, when the switch was thrown, the electrical current would enter the condemned prisoner's body through one electrode and exit through the other. If everything was done correctly, the prisoner would receive a quick and comparatively painless death, Southwick believed. And just as Thomas Edison had hoped, the chair was powered by alternating current supplied by a Westinghouse "dynamo," or generator, purchased surreptitiously, because George Westinghouse refused to sell the state any equipment that would be used for the electric chair.

THE CONDEMNED

The first prisoner selected to die in New York's electric chair was William Kemmler, 30, a vegetable peddler from Buffalo, who, in March 1888, had murdered his common-law wife with a hatchet following a long night of drinking. The execution was set for August 6, 1890, at Auburn Prison in central New York. The day before the execution was to take place, the equipment was tested by electrocuting a "gaunt, worn-out horse" to make sure it was working properly.

Shortly before 7:00 a.m. on the morning of August 6, Kemmler was ushered into the room where the electric chair had been set up. After speaking his last words, he was strapped into the chair and prepared for execution. When everything was ready,

There are 248 muscles in a caterpillar's head.

the Warden, Charles Durston, said, "Goodbye, William." Then the executioner, believed to be a man named George Irish, threw the switch.

MOMENT OF TRUTH

More than 20 witnesses were present for the execution. When the switch was thrown, they heard a click and then watched as Kemmler's body seized up, straining against the leather straps as 1,000 volts of electricity surged through him. He remained rigid for the full 17 seconds that the current was on, then slumped back in the chair after it was shut off. Alfred Southwick was there to watch his brainchild in operation. As soon as the power was cut, he exclaimed, "This is the culmination of ten years' work and study. We live in a higher civilization from this day."

His remarks were premature. It quickly became apparent Kemmler was still breathing, something that horrified many of the witnesses. "For God's sake, kill him and have it over," one newspaper reporter shouted before passing out on the floor. This time the generator was revved up to 2,000 volts and the current was applied again. "The witnesses were so horrified by the ghastly sight that they could not take their eyes off it," *The New York Times* reported:

> Blood began to appear on the face of the wretch in the chair. It stood on the face like sweat. An awful odor began to permeate the death chamber.
>
> How long this second execution lasted—for it was a second execution, if there was any real life in the body when the current was turned on for the second time—is not really known by anybody. Those who held watches were too much horrified to follow them.

IF AT FIRST YOU DON'T SUCCEED...

The execution was nothing like the quick and antiseptic process that had been promised—it was a debacle. "I would rather see ten hangings than one such execution as this," one witness, New York's Deputy Coroner, Dr. William Jenkins, told the *Times*. If the *coroner* feels that way, that's probably a bad sign.

And yet in spite of how badly the execution had gone, the state of New York did not abandon the electric chair. Mistakes had been made, the thinking went, but they could be remedied and when they were, electrocution would yet prove itself to be more humane than hanging. One physician, Dr. Alphonso Rockwell, who had helped develop the electric chair but was not present for Kemmler's execution, was so disturbed by how it had been carried out—he blamed poor placement of the electrodes on Kemmler's body—that for the rest of his life he made a point of attending executions to ensure that the electrodes were properly prepared and placed on the condemned prisoner's body, in order to minimize their suffering. By the time Rockwell died in 1933 at the age of 93, he had become an outspoken opponent of capital punishment.

The only burp in a Shakespeare play comes from a character in *Twelfth Night* called Sir Toby Belch.

HERE, THERE, EVERYWHERE

The electric chair's shortcomings aside, what was popular in New York soon spread to other states, and by the late 1940s, thirty-eight states had adopted it, making electrocution the most common form of execution in the United States. During the 20th century, more than 4,300 prisoners died in the electric chair, more than all other forms of execution combined. West Virginia was the last state to adopt the electric chair as a form of capital punishment, in 1949.

But as with the gallows before it, botched executions like William Kemmler's happened with enough frequency that the public came to see the electric chair as cruel and barbaric. In 1977, the state of Oklahoma became the first government anywhere in the world to adopt lethal injection, the method rejected in the 1880s for being *too* painless, as its method of capital punishment. Other states soon followed.

The last time New York State executed a prisoner in the electric chair was in 1963. Two years later, the state repealed the death penalty in all cases except those involving the murder of a police officer. The death penalty was reinstated in 1995, but in 2004, New York's highest court ruled that the statute violated the state constitution. The law has not been amended, so the state remains without the death penalty. It has not executed anyone since that last electrocution in 1963.

THE ELECTRIC CHAIR TODAY

As of 2021, 27 states still have the death penalty, and lethal injection is the primary or default method of execution in each of these states. Nine states still reserve the electric chair as an alternative method of execution, in some cases to be used only in the event that lethal injection is struck down as unconstitutional or becomes unworkable because pharmaceutical companies refuse to supply their drugs to be used for the deliberate killing of human beings.

TAKE YOUR PICK

Six states (Alabama, Florida, Kentucky, South Carolina, Tennessee, and Virginia) have more than one form of capital punishment on the books and allow condemned prisoners to choose the one they want. As unlikely as it may seem, even today some prisoners still opt for the electric chair over lethal injection. Reason: some condemned prisoners fear that a bungled lethal injection will be even worse than a mishap in the electric chair. With lethal injection, even when everything works perfectly, "it's about fourteen minutes of pain and horror," defense attorney Stephen Kissinger told *The New York Times* in 2020. "Then [the prisoners] look at electrocution, and [ask] how long does it take?" In February 2020, Nicholas Todd Sutton, 58, a Tennessee death row inmate and quadruple murderer who killed his own grandmother, became the fifth inmate in the state since 2018 to *choose* to die in the electric chair.

East meets West: Tumbleweed, a staple of Western movies, is actually native to Russia.

THE LAST OF IT

Everything has a beginning...and an end.

THE LAST AMERICAN TERRITORIAL ACQUISITIONS: The United States expanded from 13 American colonies in the 1770s into a global, superpower a century later. In addition to adding large landmasses such as the Louisiana Purchase (acquired from France in 1803), Texas (which became a state in 1845), and Alaska (purchased from Russia in 1867), the U.S. annexed numerous islands in the Pacific Ocean. In 1947, a United Nations Security Council's post–World War II mandate made three of Japan's holdings–the Mariana Islands, the Caroline Islands, and the Marshall Islands–American territories.

THE LAST NEW LANDMASS: Underwater volcanoes near the Tonga Islands (in the South Pacific Ocean) started erupting in December 2014, shooting out lava flows that hardened into a new island within eight weeks. It connected two preexisting islands to form one new landmass named Hunga Tonga-Hunga Ha'apai. The island was almost destroyed by another volcanic eruption in January 2022.

THE LAST IMMIGRANT ON ELLIS ISLAND: Millions of European immigrants entered the United States via New York Harbor, and were processed at the Ellis Island station. The site opened in 1892 and handled immigration inspections and paperwork for decades while also serving as a deportation center and Coast Guard training facility. Its use for handling émigrés was phased out by November 1954, when a Norwegian sailor named Arne Peterssen became the final immigrant to pass through. After overstaying his 29-day work visa by five months, he was sent to Ellis Island, where he was dispatched back to Norway.

THE LAST EUROPEAN COLONY IN AFRICA: By 1900, most of Africa was under the control of foreign countries, particularly the UK, France, Germany, Spain, Italy, Belgium, and Portugal. As those colonies developed, they sought independence, not always peacefully. By the end of the 20th century, more than 50 countries had separated from their ruling nations, the last being the Republic of Zimbabwe, which expelled the British in 1990.

THE LAST MAN IMPRISONED ON ALCATRAZ: Formerly a military outpost, Alcatraz Island (in San Francisco Bay) became a federal prison in 1934. The penitentiary became world famous for being virtually escape-proof, but it was very expensive to operate and was slowly sinking into the Pacific Ocean. The federal government shut down Alcatraz in 1963 and transferred the 1,576 prisoners to other facilities. The last inmate to board a departing boat: convicted bank robber Frank Weatherman.

The average opossum eats 20,000 ticks a year.

WEIRD CANADA

Canada—land of Mounted Police, poutine, Wayne Gretzky,
Anne Murray... and some really strange news stories.

MOOSE ON THE LOOSE

Ashley Young was driving her kids to school in Saskatoon one morning in November 2021 when her son announced that he'd just spotted a moose *inside* the school. "And of course, I'm like, 'No, there's not a moose. What are you talking about?' And he said, 'I'm not kidding.'" He really wasn't. The moose was in a community room used for student drop-offs. According to Saskatchewan Ministry of Environment inspector Steve Dobko, his office had been receiving calls about that moose all morning. Apparently, it had wandered into the neighborhood, and, after getting spooked by barking dogs, it crashed through a window and remained in the community room for hours, even while students started to arrive. Animal control officers tranquilized the moose and returned it to the wild.

BERRY BAD CRIMINALS

> They discovered that their entire crop—three acres worth of blueberries—had been quietly harvested by thieves.

Hurricane Larry made landfall in September 2021 on the Canadian coastal province of Newfoundland, leading to widespread power outages and substantial property damage. But it spared Brown's Family Farms, a large produce operation, specializing in Newfoundland blueberries. Owners thought they'd weathered the storm until, a day after the storm hit, they discovered that their entire crop—three acres worth of blueberries—had been quietly harvested by thieves. "There's not a berry left on the bush," co-owner Nancy White told reporters. "We were pretty upset and pretty much just kept walking around in disbelief." White estimates that thieves got away with as many as 3,000 pounds of blueberries.

FROM THE TOWN OF BED ROCK

Ruth Hamilton of Golden, British Columbia, was asleep in her bed one night in October 2021, when she was suddenly awakened by the sound of an explosion and the sensation of debris falling on her face. She bolted out of bed and turned on a light only to discover a large rock sitting between her pillows. It was about the size of a fist, weighed just under three pounds, and had plunged into her home, leaving a hole in her roof. After Hamilton called 911, police questioned members of a construction crew working nearby. They hadn't done any blasting that night, but said they had seen a bright light in the sky and heard an explosion. That's when authorities realized that the rock was actually a meteorite. "You're sound asleep, safe, you think, in your bed, and you can get taken out by a meteorite, apparently," Hamilton said.

Cartoon fans, can you name Speedy Gonzales's cousin?
He's Slowpoke Rodriguez, "the slowest mouse in all Mexico."

IS THERE A GOALIE IN THE HOUSE?

In February 2020, the Carolina Hurricanes of the National Hockey League traveled to Canada to play the Toronto Maple Leafs. During the game, Hurricanes goalie James Reimer was injured, so his backup, Petr Mrazek suited up. In an unlikely twist, Mrazek collided with Maple Leafs forward Kyle Clifford and was hurt so badly that he couldn't tend goal either. Fortunately, the Maple Leafs had a contingency plan: a backup goalie, 42-year-old David Ayres, who was in the stands, watching the game with his wife...while on break from his job as Scotiabank Arena's Zamboni driver. Ayres allowed two goals, but then stopped eight shots, and helped the Hurricanes to a 6–3 victory. He's the oldest goaltender in NHL history with a win in his first game (which was also his last).

HEADS UP

Jennie Steeves of New Brunswick died in 1900, at age 15. Thirty years later, her mother commissioned a statue of an angel, made out of Italian marble, to watch over her gravesite in the family's plot at the Gray's Island Cemetery in the town of Hillsborough. After being the target of multiple acts of vandalism over the years, in the mid-1990s, the head of the angel was quietly decapitated and stolen, disappearing with not a clue as to who took it or why. "There were all kinds of stories about the monument—that it was haunted, that the eyes had rubies in them—but none of that is true," Steeves descendant Kathleen Wallace told reporters. Police reports were filed and rewards offered, but nothing came of it. Until November 2021, when Wallace saw a Facebook photo of the family plot, with the statue, and it's head returned—sitting next to the body. "It was really kind of a miracle," said Wallace, who took the head home to keep it safe. "It remains a mystery. Maybe somebody had a guilty conscience."

THIS STORY IS NUTS

In 1979, Chuck and Lou Ann Best of Sanford, Florida, found an orphaned squirrel and raised it as a pet. And then they trained it to water-ski on little foam blocks pulled by a radio-controlled boat in tubs of water. The Bests took the show on the road, with Twiggy the Water-Skiing Squirrel appearing at hundreds of boat shows (and TV shows, and even a couple of Hollywood films) over the years. When Lou Ann and Chuck retired in 2018, Chuck Best Jr. took over and, in 2020, brought the spectacle to the Toronto International Boat Show—only to be rejected. The city's animal services notified show organizers that to allow Twiggy to perform would violate a city law prohibiting the domestication of Eastern gray squirrels. Toronto police informed Best that they would enforce the law. "Using a wild animal in a ridiculous display as a public attraction is archaic and cruel, and very stressful for the animal," the Toronto Wildlife Centre said. Deterred slightly, Best and Twiggy headed for a boat show in Vancouver, where animal control officials, citing similar anti-domestication laws, also prevented Twiggy from water-skiing.

In the 1800s, *cacklers* was a slang term for chickens (and eggs were *cackling farts*).

MORE EPONYMS

On page 121, we shared the histories of some well-known eponyms—words derived from people's names. Here are some less-used examples that you can add to your vocabulary. Just try not to come off as Rumsfeldian.

PECKSNIFFIAN

Who? Seth Pecksniff, a fictional character in the 1844 book *Martin Chuzzlewit*, by Charles Dickens (1812–70), an English writer and social critic.

Meaning: A description of someone who is hypocritical; they pretend to be benevolent, but behind closed doors, they don't practice what they preach.

Details: This is an offshoot of a better-known eponym, "Dickensian," which is used to describe two of Dickens's most prevalent themes: the plight of impoverished people, and the repugnant characters who lord over them, such as Ebenezer Scrooge. Here's how Dickens describes Seth Picksniff: "Some people likened him to a direction-post, which is always telling the way to a place, and never goes there." The eponym was introduced into the American lexicon by later writers, such as H. L. Mencken, who in 1919 described Philadelphia as "the most Pecksniffian of American cities."

Use It in a Sentence: "But Gen X is young enough to see the current-day Pecksniffian left-wing wokescolds trying to cancel cartoon characters and maple syrup because it 'offends' them." —*BroBible*, from the article "People Are Calling for Gen X to Save America from Cancel Culture—But Gen X Doesn't Care"

RUMSFELDIAN

Who? Donald Rumsfeld (1932–2021), Secretary of Defense under President Gerald Ford, and Secretary of Defense under President George W. Bush.

Meaning: The tendency to ignore facts when those facts go against your viewpoint.

Details: At a 2002 press conference, a reporter asked Rumsfeld whether Americans should be concerned that there were no official reports that weapons of mass destruction had been found in Iraq, despite the president's insistence otherwise. Rumsfeld's answer:

> Reports that say that something hasn't happened are always interesting to me, because as we know, there are known knowns; there are things we know we know. We also know there are known unknowns; that is to say, we know there are some things we do not know. But there are also unknown unknowns—the ones we don't know we don't know. And if one looks throughout the history of our country and other free countries, it is the latter category that tend to be the difficult ones.

Befuddling statements like that led cable news pundits to start describing any bureaucratic verbiage that uses circular logic to turn a simple concept on its head, just to make it seem not so bad after all, as "Rumsfeldian." Another example, from a letter that Rumsfeld sent to the IRS: "The tax code is so complex and the forms are so complicated, that I know that I cannot have any confidence that I know what is being requested and therefore I cannot and do not know, and I suspect a great many Americans cannot know, whether or not their tax returns are accurate."

Use It in a Sentence: "Banker: Your account is overdrawn. Rumsfeldian: I'll write a check to cover it." —**Urban Dictionary**

TRUMPIAN

Who? Donald Trump (b. 1946), mogul, TV personality, and 45th U.S. president.

Meaning: Behaving in the style of Donald Trump.

Details: "Trumpian" predates Trump's Oval Office years by more than three decades, first appearing in a 1988 issue of *Yachting* magazine. (A critic called *The Art of Winning* by Dennis Conner "within the Trumpian vein," referring to Trump's book, *Trump: The Art of the Deal*, published a few months earlier.) In the ensuing years, Trump himself was known to use "Trumpian" in an effort to make it go mainstream.

But what does it mean? That depends on who you ask. For the former president's supporters, it could mean shrewd, savvy, straight talking, tough, daring, successful, or determined. For detractors, it could mean bombastic, shameless, dishonest, narcissistic, dictatorial, ignorant, reckless, or Machiavellian. Who's correct? Only time will tell.

Use It in a Sentence: "One thing people forget...is that for decades, long before the presidency, [Trump's] whole life was a crisis and he thrived in that environment. It'd be boring if he just got blown out or won big. That would be very un-Trumpian for there not to be some calamity involved." —**senior Trump administration official, speaking anonymously a few days prior to the November 2020 election**

PYTHONESQUE

Who? Monty Python, the British sketch comedy troupe formed in 1969 by Terry Jones, John Cleese, Eric Idle, Michael Palin, Graham Chapman, and Terry Gilliam.

Meaning: Surreal, absurd comedy.

Details: Bang a couple of coconuts together while doing a silly walk and singing, "SPAM, SPAM, SPAM!" If that makes you laugh, you're a fan of Pythonesque humor. The eponym dates to 1975, after the troupe completed their groundbreaking BBC TV show *Monty Python's Flying Circus*. Today, it can also be used to describe Python-influenced torchbearers from *Saturday Night Live* to *South Park*.

Use It in a Sentence: "One of the things we tried to do with [Flying Circus] was to try and do something that was so unpredictable that it had no shape and you could never say what the kind of humor was. And I think that the fact that 'Pythonesque' is now a word in the Oxford English Dictionary shows the extent to which we failed." —**Terry Jones**

For more examples of Pythonesque humor, take your dead parrot over to page 381.

First product called an "iPhone":
A desk phone with a video screen and keyboard, capable of...

A MOST ROYALLY STRANGE DEATH

Royals–kings, princes, and such–have historically been treated like gods. But like the rest of us, they're mortals, and mortals die–although some of them still perished in bizarrely fancy and one-of-a-kind ways.

Royal: George V, King of the United Kingdom (1910–1936)
Demise: Suffering from progressively worsening health problems, primarily chronic bronchitis that made it hard to breathe, King George V was on his deathbed. His personal physician, Lord Dawson of Penn, made the decision to hasten George's demise in order to preserve what remained of the monarch's dignity. Lord Dawson administered two fatal injections–first morphine, and then cocaine. The king died just before midnight, per Dawson's plan, so that the death could be announced in the morning newspapers and not, as he wrote in his diary, the "less appropriate" and disreputable "evening journals."

Royal: Alexander, King of Greece (1917–1920)
Demise: One day in October 1920, Alexander decided to take his dog, a German shepherd named Fritz, on a walk through the grounds of one of his palaces, just outside of Athens. Unbeknownst to the king, the estate's wine steward had a pet macaque (a small monkey) who had free rein of the gardens. When the monkey encountered Fritz, it attacked. Alexander attempted to break up the scuffle, suffering two deep bites from the monkey on his leg in the

> **DID YOU KNOW?**
> King George V was the first British monarch from the House of Windsor. He took the throne in 1910 for the Saxe-Coburg-Gotha family, but in 1917, he changed the family name to Windsor. Why? The old one sounded too German, and anti-German sentiment was high because of World War I.

process. Within days, the wounds became severely infected, and Alexander's doctors considered amputating the affected leg, but ultimately decided not to because they weren't sure it would stop the spread of the infection. Wrong move. Twenty-three days after the dog-monkey fight, Alexander was dead.

Royal: Charles II, King of Navarre (1349–1387)
Demise: At the end of his life, the 54-year-old king was bedridden with various ailments and could barely move. His doctors ordered his body wrapped, like a mummy, in linen soaked in brandy, believing it would make him more comfortable.

...surfing the Web, released by a company called InfoGear in 1998. (It flopped.)

An attendant carried out the doctors' instructions, but had some loose threads at the end and wanted to remove them. Unable to find a sharp object to cut them off, she decided to burn off the ends with a lit candle. When fire comes into contact with alcohol, it tends to burn—the booze-saturated cloth enrobing King Charles II instantly ignited, along with the king himself. He lay in agony, his entire body severely burned, for two weeks until he passed away.

Royal: Martin, King of Aragon, Valencia, and Majorca (1396–1410)

Demise: Martin ate an entire goose one evening in 1410, which gave him such an upset stomach he was unable to sleep. Late into the night, he called for his jester to distract him by way of entertainment. The jester took more than an hour to arrive, and when Martin demanded an explanation for the delay, the entertainer quipped that he was "in the vineyard, where I saw a young deer hanging by his tail from a tree, as if he'd been punished for stealing figs." Martin reportedly thought that was so funny that he broke into uproarious laughter...and then couldn't stop. According to historians, he laughed for three hours, at which point he fell out of bed and died. It's likely that the king's indigestion and the frenetic behavior indicated by his laughing fit were actually symptoms of a heart attack.

Royal: Pyrrhus, King of Epirus (297–272 BC)

Demise: In addition to serving as the king of an Ancient Greek city-state, Pyrrhus was a notable general. (The phrase "Pyrrhic victory," which describes a win that comes at a cost so great that it's almost a loss, is named for him.) In 272 BC, he led soldiers in what was planned as a surprise invasion of the city-state Argos, but when Pyrrhus arrived, he was met with hundreds of Argive troops, ready to defend their homeland. As the Battle of Argos progressed, Pyrrhus—on horseback—was caught with his back against the wall of a home, engaged in combat with an Argive soldier. As they squared off, the soldier's mother, standing on a nearby roof, picked up a tile and threw it at Pyrrhus, who fell off his horse and fractured his spine. As the fallen king lay paralyzed and barely alive, a Macedonian soldier named Zopyrus took pity on Pyrrhus and beheaded him.

Royal: Béla I, King of Hungary (1060–1063)

Demise: This Hungarian ruler commissioned a large wooden throne for himself, along with an ornate wooden canopy to surround and cover the throne. One day in 1063, on the eve of battle with Holy Roman emperor Henry IV, Béla was sitting on his throne when the wooden canopy spontaneously collapsed. Historians speculate that the throne had been sabotaged, but whatever the cause, the result was that the collapsing timbers struck and crushed the ruler.

Hello! The energy expended during a professional tennis match could power a smartphone for a year.

SURVIVAL STORIES

Never underestimate the power of the human spirit.

BURIED ALIVE

At a ski resort in the French Alps on December 26, 2018, a group of seven skiers had ventured *off-piste* (away from prepared ski runs) on a steep "Black Diamond" slope. A 12-year-old boy (unnamed in press reports) skied ahead of the pack and was all alone when he was swept down the mountain in a sudden avalanche of snow, ice, and rocks. After the snow settled, his group looked but could not see him anywhere. The boy's father frantically called for help; the rescuers knew there wasn't a minute to waste. Buried avalanche victims can usually remain alive for about 15 minutes. After that, their chances diminish steadily as the weight of the snow slowly suffocates them. The family's only hope was that the boy had come to rest in an air pocket, and hadn't suffered major trauma. Making matters more dire, he wasn't wearing an avalanche transceiver that emits a signal for rescuers.

A search-and-rescue team arrived via helicopter with a dog that's specially trained to find human scents. Half an hour passed without any success. At 45 minutes, the boy's chances of survival would fall to 30 percent or less. Then, around 40 minutes into the search, the dog picked up the boy's scent and rescue workers found him buried in the snow more than 100 yards from where he fell. Other than a broken leg, the boy wasn't seriously injured. The rescuers called his survival a "Christmas miracle."

IN AND OUT

At 69 years old, Harry Burleigh knew that an experienced outdoorsman must always implement the seven P's: "Proper prior planning to prevent piss-poor performance." But in May 2021, on his way home from an overnight fishing trip in rural Oregon, he disregarded those first three P's when he made a rash decision to try his luck at another lake. It was just a 10-mile drive up a windy forest road, followed by a 1.25-mile hike to the fishing spot. "In and out," as Burleigh later described it. He parked at the trailhead at 4:00 p.m. and took only his rod and reel. No water. No compass. No hat. Not even boots—just sandals and wool socks. And there was no cellular service that deep in the wilderness. About a mile into the hike, the ground was covered in snow, and by the time Burleigh realized he wasn't on the trail anymore, it was getting dark. He'd have to spend a cold night in the woods.

The next morning, Burleigh got even more lost and slipped down a ravine. He fell hard onto a log, injuring his leg and breaking his fishing pole. When the day ended and he still hadn't found the trail, he realized he could be in serious trouble. Over the

In the 14th century, kids in Herefordshire, England, were baptized in cider, because it was believed to be cleaner than water.

next several days, Burleigh's struggles only worsened as he lived off creek water (or his own urine, when water was scarce) and the occasional grub, millipede, snail, or scorpion. It got so cold at night that he used fern leaves as bedding and wore his underwear on his head to retain body heat. A few times, Burleigh saw a plane or a helicopter flying low overhead, but he couldn't get their attention. He was hurting and famished. About 50 miles away in the town of Roseburg, his worried wife Stacy wasn't doing much better. "It would get hard," she said, "but every morning would be a new day. I had hope." More than 100 people joined in the search.

> **It got so cold at night that he used fern leaves as bedding and wore his underwear on his head to retain body heat.**

One week passed. Then two. On day 17, rescuers finally located Burleigh. He was disoriented, had lost almost 30 pounds, and could barely walk. But he was alive. How'd he do it? "It became about 'one more day.' One more day to be here. One more day to see my wife."

SWEPT AWAY

Tonga is a South Pacific nation comprised of more than 150 islands, 36 of which are inhabited by 100,000 people...who live dangerously close to an undersea volcano called Hunga Tonga-Hunga Ha'apai. In January 2022, a massive eruption created a volcanic plume nearly 20 miles high and sent tsunami waves as far away as Alaska. Near the epicenter, there wasn't much time for Tongans to make it to safety. The eruption's shock wave was soon followed by a smoke cloud, then a rain of rocks, and then a series of increasingly massive tsunamis. On one small island, a 59-year-old retired carpenter named Lisala Folau, who's disabled and has trouble walking, was separated from his family by a 20-foot wave. "The sea kept twirling me and taking me underwater," said Folau, who could hear his son yelling for him. But he didn't answer because he didn't want anyone risking their own life to save him.

Folau clung desperately to a log as it dragged him out to sea. After floating all night, he made landfall on a small, uninhabited island. He tried waving down a police patrol boat, but without success, so he decided to swim to Tonga's main island...nearly five miles away. Eight hours later, more than a day since the tsunami swept him away, Folau finally washed up on an abandoned beach. He crawled to a road, found a stick to use as a cane, and then wandered until he found help. Folau's harrowing tale of survival made news all over the world. The press dubbed him "the real-life Aquaman."

* * *

RANDOM FACT: Before he designed his first car, Ferdinand Porsche was a chauffeur for Archduke Franz Ferdinand. The archduke's assassination, while riding in a car, triggered World War I. (Porsche wasn't driving.)

You've seen 'em, now you know their names: The "see no evil, hear no evil, speak no evil" monkeys are named Mizaru, Kikazaru, and Iwazaru.

THE SMART HISTORY OF CRASH TEST DUMMIES

One thing that all new passenger cars sold in the United States since the late 1960s have in common: nobody gets to drive them until crash test dummies have "driven" them first. Here's the story of how those dummies came to be.

JET-SETTER

In March of 1947, a U.S. Army Air Force surgeon named Dr. John Paul Stapp was assigned a project to study the effects of sudden deceleration on human beings. World War II had ended just a year and a half earlier, but it was already clear where the future of military aviation was headed: propeller-driven aircraft were giving way to jet airplanes, which someday might even fly faster than the speed of sound (767 miles per hour). At such tremendous speeds, if something went wrong, a pilot would be unable to just unbuckle their safety harness, slide open the canopy, and clamber over the side of the plane with their parachute as they'd done in World War II.

One possible new means of escape being considered was to blast the entire pilot seat, with the pilot still strapped in it, up and out of the aircraft using small rocket motors—an "ejection seat," as it would come to be known. But the idea would have to be tested first: could pilots even survive being rocketed out of an aircraft this way? And at such high speeds? The instant they cleared the cockpit, they would be hit with powerful wind resistance, causing rapid deceleration. (Remember what it felt like as a kid to stick your hand out the window of a moving car and feel the air pushing against your hand? That's wind resistance. Now imagine what it would have felt like if the car was traveling over 700 miles an hour, and you stuck your *entire body* out of the window.)

What was the maximum speed at which a pilot could eject from an aircraft and expect to survive? If the airplane crashed, what was the maximum amount of force the pilot could absorb on impact without being injured or killed? Which types of safety harnesses did the best job of keeping a pilot safe and secure during an ejection or a crash? These were the kinds of questions that Stapp needed to answer.

TOUGH SLEDDING

Rather than conduct such tests from an aircraft, the U.S. Air Force used testing facilities at the Holloman Air Force Base in the New Mexico desert, and later at Muroc Air Force Base (now Edwards Air Force Base) in Southern California, using rocket-powered sleds on standard gauge railroad tracks. Stapp or another volunteer would strap himself into the seat on the rocket sled, then blast off down the track. Once

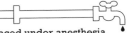
Weird plant fact: The carnivorous Venus flytrap plant can be placed under anesthesia. While sedated, it will not eat bugs.

it reached maximum speed, the sled would brake rapidly, subjecting the volunteers to rapid deceleration to see how well their bodies tolerated the stress of coming to a sudden, violent stop. Different configurations of pilot seats and harnesses were tested.

Stapp took his first ride in the winter of 1947–48, reaching a speed of 90 miles per hour before slamming to a halt. Over the next seven years he subjected himself to another 28 more test runs, increasing the top speed with every test—first to 150 miles per hour, then to 200, and up from there. As the speeds increased, so did the risk of injury or even death. In the later (faster and more violent) tests, Stapp suffered severe headaches, blackouts, and concussions. He also cracked ribs and broke his left wrist twice, and had six fillings in his teeth pop out.

But the worst sled ride of all was Stapp's very last one: On December 10, 1954, his sled accelerated from zero to *632 miles per hour* in five seconds—faster than a .45-caliber bullet fired from a pistol—then braked to a complete stop in 1.4 seconds. In the process, Stapp broke the world land speed record (it has since been broken many times), earning himself the nickname "Fastest Man Alive." He also broke the record for the greatest amount of (voluntary) deceleration: 46.2 g, or 46.2 times the force of gravity, the equivalent of crashing into a wall at 120 miles per hour. That record has never been broken; Stapp holds it to this day.

He paid quite a price for it: this time he broke both wrists, suffered two collapsed lungs, and his eyes nearly popped out of their sockets, which he described as feeling "somewhat like the extraction of a molar without anesthetic." So many blood vessels burst in his retinas that he was temporarily blinded. His vision returned later that same day, but Stapp had been so concerned about being permanently blinded that in the days leading up to the test, he had practiced getting dressed in the dark—just in case. By taking the risk, he demonstrated that pilots could survive the equivalent of ejecting from an aircraft traveling 1,000 miles per hour at an altitude of 35,000 feet, and that when properly restrained, they could withstand sudden deceleration up to 45 g.

BODY DOUBLE

In spite of his injuries, Stapp believed he could go even faster and brake even harder. He wanted to travel as fast as 1,000 miles per hour, well past the speed of sound, and brake to a sudden stop again. While he recovered from his injuries, he began making preparations for just such a sled test. But his commanding officer intervened: The tests were getting too dangerous, and Stapp was worth more to the military as a researcher than as a test subject who might be killed at any moment. He ordered Stapp to come up with an alternative to human testing.

Primitive "dummies" were already being put to use in other military programs, but they hadn't advanced much beyond human-shaped sacks filled with sand or other ballast to give them the approximate weight and center of gravity of a human being.

How popular was the Doritos Locos taco when it was added to the Taco Bell menu in 2013? The fast-food chain had to hire 15,000 new employees to meet the demand.

Stapp needed something better. He turned to an engineer named Sam Alderson, who had made a name for himself designing artificial limbs for U.S. soldiers who'd been injured in the war. "Being involved in replacement parts for a human, I found it very fascinating to go ahead and duplicate the entire human," Alderson later recounted.

Working from U.S. Air Force statistics, Alderson created a dummy, more properly known as an "anthropomorphic test device," with the weight and measurements of an average air force pilot. He gave the dummy movable limbs that replicated some but not all of the movements of human beings. Sensors in the chest and head recorded measurements of the stresses the dummy was subjected to during testing.

DRIVEN

In the years that followed, this dummy and others designed by Alderson's company, Alderson Research Laboratories, as well as dummies designed by another company, Sierra Engineering, helped the U.S. Air Force design safety harnesses, ejection seats, parachutes, and other equipment that solved the problem of how best to get pilots out of malfunctioning jet aircraft and safely back on the ground. But just how successful the program was didn't become clear until Stapp began reviewing air force accident statistics and discovered that more pilots were injured driving their cars to their bases than they were while flying their aircraft.

That fascinated Stapp, so he started using his military dummies in automobile crash tests. In other tests, he used live, anesthetized hogs, because they are at least somewhat anatomically similar to humans, and they can be strapped into a "sitting up" position in a car seat similar to humans in crash tests. (After each of the hog tests, the anesthetized animals were slaughtered, butchered, and served up as barbecue for the researchers.)

When these crash tests became public knowledge, they were disturbing to both the public and the U.S. auto industry, not because of how the hogs had been treated, but because the tests had shined a spotlight on the dangers inherent in driving automobiles. Pressure from the auto industry soon caused the air force to bring Stapp's auto crash testing to an end.

UNSAFE AT ANY SPEED

And that might well have been the end of all auto crash testing, at least for a while, had a brash young consumer advocate named Ralph Nader not published an exposé of the U.S. auto industry, called *Unsafe at Any Speed*, in 1965. Among other things, the book demonstrated just what little attention domestic automakers paid to improving the safety of their vehicles. At General Motors, unnecessary styling changes added about $700 to the price of a new car; by comparison, safety improvements averaged just 23 cents per car, at a time when not even seat belts were offered as

Longest tapeworm ever pulled out of a human being: 59 feet.

> **Now that GM had no choice, it decided to use the most sophisticated test dummies possible.**

standard equipment. This and other revelations in the book prompted the U.S. Congress to play a larger role in regulating automobile safety, including instituting the first mandatory crash tests.

Now that GM had no choice, it decided to use the most sophisticated test dummies possible. The company looked at various test dummies produced for the military by Alderson Research Labs and Sierra Engineering, but none of the dummies met their needs. So it financed the development of its own dummy called the Hybrid I, so named because it combined all the most desirable features of the earlier dummies. Introduced in 1971, the Hybrid I was designed to model an average American male in height, weight, and weight distribution. Improved articulation of the limbs meant that the dummy sat in car seats more realistically than earlier dummies and responded to crash tests more realistically. Instruments in the head and chest cavity measured the forces that the dummy was subjected to during crash tests.

Unlike on earlier crash test dummies, the head, rib cage, and other parts of the Hybrid I dummy could be recalibrated between crash tests to make sure that its performance did not vary from one crash test to the next. This was an important feature: if, for example, different seat belt configurations were being studied in a series of crash tests, and the crash test dummies' responses varied from one test to the next, there was no way to tell what was responsible for changes in the test results—the dummy or the seat belt configuration.

In 1973, the Hybrid I was followed up by an improved version called the Hybrid II, which had more realistic crash responses in the shoulder, spine, and knee. The Hybrid II was replaced in 1977 by the Hybrid III, which boasted further improvements in the spine and neck, and better instrumentation in the head, rib cage, and thigh bone. More than 40 years later, the Hybrid III crash test dummy remains the international standard for frontal crash tests. Today, there's an entire Hybrid III "family," available in five different sizes representing a standard adult male (5'9" and 170 pounds), a larger adult male (6'2" and 223 pounds), an adult female (5' and 110 pounds), and two children, ages three (33 pounds) and six (47 pounds). Other specialized dummies have been developed for side impact crash tests and rear impact crash tests.

BODY(S) OF EVIDENCE

Crash test dummies are designed to measure the forces that would break human bones and cause other injuries, and to do it without themselves breaking. But how do researchers know how much force is enough to break a rib or fracture a skull? Unfortunately, the only way to find out is by actually breaking a human rib or skull,

Nothing to sniff at: 3 percent of all people suffer from *anosmia*, the inability to smell.

and measuring the forces required to do it. Since this can't be done with living human test subjects, cadavers donated for medical research are used.

Detroit's Wayne State University, located near the heart of the U.S. auto industry, was an early pioneer in this field. In the late 1930s, they began performing crash tests using human heads, and later began devising crash tests using entire cadavers. The early full-cadaver tests were primitive: the bodies were dropped down elevator shafts onto metal plates that measured the force of the impact. Autopsies and X-rays were then used to see if that amount of force had been enough to break the bones being studied. If the bones were not broken, then during the next test the cadaver would be dropped from higher up in the elevator shaft, causing the body to reach a greater speed before striking the metal plate at the bottom of the shaft. The test was repeated (using a different cadaver each time) until the bones were broken. Later cadaver tests were more sophisticated and were conducted using sleds that were designed to mimic car crashes.

In the past, Wayne State used to conduct cadaver tests on average about once a month, but as the body (so to speak) of information collected from the tests has grown over the years, the need to conduct further cadaver tests has diminished considerably; today the university conducts cadaver tests only a couple of times a year. It's estimated that the automobile safety improvements that have been made possible by cadaver testing have saved more than 8,500 lives a year since 1987.

* * *

WHY GEORGE MARTIN DECIDED TO PRODUCE THE BEATLES IN 1962

This is how he explained it, late in his life, to his four-year-old granddaughter:

"There were four of them. And I said, 'Who are they, what are they?' And [Beatles manager Brian Epstein] said 'Well, they're a group. We call them the Beatles.' And I said, 'Well, that's a silly name for a start. Who would ever want a group with the name "beetles"?' And he said, 'Well, it isn't the beetles you think of. It's "Beatles" with an "a" in it, like "Beat-les."' So I listened to what he said and I said, 'Well, I'll have to hear them first of all.'

"So he sent them down from Liverpool, which is quite a long way, and I met them in London. And when I listened to what they did, it was OK, but it wasn't brilliant. It was OK. So I thought well, *Why should I be interested in this?*

"But the magic came when I started to get to know them because they were terribly good people to know. They were funny, they were very clever, they said all the lovely things. They were the kind of people that you like to be with. And so I thought, *Well, if I feel this way about them, other people will feel this way about them.* So therefore they should be very popular. And I made records with them."

Makes sense: *The Newlywed Game* host Bob Eubanks is married to a wedding planner.

THE ANTARCTICA TIMELINE, PART II

*On page 267, we traced the history of Antarctica from its formation to the first
people to go there, which, on a geologic time scale—counting the history
of Earth as one day—happened less than a second ago.*

PLANET ANTARCTICA

"Antarctica has this mythic weight," wrote *Into the Wild* author Jon Krakauer. "It resides
in the collective unconscious of so many people, and it makes this huge impact, just
like outer space. It's like going to the Moon." And just as it was with the Space Race,
there was a lot at stake in the race to Antarctica: bragging rights and national pride
awaited whoever got there first and planted their flag. But as these firsts unfolded—
reaching the mainland, establishing a base, walking on the South Pole—it would soon
become clear that Antarctica's true worth lay not in any strategic advantage, but for
what this barren landscape has to teach us about our planet's past, present, and future.
In a way, Antarctica has become the world's largest laboratory; it has no permanent
residents or ruling government, but at any given time there are about 5,000 scientists
and 30,000 tourists down there. Here are the heroes who paved the way.

1895   The "Heroic Age" of Antarctic exploration begins. While the Swedish
steamship *Antarctic* is on its way to the first verified landing on the
southern continent, the Sixth International Geographical Congress
convenes in London to pass a general resolution promoting Antarctica as
a land of exploration and research. But for the most part, whaling, sealing,
and krill harvesting will be the main draws during the Heroic Age.

1898   Belgium's Adrien de Gerlache leads the first purely scientific expedition to
Antarctica. After getting stuck in the ice, he and his crew become the first
people to winter there, albeit on a ship. (Some of the men go mad.)

1899   England's *Southern Cross* expedition arrives at Cape Adare. Led by Carsten
Borchgrevink, 10 men are left behind to spend the first winter on the
mainland. They bring pre-fabricated wooden huts, enough food for
three years, 20 tons of coal, scientific instruments, and weapons to hunt
polar bears (which they didn't find because Antarctica has no native
land mammals). Australian physicist Louis Bernacchi is there to study
the region's magnetic properties. He will later write the first book about
Antarctica by someone who was there. Another first: sled dogs. They will
soon become Antarctica's primary mode of transportation.

The last surviving veteran of the American Revolution,
Samuel Downing, was also the only one to be...

1901 | The race to become the first country to discover the South Pole officially begins. Englishman Robert Falcon Scott's *Discovery* expedition is forced to turn back after two months on the tundra. The *Guardian* will later report: "The expedition was caught in blizzards and dense fog, Ernest Shackleton burst a blood vessel in one of his lungs, while some men showed symptoms of scurvy." One milestone: Scott flies over the Ross Ice Shelf in a hydrogen balloon, becoming the first person to see Antarctica from the air.

1903 | The Scottish National Antarctic Expedition installs the region's first permanent meteorological station on the South Orkney Islands.

1907- 1909 | England's Ernest Shackleton (third mate on Scott's failed mission to the South Pole), returns on the *Nimrod*, this time with motorized vehicles, but his team makes it only to within 100 miles of the South Pole. On the same expedition, Australia's Douglas Mawson leads the first team over Mount Erebus, and he claims to have located the South Magnetic Pole. (Later measurement will show that he was pretty close.)

1911 | On December 14, the race to the South Pole is won by Norway's Roald Amundsen and four other men, and their sled dogs. "It is like a fairy tale," writes Amundsen. A month later, Captain Scott and his team arrive...only to find Amundsen's flag. "The worst has happened," writes Scott, "Great God! This is an awful place!" Scott sets off for the 862-mile journey back to the coast—on foot. A year later, Scott's and his team's frozen corpses are discovered only 11 miles from base camp. But on their ill-fated journey, they had collected tree fossils from the exposed rock, giving scientists their first clue that Antarctica was once a forested continent in a much more temperate region.

1914 | Douglas Mawson returns to lead the Australasian Antarctic Expedition, which catalogs more flora and fauna, and maps more of the coastline than ever before. His words paint a vivid picture: "On those rare summer days the sun blazed down on the blue ice; skua gulls nestled in groups on the snow; sly penguins waddled along to inspect the building operations; seals basked in torpid slumber on the shore; out on the sapphire bay the milk-white bergs floated in the swell." On the return trip, all of Mawson's companions die, and he completes the monthlong journey back to Commonwealth Bay alone. Other firsts: the use of radio, and the discovery of meteorites. (They're quite easy to spot because there are literally no other rocks on the glaciers.)

1915- 1917 | Shackleton attempts the first crossing of Antarctica but doesn't make it. He and what's left of his team won't be rescued for two years.

...photographed—he had his picture taken in 1864, at the age of 99.
(He died three years later.)

1923	Shackleton attempts one more Antarctic expedition but dies of a heart attack en route. Thus ends the Heroic Age, and begins the "Mechanical Age"—when air travel will open up the continent, and fleets of ships will conduct large-scale whaling operations.
1928	With funding from American magnate William Randolph Hearst, aviators Hubert Wilkins of Australia and Carl Benjamin Eielson of the U.S. fly a Lockheed Vega 1 monoplane over Antarctica, but not the South Pole. Richard E. Byrd achieves that milestone a year later.
1935	Caroline Mikkelsen, wife of a Norwegian whaler, becomes the first woman to travel to Antarctica, though whether she actually sets foot on the mainland or one of the islands is unknown. Also, American Lincoln Ellsworth completes the first flight across the continent.
1943-1946	During World War II, the British military conducts a top-secret mission code-named Operation Tabarin at the Falkland Islands, located 750 miles from the northern tip of the Antarctic Peninsula. According to the British Antarctic Survey, its objective is "to deny safe anchorages to enemy raiding vessels and to gather meteorological data for allied shipping in the South Atlantic." The "raiding vessels" are from Argentina and Chile, which have made similar claims to the Falklands. Militarily, the three-year operation marks the beginning of decades-long tensions in the region. Scientifically, it establishes England's first three permanent bases (where people can live year-round) on islands within the Antarctic Peninsula: Port Lockroy, Deception Island, and Hope Bay, none of which will still be active in 2021.
1946-1957	Antarctic exploration picks back up again after the war. The first major endeavor is the U.S. Navy's Operation HIGHJUMP. Led by Admiral Byrd, its official objective is to "amplify existing stores of knowledge of electromagnetic, geological, geographic, hydrographic, and meteorological propagation conditions in the area." Its other objective, which requires 4,700 men on 13 ships and 33 airplanes, is to test the American war machine's "efficacy in frigid conditions."
1947	Americans Edith Ronne and Jennie Darlington become the first documented women to not only visit the mainland, but spend a winter there (while accompanying their husbands on the Ronne Antarctic Research Expedition). Darlington later writes, "Taking everything into consideration, I do not think women belong in Antarctica."
1952	The "Hope Bay Incident." As post–World War II tensions rise, the Argentinian military fires warning shots at a British ship in Argentina-claimed Hope Bay—which is 700 miles away from the southernmost South

American country. The UK dispatches a warship in response, and Argentina apologizes. (Back home, the Argentinian sailors receive a hero's welcome.)

1955 McMurdo Station (named for a crewmember on the *Terror*) is built on Ross Island, notable as the southernmost rocky ground—as opposed to ice-covered—reachable by ship. Today it's Antarctica's largest facility, with 85 buildings, a harbor, landing strips, and a helicopter pad. It's also the headquarters of NASA's Antarctica Analog Studies program, which utilizes the "extreme temperatures, harsh winds, and atypical seasons of daylight and darkness" to prepare astronauts for living on Mars.

1956 Although there have been several flyovers, no one has set foot at the South Pole since 1912. Forty-four years later, the U.S. Navy lands a military transport aircraft nearby.

1957-1958 A cooperative research program called the International Geophysical Year (IGY) sends scientists from 12 nations to establish 60 research stations. The IGY marks the start of widespread drilling for ice core samples, a crucial tool to understanding Antarctica's past.

1957 Several IGY scientists join the Commonwealth Trans-Antarctic Expedition, which completes the first overland crossing to the South Pole since 1912. On this expedition is New Zealand's Edmund Hillary, who five years earlier became the first person (along with his Sherpa) to summit Mount Everest.

1959 Propelled by the success of the IGY, the Antarctic Treaty is signed by 12 nations, establishing that the southern continent "shall be used for peaceful purposes only" and "scientific observations...shall be exchanged and made freely available." What's remarkable about this is that two of these nations are Cold War enemies: the U.S. and the U.S.S.R. Unlike Alaska, which becomes a U.S. state this same year, Antarctica offers no military advantage. The treaty formally establishes Antarctica as all the land and ice shelves south of 60°S latitude. (The other signatories: Argentina, Australia, Belgium, Chile, France, Japan, New Zealand, Norway, South Africa, and the UK.)

1960s Scientists from the U.S., Belgium, and Norway embark on the South Pole-Queen Maud Land Traverse, which over five years will take a zigzag course across the Antarctic Plateau to the South Pole. This endeavor is notable for the deepest ice core sample ever retrieved up to that point: 7,100 feet at Byrd Station.

1969 Just a few months after three men land on the Moon, Pamela Young, Jean Pearson, Lois Jones, Eileen McSaveney, Kay Lindsay, and Terry Tickhill become the first women to reach the South Pole.

1978	Fortín Sargento Cabral is the first baby born in Antarctica. Because his parents are both Argentinian, and he is born at Esperanza Base in the claimed "Argentine Antarctica," he is granted Argentinian citizenship. There have been fewer than a dozen births on the continent since then.
1982	The Commission for the Conservation of Antarctic Marine Living Resources is established in response to decades of unchecked sealing and whaling. The multinational commission is based on an "ecosystem-based management" approach that "does not exclude harvesting as long as such harvesting is carried out in a sustainable manner."
1983	The United Nations General Assembly addresses the "Question of Antarctica," the main issues being: 1) are the 12 Antarctic Treaty nations doing enough to protect the land; and 2) should the treaty include developing countries? After the 1982 Falkland Islands War (between Argentina and the UK), an uneasy peace is reached. To this day, there are overlapping claims in the Antarctic Peninsula among Argentina, Chile, and England.
1983	The thermometer at the Vostok station in the Australian Antarctic Territory displays a reading of -128.6°F, the lowest temperature ever recorded on Earth.
1985	Researchers from the British Antarctic Survey report "abnormally low levels of ozone" over the Antarctic stations Halley and Faraday. This discovery of the so-called Ozone Hole sets off a global initiative to reduce greenhouse gases.
1994	The last sled dog leaves Antarctica. Their removal is part of the Environmental Protocol, an initiative calling for all nonnative species to be banned from Antarctica. Dogs have proven to be especially problematic due to their ability to pass canine distemper to seals, and when they run free, they can disturb sensitive habitats.
1997	Norwegian explorer Børge Ousland becomes the first person to reach the South Pole on an unsupported solo trip. Using skis and kites to propel him, he traverses 1,864 miles in 34 days from the Ronne Ice Shelf to the Ross Ice Shelf.
2000	B-15, the largest iceberg in recorded history, is born when a piece of the Ross Ice Shelf detaches—in a process called *calving*—and floats off into the ocean. Originally 159 miles long and 25 miles wide, B-15 has since broken up into smaller (but still enormous) pieces.
2005	"In the harshest place on Earth, love finds a way," narrates Morgan

Peter Weller, the star of *RoboCop*, has a PhD in Italian Renaissance art history.

Freeman in *March of the Penguins*. Filmed entirely in Antarctica, French director Luc Jacquet follows a family of Emperor penguins on their struggle to survive. The film becomes a worldwide phenomenon, not only winning the Oscar for Best Documentary Feature, but outgrossing every Best Picture nominee.

2007-2009	The International Polar Year (IPY) is a global scientific effort to study the effects of climate change on both polar regions. The endeavor launches a five-year project called the Census of Antarctic Marine Life with the objective "to study the evolution of life in Antarctic waters, to determine how this has influenced the diversity of the present biota, and to use these observations to predict how it might respond to future change."
2012	The British horror film *South of Sanity* is the first fictional movie filmed entirely in Antarctica. The plot: a rescue team is dispatched to a remote outpost where they find no one alive...except a ruthless killer.
2016	A station at the South Pole that measures carbon dioxide becomes the last place on Earth where CO_2 levels have surpassed 400 parts per million, levels not present there for four million years. The National Oceanic and Atmospheric Administration reports that, after rising steadily since the Industrial Revolution, "Global CO_2 levels will not return to values below 400 ppm in our lifetimes, and almost certainly for much longer."
2021	The world's (currently) largest iceberg—A-76—is born when a chunk of the Ronne Ice Shelf calves into the Weddell Sea. It's 105 miles long and 15 miles wide...and it doesn't bode well for the future.

EPILOGUE

More than a century of scientific study has shown unequivocally how crucial Antarctica is to Earth's climate. It contains 90 percent of the ice...which is melting as you read this. In the last 50 years, temperatures at the Antarctic Peninsula have risen by 5.4°F. That's *five times* the global average. As warming seas cause more ice shelves to break off, predictions range from bad to worse. Of particular interest is Thwaites Glacier. Nicknamed the "Doomsday Glacier," it's 74,000 square miles and could break off in a few years or a few decades. If the worst-case scenario occurs, a major calving event would be like a cork letting all of West Antarctica's ice out into a warming ocean, causing sea levels to rise by as much as 10 feet.

* * *

"I am as frustrated with society as a pyromaniac in a petrified forest."
—A. Whitney Brown

A relaxing night by the fire: Watching one burn has been shown to lower blood pressure.

CRÈME DE LA CRUD: BAD MUSICALS

Not every song-and-dance spectacular that hits Broadway can be Hamilton
or Les Misérables. *Here are some of the worst, and worst-received,
musicals to ever play (however briefly) on the Great White Way.*

HOT FEET

On paper, it must have seemed like a surefire hit. It was a musical adaptation of a
familiar story—Hans Christian Andersen's 1845 fairy tale *The Red Shoes*, about an
aspiring dancer and the magical (and cursed) shoes that take control of her body—but
taking place in contemporary New York City and set to songs by the legendary
R & B group Earth, Wind & Fire. *Hot Feet* producers staged a trial run in
Washington, DC, in March 2006, and after critics savaged it, author Heru Ptah
rewrote the entire show in anticipation of a Broadway debut. After two delays
(because Ptah had so much trouble with the rewrite), *Hot Feet* finally opened in New
York...where critics still hated it. Charles Isherwood of the *New York Times* called
Hot Feet a "dancing encyclopedia of cliches" and likened it to "a two-and-a-half-hour
episode of *Soul Train*." *Talkin' Broadway* was harsher, calling it "a nuclear meltdown."
After 97 performances, *Hot Feet* closed. The end came so quickly that an original cast
album—which preserves even the worst Broadway failures—was never recorded.

METRO

What if somebody turned the classic 1970s musical *A Chorus Line* into a Polish-
language show about homeless Polish teenagers...and then translated it into English
and presented it on Broadway, where *A Chorus Line* held the record as the longest-
running show in American musical theater history? Well, then they'd have *Metro*,
which tells the story of young Polish men and women who live in the subway tunnels
of Warsaw while trying to get cast in a big theatrical production. *Metro* was a massive
hit when it opened in Warsaw in 1991, so producers hired English writers to translate
the script from Polish, and then spent $5 million (a near-record at the time) to bring
it to Broadway. Bad idea. With attendance figures of just 35 percent capacity at the
Minskoff Theatre, *Metro* closed after 13 performances in April 1992. The reviews
certainly didn't help. Frank Rich of the *New York Times* did compare it to *A Chorus
Line*—but to "a faded 10th-generation bootleg videocassette of the film version of its
Broadway prototype, with a reel of *Hair* thrown in by mistake."

How about you? Nine in 10 Americans live within 10 miles of a Walmart.

IN MY LIFE

In 1977, former advertising jingle composer Joseph Brooks wrote and directed the movie *You Light Up My Life*, a commercial bomb and a totally forgettable project apart from Brooks's title song, which, as sung by Debby Boone, was the best-selling single of the 1970s. After working on a handful of other projects, Brooks wrote a couple of stage musicals—the 1989 British production *Metropolis*, and *In My Life*, a follow-up that took him 16 years to get off the ground. He wrote the book, music, and lyrics as well as producing, directing, and financing *In My Life*. The plot: J. T., a singer-songwriter who suffers from Tourette's syndrome (meaning he swears uncontrollably and screams "LEMON!" when he gets excited), falls in love with Jenny, a personal-ads processor for a New York City newspaper who has obsessive-compulsive disorder. They're unaware that the strings of their relationship are being pulled by a heavenly angel named Winston, who decides to make a "reality opera" out of the romance with the help of God, who also writes advertising jingles. Because operas have to be tragic, Winston and God give J. T. a fatal brain tumor. Theater critics hated *In My Life*; the *New York Times* called it "jaw-dropping," *Variety* labeled it "an astonishing misfire," and the Associated Press found it "strange, strange, strange" and "tedious." *In My Life*'s life ended after 64 performances.

> **He swears uncontrollably and screams "LEMON!" when he gets excited.**

LEGS DIAMOND

Australian entertainer Peter Allen wasn't exactly a household name in the United States. He was a successful songwriter, penning '70s soft rock hits (Olivia Newton-John's "I Honestly Love You" and Melissa Manchester's "Don't Cry Out Loud"); he was briefly married to Liza Minnelli; and he had a nightclub-style act that was popular almost exclusively in New York City (he even sold out Radio City Music Hall with his one-man show a few times). In 1988, Allen made his Broadway debut as a lead performer with *Legs Diamond*. He'd started work on the show in 1983, teaming up with fashion designer Charles Suppon to write a dark, violent script based on the movie *The Rise and Fall of Legs Diamond*, about a Prohibition-era gangster (and killer). Tony Award–winning writer and actor Harvey Fierstein saw a workshop performance of *Legs Diamond* in 1987 and came on board to write an entirely new script, adding a new, fictional element: Legs Diamond (played by Allen) really wanted to be a Broadway dancer, and uses his criminal enterprises to help fulfill that dream. A pre-Broadway debut tour was canceled when the show's elaborate set proved impossible to move, and so *Legs Diamond* opened for a preview period of two months in New York, with Allen, Suppon, and Fierstein constantly revising the show based on critical feedback. After one writer said that Allen couldn't act, Fierstein suggested adding long, improvised monologues where Allen interacted with the audience, essentially reprising his nightclub act. Finally opening on December 26, 1988, *Legs Diamond* went dark after 64 performances.

Since 1990, Grammys have been made from a special zinc alloy called Grammium.

SPIES IN THE BATHROOM

You'll probably never see it in a James Bond film, but spying on world leaders when they go to the bathroom is more common than you may realize.

STOOL PIGEON

When the North Korean leader Kim Jong-un traveled to Singapore in 2018 for a summit with President Donald Trump, the trip was remarkable in that it was the first meeting of its kind between a North Korean head of state and a United States president. Equally as interesting (at least as far as Uncle John is concerned) were the news reports that Kim Jong-un brought his own portable toilet to the summit. During his entire visit, Kim used no toilet other than his own, not even the one in his five-star luxury hotel suite. When he returned to North Korea, the toilet and its contents returned home with him.

Why would he do that? It definitely wasn't because Kim feared that the facilities in Singapore would be subpar. According to the South Korean newspaper *The Chosun Ilbo*, the portable toilet's purpose was to "deny determined sewer divers insights into the supreme leader's stools." North Korea, nicknamed the "Hermit Kingdom," is one of the most secretive countries on Earth, and this rare trip abroad presented a tantalizing opportunity for Western intelligence agencies to gain insights into what is perhaps the regime's most closely guarded secret: the current state of Kim's health. Does he have high blood pressure? Is he diabetic? Does he drink too much? Does he take antidepressants? Sleeping pills? Any other prescription drugs? What about recreational drugs? How healthy is his diet? Is he constipated? These and other questions could be answered by analyzing Kim's urine and stool samples, which is why the regime went to such great lengths to prevent them from falling into the wrong hands (so to speak).

According to Lee Yun-keol, a high-ranking North Korean official who defected to South Korea in 2005, even when Kim travels inside his own country, his motorcade includes a special toilet vehicle that he uses instead of restrooms at the sites he visits. "The leader's excretions contain information about his health status so they can't be left behind," not even in North Korea, Lee says. (Avoiding public restrooms also helps to perpetuate the state propaganda myth that the godlike Kim Jong-un's body, like that of his father and grandfather who ruled the country before him, is "so well-calibrated" that it does not produce any bodily wastes to begin with.)

NOT SO ODD

As crazy as it sounds, stealing the urine and excrement of world leaders for one reason or another is something that has gone on for decades, and perhaps much longer than that. Here are some examples:

If your name is Isabella, you receive free admission to the Isabella Stewart Gardner Museum in Boston. (Anyone accompanying you has to pay full price.)

- Joseph Stalin (1878–1953). Stalin, who ruled the Soviet Union from the early 1920s until his death, had a special "scatology" lab set up to analyze the excrement of foreign leaders who visited the communist country, in the hope of gaining insight into their *personalities*, not their health. Special toilets that were set up for the foreigners sent the waste directly into collection boxes, which were whisked off to the secret lab after every bathroom visit. High levels of the amino acid tryptophan, if found, were thought to indicate that the subject was "calm and approachable," for example, but a lack of the chemical element potassium was associated with insomnia and a nervous disposition. Each fecal analysis was given to Stalin, who tailored his policies toward the foreign leaders accordingly. It's not clear how many visitors were subjected to this treatment before Stalin's successor Nikita Khrushchev shut the lab down in the late 1950s.

> **DID YOU KNOW?**
>
> First president to have an indoor toilet in the White House: Thomas Jefferson (1801–09), who had the outdoor privies demolished and replaced with two "water closets" that were fed water via wooden pipes connected to a cistern in the attic.

- Leonid Brezhnev (1906–1982). It turns out the Soviets weren't just the instigators of bathroom spying—on at least one occasion they were the victims of it. According to Alexandre de Marenches, former head of the French secret service, when Khrushchev's successor, Leonid Brezhnev, visited Sweden in the mid-1970s and stayed in a Copenhagen hotel, French agents booked themselves into the suite directly beneath his and took apart the plumbing to "intercept" the contents of Brezhnev's toilet after it was flushed, then sent the samples to Paris for analysis. De Marenches never revealed much about what was discovered, but Brezhnev, a heavy drinker and smoker, was in declining health and addicted (we now know) to tranquilizers and sleeping pills. He had already suffered the first of several heart attacks and at least one stroke, so there would likely have been plenty there for the lab technicians to find.

- Hafez al-Assad (1930–2000). When King Hussein of Jordan died in February 1999 at the age of 63 and Assad, the ruler of neighboring Syria, traveled to Amman for the funeral, he was flattered to learn that a special toilet had been set up for his exclusive use. But flattery was not its intent: the pot was constructed by Mossad, the Israeli intelligence agency, and its Jordanian counterpart for the express purpose of collecting Assad's urine and excrement for study. Every time Assad used the toilet, his specimens were collected and "sped to a hospital in Israel, where a team of pathologists and biochemists was waiting to analyze it," the Jewish Telegraphic Agency reported in January 2000.

  The analysis, which found that Assad suffered from diabetes, heart disease, and cancer, concluded that he was so incapacitated by illness that he was probably

All the electrons that fuel the internet weigh a total of 1.76 ounces, about the same as an egg.

unable to work for more than a few hours a day, and would probably die soon. The sorry state of Assad's health prompted the Israeli government to speed up its efforts to reach a peace agreement with Syria before he died, fearing that whoever replaced him would be worse. But those efforts were unsuccessful; Assad died in June 2000 before any peace agreement could be signed. The two countries have remained locked in a perpetual state of war with each other since the founding of the state of Israel in 1948.

• George W. Bush. Does this story sound familiar? When President Bush traveled to Vienna, Austria, in June 2006, he brought a special portable toilet with him to protect his bodily waste from being intercepted by a foreign intelligence agency. The U.S. Secret Service is mum on the subject—it's a *secret* service, after all—but it reportedly refers to such precautions as TOILSEC, short for "toilet security."

* * *

PLEONASMS

A pleonasm is a two- or three-word phrase in which one word provides information that's already implied by the other word. For example, a shout is loud, so you don't need to say that someone "shouted loudly." Here are a few more.

• Molten lava

• Little baby

• Blend together

• Chocolate brownie

• Closed fist

• Horribly bad

• Safe haven

• Arid desert

• Yellowish gold

• Grayish silver

• Bright white

• Tired cliché

• Heard it with my own ears

• Empty void

• Restful sleep

• It may be possible

• Cash money

• Revert Back

• Plan Ahead

• True fact

• Unexpected surprise

• False pretense

• Veer off course

• PIN number

• ATM machine

• Prepay in advance

• Fuse together

• The Los Angeles Angels (This means they're the angels of "the angels")

• Sahara Desert ("Sahara" is Arabic for "desert")

• Gobi Desert ("Gobi" is Mongolian for "desert")

• Head honcho ("honcho" comes from a Japanese word for "boss")

• Chai tea ("Chai" means "tea" in multiple languages)

When you're sleeping, your sense of smell is temporarily disabled.

NOTABLE NATIVE AMERICANS

"American history" goes back way past the Founding Fathers. Before European settlers arrived, the continent was occupied by millions of indigenous people, and the leaders and warriors of many of those tribes became legends. Here's a look at the lives of some of those Native Americans that you may have learned about in school (or should have).

CHIEF SEATTLE

Seattle is believed to have been born around 1786 in the area of Puget Sound, near what is now the city named after an Anglicized version of his real name, Si'ahl. His mother was a member of the Duwamish tribe and his father was a chief of the Suquamish. He inherited his father's position, but because he had ties to power in both groups, he was able to forge an alliance between the two tribes. Si'ahl was friendly and helpful to white settlers who established settlements in his ancestral homeland. Having first encountered Europeans in the 1790s when Captain George Vancouver's ships anchored at the nearby Bainbridge Island on their way to Canada, Si'ahl was not startled when White settlers began to arrive in large numbers in the 1850s. Instead, Si'ahl helped ill-prepared settlers survive. When cow's milk was unavailable to feed their children, Si'ahl and the Suquamish introduced them to the juice of the clams that populated the bays, taught them how to get housing-suitable long boards out of cedar trees, and traded venison, furs, and potatoes. The growing European American community was so grateful (at the time) that they named the largest permanent settlement in the area after him—Seattle.

Si'ahl knew that White settlers would eventually mean the end of his tribe's occupation of their homeland, but theorized that resistance would only provoke violence, and bring about a quicker end. He and his people ingratiated themselves to Whites by assimilating somewhat. Si'ahl even converted to Catholicism after meeting with Jesuit missionaries. He died on Suquamish land in 1866 at age 80.

COCHISE

Born circa 1805 in what's now the American Southwest in territory under Spanish occupation, Cochise aggressively resisted intrusion by both the U.S. and Mexican governments. A leader and warrior in the Chiricahua Apache (specifically the Chokonen band), Cochise led retaliatory raids on both Mexican and American settlements when representatives of those nations encroached on Apache land in southern Arizona and northern Mexico. Settlers called on governments to send

---

Good to know: According to the USDA, a sandwich is legally defined as
"meat or poultry filling between two slices of bread, a bun, or biscuit."

the military to stop Cochise and punish him accordingly, particularly after an 1861 Apache raid on a ranch owned by John Ward in which Ward's adopted 12-year-old son, Felix, was kidnapped. Ward believed Cochise was behind it, and called upon the U.S. Army to rescue his son. Under the command of Lt. George Bascom, a squadron arrived at a stagecoach station in Arizona and invited Cochise to a meeting. But when the Apache men arrived, Bascom's men arrested Cochise for the kidnapping. He swore innocence (he really didn't have anything to do with it), but the Americans vowed to hold him prisoner until Felix was released. Instead, Cochise broke out of the encampment and, realizing that he'd have to escalate the violence if he really wanted to keep White settlers out of his peoples' lands, ramped up the raids, killing hundreds of civilians and burning villages to the ground. By 1872, after more than a decade of near-constant war, Cochise surrendered, agreeing to take his tribe to a reservation. Two years later, he died of what was likely stomach cancer. His most trusted lieutenants painted his body yellow, black, and red, and lowered it into a crevice in the Dragoon Mountains, now called Cochise Stronghold. (Note: Felix Ward resurfaced in the 1880s—he had been kidnapped by a different Apache group with little affiliation with Cochise, was raised as an Apache, and was working as an Apache-speaking scout for the U.S. Army under the name "Mickey Free.")

CRAZY HORSE

The son of an Oglala Sioux shaman named Crazy Horse, the younger, more famous Crazy Horse was called "Curly" (because he had curly hair) after his birth, circa 1841, in the Black Hills of what would become South Dakota. But after he demonstrated bravery in a battle with the Arapaho as a young man, his father gave him his name (and renamed himself "Worm"). Crazy Horse's fighting journey began in 1851. All of ten years old, he embarked on a two-day solo vision quest, where a ghostly horseman told him to wear a single feather instead of a war bonnet, to toss dust on his horse before going into battle, and to never personally partake of war spoils. He abided by those rules for the rest of his life. In the years after gold was discovered in Montana in 1862—on Sioux land—General William Tecumseh Sherman led his followers to establish protective forts in the area. A collective of Sioux and Cheyenne warriors fought back, with Crazy Horse acting as a decoy and ambushing 80 American troops. Crazy Horse ordered the dead soldiers cut up and sent to Sherman as a message to back off. After another attack in 1867, Sherman brokered a peace with the Sioux and gave them ownership of the Black Hills and areas west of Missouri and into Wyoming. Non-Sioux didn't abide by the treaty for long. When gold was found in the Black Hills, thousands of White miners arrived, outnumbering the Sioux and supported by the military might of General George Custer and a battalion of troops. Angling for a fight in 1876 at the Battle of Little Big Horn, Crazy Horse led 1,000 warriors

All members of the British royal family are descendants of Vlad the Impaler, the 15th-century Romanian despot who was the inspiration for Bram Stoker's *Dracula*.

and surrounded the American forces, defeating them and killing Custer. Over the following year, Crazy Horse continued to attack miners...until an onslaught from Col. Nelson Miles at the Battle of Wolf Mountain and a particularly harsh winter ended his resistance. Crazy Horse surrendered and took the offer of a reservation for his starving Sioux brethren. But he tried one more time to fight White advancement. In 1877, while helping the Nez Perce tribe escape from their reservation, Crazy Horse was captured and jailed. After pulling a knife on an intermediary, a soldier stabbed him with a bayonet and killed him. Crazy Horse was 35.

GERONIMO

During World War II, American paratroopers jumped out of airplanes while yelling "Geronimo!", the name of a 19th-century Chiricahua Apache leader and medicine man. Born in what's now Arizona in 1829, his name was actually Goyahkla, or "one who yawns." (The name "Geronimo" probably comes from frightened Mexican troops loudly invoking intercession from Saint Jerome—*San Jerónimo*—when they faced the warrior.) Geronimo resisted all invaders who tried to remove him and his people from their lands in southwestern America. In 1851, while Geronimo was away on a trading voyage, Mexican militiamen raided his family's camp, killing his children, his wife, and his mother. He successfully hunted down the men responsible and, from then on, devoted his life to the twin pursuits of defending his people against Mexico and the U.S., and exacting vengeance for his family's murder. By 1872, the government sent the Chiricahua Apache to a reservation, only to kick them out and send them into a reservation with other Apache groups in Arizona. Over the next 10 years, Geronimo led three rebellions, breaking out of the reservation with troops each time. He was unafraid of death because, on a vision quest, he had come to believe that he was impervious to bullets. After embarrassing the American government for years for its inability to capture him (and becoming a folk hero in the process), Geronimo surrendered, but then led one more revolt, absconding with more than 130 other Apache and moving 70 miles per day, fortifying themselves by raiding Mexican and American villages while also killing civilians. In 1886, facing a unified army of 5,000 American and 3,000 Mexican troops, Geronimo surrendered at Skeleton Canyon, Arizona. He was imprisoned at a Comanche and Kiowa reservation near Fort Sill, in what became Oklahoma, leaving occasionally for forced participation in World's Fair and Wild West traveling shows. He died of pneumonia in 1909, going down in history as the last Native American leader to surrender to the U.S. government.

*   *   *

It is better to have less thunder in the mouth and more lightning in the hand.

–Apache proverb

First marketing slogan for Nerf foam balls: "You can't hurt babies or old people."

🗣 MOUTHING OFF 🗣

COACHING WISDUMB

Coaching and managing at sporting's highest levels requires a keen wit and superior communication skills—which makes these bewildering utterances all the more...bewildering.

"He speaks English. Spanish. and he's bilingual. too."

—Don King, boxing promoter

"We didn't underestimate them. They were a lot better than we thought."

—Bobby Robson, soccer coach

"I will personally challenge anyone who wants to get rid of fighting to a fight."

—Brian Burke, hockey general manager

"All he does is catch touchdowns."

—Buddy Ryan, football coach, on why he cut a player

"A LOT OF HORSES GET DISTRACTED. IT'S JUST HUMAN NATURE."

—Nick Zito, horse trainer

"FOOTBALL IS AN INCREDIBLE GAME. SOMETIMES IT'S SO INCREDIBLE, IT'S UNBELIEVABLE."

—Tom Landry, football coach

"I told them three things last night: fight until the end, believe in yourself, believe in your teammates, and sparkle out there."

—Matt Whitcomb, skiing coach

"I've never criticized my players in public, and I'll never do it again."

—Bobby Valentine, baseball manager

"This team is one execution away from being a very good basketball team."

—Doc Rivers, basketball coach

"You have to have a catcher, otherwise you will have a lot of passed balls."

—Casey Stengel, baseball manager

"We're not attempting to circumcise rules."

—Bill Cowher, football coach

THE REAL-LIFE INDIANA JONES, PART II

Here's Part II of our story of Hiram Bingham III's expeditions as he risked life and limb to track down remnants of the lost Inca civilization. (Part I is on page 225.)

CANYON OF DOOM

In the summer of 1911, Bingham's search brought him to the formidable Urubamba River canyon in Peru. It was a "most difficult place to explore," he wrote. "In places the mighty precipices of solid granite rise five thousand feet sheer from the rapids to the clouds, and then continue upward to glaciers and snow-capped peaks." His team feared mosquito-borne illnesses such as malaria and yellow fever, and they narrowly dodged poisonous vipers in the brush. Then there was the winding Urubamba River itself, which was up to 300 feet wide and had to be crossed more than once. Bingham knew Vitcos and Vilcabamba could be accessed only by suspension bridges, but because those had washed out, the group had to ford the roaring river; other times they crossed on handmade log rafts. Tragically, a young crewmember drowned on one such crossing, raising the team's doubts about whether the peril was worth it.

A few days later, their luck changed. A drunken farmer told Bingham about "fine" ruins on a mountain. The rest of the team dismissed the story, assuming he just wanted to get paid to guide them. But Bingham took him at his word. The next morning, he joined the farmer on a harrowing climb. Like in the rope bridge scene in *Indiana Jones and the Temple of Doom*, they crossed the river on a precarious bridge of sticks bound with vine. Bingham crawled over it, inch by inch, then scaled steep, muddy slopes, clinging to plants for dear life. Before reaching the top of the mountain, the farmer quit and left him with a young boy. Bingham, just as reluctant as Indiana Jones is with his young sidekick Short Round, dubiously followed the child up the peak.

CITY IN THE CLOUDS

Bingham's commitment paid off. On July 24, 1911, he was greeted with a spellbinding sight. A stone village, overgrown with vines and bamboo thickets, lay in the side of the mountain opposite him. At 8,000 feet elevation, it rose above the clouds. According to locals, the city, likely built around 1450 by the emperor Pachacuti, was called Machu Picchu, after the mountain it sits on. For centuries, the walls, buildings, and 3,000 steps all made of white granite remained undisturbed. There are 700 terraces for growing corn and potatoes, and an incredible network of water channels to irrigate them. Four temples still stand, one of which is an intricately carved tower that honors the Inca sun god. On examining it, Bingham recalled, "I began to realize that this wall and its adjoining semicircular temple over the cave were as fine as the finest stonework in the world. It fairly took my breath away." The tower has a rare curved wall, one of the only ones in the entire Inca empire, and its windows are aligned with the sun's rays on solstices. Also noteworthy is the city's Intihuatana, which is similar to a sundial and translates from Quechua as the "Hitching Post of the Sun." Remarkably, this one was found intact, while conquistadors had destroyed the others.

Bingham noted that Machu Picchu was exquisitely constructed. How the Inca accomplished this is mind-blowing. Without having the wheel, the indigenous people must have moved all those tons of rocks up the mountain by...pushing them. Lacking iron technology, they had to painstakingly chisel the rock using stone tools. And even without mortar, the workers arranged the stones so tightly that a knife can't fit between them. Seeing the white granite temples, Bingham suspected this must be Vitcos, home of King Manco's White Palace. Yet Bingham spent only one afternoon there, eager to look for more ruins.

DESCENT INTO THE AMAZON

After a few dead-end leads, Bingham went west to the highlands, where he arrived at the village of Pucyura on August 7. Nearby was an Incan town, and, to his surprise, the rumors he'd heard about it hadn't been inflated. It was magnificent. Most notable was a palace of white granite with 30 beautifully carved doors—which had been mentioned by a Spanish captain who saw it in the 1570s. Excitement set in when Bingham found something else he'd read about: overhanging a spring was a giant white rock with carved steps and seats and a large crack that, he theorized, drained the blood of sacrificial victims. It was clear to him that he'd found Vitcos! And this meant that Machu Picchu was actually the Lost City.

Fueled by his discoveries, Bingham moved on to the toughest leg of his journey. A rubber tree prospector had claimed in 1902 to have found an Inca village in the Amazon rain forest. It took days for Bingham to find a guide, and nearly everyone was against this next venture: that area was jaguar territory, and there were indigenous tribes who would shoot poisoned arrows at white men. Bingham was undeterred. As the team trudged along, they had to abandon their dogs and mules. It rained constantly, and the humidity was so high that their leather got moldy. But instead of hostiles, they found hospitable natives who fed them (sheep's entrails and guinea pigs). The locals even helped chop their path through the jungle. After five days, the expedition reached ruins 50 miles west of Machu Picchu. Indigenous people called it Espiritu Pampa, or the "Plain of Ghosts." Bingham identified it as the home of Manco's second son. He catalogued stone houses, a temple with 24 doors, a fountain with three spouts, and pottery. But exhausted and missing his family, he was ready to find a real bed. He left Espiritu Pampa and never returned.

RAIDERS OF THE LOST TOWN

Over the next few years, though, Bingham did revisit Machu Picchu. His crew risked their lives to build bridges and clear routes through thorny brush and dense forest. Once, a clearing fire they set went wild, and Bingham had to race down a mountainside to escape. Another time, he slid down a cliff and would've fallen more than 200 feet into the river if he hadn't grabbed onto a mesquite bush a few feet from the edge, tearing the ligaments in his arm. With the other arm, he hauled himself up the 70-degree slope in true adventure-movie fashion.

The risks were worth it. Bingham found a treasure trove—40,000 Inca artifacts in buildings and caves. The haul included silver statues, bronze pendants, ceramics, ceremonial knives, and many human bones. In 1913, *National Geographic* devoted an entire issue to Bingham's photos and findings. As the *New York Times* described him, "One member of the daredevil explorers' craft has 'struck it rich,' struck it so dazzlingly rich, indeed, that all his confreres may be pardoned if they gnash their teeth in chagrin and turn green with envy." Most important, his discoveries kick-started scientific interest in South America, which, until then, had been largely ignored.

> The risks were worth it. Bingham found a treasure trove—40,000 Inca artifacts in buildings and caves.

Bingham's mission was controversial, however. He had the support of Peru's president, but many ordinary Peruvians were aghast that Americans had "stolen" their precious artifacts for display at Yale. Though the government agreed only to loan the items to Bingham, he never returned them, which caused an international uproar that lasted a century. (Yale finally returned them in 2012.) Locals feared curses from the excavated graves, and some stormed Bingham's office. In one eerie photo, a team member poses in a pile of 200 human skulls they'd removed from a cave, a reminder that they kind of *were* glorified grave robbers.

Only after Bingham's death in 1956 was the shocking truth proven: Machu Picchu was *not* Vilcabamba, and not even a capital city. Bingham believed that Machu Picchu was originally a nunnery and had been used for centuries. In reality, it was probably a retreat for aristocrats and was occupied for only 80 years. Ironically, Bingham *had* discovered the Lost City, but he never knew it. The Lost City was actually the jungle village, Espiritu Pampa. Had Bingham ventured half a mile farther, he might have seen the main city. It wasn't until 1964 that experts discovered, under moss and vines, 350 buildings—and the town's true significance. After all, they note, Bingham was a historian with little knowledge of archaeology, anthropology, or agriculture. According to Bingham's own research, Vilcabamba was northeast of Vitcos in a valley with cattle pastures and a tropical climate. That description matches Espiritu Pampa, not Machu Picchu. Not only that, but Bingham's assumption that Espiritu Pampa was built by the Inca was wrong. It was built hundreds of years before, by a tribe called Wari. Lastly (and most disappointing), the real Vilcabamba had no Inca treasures. When they fled Cuzco, the Incas likely grabbed only useful items, not metal ornaments.

INDY IS BORN

Despite these inaccuracies, Hiram Bingham was widely admired. He was an early aviator and joined the U.S. Air Service during World War I, rising to the rank of lieutenant colonel. He later served as governor of Connecticut and then as a U.S. senator. He even served as the model for a character played by Charlton Heston (named Harry Steele) in the 1954 film *Secret of the Incas*.

In 1981, more comparisons to Bingham were drawn when Harrison Ford played Henry Walton "Indiana" Jones Jr., the bullwhip-brandishing archaeology professor in *Raiders of the Lost Ark*. Jones is the spitting image of Bingham: tall, dressed in khakis, leather jacket, and fedora—and ruggedly handsome. Nevertheless, Indy's creators deny the character was inspired by Bingham. (They do not deny that he was inspired by Charlton Heston's Harry Steele in *Secret of the Incas*.) Besides, Bingham didn't demolish temples or use a human bone as a torch like Indy has. Rather, he researched meticulously, set lofty goals, and stuck to his mission despite the hardships, all so that an ancient culture wouldn't be forgotten by history. *That's* what makes him a hero— now cue the Indiana Jones theme song.

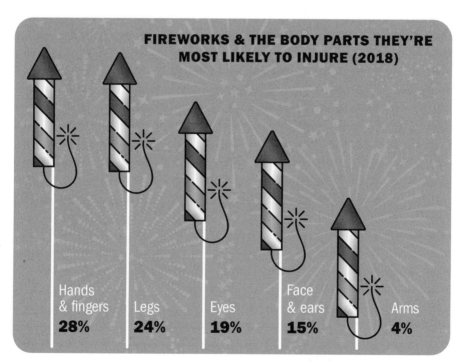

FIREWORKS & THE BODY PARTS THEY'RE MOST LIKELY TO INJURE (2018)

Hands & fingers	Legs	Eyes	Face & ears	Arms
28%	24%	19%	15%	4%

Supernumerary phantom limb is a rare-but-real medical phenomenon in which a stroke victim feels the presence of a nonexistent third arm or leg.

AND NOW FOR SOME MORE MONTY PYTHON

Enjoy some Pythonesque trivia we couldn't cram into "Pythonesque" on page 37.

WHERE'S THE CIRCUS?

At the first live taping of *Monty Python's Flying Circus* in September 1969, the BBC filled the studio audience with OAPs (old age pensioners) who were expecting to see an actual circus. According to Barry Cryer, a British comedian who warmed up the crowd that night, "They saw sketches with a dead body in a bin bag and undertakers and God knows what, the atmosphere was amazing! These dear old souls–'Oh yes, a circus, that'll be interesting!'"

(Speaking of Cryer: What do Jack Benny, George Burns, Tommy Cooper, David Frost, Bob Hope, Richard Pryor, and Spike Milligan have in common? At one point or another, Barry Cryer wrote material for each of these legendary comedians, and many more.)

HOW MUCH FOR THAT PYTHON IN THE WINDOW?

A leaked memo from the BBC revealed how much the troupe was paid for *Monty Python's Flying Circus*: £160 ($220) each. That's about $2,500 in today's money, which would be pretty good if it were per episode–but that's how much each member earned for a 13-episode series (what they call a season in England).

After *Flying Circus* was canceled in 1974, the poor Pythons didn't have a lot to their name, so they turned to some of their biggest fans–rock stars–to help pay for *Monty Python and the Holy Grail*. Led Zeppelin pitched in £31,500 ($43,000), Pink Floyd paid £21,000 ($29,000), and Ian Anderson of Jethro Tull paid £6,300 ($8,700). That's over $80,000 in today's money. (Unlike the first two bands, whose labels ponied up, Anderson used his own money.) All in all, it was enough for Python to make *Holy Grail*, but they had to do it on the cheap–which explains why King Arthur and his knights knock coconuts together in lieu of riding around on very expensive horses.

LIFE OF GEORGE

In 1979, a few weeks prior to filming *Monty Python's Life of Brian*, the financiers (EMI Records) backed out. Eric Idle asked his old friend, the Beatles' George Harrison, if he could help. "Done," replied Harrison. He mortgaged his home for $4.5 million to launch HandMade Films. Its first project: *Life of Brian*, which Idle called "the most anybody's ever paid for a cinema ticket in history." The *Guardian* called *Life of Brian*

Yule logs: The average Christmas fruitcake is as dense as mahogany wood.

"the Pythons' masterpiece: a 90-minute sketch elevated to an entirely consistent, hugely audacious and ambitious film." Harrison's HandMade Films went on to produce dozens of movies, including *The Long Good Friday* (1980), *Time Bandits* (1981), *A Private Function* (1984), *Mona Lisa* (1986), and *Lock, Stock and Two Smoking Barrels* (1998).

One reason that Idle and Harrison hit it off, according to Idle: "We were the outsiders, playing similar roles in our groups." In Python, the two main writing teams were Cleese and Chapman, and Palin and Jones, which meant that Idle often had to battle to get a word in edgewise. When Idle complained about this to the former Beatle, Harrison replied, "Well, imagine what it's like trying to get studio time with Lennon and McCartney."

WHO'S YOUR FAVORITE PYTHON?

According to a 2019 poll conducted by the British government, John Cleese and Michael Palin nearly tied for the fans' favorite member of Monty Python, with 63 percent of respondents giving them both a favorable rating. However, Palin edged out Cleese because more fans have a negative opinion of Cleese (9 percent) than Palin (5 percent). Who knows why?

4 JOHN CLEESE QUOTES

- "Comedy always works best when it is mean-spirited."
- "Loving your neighbor as much as yourself is practically impossible."
- "Some actors want to feel that they are as creative as the writer. And frankly, they're not."
- "No hope for the planet at all. But I will be gone before the planet is gone, so it's your problem."

THE SEVENTH PYTHON

Just as you'll hear talk of a "fifth Beatle," there are also contenders for the "seventh Python"—including Neil Innes, who wrote much of their music and appeared in the films, and a few celebrities who joined the troupe on stage—including Eddie Izzard, Robin Williams, and Tom Hanks.

But for true fans there's really only one seventh Python, and that's Carol Cleveland. She appeared in nearly all the *Flying Circus* episodes (including the first one), all the movies, and most of the tours. Fans may know her best as the beautiful Zoot (and her twin sister Dingo) of the Castle Anthrax in *The Holy Grail*. Typecast from the start, Cleveland's first Python character was written in the script as "a blonde buxom wench in the full bloom of womanhood."

Born in 1942 in England and raised in Texas and California, Cleveland moved to London in the '60s and, as she recalled, "Word got around there was this glamorous

Map fact: Colorado isn't a rectangle, it's a *hexahectaenneacontakaiheptagon*— a 697-sided polygon.

lady who could also be funny." Her time with Monty Python did have its challenges. She described herself as a "glamour stooge" who served as "the straight feed for the comedian, which was fun but not particularly rewarding." It also didn't help that Cleveland was often referred to as "Carol Cleavage" by some of the Pythons...but not all of them. In 2019, when Cleveland joined an online dating site at age 77, the *Mirror* asked her to describe her ideal man: "I'd like someone who's charming, witty, bright, and good fun to be with...My ideal man is Michael Palin, but he's never been available." (Palin's been married since 1966.)

THE FIRST GAY SITCOM

In 1973, a few months after coming out as gay to his fellow Pythons, Graham Chapman became one of the first celebrities to do so publicly (in a drunken diatribe on a talk show). Known for serious characters such as the earnest King Arthur in *Holy Grail* and the incredulous Brian in *Life of Brian*, behind the scenes, Chapman was considered the most "anarchic" of the bunch. One example: Cleese came up with a sketch idea about a man who tries to return a broken toaster, but Chapman, his writing partner, changed the toaster to a dead parrot.

Along with his romantic partner of 24 years, writer David Sherlock (they adopted a son), Chapman was an activist who helped launch the advocacy magazine *Gay News*. Outside of Python, the project Chapman was most passionate about was *Frank & Ernest*, which would have been the first sitcom with gay lead characters. The semiautobiographical plot centered on a young gay couple in the mid-1970s navigating life in the closet—like pretending to just be friends when Frank's parents come around. Chapman pitched *Frank & Ernest* to legendary BBC comedy producer Humphrey Barclay. His response: "I love this. Too soon. We will never get this on. Too soon."

Speaking of too soon, Chapman was the first member of Monty Python to die, succumbing to cancer in 1989 on the eve of the 20th anniversary of *Flying Circus*. Terry Jones called Chapman's poor timing "the worst case of party-pooping in all history."

WALK THIS WAY

The season 2, episode 1, sketch "The Ministry of Silly Walks"—which features a high-stepping, bowler-hat-wearing bureaucrat played by John Cleese—is the only comedy sketch that has its own holiday. International Silly Walks Day was created in 2012 in the Czech Republic, and is observed every January 7 with a Silly Walk March. So if it's the seventh of January and you come across this sign, it's requested that you do your utmost to follow suit.

(Want to organize a Silly Walk March where you live? Find out how on the "Silly Walks – The International March" Facebook page.)

For emotional support? Sigmund Freud brought his pet chow chow dog, Jo-Fi Ling, to all of his therapy sessions.

THE STRANGE FATE OF IRON MIKE MALLOY

Some people are famous for how they lived, others for how they died. Mike Malloy is famous for how he didn't *die...over and over again.*

HARD TIMES

Running a "speakeasy" or illegal drinking establishment wasn't exactly an easy way to make a living in the early 1930s. The end of Prohibition was clearly in sight, and when it arrived, people would have a lot more taverns and bars to spend their money in. The days when people would crowd into a dingy, rundown storefront like Marino's on Third Avenue near East 177th Street in the Bronx and order overpriced drinks at a makeshift bar would soon be over. Perhaps that's the reason that owner Tony Marino and some of his associates came up with another way to make money: taking out life insurance policies on some of the speakeasy's regulars...and then killing them.

> **DID YOU KNOW?**
>
> Where is the oldest brewery in the world? In a cave near Haifa, Israel. Archeological evidence suggests that a wheat- and barley-based alcohol was brewed there more than 13,000 years ago. The beer is believed to have been served during ritual feasts honoring the dead.

The first person to fall victim to this scheme was an indigent woman identified in some newspaper accounts as Mabelle Carson. Marino and three of his cronies—his bartender Joseph "Red" Murphy, undertaker Francis Pasqua, and fruit peddler Daniel Kreisberg—pooled their money and took out a life insurance policy on Carson that named Marino as the beneficiary. Then, on a freezing cold night when Carson was drunk at Marino's, they accompanied her home. When she passed out on her bed, the conspirators stripped off her clothes, poured cold water all over her body, and opened the window to let in the frigid winter air. Then they left. By the time Carson's body was found the next morning, she was dead from hypothermia. With foul play ruled out as the cause of death, the insurance company paid Marino $2,000 (about $39,500 today), which he split with his coconspirators.

LAST CALL

By July 1932, Marino was ready to try again. This time the target was Michael Malloy, an Irishman in his early sixties, who years earlier had been a firefighter but who was now a hopeless, destitute drunk. He hung around Marino's and other watering holes, sweeping up and doing other chores in exchange for drinks. He was rarely sober enough for any other kind of employment. Decades of alcohol abuse had taken their toll: he was frail, jaundiced, skeletal, and looked about as close to death as a person could without actually *being* dead. He seemed like the perfect victim.

Pasqua, the undertaker, arranged the insurance. It took nearly six months to do it, but with a little help from a crooked insurance broker who didn't ask too many questions, he took out three different life insurance policies on Malloy—one from Metropolitan Life that would pay out $800 upon his death, and two more from Prudential Life that would pay $494 each. Because each policy had what was known as a "double indemnity" clause, if Malloy died by accident then the payout would double from $1,788 to $3,576 (about $70,500 today). To allay any possible suspicion, this time Red Murphy was listed as the policies' beneficiary instead of Marino.

ON THE HOUSE

Once the life insurance policies were in place, Marino let Malloy drink as much as he wanted. The Irishman looked so deathly ill that Marino assumed he'd drink himself to death in a week or two at most. But it didn't happen. Each day Malloy arrived at the speakeasy soon after it opened and downed one drink after another until the bar closed. The next day he'd return and be right back at it. His health even appeared to improve a bit, perhaps because he was filling up on the complimentary crackers and sardines that the bar served along with all those free drinks.

Marino became very annoyed: the old derelict was drinking prodigious amounts of free whiskey and gin, and now it looked like he might actually stick around for a while. If Malloy wasn't going to be courteous enough to drop dead on his own, Marino and the other conspirators decided they would help him along, just as they'd helped poor Mabelle Carson.

NAME YOUR POISON

Red Murphy suggested serving Malloy *methanol,* or wood alcohol, which in those days was used both as paint thinner and as antifreeze in automobiles. Unlike *ethanol,* the kind of alcohol that people drink, methanol is toxic. Consuming as little as two teaspoons can cause irreversible blindness; drinking less than half a cup can be fatal. The next day, as soon as Malloy set foot in Marino's, Murphy served him a few shots of regular alcohol to dull his senses, then switched to wood alcohol and served him at least half a dozen more shots. Nothing happened—although Malloy did say he liked the taste of the stuff. He returned the following day, and the day after that, and the day after that. Each time they served him wood alcohol, and each time it seemed to have no effect. He was impervious to the stuff.

Or was he? A few nights later, Malloy was drinking wood alcohol again when he suddenly crumpled to the floor, unconscious. Pasqua was there, and when he detected only a weak pulse, he predicted Malloy would be dead within an hour. The hour passed, and then another. After about three hours Malloy regained consciousness, sat up, and said, "Gimme some of the old regular, me lad!"

After more days passed without the wood alcohol taking its toll, Red Murphy began serving Malloy another toxic paint thinner called turpentine, then horse liniment, and finally horse liniment spiked with rat poison. It didn't seem to matter what he served: Malloy just drank it down and asked for more.

TAKE-OUT FOOD

If they couldn't kill Malloy with drinks, what about food? Marino served Malloy some tainted raw oysters marinated in wood alcohol, and when that didn't work, he fed him a sandwich made with rat poison, carpet tacks, metal shavings, and a tin of rancid sardines that had sat out for several days. Malloy wolfed the sandwich down, chased it with a few shots of wood alcohol, then bade Murphy good evening and shuffled out the front door. Murphy figured he'd never see Malloy alive again, but the next day he was back, asking for another drink and another one of those delicious sandwiches.

> He fed him a sandwich made with rat poison, carpet tacks, metal shavings, and a tin of rancid sardines.

COLD COMFORT

By now it seemed that Malloy could not be destroyed by any kind of poisoning, so the conspirators began thinking up other ways to kill him. One night when the temperature dropped below zero, they waited until Malloy passed out drunk, then they took him to a nearby park and laid him on a bench. Then they poured water over him and left him there, certain that he'd freeze to death. But he didn't: The next day when Marino arrived at the speakeasy, Malloy was already there. He'd awakened in the middle of the night and found his way back to the bar, where he was now curled up asleep on the floor. As soon as he woke up, he complained of a "wee chill" and asked for a drink.

Next the conspirators tried to kill Malloy by running him down with a car. Once again, they waited for him to drink himself senseless, and then loaded him into a taxi owned by a man named Harry Green. Green drove to a quiet street a few blocks away where Marino and another man named "Tough Tony" Bastone took Malloy out of the car and stood him up in the middle of the street, jumping out of the way just as Green slammed into him at about 50 miles per hour. After Green backed over Malloy's body for good measure, the conspirators piled into the cab and sped off, certain that Malloy was finally dead. For his part in the conspiracy, Green was promised $150 as soon as the insurance companies paid up.

HERE WE GO AGAIN

Two weeks passed, by which time Red Murphy, posing as Malloy's next of kin, had called every morgue and hospital in the city looking for the man he claimed was his missing brother. But Malloy was nowhere to be found. Another week passed.

A month before he died in 1953, Hank Williams released his final single, "I'll Never Get Out of This World Alive."

Then one day the door opened at Marino's speakeasy and in limped Michael Malloy. He said he vaguely remembered being hit by a car, and had been recovering in the hospital with a broken shoulder, a concussion, and other injuries. Perhaps because he hadn't been carrying identification, the hospital had not registered him under his own name, which was why Red Murphy had not been able to find him.

IF AT FIRST YOU DON'T SUCCEED...

It's not clear exactly how many times Marino and his associates tried to kill Malloy. According to one estimate, if you include all the days he was served wood alcohol and other poisonous drinks, at least *thirty* attempts were made on his life, to no avail. Finally, in February 1933, Red Murphy and Daniel Kriesberg waited for Malloy to drink himself senseless one more time. Then they helped him to a nearby tenement house where the two men had rented a room just a few days earlier. The room was lit with gas lamps: after laying Malloy down on the bed, where he promptly passed out, Murphy and Kriesberg attached one end of a rubber hose to the nozzle of the gas lamp and put the other end of the hose in Malloy's mouth. Then they covered Malloy's face with a towel to prevent him from breathing through his nose and turned on the gas. In those days gas used for lighting contained significant quantities of carbon monoxide, which is lethal. Within five minutes of the gas being turned on, Malloy was dead from carbon monoxide poisoning—this time for real.

The following morning, Malloy's body was discovered, and a crooked doctor named Frank Manzella, who was promised a $50 cut of the insurance money, provided a false cause of death: pneumonia complicated by alcoholism. Pasqua, the undertaker, arranged a quick burial in a pauper's grave in the Ferncliff Cemetery in Westchester County.

SPEAK EASY

That might well have been the end of it, and Michael Malloy might be long forgotten today, were it not for the fact that his story was too good not to tell. The conspirators simply couldn't help themselves. Considering how long it took to kill Malloy and how many people were involved, it's possible that some of the other regulars in Marino's speakeasy figured out what was going on. Whatever the case, the legend of Michael Malloy—soon to be known as Iron Mike, Mike the Durable, the Juggernaut, and the Irish Rasputin, among other nicknames—began to grow and spread to speakeasies all over the city as drinkers made the rounds.

Rumors of the murder soon found their way to the police, who also learned about the insurance policies. Metropolitan Life had promptly paid the $800 due, but Prudential never paid a cent—they were too suspicious of the circumstances surrounding Malloy's death. It didn't help that the taxi driver Harry Green only received $20 of the $150 he was promised and was loudly complaining to anyone who would listen.

Least common flag color: purple. It's used on only the flags of Nicaragua and Dominica.

In May 1933, the district attorney dragged Marino, Murphy, Pasqua, Kriesberg, and Green before a grand jury to have them testify under oath about Malloy's death. The conspiracy quickly unraveled and within days all five were charged with first-degree murder. Green, the taxi driver, copped a plea and turned state's witness. While the defendants sat in jail awaiting trial, Malloy's body was exhumed. An autopsy revealed that he had died from carbon monoxide poisoning.

MUSICAL CHAIRS

The conspirators went on trial in October 1933. The jury deliberated just seven hours before finding Marino, Murphy, Pasqua, and Kriesberg guilty of murder; the following day, the judge sentenced all four to die in the electric chair. As part of his plea deal, Harry Green pled guilty to an assault charge and received a ten-year sentence. Doctor Manzella, who was charged with being an accessory after the fact, pled guilty to the lesser charge of failing to report a suspicious death and was sentenced to an indeterminate prison term.

If the condemned prisoners were hoping that their deaths would take as long as Malloy's had, they were soon disappointed: in June 1934, Marino, Pasqua, and Kriesberg were all executed on the same day, dying minutes apart from each other in the same electric chair in New York's Sing Sing prison. Red Murphy was executed a month later when the last of his legal appeals was denied.

*   *   *

SECRET SERVICE CODE NAMES

- John F. Kennedy: *Lancer*
- Jacqueline Kennedy: *Lace*
- Rose Kennedy: *Coppertone*
- Lyndon B. Johnson: *Volunteer*
- Lady Bird Johnson: *Victoria*
- Lynda Bird Johnson: *Velvet*
- Richard Nixon: *Searchlight*
- Pat Nixon: *Starlight*
- Patricia Nixon: *Sugarfoot*
- Julie Nixon: *Sunbonnet*
- Gerald Ford: *Passkey*
- Betty Ford: *Pinafore*
- Jimmy Carter: *Deacon*
- Amy Carter: *Dynamo*
- Ronald Reagan: *Rawhide*
- Nancy Reagan: *Rainbow*
- George H. W. Bush: *Timberwolf*
- Barbara Bush: *Snowbank*
- Jeb Bush: *Tripper*
- Bill Clinton: *Eagle*
- George W. Bush: *Trailblazer*
- Laura Bush: *Tempo*
- Jenna Bush: *Twinkle*
- Barack Obama: *Renegade*
- Michelle Obama: *Renaissance*
- Malia Obama: *Radiance*
- Sasha Obama: *Rosebud*
- Donald Trump: *Mogul*
- Melania Trump: *Muse*
- Eric Trump: *Marksman*
- Joe Biden: *Celtic*
- Jill Biden: *Capri*

Clothing designs can't be copyrighted.

A HART-FELT LIE

*Here's the story of a teenage imposter who conned his way
onto a major college football team...almost.*

ALERT THE MEDIA

On February 1, 2008, in front of the entire 900-person student body of Fernley High School in Fernley, Nevada, and with various members of the media present, star offensive lineman Kevin Hart answered the question on everyone's minds: at what college would he be playing football that fall? Picking up two hats, one bearing the name of the University of Oregon and the other, the University of California, Berkeley, Hart put on the UC hat to thunderous applause, thereby announcing his intention to hit the field for the Cal Golden Bears. Only problem: Cal hadn't recruited Hart. In fact, they'd barely heard of the 18-year-old.

GROWING PAINS

Kevin Hart spent the first 14 years of his life in Oakley, California, about 50 miles from UC Berkeley, and grew up rooting for the Golden Bears. Like many young fans, he signed up to play Pop Warner football, but by age 10 he was so big and tall that he exceeded the league's size limits and wound up playing in a YMCA flag football league instead. Then his family moved to Fernley, a tiny town of 13,000 where the cost of living was lower and the high school football team didn't have any size restrictions. As a freshman in 2004, Hart, standing 6'4" and weighing 300 pounds, earned a spot on the school's junior varsity squad as an offensive lineman.

Fernley's football program wasn't exactly elite—the varsity team hadn't had a winning season in more than 20 years and had never produced a Division I college scholarship athlete. Fernley High recruited Mark Hodges, a veteran of college and high school programs in southern Oregon, to turn things around. He put Hart on a weight-lifting regimen, which made him a stronger athlete, but Hodges's first season, and Hart's sophomore campaign with the JV squad, was negated by the Nevada state athletics board for recruiting violations and for holding illegal Sunday practices.

LETTER MAN

Nevertheless, Hart developed into a better player. In his junior year (2006), he made varsity and was named to the all-state squad; in the following spring, he started to receive recruitment letters from big colleges, including the University of Oregon, the University of Washington, and the University of Nevada.

Hart was excited by the possibility of playing for a Division I program—and on a full-ride scholarship. He started referring to himself as "D1," convinced that this next step was a done deal. What he didn't realize: the correspondence he received from

Makes sense: The area code for Cape Canaveral, Florida,
where NASA counts down and launches spacecraft, is 3...2...1.

colleges weren't offers. College football programs send out similar letters in bulk to thousands of high school athletes all over the country—they're essentially advertising. Actual recruitment for a college sports program involves the student visiting the campus, coaches coming to the player's home to meet with their parents, and several other precise, tried-and-true steps.

THE OLD COLLEGE TRY

Another aspect of the application process that Hart didn't quite grasp: the academic side. The state of Nevada required student athletes to maintain a grade point average of 2.0. But because of a loophole in the rules, Fernley High students needed only a 1.5 GPA, and Hart's GPA was 1.8. Most colleges, or at least the ones Hart was interested in (or, rather, the ones he thought were interested in *him*) require athletes to have a 3.0 or better. In other words, even if big colleges had recruited Hart for his football skills, there was no way he would have actually been admitted.

Nevertheless, Hart started to lie to his coaches, friends, and family members. In the spring of 2007, he announced that he was flying to Seattle to meet with the football team at the University of Washington. On his return, Hart told his grandfather (who paid for the trip) that he participated in a practice session. What actually happened: prior to the trip, he'd sent his academic transcript and a tape of himself playing football to the school...and never heard back, their silence implying his athletic ability and his academic record were both subpar. On his trip to Seattle, Hart wandered around the city, attended a Seattle Mariners game, and then came home.

A couple of months later, Hart visited the University of Oregon, where an assistant coach told the young athlete that the school wasn't interested in him presently, but might be a year later after he'd developed his skills more, and to send in his academic transcripts in the meantime. Knowing his grades wouldn't be good enough, Hart never sent the transcripts. A session with the University of Nevada ended pretty much the same way—a coach said his skills weren't up to snuff, but they never asked for his school records, the college's quiet, polite way of telling him they didn't want him.

HOMETOWN HERO

Back in Fernley for his senior year and final season of high school football, Hart continued to lie to his coaches and friends, making up stories about how the schools he'd visited—along with several others with which he had zero connection—were all vying to have him on their teams. "Right now, there are a number of colleges recruiting me to play football: Nevada, Boise State, Washington, Oregon, California and Oregon State," Hart told his high school newspaper, the *Vaquero Voice,* in the fall of 2008. "But the schools that I am in contact with are Nevada, Oregon and Washington. Oregon and Washington have offered me full-ride scholarships."

That was all nonsense, of course. Hart told his excited parents that his coaches were handling the recruitment, and told the coaches that his parents were in touch with the colleges. On the field, however, Hart played like he was actually being recruited—he led Fernley to the state football semifinals and was named the top high school lineman in the state of Nevada.

PRESS TO IMPRESS
National Signing Day is when the top recruits in American high schools announce what college they'll be playing football for in the fall. In 2008, that event fell on February 1, and across the country, it played out the same way hundreds of times. It's a combination pep rally and press conference, staged in the recruits' school gyms. The star player sits behind a desk adorned with baseball caps representing their final choice schools. Then, they put on one of the hats, indicating the college they've chosen, and everyone cheers. At Fernley High, football coach Mark Hodges arranged such a spectacle for Hart.

A few days before the ceremony, Hart told Fernley offensive line coach Chris Kribs that he'd narrowed down his choices to the University of Oregon and the University of California, Berkeley, and that he'd play for the UC because he considered the San Francisco Bay Area home. Kribs emailed Cal's offensive line coach Jim Michalczik, to thank him for accepting Hart, as well as for giving him a four-year scholarship. In response, Michalczik wrote back, "I think there is some misunderstanding here. We have not offered Kevin a full ride. Are you sure he's not going to Oregon?" Kribs questioned Hart, who told his coach that Cal had to deny any knowledge of the situation, because it was an ethics violation to comment on recruits before National Signing Day.

A LATE FUMBLE
That made sense to Kribs, and he believed it. So on February 1, Hart entered his gym, and put on the University of California cap. "Coach Tedford and I talked a lot, and the fact that the head coach did most of the recruiting of me kind of gave me a real personal experience with that coach. And we had like a really good relationship," Hart told reporters about his rapport with Cal head coach Jeff Tedford—a man he'd never met and never even spoken to.

When the news hit, Cal coach Michalczik got back in touch with Kribs, reiterating the fact that there was no invitation and no scholarship for Hart. Kribs called Hodges, who called Hart's parents. They all confronted the teenage athlete together, and called him out on his long-running web of lies. Hart, however, continued the ruse. He admitted that Cal had not offered him a scholarship, and claimed that a man he'd hired to talk him up to recruiters had taken his money and scammed him, having never promoted him to colleges. When asked by his parents and coaches for a name and contact information, Hart blurted out the first name he could think of: Kevin Riley, which was also the name of Cal's quarterback at the time.

In the UK, baby carrots are called "carrot nibblers."

Police obviously couldn't track down this nonexistent scam artist.

Police obviously couldn't track down this nonexistent scam artist, and within a week of National Signing Day, Hart had confessed to everything, issued an apology, and was suspended from school.

OVERTIME

Hodges was fired by the Lyon County School District, but ironically, the media attention elevated Hart's profile. Feather River College, a small, two-year institution in northern California, extended an offer to the controversial student athlete. After sitting out his first year of eligibility due to a knee injury, Hart played for two years for the school. In 2012, Hart transferred and played his final two years of college ball at the slightly larger Missouri Western State University. He majored in sports management and in his first season with MWSU, his team made it into the NCAA Division II football playoffs. After the 2012–13 season, however, Hart was done with school, and never played another game of football—college or professional—and settled into a quiet life off the gridiron.

Amazingly, Hart's saga wasn't the last story of a would-be college football player with a story that didn't add up.

- In 2017, a wide receiver from New York state named Unique Brissett II claimed on Twitter that he'd been recruited by five big colleges, including the Universities of Michigan and Miami, and that he'd made a campus visit to Michigan State University. Then a reporter from the sports news website Land of 10 realized that the photos Brissett had posted were actually another player, someone he recognized. It quickly became evident that everything Brissett said was a lie—the coaches he'd said were scouting him had never heard of him, the highlight reel he'd shared was that of a different guy, and his high school didn't even have a team. Brissett was actually a 20-year-old man who staged the entire hoax as a bet with a cousin...to see if he could convince the world that he was a star high school athlete.

- In the 1980s, Ron Weaver played football for Monterey Peninsula College and Sacramento State College, but tryouts with the CFL's B.C. Lions and the NFL's Houston Oilers didn't get him a spot on either team. So, at the age of 30, he went back to school, enrolling at Pierce College in Los Angeles. Because he'd used up all his years of college sports eligibility, Weaver joined the team under the name (and Social Security number) of a friend, Joel McKelvey. Claiming to be 21, Weaver/McKelvey played two years at Pierce before transferring to the University of Texas and receiving a full scholarship. On the day before the 1995 Sugar Bowl, in which "McKelvey" was supposed to play, a reporter exposed his scheme. Ron Weaver never played football again, but he did plead guilty on a federal charge of illegal use of a Social Security number.

Can you name all the vice presidents who died in office?
Neither can we, but so far there have been seven of them.

THE CHAUCER OF CHEESE

Have you heard of one James McIntyre? His unusual verses set the world afire. Think of this while eating your Cheerios: In the 1800s he was the bard of southwestern Ontario. His work is published this day still, If you read his poems, they'll make you ill.

A BARD IS BORN

James McIntyre (1827–1906), known to his admirers as the "Chaucer of Cheese," was born in the Scottish village of Forres. He moved to Canada when he was 14 and lived most of his life in Ingersoll, a small town in Ontario, where he worked as a furniture and coffin maker. But what earned him his reputation was his hobby—writing poetry. McIntyre wrote poems on a variety of topics: He described Ontario towns, saluted his favorite authors, and sang the praises of farming and country life. He even composed tributes to his furniture.

WHAT RHYMES WITH GOUDA?

Most famously, he wrote poems to promote the local economy. And in the mid-1800s, the economy of southwestern Ontario was cheese. In 1866, for example, Ontario dairy farmers produced what was then the world's largest block of cheese—it measured more than 21 feet across and weighed 7,300 pounds. The giant inspired two of McIntyre's best-known poems: "Ode on the Mammoth Cheese" and "Prophesy of a Ten Ton Cheese."

When the *Toronto Globe* printed some of his work, including such poems as "Oxford Cheese Ode," "Hints to Cheesemakers," "Dairy Ode," and "Father Ranney, the Cheese Pioneer," his fame spread across Canada and then around the world. What makes McIntyre's poetry fun to read isn't just his choice of subject matter (cheese) or his weird rhymes (pairing "fodder" with "Cheddar," or "shoes Norwegian" with "narrow toboggan").

"If you read his poetry, what comes out is his enthusiasm," says Michael Hennessy, mayor of Ingersoll. "People might say they are terrible poems, but McIntyre was a trier, and that is a great quality in a writer."

What's a *quockerwodger*? It's 19th-century slang for a politician controlled by special interests.

WHO IS THE WORST?

Giving new meaning to the term cheesy, many of McIntyre's admirers argue that he, not Scotland's William McGonagall, deserves the title of World's Worst Poet. But McGonagall's fans steadfastly disagree. "McGonagall is by far the worst poet in the English language," says Scottish poet Don Paterson. "He could write a bad poem about anything. This cheese guy may be a bad poet, but it seems he could write bad poetry about only one subject."

A MCINTYRE SAMPLER

A few excerpts from our favorite McIntyre poems:

"Hints to Cheesemakers"

All those who quality do prize
Must study color,
taste and size,
And keep their dishes
clean and sweet,
And all things round
their factories neat,
For dairymen insist that these
Are all important points
in cheese.
Grant has here a
famous work
Devoted to the cure of pork,
For dairymen find it doth pay
To fatten pigs
upon the whey,
For there is money
raising grease
As well as in the
making cheese.

"Dairy Ode"

Our muse it doth
refuse to sing
Of cheese made early
in the spring.
When cows give milk
from spring fodder
You cannot make
a good cheddar.

The quality is often vile
Of cheese that is
made in April,
Therefore we
think for that reason
You should make cheese
later in the season.

Cheese making
you should delay
Until about the first of May.
Then cows do feed
on grassy field
And rich milk they
abundant yield.

Pro tip: Warming balls during a round of golf is against the rules, but doing it beforehand is perfectly legal.

Utensils must be
clean and sweet
So cheese with first class
can compete,
And daily polish up
milk pans,
Take pains with vats
and with milk cans.

And it is important matter
To allow no stagnant water,
But water from
pure well or stream
The cow must drink
to give pure cream.

Though 'gainst spring cheese
some do mutter,
Yet spring milk also makes
bad butter,
Then there doth
arise the query
How to utilize it in the dairy.

"Oxford Cheese Ode"

The ancient poets
ne'er did dream
That Canada was
land of cream
They ne'er imagined
it could flow
In this cold land
of ice and snow,
Where everything
did solid freeze,
They ne'er hoped or
looked for cheese.

"Ode on the Mammoth Cheese"

We have seen thee,
queen of cheese,
Lying quietly at your ease,
Gently fanned by
evening breeze,
Thy fair form no flies dare seize.

All gaily dressed soon you'll go
To the great Provincial show,
To be admired by many a beau
In the city of Toronto.

Cows as numerous
as a swarm of bees
Or as the leaves upon the trees,
It did require to
make thee please,
And stand unrivalled,
queen of cheese.

May you not receive a scar as
We have heard that Mr. Harris
Intends to send you off as far as
The great world's show at Paris.

Of the youth beware of these,
For some of them might
rudely squeeze
And bite your cheek,
then songs or glees
We could not sing, oh!
queen of cheese.

We'rt thou suspended
from balloon,
You'd cast a shade
even at noon,
Folks would think
it was the moon,
About to fall
and crush them soon.

HEEERE'S JOHNNY!

Johnny can be good. He can be rotten. Or a robot, or a poet...

Johnny Cash: In 1932, Ray Cash wanted to call his baby boy Ray, after himself; his wife, Carrie, preferred John, after her father. They settled on J. R. When young Cash joined the U.S. Air Force in 1950, initialed names weren't allowed, so he became John R. Cash. Four years later (after buying his first guitar while stationed in Germany), Cash went to Sun Records in Memphis, Tennessee, and sang gospel songs to producer Sam Phillips. "Go home and sin," said Phillips, "then come back with a song I can sell." Cash came back with a rockabilly weeper called "Cry, Cry, Cry." Phillips liked the song...but not the name "John Cash." He insisted on changing it to "Johnny." The singer protested at first— only his girlfriend called him Johnny—then acquiesced to the man who was offering him a contract. Over the next 50 years, Johnny Cash sold more than 90 million records.

Johnny Unitas: Today, the National Football League is the most watched sport on American TV. Back in the 1950s, baseball reigned supreme (followed by boxing, horse racing, and college football). Then came Johnny "the Golden Arm" Unitas. Considered the first "marquee quarterback," his Baltimore Colts' 23–17 championship win over the New York Giants at Yankee Stadium on December 28, 1958, is still regarded as the NFL's greatest game ever played. Featuring 12 future Hall of Fame players, it was the first nationally televised NFL game. More than 45 million sports fans were glued to their couches as Unitas led the Colts all the way down the field in the final two minutes to tie the game, and then, in sudden-death overtime (another NFL first), he put together another gutsy drive to win the championship. Unitas's heroics made the game an instant classic and began the NFL's rise to ratings dominance.

Johnny Hendrix: On November 27, 1942, at 10:15 a.m., Johnny Allen Hendrix was born in Seattle, Washington. That was the name his mother Lucille gave him. But when the toddler was just shy of four, his father, Al (full name: James Allen Hendrix) reentered the picture and thought that "Johnny Allen" sounded like someone his wife would have an affair with. So Al changed his son's name to the more dignified...James Allen Hendrix. The boy went by Jimmy. After teaching himself the guitar, his first stage name was Jimmy James. It was during Hendrix's star-making stint in England in 1967 that his manager changed the spelling to Jimi.

Johnny Bench: Ask any diehard baseball fan to name the greatest catcher of all time, and they'll answer Johnny Bench, who, along with Pete Rose and Joe Morgan, made Cincinnati's "Big Red Machine" nearly unbeatable in the 1970s. On offense, Bench hit more home runs than any other catcher of his time. On defense, he was the very definition of a "clutch player." In 45 postseason games, opposing teams stole only six

Annapurna is a group of mountains in Nepal. As of 2020, 157 climbers have reached the top...and another 60 have died in the attempt, for a fatality rate of 38%.

bases from him out of 19 attempts. Speaking of clutch, Bench explained the secret to his throwing success: "It helps to have a big hand and long fingers." To demonstrate, he famously clutched seven baseballs in his throwing hand. In 2021, at 73 years old, he issued the "Bench Challenge" to find out if any modern Major Leaguers could hold more baseballs. Not only did Bench's (unofficial) record stand, while filming a TV commercial, he set a new (also unofficial) record by holding seven cheeseburgers in one hand.

Johnny Appleseed: True or false? Johnny Appleseed walked throughout the Midwest in the early 19th century tossing seeds into fields that grew into orchards. False. He planted them in fenced-in nurseries. True or false? Johnny Appleseed planted delicious apples. False. The apples were so tart that they were called "spitters," but they were perfect for making cider. Not only were they more profitable to grow than regular apples, but the cider was safer to keep for long periods of time because cider doesn't harbor bacteria like tea and water do. (That's why he's so revered.) True or false? His name was Johnny Appleseed. False. He was born John Chapman in Massachusetts in 1774. He got the "Appleseed" nickname in the 1820s.

"Johnny B. Goode": When rock 'n' roll was just getting going in 1955, Chuck Berry, a hairdresser by trade, wrote this semiautobiographical song about a poor "country boy" who could "play a guitar just like ringin' a bell." Johnny's surname comes from 2520 Goode Avenue, where Berry grew up in

> **DID YOU KNOW?**
>
> Chuck Berry was a huge influence on the Beatles. How huge? From 1956 (when they were still the Quarrymen) until their final stadium concert in 1966, the Fab Four covered at least 15 Berry songs. "If you tried to give rock 'n' roll another name," said John Lennon, "you might call it 'Chuck Berry.'"

St. Louis. His first name was inspired by local blues pianist Johnnie Johnson (who would later play on all of Berry's hit records, including "Maybellene," "Rock and Roll Music," "Memphis, Tennessee," "No Particular Place to Go," and "Roll Over Beethoven"). Released in 1958, "Johnny B. Goode" became *the* quintessential rock song...thanks in part to one minor revision. "The original words," recalled Berry, were "'that little colored boy could play.' I changed it to 'country boy'—or else it wouldn't get on the radio."

"Johnny Get Angry": In 1962, the songwriting team of Hal David and Sherman Edwards wrote a song about a much more troubled Johnny. Cheerfully sang by Joanie Sommers, she begs her meek boyfriend Johnny to show her he's the boss in their relationship. The song's most memorable line: "I want a brave man. I want a cave man. Johnny, show me that you care, really care, for me." Then there's a kazoo solo. Amazingly, "Johnny Get Angry" hit #7 on the charts, one spot *higher* than "Johnny B. Goode," which hit only #8 on the *Billboard* Top 100. Later that year, a singer named Vinnie Monte followed that up with "Joanie Don't Be Angry" (he's "sorry as can be" for leading her on). It failed to chart.

Johnny 5: Ah, movies of the 1980s, when a bolt of lightning was all it took to transform a "robot of war" into the adorable Johnny 5—the hero of the 1986 sci-fi comedy, *Short Circuit*, starring Steve Guttenberg as the scientist who lost the robot. For most of the movie's run, the robot is simply called Number 5. But as his self-awareness grows—"Number five is ALIVE!"—he starts referring to himself in the first person. The robot finally chooses a name while listening to the song "Who's Johnny" by R & B singer El DeBarge. The filmmakers reportedly didn't have enough money for the song they originally wanted: "Money for Nothing" by Dire Straits. (Would the robot have then chosen "Money 5"?)

Johnny Rotten: John Joseph Lydon's stage name was bestowed upon him in 1975 at age 19. Why? He had rotten teeth. But who has time for dentists? Johnny Rotten apparently didn't—he was too busy leading the punk band Sex Pistols ("Anarchy in the UK"), and then the post-punk anti-rock band Public Image Ltd, on his way to being named by the BBC as one of the "100 Greatest Britons" in 2002 (he was #87). In 2008, Lydon, 52, did find the time for a dentist...at a cost of $22,000. "All those rotten teeth were seriously beginning to corrupt my system," he said. Later that year, Lydon had to defend his punk cred after he starred in an ad campaign for Country Life Butter: "It's bizarre and odd, but [it was] the only way to buy my way out of the stifling contracts from the Sex Pistols. The working-class chap in me wasn't going to turn away a gift horse." The ad campaign led to an 85 percent increase in butter sales (and more than paid for Lydon's dental bills).

Johnny Depp: Because his father was John Depp, the boy—born John Christopher Depp II in Kentucky in 1963—was called Johnny. (His friends called the aloof teen Johnny Dipp.) Depp's first love wasn't acting, it was guitar. In 1981, he was in a band called the Kids that opened for big-name acts like the Talking Heads, the B-52s, and Iggy Pop...who happened to be Depp's childhood hero. One night after a concert, while Pop was walking his dog, the 17-year-old Depp approached him (after drinking vodka to get his courage up). "I started screaming 'Iggy Flop, Piggy Slop!'" Depp recalled. "He walked toward me with the beagle on a leash, and he got like that close to my face, and I'm looking at Pop's blue eyes...and he just says, 'You little turd.' To this day, it's one of the best moments in my life."

> "I started screaming 'Iggy Flop, Piggy Slop!' "

Johnny Galecki: Although he's known for playing physicist Dr. Leonard Hofstadter on *The Big Bang Theory* (2007–19), in real life, Galecki dropped out of high school after his first day and never went back. That was in 1990, two years before landing his breakout role of David on *Roseanne*. His family was moving away from southern California, but Johnny had just been cast in a sitcom called *American Dreamer*. Incredibly (and somewhat horrifyingly), his parents let him live all by himself in

Geometry quiz: What's a *triacontagon*? Answer: a 30-sided polygon.

a Burbank apartment for a few months. "I was 14 and looked like I was nine," he recalled, which was a problem considering the TV studio was a 20-minute drive away. Solution: Galecki bought a motorcycle—and a mirrored helmet to hide his boyish face—and started down the road to success.

Johnny Carson: Born in Iowa in 1925, the future "King of Late Night" got his first paid gig at 14 performing magic tricks as "The Great Carsoni." But he was better at making people laugh than fooling them, so he dedicated his life to comedy. In fact, Carson's senior college thesis was titled "How to Write Comedian Jokes." After entertaining World War II troops with his ventriloquist dummy act, Carson got his first talk show on the radio in 1949. After moving to California (from Nebraska) in 1951, he hosted a sketch-comedy TV show called *Carson's Cellar* that caught the attention of comedian Red Skelton, who hired him as a writer. Over the next decade, Carson became a mainstay on game shows and panel shows before landing *The Tonight Show* job in 1962. By the 1980s, he (and *The Tonight Show*) had become so influential that he could jumpstart a young comedian's career based on whether he invited them to the couch after their routine. "It was like the Pope blessing you," said Carl Reiner. Some famous couch invitees: Ellen DeGeneres, David Letterman, Joan Rivers, Eddie Murphy, Roseanne, and Drew Carey (but not Jim Carrey).

"Heeere's Johnny!" In 2006, *TV Land* compiled the Top 100 TV catchphrases of all time. Coming in at #1: The *Tonight Show's* "Heeere's Johnny." (Number 2 was Neil Armstrong's "One small step for a man.") The booming-voiced Ed McMahon, Johnny Carson's sidekick, introduced his friend with this line more than 4,000 times from 1962 to '91. The catchphrase caught on so well that a portable toilet company started using it as their slogan. (Carson sued.)

The catchphrase lives on—mainly in meme form...thanks to Jack Nicholson. While filming the 1980 horror movie, *The Shining*, Nicholson smashed a door with an axe, pressed his crazed face through the splinters, and ad-libbed the line, "Heeere's Johnny!" Director Stanley Kubrick was an American expatriate living in England and didn't get the reference, so he nearly cut the line. But he didn't, and it's taken on a life of its own, having been parodied hundreds of times on shows and in movies. "Heeere's Johnny" even took the #1 spot on Screen Rant's "15 Most Iconic Quotes from Horror Movies."

Johnny Paycheck: The name of the "Outlaw" country singer best known for singing "Take This Job and Shove It" (because he ain't working there no more) was not, as many have assumed, a parody of Johnny Cash's name. Born Donald Eugene Lytle, he changed his name in 1963. His inspiration: a St. Louis boxer named John J. Pacek (pronounced "Paychek") who fought Joe Louis for the Heavyweight Championship in 1940 and lost by a knockout in the second round. Paycheck really was an outlaw; he served numerous jail terms throughout his troubled life.

Botox was initially developed as a treatment for cross-eyes.
It is used to weaken "too strong" muscles that pull an eye out of alignment.

Johnny Poet: What do you call a college's sports teams when the college is named after a poet? The Poets! Southern California's Whittier College was founded in 1901 and named for Massachusetts-born Quaker and abolitionist—and poet—John Whittier. (One famous football-playing Whittier Poet: Richard Nixon.) The school's mascot is called Johnny Poet, and he carries a mascot-sized pen...which inspired us to present the rest of the Johnnys on our "Famous Johnnys" list as a poem. (Please keep in mind that we usually write prose.)

"AN ODE TO JOHNNY"

An ode to Johnny, that affectionate diminutive of a masculine given name,
Like baseball's Bench and football's Unitas, here's the Johnny Hall of Fame.*
   (*Excluding all the Johnnys we covered in the previous sections.
   Think of these other famous Johnnys as the Johnny-rable mentions.)

Olympic skater Johnny Weir made the semis on *Dancing with the Stars*, and
Olympic swimmer Johnny Weissmuller was the man who starred as Tarzan.
   Old West outlaw Johnny Ringo was arrested near the Mason County line.
   The oft-covered "Frankie and Johnny" was inspired by a murder in 1899.

Jonny Quest embarked on his animated adventures back in 1964.
Johnny Bravo made the Cartoon Network cool from '97 till 2004.
   Like his brother Edgar, blues great Johnny Winter had hair as white as snow.
   Johnnie Cochran made a rhyme about a glove, and the jury let O. J. go.

Johnny Marr of the Smiths dropped his first ever solo record in 2013,
Rowan Atkinson's Johnny English was just a big-budget *Mr. Bean.*
   "Do it for Johnny!" yelled *The Outsiders*' Matt Dillon (who played Johnny in Capone).
   The Fantastic Four's Human Torch (Johnny Storm) died in the Negative Zone.

In 1954, crooner Johnny Ace accidentally shot himself on Christmas Day.
In 1967, the Fantastic Johnny C had a hit with "Boogaloo Down Broadway."
   Johnny Mathis sold 350 million records; only Sinatra and Elvis sold more.
   "Come on down!" yelled Johnny Gilbert to *The Price Is Right* contestants galore.

Johnny Lawrence got "craned" by *The Karate Kid* and brought shame to *Cobra Kai.*
Johnny Knoxville did tons of stunts on *Jackass* and somehow didn't die.
   The Foo Fighters' "Hey, Johnny Park!" was Dave Grohl looking for a lost friend.
   Tommy Wiseau played Johnny in *The Room*, and now this poem must end.

Of all UFOs that are investigated, 98.2 percent are ultimately explained.
As for the other 1.8 percent...

ANSWERS

CLASSIC BRAINTEASERS (Answers for page 113)

1. 12 (January 2nd, February 2nd, March 2nd, etcetera.)

2. February, because it has the least number of days.

3. Each of their names includes a body part: Britney Sp**ears**, Fred **Arm**isen, Denzel Wa**shing**ton, Jack **Hand**ey, and John **Leg**uizamo.

4. Remove the "f" and "e" from "five" and you're left with "iv," the Roman numeral for 4.

5. Stop imagining.

6. Their surname.

7. Nine. Two parents, six sons, and one daughter.

8. Each car turned right.

9. When you add those numbers on a clock. 8:00 a.m. + 8 hours = 4:00 p.m.

10. 888 + 88 + 8 + 8 + 8 = 1000

11. Timmy and Tammy cross first. Timmy stays there, and Tammy rows back alone. Tommy crosses alone, and stays there while Timmy rows back to get Tammy, and then Timmy and Tammy cross together.

12. An hourglass, which contains thousands of grains of sand.

13. There are three ducks.

14. Remove one letter, and still have it be a word, until there's only one letter left, which is also a word: startling - starting - staring - string - sting - sing - sin - in - I.

15. It would take 47 days.

16. He was on only the first rung of the 50-foot ladder when he fell.

17. The next letters are: I-T-S. (The series consists of the first letters of each word in the sentence "Guess the next three letters in the series."

18. Noon. (And time to fix the clock.)

ARE YOU A POLYGLOT? (Answers for page 182)

1. f. Some people use "ketchup" and others use "catsup," but they're just two different spellings for the same tasty condiment—and both come from the same word in Hokkien Chinese, a dialect from southeastern China. *Kê-tsiap* was a sauce made from fermented fish in that region, probably as early as 300 BC. Later, the British version of *katchup* (or *ketchup*) used mushrooms, anchovies, or oysters. By the early 1800s, Americans made *catsup* using tomatoes. The Heinz company added vinegar to prevent spoilage in 1876, creating the ketchup we love today.

2. c. Since the 1990s, people have used images such as a heart to convey emotion in electronic communication. But if you thought the *emo-* came from *emotion* or *emote*, you're wrong. It stems from the ancient Japanese word *e* for "picture," plus *moji* for "letter" or "character."

3. k. The Czech word *robota* means "forced labor." In 1921, Czech author Karel Čapek introduced the word "robot" in his play *R.U.R.*, which centers on the manufacture of artificial people. Today, *robots* are machines that emulate the motions of living beings, while *androids* are more human, like those in the play—in which they revolt against their human slavers, just like they do in most of the robot stories that have been written since then.

4. g. *Cafetería* in Spanish is a coffee shop. But by 1894, in English it meant a self-serve lunch counter or dining hall where people take their food to their table. (While you're there, get *nachos*, *salsa*, and maybe a *daiquiri*—all words that originated from Spanish.)

5. j. Long before the James Cameron blockbuster film, *avatar* had roots in Hinduism; *avatāra* meant "descent." When *avatar* was adopted in English in 1784, it usually referred to the descent of a Hindu deity to Earth in human or animal form. Later, it described any incarnation in any form, and it's now the image we choose to represent us in social media, video games, and text messages.

6. l. Europe may be known for its chocolate, but the word comes from the language of the Aztecs in what's now Mexico and Central America. In the 1400s, the Aztecs (and before them, the Mayans) roasted and ground cacao beans, and then mixed them with water to make a bitter chocolate drink. Many sources say *chocolate* derives from their word *xocolatl*, meaning "sour water," but more likely it's from *chikolātl*, referring to the hooked stick—the *chikolli*—used to beat cacao, and *atl*, which means "water." Indigenous people used cacao for rituals, medicine, and even currency before Spanish explorers brought it back to Europe, where it became *chocolate* around 1600.

7. d. After gaining independence from Britain, the rebellious Americans disliked the British term *master*. So, American author Washington Irving used a variation of the Dutch word for it, *baas*, becoming first to put *boss* in writing in 1806.

8. a. Meaning "hurry" or "quick," *wiki* was first used in English in 1995 when a programmer named his collaborative website WikiWikiWeb. After that came more wikis—websites that let anyone write or edit content—such as Wikipedia, plus fan wikis for every topic imaginable, including a wiki for Hypothetical Hurricanes ("not real or fictional").

9. h. *Zombie* actually arose from words in several West African languages. One is *ndzumbi*, which is "corpse" in the Tsogo language spoken by the Bongo people of Gabon. Another is *nzambi*, meaning "god" or "spirit of a dead person" in the Kimbundu language. Starting in the 1600s, many West Africans were enslaved by Europeans and shipped to Haiti, where they believed that if they committed suicide, they'd become zombies—in a nightmarish state of being a slave working plantations for eternity, unaware that they're dead and denied their afterlife. The word entered English in the 1800s, but it wasn't until the *Night of the Living Dead* film franchise in the 1960s and '70s that zombies became the soulless flesh-eaters we know today.

10. b. The game of chess got some of its terms from Persia, where an early version of it was played in the first millennium. *Checkmate* derives from *shāh māt*, meaning "the king is helpless." (*Rook* comes from *rukh*, for "war-chariot.")

11. i. In Polynesian culture, *tapu* is something that's prohibited or requires "spiritual restriction" based on societal rules. In the 1770s, it spread from Tonga to Britain thanks to British explorer Captain James Cook, who spelled it *taboo* and found it interesting enough to write about in his journals.

12. e. *Restaurant* derives from the French *restaurer*, meaning "to restore." Eventually, restaurant became the name for a restorative soup, and the person who made it was the restaurateur. People commonly think the restaurant's owner should be spelled "restauranteur" because they incorrectly assume that *restaurateur* derives from *restaurant*. In fact, they both derive from the same root word (*restaurer*), so they are spelled *restaur-* with two different suffixes: *-ant* and *-ateur*.

THE RIDDLER (Answers for page 289)

1. The future.

2. By getting up and walking to another spot.

3. Tug-of-war.

4. He was dead.

5. Growing older.

6. Water. (Flowing, it can crack stone; frozen, it can stop traffic; as a vapor cloud, it can fly high in the sky.)

7. Fallen leaves.

8. Darkness.

9. A coat of paint.

10. A hole.

11. Throne. (Remove three letters—T-H-R—and there is "one" left.)

12. A book.

13. A cold.

14. A sewing needle.

15. A mask.

16. Salt and pepper.

17. Love.

18. The two letter symbols n and g will make "you" "young."

MATCH THE ROCK STAR TO THE SUPERMODEL (Answers for page 320)

1. e. Mick Jagger has been romantically linked with numerous models, including Anita Pallenberg, Edie Sedgwick, and Janice Dickinson. In 1977, the Texas-born Jerry Hall was dating Bryan Ferry (Roxy Music) when she left him for the Rolling Stones' frontman. Jagger and Hall dated on-and-off over the next decade, and had two kids. They wed in 1990 in a Hindu ceremony, then had two more kids before divorcing in 1999. (A judge ruled their marriage wasn't even legal.) Jagger was later linked to designer L'Wren Scott and ballet dancer Melanie Hamrick; in 2015, Hall married the head of Fox News, Australian billionaire Rupert Murdoch.

2. k. From 1979 to 1984, Rod Stewart (formerly of the Faces) was married to model and actress Alana Hamilton. Then he spent seven years with *Sports Illustrated* swimsuit model Kelly Emberg. In 1990, Stewart married Rachel Hunter...and they split in 1999. Since 2007, he's been married to British model and TV personality Penny Lancaster.

3. i. Ric Ocasek and Paulina Porizkova met while filming the music video for the Cars' 1984 hit, "Drive." Porizkova played the singer's love interest. Soon after, Ocasek separated from his second wife and married Porizkova in 1989. They divorced in 2017, but Porizkova stayed with Ocasek and took care of him through a series of health issues. After he died in 2019, Porizkova learned that she'd been left out of his will for "abandoning" him. She sued Ocasek's estate and was awarded a settlement worth millions.

4. g. Seal, the 1990s British singer best known for soft rock anthems like "Crazy" and "Kiss from a Rose," met German-born Heidi Klum at the 2003 GQ Awards in London, but they didn't really connect until a year later in New York. Klum had just split from Italian businessman Flavio Briatore and was expecting his child. She married Seal in 2005 and had three kids with him. Seal adopted Klum's first born, future model Leni Klum. Heidi filed for divorce in 2012.

5. b. In 1991, John Mellencamp was 40 years old and twice-divorced when he met 23-year-old Elaine Irwin, the cover model for his album *Whenever We Wanted* and star of the video for "Get a Leg Up." They married in 1992 and divorced in 2011. After a three-year relationship with actress Meg Ryan, Mellencamp briefly dated model Christie Brinkley (Billy Joel's ex-wife).

6. j. When the hard-rocking White Stripes hit the big time in the early 2000s, singer and guitarist Jack White alternately said that drummer Meg White was his sister, his wife, and his former wife. The latter was true—they married in 1996 (with Jack Gillis taking his wife's name) before divorcing amicably in 2000. Five years later, White married English model and musician Karen Elson. They had two kids and divorced eight years later.

7. a. In 1970, Billy Joel was playing piano in a psychedelic band called Atilla when he had an affair with drummer Jon Small's wife, Elizabeth Weber. She divorced Small, married Joel in 1973, and then divorced him in 1982. After the divorce, Joel hopped on to the piano at a bar in St. Bart's, where other superstars were hanging out—including singer Whitney Houston and models Elle Macpherson and Christie Brinkley. Joel dated Macpherson (he wrote "Uptown Girl" for her) but later left her for Brinkley. They married in 1985 and divorced in 1994.

8. c. In 1987, Axl Rose wrote Guns N' Roses' #1 single, "Sweet Child o' Mine" (from their 30-million selling debut album, Appetite for Destruction), about his girlfriend, Erin, whose dad was Don Everly of the Everly Brothers. In 1990, the couple wed in Las Vegas. Rose filed for divorce a month later but then retracted the paperwork. In early 1991, he allegedly assaulted Everly, so she had the marriage annulled. Rose later dated model Stephanie Seymour and gave her a starring role (as his wife) in two Guns N' Roses videos. In real life, they got engaged, called it off, and then sued each other in 1993. Rose accused Seymour of stealing $100,000 worth of his jewelry; Seymour accused Rose of physical abuse. (Both suits were settled out of court.)

9. d. George Harrison met 19-year-old model Pattie Boyd in 1964 when she was cast as a screaming fan in the Beatles' movie *A Hard Day's Night*. After Harrison and Boyd were married in 1966, she was openly courted by Mick Jagger and John Lennon. In 1973, she had an affair with Ron Wood of the Rolling Stones. Harrison retaliated...with Wood's wife. Boyd shared her marriage woes with Harrison's best friend, Eric Clapton, who fell in love with her. After more carousing on Harrison's part, Boyd filed for divorce in 1977 and married Clapton two years later.

10. l. Scott Weiland and Mary Forsberg dated briefly in the 1980s when he was still an up-and-coming singer and she was launching her modeling career. In 1994, Weiland married Janina Casteneda (for whom he wrote the Stone Temple Pilots' hits "Sour Girl" and "Interstate Love Song"). After they divorced in 2000, Weiland rekindled his romance with Forsberg and married her later that year. They had two sons together and divorced in 2007. (Weiland died in 2015.)

11. h. Liv Tyler is the daughter of a model and a rock star. Her mother: *Playboy* Playmate Bebe Buell. Her father: Steven Tyler of Aerosmith. Until Liv was a teenager, she thought her father was Buell's boyfriend, rocker Todd Rundgren. Tyler modeled in the early 1990s and acted in Aerosmith videos before making it big in the movies *Empire Records* and *The Lord of the Rings*. From 2003 to 2008 she was married to Royston Langdon, bassist and singer of the alt-rock band Spacehog.

12. f. British supermodel Kate Moss dated some of show business's most eligible bachelors—including Mark Wahlberg, Leonardo DiCaprio, John F. Kennedy Jr., Lenny Kravitz, and Johnny Depp. But the only man she married—in 2011—was Jamie Hince, guitarist of the rock duo the Kills. They divorced in 2016.

13. r. Pianist, singer-songwriter, and *The Voice* coach John Legend is the second-youngest performance artist to ever "EGOT," win an Emmy, Grammy, Oscar, and Tony Award. In 2006, while filming a video for his song "Stereo," his dance partner and love interest was lingerie-clad Chrissy Teigen. They were engaged in 2011 and married in 2013.

14. n. Iman (born Zara Mohamed Abdulamajid in 1955) married a hotel executive named Hassan in her native Somalia at age 18, and then left him to move to America and become a model. In the late 1970s, she dated Warren Beatty and then married NBA star Spencer Haywood. In 1990, three years after her second divorce, Iman met David Bowie (also divorced) on a blind date. They married in 1992 and remained together until Bowie's death in 2016.

15. s. In 1989, 22-year-old piano prodigy Harry Connick Jr. hit it big with his album of standards for the *When Harry Met Sally* soundtrack. He landed a small role in the 1990 movie *Memphis Belle* alongside actor D. B. Sweeney, who was dating Texas-born Victoria's Secret model Jill Goodacre. Connick and Goodacre married in 1994 and have three daughters together.

16. p. In 1984, Duran Duran lead singer Simon Le Bon had just split up with model Claire Stansfield when he was flipping through a magazine and saw model Yasmin Parvaneh. Instantly smitten, he used his contacts to find her and ask her out. A year later, they were married.

17. o. Following a 13-year relationship with German-Italian model Anita Pallenberg, Keith Richards married American model Patti Hansen, who's graced the covers of *Seventeen*, *Vogue*, *Glamour*, and *Cosmopolitan*. The couple wed in Mexico in 1983 on Richards's 40th birthday. As of 2022, they're still married.

18. t. Caleb Followill, leader of the Southern rock band Kings of Leon, met supermodel Lily Aldridge backstage at the Coachella Valley Music and Arts Festival in 2007. They wed four years later.

19. m. Adam Levine, son of M. Fredric department store founder Fredric Levine, formed a high school band called Kara's Flowers that later changed its name to Maroon 5. Just weeks after Levine (named *People*'s "Sexiest Man Alive" in 2013) ended a two-year relationship with *Sports Illustrated* swimsuit model Anne Vyalitsyna, he started dating Victoria's Secret model Behati Prinsloo. They married in 2014, with Levine's childhood friend, actor Jonah Hill, officiating.

20. q. McCartney married American photographer Linda Eastman in 1969. Virtually inseparable, their marriage ended when Linda died of breast cancer at age 56 in 1998. In early 2000, McCartney started accompanying model and prosthetics-wearing, anti-landmine advocate Heather Mills to events, leading to their marriage in 2002. After a messy public divorce in 2006, McCartney married transportation company executive Nancy Shevell.

We are pleased to offer over 150 ebook versions of Portable Press
titles—some currently available only in digital format!
Visit *www.portablepress.com* to collect them all!

- Bathroom Science
- The Best of the Best of Uncle John's Bathroom Reader
- Best Movies of the 80s
- The Best of Uncle John's Bathroom Reader
- The Biggest, Funniest, Wackiest, Grossest Joke Book Ever!
- Dad Jokes
- Dad Jokes Too
- Do Geese Get Goose Bumps?
- The Funniest & Grossest Joke Book Ever!
- The Funniest Joke Book Ever!
- The Funniest Knock-Knock Jokes Ever!
- Great TED Talks: Creativity
- Great TED Talks: Innovation
- Great TED Talks: Leadership
- The Grossest Joke Book Ever!
- History's Weirdest Deaths
- How to Fight a Bear...and Win
- Instant Engineering
- Instant Genius
- Instant Genius: Smart Mouths
- Instant History
- Instant Mathematics
- Instant Science
- OK, Boomer: And Other Age-(In)appropriate Jokes
- Potty Humor: Jokes That Should Stink, But Don't
- Mom Jokes: Like Dad Jokes, Only Smarter
- See Ya Later Calculator
- Show Me History! Abraham Lincoln
- Show Me History! Albert Einstein
- Show Me History! Alexander Hamilton
- Show Me History! Amelia Earhart
- Show Me History! Babe Ruth
- Show Me History! Benjamin Franklin
- Show Me History! George Washington
- Show Me History! Harriet Tubman
- Show Me History! Jesus
- Show Me History! Martin Luther King Jr.
- Show Me History! Muhammad Ali
- Show Me History! Sacagawea
- Show Me History! Susan B. Anthony
- Show Me History! Walt Disney
- The Spookiest Tricks & Treats Joke Book Ever!
- Strange Crime
- Strange History
- Strange Hollywood
- Strange Science
- Uncle John's Absolutely Absorbing Bathroom Reader
- Uncle John's Actual and Factual Bathroom Reader
- Uncle John's Ahh-Inspiring Bathroom Reader
- Uncle John's All-Purpose Extra Strength Bathroom Reader
- Uncle John's Bathroom Reader Attack of the Factoids
- Uncle John's Bathroom Reader Book of Love
- Uncle John's Bathroom Reader Cat Lover's Companion
- Uncle John's Bathroom Reader Christmas Collection
- Uncle John's Bathroom Reader Dog Lover's Companion
- Uncle John's Bathroom Reader Extraordinary Book of Facts
- Uncle John's Bathroom Reader Fake Facts
- Uncle John's Bathroom Reader Flush Fiction
- Uncle John's Bathroom Reader For Girls Only!
- Uncle John's Bathroom Reader For Kids Only!
- Uncle John's Bathroom Reader For Kids Only! Collectible Edition
- Uncle John's Bathroom Reader Germophobia
- Uncle John's Bathroom Reader Golden Plunger Awards
- Uncle John's Bathroom Reader History's Lists
- Uncle John's Bathroom Reader Horse Lover's Companion
- Uncle John's Bathroom Reader Impossible Questions
- Uncle John's Bathroom Reader Jingle Bell Christmas
- Uncle John's Bathroom Reader Nature Calls
- Uncle John's Bathroom Reader Plunges into California
- Uncle John's Bathroom Reader Plunges into Canada, eh
- Uncle John's Bathroom Reader Plunges into Great Lives
- Uncle John's Bathroom Reader Plunges into History
- Uncle John's Bathroom Reader Plunges into History Again
- Uncle John's Bathroom Reader Plunges into Hollywood
- Uncle John's Bathroom Reader Plunges into Michigan
- Uncle John's Bathroom Reader Plunges into Minnesota
- Uncle John's Bathroom Reader Plunges into Music
- Uncle John's Bathroom Reader Plunges into National Parks
- Uncle John's Bathroom Reader Plunges into New Jersey
- Uncle John's Bathroom Reader Plunges into New York
- Uncle John's Bathroom Reader Plunges into Ohio
- Uncle John's Bathroom Reader Plunges into Pennsylvania
- Uncle John's Bathroom Reader Plunges into Texas
- Uncle John's Bathroom Reader Plunges into Texas Expanded Edition

THE LAST PAGE

FELLOW BATHROOM READERS:

The fight for good bathroom reading should never be taken loosely—we must do our duty and sit firmly for what we believe in, even while the rest of the world is taking potshots at us.

We'll be brief. Now that we've proven we're not simply a flush-in-the-pan, we invite you to take the plunge: Sit Down and Be Counted! To find out what the BRI is up to, visit us at *www.portablepress.com* and take a peek!

GET CONNECTED

Find us online to sign up for our email list, enter exciting giveaways, hear about new releases, and more!

Website: www.portablepress.com

Facebook: www.facebook.com/portablepress

Pinterest: www.pinterest.com/portablepress

Twitter: @Portablepress

Well, we're out of space, and when you've gotta go, you've gotta go. Tanks for all your support. Hope to hear from you soon.

Meanwhile, remember...

Keep on flushin'!